Sustainable Perspectives in Business, Economics and Education

Venelin Terziev (ed.)

Sustainable Perspectives in Business, Economics and Education

Theoretical and Empirical Approaches

PETER LANG

Berlin - Bruxelles - Chennai - Lausanne - New York - Oxford

Library of Congress Cataloging-in-Publication
A CIP catalog record for this book has been applied for at the Library of Congress.

Bibliographic information published by the Deutsche Nationalbibliothek
The Deutsche Nationalbibliothek lists this publication in the Deutsche Nationalbibliografie; detailed bibliographic data is available on the Internet at http://dnb.d-nb.de.

ISBN 978-3-631-92917-9 (Print)
E-ISBN 978-3-631-93534-7 (E-PDF)
E-ISBN 978-3-631-93535-4 (E-PUB)
DOI.10.3726/b22751

Published by Peter Lang GmbH, Berlin, Germany

info@peterlang.com - www.peterlang.com

This publication has been peer-reviewed.

Venelin Terziev

Foreword

Our book called "Sustainable Perspectives in Business, Economics and Education Theoretical and Empirical Approaches" consists of 30 chapters, 76 authors have contributed to our book. This book contains trends and innovations in the field of economy and business. The target audience of this book is researchers, students and academics interested in business and economics. We think that it is a book in which you can find various topics and read with pleasure. We would like to express our gratitude to our publisher PETER LANG for the care they have taken in the preparation of the book.

Table of Contents

List of Contributors

Abdurashid Kadirov
Research center "Scientific bases and issues of economic development of Uzbekistan" under the Tashkent State University of Economics, Uzbekistan

Alanood Alshamsi
Zayed University, College of Humanities and Social Science, Dubai, United Arab Emirates

Ali Rakipi
University of Prishtina "Hasan Prishtina", Prishtine, Kosovo

Aliya Akhmedieva
Tashkent State University of Economics, Uzbekistan

Anita Zenuni
Academy of Public Safety, Vushtrri, Kosovo

Areej El Sayary
Zayed University, Faculty of College of Interdisciplinary Studies, Dubai, United Arab Emirates

Arta Morina
MA, University of Prishtina "Hasan Prishtina", Prishtina, Kosova

Bahtiyor Mamurov
Research center "Scientific bases and issues of economic development of Uzbekistan" under the Tashkent State University of Economics, Uzbekistan

Baizhuman Kashkhynbay
Eurasian National University, Astana, Kazakhstan

Cátia Susana Claro Chasqueira
INDEG-ISCTE, Executive Education, Lisboa, Portugal

Constantinos Challoumis
N.K.U.A. (National and Kapodistrian University of Athens), Athens, Greece

Daniele Grechi
DiDEC, University of Insubria, Como, Italy and DIMSEFA, Catholic University of the Sacred Heart, Milano, Italy

Dawood Ahmad
International Open University, Department of Education, Gambia

Dijana Vuković
University of North, Croatia

Dilnur Mukhambek
Eurasian National University, Astana, Kazakhstan

Dilobar Ruzieva
Tashkent State University of Economics, Tashkent, Uzbekistan

Dora Naletina
University of Zagreb, Zagreb, Croatia

Edona Berisha Kida
University of Prishtina "Hasan Prishtina", Prishtine, Kosovo

Eka Sepashvili
Tbilisi State University, Tbliisi, Georgia

Elena Linca
University "1 Decembrie 1918" Alba Iulia, Romania

Ema Peternel
School of Economics and Business, University of Ljubljana, Slovenia

Eneken Titov
Estonian Entrepreneurship University of Applied Sciences

Enes Akkurt
Ankara Haci Bayram Veli University, Türkiye

Erita Hoxha
University of Prishtina "Hasan Prishtina", Prishtine, Kosovo

Fatima AlMohsen
Zayed University, College of Humanities and Social Science, Dubai, United Arab Emirates

Fatlume Berisha
University of Prishtina "Hasan Prishtina", Prishtine, Kosovo

Fatma AlMaghribi
Zayed University, College of Humanities and Social Science, Dubai, United Arab Emirates

Georg Ikoro
Estonian Entrepreneurship University of Applied Sciences

Hena Oak
Miranda House, University of Delhi, India

Ileana Hamburg
Institut Arbeit und Technik, Westfälische Hochschule, Gelsenkirchen, Germany

Ivana Štulec
University of Zagreb, Zagreb, Croatia

Jehona Shkodra
University of Prishtina, Kosovo

Katarzyna Sanak-Kosmowska
University of Economics in Krakow, Poland

Laila Mohebi
Zayed University, College of Humanities and Social Science, Dubai, United Arab Emirates

Lawrence Meda
Department of Educational Leadership, Sharjah Education Academy

Luís Barbosa
Centre for Research in Applied Communication and New Technologies, Universidade Lusófona, Porto, Portugal

Luisa Anderloni
University of Milan, Milan, Italy

Manuel Bogalheiro
Centre for Research in Applied Communication and New Technologies, Universidade Lusófona, Porto, Portugal.

Maria da Conceição dos Santos Contreiras Salema Aleixo
Setúbal Polytechnic University, School of Business, Setúbal, Portugal

Mariam AlHammadi
Zayed University, College of Humanities and Social Science, Dubai, United Arab Emirates

Marin Georgiev
Vitalis Ruse, Ruse, Bulgaria

Marin Marinov
Georgi Benkovski Bulgarian Air Force Academy, Dolna Mitropolia, Bulgaria

Marusya Lyubcheva
Black Sea Institute, Bourgas, Bulgaria

Marziya Assylbekova
Eurasian National University, Astana, Kazakhstan

Milen Dimitrov
Black Sea Institute, Bourgas, Bulgaria

Muharrem Umut
Ankara Haci Bayram Veli University, Türkiye

Enes Akkurt
Ankara Haci Bayram Veli University, Türkiye

Muna Mohamed Alhammadi
Zayed University, Dubai, United Arab Emirates

Nikolina Filipović
Sales Consultant at Volvo Financial Services, Zagreb, Croatia

Norbert Laurisz
University of Economics in Krakow, Poland

Ornella Moro
University of Sassari, DISEA, Sassari, Italy

Patrizia Gazzola
DiECO, University of Insubria, Varese, Italy

Pedro Fernandes da Anunciação
Setúbal Polytechnic University, School of Business, Setúbal, Portugal

Peter Schmunkamp
Alexandru Ioan Cuza University, Iaşi, Romania

Reem Thani AlDhaheri
Zayed University, Dubai, United Arab Emirates

Rimma Yunusova
Tashkent State University of Economics and Ural State University of Economics, Tashkent, Uzbekistan

Roman Pantin
Tashkent State University of Economics, Tashkent, Uzbekistan

Roxana Maria Stejerean
University "1 Decembrie 1918" Alba Iulia, Romania

Simeon Simeonov
University Hospital Kaneff, Rousse, Bulgaria

Sirojiddin Abrorov
Research center "Scientific bases and issues of economic development of Uzbekistan" under the Tashkent State University of Economics, Tashkent, Uzbekistan

Sitora Khaydarova
Tashkent State University of Economics, Tashkent, Uzbekistan

Suha Karaki
Zayed University, Faculty of College of Interdisciplinary Studies, Dubai, United Arab Emirates

Tamar Mermanishvili
Tbilisi State University, Tbliisi, Georgia

Tanja Grmuša
University of North, Croatia

Tanja Unterwegs
University of North, Croatia

Tatiana Dănescu
Dr. George Emil Palade University of Medicine, Pharmacy, Science, and Technology of Targu Mures, Romania

Venelin Terziev
Black Sea Institute, Bourgas, Bulgaria

Vjollca Ahmedi
University of Prishtina "Hasan Prishtina", Prishtina, Kosova

Vladimir Bukvič
GEA College Faculty of Entrepreneurship Ljubljana, Slovenia

Zhaniyat Baltabayeva
Eurasian National University, Astana, Kazakhstan

Zulkhumor Fazliddinova
Research center "Scientific bases and issues of economic development of Uzbekistan" under the Tashkent State University of Economics, Uzbekistan

Rozafa Ferizi Shala
University of Prishtina "Hasan Prishtina", Kosova

Violeta Buza
Faculty of Social Science, AAB College, Kosova

Teodora Petrova
Trakia University-Stara Zagora, Bulgaria

Zhivo Petrov
National Defence College -Sofia, Bulgaria

Donghui Zhao
Graduate School of Business, The National University of Malaysia, Malaysia

Sue Lin Ngan
Graduate School of Business, The National University of Malaysia, Malaysia

Ainul Huda Jamil
Graduate School of Business, The National University of Malaysia, Malaysia

Mohd Fairuz Md Salleh
Graduate School of Business, The National University of Malaysia, Malaysia

Wan Sallha Yusoff
Centre of Excellence Social Innovation and Sustainability, Faculty of Business & Communication, University Malaysia Perlis, Malaysia

List of Figures and Graphs

The Concept of Test City from a Modern Smart City Perspective

Professional Support for Educators through Training and Follow-Up of Changes in Practices of Working with Children of Ages Up to 3 Years Old

The Evolution of ESG Integration in Finance: A Two-Decade Bibliometric Analysis

List of Tables

Financial Literacy, Digital Literacy and Sustainability in Small-Scale Entrepreneurship

The Roleand Importance of Construction Completion Insurance in Türkiye

Communication about the Sustainability of Fashion Brands – True Desire for Change in Fashion

Effects of Social Media Usage with Academic Performance of University Students: A Comparative Study of UAE and Pakistan

Has the World Become Truly Sustainable? Evidence from the Top Carbon Emitters of 2022

Pioneering Sustainable Transport: A Case Study on the Adoption of Electric Trucks

Victimization and Victim Behavior among Adolescents in Central Asian Country

The Evolution of ESG Integration in Finance: A Two- Decade Bibliometric Analysis

Peter Schmunkamp

How Does Voluntary Disclosure of ESG Information Influence IPO'S Performance?

1. Introduction

Climate change, social injustice and financial crimes are scenarios which influence investors choice and lead to an increasing interest in sustainability in the financial market, as well as the economy itself (Hartzmark & Sussman, 2017). There may be several reasons for this: On the one hand, an expectation of market participants and clients towards financial institutions and companies is assumed; on the other hand, this interest can also be understood as risk management and preparation for changing market paradigms (Landi et al., 2022). In addition to that, the goal of creating value for future generations and preserving it could be another reason (Signori et al., 2021). Deriving from this, financial market participants try to integrate environmental, social und governance (ESG) in their strategy in order to participate from positive financial effects (Hussain, 2015).

Not only are ESG ratings and sustainability strategies finding their way into investors' decision-making processes, but interest in the academic and scientific community has also surged in recent years, leading to the abandonment of the maxims of classic economics, market regulation and market efficiency (Friede et al., 2015). Investors use ESG-criteria to find potential investments and companies in order to avoid companies which work against the investors sustainability perception or to find valuable companies in a ESG context (Nakajima et al., 2021).

Focusing on Initial Public Offerings (IPOs) ESG criteria and reporting are critical information sources which are taken account into communication strategies in the term of IPO processes in order to ensure adequate analysis for the investors (Ferri et al., 2023). On the same side, communication is a key tool to facilitate the best possible IPO and strengthen the capital base of the respective companies. The underpricing, as a compensation, of IPOs can be an indicator to identify disturbed communication which leads to information asymmetry on capital markets (Rock, 1986). IPOs underpricing can be identified as a market specific behavior in which the offering price, chosen by the companies, and the price on the second market are spread even in a short-term period independent of the stock marketplace (Rehkugler & Schenek, 2001). Deriving from this, there could be a significant relationship between voluntary ESG disclosure and IPOs underprcing effect.

This study uses a model which indicates the quantity of voluntary ESG information disclosure by focusing on the information that is given by the companies before the IPO release date. Hence, the research focuses on the quantity of ESG information in the S-1 prospectuses, whereas these documents are a fundamental information source for institutional investors, which represents the largest group of IPO investors (Barrios et al., 2020).

2. Research Hypothesis

The main hypothesis of this research assumes a negative correlation between underpricing and ESG information content in the IPO process, regardless of whether this information originates from a subarea of sustainability or whether they are considered together. This is coherent with theories about the reduction of information asymmetry, in which disclosure of new information reduces the asymmetry between the investors and companies (Ajina et al., 2015). In addition to that, disclosure ESG information can also bring positive effects regarding company's financial performance (Cek & Eyupoglu, 2020).

This leads to the following hypothesis:

H1: The voluntary exposure of ESG-related information is negatively associated with the information asymmetry in an IPO market.

Deriving from the main hypothesis the sub-hypothesis concentrates on the single ESG elements. According to Friede, Bush and Bassen (2015), there is a ranking depending on the degree of influence on the IPO underpricing. The greatest influence on the information asymmetry is represented by the Governance disclosure, followed by Environmental and Social. The ESG disclosure as a whole has the least effect on underpricing (Friede et al., 2015):

H2: The information asymmetry in an IPO market is influenced, in order of magnitude, by Governance-, Environmental- and Social-disclosure.

3. Methodology and Data

3.1. Textual and Sentiment Analysis

As mentioned before, this study analyzes the S-1 forms of IPOs. In accordance with Loughran and McDonald (2011) textual mining is used to find words from a list which is corresponding with sentiment characteristics like positivity, uncertainty or negativity in relation to ESG (Loughran & McDonald, 2011). RStudio as a statistic tool is used to collect the data via the "edgar"-package (Lonare et al., 2021).

3.2. Data Sample

As this study is focused on the influence of voluntary ESG disclosure and IPO underpricing, a sample of IPOs on the US market is taken, based on the date of the first issuing date. The primary source for the IPO data over the period from 2003 till 2022 was Refinitiv Eikon. Essentially, the database provided information on issue date, stock market, economic sector, offer price, first closing price and other financials. Companies from the banks and insurances and utilities sectors were excluded from the sample. The reason for this is that insurance companies and banks must fulfill a high degree of regulation regarding capital requirements. Utilities companies are also very dependent on regulatory intervention, meaning that these groups of companies have very specific reasons for accessing the capital markets (Kennedy et al., 2006).

To map the degree of publication of ESG information, the respective IPO prospectuses were analyzed with the help of text analyzes. The IPO prospectuses represent a key source of information for potential investors and can help to reduce information asymmetries (Hanley & Hoberg, 2009). During the IPO process the prospectuses (S-1 files) are collected by the Security Exchange Commission (SEC). To investigate the respective prospectuses further, the respective document was collected and analyzed for each company with the help of the EDGAR database. As companies update their data and file new S-1 forms as part of the IPO process, this was also considered by analyzing the entire history of filings.

With the support of the Application Programming Interface (API) EDGAR package, prospectuses from 2003 to 2022 in the form of HTML-format were downloaded. Subsequently, each text file was analyzed using the ESG word list shown in Appendix 1. Non-relevant stop words were removed in advance of the analysis.

3.3. Variables

3.3.1. Dependent Variables

In the part of the development of the research hypothesis, it has already been explained that the aim is to examine which specific factors influence the degree of disclosure of companies, which is why the disclosure of information is a dependent variable. Before being used as a variable the absolute information disclosure will be logarithmically trans-formed. A normal distribution is assumed for the disclosure of information. Neverthe-less, this variable is also used as an independent variable to determine whether it has a negative influence on underpricing.

In addition to the voluntary disclosure of ESG information, underpricing is to be used as a dependent variable to represent the degree of uncertainty as a proxy. To determine the underpricing and the resulting potential loss of opportunity for issuers, a quantitative assessment is required, which should be carried out using the initial return (IR). The unadjusted initial return is calculated as follows:

$$IR = \frac{\left(P_{o,t} - E_i\right)}{E_i}$$

As the unadjusted IR is only of limited use for analyzing the excess return, it is adjusted by taking into account an approximate market portfolio (Beatty & Ritter, 1985). No historical share price data is available at the time of the initial issue, which is why a beta of one is assumed. However, the formation of a market portfolio can be achieved by comparing similar companies. The IR can be adjusted for the performance of an already traded company that has comparable key figures or characteristics in terms of company size, sector affiliation or price-to-book ratio. As this procedure requires a very large number of comparable companies and would take up too much of the work due to the resources required, it is not used here.

Instead of adjusting for peer companies, the equity market adjustment method is used. The S+P 500 Index will be used as the benchmark to adequately represent market developments. This index, also known as the Standard and Poor's 500, comprises the 500 largest listed companies in the USA, which are determined by the rating agency Standard and Poor's Corp. based on their respective market capitalization. As the development of the stock market is reflected in this index, the S+P 500 is chosen as an indicator of market development.

The adjustment by the above-mentioned benchmark therefore leads to the extension of the IR formula:

$$IR_{ad} = \frac{\left(P_{o,t} - E_i\right)}{E_i} - \frac{\left(M_{t0} - M_{t-1}\right)}{M_{t-1}}$$

3.3.2. Independent Variables

The primary independent variable in this research project is the publication of ESG information, which is determined from the IPO prospectuses of the respective companies. The number of relevant ESG words per prospect is to be counted using the frequency term method. According to Loughran and McDonald it is important to include a weighted scheme in order to relativize words to other content in the IPO prospectuses (Loughran & McDonald, 2016).

The weighted term frequency method is used to examine the importance of terms in the sample. This leads to, that words found in more prospectuses are more weighted compared to others:

$$W_{i,j} = \frac{1+\log\left(tf_{i,j}\right)}{1+\log\left(aj\right)} * log\frac{N}{df_i} if\ tf_{i,j} > 0$$

3.3.3. Control Variables

The control variables are divided into three different categories: firm characteristics, offer characteristics and market characteristics.

A proxy that reflects the size of a company are the revenues, which can influence the investors decision. Most investors consider the uncertainty to be lower for larger companies, which is why it can be assumed that companies with high revenues will be less underpriced (Leone et al., 2007). The total assets of a company can also influence uncertainty in the same way as revenues and are therefore also analyzed as a control variable. Another variable which reduces IPOs underpricing is firm age, which is the difference between the foundation year of a company and the year of offering. It is argued that older firms have a longer financial history and more published information leading to reduce the ex-ante uncertainty (Engelen & van Essen, 2010).

A market based controlling variable is the venture capital (VC) involvement. IPOs, which have a prior venture capital owner structure might be more underpriced compared to companies without VC involvement (Lowry & Schwert, 2004). In addition to that, shares offered on the NASDAQ tend to be more underpriced. An argument to this is, that this stock market has specific issuers which tend to be smaller, younger, and more focused on high technology (Corwin, 2003).

Companies that are accompanied by established bookrunners as part of the IPO process tend to be less underpriced. The reason for this is the reputation of the respective underwriter, which can be a positive signal for investors. This study therefore focuses on the ranking of the respective underwriter that is named first in the dataset. The scale is from 0 until 9.1 based on Ritter`s underwriter ranking.

3.4. Methodology

To determine the hypothesized effects of the dependent variables, Ordinary Least Squares (OLS) is used, as this can be used for the IPO-relevant data. A linear regression is then used to determine the correlation between the dependent variable and the other variables. The following regression is used to test the hypothesis:

$$IR_{ad} = \alpha + \ln(WE, j) + \ln(WS, j) + \ln(WS, j) + \ln(\text{Assets}) + \ln(\text{revenues}) \\ + \ln(age) + VC_{dummy} + StockExchange_{dummy} + UW_{ranking}$$

3.5. Descriptive Statistics

The table below (Table 1) shows an overview of the descriptive statistics including ESG information, transaction, and firm characteristics.

Table 1: Summary statistics

	N	Mean	sd	IQR	Min	p25	Median	p75	Max
ESG information disclosure characteristics									
E word count	1803	17,944.550	15,421.991	11,956.500	-	9,237.000	12,992.000	21,193.500	218,769.000
S word count	1803	20,008.360	30,140.637	13,236.000	-	8,882.500	12,932.000	22,118.500	651,031.000
G word count	1803	8,438.910	7,620.326	5,517.500	-	4,485.000	6,176.000	10,002.500	108,762.000
ESG word count	1803	46,424.810	30,140.637	13,236.000	-	8,882.500	12,932.000	22,118.500	651,031.000
Transaction characteristics									
Total Assets	1803	695.641	3,909.670	325.900	0.000	15.850	74.000	341.750	137,238.000
Total Revenues	1803	423.889	2,314.637	151.950	0.000	0.000	5.600	151.950	66,468.300
Underpricing	1803	0.056	0.434	0.233	-1.000	-0.018	0.033	0.215	5.330
Underpricing adjusted	1803	0.056	0.434	0.236	-1.029	-0.022	0.033	0.214	5.337
Offer Price	1803	14.070	5.849	7.000	3.500	10.000	14.000	17.000	65.000
Bookrunner ranking	1803	7.643	1.190	2.113	1.001	6.888	8.376	9.008	9.001
Firm and market characteristics									
Company age	1803	13.144	18.416	11.000	1.000	3.000	8.000	14.000	187.000
High Technology	1803	0.657	0.475	1.000	-	-	1.000	1.000	1.000
Venture Capital	1803	0.663	0.473	1.000	-	-	1.000	1.000	1.000

Source: By author

The average ESG word count is at 46,425 words per company. The majority of this is attributable to the Environmental (17,945) and Social (20,008) divisions. With 8,439 words per company, the area of governance only accounts for around 18 % of information disclosures. If the weighted disclosure levels are considered, then Environmental has a value of 0.029, Social 0.030 and Governance 0.014. According to that, environmental and social words are more unique in the prospectuses, thus they can be seen as important.

If the transaction characteristics are analyzed, there are hardly any differences between unadjusted and adjusted underpricing. This indicates that the IPOs in the sample were not influenced by strong market fluctuations on their publication date. The average underpricing in the overall sample is 5.6 %. On average, the companies reported an asset volume of USD 695,641 million and revenues of USD 423,889 million before their first day of trading on the hospital market. However, it should be noted that some companies either did not report any financials before the IPO or were not yet able to present any.

The bookrunner ranking is 7.643, which is relatively high compared to the range from 0 to 9.1. About 66.3 % of the sample are backed by venture capital (VC) and around 65.7 % have published on the NASDAQ. The average company age is 13.14 years.

As can be seen in the chart below, the number of IPOs fell sharply during the 2008 financial crisis but recovered over the following years. A further decline can be seen in 2020, which was caused by the COVID-19 pandemic.

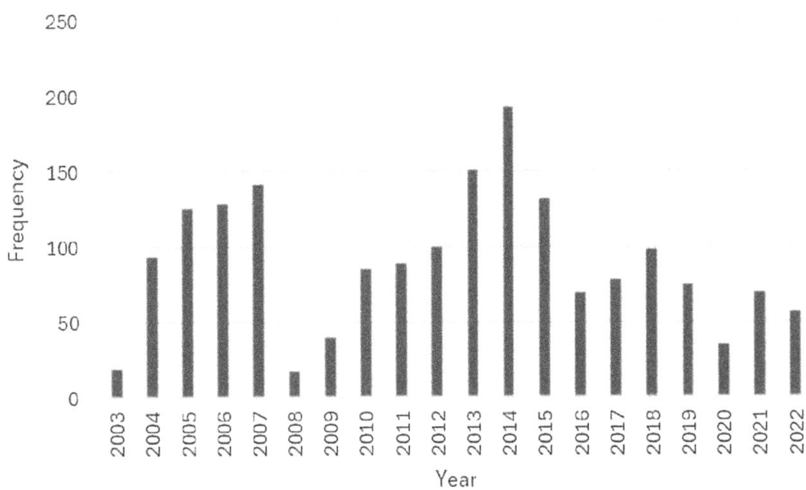

Figure 1: IPO frequency
Source: By author

In Table 2 below the sample is shown by business sector. The table shows that, at 20.97 %, companies from the Pharmaceuticals & Medical Research sector are the most strongly represented. This is followed by Software & IT Services with 11.98 % and Investment Holding Companies with 11.76 %.

Table 2: Underpricing by business sector

	N	N %	Mean	sd	IQR	Min	p25	Median	p75	Max
Academic & Educational Services	11	0.61%	0.210	0.206	0.212	-0.072	0.078	0.170	0.290	0.674
Applied Resources	10	0.55%	0.056	0.138	0.163	-0.176	-0.022	0.049	0.141	0.299
Automobiles & Auto Parts	15	0.83%	-0.106	0.417	0.131	-1.005	-0.052	0.019	0.079	0.433
Chemicals	27	1.50%	-0.012	0.297	0.124	-1.005	-0.004	0.034	0.121	0.265
Collective Investments	11	0.61%	-0.011	0.371	0.091	-1.004	-0.013	0.001	0.078	0.518
Cyclical Consumer Products	40	2.22%	0.123	0.371	0.315	-1.004	-0.005	0.103	0.310	1.007
Cyclical Consumer Services	89	4.94%	0.142	0.487	0.366	-1.019	-0.041	0.088	0.325	1.307
Energy - Fossil Fuels	176	9.76%	-0.011	0.311	0.151	-1.029	-0.024	0.036	0.128	0.509
Food & Beverages	22	1.22%	-0.060	0.426	0.174	-1.011	-0.051	0.030	0.123	0.662
Food & Drug Retailing	12	0.67%	0.315	0.320	0.302	-0.027	0.100	0.244	0.402	1.209
Healthcare Services & Equipment	141	7.82%	0.099	0.388	0.289	-1.005	-0.018	0.068	0.271	2.191
Industrial & Commercial Services	83	4.60%	0.098	0.404	0.214	-1.010	0.001	0.107	0.215	1.860
Industrial Goods	62	3.44%	0.062	0.274	0.175	-1.001	-0.010	0.069	0.165	0.712
Investment Holding Companies	212	11.76%	-0.182	0.397	0.031	-1.021	-0.018	0.000	0.013	0.192
Mineral Resources	20	1.11%	0.040	0.121	0.169	-0.119	-0.047	0.014	0.122	0.351
Personal & Household Products & Services	11	0.61%	0.136	0.145	0.293	-0.027	-0.011	0.134	0.282	0.309
Pharmaceuticals & Medical Research	378	20.97%	0.064	0.485	0.277	-1.019	-0.056	0.014	0.221	5.337
Real Estate	24	1.33%	0.033	0.383	0.271	-0.999	-0.035	0.056	0.236	0.661
Renewable Energy	17	0.94%	0.104	0.660	0.210	-1.022	-0.035	0.076	0.175	2.112
Retailers	60	3.33%	0.151	0.413	0.345	-1.000	0.003	0.141	0.348	1.226
Software & IT Services	216	11.98%	0.246	0.498	0.411	-1.013	0.015	0.199	0.426	4.101
Technology Equipment	96	5.32%	0.062	0.376	0.297	-1.007	-0.036	0.075	0.261	0.953
Telecommunications Services	37	2.05%	-0.013	0.400	0.304	-1.011	-0.061	0.026	0.243	0.637
Transportation	33	1.83%	-0.054	0.386	0.129	-1.005	-0.047	0.005	0.081	0.509

Source: By author

It can also be seen that the underpricing for the Food & Drug Retailing (31.5 %), Software & IT Services (24.6 %) and Academic & Education Services (21.0 %) sectors is significantly higher compared to other sectors. The observation about the Software & IT Services sector is therefore consistent with the statement that high-tech companies are more underpriced than other sectors in comparison (Corwin, 2003).

4. Results

The table (Table 3) below shows the dependence of the variable underpricing on the independent variables. There is a strong significance in the correlation between underpricing and the use of venture capital. The positive expected value is consistent with the assumption that IPOs supported by VC tend to be underpriced more than companies without VC (Francis & Hasan, 2001).

Table 3: Summary underpricing correlation

	Estimate	Std. Error	t value	Pr(>|t|)
(Intercept)	-0.174995	0.073246	-2.389	0.016991 *
Bookrunner.ranking	0.01249	0.006178	2.022	0.043348 *
Dummy.Nasdaq	0.041623	0.02281	1.825	0.068194 .
ln_age	0.052121	0.022284	2.339	0.019446 *
ln_assets	0.009906	0.0042	2.359	0.018456 *
ln_E_weighted	-0.307303	0.11063	-2.778	0.005531 **
ln_G_weighted	0.157865	0.087674	1.801	0.071936 .
ln_revenues	0.004268	0.002309	1.848	0.064771 .
ln_S_weighted	0.115379	0.078116	1.477	0.139843
VC.Dummy	0.091533	0.025086	3.649	0.000271 ***

Signif. codes: 0 '***' 0.001 '**' 0.01 '*' 0.05 '.' 0.1 ' ' 1

Source: By author

In addition to the VC, the correlation between the underpricing and the published environmental information is also significant. However, this significance is given at a confidence level of 99 %. Nevertheless, this aspect is consistent with the hypothesis, as the publication of e-information has a negative influence on underpricing. The variable assets also show significance, which is somewhat lower in comparison, but is nevertheless in line with the assumptions and previous observations of other studies (Karami et al., 2014). The bookrunner ranking also has a positive influence on underpricing and is in line with the observations of Liu and Ritter (2011), as companies tend to be more underpriced if the underwriter offers higher quality or industry experience (Liu & Ritter, 2011). Another variable that has a positive influence on underpricing is the age of the companies. However, this observation is not consistent with the expectations and previous observations of other studies. The variables NASDAQ dummy, governance information and revenues also show significance, but these are at a rather low level, so they are not considered further.

4.1. Robustness Check

Appendix 2 shows the results of the statistical tests. The test for multicollinearity was determined using the Variance Inflation Factor (VIF). Depending on the current literature, a VIF of 5 or 10 is considered critical (Cleff, 2012). The VIFs for the individual variables are shown in the upper part of the table. It can be seen that the variables representing the ESG information levels have a value above 5. The variable ln_E_weighted contains a value of 11.853. From this it can be concluded that these variables are dependent on other variables in the model. Considering that the ESG information grades are calculated depending on their frequency in the respective prospectuses, it is causally correct that these three variables influence each other. This can be seen in particular from the correlation table shown in Appendix 2.

In addition to multicollinearity, autocorrelation and misspecification were also tested. The Durbin-Watson (DW) test was used to check the autocorrelation. The result is a DW value of 1.9095 and is therefore close to the target value of 2.0. An autocorrelation can therefore be rejected. Ramsey's Regression-Specification-Error-Test (RESET) was used to determine the misspecification. The p-value calculated from this is 0.5466 and is therefore sufficiently large to reject a specification error.

As a further statistical robustness test, the studentized Breusch-Pagan test was used to test the heteroscedasticity of the previous model. The result of the test is a p-value of 11.84 % The null hypothesis of homoscedasticity therefore does not have to be rejected.

5. Conclusion

This paper has analyzed the publication of ESG information as part of the IPO process. The aim was to analyze whether the publication of this information can contribute to the reduction of information asymmetries and thus provide an explanation for the underpricing effect. Variables from the company, market and transaction characteristics were used. The variables were bookrunner ranking, firm age, VC involvement, industry, year of IPO and financials. Information on the publication of ESG information prior to the IPO was used to consider ESG aspects within the IPO prospectuses by using the term frequency method.

The findings of this work are essentially in line with current research. A direct link can be established between the underpricing of IPOs and the voluntary publication of ESG information. Thus, the theory presented in the literature review is consistent with the thesis that the reduction of information symmetry leads to lower underpricing. However, it must be considered that this only applies to information on the subject area "Environmental." No significant correlation was found for the "Social" and "Governance" areas. Furthermore, there is only a further significance to be considered for the VC dummy as a control variable. This is also in line with the theories that the involvement of venture capital increases uncertainty in relation to the issuing company and consequently increases underpricing. Even if the significance of the variables age, assets and bookrunner ranking are only of secondary importance, the positive influence of these variables on the underpricing can be justified with the signaling theory. Hypothesis 1 can therefore be answered conditionally in the affirmative. However, the situation is different for hypothesis 2, which was intended to analyze the interdependence of the individual ESG aspects. No clear statement could be made here due to the lack of significance. The second hypothesis must therefore be rejected.

In principle, this work represents a contribution to explaining the relationship between underpricing and the publication of ESG information. The hypothesis that ESG information has a negative influence on information asymmetry can only be answered to a limited extent, as only information from the "environmental" area has a significant influence.

The second hypothesis, which gives the individual ESG aspects an order in which "governance" followed by "environmental" and "social" influence the underpricing, must be rejected. No actual order can be recognized from the observation of the data, as only the significance of "E" could be demonstrated. Further research is needed to investigate the relationship between underpricing and the voluntary disclosure of ESG information.

If the method of determining the level of disclosure is considered, it can be stated that there are several methods of determining this. Information is often extracted from official documents such as the IPO prospectuses used in this study but can also come from specialized ESG databases or announcements via the press channels of individual companies. Future research should utilize other sources to further investigate the influence of ESG information.

The list of words shown in Appendix 1 also represents a limitation of this research, as it significantly influences the calculation of term frequencies. As the list of words is the same for all companies regardless of their respective organization, this can lead to distortions with regard to the calculation of the disclosure level. In addition, the weighted consideration of these words leads to a dependency between the ESG disclosure of each company and the entire sample. In order to obtain more precise findings on ESG furnace disclosure, this study would have to be repeated with an extended or different sample.

It should also be mentioned that not all companies that started the IPO process in the period under review could be included in the observation, as some of them canceled the IPO process before the first trading day or the required information about the financials was not provided.

Future research should develop alternative methods for measuring the degree of ESG disclosure and utilize alternative sources of information. Furthermore, additional factors from the company, market and transaction characteristics should be included in future modeling. The influence of ESG information on a short-term effect such as underpricing should also be analyzed, as well as other capital markets (especially emerging markets).

Appendix 1: Word Catalog

Environmental: accountability institute, acute risk, adverse weather, agri business, agricultural, agriculture, air, airquality, animal, arctic drilling, ash, biodiverse, biodiversity, biological, biology, business, calamitous, carbon, catastrophe, catastrophy, celsius, clean, climate, co, co2, coffee, commodity, compensation, construction, contamination, damage, death, degradation, degree, depletion, diversity, drought, earth, earthquake, eco, ecological, electricity, emission, emissions, energy, environment, environmental, erisk, erosion, esg, explosion, fahrenheit, fatality, fine, fire, flood, food, footprint, forest, fuel, gas, geographic, grape, green, greenhouse, health, heat, hurricane, hybrid, hydrocarbon, imported energy, innovation, jungle, landuse, leakage, local, loss of export, mark carney, material, material, materials, medical spending, mine, mining, morbidity, mortality, natural, natural, nature, ocean, organism, packaging, ph, physical, planet, pollute, pollution, protection, protect, rain, rainforest, recycle, recycled, recycling, reduce, reducing, reduction, renewable, renewable, resilience, resilient, resource, resources, scarce, scarcity, sealevel, sewer, sids, soil, stern review, stewardship, storm, sun, suppliers, surge, sustainable, sustainability, task force on climate, tcfd, technologies, technology, temperature, timber, toxic, transition risk, typhoon, underwritingloss, utility, vulnerable 20, warmup, waste, waste, water, water, weather, wildfire, wind, zero

Social: absenteeism, abuse, abusive, acceptance criteria, accident, accountability, activism, adapt, adjust, affordability, affordable, age, aging, animal, anticipate, audience, aware, behavior, behavior, bisphenol, bonus, boycott, brandname, buyer beware, care, career, cave atemptor, circular economy, civic organization, civil society, class action, clinical, client, cohesion, cohesiveness, combat, community, community-related, compensation, complaint, compliance, comply, conflict, consumer, controversy, corruption, credible, credibility, crime, cultural, culture, customer, damage, danger, death, deficiency, deficient, demographic, demography, demonstration, diploma, diplomacy, disclose, disclosure, dispute, disrupt, diverse, diversity, due diligence, economic development, education, effectiveness, employee, employee, employees, engage, enhanced business, ethical, ethical, ethics, ethnic minority, excessive, explosion, facilities, fatal, fight, fine, flexible, free, gender, gender, geopolitic, global compact, gmo, group, hazard, health, health, healthcare, healthcare, healthy, helping, hospital, human,

human capital, inclusion, inclusion, income disparity, income distribution, indigenous, inequalities, infrastructure, innovation, insight, instability, institutional assessment, institutional profile, institutional quality, insurance, investigation, labor, labor, labor, lawsuit, legal, liability, liabilities, license to operate, literacy, living standard, long horizon investment, management practice, management shortcoming, management team, medical, medical spending, middle class, migration, misconduct, mis-selling, mission, money laundering, non-profit, non-traditional, not-for-profit, old, openness, operational performance, operational risks, order, oversight, pay, pay-gap, pay gap, penalties, pension, personnel, philanthropy, policy, political, poor transparency, population, poverty, predictability, pressure, privacy, procedure, product defect, product recalls, protest, prudential, public good, public opinion, public resources, public service, public transport, punish, qualification, quality, quality of life, race, racial, regulation, regulator, relation, remuneration, representation, representative, reputable, reputation, responsible investment, restructuration, right, safe, safety, safety, sanction, satisfaction, scandal, school, security, self-sustaining, sign-up process, skill, social, social, societal priorities, socio-economic, sri, stability, staff turnover, stakeholder, standards of living, statutory, strategic, strategy, strike, stringent, substitution, suicide, supervision, supporting, sustainable, talent, taste, tax evasion, taxation, technological change, teams, team, terror, top management, together, trend, tribal, tribe, treatment, union, united nations, unrest, urbanization, values, violation, violence, violent, vision, vulnerable clientele, war, welfare, women, workforce, workforce, working conditions, workplace, world bank group, young

Governance: abuse, abusive, accountability, accountable, accuracy, activism, adjust, aggressive, allegation, audit, authority, aware, background, bankruptcy, board, board independence, board inefficiency, board membership, board skillsets, board turnover, board-related factor, bonus, breach, breadth, brexit, bribery, budgetary flexibility, budgetary performance, budgetary pressure, business environment, business plan, cease-and-desist, ceo, combat, communicate, communication, committee, community-related, compensation, compliance, comply, composition, comprehensive, conduct, conflict, control, controversy, corporate, corporate behavior, corporate value, corruption, council, credibility, credible, culture, deficiencies, deficiency, deficient, diplomacy, director, disclosure, disclosures, dissent, diverse skill, diversity, divestiture, duality, due diligence, effectiveness, efficiency of the board, electricity subsidy, employee, engagement, equator principles, erm, excessive, execution, executive, experience, expertise, extraordinary support, fine, framework, fraud, geopolitical, governance, governing body, government, implementation support, independent, independent board, independent institution, independent, institution, institutional assessment, institutional framework, institutional investor, institutional profile, institutional quality, investigation, irregularities, key institution, leaders, leadership, lawsuit, laws, legal, liquidity risk, litigation, manage, manage risk, management, managing risks, member, misconduct, mission, money laundering, monitoring, national, new focus, openness, operational goal, operational performance, operational risk, organization, organizations, oversight, partner, party, penalties, penalty, planning, policies, policy, policy flexibility, policy framework, policy making, policy support, political, political institution, principles, practices, predictability, procedure, prudential, prudently mitigate, public opinion, punish, realistic budgeting, referendum, regulation, regulator, relation, reliability, remuneration, report, reported, reporting, representation, reputable, reputation, responsible investment, restructuring, risk appetite, risk framework, risks, robust, rule of law, ruling, sanction, scandal, shareholder initiative, societal priorities, stability, stakeholder, stakeholders, standards, standard, standards, stakeholder, stakeholders, stability, stake, stability, stewardship, strategic, strategies, strategy, structure, supervisory, tax, technical advice, tolerance, track, transparency, transparent, union, unrest, values, violation, vision, vote, voting

Appendix 2: Statistical Tests

Variance Inflation Factor (VIF) test

Bookrunner.ranking	Dummy.Nasdaq	ln_age	ln_assets	ln_E_weighted	ln_G_weighted	ln_revenues	ln_S_weighted	VC.Dummy
1.37804	1.173807	1.2075	1.356416	11.835273	9.248781	1.36353	6.29879	1.408639

	(Intercept)	Bookrunner.ranking	Dummy.Nasdaq	ln_age	ln_assets	ln_E_weighted	ln_G_weighted	ln_revenues	ln_S_weighted	VC.Dummy
(Intercept)	1	-0.563	-0.31	-0.159	0.007	-0.02	0.269	0.147	-0.024	0.095
Bookrunner.ranking	0.563	1	0.293	-0.005	-0.042	-0.042	-0.04	-0.065	0.146	-0.377
Dummy.Nasdaq	-0.31	0.293	1	-0.04	0.066	0.045	-0.021	0.151	-0.022	-0.19
ln_age	-0.159	-0.005	-0.04	1	-0.078	-0.071	0.118	-0.121	-0.043	-0.28
ln_assets	0.007	-0.042	0.066	-0.078	1	-0.034	0.029	-0.398	0.032	-0.134
ln_E_weighted	-0.02	-0.042	0.045	-0.071	-0.034	1	-0.703	0.002	-0.499	0.009
ln_G_weighted	0.269	-0.04	-0.021	0.118	0.029	-0.703	1	0.018	-0.195	-0.004
ln_revenues	0.147	-0.065	0.151	-0.121	-0.398	0.002	0.018	1	-0.032	-0.042
ln_S_weighted	-0.024	0.146	-0.022	-0.043	0.032	-0.499	-0.195	-0.032	1	-0.03
VC.Dummy	0.095	-0.377	-0.19	-0.28	-0.134	0.009	-0.004	-0.042	-0.03	1

Durbin-Watson test

DW	p-value
1.9095	0.02612

RESET test

RESET	df1	df2	p-value
1.5896	18	1775	0.05466

Studentized Breusch-Pagan test		
BP	df	p-value
2.4387	1	0.1184

References

Ajina, A., Sougne, D., & Lakhal, F. (2015). Corporate Disclosures, Information Asymmetry and Stock-Market Liquidity in France. *Journal of Applied Business Research (JABR), 31*(4), 1223. https://doi.org/10.19030/jabr.v31i4.9297

Barrios, J. M., Choi, J. H., Hochberg, Y. V., Kim, J., & Liu, M. (2020). *Informing Entrepreneurs: Public Corporate Disclosure and New Business Formation.* https://doi.org/10.2139/ssrn.3640736

Beatty, R. P., & Ritter, J. R. (1985). *Investment Banking, Reputation, and the Underpricing of Initial Public Offerings. Working paper (Rodney L. White Center for Financial Research).* Rodney L. White Center for Financial Research. https://books.google.de/books?id=XPPptgAACAAJ

Cek, K., & Eyupoglu, S. (2020). Does Environmental, Social and Governance Performance Influence Economic Performance? *Journal of Business Economics and Management, 21*(4), 1165–1184. https://doi.org/10.3846/jbem.2020.12725

Cleff, T. (2012). *Deskriptive Statistik und moderne Datenanalyse: Eine computergestützte Einführung mit Excel, PASW (SPSS) und STATA* (2., überarbeitete und erweiterte Auflage). Gabler. https://doi.org/10.1007/978-3-8349-7071-8

Corwin, S. A. (2003). The Determinants of Underpricing for Seasoned Equity Offers. *The Journal of Finance, 58*(5), 2249–2279. https://doi.org/10.1111/1540-6261.00604

Engelen, P.-J., & van Essen, M. (2010). Underpricing of IPOs: Firm-, Issue- and Country-specific Characteristics. *Journal of Banking & Finance, 34*(8), 1958–1969. https://doi.org/10.1016/j.jbankfin.2010.01.002

Ferri, S., Tron, A., Colantoni, F., & Savio, R. (2023). Sustainability Disclosure and IPO Performance: Exploring the Impact of ESG Reporting. *Sustainability, 15*(6), 5144. https://doi.org/10.3390/su15065144

Francis, B. B., & Hasan, I. (2001). The Underpricing of Venture and Nonventure Capital IPOs: An Empirical Investigation. *Journal of Financial Services Research, 19*(2), 99–113. https://doi.org/10.1023/A:1011134715911

Friede, G., Busch, T., & Bassen, A. (2015). ESG and Financial Performance: Aggregated Evidence from More than 2000 Empirical Studies. *Journal of Sustainable Finance & Investment, 5*(4), 210–233. https://doi.org/10.1080/20430795.2015.1118917

Hanley, K. W., & Hoberg, G. (2009). *The Information Content of IPO Prospectuses.*

Hartzmark, S. M., & Sussman, A. B. (2017). *Do Investors Value Sustainability? A Natural Experiment Examining Ranking and Fund Flows.* https://doi.org/10.2139/ssrn.3016092

Hussain, N. (2015). *Impact of Sustainability Performance on Financial Performance: An Empirical Study of Global Fortune (N100) Firms.*

Karami, G., Kordlar, A. E., Amini, Y., & Hajipour, S. (2014). Earnings Management and Underpricing of Initial Public Offerings (IPO), Evidence from Iran. *International Business Research.* https://www.semanticscholar.org/paper/Earnings-Management-and-Underpricing-of-Initial-Karami-Kordlar/2df0aa6971f219857a9ecf08602f0604f8c096d5?p2df

Kennedy, D. B., Sivakumar, R., & Vetzal, K. R. (2006). The Implications of IPO Underpricing for the Firm and Insiders: Tests of Asymmetric Information Theories. *Journal of Empirical Finance, 13*(1), 49–78. https://doi.org/10.1016/j.jempfin.2004.10.003

Landi, G. C., Iandolo, F., Renzi, A., & Rey, A. (2022). Embedding Sustainability in Risk Management: The Impact of Environmental, Social, and Governance Ratings on Corporate Financial Risk. *Corporate Social Responsibility and Environmental Management, 29*(4), 1096–1107. https://doi.org/10.1002/csr.2256

Leone, A. J., Rock, S., & Willenborg, M. (2007). Disclosure of Intended Use of Proceeds and Underpricing in Initial Public Offerings. *Journal of Accounting Research, 45*(1), 111–153. https://doi.org/10.1111/j.1475-679X.2006.00229.x

Liu, X., & Ritter, J. R. (2011). *Local Underwriter Oligopolies and IPO Underpricing.* https://doi.org/10.2139/ssrn.1512554

Lonare, G., Patil, B., & Raut, N. (2021). Edgar: An R Package for the U.S. SEC EDGAR Retrieval and Parsing of Corporate Filings. *SoftwareX, 16*, 100865. https://doi.org/10.1016/j.softx.2021.100865

Loughran, T. I., & McDonald, B. (2016). Textual Analysis in Accounting and Finance: A Survey. *Journal of Accounting Research, 54*(4), 1187–1230. https://doi.org/10.1111/1475-679X.12123

Loughran, T., & McDonald, B. (2011). When Is a Liability Not a Liability? Textual Analysis, Dictionaries, and 10-Ks. *The Journal of Finance, 66*(1), 35–65. https://doi.org/10.1111/j.1540-6261.2010.01625.x

Lowry, M., & Schwert, G. (2004). Is the IPO Pricing Process Efficient? *Journal of Financial Economics, 71*(1), 3–26. https://doi.org/10.1016/S0304-405X(03)00205-8

Nakajima, T., Hamori, S., He, X., Liu, G., Zhang, W., Zhang, Y., & Liu, T. (Eds.). (2021). *Springer Briefs in Economics: ESG Investment in the Global Economy*. Singapore: Springer. https://doi.org/10.1007/978-981-16-2990-7

Rehkugler, H., & Schenek, A. (2001). Underpricing oder Overpricing? IPOs am deutschen Kapitalmarkt. In B. W. Wirtz & E. Salzer (Eds.), *IPO-Management: Strukturen und Erfolgsfaktoren* (pp. 277–308). Gabler Verlag. https://doi.org/10.1007/978-3-322-92966-2_13

Rock, K. (1986). Why New Issues Are Underpriced. *Journal of Financial Economics, 15*(1), 187–212. https://doi.org/10.1016/0304-405X(86)90054-1

Signori, S., San-Jose, L., Retolaza, J. L., & Rusconi, G. (2021). Stakeholder Value Creation: Comparing ESG and Value Added in European Companies. *Sustainability, 13*(3), 1392. https://doi.org/10.3390/su13031392

Jehona Shkodra and Njomza Mehmeti

Rural Enterprises and Their Impact on Economic Development: The Case of Kosovo

1. Introduction

Entrepreneurship is an important driver of economic growth. It creates new jobs and new economic opportunities, drives innovation and stimulates competition.

Entrepreneurs in the agricultural sector can introduce new technologies and practices that improve agricultural productivity and efficiency, leading to higher yields and profitability (Kharga et al., 2021).

Research has shown that by introducing innovation and knowledge spillovers, entrepreneurship can significantly contribute to economic growth, by increasing diversity and competition between firms (Ahlstrom et al., 2019; Si et al., 2020; Tomzawa et al., 2020; Muhammad et al., 2017; He et al., 2019; Hongbin et al., 2009). Rural entrepreneurs differ from other types of entrepreneurs in that they use and develop local resources to promote the local economy (Muller & Korsgaard, 2018; Soleymani et al., 2021; Pato & Teixeira, 2018; Saadatmandy & Barberi, 2019).

However, some studies report that entrepreneurship and economic development are negatively correlated. For example, it has been reported that entrepreneurial activities have a heterogeneous impact on economic growth in some provinces (Xu et al., 2021), and entrepreneurship has no significant impact in high-income countries, but a significantly positive impact in low-income countries (Stam et al., 2011). Other studies have reported mixed findings on the role of entrepreneurship in economic growth (Stam, 2008; Parker, 2009).

In Kosovo, as in many other European countries, agriculture is comprised of family farms that are part of a broader structure that includes forestry and rural development, all managed and overseen by families. This dynamic means that the entire burden of risk rests on the shoulders of these families, underscoring their central role. Therefore, agriculture is the most prominent segment of the economy and occupies a special place in Kosovo's development policy. Agricultural enterprises form a 'golden triangle' between farmers, the processing industry and consumers.

In the annals of Kosovo's economic history, agriculture has always been a cornerstone. It is characterized by small livestock, high expenditure on inputs, below-average productivity, inadequate infrastructure and a lack of effective extension services (Miftari et al., 2011). Furthermore, accounting plays a subordinate role in farming in Kosovo (Shkodra et al., 2011), and the fact that rural businesses often do not realize the importance of analyzing financial statements is a recurring theme in various studies (Shkodra et al., 2011; Ismajli & Shkodra, 2012; Shkodra et al., 2016). This problem is exacerbated by the fact that credit is touted as a key tool to increase agricultural production and revenue; paradoxically, interest rates for agricultural loans in Kosovo are consistently higher than those for other sectors of the economy (Shkodra & Shkodra, 2018).

In essence, entrepreneurship serves as an economic engine that transforms knowledge into innovative products, new employment opportunities and emerging businesses. There are a large number of studies that examine the relationship between entrepreneurship and economic growth (Urbano & Aparicio, 2016; Boudreaux, 2019; Abebe & Gebremariam, 2021; Yeboah et al., 2015; Gyimah & Lussier, 2021). Rural entrepreneurship manifests as a channel for using local resources to stimulate local development. This lends itself to efficient resource allocation in rural areas, which is impervious even to economic policies. Beyond their local influence, rural entrepreneurs have a significant impact on national economic development. This undoubtedly means that rural entrepreneurs are key players in driving a country's economic progress. Burgeoning rural entrepreneurship promotes self-employment opportunities and the expansion of industrial and economic activities while optimizing the use of resources and the local labor pool (Abey & Velmurugan, 2020; Koyana & Mason, 2017).

Agricultural entrepreneurship equips unemployed rural youth with the skills to start businesses and excel in agricultural businesses. Agricultural entrepreneurs can be defined as farmers who are engaged full-time or part-time in a variety of agricultural tasks as their main source of income. These visionaries are characterized by their ownership of farms, their constant vigilance and their tireless zeal for innovation. Their technological skills, coupled with their unwavering commitment to continuous professional development, enable them to recognize market trends and contemporary innovations. The vitality of entrepreneurship proves essential for farmers seeking to add value to their farms. Such endeavors require adaptation to new technologies. This development underscores the fact that the role of agriculture is evolving beyond mere food production to become an active participant in the holistic development of rural regions (Choudhury & Easwaran, 2019).

A review of the literature reveals a large number of studies that examine the relationship between entrepreneurship and sustainable, long-term economic growth (Abebe & Gebremariam, 2021; Boudreaux, 2019; Boohene & Agyapong, 2017; Deller et al., 2019; Dunne et al., 2016; Starchenko et al., 2024), question whether new rural ventures constitute effective rural entrepreneurship or are merely entrepreneurial ventures in rural settings (Pato & Teixeira, 2018) and explore rural interpreters and poverty alleviation (Sarkar, 2018; Sutter, et al., 2019; Si et al., 2020; [36–38]). This is particularly evident in poverty alleviation, where agricultural efforts have multiple benefits. The economic contribution of agriculture is widely recognized.

Beyond the agricultural sector, the emergence of microfinance institutions has proven to be a transformative force in the alleviation of poverty and a catalyst for economic development. One pioneering study highlights the significant progress made through these institutions, particularly in the context of rural areas, where their influence has been a beacon of change (Shkodra, 2019).

Scholars agree on the central role of entrepreneurship in economic growth. A wealth of research highlights the central role of entrepreneurship in rural areas, its contribution to the livelihoods of rural people and its crucial role in overall economic growth. Entrepreneurship acts as a catalyst for economic progress by fostering increased competition, knowledge diffusion and diversified economic landscapes (Yeboah et al., 2015). This is echoed in further research that highlights the transformative power of rural entrepreneurship in shaping the recovery of impoverished areas (Chandrahasa, 2016). Another study portrays the design and implementation of a rural entrepreneurship strategy in a depopulated area, engaging civil society to participate by adapting the 'Working with People' model to the idiosyncratic conditions of the context (Lopez et al., 2019). This study then considers the main factors of this strategy by analyzing its application in a wider area in the province of Ávila, Spain. We note that rural entrepreneurship can be enriched by strategies designed and evaluated by its beneficiaries in the early stages of development.

These studies deal with the vast tableau of rural development, which is a complex subject that not only involves agricultural investments but also infrastructural development, education and healthcare. It is clear that rural development can suffer if rural youth are unable to pursue entrepreneurship as a career path. Ways to increase motivation, and provide better education and a supportive infrastructure are critical to promote entrepreneurship. Rural development is also impacted by market regulation and government funding. Although evaluation and standardization can refine and enhance the impact of rural development, this is not limited to the government's involvement. The rural community interacts with social clubs, educational institutions and non-governmental organizations, which all promote rural entrepreneurs and offer them a sustainable opportunity to contribute to the macro-economic development of their home countries. Thus, rural entrepreneurs do not act alone, but as a collective; every effort and innovation contributes to national progress. Rural landscapes become epicenters of economic activity, rich with potential and reflecting the vibrancy of diverse communities.

To summarize, the existing literature in developed and developing countries has thoroughly examined the impact of entrepreneurship on economic development, providing a solid foundation for the research of this paper, which is the first to examine Kosovo.

Our study contributes to the literature on agricultural entrepreneurship and economic growth in two ways. First, we provide new insights into the impact of agricultural enterprises on economic growth. Second, we focus on socioeconomic variables and examine how the impact of agricultural entrepreneurship on economic growth varies over time.

2. Material and Methods

The successful realization of this study's objectives was supported by a methodological approach, in which descriptive and analytical elements were seamlessly intertwined to achieve a multi-layered panorama of findings. These two facets were combined to explore the intricate dynamics of the influence of rural businesses on Kosovo's economic development from 2008 to 2020.

The study hypothesizes that rural businesses contribute to economic development in general and in rural areas in particular. Specifically, it addresses questions such as: What is the impact of agricultural enterprises on economic development? How do agricultural enterprises contribute to employment, exports and economic development?

The descriptive dimension of the methodology served as a gateway to understanding the scope and nuances of the influence of rural businesses. Descriptive data was gathered to describe the rural businesses environment. These data spanned multiple dimensions and highlighted the evolution, challenges and successes of businesses. These data were sourced from annual reports from the Ministry of Agriculture and publications by the World Bank, Eurostat and statistical offices. The data form a comprehensive mosaic of the development of rural enterprises.

The analytical component of the methodology of this study was adapted from previous research (Aparicio et al., 2016; Khyareh & Amini, 2021). Of central importance was the careful econometric analyzes, a challenging task that was performed using Minitab 20 software. The focus was on multiple regression (Stanic & Racic, 2019; Samiyu, 2021) and correlation analysis (Shkodra et al., 2022) to analyze and understand the complicated relationships between the variables. The analysis provided the key to deciphering the web of influences and interactions linking rural factors to broader economic growth. The compilation of research sources from an extensive literature on the topic, is an example of a careful synthesis of knowledge. Annual reports from government agencies, such as the Ministry of Agriculture, and scientific publications from global institutions, such as the World Bank, Eurostat and statistical offices, enriched the basis of the study. This mixture of different sources lent the study credibility, emphasized its comprehensive character and enabled a fusion of insights from different fields.

Minitab was used for statistical analysis. Multiple regression analysis was performed to decipher the intricate relationships and causal connections between the variables. In parallel, correlation analysis was used to understand how the different factors interacted. This methodology acted not just as an academic endeavor, but as a living exploration that impacted the real world. By employing a sophisticated method of analysis, the study was able to go beyond the theoretical realm to provide a tangible account of how rural factors contribute to economic growth in Kosovo.

The methodology of our study involved a comprehensive examination of a wide range of demographic data, selected to decipher the intricate dynamics of economic development in the chosen context. These data were carefully selected to identify variables and to capture the essence of economic progress and its multi-layered interplay.

We used GDP as a dependent variable, because it is an important indicator of a nation's economic vitality. This choice was based on the use of GDP as a barometer of economic health, capturing the total value of goods and services within a nation's borders. This, in turn, allowed us to investigate the history of Kosovo's economic development.

In parallel, we examined the themes of economic and rural enterprises, which were carefully selected to reflect the scope of our research topic. The history of economic growth is often closely intertwined with the history of entrepreneurship, and our study took this connection into account by positioning economic and rural enterprises as meaningful indicators for this thematic underpinning. These elements were deliberately chosen to represent the entrepreneurial backbone of our chosen context, fitting into the overarching narrative of our study and seamlessly reinforcing the multi-layered dynamics at play.

The study also covered the important aspect of employment, which is a measure of the companies' effectiveness in creating wealth. This dimension was carefully examined to determine the extent to which economic and rural enterprises tangibly benefit the population. By examining employment, we sought to understand how these businesses were translating their economic contributions into real improvements, underlining their role as drivers of prosperity.

Because exports are one of the foundations of a nation's economy, we took exports as an independent variable. This decision was based on the realization that exports in the intricate web of global trade contribute to a nation's economic vitality. By looking at exports as a standalone variable, our methodology allowed us to understand the nuanced interplay between this fundamental economic pillar and the broader fabric of development.

3. Results and Discussion

There is a perfect correlation (p = 0.000) between GDP and employment, with a correlation of 0.892, and between economic enterprise and rural enterprises, with a strong correlation of 0.937. We also report a strong positive correlation between GDP and economic enterprises (p = 0.00; correlation = 0.869); GDP and rural enterprises (p = 0.003; correlation = 0.805); GDP and exports (p = 0.001; correlation = 0.861); economic enterprises and employment (p-value = 0.023; correlation = 0.673); business enterprises and exports (p = 0.033; correlation = 0.644); rural enterprises and employment (p = 0.043; correlation = 0.617) and employment and exports (p = 0.006; correlation = 0.769) (Table 1).

Table 1: Correlation

	GDP	GDP in Agriculture	Economic enterprise	Agriculture enterprise	Employment
GDP in Agriculture	-0.187 0.583				
Economic enterprise	0.869 0.001	0.055 0.872			
Agriculture enterprise	0.805 0.003	0.271 0.420	0.937 0.000		
Employment	0.892 0.000	-0.182 0.591	0.673 0.023	0.617 0.043	
Export	0.861 0.001	-0.056 0.869	0.644 0.033	0.612 0.045	0.769 0.006

Pearson Correlation and P-value

Determination involves how changes in the dependent variables are explained by the independent variables. The coefficient of determination R-squared is 98.16 % (Table 2). This means that 98.16 % of the change in GDP (dependent variable) is explained by the GDP of agriculture, business enterprises, rural enterprises, employment and agriculture exports (independent variables), while 1.84 % of the factors in the model remain unexplained.

Table 2: Model summary

S	R-sq	R-sq (adj)	R-sq (pred)
164447	98.16 %	96.93 %	90.82 %

Source: Prepared by the author.

Based on the model $Y_i = \beta_{0+}\ \beta 1X1+\beta 2X2+\beta 3X3+\beta 4X4+ e_i$
results in:

$$GDP = 2384315 - 4.93\ GDP\ in\ agriculture + 1411\ Agriculture\ enterprise + 11.74\ Employment + 4.57\ Agriculture\ export$$

The most important factors influencing economic growth are agricultural holdings, employment and agriculture exports. With the increase in GDP per unit, rural farms increase by 141, with the increase in GDP per unit, employment increase by 11.74, while exports increase by 4.57 for every increase in GDP. However, we see that the value of GDP in agriculture is (-4.93), which shows that the increase in GDP per unit has an impact on the decrease in GDP in agriculture.

Multiple regression analysis was performed with GDP as the dependent variable and GDP of agriculture, business enterprises, rural enterprises, employment and agriculture exports as independent variables (Table 3). This analysis allowed us to understand the role of rural activities, especially rural enterprises, in the economic development of Kosovo. From the analysis, the significant variable in the model is each, with the p-value of rural enterprises being 0.001, indicating that it plays an extremely significant role. GDP also plays a significant role, followed by the other variables, as shown in Table 3, where other indicators, such as the coefficient, SE coefficient, and value of T and VIF, are listed.

Table 3: Regression analysis

Term	Coefficient	SE Coefficient	T-Value	P-Value	VIF
Constant	2384315	1439388	1.66	0.149	
GDP in agriculture	-4.93	1.29	-3.83	0.009	1.37
Agriculture enterprise	1411	238	5.93	0.001	2.28
Employment	11.74	3.82	3.07	0.022	3.11
Export	4.57	1.32	3.47	0.013	2.65

Source: Prepared by the author.

4. Conclusions

This study created a model based on the background of agricultural enterprises in economic development in Kosovo, to empirically examine the impact of rural entrepreneurship on economic development, using selected variables for the years 2008–2020. The main conclusions of the study are:

First, the results of the correlation tests showed that the development of agricultural enterprises in Kosovo has a significantly positive effect on economic development and is highly clustered, while the correlation of agricultural enterprises in rural areas is low clustering. This demonstrates that, although there is a strong development dynamic of rural entrepreneurship in rural areas, it is still in the initial phase and the model of rural entrepreneurship needs to be further optimized. Second, the regression results indicated that agricultural enterprises in rural areas have a significant direct effect on promoting local economic growth and also have a significant impact on the economic development of the country as a whole. Third, the results of the coefficient of determination R-squared indicated that agriculture, business enterprises, rural enterprises, employment and exports have a significant relationship with GDP, which shows that agricultural enterprises have a great weight in economic development.

4.1. Policy Recommendations

Based on our research, we propose the following policy measures:

The government should provide incentives and special support measures to create a favorable environment for agricultural enterprises, such as favorable tax policies or the creation of a rural enterprise support group. Furthermore, the government should start a fund to mitigate the risks involved in agricultural enterprises. Such a fund could reduce the entry barriers for agricultural enterprises, increase the enthusiasm of agricultural workers and attract new entrepreneurs.

4.2. Limitations and Scope for Future Research

Although this study provides some important results and contributes to the existing literature, there are still some limitations and scope for future research. First, efforts must be made to find more objective indicators that represent the economic development of farms. Second, the impact of innovation on the development of rural enterprises and its impact on economic development should be investigated.

4.3. Acknowledgments

This research received no external funding.

4.4. Conflict of Interest

There was no conflict of interest in the submission of this manuscript, and the manuscript was approved for publication by all authors.

References

Abebe, G. K., & Gebremariam, T. A. (2021). Challenges for Entrepreneurship Development in Rural Economies: The Case of Micro and Small-scale Enterprises in Ethiopia. *Small Enterprise Research*, *28*(1), 36. https://doi.org/10.1080/13215906.2021.1878385

Abey, J., & Velmugan, R. (2020). Obstacles Mentioned by the Rural Entrepreneurs in Central Districts of Tamilandu. *Journal of Critical Reviews*, *7*(3), 230. http://dx.doi.org/10.31838/jcr.07.03.42

Ahlstrom, D., Chang, A. Y., & Cheung, J. S. (2019). Encouraging Entrepreneurship and Economic Growth. *Journal of Risk and Financial Management*, *12*(4), 178. https://doi.org/10.3390/jrfm12040178

Aparicio, S., Urbano, D., & Audretsch, D. (2016). Institutional Factors, Opportunity Entrepreneurship and Economic Growth: Panel Data Evidence. *Technological Recasting and Social Change*, *102*, 45. https://doi.org/10.1016/j.techfore.2015.04.006

Boohene, R., & Agyapong, D. (2017). Rural Entrepreneurship in African Countries: A Synthesis of Related Literature. *Journal of Small Business and*

Entrepreneurship Development, *5*(1), 43. https://doi.org/10.15640/jsbed.v5n1a5

Boudreaux, C. J. (2019). Entrepreneurship, Institutions, and Economic Growth: Does the Level of Development Matter? https://doi.org/10.48550/arXiv.1903.02934

Chandrahasa, R. (2016). Challenges, Problems, Opportunities and Skills for Successful Rural Entrepreneurship in India. *Indian Journal of Research*, *5*, 405.

Choudhury, K., & Easwaran, K. (2019). Agricultural Entrepreneurship in Lower Brahmaputra Valley, Assam. *Journal of Global Entreprenuership Research*, *9*(59). https://doi.org/10.1186/s40497-019-0179-x

Deller, S., Kures, M., & Contoy, T. (2019). Rural Entrepreneurship and Migration. *Journal of Rural Studies*, *66*, 30. https://doi.org/10.1016/j.jrurstud.2019.01.026

Dunne, T. C., Aaron, J. R., Mcdowell, W. C., Urban, D. J., & Geho, P. R. (2016). The Impact of Leadership on Small Business Innovativeness. *Journal of Business Research*, *69*(11), 4876. https://doi.org/10.1016/j.jbusres.2016.04.046

Gyimah, P., & Lussier, R. N. (2021). Rural Entrepreneurship Success Factors: An Empirical Investigation in an Emerging Market. *Journal of Small Business Strategy*, *31*(4), 5. https://doi.org/10.53703/001c.29470

He, C., Lu, J., & Qian, H. (2019). Entrepreneurship in China. *Small Business Economics*, *52*(3), 563. https://doi.org/10.1007/s11187-017-9972-5

Hongbin, L., Zheyu, Y., Xianguo, Y., & Junsen, Z. (2009). *Entrepreneurship and Growth: Evidence from China*. Discussion Papers, Chinese University of Hong Kong, Department of Economics.

Ismajli, H., & Shkodra, J. (2012). The Analysis of Business Failure for Small and Medium Businesses in Kosovo. *International Journal of Economics and Finance Studies*, *4*(1), 101.

Kharga, B. D., Anindita, S., Pradhan, K., & Rakesh, R. (2021). Focusing the Relationship of Net Profit with the Determinant Attributes of Rural Entrepreneurs. *Indian Journal of Extension Education*, *57*(2), 135.

Khyareh, M. M., & Amini, H. (2021). Governance Quality, Entrepreneurship and Economic Growth. *Journal of Competitiveness*, *13*(2), 41. https://doi.org/10.7441/joc.2021.02.03

Koyana, S., & Mason, R. B. (2017). Rural Entrepreneurship and Transformation: The Role of Learnerships. *International Journal of Entrepreneurial Behavior, Research*. https://doi.org/10.1108/IJEBR-07-2016-0207

Lopez, M., Cazorla, A., & Panta, M. D. P. (2019). Rural Entrepreneurship Strategies: Empirical Experience in the Northern Sub-Plateau of Spain. *Sustainability*, *11*(5), 1243. https://doi.org/10.3390/su11051243

Miftari, I., Ahmeti, S., Gjonbalaj, M., & Shkodra, J. (2011). The Role of Demographic and Socioeconomic Factors on Consumption Patterns and Demand for Dairy Products in Kosovo. Anadolu International Conference in Economic.

Muhammad, N., Mcelwee, G., & Dana, P. (2017). Barriers to the Development and Progress of Entrepreneurship in Rural Pakistan. *International Journal of Entrepreneurial Behavior Research*. https://doi.org/10.1108/IJEBR-08-2016-0246

Müller, S., & Korsgaard, S. (2018). Resources and Bridging: The Role of Spatial Context in Rural Entrepreneurship. *Entrepreneurship, Regional Development*, (30), 224. https://doi.org/10.1080/08985626.2017.1402092

Parker, S. (2009). *The Economics of Entrepreneurship*. London, Cambridge University Press.

Pato, L., & Teixeira, A. A. C. (2018). Rural Entrepreneurship: The Tale of a Rare Event. *Journal of Place Management and Development*, *11*(1), 46. https://doi.org/10.1108/JPMD-08-2017-0085

Saadatmand, Y., & Barberi, D. (2019). Globalization, Gender and Entrepreneurial Activities in Latin America. *Journal of Developmental Entrepreneurship*, *24*(04), 36–45.

Samiyu, M. (2021). Multiple Regression Model for Predicting GDP Using Macroeconomic Variables. *1*, 13. https://doi.org/10.1142/S1084946719500249

Sarkar, S. (2018). Entrepreneurs and Social Change at the Bottom of the Pyramid: The Role of Bricolage. *Entrepreneurship, Regional Development*, *30*(4), 421. https://doi.org/10.1080/08985626.2017.1413773

Shkodra, J. (2019). Financial Performance of Microfinance Institutions in Kosovo. *Journal of International Studies*, *12*(3), 31. https://doi.org/10.14254/2071-8330.2019/12-3/3

Shkodra, J., & Shkodra, L. (2018). Impact of Agricultural Finance in Rural Areas–Case Study Kosovo. *Bulgarian Journal of Agricultural Science*, *24*(5), 737.

Shkodra, J., Gjonbalaj, M., Beqiri, V., & Miftari, I. (2011). The Role of Financial Analysis in Agriculture Farms in Kosovo. *International Journal of Arts, Sciences*, *4*(26), 157.

Shkodra, J., Ismajli, H., & Rexhepi, S. (2011). Implementing Accounting in Agricultural Farms in Kosovo. *Revista Economica*, *6*(59). https://ssrn.com/abstract=2847870.

Shkodra, J., Krasniqi, A., & Ahmeti, N. (2022). The Impact of Government Expenditure on Economic Growth in Southeast European Countries. *Journal of Management Information and Decision Sciences*, *25*(S1), 1.

Shkodra, J., Pllana, M., & Gjoka, E. (2016). The Lack of Financial Statement Application in Kosovo's Farms and Its Consequences. *ILIRIA International Review, 3*(2), 391. https://ssrn.com/abstract=2851500

Si, S., Cullen, J., Ahlstrom, D., & Wei, J. (2020). Business, Entrepreneurship and Innovation Toward Poverty Reduction. *Entrepreneurship, Regional Development, 32*(1–2), 1. https://doi.org/10.1080/08985626.2019.1640485

Soleymani, A., Farani, A. Y., Karimi, S., Azadi, H., Nadiri, H., & Scheffran, J. (2021). Identifying Sustainable Rural Entrepreneurship Indicators in the Iranian Context. *Journal of Cleaner Production, 290*, 125186. https://doi.org/10.1016/j.jclepro.2020.125186

Stam, E. (2008). *Entrepreneurship and Innovation Policy: Micro-Foundations for Innovation Policy* (p. 135). Amsterdam/Chicago: Amsterdam UniversityPress/Chicago University Press. https://hdl.handle.net/10419/25694

Stam, E., Hartog, C., Van, S. A., & Thurik, R. (2011). *Ambitious Entrepreneurship, High-growth Firms and Macroeconomic Growth in the Dynamics of Entrepreneurship: Evidence from Global Entrepreneurship Monitor Data* (p. 231). Oxford, UK: Oxford University Press. https://doi.org/10.1093/acprof:oso/9780199580866.003.0011

Stanic, S., & Racic, Ž. V. (2019). Analysis of Macroeconomic Factors Effect to Gross Domestic Product of Bosnia and Herzegovina Using the Multiple Linear Regression Model. *Economics, 7*(2), 91. https://doi.org/10.2478/eoik-2019-0022

Starchenko, G., Ostrovska, N., Garbazhii, K., Kotelevets, D., Nykoniuk, K., & Amirkhanian, H. (2024). Tools of the State Business Support in the Context of Sustainable Development. *Management Theory and Studies for Rural Business and Infrastructure Development, 46*(1), 15–22. https://doi.org/10.15544/mts.2024.02

Sutter, C., Bruton, G. D., & Chen, J. (2019). Entrepreneurship as a Solution to Extreme Poverty: A Review and Future Research Directions. *Journal of Business Venturing, 34* (1), 197. https://doi.org/10.1016/j.jbusvent.2018.06.003

Tomizawa, A., Zhao, L., Bassellier, G., & Ahlstrom, D. (2020). Economic Growth, Innovation, Institutions and the Great Enrichment. *Asia Pacific Journal of Management,* (37), 7. https://doi.org/10.1007/s10490-019-09648-2

Urbano, D., & Aparicio, S. (2016). Entrepreneurship Capital Types and Economic Growth: International Evidence. *Technological Forecasting and Social Change, 102*, 34. https://doi.org/10.1016/j.techfore.2015.02.018

Xu, B., Yu, H., & Li, L. (2021). The Impact of Entrepreneurship on Regional Economic Growth: A Perspective of Spatial Heterogeneity. *Entrepreneurship, Regional Development*, 33, 309. https://doi.org/10.1080/08985626.2021.1872940

Yeboah, A. E., Mussah, S. I. J., Bawole, J. N., & Nurudeen S. (2015). The "third sector" and Poverty Reduction in Developing Societies: The Experience of Hunger Project in Selected Rural Communities of Ghana. *International Journal of Rural Management, 11*(2), 85. https://doi.org/10.1177/0973005215601944

Constantinos Challoumis

Comparing the Cycle of Money: Rewarding Taxes and the Impact Factor of Education

1. Introduction

This chapter compares the cycle of money firstly with the implementation of rewarding taxes considering the impact factor of education and secondly without them. The impact factor of education facilitates uncontrolled transactions, making it essential for driving the economic dynamics of any economy. The analysis leads to conclusions on the significance of this impact factor, employing the Q.E. method (Challoumis, 2018b, 2018c). The chapter aims to compare the cycle of money with all rewarding taxes and without the impact factor of education. It examines two scenarios: one incorporating the impact factors of education and one excluding them. By analyzing these cases, conclusions are drawn on the importance of the education impact factor in the economy using the Q.E. method. This impact factor relates to the administration of the public sector's influence on the private sector and the return of taxes to the market through education.

The education system is a cornerstone of societal development and economic prosperity. It equips individuals with the knowledge, skills, and critical thinking abilities necessary to navigate and contribute to an increasingly complex world (Challoumis, 2019a, 2021a; Leimbach, Kriegler, Roming, & Schwanitz, 2017; Miailhe, 2017; Moreno-Jiménez, Pérez-Espés, & Velázquez, 2014; Spiel, Schober, & Strohmeier, 2018; Woody & Viney, 2017). Quality education fosters innovation, drives economic growth, and enhances the overall quality of life. It serves as a foundation for a skilled workforce, which is essential for industries to thrive and compete globally. Additionally, education promotes social cohesion and reduces inequalities by providing equal opportunities for all individuals to succeed. Investment in education not only benefits individuals but also strengthens communities and nations, making it a pivotal element in building a sustainable and prosperous future (Acs, Åstebro, Audretsch, & Robinson, 2016; Androniceanu, Gherghina, & Ciobănașu, 2019; Engström et al., 2020; Kartini, Mulyawan, & Muradi, 2019; Khan & Liu, 2019; Kroth, Geremia, & Mussio, 2020; Marenco, Strohschoen, & Joner, 2017; Noland, 2020).

2. Literature Review

It should be noted that companies involved in controlled transactions, as well as tax authority inspections, operate under the condition of proportional adjustments. This means that companies engaged in controlled transactions often lack appropriate data and comparable uncontrolled transactions under similar circumstances. As a result, they adjust their data proportionally. If the tested companies determine that the profits and losses from uncontrolled transactions are significantly higher or lower, they apply a proportional analogy to compare these figures with their data. The production of goods or services generates profits and costs for the companies.

$$u = s(zf + \tilde{z}d) \tag{1}$$

$$z = |\tilde{z} - 1| \tag{2}$$

The symbol u represents the impact factor of the comparability analysis applied to $\boldsymbol{s}$. The symbol z is a coefficient ranging between 0 and 1, with its value determined by the influence of the method (using the best method rule) on $\boldsymbol{s}$. The symbol $\boldsymbol{f}$ denotes the cost arising from the production of goods, while the symbol $\boldsymbol{d}$ denotes the cost associated with the distribution of goods.

$$u_c = zf + \tilde{z}d \tag{3}$$

$$\mathrm{b} = (\mathrm{p} - u_c) * j_1 \tag{4}$$

The symbol of b in the prior equation is about the amount of taxes that should be paid to the companies of controlled transactions in the application of the arm's length principle. The u_c is the amount of tax obligations that can be avoided through the allocations of profits and losses. Moreover, j_1 is a coefficient for the rate of taxes. Then, the equation (4) shows the case of the arm's length principle.

$$v = \mathrm{p}^* j_2 \tag{5}$$

The symbol of v in the previous equation shows the taxes that should be paid to the enterprises of controlled transactions in the application of the fixed length principle. Then, j_2 is a coefficient for the rate of taxes in the case of the fixed length principle.

$$v \geq b \tag{6}$$

The tax for the companies that participate in controlled transactions of transfer pricing in the case of the fixed length principle is higher or at least equal to that of the case of the arm's length principle. According to the fixed length principle, it is plausible to recover the tax losses of the global tax revenue from the controlled transactions of the transfer pricing. The next scheme illustrates the procedure that companies of controlled transactions follow for their allocations of profits and losses, the proportional adjustments of data, and the fixed length principle.

3. The Cycle of Money

The tax revenues correspond to the savings that the companies could have if the taxes were avoided. The way that these savings are administrated is different from case to case. Then the benefits of the companies could be managed in a completely different way, as could be saved or could be taxed. The theory of cycle of money shows when the savings robust the economy and when the taxes robust the economy. There is a separation of savings into the non-returned savings (or escaped savings) and the returned savings (or enforcement savings). For the scope of this analysis below are demonstrated the equations which are:

$$\alpha = \alpha_s + \alpha_t, \text{or}, \ \frac{1}{v} + \alpha_t \tag{7}$$

$$x_m = m - a \tag{8}$$

$$\mathrm{m} = \mu + \alpha_p \tag{9}$$

$$\mu = \sum_{\iota=0}^{n} \mu_\iota \tag{10}$$

$$\alpha_p = \sum_{j=0}^{m} \alpha_{pj} \tag{11}$$

$$c_m = \frac{dx_m}{da} \tag{12}$$

$$c_\alpha = \frac{dx_m}{dm} \tag{13}$$

$$c_y = c_m - c_\alpha \tag{14}$$

The variable of α is symbolized the case of the escaped savings (Challoumis, 2022, 2023a, 2023c, 2023f, 2024d). This means that there are savings that are not returning to the economy or come back after a long-term period. The variable of α_s symbolizes the case that there are escaped savings that come from transfer pricing activities (Challoumis, 2018a, 2019b, 2021b, 2023b, 2023d, 2023e, 2024a, 2024b, 2024c). The variable of α_t is symbolizes the case that the escaped savings not from transfer pricing activities but from any other commercial activity. For instance α_t could refer to the commercial activities that come from uncontrolled transactions. The variable of m symbolizes the financial liquidity in an economy. The variable of μ symbolizes the consumption in an economy. The variable of α_p symbolizes the enforcement savings, which come from the citizens and small and medium-sized enterprises. The variable of x_m symbolizes the condition of financial liquidity in an economy. The variable of c_m symbolizes the velocity of financial liquidity increases or decreases. The variable of c_α symbolizes the velocity of escaped savings. Therefore, the variable of c_y symbolizes the term of the cycle of money. Thereupon, the cycle of money shows the level of the dynamic of an economy and its robustness. It is observed that the cycle of money expands when a tax system is implemented that follows the fixed length principle, allowing for lower taxation of uncontrolled transactions and higher taxation of controlled transactions. It should be noted that uncontrolled transactions include financial liquidity for citizens and small to medium-sized companies.

4. Analysis and Results

For the mathematical approach to the cycle of money:

$$\alpha_p = \alpha_r + \alpha_n * h_n + \alpha_m * h_m \tag{15}$$

$$\alpha_r \geq \alpha_n * h_n \geq \alpha_m * h_m \tag{16}$$

In the prior two equations used some impact factors, which are the a_p, and the variables α_r, α_n, h_n, α_m and the h_m. The variable α_r symbolizes the impact factor of the rest rewarding taxes. The symbol of α_n is the impact factor of education and any technical knowledge. The symbol of α_m is about the impact factor of education anything relevant and supporting of this issue. The symbol of h_n, and of the h_m, are the coefficients of the education and the education impact factor accordingly.

Table 1: Compiling coefficients (author's results)

Factors	**Values**	**Values'**
α_s	0.6	0.6
α_t	0.7	0.7
μ	0.9	0.9
α_r	0.4	0.4
α_n*h_n	0.3	-
α_m*h_m	0.2	0.2

The generator of this procedure used the coefficients which appeared in the previous table. Therefore, the factors have an upper limit of 1, and a lower limit of 0, (see Table 1) but s and $\tilde{s}$ are plausible to receive values greater than one as their mathematical structure allows this. After 461 iterations the following diagram:

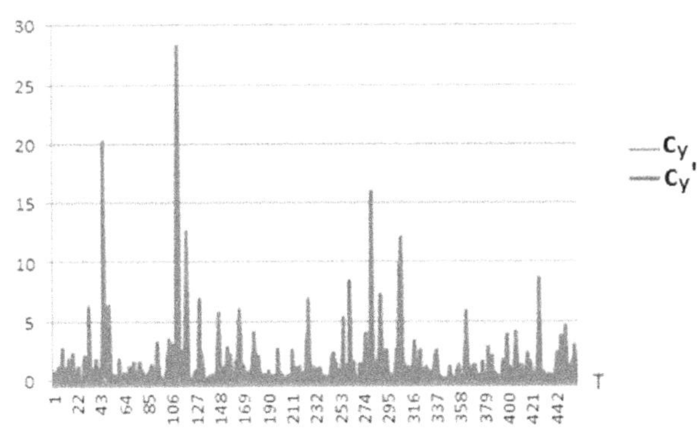

Figure 1: Money cycle with and without the impact factor of education (author's results)

The applied method is the Q.E. (see Figure 1) methodology. An economy with structural education issues exhibits diminished economic dynamism. This indicates that education-related taxes are classified as supportive taxes within the economy.

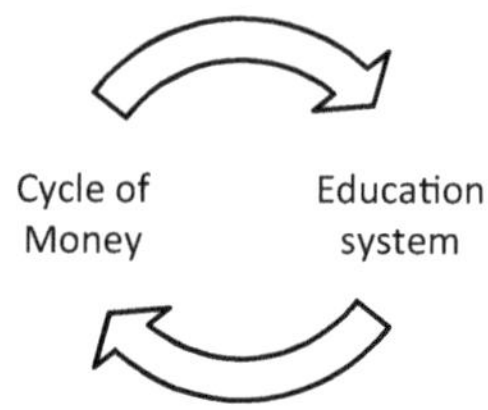

Figure 2: Money cycle and education system (author's results)

Consequently, an economy with limited education infrastructure at any level experiences a negative impact on its overall robustness (see Figure 2).

Table 2: Education on the money cycle (author's table)

Aspect	Observation
Impact Factor of Education	Significantly influences the cycle of money.
Economic Dynamism	Diminished in economies with structural education problems.
Classification of Education-Related Taxes	Considered supportive taxes that bolster the economy.
Education Infrastructure	Limited education infrastructure at any level adversely affects economic robustness.
Overall Economic Robustness	Negatively influenced by inadequate education infrastructure, weakening the economic structure and performance.

5. Conclusions

It is observed that education supports the private sector and strengthens the economy as anticipated. Thus, the impact factor of education contributes significantly to economic growth. An educated society enhances the market and the economic dynamics of any environment. Consequently, the education system positively impacts market expansion (Bowling, Boyland, & Kirkeby, 2019; Delgado Rodríguez & de Lucas Santos, 2018; Montmarquette, 2020; Nicoleta Dospinescu, 2019; Oueslati, 2015; Silva, Silvestre, & Amaral, 2020; Tvaronavičienė, Tarkhanova, & Durglishvili, 2018).

The tax for this purpose is considered one of the few taxes that significantly aid economic growth. The impact of education on the economy extends beyond direct support to the private sector. Improved education infrastructure leads to increased productivity, reduced absenteeism, and a more resilient workforce. These factors collectively enhance the efficiency and output of businesses, thereby driving economic performance. Additionally, a robust education system attracts investment, as companies prefer stable environments with accessible education for their employees.

Moreover, the economic benefits of a strong education system are reflected in the long-term sustainability of the economy. Education-related expenditures, while initially a cost, ultimately result in savings by preventing expensive treatments and managing chronic diseases effectively. This proactive approach reduces the economic burden on both the public and private sectors. In conclusion, the education system's role in supporting and expanding the economy is multifaceted. It not only boosts the private sector and market dynamics but also contributes to a stable and sustainable economic environment. The positive effect of education-related taxes underscores their importance in economic policy, highlighting the need for continued investment in education to ensure ongoing economic growth and resilience.

References

Acs, Z., Åstebro, T., Audretsch, D., & Robinson, D. T. (2016). Public Policy to Promote Entrepreneurship: A Call to Arms. *Small Business Economics*, *47*(1). Retrieved from https://doi.org/10.1007/s11187-016-9712-2

Androniceanu, A., Gherghina, R., & Ciobănașu, M. (2019). The Interdependence between Fiscal Public Policies and Tax Evasion. *Administratie Si Management Public*, *2019*(32). Retrieved from https://doi.org/10.24818/amp/2019.32-03

Bowling, S. J., Boyland, L. G., & Kirkeby, K. M. (2019). Property Tax Cap Policy in Indiana and Implications for Public School Funding Equity. *International Journal of Education Policy and Leadership*, *15*(9). Retrieved from https://doi.org/10.22230/ijepl.2019v15n9a881

Challoumis, C. (2018a). Methods of Controlled Transactions and the Behavior of Companies According to the Public and Tax Policy. *Economics*, *6*(1), 33–43. Retrieved from https://doi.org/10.2478/eoik-2018-0003

Challoumis, C. (2018b). Q.E. (Quantification of Everything) Method and Econometric Analysis. *SSRN Electronic Journal*. Retrieved from https://doi.org/10.2139/ssrn.3150101

Challoumis, C. (2018c). Quantification of Everything (A Methodology for Quantification of Quality Data with Application and to Social and Theoretical Sciences). *SSRN Electronic Journal*, 1–8. Retrieved from https://doi.org/10.2139/ssrn.3136014

Challoumis, C. (2019a). The Issue of Utility of Cycle of Money. *Journal Association SEPIKE*, *2019*(25), 12–21. Retrieved from https://5b925ea6-3d4e-400b-b5f3-32dc681218ff.filesusr.com/ugd/b199e2_dd29716b8bec48ca8fe7fbcfd47cdd2e.pdf

Challoumis, C. (2019b). The R.B.Q. (Rational, Behavioral and Quantified) Model. *Ekonomika*, *98*(1), 6–18. Retrieved from https://doi.org/10.15388/ekon.2019.1.1

Challoumis, C. (2021a). Index of the Cycle of Money – The Case of Latvia. *Economics and Culture*, *17*(2), 5–12. Retrieved from https://doi.org/10.2478/jec-2020-0015

Challoumis, C. (2021b). Index of the Cycle of Money – The Case of Bulgaria. *Economic Alternatives*, *27*(2), 225–234. Retrieved from https://www.unwe.bg/doi/eajournal/2021.2/EA.2021.2.04.pdf

Challoumis, C. (2022). Conditions of the CM (Cycle of Money). In Social and Economic Studies within the Framework of Emerging Global Developments, Volume – 1, V. Kaya (pp. 13–24). Retrieved from https://doi.org/10.3726/b19907

Challoumis, C. (2023a). A Comparison of the Velocities of Minimum Escaped Savings and Financial Liquidity. In Social and Economic Studies within the Framework of Emerging Global Developments, Volume – 4, V. Kaya (pp. 41–56). Retrieved from https://doi.org/10.3726/b21202

Challoumis, C. (2023b). From Savings to Escape and Enforcement Savings. *Cogito*, *XV*(4), 206–216.

Challoumis, C. (2023c). Impact Factor of Liability of Tax System According to the Theory of Cycle of Money. In Social and Economic Studies within the Framework of Emerging Global Developments Volume 3, V. Kaya (Vol. 3, pp. 31–42). Retrieved from https://doi.org/10.3726/b20968

Challoumis, C. (2023d). Index of the Cycle of Money: The Case of Costa Rica. *Sapienza*, *4*(3), 1–11. Retrieved from https://journals.sapienzaeditorial.com/index.php/SIJIS

Challoumis, C. (2023e). Risk on the Tax System of the E.U. from 2016 to 2022. *Economics*, *11*(2), 55–72.

Challoumis, C. (2023f). Utility of Cycle of Money without the Escaping Savings (Protection of the Economy). In Social and Economic Studies within the

Framework of Emerging Global Developments Volume 2, V. Kaya (pp. 53–64). Retrieved from https://doi.org/10.3726/b20509

Challoumis, C. (2024a). From Economics to Economic Engineering (The Cycle of Money): The Case of Romania. *Cogito, XVII*(2), 161–70.

Challoumis, C. (2024b). *Impact Factor of Liability Using the Sensitivity Method.* Peter Lang, Zurich.

Challoumis, C. (2024c). Index of the Cycle of Money – The Case of Switzerland. *Risk and Financial Management, 17*(4), 1–24. Retrieved from https://doi.org/https://doi.org/10.3390/jrfm17040135

Challoumis, C. (2024d). *Rewarding Taxes on the Cycle of Money: Social and Economic Studies within the Framework of Emerging Global Developments* (Vol. 5), Peter Lang, Zurich.

Delgado Rodríguez, M. J., & de Lucas Santos, S. (2018). Speed of Economic Convergence and EU Public Policy. *Cuadernos de Economia, 41*(115). Retrieved from https://doi.org/10.1016/j.cesjef.2017.01.001

Engström, G., Gars, J., Jaakkola, N., Lindahl, T., Spiro, D., & van Benthem, A. A. (2020). What Policies Address Both the Coronavirus Crisis and the Climate Crisis? *Environmental and Resource Economics, 76*(4). Retrieved from https://doi.org/10.1007/s10640-020-00451-y

Kartini, D. S., Mulyawan, R., & Muradi, M. (2019). Public Policy Pragmatism on Special Economic Zone in Tanjung Lesung, Pandeglang Regency. *MIMBAR : Jurnal Sosial Dan Pembangunan, 35*(1). Retrieved from https://doi.org/10.29313/mimbar.v35i1.4283

Khan, S., & Liu, G. (2019). Socioeconomic and Public Policy Impacts of China Pakistan Economic Corridor on Khyber Pakhtunkhwa. *Environmental Management and Sustainable Development, 8*(1). Retrieved from https://doi.org/10.5296/emsd.v8i1.13758

Kroth, D. C., Geremia, D. S., & Mussio, B. R. (2020). National School Feeding Program: A Healthy Public Policy. *Ciencia e Saude Coletiva, 25*(10). Retrieved from https://doi.org/10.1590/1413-812320202510.31762018

Leimbach, M., Kriegler, E., Roming, N., & Schwanitz, J. (2017). Future Growth Patterns of World Regions – A GDP Scenario Approach. *Global Environmental Change, 42*. Retrieved from https://doi.org/10.1016/j.gloenvcha.2015.02.005

Marenco, A., Strohschoen, M. T. B., & Joner, W. (2017). Capacidade estatal, burocracia e tributação nos municípios brasileiros. *Revista de Sociologia e Politica, 25*(64). Retrieved from https://doi.org/10.1590/1678-987317256401

Miailhe, N. (2017). Economic, Social and Public Policy Opportunities Enabled by Automation. *Field Actions Science Reports. The Journal of Field Actions*, Actions, *Vol. 71*(6), pp. 943–961.

Montmarquette, C. (2020). From Economic Analysis to Public Policies in the Economics of Education. *Revue Economique*. Retrieved from https://doi.org/10.3917/reco.716.0943

Moreno-Jiménez, J. M., Pérez-Espés, C., & Velázquez, M. (2014). E-Cognocracy and the Design of Public Policies. *Government Information Quarterly*, *31*(1). Retrieved from https://doi.org/10.1016/j.giq.2013.09.004

Nicoleta Dospinescu, O. D. (2019). A Profitability Regression Model in Financial Communication of Romanian Stock Exchange's Companies. *Asociația de Cooperare Cultural-Educațională Suceava*, *1(8)*, 1–4.

Noland, M. (2020). Protectionism under Trump: The China Shock, Deplorables, and the First White President. *Asian Economic Policy Review*. Retrieved from https://doi.org/10.1111/aepr.12274

Oueslati, W. (2015). Growth and Welfare Effects of Environmental Tax Reform and Public Spending Policy. *Economic Modelling*, *45*. Retrieved from https://doi.org/10.1016/j.econmod.2014.10.040

Silva, D. S., Silvestre, B. M., & Amaral, S. C. F. (2020). Assessing the Timemania Lottery as a Sports Public Policy. *Journal of Physical Education (Maringa)*, *31*(1). Retrieved from https://doi.org/10.4025/JPHYSEDUC.V31I1.3131

Spiel, C., Schober, B., & Strohmeier, D. (2018). Implementing Intervention Research into Public Policy – the "I3-approach." *Prevention Science*, *19*(3). Retrieved from https://doi.org/10.1007/s11121-016-0638-3

Tvaronavičienė, M., Tarkhanova, E., & Durglishvili, N. (2018). Sustainable Economic Growth and Innovative Development of Educational Systems. *Journal of International Studies*, *11*(1). Retrieved from https://doi.org/10.14254/2071-8330.2018/11-1/19

Woody, W. D., & Viney, W. (2017). A History of Psychology: The Emergence of Science and Applications, Sixth Edition. *A History of Psychology: The Emergence of Science and Applications, Sixth Edition*, 1–599. Retrieved 31 October 2022 from https://doi.org/10.4324/9781315544403/HISTORY-PSYCHOLOGY-WAYNE-VINEY-WILLIAM-DOUGLAS-WOODY

Eka Sepashvili, Tamar Mermanishvili, Patrizia Gazzola, and Daniele Grechi

The Relevance of Migration Processes on the Sustainable Development of the European Union

1. Introduction

Migration of People is one of the essential components of the modern global world and itis accompanied by both positive and negative results and consequences and comprises many interrelated factors such as political, economic, social and cultural. The 2030 Agenda for Sustainable Development identifies a recognized connection between the contribution of migration to the achievement of sustainable development and adequate governance policies can lead to benefits in the development of both the countries of origin and those of destination. Migrants enable the creation of trade and investments, they bring innovation, skills and knowledge to their countries of origin and those of destination (Gavonel et al., 2021). Migration of people is not just a result of recent global processes. On the contrary, population movement across regions and continents has been part of human history since its beginning. Individuals have been relocating from one place to another, from one region or country to another, and even between continents. There are plenty of examples when population was moving within the same country's region. Consequently, the term "migration" can be defined as a process of movement of people both across the international national borders and within a country. The term means and describes any type of movement of people regardless of reason or distance and under this term it is possible to include refugees, displaced persons, internally displaced persons as well as persons displaced by economic or environmental reasons. The phenomenon of migration has been indispensable for human history, culture, and civilizations. The increasing and long-term proofs on people mobility and mobility demonstrations that migration is, for the most portion, linked to broad political, economic, global, social, cultural and technological transformations that also affect high priority political issues. International and domestic migration over the centuries has played a role in shaping the world as it is today. Most people migrate for reasons related to family and education (IOM, 2020). In addition, there are contrasting reasons for migration, such as forced and tragic reasons such as conflict, persecution, disaster, and others. Refugees and internally displaced persons (IDPs) constitute a relatively small percentage of migrants and are most in necessity of support and care. In light of the current scientific and political discussions surrounding migration, the objective of this work is to examine and deliberate upon global migration patterns and assess how they align with the realities of the European Union. The theoretical methodological basis of the document were the scientific papers represented by scholars in international journals and books, international research, publications and statistical data represented by international organizations such as: International Organization for Migration IOM, International Labour Organization ILO, European Commission, Eurostat, European Parliamentary Research Service, The World Bank, United Nations, and other. Section 2 discusses migration flows divided by periods, followed by a section which is focused on the European Union and migration trends, considering the nationalities of migrants. Subsequently, motivations and main entry points are analyzed in the followed section on employment. The last section on pandemic impact on migration, analysis data on migrants that show, how they were affected by the COVID19 pandemic. The primary aim is to provide a comprehensive and detailed overview of the intricate situation of migration in Europe. Through a thorough analysis of migration trends, patterns, and their multifaceted impacts on the European Union, this work seeks to paint a vivid and accurate picture of the dynamic relationship between migration and the continent. By examining factors such as the scale of migration flows, emerging trends, the origins and motivations of migrants, key entry points, and the occupational roles they assume, this study aims to offer a holistic understanding of the complexities involved in European migration. Additionally, the chapter also addresses the unique challenges posed by the COVID19 pandemic, which have further shaped and intensified the migration landscape in Europe.

2. The Magnitude of Current Flows of Migration

Recently, substantial modifications have been made in regard with the management of world migration. Namely, the member states of the United Nations have decided to initiate and develop two important global agreements on international manifestations of migration and displacement: "The Global Compact for Safe, Orderly and Regular Migration" (UN, 2021) and "Global Compact on Refugees" (UN, 2018). The signature these agreements is the outcome of year of efforts by activists, states, specific international organizations, civil society organizations and other actors (e.g., private organizations, scientists and est.), and aims to improve migration management at the international level. According to recent trends, international migration is increasing. The number of international migrants worldwide is 272 million (IOM, 2020), where almost two thirds are labor migrants. This figure is a very small percentage of the world's population (3.5 %), which means that many people globally (96.5 %) live in the country where they were born. However, this figure is already higher than some predictions made for 2050, which was 2.6 % of the world's population, or 230 million. Predicting the scale and pace of international migration is difficult due to its ties to acute events like instability, economic crises, or conflicts, as well as long-term trends such as demographic changes, economic development, and advances in communication and transportation. Long-term data shows that migration is not uniform globally, being driven by diverse political, historical, economic, social, geographic, ecological, and demographic factors. This has resulted in different migration patterns, such as established migration "corridors" formed over many years. The largest "corridors" were formed from developing countries to countries with larger economies, such as the United States of America, France, the Russian Federation, the United Arab Emirates, and Saudi Arabia. These examples are likely to remain the same for many years, especially as populations in developing regions and countries are projected to increase over the next decade, putting migration pressure on future generations (Mermanishvili, 2022; Ahlmeyer & Volgmann, 2023). It is a sad reality, that the last two years have seen major migration and displacement events, which have caused great hardship and trauma, such as deaths. Millions of people have been displaced by conflicts such as aggression war against Ukraine, the Syrian conflict, conflicts in Yemen, the Central African Republic, South Sudan and the Democratic Republic of Congo. Also, displacement due to extreme violence, such as the Rohingya population seeking safe haven in Bangladesh, and the severe economic and political instability experienced by millions in Venezuela. In addition, increasing displacement due to climate and environmental changes was observed. Also, in 2018–2019, many parts of the world saw increasing mobility due to threats related to climate and environmental changes in countries such as the Philippines, Mozambique, China, India, and the United States of America. Even though the share of international migrants has increased globally, a huge number of people still live in the countries where they were born. The diagram below shows the number of international migrants worldwide and their share of the world population from 1970 to 2022.

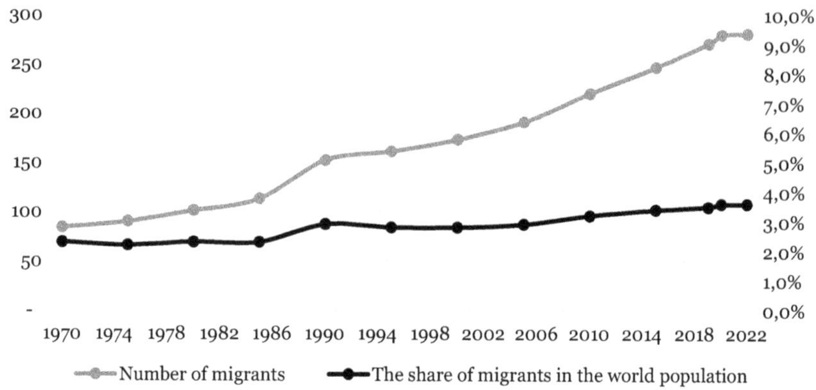

Figure 1: International migrants in 1970–2022. Source: International Organization for Migration

Although the migrant population has increased globally (as seen in figure 1) the proportion of the world population has remained stable. Also, it is noteworthy that 74% of the international migrants are of working age, approximately between 20 and 64 years old (IOM, 2022). In 2019, Europe received 82 million migrants, meanwhile Asia received 2 million more, and 84 million migrants. All together these migrants accounted 61 % of global migrants. The third largest number of migrants, approximately 59 million, moved to North America and amounted 22 % of total world migrants' number. Africa received 10 % of total number of international migrants, Latin America and the Caribbean, both received 4 % and the Oceania region had followed them with 3 %. When the number of migrants was compared to the population of these regions, the largest shares in 2019 were in Oceania (21 %), North America (16 %) and Europe (11 %). A relatively small share of migrants was recorded in Asia (1.8 %), Africa (2 %), Latin America and the Caribbean (1.8 %). However, migration to Asia experienced the most significant increase from 2000 to 2019, by 69 %, which is about 34 million people. And Europe is on the second place with the rate of growth of migrants during this period, which is 25 million migrants, followed by North America where the number of migrants increased by 18 million, and by 11 million in Africa (UN, 2021). The first Report on World Migration was issued 20 years ago and from the very beginning it was a one-off report intended at improving the knowledge and essence meaning of migration and was supposed to help politicians and the public to profoundly understand the effects and results of globalization, which were happening in many and various parts of the world and in numerous means. The first World Migration Report affirmed that part of its origin is lays on to the influence of globalization on migration designs. Therefore, the report resumes "a growing economy that has led to unprecedented inflows of new migrants in many countries." The report emphasized the new reality that, despite being an "ancient phenomenon," migration processes were accelerated due to the broad global transformation of the world economic and trade relations, allowing greater movement of goods, services, labor, and capital within the countries and across the national borders. In 2018, international remittances reached up to 689 billion US dollars. The top three largest remittance-receiving countries were: India receiving $78 billion, China – $67.4 billion and Mexico – $35.7 billion. International remittances have increased from the depression in 2020 caused by the COVID-19 pandemic. Migrants sent a projected USD 831 billion as international remittances worldwide in 2022. This was a growth from USD 791 billion in 2021 and to more than USD 717 billion in 2020 (World Bank, 2023). Like earlier years, low- and middle-income countries received huge portion of remittance inflows. Worth to mention that these inflows grew by 8 % from 2021 to 2022, namely, in 2021 the amount comprised USD 599 billion and in 2022 reached USD 647 billion. The United States is the largest remittance-sending country, which sent $68 billion. It is followed by the United Arab Emirates, sending $44.4 billion and Saudi Arabia – $36.1 billion (IOM, 2020; UN, 2018, 2021). The table below delivers an overview of key statistical data from the World Migration Report 2022 (IOM, 2022). It illustrates that some features have remained constant, for example the rates of female international migrants, as well as the share of migrants in the world's population are the same during reported period, meanwhile other aspects have changed dramatically (IOM, 2020; UN, 2021).

Table 1: Key trends from the World Migration Report in 2000–2022

	2000 Report	2020 Report	2022 Report
Estimated number of international migrants	150 million	272 million	281 million
Estimated proportion of world population who are migrants	2.8 %	3.5 %	3.6 %
Estimated proportion of female international migrants	47.5 %	47.9 %	48.0 %

(continued)

Table 1: Continued

	2000 Report	2020 Report	2022 Report
Estimated proportion of international migrants who are children	16.0 %	13.9 %	14.6 %
Region with the highest proportion of international migrants	Oceania	Oceania	Oceania
Country with the highest proportion of international migrants	United Arab Emirates	United Arab Emirates	United Arab Emirates
Number of migrant workers	-	164 million	169 million
Global international remittances (USD)	126 billion	689 billion	702 billion
Number of refugees	14 million	25.9 million	26.4 million
Number of internally displaced persons	21 million	41.3 million	55 million

Source: World Migration Report, 2022

For example, international remittances increased from 126 billion USD to 689 billion USD from 2000 to 2020, highlighting the development of international migration (Abdullah et al., 2021) This partly supports to clarify the appearance of migration as a first-rate global issue, because of which UN member states have taken several steps to strengthen global migration governance, especially since 2000. It is not surprising that the number of member states of the International Organization for Migration (IOM, 2020, 2022) has increased from 76 countries to 173 countries in the last two decades. Also noteworthy in the table is the increase of international migrants worldwide (about 85 %), in addition to the increase of refugees (about 80 %) and internally displaced persons (97 %); But despite this, these numbers remain a very small part of the world population. The share of migrants in 2000 is about 2.8 % of the world's population, and in 2022 it was 3.5 %, and in 2022 reached 3.6 %. According to the Table 1, the data of female international migrants is almost the same for 20 years, while the share of child migrants has decreased, it was 16 % in 2000, and 13.9 % in 2020, and was approximately the same in 2022, 14.6 %. The region with the highest share of international migrants in both 2000 and 2020 is the Oceania region, and the United Arab Emirates is the country with the highest share of international migrants in 2000 and 2020. 2000 data on migrant workers are not recorded, and in 2020 their number is 164 million. As for the number of refugees and the data of internally displaced persons, compared to the data of 2000, an increase has been recorded. In particular, the number of refugees was 14 million in 2000, and in 2020 it was 25.9 million. The number of internally displaced persons has increased by 20.3 million in 20 years (21 million in 2000), 41.3 million in 2020. As for the number of stateless persons, this data was not recorded in 2000, and in 2020, their number was 3.9 million (IOM, 2022). The contribution of the World Migration Report to immigration or emigration policy as well as migration studies/research was timely. Twelve World Migration Reports have been published by the International Organization for Migration (IOM) since 2000 and have become the organization's flagship publication series. The report consistently focuses on appropriate, wide-ranging and evidence-based contributions that support the consideration of migration nature by policymakers, decision-makers, practitioners, civil society, researchers and the broader public. Over time, the growth of numbers of international migrates in certain regions has influenced population change. Although Europe has usually been one of the main destination regions for internationally moved population, it had the lowest rate of comparative population modification during this period, at just above 1 %. Though, this figure is expected to be much lower without international migrants, which have moderated population decline in some European countries, such as decreasing birth rates. By comparison, Africa experienced the most important modification, namely the growth of its population by approximately 30 % during this period, caused by high fertility rate and improved life conditions, which resulted in longer life expectancy. Since 1970, the United States of America has been the main destination country for international migrants. From 1970 to 2019, the number of foreign-born people living in the country increased fourfold – from 12 million to 51 million. Germany is the second largest destination for migrants worldwide, with the increase in migrants from 8.9 million to 13.1 million between 2000 and 2019. The world ranking of migrant destination countries is as follows: (1) United States of America, (2) Germany (3) Saudi Arabia, (4) Russian Federation (5) United Kingdom (6) United Arab Emirates (7) France (8) Canada (9) Australia (10) Italy (11) Spain (12) Turkey (13) India (14) Ukraine (15) (IOM, 2020, 2022; UN, 2021). And as for the countries of origin of migrants, in 2019 more than 40 % of migrants (9,112 million) were born in Asian countries, mainly in China, India and South Asian countries such as Pakistan, Bangladesh, and Afghanistan, followed by Mexico and the Russian Federation (IOM, 2020). Three main periods can be distinguished from the point of migration processes development in the history of the European Union. The first period falls in the years of 1950–1974. This is the period before the oil crisis have been developed and this period is considered as the stable one due to the steady economic growth and overall development. Movements of people from east part to west was dominated in this period, including migration from former colonies to homelands and refugees' migration. The second period started with the oil crisis and finished with the fall of the Iron Curtain dividing former Soviet Union from the rest of the world in the late 1980s. Throughout this time, the governments of northwestern European countries progressively restricted migration (Van Mol, 2016). During this period, the main reason and way of migrants' entry into these countries were family reunion and family creation with an increase of asylum seekers. Towards the end of the period, migrants' flows began to change the destination, namely they moved to the Southern European countries of former emigration. The third period is counted from the fall of the Iron Curtain up to the present period. This time is distinguished by the growing influence of the European Union at the international level. This period the EU started to implement the policies, aiming at controlling migration flows from the third countries into the EU and boosting Intereuropean mobility (Van Mol, 2016; Van Mol & de Valk, 2016; Czaika & Reinprecht, 2022) of people and workers

2.1. 1950s to 1974: Workers' Schemes and Decolonization

After the Second World War, the economic development of North-West Europe is characterized by a sharp rise. For example, in 1953–1958, industrial production in-creased by 30 % (Dietz & Kaczmarczyk, 2008). Indigenous workers of the region have become more and more educated and increasing opportunities for so-called social mobility have allowed majority of them to change their jobs into white-collar ones (Boyle et al., 1998). Therefore, native workers could not occupy the vacancies because the labor pool were restricted. In addition, the local population did not want any more to work on unhealthy jobs, which at the same time, were poorly paid, namely in the sphere of agriculture, home cleaning, mining, construction and etc. As a result, the governments of northwestern European countries had to hired workers from peripheral countries. These countries, which used this practice, were mainly France, Belgium, Germany, Netherlands, Luxembourg, Switzerland and Sweden. Employed foreign workers were obligated to return to their home countries after accomplishing their work. So, they were given limited social and labor rights, consequently, they no or little access to health care system or social assistance (Boyle et al., 1998; Boyle & Norman, 2009). At the end of this period, majority of the migrants living in North-West Europe came from Algeria, Italy, Greece, Portugal, Morocco, Spain, Turkey, Tunisia and Yugoslavia. During this period, international movement of workers was generally regarded as positive process as the economic benefits were clear and tangible for both perspectives, of sending and receiving countries (Bonifazi, 2008; Bonifazi et al., 2021).

2.2. 1974 to the Late 1980s: The Oil Crisis and International Migration Control

The oil crisis of 1973–1974 had a substantial effect on the economic performance of Europe. The crisis gave new impetus to economic and social restructuring and severely reduced the demand for labor force (Boyle et al., 1998). During this period, the confidence, that the economic growth was unlimited, significantly weakened. In 1970–1972, Sweden and Switzerland were the first countries, which demanded to pause the migration. In 1973–1974, other countries such as France, Germany and the Benelux used the same approach (Rella & Vadala, 1984; Hudson & Lewis, 2022). Policies aimed at controlling and reducing migration have been transformed into policies that stop migration. The number of foreign residents has been constantly increasing, because the change of European migration management systems, that moved from circular migration to chain migration and caused the natural growth of the migrant population. Migrants from non-European countries who came to work in European countries became more and more permanently settled, and they were afraid to return to their home country for a long time no to lose their permissions. Many migrants began to bring their family members to Europe (Beck-Gernsheim, 2007; Strasser et al., 2009). From the beginning, European governments tried to restrict family unifications, but this practice met little success (Castles & Ozkul, 2014; Hansen & Donohoe, 2003). Later, according to Article 19 of the European Social Charter of 1961, family reunification of working migrants was acknowledged as the fundamental right of migrants. During this period, the configuration of the local migrant population similarly changed. In the first period, European migrants were the majority, meanwhile in the second period, the share of non-European migrants in the total population significantly increased. For example, in 1999, 40 % of the foreign-born population in Sweden were non-European, while this showing was 7.6 % in 1970 (Goldscheider et al., 2008).

2.3. 1990s to Present: Recent Trends in Migration in Europe

Since 1990, migration to and from Europe has undergone significant changes. The collapse of the Iron Curtain and the opening of Eastern European borders led to new migration flows to European countries. The collapse of the Soviet Union, the end of the Cold War and the raised wars in the countries of the former Yugoslavia boost new flows of people, who were registered as asylum seekers trying to find shelters in West-ern European countries. During this period the top countries of origin of migrants were from the Federal Republic of Yugoslavia, reaching almost 836,000 immigrants, 400,000 immigrants were moved from Romania, 356,000 immigrants from Turkey, 211,000 immigrants from Iraq and 155,000 immigrants from Afghanistan relocated from their homelands (Hansen & Donohe, 2003). In the first decade of the 21st century, the EU countries introduced several admission restrictions to new asylum. The new situation entailed violent conflicts. During the third period, integration became a key policy issue (Doomernik & Bruquetas-Callejo, 2016; Doomernik et al., 2023). Many European countries have stepped up efforts to attract educated or highly skilled workers as migrants. Currently, this goal is still a central subject of a number of national programs, including but not limited to Denmark, Sweden, Germany, thy Great Britain and est. The European Union has established the Blue Card scheme, which involves and deals with residence and work permits across the EU (Eurostat, 2011). Moreover, the migration of students from the third countries to the EU has become a progressively vital is-sue in certain EU countries. Governments in some countries have actively recruited students to work after graduation to integrate the best of hard work (Lange, 2013). Higher education institutions have introduced special policies in the form of high tuition fees to boost these efforts as far as the economic benefits from the involved international students was evident and clear (Findlay, 2011a, 2011b). For this reason, several European countries, including France, the Netherlands, Germany and Great Britain, made easier relevant procedures for international students (Tremblay, 2005; Van Mol, 2014). As of January 1, 2021, the EU population was 447.7 million, which were living in the territory covering above 4 million km^2. 4.7 % of the total EU population, consisting of 20.9 million inhabitants, were from non-EU countries. Moreover, 34.2 million people, 7.7 % of the total EU population, was born outside the EU (European Commission, 2020). Migration is a very important phenomenon for the European Union. According 2022 EU commission data, 2.26 million immigrated to the EU in 2021 and 2.2 million were entered the territory of the European Union, in 2019. In 2012, approximately, 1.12 million persons emigrated from the EU. Thus, 1.14 million persons consisted net immigration to the EU. Meanwhile, in 2019 0.9 million people emigrated from the borders of the European Union. Total net immigration to the EU was 1.3 million people. Taking into consideration, that in 2019, 4.2 million babies were born, and 4.7 million people died in the EU, without migration Europe's population would decrease by half a million (European Commission, 2022).

3. The Trends of EU Migration

Over the years EU population has increased, but at slow rate, with most of the growth attributed to immigration rather than natural increase. One of the main factors driving population growth in the EU is immigration, as many people from outside the EU come to work or study in member states. The migration trends in the European Union (EU) are constantly evolving and this matter is a very important phenomenon for the EU.

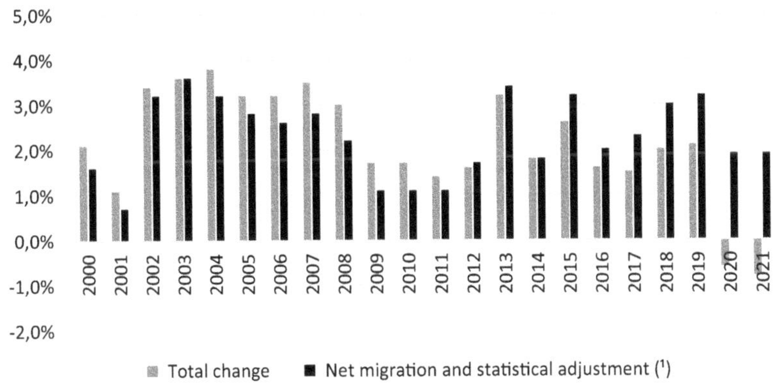

Figure 2: Dynamics of the EU population and net migration change 2000–2021
Source: Eurostat

According to recent data (Eurostat, 2021), in 2021 the total change of EU population was -0.4 % and the net migration rate was 2.4 % which significantly exceeds the population change rate. If we look at EU population and Net migration change during the 2000–2021 years (Figure 2), we will see that net migration rate is increased by 50 % and the EU population change is decreased by 19.04 % (Figure 2).

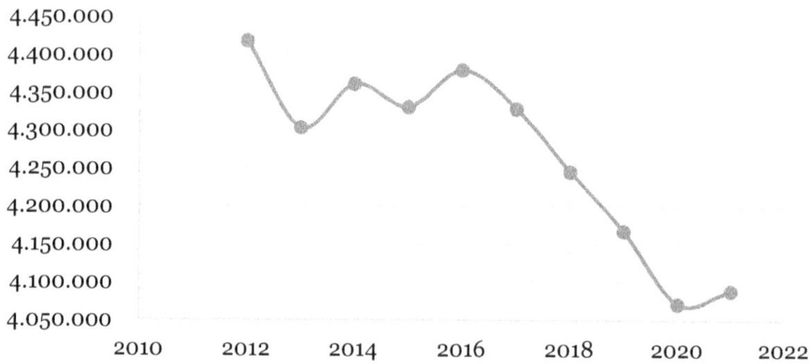

Figure 3: Dynamics of birth rates in Europe 2012–2021 years
Source: Eurostat

The birth rate in the EU has been declining in recent years. If we look at the birth rates from 2012 to 2021, there is a sharp decrease from 2016 to 2020. Since 2020, the birth rate has started to increase, which continues until 2021, however, it is a remarkable fact that this increase cannot equal the birth rates from 2013 to 2016 (see Figure 3). The World Health Organization declared a pandemic on March 11, 2020 (Who, 2020), which had a huge impact on the world in all directions. Of course, the corona virus pandemic had a great impact on migration not only in the EU countries, but throughout the world. Data collected by the International Organization for Migrants' Movement Monitor from March 13, 2020, to January 28, 2021, demonstrate that internal mobility restrictions in countries everywhere affected regular travelers and citizens by 61 % and 59 % of the estimated percentage of internal transit points respectively (2021). According to a survey conducted by the Center for Mixed Migration (Center for Fixed Migration, 2021), among 33,393 respondents, almost 28 % stated that the pandemic did not make it difficult to cross borders, while 25 % declared that it influenced internal mobility. As a result of the lockdown, internal migrants have been left unemployed and home-less, thousands of informal sector workers have left cities (e.g., New Delhi, India) and returned to their hometowns (UN, 2020). As of March 1, 2021 (UN DESA, 2020), the highest number of cumulative cases of COVID-19 were reported in countries where migrants represented a significant proportion of their population. For example, the specific share of migrants in Germany was 19 % of the population, little bit less, 15 %, in the United States, the same,15 %, in Spain, in the United Kingdom – 14 %, and in France – 13 %. The main areas of employment for migrants in these countries are healthcare and services. Consequently, there was an increase in the return of migrants from these countries to their countries of origin. In 2017, 164 million people were migrant workers (ILO, 2018) moreover, migrant workers account up to 20.6 % of the total workforce in North America and 17.8 % in South-West Europe (ILO, 2017). Living in overcrowded housing poses a specific risk for the spread of Covid-19 amongst migrant workers and their family members (Tzoraki et al., 2021). Migrants, regardless of their workplace, are making an essential contribution to tackling the pan-demic, as they face higher risks of exposure to the virus. Situation as of March 1, 2021, listed the world's 20 countries with the highest number of Covid-19 cases. Available international data shows that several countries – the United States, France, United Kingdom, Italy, Spain, Germany, and the Czech Republic – have a critical health care sector dependent on foreign-born workers. For example, in the UK in 2015–2016, 33 % of doctors and 22 % of nurses were foreign-born (OECD, 2019). At the same time, health worker shortages have been occurring globally for numerous years, and the demand for skilled health workers is expected to be aggravated by the current pan-demic. In particular, the countries of origin of educated/skilled migrants suffer from a lack of access to the health sector. This problem is more complex than simply the big numbers of emigrant workers. Twenty-nine percent of doctors in the United Kingdom and 25 % of doctors in the United States have gained their qualification abroad (OECD, 2015, 2020). Migrants represent a significant share in critical sectors, as well as in the sectors most damaged by the global health crisis: for example, more than 1 % of sales and service workers were foreign-born in 7 countries from those 20 countries, which registered the highest number of Covid-19 cases. Additionally, available data showed, that in 5 countries of the 20 countries with the highest number of Covid-19 cases, more than 9 % of skilled agricultural, forestry and fisheries professionals were foreign-born (OECD, 2020). Due to the pandemic, the situation has certainly changed in the EU countries as well. EU data on asylum-seekers and irregular border crossings cases for the first 10 months of 2020 showed the effect of the pandemic on migration to the EU. A 33 % de-crease in asylum requests is recorded in the EU (EUAFR, 2020). In the same period 390,000 asylum applications were submitted to the EU (including 349,000 first-time applications).EU member states have also reduced asylum proceedings. At the end of October 2020, the number of cases was 786,000, which is 15 % less than at the end of 2019. In April 2020, 90 % of asylum seekers were rejected due to the corona virus, the lowest rate since 2008. Asylum procedures are gradually being reformed in many countries, but challenges remain. Access to information remains problematic in many countries (EUAFR, 2020). In the period January-November of 2020, there was 114,300 irregular EU border crossing cases. This is a 10 % decrease to compare to the same period in 2019 and is the lowest in the last 6 years. There were 19,300 of cases of irregular arrivals in the Eastern Mediterranean countries. This was a significant decrease, comprising -74 %. This decline decrease was caused by to less numbers of arrivals from Turkey to Greece, where the situation changed due to numerous factors affecting country's political and economic developments (European Commission, 2020). Despite the decrease in total number of migrations, irregular arrivals via the Mediterranean countries (Malta and Italy) significantly increased (+ 154 %) compared to the same period in 2019. In 2020, 34,100,000 arrivals were recorded, which is higher than 11,500 cases of 2019, with the majority of destinations in Lampedusa. Exception for the period of March, the numbers consistently exceeded the level of 2019. Compared to 2019, arrivals to Spain and the Canary Islands increased significantly, by 46 %, and reached 35,800 cases in 2020. Nevertheless, crossing the Mediterranean is still dangerous. Despite the decrease in departures in 2020, 1,754 people died or went missing, compared to 2,095 in 2019 (European Commission, 2020). The spread and pandemic of Covid-19 has certainly had a significant impact on international students as well. As of 2017, there are 5.3 million international students in the world, of which 3.3 million come from North America and Europe. For international students, the impact of the corona virus pandemic has been manifested in the closure of campuses, the loss of jobs for students, as well as the restrictions on mobility imposed by both the countries of origin of international students and the countries where they have been (Koris et al., 2021). The World Health Organization published data in March 2021 showing the percentage of migrants in countries with the highest confirmed cases of Covid-19. In these countries of the world, the EU member states occupy leading positions: the 6th country in the list is France, where 13.1 % of the confirmed cases of Covid-19 come from migrants, the 7th is Spain with 14.6 %, the 8th is Italy with 10.6 %, I -10 Germany with 18.8 % and so on. Thus, due to the pandemic, the situation has changed in terms of the number of migration and asylum seekers in the EU countries, in particular, the EU official data on asylum-seekers and irregular border crossing cases for the first 10 months of 2020 showed that migration to the EU has decreased due to the impact of the pandemic. A 33 % de-crease in asylum requests is recorded in the EU (EUAFR, 2020; McAuliffe et al., 2021). According to EU data (Eurostat, 2021), in the period January-November 2020, there were 114,300 cases of irregular EU border crossings. This figure is the lowest in the last 6 years and is 10 % decrease compared to the same period in 2019.

4. The National Origins of Migrants

In recent years, the EU has experienced a significant increase in the number of asylum seekers, with the majority of migrants coming from Africa and the

Middle East. First-time asylum seekers by continent of origin in 2019 were 25 % (158,215 people) from Asian countries, 24 % (153,065 people) from the African continent, 19 % (118,010 people) from Latin America, 18 % (114,105 people) from the Middle East, 12 % (78,500 people) from Europe and 2 % (9,410 people) from the rest (Eurostat, 2020). In the following figure (Figure 4) are represented the Asylum seekers in the European Union by region.

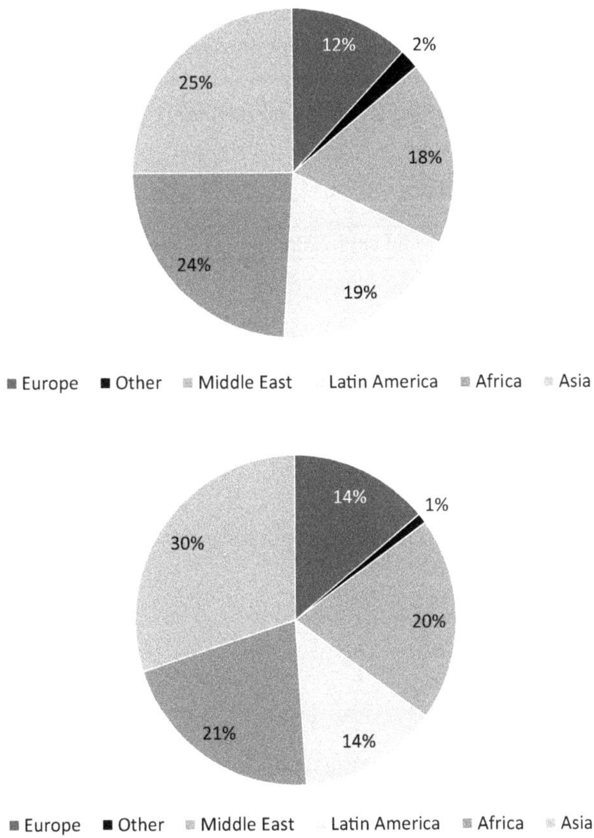

Figure 4: Asylum seekers in the European Union by region%/Share of regions in world population % as of 2019 and Asylum seekers in the European Union by region in 2022

Source: Eurostat

In 2019, asylum seekers came from 150 countries and in 2022 from 140 countries. 699,000 applications were requesting asylum in the EU, among them 631,000 were the first-time applicants. This was 12 % increase to compare to 2018 data. In 2022 the number of asylum-seekers, who were lodged, reached 962,200, among them 881,200 applicants were first time submitting the claim. This was 52 % increase in comparison to 2021, and of 38 % increase in comparison to in 2019, before COVID (Eurostat, 2020). An increasing share of asylum seekers were from countries with visa-free access to the EU. According to Eurostat data, in 2019 the share of primary applicants was 27 %, it was 15 % in 2021 and 22 % of first-time applicants in 2022, because of increased number of applicants from Latin America, who crossed the EU border legally. These countries are represented in Table 2.

Table 2: Application per countries

Country	**% of all initial application**	**% of all initial application**
Year	2019	2022
Venezuela	7.1	5.7
Colombia	5.0	4.8
Georgia	3.2	2.9
Albania	2.7	1.4
Ukraine	N/A	2.8

The most initial applications come from the following countries:

- Germany (142,450);
- France (138,290);
- Spain (115,175);
- Greece (74,910);
- Italy (35,005).

In 2019, among asylum seekers, 207,000 persons were under the age of 18. 14,000 of them (7 %) were children traveling without accompanied persons. In 2022, this showing increased up to 239,500. About one in six of them, 39,500 where unaccompanied children Majority of unaccompanied children came from Syria, Afghanistan, Somalia and Pakistan.

4.1. Recognition of Refugees

From 2019 to 2022, the European Union experienced significant changes in its asylum and protection landscape. Initial asylum decisions rose notably from

541,000 to 632,400, with the proportion of positive outcomes increasing from 38 % to 49 %. This trend is underscored by specific increases in refugee status grants from 109,000 to 142,800 and auxiliary protection status from 52,000 to 101,700. Humanitarian status grants also saw an uptick from 45,000 to 65,900. Appeals decisions totaled 297,000, showing fluctuations in positive outcomes across categories. Overall, EU member states granted protection to approximately 300,000 individuals in 2019 and 384,200 in 2022, with Syria, Afghanistan, and Venezuela being the most prevalent nationalities. The EU also saw shifts in asylum applications, with a decrease in 2020 followed by a rebound to 962,200 in 2022. In 2020 a decrease in asylum applications was observed in the first ten months of 2020, 390,000 asylum applications were made in the EU (including 349,000 initial applications), which is 33 % less than in the same period of 2019. In October, the number of cases reached 786,000, which is 15 % less than the last data of 2019. But in 2022 962,200 applications entered the appropriate EU institution (European Commission, 2022, European Commission, 2020; Eurostat, 2021). In 2019, approximately 21,200 persons in need of international protection were relocated from non-EU countries to EU member states. This was 12 % more than in 2018. In 2022 approximately, 17,300 people in need of international protection moved from third countries to EU Member States. It was 27 % less than numbers in 2021, but 496 % more than in 2020. Obviously, such increase was due to the covid restriction abolishment. The highest number of departures was recorded in Turkey. Syrian was the main nationality, accounting for 60 % of the displaced people in 2019 and 63 % in 2022 according EUstat data. Since 2015, more than 75,000 persons received protection in the EU by means of joint EU resettlement schemes. By 2022 this number increased up to 115 000 persons. In addition, since 2021, more than 40,000 persons, mostly people of Afghanistan, resettled in the EU by help of humanitarian admission. This new humanitarian scheme, meaning issuing resettlement and humanitarian admissions, envisages certain financial assistance from the EU budget to the member states (European Commission, 2022, European Commission, 2020; Eurostat, 2021).

5. The Reasons for Migrating

It is quite difficult to predict such events as the current political-economic or socio-cultural developments in the countries, therefore it is possible to discuss the existing reality and make decisions only from the current situation.

Migrants can be divided into two broad categories: humanitarian and economic. Humanitarian migrants include asylum seekers and refugees. These individuals usually migrate to countries geographically close to their country of origin. Economic migrants migrate in search of work or to improve their financial situation. In the past, these migrants moved from poorer countries to relatively richer countries (Lee, 1966; Migali et al., 2018; Hatton & Williamson, 2005; Selod & Shilphi, 2021). Socio-political factors can also become an impetus for migration. Such factors may include ethnic, religious, racial, and cultural persecution and, moreover, war or the threat of conflict are also important push factors (Lee, 1966; Mermanishvili, 2022). The politicization of religious and ethnic identity can lead to significant levels of conflict within states. According to empirical evidence, states that transition from authoritarian rule to democracy in politics are more prone to instability and internal conflict, and often these states lack the capacity to respond appropriately to social instability. Accordingly, such states give birth to migrants, who turn to emigration to seek asylum (The Economist, 2018). Subsequently, there are ecological migrants whose migration is caused by ecological factors and other ecological disasters. Of the environmental factors driving individuals to mi-grate, climate change is arguably the most serious. Even if people affected by climate change move only a short distance, it can change social, political, and economic dynamics. The economic drivers of migration are related to countries' labor markets, their unemployment rates, and the health of the economy as a whole. If economic conditions are not favorable and if the economy is in danger of shrinking, more people are more likely to immigrate to a country with a better economy. These migrants are likely to come from middle-income countries with increasingly well-educated populations. Economic recessions often lead to people moving from rural areas to urban areas (Kerwin, 2020; Gečienė-Janulionė, 2018; Manyika et al., 2013). Economic migrants migrate internationally for higher wages and better opportunities or at least to escape the social and political situation in their country. Economic migrants have more choice than humanitarian migrants in determining their destination. Technological advances, both in communications and transportation, along with the liberalization of labor markets, have tended to induce circular migration. This type of migration occurs when individuals migrate between places of origin and destination on several separate occasions. Generally, economic forces induce individuals to move to countries where employment prospects are better. Research has shown that circular migration can have positive development consequences. More importantly, circular migrants send more remittances to their country of origin than those who settle permanently in the country of destination. Additionally, issues related to brain drain and workforce withdrawal are largely avoided. However, problems of exploitation remain, suggesting that efforts are needed to adopt standardized regulations on the rights of circular migrants (Bedianashvili, 2016). Thus, economic inequality between countries, rising levels of intolerance, as well as the threat of climate change and related impacts are all important factors driving migration and population movements. In 2019, 13,763,319 persons moved to the EU (Figure 5) and gained residence permit. 38 % of then noted family as a reason for resettlement in the EU. For 17 % of those people the primarily reason related to work/jobs. (the reason for coming to the EU for people with a residence permit (total 13,763,319 people) was family for 38 %, work for 17 %, asylum for 9 %, education for 4 % and other reasons for 32 % (European Commission, 2020).

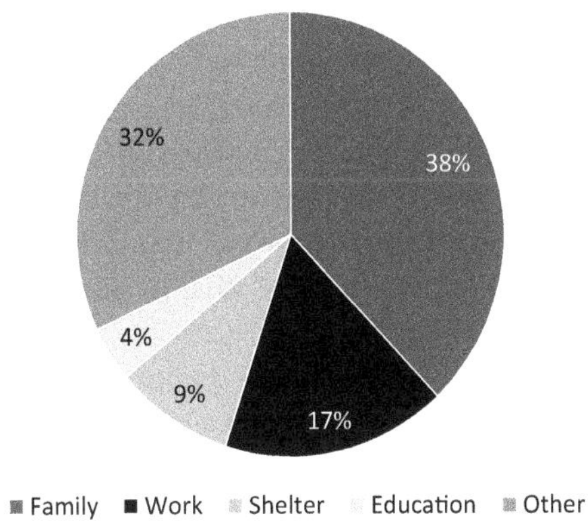

Figure 5: Reasons for coming to the EU
Source: Eurostat

Three million first-time residence permit applications were issued in the EU for the following reasons: work-41 %, family 27 %, education 14 %, asylum 9 %, and 9 % for other reasons (Eurostat, 2021). The average employment rate among the working-age population is higher for EU citizens (73.8 %) than for non-EU citizens (60 %) in 2019 (European Commission, 2022).

6. Illegal Migration

Thus far, the focus has been on the data concerning migrants who have legally crossed the borders of the European Union. Nonetheless, illegal border crossings by migrants are also prevalent in the EU, with sea and land borders being the main points of unauthorized entry. In the last decade, 2015 year was mentioned with highest number of illegal migrants crossing the EU border illegally (Guild et al., 2015). The EU's border agency, Frontex reported above 1.8 million illegal border crossing in 2015 (Frontex, 2015). However, after this year the number of illegal migrants significantly decreased (Sachseder et al., 2022).

To handle the refugee crisis of 2015, the European Commission proposed a reform for the Common European Asylum System in 2016, which included reforming of the Dublin System to better deal with asylum seekers by EU countries. According to the initiated system, significant duty posed on EU countries which have external borders as they were the countries responsible treating asylum claims. However, as the illegal migration is comprehensive problem, EU countries did not reach an agreement on how to share responsibilities.

In 2020, the Commission projected a new a New Pact on Migration and Asylum. The innovative asylum system objects to backing front line countries by announcing a new system of flexible aids from other EU countries, fluctuating from the relocation of asylum seekers from the country of first entry, to returning people believed to have no right to stay (De Bruycker, 2022). The new system is grounded on voluntary cooperation and different forms of support. European Parliament decided on its negotiating position on the re-view of the Regulation on Asylum and Migration Management in April 2023. Currently it is to start consultations with EU countries and hopefully the process will be finished in February 2024. Meanwhile the figures of illegal migration fluctuate. In 2019, 141,700 illegal border crossings were recorded at the border areas of the EU, which is 5 % lower than in 2018 and the lowest in the last 6 years. Of these, 106,200 illegal border crossings were by the sea, which is 7 % less than in 2018, and 35,500 land illegal border crossings, which is the same figure as in 2018. In 2020, 557 500 non-EU citizens illegally cross the EU border at one of the EU Member States (Frontex, 2022). Compared with 2019, declines are detected for all main indicators. This situation reflects the impact of the COVID-19 pandemic, which with many other reasons influenced through temporary closures of borders and imposing traveling restrictions. In 2021, about 140,000 people entered the EU illegally (Frontex, 2022). In this case, the decrease is caused by several factors, such as the EU's reinforced border control measures, collaboration among EU countries and the drop in the number of refugees escaping conflict zones period of 2019. In 2022, about 1.08 million persons were revealed to be illegally living in the EU. This was 59 % growth in comparison with 2021. In 2021 the number of such persons were 679 730. In the same 2022 year, about 330 000 illegal border crossings were identified at EU's border. This is the highest amount since 2016 and a rise of 64 % from the previous year. After the pandemic encouraged decline in 2020, this was another second year distinguished with a sharp rise in the number of irregular migrants (Frontex, 2022). In the previous period, EU and Schengen associated countries confronted extraordinary challenges at their external borders. These were the state-organized migration performed by Belarus from 2021 and due to Russia's invasion and aggressive war in Ukraine in February 2022. The later caused huge number of refugees arriving in the European Union. At the same time, almost 13 million Ukrainian refugees were calculated to enter the EU's external land borders from Ukraine and Moldova between 24 February 2022 until the end of the year. This Amount is not included in these figures (De Coninck, 2023; Kulu et al., 2023). In the same period, 10 million Ukrainian nationals were informed to departure at the same border sections. These events, along with the progressively growing number of irregular crossings, prove the need for stronger and effective European Border and Coast Guard of EU Member States.

7. The Occupation Niches

Considering workforce, Eurostat data suggest, that in 2021, 4,7 % of total EU working-age citizens (from 20 to 64) were immigrants. Their number reached 8,84 mln meanwhile the EU citizen working-age population number was 189.7 mln in the same year. The employment rate for non-EU citizens was 59,1 % and was much less than employment rate for EU citizen population that reached 74 % (European Commission, 2021). In 2019, non-EU citizens were over-represented in some specific economic sectors, as shown in the table 3 below:

Table 3: Distribution of non-EU citizens in work sectors – 2019–2022

Sector	**Common employment of non-EU citizens**		**Common employment of EU citizens**	
Year	2019	2022	2019	2022
Accommodation and catering facilities	13.2 %	11.3 %	4.4 %	4.2 %
Administrative and support activities	7.5 %	7.6 %	4.0 %	3.9 %
Household activities	7.5 %	7.9 %	0.8 %	0.7 %

Source: Eurostat

As data demonstrations in the above table, the minor changes took place during the 3-year period. Thus, we can conclude this trend as established tendency for non-EU citizens. As for activity sphere, non-EU citizens were mostly represented in the so-called "black jobs," such as services in households, support staff and cleaners, food preparation assistants, construction workers, etc. (see Table 4).

Table 4: Distribution of non-EU citizens by activity in 2019–2022

Sector	Common employment of non-EU citizens		Common employment of EU citizens	
Year	2019	2022	2019	2022
Cleaners and helpers	13.3 %	11.4 %	3.2 %	2.9 %
Personal service workers	9.5 %	7.3 %	4.7 %	4.1 %
Personal hygiene workers	5.3 %	5.5 %	2.9 %	3.0 %
Construction workers	6.5 %	6.1 %	3.8 %	3.7 %
Manpower in mining, construction, manufacturing and transport	6.1 %	6.0 %	2.6 %	2.5 %
Food preparation assistants	3.0 %	2.6 %	0.6 %	0.6 %
Agricultural and fishery workers	2.5 %	2.4 %	0.7 %	0.7 %

Source: Eurostat

Non-EU citizens were underrepresented in such economic sectors as public sector and education sector. Similarly, the difference of 2019 data and 2022 data is very little and illustrated the sound tendency. Their participation is even less among business administration and agriculture professionals (see Table 5). The second tendency that is observed in immigrants' employment is that employers in EU countries prefer to hire highly educated non-EU workers to conduct duties on the jobs for which they are over-qualified rather than their host-country peers. EU-wide, 42 % are over-qualified, against 22 % of nationals. This tendency is clearly detected in Southern Europe, where many immigrants have arrived prior to the economic crisis. They mainly perform low-skilled work and usually are over-qualified, consisting at least two-thirds of highly educated third-country nationals. The gap be-tween host- country workers and non-EU national workers is the widest in Italy, where over-qualification is 4 times more among immigrants, and in Portugal, where this showing is 5 times greater. In the north of the EU, in particular in Luxembourg and the United Kingdom non-EU national workers' over-qualification rates are less than 10 % in comparison with these countries' nationals (Oecd, 2018).

8. Impact of the Pandemic on Migration

It is not yet known what effect Covid-19 will have on migration trends in the long term. The following table offers a list of counties, with the highest number of Covid-19 cases and the highest percentage of migrants.

Table 5: Number of cases of infection with Covid-19 among migrants by age in 2020

Country	**Confirmed Covid-19 cases for whole population (mln)**	**Migrants number among whole population, confirmed covid 19 cases.**	**Share of working-age migrants (20–64 years old) (%), mid-2020**
US	79,070	12,098	77.2 %
India	7,828	31	70.7 %
Brazil	43,938	220	59.3 %
Russia	26,847	2,148	76.7 %
UK	57,034	7,871	77.4 %
France	48,994	6,418	67.6 %
Spain	61,672	9,004	80.7 %
Italy	42,734	4,530	84.4 %
Turkey	29,655	2,135	70.9 %
Germany	26,879	5,053	70.2 %
Columbia	41,775	1,546	57.6 %
Argentina	43,206	2,160	68.4 %
Mexico	14,630	132	34.8 %
Poland	40,519	891	36.9 %
South Africa	24,668	1,184	81.8 %
Iran	17,208	568	51.4 %
Ukraine	28,176	3,212	72.9 %
Peru	35,131	1,300	61.4 %
Indonesia	4,106	4	78.5 %
Czech Republic	94,626	4,826	87.6 %

Source: World Health Organization, 2021

As the table shows, France, Italy, Germany, Poland, Spain and the Czech Republic are leader according to this data. On average, 13 % of key workers in Europe are immigrants (Fasani & Mazza, 2020). In 2017, the United States hired 161,583 foreign workers on seasonal jobs issuing special work permits (OECD, 2019), meanwhile seasonal workers are often not even counted in the European Union. According to the data of the World Health Organization in February 2020, the number of people infected with the corona virus is 112,456,453 million, and the number of deaths is 2,497,514 million (Center for Fixed Migration, 2021). Of these, 38,176,678 cases come from Europe, with the UK leading the way (4,144,581 confirmed cases and 121,747 deaths), France (3,597,495 confirmed cases and 84,894 deaths), Spain (3,180,212 cases and 68,813 deaths),

Italy (2,868,435 and 496 confirmed deaths) Germany (2,424,684 confirmed and 69,519 accidental deaths). The number of confirmed cases in Georgia is 270,137, and the number of deaths is 3,485. The Covid-19 pandemic has created border restrictions, which of course have affected the mobility of people, among them migrants. This situation affected the role of humanitarian organizations too. From 11 March 2020, when the World Health Organization declared the Covid-19 pandemic, till 22 February 2021, approximately 105,000 movement restrictions were imposed worldwide (Global Migration Indicators Report, 2021). At the same time, 795 countries out of 189 have granted exemptions to the restrictions, allowing for mobility. From March 1 to July 1, 2020, estimates show zero growth in the number of migrants, representing a global decrease of almost 2 million international migrants (United Nations, 2020). Most of the countries of the world have closed their borders completely or partially for the citizens of foreign countries in order to prevent the spread of the corona virus. Nine-tenths (91 %) of the world's population, or 7.1 billion people, live in countries that restrict the entry of non-residents and non-citizens from other countries, such as tourists, business travelers, and new immigrants (Pew research Center, 2020). According to the Pew Research Center's analysis of border closure announcements and UN population data, about 3 billion people, or 39 %, live in countries where borders are completely closed to non-citizens and non-residents. Travel restrictions vary by country, but all aim to reduce travel. As a result, airlines reduced their flight routes and tourism fell. Some countries such as Ecuador and Central Asian countries have even closed their borders to their own citizens (Pew research Center, 2020). Migrants flows to OECD countries, as is measured by new permits issued, fell by 46 % in the first half of 2020. In 2020 it is expected to see historically low migration level in the above-mentioned countries (International Migration Outlook, 2020). Such declines in migration may also have demographic implications for countries that depend on migration for population growth. For example, according to 2020 estimates, the German population did not in-crease for the first time in a decade due to a decrease in immigration (German Federal Office, 2021). In Australia, by 2020/2021 net migration is expected to be negative since 1945, causing in the lowest population growth (Australian Population Centre, 2020). In 2013, there were approximately 11.5 million migrant workers (MDW) world-wide, of which approximately 8.5 million were women (ILO, 2015). Covid-19 has really created problems for migrant workers. For example, during the Covid-19 pandemic, employers of migrants may become infected, transmit the disease to them, or die, and this poses a threat to migrant workers, as their income and work permits are directly linked to their employers. Due to border closures and economic limitations, return to countries of origin is often impossible or very difficult, and therefore, migrants are trapped in the destination countries without housing or income. As we see from the discussed Eurostat data above (Table 5), migrants are the workers that have occupied lower paid jobs and are mainly in irregular positions. Therefore, they were person who were more or mostly affected by and vulnerable to the spread of COVID-19. Simultaneously, migrants also made significant contributions to the COVID-19 response by actively employed in essential sectors like childcare, domestic work, and healthcare. COVID-19 Pandemic connected restrictions have an impact on the mobility of migrants. During 10 March 2020 (when the World Health Organization declared pandemic status) – 28 February, 2022, period altogether 122,823 movement restrictions were realized over the globe (IOM, 2022). If we assume the zero growth of the quantity of migrants in the period 1 March-1 July 2020, estimations propose a reduction of about 2 million migrants compared to the originally predicted growth during the period of mid-2019 and mid-2020 (European Commission, 2022; IOM, 2022). In 2020, migration inflows to OECD countries were fallen by more than 30 %. This was the historical lowest level of migration to OECD countries since 2003 (OECD, 2021). Mean-while, the largest declines were observed in terms of family migration, which reached 35 % by the end 2020. Such decline of migration inflows in EU countries had demo-graphic effect on EU population. For instance, in 2020 population growth in Germany was zero for the first time in the current decade, which was caused by the limited immigration. Migrant workers play a dual role, addressing two crucial voids. Firstly, they contribute to the workforce, stimulating the economies of host nations, leading to job creation and increased tax revenue. Secondly, migrants play a pivotal role in bridging demographic disparities in aging societies (Molinero-Gerbeau et al., 2021; Al-Husban & Adams, 2016). The similar effects were demonstrated in other countries. In Australia high migration outflow resulted in the lower growth of population in comparison with the rate during almost century. The mobility of international students has also been restricted. For example, the USA and the UK, which are the most frequent choice for destination to study abroad, – issued 69 % and 40 % less first permits to students in 2020 correspondingly to compare the numbers of 2019 year (Migration Data Portal, 2023). Because international migrants are an extremely heterogeneous group, the effects and impact on their health condition were also diverse. An overview of relevant publications reveals that covid-19 disease incidence among migrants were constantly higher than among non-migrant groups. At the same time, immigrants stayed at a higher risk to be infected due to the poor working and living conditions even in high-income countries. Another reason of their higher rate of infection was migrants' to limited access to healthcare

(Hintermeier et al., 2021; Hayward et al., 2021). In 2020 due to the Covid -19 the unemployment rates of migrants significantly in-creased by more than 75 % in every OECD country (OECD, 2021). Despite this fact, migrants played significant role in addressing the pandemic and were showing the higher risks of contracting the virus. Appropriate data shows that seven countries – the United States, the United Kingdom, France, Germany, Spain, Italy and the Netherlands, depended on foreign or migrant workers in the essential sector of healthcare services. Moreover, in UK 33 % of doctors and 22 % of nurses were foreign-born according the 2015–2016 data (OECD, 2021). Though in 2021, deaths among migrants globally move toward the pre-pandemic levels.

9. Conclusions

This comprehensive exploration of the influence of migration on the demographic situation and development of the European Union illustrates the intensive dynamics of this multifaceted and very complex issue. By meticulously analyzing global migration trends and dissecting various facets of migration patterns, this chapter has provided a nuanced understanding of the complex relationship between migration and the EU's population landscape. The examination of migration patterns, including the scale of migration flows, evolving trends, the diverse national origins of migrants, their motivations for relocating, primary entry points into the EU, and the occupational niches they occupy, underscores the diversity and depth of this phenomenon. Migration is not a monolithic process; it is influenced by a myriad of factors, each contributing to the complex tapestry of demographic change within the EU. Moreover, the work has underscored the critical impact of the COVID-19 pan-demic on migration dynamics. The pandemic has exacerbated pre-existing migration challenges and introduced new layers of complexity. Migrants, already vulnerable, have faced heightened risks and hurdles, necessitating adaptive and human policies to address their unique needs. As the European Union grapples with the ongoing challenges and opportunities presented by migration. The contribution of migrants in the destination countries is obviously commensurate with the level of integration achieved, where the person can better express their work potential and entrepreneurial ability (Aniche, 2020). In USA, the countries where migrants contribute to economic development in a decisive way, they stimulate the demand for goods and services, paying taxes for the continuous improvement of basic services such as healthcare and schools. Many studies agree on a high rate of entrepreneurship, initiative and innovation among migrant populations. And it is a visible impact not only in a small or local micro-commerce dimension: for example, 44 % of the largest and most important Fortune 500 companies in 2021 were founded by migrants or their children, providing employment to around 14 million people. This is very important example of sustainable development. This work serves as an invaluable resource for policymakers, to implement the migration aspects of the SDGs, to integrate migration into local or national development planning, by designing and implementing interventions that relate to migration in the context of the SDGs (Jakovljevic et al., 2021; Bălăcescu et al., 2022). It not only provides historical context and a com-prehensive view of migration trends but also emphasizes the urgent need for thoughtful, evidence-based policies to navigate this evolving landscape. In a world where migration is an integral part of the global tapestry, the demo-graphic future of the European Union is undeniably intertwined with its ability to effectively manage and harness the potential of international migration. To do so successfully requires a holistic approach that considers the diverse motivations and aspirations of migrants while addressing the social, economic, and political implications of demographic change.

9.1. Limitations and Future Developments

Recognizing its limitations, it is crucial to emphasize that a more thorough examination of migration patterns at the regional level within the EU could uncover distinct challenges and opportunities. Additionally, a longitudinal study could shed light on how migration dynamics have evolved over time. Given the ever-changing nature of migration data, this chapter provides an update as of 2023. A key advancement would be to perform new analyzes with the most recent data available. Furthermore, considering future developments, the dynamic nature of migration and the possibility of unforeseen global events necessitate that future research remain adaptable to new circumstances. Continual updates and revisions to migration policies, along with responses to emerging crises, will be essential to maintaining a current understanding of migration issues.

Acknowledgment

This chapter is part of the project NODES (D.G and P.G) which has received funding from the MUR – M4C2 1.5 of PNRR funded by the European Union – NextGenerationEU (Grant agreement no. ECS00000036).

References

Ahlmeyer, F., & Volgmann, K. (2023). What Can We Expect for the Development of Rural Areas in Europe? – Trends of the Last Decade and Their Opportunities for Rural Regeneration. *Sustainability*, *15*(6), 5485.

Al-Husban, M., & Adams, C. (2016). Sustainable Refugee Migration: A Rethink towards a Positive Capability Approach. *Sustainability*, *8*(5), 451.

Aniche, E. T. (2020). Migration and Sustainable Development: Challenges and Opportunities. *Migration Conundrums, Regional Integration and Development: Africa-Europe Relations in a Changing Global Order*, 37–61.

Australian Population Centre. (2020). Available Online: https://population.gov.au/sites/population.gov.au/files/2021-09/population_statement_2020.pdf (accessed on 01 September 2023)

Bălăcescu, A., Zaharia, M., Gogonea, R. M., & Căruntu, G. A. (2022). The Image of Sustainability in European Regions Considering the Social Sustainability Index. *Sustainability*, *14*(20), 13433.

Beck-Gernsheim, E. (2007). Transnational Lives, Transnational Marriages: A Review of the Evidence from Migrant Communities in Europe. *Global Networks*, *7*(3), 271–288.

Bedianashvili, G. (2016). The Global Business Environment, European Integration and the Cultural Potential of Social-economic Development of Georgia. *Globalization & Business*, № 1, pp. 19–25.

Bonifazi, C. (2008). Evolution of regional patterns of international migration in Europe. In C. Bonifazi, M. Okólski, J. Schoorl, & P. Simon (Eds.), *International migration in Europe: New trends and new methods of analysis* (IMISCOE research, pp. 107–128). Amsterdam: Amsterdam University Press.

Bonifazi, C., Heins, F., Licari, F., & Tucci, E. (2021). The Regional Dynamics of Internal Migration Intensities in Italy. *Population, Space and Place*, *27*(7), e2331.

Boyle, P. J., Flowerdew, R., & Shen, J. (1998). Modelling Inter-ward Migration in Hereford and Worcester: The Importance of Housing Growth and Tenure. *Regional Studies*, *32*(2), 113–132.

Boyle, P., Norman, P., 2009. Migration and health. In: Brown, T., McLafferty, S., Moon, G. (Eds.), *A Companion to Health and Medical Geography*. Wiley-Blackwell, London, pp. 346–374.

Castles, S., & Ozkul, D. (2014). Circular Migration: Triple Win, or a New Label for Temporary Migration?. In Mixed Migration Centre, *Global and Asian Perspectives on International Migration* (pp. 27–49). Cham: Springer International Publishing.

Center for Fixed migration. Available Online: https://mixedmigration.org/wp-content/uploads/2023/01/208_annual_catalogue_2021.pdf (accessed on 01 September 2023).

Czaika, M., & Reinprecht, C. (2022). Migration drivers: Why do people migrate. In P. Scholten (Ed.), *Introduction to migration studies: An interactive guide to the literatures on migration and diversity* (pp. 49–82). Cham, Switzerland: Springer.

De Bruycker, P. (2022, February). The New Pact on Migration and Asylum: What It Is Not and What It Could Have Been. In Brill - Leiden (NL), *Reforming the Common European Asylum System* (pp. 33–42). Nomos Verlagsgesellschaft mbH & Co. KG.

De Coninck, D. (2023). The Refugee Paradox during Wartime in Europe: How Ukrainian and Afghan Refugees Are (Not) Alike. *International Migration Review*, *57*(2), 578–586.

Dietz, B. & Kaczmarczyk, P. (2008). On the demand side of international labour mobility: The structure of the German labour market as a causal factor of seasonal Polish migration. In: Simon, P., Bonifazi, C., Okólski, M., & Schoorl, J. (Eds.) *International Migration in Europe. New Trends and New Methods of Analysis*. Amsterdam University Press, pp. 37–64.

Doomernik J, Bruquetas-Callejo M (2016) National immigration and integration policies in Europe Since 1973. In: Garcés-Mascareñas B, Penninx R (eds) *Integration processes and policies in Europe: contexts, levels and actors*. Springer International Publishing, Cham, pp. 57–76.

Doomernik, J., Garcés-Mascareñas, B., & Güell, B. (2023). Seasonal Workers in Agriculture: The Cases of Spain and The Netherlands in Times of Covid-19. In European Commission, *Migration Control Logics and Strategies in Europe: A North-South Comparison* (pp. 209–226). Cham: Springer International Publishing.

EUAFR. (2020). Available Online: https://ec.europa.eu/commission/presscorner/detail/en/ip_21_232 (accessed on 01 September 2023).

European Commission. (2020). Available Online: https://ec.europa.eu/eurostat/documents/3217494/12278353/KS-06-20-184-EN-N.pdf/337ecde0-665e-7162-ee96-be56b6e1186e?t=1611320765858 (accessed on 01 September 2023).

European Commission. (2021). Available Online: "Statistics on migration to Europe" at https://commission.europa.eu/strategy-and-policy/priorities-2019-2024/promoting-our-european-way-life/statistics-migration-europe_en (accessed on 20 November 2023).

European Commission. (2022). Available Online: https://commission.europa.eu/system/files/2023-01/report-migration-asylum-2022.pdf (accessed on 01 September 2023).

Eurostat. (2011). https://ec.europa.eu/eurostat/web/products-statistical-books/-/ks-31-10-539 (accessed on 01 September 2023).

Eurostat. (2020). Available Online: https://ec.europa.eu/eurostat/statistics-explained/index.php?title=Migration_and_migrant_population_statistics (accessed on 01 September 2023).

Eurostat. (2021). Available Online: https://ec.europa.eu/eurostat/web/migration-asylum (accessed on 01 September 2023).

Fasani, F., & Mazza, J. (2020). Immigrant Key Workers: Their Contribution to Europe's COVID-19.

Findlay, A. M. (2011a). An Assessment of Supply and Demand-side Theorizations of International Student Mobility. *International Migration*, *49*(2), 162–190.

Findlay, A. M. (2011b). Migrant Destinations in an Era of Environmental Change. *Global Environmental Change*, *21*, S50–S58.

Frontex. (2015). Available Online: https://frontex.europa.eu/assets/Key_Documents/Annual_report/2015/General_Report_2015.pdf (accessed on 01 September 2023).

Frontex. (2022). Available Online: https://prd.frontex.europa.eu/document/eus-external-borders-in-2022-number-of-irregular-border-crossings-highest-since-2016/ (accessed on 01 September 2023).

Gavonel, M. F., Adger, W. N., de Campos, R. S., Boyd, E., Carr, E. R., Fábos, A., … & Siddiqui, T. (2021). The Migration-sustainability Paradox: Transformations in Mobile Worlds. *Current Opinion in Environmental Sustainability*, *49*, 98–109.

Gečienė-Janulionė, I. (2018). Migration and Welfare State: The Coherence between Welfare State, Migratory Regimes and Migration Flows. *Filosofija. Sociologija*, *29*(4), 38–56.

German Federal Statistical Office. (2021). Available Online: https://www.destatis.de/Europa/EN/Topic/Population-Labour-Social-Issues/Demography-migration/_node.html (accessed on 01 September 2023).

Global Migration Indicators Report. (2021). https://publications.iom.int/system/files/pdf/Global-Migration-Indicators-2021_0.pdf (accessed on 01 September 2023).

Goldscheider, C., Bernhardt, E., & Goldscheider, F. (2008). What Integrates the Second Generation? Factors Affecting Family Transitions to Adulthood in Sweden. *International Migration in Europe: New Trends and New Methods of Analysis*, 225–246.

Guild, E., Costello, C., Garlick, M., & Moreno-Lax, V. (2015). *The 2015 Refugee Crisis in the European Union* (pp. 4–9). Brussels: Centre for European Policy Studies.

Hansen, E., & Donohoe, M. (2003). Health Issues of Migrant and Seasonal Farmworkers. *Journal of Health Care for the Poor and Underserved, 14*(2), 153–164.

Hatton, T. J., & Williamson, J. G. (2005). What Fundamentals Drive World Migration?. In *Poverty, International Migration and Asylum* (pp. 15–38). London: Palgrave Macmillan UK.

Hayward, S. E., Deal, A., Cheng, C., Crawshaw, A., Orcutt, M., Vandrevala, T. F., … & Hargreaves, S. (2021). Clinical Outcomes and Risk Factors for Covid-19 among Migrant Populations in High-Income Countries: A Systematic Review. *Journal of Migration and Health, 3*, 100041.

Hintermeier, M., Gencer, H., Kajikhina, K., Rohleder, S., Hövener, C., Tallarek, M., … & Bozorgmehr, K. (2021). SARS-CoV-2 among Migrants and Forcibly Displaced Populations: A Rapid Systematic Review. *Journal of Migration and Health, 4*, 100056.

Hudson, R., & Lewis, J. (Eds.). (2022). *Uneven Development in Southern Europe: Studies of Accumulation, Class, Migration and the State*. Routledge. London, UK.

ILO. (2017). Available Online: https://www.ilo.org/wcmsp5/groups/public/---dgreports/---dcomm/---publ/documents/publication/wcms_652001.pdf (accessed on 01 September 2023).

ILO. (2018). Available Online: https://www.ilo.org/global/publications/books/WCMS_652001/lang--en/index.htm (accessed on 01 September 2023).

International Labour Organization (ILO). (2015). Available Online: Global Estimates on Migrant Workers-Results and Methodology. https://www.ilo.org/wcmsp5/groups/public/---dgreports/---dcomm/documents/publication/wcms_436343.pdf (accessed on 20 November 2023).

International Migration Outlook. (2020). https://www.oecd-ilibrary.org/social-issues-migration-health/international-migration-outlook-2020_ec98f531-en (accessed on 01 September 2023).

IOM. (2015). Available Online: https://publications.iom.int/books/global-migration-trends-factsheet-2015 (accessed on 01 September 2023).

IOM. (2020). Available Online: https://publications.iom.int/system/files/pdf/wmr_2020.pdf (accessed on 01 September 2023).

IOM. (2022). World Migration Report-2022. ISSN 1561-5502 ISBN 978-92-9268-076-3 (PDF).

Jakovljevic, M., Cerda, A. A., Liu, Y., García, L., Timofeyev, Y., Krstic, K., & Fontanesi, J. (2021). Sustainability Challenge of Eastern Europe – Historical Legacy, Belt and Road Initiative, Population Aging and Migration. *Sustainability, 13*(19), 11038.

Kerwin, D. (2020). International Migration and Work: Charting an Ethical Approach to the Future. *Journal on Migration and Human Security*, *8*(2), 111–133.

Koris, R., Mato-Díaz, F. J., & Hernández-Nanclares, N. (2021). From Real to Virtual Mobility: Erasmus Students' Transition to Online Learning Amid the COVID-19 Crisis. *European Educational Research Journal*, *20*(4), 463–478.

Kulu, H., Christison, S., Liu, C., & Mikolai, J. (2023). The War, Refugees, and the Future of Ukraine's Population. *Population, Space and Place*, *29*(4), e2656.

Lange, T. (2013). Return Migration of Foreign Students and Non-resident Tuition Fees. *Journal of Population Economics*, *26*, 703–718.

Lee, E. S. (1966). A Theory of Migration. *Demography*, *3*, 47–57.

Manyika, J., Chui, M., Bughin, J., Dobbs, R., Bisson, P., & Marrs, A. (2013). *Disruptive Technologies: Advances That Will Transform Life, Business, and the Global Economy* (Vol. 180, pp. 17–21). San Francisco, CA: Mckinsey Global Institute.

McAuliffe, M., Blower, J., & Beduschi, A. (2021). Digitalization and Artificial Intelligence in Migration and Mobility: Transnational Implications of the COVID-19 Pandemic. *Societies*, *11*(4), 135.

Mermanishvili, T. (2022). Migration to the EU: Some Aspects of Georgian Population Attitude and Baltic States Experience. *Filosofija. Sociologija*, *33*(2), 97–106.

Migali, S., Natale, F., Tintori, G., Kalantaryan, S., Grubanov-Boskovic, S., Scipioni, M., … & Barbas, T. (2018). *International Migration Drivers*. Ispra, Italy: Joint Research Centre.

Migration Data Portal. (2023). Available Online: https://www.migrationdataportal.org/international-data (accessed on 01 September 2023).

Molinero-Gerbeau, Y., López-Sala, A., & Şerban, M. (2021). On the Social Sustainability of Industrial Agriculture Dependent on Migrant Workers. Romanian Workers in Spain's Seasonal Agriculture. *Sustainability*, *13*(3), 1062.

OECD. (2015). Available Online: https://www.oecd.org/els/mig/Migration-data-brief-4-EN.pdf (accessed on 01 September 2023).

OECD. (2018). Available Online: https://www.oecd.org/publications/indicators-of-immigrant-integration-2018-9789264307216-en.htm (accessed on 01 September 2023).

OECD. (2019). Recent Trends in International Migration of Doctors, Nurses and Medical Students, https://www.oecd.org/content/dam/oecd/en/publications/reports/2019/07/recent-trends-in-international-migration-of-doctors-nurses-and-medical students_dbd9ed7f/5571ef48-en.pdf (accessed on 12 February 2025).

OECD. (2020). Available Online: International Migration Outlook 2020, https://www.oecd-ilibrary.org/social-issues-migration-health/international-migration-outlook-2020_ec98f531-en (accessed on 01 September 2023).

OECD. (2021). International Migration Outlook 2021, Available Online: https://doi.org/10.1787/29f23e9d-en (accessed on 01 September 2023).

Pew Research Center. (2020). Available Online: Coronavirus Disease (COVID-19), https://www.pewresearch.org/fact-tank/2020/04/01/more-than-nine-in-ten-people-worldwide-live-in-countries-with-travel-restrictions-amid-covid-19/ (accessed on 20 November 2023).

Rella, P., & Vadala, T. (1984). Sociological Literature on Migration in Italy. *Current Sociology*, *32*(2), 143–174.

Sachseder, J., Stachowitsch, S., & Binder, C. (2022). Gender, Race, and Crisis-driven Institutional Growth: Discourses of "migration crisis" and the Expansion of Frontex. *Journal of Ethnic and Migration Studies*, *48*(19), 4670–4693.

Selod, H., & Shilpi, F. (2021). Rural-Urban Migration in Developing Countries: Lessons from the Literature. *Regional Science and Urban Economics*, *91*, 103713.

Strasser, E., Kraler, A., Bonjour, S., & Bilger, V. (2009). Doing Family: Responses to the Constructions of "the migrant family" across Europe. *The History of the Family*, *14*(2), 165–176.

The Economist. (2018). Available Online: URL Europeans Remain Welcoming to Immigrants. Available at: https://www.economist.com/graphic-detail/2018/04/19/europeans-remain-welcoming-to-immigrants (accessed on 01 September 2023).

Tremblay, K. (2005). Academic Mobility and Immigration. *Journal of Studies in International Education*, *9*(3), 196–228.

Tzoraki, O., Dimitrova, S., Barzakov, M., Yaseen, S., Gavalas, V., Harb, H., … & Trajanovic, M. (2021). The Impact of the COVID-19 Pandemic on the Working Conditions, Employment, Career Development and Well-being of Refugee Researchers. *Societies*, *11*(3), 71.

UN DESA. (2020). Available Online: https://www.un.org/development/desa/pd/sites/www.un.org.development.desa.pd/files/undesa_pd_2020_international_migration_highlights.pdf (accessed on 01 September 2023).

UN. (2018). Available Online: https://www.unhcr.org/media/global-compact-refugees-booklet (accessed on 01 September 2023).

UN. (2020). Available Online: https://www.un.org/development/desa/pd/content/international-migrant-stock (accessed on 01 September 2023).

UN. (2021). *The Global Compact for Safe, Orderly and Regular Migration*. Report of the Secretary-General (A/76/642) (accessed on 01 September 2023).

United Nations. (2020). Available Online: “International Migrant Stock,” https://www.un.org/development/desa/pd/content/international-migrant-stock (accessed on 01 September 2023).

Van Mol, C. (2014). *Intra-European Student Mobility in International Higher Education Circuits: Europe on the Move*. Springer, Switzerland.

Van Mol, C. (2016). Migration Aspirations of European Youth in Times of Crisis. *Journal of Youth Studies*, *19*(10), 1303–1320.

Van Mol, C., and de Valk, H. (2016). “Migration and immigrants in Europe: a historical and demographic perspective,” in *Integration Processes and Policies in Europe*, IMISCOE Research Series (Cham: Springer), 31–55. doi: 10.1007/978-3-319-21674-4_3”

Who. (2020). Available Online: https://apps.who.int/iris/rest/bitstreams/1354489/retrieve (accessed on 01 September 2023).

World Bank. (2023). World Bank, FDI and ODA Data from World Development Indicators. https://data.worldbank.org/ (accessed 12 february 2025).

Ema Peternel and Vladimir Bukvič

Investment Strategies of Some of the Most Successful Investors in the World's Stock Markets and a Comparison of Their Profitability with Slovenian Funds

1. Introduction

The efficient market hypothesis states that stocks are always traded on stock exchanges at their fair value. It argues that without inside information, no one can generate risk-adjusted excess returns consistently enough. Thus, it seems that the only real approach to achieving higher returns is to invest in riskier investments (Downey, 2023). Despite this, financial moguls like Warren Buffett, Bill Ackman and Chamath Palihapitiya consistently manage to achieve returns that exceed the market average. We wonder what the secret of their success is.

The aim of the paper is to study and present the investment philosophies and methods of three globally recognized investors – Warren Buffett, Bill Ackman and Chamath Palihapitiya. We will examine their philosophies and approaches to investing. Theoretical concepts will be supported by empirical data and case studies. As part of the research, we conducted three case studies that were not included in the article due to their limited scope (Buffett, 2013; Canadian Pacific, 2012; Dinner, 2023; Greenslade, 2014; Sheetz, 2021; USSEC, 2019; Virgin Galactic, 2019, 2022a, 2022b, 2023). The following investments were discussed: Buffett's investment in The Washington Post, Ackman's investment in The Canadian Pacific Railway, and Palihapitiya's investment in Virgin Galactic. A more detailed discussion of the studies is available in the author's thesis (Peternel, 2023). In the research, we conducted a comparative analysis, comparing the financial indicators of Berkshire Hathaway and Pershing Square with the returns of the S&P 500 index and the selected Slovenian mutual funds. We have prepared the calculations necessary for the comparative analysis. We obtained the data from the Yahoo Finance databases. An important part of this paper is the Monte Carlo simulation, which enables the modeling of potential returns for continuous annual investments. We have estimated the expected returns using the CAPM model.

With this paper, we want to determine whether and to what extent the principles and philosophies of the selected investors influence their investment decisions, whether the selected mutual funds exceed the return of the S&P 500 index and, if so, we aim to analyze the factors that contributed to their higher return, how the investment strategies are reflected in the profitability and risk of the fund, what is the profitability of the selected American funds compared to the selected Slovenian funds and, last but not least, what influence do knowledge and tracking of the intrinsic value of the company have on the final investment profitability.

2. Literature Review

2.1. Investment Philosophies and Strategies

2.1.1. Warren Buffett's Investment Strategy

In order to effectively manage Berkshire Hathaway and its investments, Buffett wrote twelve principles in a 2013 letter to the company's shareholders, which are classified into four main groups: (1) Business principles, (2) Management principles, (3) Financial principles and (4) Market principles. In summary, the short-term performance of an investment does not mean that the portfolio managers are good or bad. The period in which we measure the ability to generate returns is simply too short to draw any meaningful conclusions. However, if we look at the company's operating results, we can assess progress when the share price deviates from expected returns. Buffet emphasizes that the key to a successful investment is a competitive advantage and a favorable price compared to the internal value (margin of safety) (Buffett, 2014; Hagstrom, 2014; Klarman, 1999; Buffett, 1985).

2.1.2. Bill Ackman's Investment Strategy

Bill Ackman is a hedge fund manager and investor known for his use of activist investing (Dallas, Bainbridge & Bohinc, 2001). Ackman's activist investment approach is based on acquiring large stakes in undervalued companies through his hedge fund Pershing Square Capital Management. It works with the management of these companies to drive change that can increase shareholder value. Changes can be reflected in operational improvements, reallocation of capital, or in the restructuring of the management team. Ackman often expresses his opinion publicly. He prepares presentations or writes open letters to the company's stakeholders in which he explains his investment strategy (Tenorio, 2021).

2.1.3. Chamath Palihapitiya's Investment Strategy

Chamath Palihapitiya focuses on investing in high-tech companies with high growth and transformation potential. He looks for opportunities in undervalued companies with long-term competitive advantages. His strategy focuses on making unconventional decisions that deviate from market trends, thorough data analysis, and trust in management with a proven ability to lead and make decisions effectively. He believes in the power of technology to solve social problems and promotes companies that have a positive impact on society. He supports ethical behavior, transparency and socially responsible investing. Issues of diversity, equality and inclusion are also of critical significance. As the co-founder of Facebook, he promotes a form of capitalism where success is measured not only by profit, but also by social impact (Dure, 2023).

3. Research Methodology and Research Hypothesis

With our research, we set the following research hypotheses:

H1: Proper assessment and monitoring of the company's future intrinsic value enables above-average investment returns.
H2: The fund's profitability and risk are a reflection of the chosen investment strategy. Investment funds that are willing to take on more risk often aim for higher returns, while more conservative funds aim for lower, but more stable returns.
H3: The most important factors in investing are time and patience.
H4: The stock market does not always accurately reflect the value of an individual company, so it is important to critically evaluate every decision and not blindly follow market trends.

In the theoretical part of the research, we used the scientific method of description as well as the scientific methods of classification, comparison, analysis and synthesis.

In the empirical part of the research, we used statistical methods (arithmetic mean, standard deviation) and analyzed the data using the Sharpe ratio, performed a Monte Carlo simulation and used the CAPM model.

For the research, we used secondary data from the Yahoo Finance database and secondary data for the Slovenian mutual funds. The research covers the 2018–2022 period.

At this point, we should also mention the limitations we encountered during the research. The first limitation stems from the non-random sample size. We limited the research to two large foreign joint-stock companies, whose shares are listed on world stock exchanges, and to a few Slovenian mutual funds. The research could cover a longer period. We would also like to point out that our analysis of returns and risks does not cover all relevant factors, such as macroeconomic and regulatory conditions.

4. Profitability and Risk of Investments: The Eternal Dilemma of Investors

Investors generally expect higher returns from riskier investments. The risk is not the same for all investors. Different investors take different risks. We are talking about risk appetite. Risk appetite is the degree of broad-based risk that an investor is willing to accept in pursuit of their strategic goals. Risk appetite reflects the risk management philosophy an investor wants to adopt and consequently influences their risk culture, way of operating and decision-making (The Global Fund, 2018). When it comes to a low-risk investment, the return is generally low as well. Similarly, high risk brings with it the possibility of high losses. Therefore, investors should diversify their portfolio. Diversification of investments has a statistical effect in terms of reducing overall risk. Investors, especially beginners, are often advised to diversify their portfolio (Bukvič, 2024).

4.1. Profitability of Shares of Joint-Stock Companies on Global Stock Exchanges and Slovenian Mutual Funds

4.1.1. The Return on Shares of Two Companies Listed on Global Stock Exchanges

The value of a hypothetical $10,000 investment in Berkshire Hathaway (BRK – A) stock from 2018 to 2022 would increase to about $15,890. The investment would therefore increase by 59 % in five years.

Figure 1 shows Berkshire Hathaway's annualized return and the performance of a hypothetical $10,000 investment in Berkshire Hathaway stock in the 2018–2022 period.

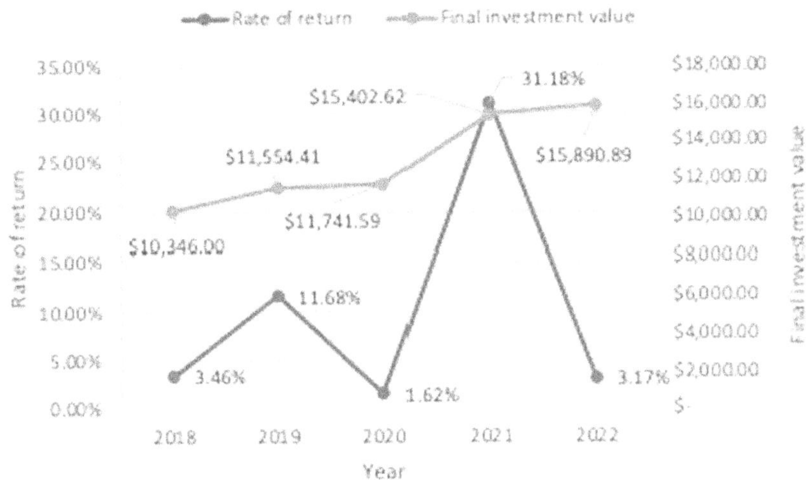

Figure 1: Graphic representation of Berkshire Hathaway's annualized return and the performance of a hypothetical $10,000 investment in Berkshire Hathaway's stock in the 2018–2022 period

Source: Yahoo Finance (2023a).

The value of a hypothetical $10,000 investment in Pershing Square (PSH.AS) stock would increase to about $26,500 from 2018 to 2022, a 165 % increase. Short-term losses do not reflect long-term trends, as high returns in other years more than offset these losses. Although the path has been unpredictable, the company's long-term strategy is successful in uncertain market conditions.

Figure 2 shows the annualized return of Pershing Square stock and the performance of a hypothetical $10,000 investment in Pershing Square stock in the 2018–2022 period.

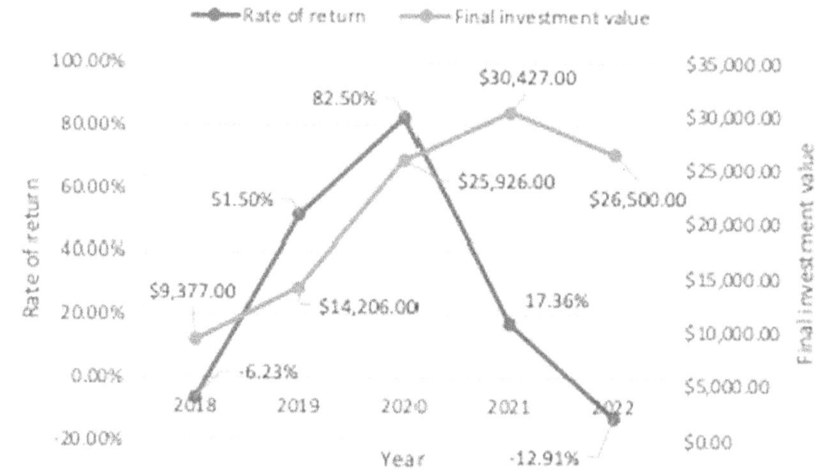

Figure 2: Graphical representation of Pershing Square's annualized return and the performance of a hypothetical $10,000 investment in Pershing Square in the 2018–2022 period

Source: Yahoo Finance (2023b).

An analysis of Berkshire Hathaway and Pershing Square's 2018–2022 stock returns highlights the importance of a long-term strategy and patience, which are key for investors. Despite short-term fluctuations and negative returns in some years, high positive returns in other years led to overall investment growth. Pershing Square's stock stood out for its outstanding returns, which more than offset short-term losses. These fluctuations show that the stock market does not always reflect the true value of companies, which requires critical judgment from investors.

4.1.2. *Average Return on Shares of Selected Companies, Mutual Funds and the S&P 500 Index*

Among the selected companies and mutual funds, the shares of *Pershing Square (PSH.AS)* achieved by far the highest average annual return of 21.74 % over the five-year period under review.

The shares of *Berkshire Hathaway (BRK-A)* achieved an average return of 9.65 % over a five-year period, outperforming the S&P 500 but trailing Pershing Square. The lower return of the shares (BRK-A) can be attributed to the company's conservative strategy, which strives for long-term stability and growth.

The NLB Developed Europe equity mutual fund, which focuses on investments in established European companies and is managed by NLB funds, recorded an average annual return of 1.40 % in the period under review. This allows us to draw conclusions about the fund's less successful investment strategy. However, a lower return does not necessarily mean that the fund is a poor choice for investors. Its long-term profitability depends on the performance of the European economy.

The NLB Global equity mutual fund, managed by NLB funds, achieved an average annual return of 5.07 % over the five years in question. The annual return is below that of the S&P 500 index.

TRIGLAV North America, a mutual fund managed by Triglav funds, achieved an average annual return of 8.96 %, which exceeds the return of the S&P 500 index. The fund is categorized as high risk, so it is important to assess its ability to create value relative to the risk taken (Triglav skladi, 2023b).

The TRIGLAV Europe mutual fund, managed by Triglav funds, achieved the lowest average annual return of 1.36 %. The fund focuses on investments in European companies, but the regional focus has not brought the desired results during this period. Possible reasons for such a low return may include worse economic performance in Europe or an unsuccessful investment strategy of the mutual fund (Triglav skladi, 2023a).

The S&P 500 index achieved an average annual return of 7.33 % during the period under review. Investments in funds that track this index are often considered less risky because of the broad diversification among the 500 companies. However, diversification does not eliminate all the risks. The S&P 500 index is a frequent benchmark for assessing profitability and will serve as a basis for comparing the performance of the funds and companies in question.

Figure 3 shows a comparison of the average annual return of selected mutual funds, company shares and the S&P 500 index for the last five-year period.

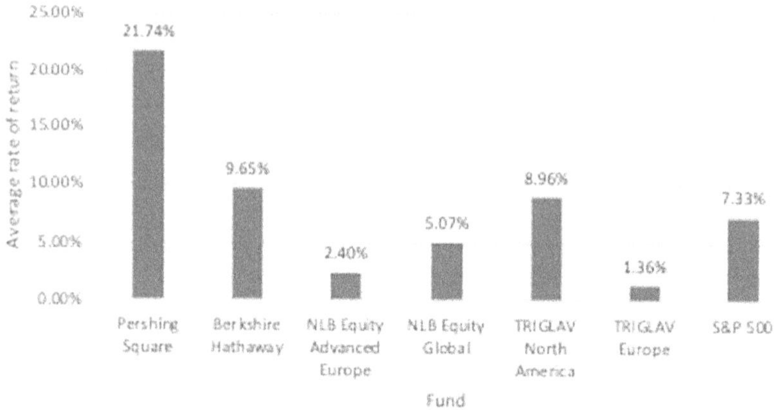

Figure 3: Graphic representation of the average annual return on shares of selected companies, mutual funds and the S&P 500 index in the 2018–2022 period

Source: NLB funds (2023b), Triglav skladi (2023b), Yahoo Finance (2023c).

The quantitative analysis of the average return on mutual funds and company shares in the selected period reveals the impact of investment strategy and geographic focus. Different strategies produced varied results, with higher risk often leading to higher returns but also higher volatility.

4.2. The Risk of Investments of Joint-Stock Companies on Global Stock Exchanges and in Slovenian Mutual Funds

In the investment world, there is no return without risk. In this subsection, we focus on a tool that is often used in financial analyzes to measure this risk: the annual standard deviation.

The standard deviation for the *S&P 500* in the 2018–2022 period was 0.219. The annual returns on the S&P 500 have fluctuated with a volatility of 21.9 % around the average annual return.

The standard deviation for the *Pershing Square* stock in the 2018–2022 period was 0.275. The stock's returns have fluctuated with a volatility of about 27.5 % around the average annual return. The returns have fluctuated widely between 82.5 % in 2022 and −12.91 % in 2022.

The standard deviation for the *Berkshire Hathaway* stock was 0.224 during the period under review, which means that the stock's returns have fluctuated with a volatility of about 22.4 % around its average annual return. Since the standard deviation of Berkshire Hathaway's stock is only slightly above the standard deviation of the S&P 500, this indicates a relatively low risk investment in the company.

The standard deviation of the units of the NLB Razvita Evropa Delniški mutual fund was 0.180, which means that the returns of the mutual fund have fluctuated with a volatility of approximately 18 % around the average annual return during the period under review.

The shares of the NLB Globalni Delniški mutual fund also had a lower annual standard deviation than the S&P 500 index. This was 0.173 and it reflects that the returns of the mutual fund have fluctuated with a volatility of 17.3 % around the average annual return during the period under review. Smaller fluctuations in returns are attractive to investors looking for more stable investments.

The TRIGLAV North America mutual fund recorded a standard deviation of 0.223. This value reflects the volatility of the fund's return, which was approximately 22.3 % around the average annual return. The mutual fund was very similar to the stock market in terms of volatility, but outperformed the S&P 500 index with an 8.96 % average annual return.

The standard deviation of the assets of the TRIGLAV Europe mutual fund amounted to 0.172 in the considered period. The mutual fund's return volatility has hovered around 17.2 % around its average annual return. We can conclude that their returns were more stable and less volatile.

Figure 4 illustrates the investment risks of selected shares of foreign companies and Slovenian mutual funds in the period under consideration.

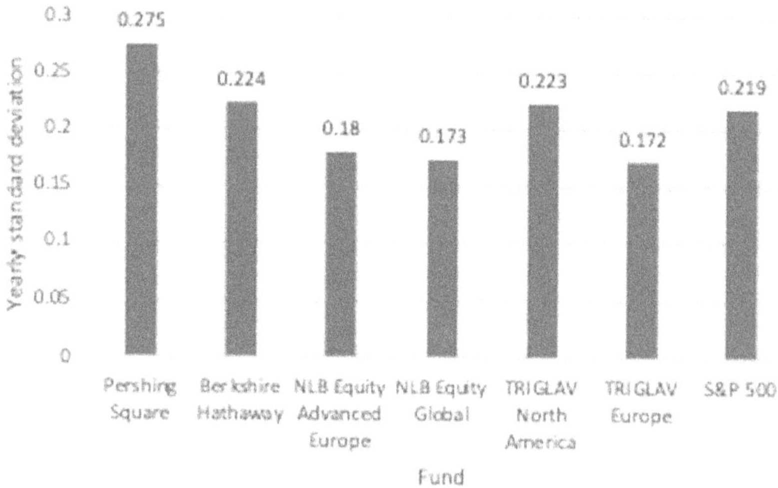

Figure 4: Graphic representation of investment risks of selected company shares, mutual funds and the S&P 500 index (2018–2022)

Source: NLB funds (2023b), Triglav skladi (2023b), Yahoo Finance (2023c).

We can conclude that the return and risks of the fund and the company's shares are a reflection of its chosen investment strategy. While Pershing Square pursues a strategy focused on achieving high returns, which is reflected in its share price, mutual funds such as NLB Razvita Evropa Delniški, NLB Globalni Delniški and TRIGLAV Evropa have chosen a strategy that favors lower risk and more stable returns.

4.3. Profitability Compared to the Risk of Investments of Joint-Stock Companies on Global Stock Exchanges and in Slovenian Mutual Funds

4.3.1. The Sharpe Ratio

The Sharpe ratio for the *S&P 500* was 0.24 during the period under review. For every unit of risk assumed, the S&P 500 gained 0.24 units of excess return above the risk-free interest rate. A higher Sharpe ratio means higher risk-adjusted returns, so in this case it can be argued that the S&P 500 has performed relatively well compared to the risk taken.

The Sharpe ratio for shares of *Pershing Square* was 0.71. The stock is better adjusted to the risk compared to the capital market. Investing in Pershing Square shares has by far the highest average returns, is highly volatile and therefore riskier.

The Sharpe ratio for *Berkshire Hathaway* stock was 0.34. The stock generated 0.34 units of excess return for every unit of risk assumed. Although the company's stock has not achieved as high a ratio as Pershing Square's stock, it has managed to generate better returns relative to the risk taken compared to the equity market (S&P 500).

For the *NLB Razvita Evropa Delniški mutual fund*, the Sharpe ratio was barely 0.02 in the considered time period. That's significantly less than the ratio for S&P 500. It has generated extremely low risk-adjusted returns compared to others.

For the mutual fund *NLB Globalna Delniški*, the Sharpe ratio was 0.17. For each unit of risk assumed, the mutual fund generated 0.17 units of excess return above the risk-free interest rate. Adjusted for risk, it underperformed the S&P 500.

The TRIGLAV North America mutual fund had a slightly better Sharpe ratio of 0.31. The mutual fund outperformed the ratio achieved by the S&P 500 index during the period under review. For every unit of risk, the mutual fund generated 0.31 units of excess return.

The mutual fund TRIGLAV Europe created the worst Sharpe ratio of all mutual funds and companies, which amounted to –0.04. Therefore, mutual fund Triglav Evropa generated lower returns than the risk-free rate of return (it is a systematic risk).

Figure 5 visualizes the Sharpe ratios as shown in Table 5 and represents the return-to-risk ratio for selected mutual funds and companies.

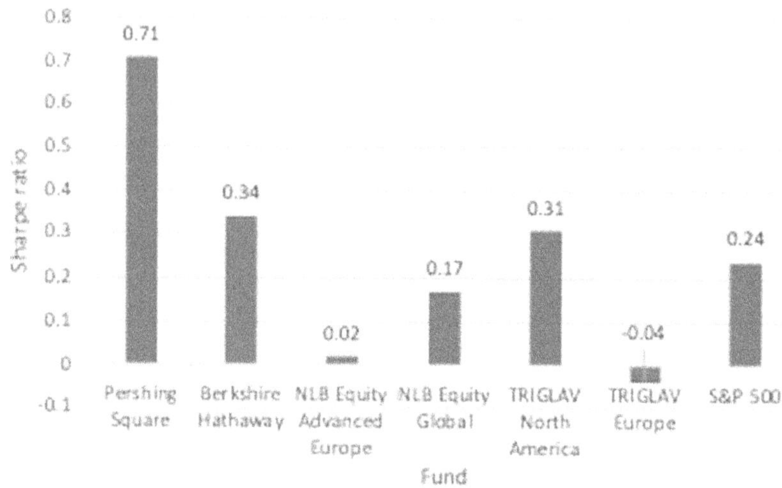

Figure 5: Display of the Sharpe ratio for shares of selected companies, mutual funds and the S&P 500 index

Source: NLB funds (2023b), Triglav skladi (2023b), Yahoo Finance (2023c).

The Sharpe ratio analysis offered a thorough insight into their return in relation to the risk taken. The differences in ratios showed a clear divide between individual investment strategies of mutual funds and companies. From the perspective of an investor seeking the optimal combination of return and risk, this analysis helps identify potential opportunities and pitfalls within available investment options.

4.3.2. The Monte Carlo Simulation

A Monte Carlo simulation is based on random sampling to simulate the range of possible outcomes for an uncertain event. The results shown are only simulated and do not exactly represent the predicted outcomes, but rather serve as a tool for evaluating different possible scenarios (Kenton, 2023).

In our example, we run a Monte Carlo simulation that considers an annual investment of $6,000 over a period of 40 years (2022–2062). We run 10,000 scenarios for each share of the selected company and asset unit of the mutual fund. The results of the Monte Carlo simulation are shown in Table 1.

Table 1: Combined Monte Carlo simulation results for selected mutual funds, corporate stocks and the S&P 500 index

				in $
Shares, Fund, Index/Percentile	**5 %**	**25 %**	**75 %**	**95 %**
PSH.AS	3,934,025	14,626,639	89,513,017	326,300,383
BRK-A	290,724	761,113	3,041,195	8,812,753
NLB Razvita Evropa Delniški	102,555	191,997	491,570	1,041,253
NLB Globalni Delniški	182,646	357,329	958,234	2,047,977
TRIGLAV Severna Amerika	250,877	644,925	2,578,724	7,260,077
TRIGLAV Evropa	92,492	162,139	385,506	766,662
Indeks S&P 500	183,454	441,362	1,650,003	4,384,542

Source: NLB funds (2023b), Triglav skladi (2023b), Yahoo Finance (2023a, 2023b, 2023c).

The distributions are right-skewed with a high skewness coefficient. The asymmetry strongly affects mean values and the standard deviation. Distributions have a high kurtosis coefficient. Distributions are characterized by a leptokurtic shape, with a higher concentration of values near the middle and extreme values at the tails of the distribution.

The Monte Carlo simulation revealed the dynamics of long-term investments in shares of selected companies and mutual funds. The long-term approach allowed the capital to develop and grow without the investment being exposed to momentary market reactions. Time and patience are essential factors in building a successful investment portfolio and reinforce the mindset that long-term investment patience often yields more stable and positive results.

Pershing Square's stock achieved high closing values with an aggressive strategy, while *Berkshire Hathaway's* conservative approach showed lower but still high closing values for the investment. Mutual funds *TRIGLAV Europe*, *NLB Developed Europe Equity* and *NLB Global Equity* showed lower final investment values, reflecting a different approach to the investment strategy.

4.3.3. *The CAPM Model*

In Table 2, we show the results of the CAPM model.

Table 2: Display of Beta and CAPM values for selected mutual funds, company shares and the S&P 500 index

Indicator	PSH.AS	BRK-A	NLB Razvita Evropa	NLB Globalni Delniški	TRIGLAV Severna Amerika	TRIGLAV Evropa
BETA	0.9700	0.870	0.6274	0.4631	0.3974	0.5437
CAPM	8.8 %	8.4 %	7.3 %	6.6 %	6.3 %	7.0 %

Source: NLB funds (2023b), Triglav skladi (2023b), Yahoo Finance (2023a, 2023b).

The beta coefficient for *Pershing Square (PSH.AS)* is 0.97. The return on this company's share moves in line with the return on the *S&P 500 index*. The CAPM model shows a return of 8.8 %. It should be noted, however, that the CAPM model only takes into account systematic risk (beta), but not non-systematic risk or specific characteristics of investments. Pershing Square exploits market inefficiencies, so the CAPM model may not reflect realistic future returns for this stock.

The beta coefficient for *Berkshire Hathaway (BRK-A)* is 0.87. Therefore, the return on the share is slightly less sensitive to market movements than the *S&P 500 index*. According to the CAPM model, we can expect an annual return of 8.4 %. Again, the CAPM model does not take into account the specifics of Berkshire Hathaway's strategy, which exploits market irrationalities and has a highly diversified investment policy. The CAPM model may not reflect the true expected return of a stock.

The beta coefficient for the *NLB Developed Europe Equity fund* is 0.63, which means that the mutual fund's performance is not that strongly correlated with the general movement of the market. Using the CAPM model, we can conclude that the expected return could be 7.3 %.

The beta coefficient for *NLB Global Equity Fund* is 0.46. Based on the CAPM model, we would expect a return of 6.6 %.

The TRIGLAV North America fund unit has a beta coefficient of 0.40. According to the CAPM model, a return of 6.3 % could be expected.

The beta coefficient of the *TRIGLAV Europe fund* unit is 0.54. According to the CAPM model, we can expect an annual return of 7 %.

In conclusion of this subsection, we can note that the CAPM model is a useful and effective tool for understanding risks and returns in the context of systematic market risk. However, its use is best in combination with other tools and analytical approaches that can better include the complexity and dynamics of individual investments.

5. Findings and Conclusion

Our research shows that the ability to monitor and assess a company's intrinsic value can lead to extraordinary returns. Using fundamental analysis, Buffett, Ackman and Palihapitiya found undervalued companies, invested in them and made money by increasing their market value.

We confirm the first hypothesis *H1: Proper assessment and monitoring of the company's future intrinsic value enables above-average investment returns.*

The financial analysis confirmed the fact that the capital fund's profitability and risk are a reflection of its chosen strategy. The ability of Pershing Square and Berkshire Hathaway to achieve above-average returns also stems from the acceptance of higher risks, which both companies managed by diversifying their investments. NLB funds followed more conservative strategies, which is why they generated lower but more stable returns.

We confirm the second hypothesis *H2: The fund's profitability and risk are a reflection of its chosen investment strategy.*

Funds that are prepared to accept more risk often aim for higher returns, while more conservative funds focus on achieving more stable but lower returns.

All three investors are well-aware that to achieve truly high returns, it is necessary to take a strategic, long-term view of investments. They focus on the long-term performance of the company rather than on short-term market fluctuations. They warn that a short-term view leads to extremely risky speculative investments, which confirms the third hypothesis *H3: The most important factors in investing are time and patience.*

In the financial world, opinions on the accuracy of stock market values remain divided. Some financial experts believe that markets always reflect all available information consistent with the efficient market hypothesis. Nevertheless, it should be noted that Buffett, Ackman and Palihapitiya, with their good understanding of individual companies and their excellent knowledge of how the stock market works, managed to identify investment opportunities well. We partially confirm the fourth hypothesis *H4: The stock market does not always reflect the real value of an individual company, so it is important to critically evaluate every decision and not blindly follow market trends.*

References

Buffett, W. E. (1985). *Berkshire Hathaway Inc.* Acquired from: https://www.berkshirehathaway.com/letters/1984.html.

Buffett, W. E. (2013). *Berkshire Hathaway Inc.* Acquired from: https://www.berkshirehathaway.com/letters/2012ltr.pdf.

Buffett, W. E. (2014). *Shareholder Letter.* Acquired from: https://www.berkshirehathaway.com/letters/2013ltr.pdf.

Bukvič, V. (2024). Strateške investicije v luči njihove dinamike in financiranja: primer slovenskih podjetij v obdobju 2010 do 2017 = Strategic investments in the light of their dynamics and financing: an example of Slovenian companies in the period from 2010 to 2017. *Poslovodno računovodstvo.* [Spletna izd.]. 2024, letn. 17, št. 1, pp. 153–218.

Canadian Pacific. (2012). *Canadian Pacific Annual Report 2011.* Acquired from https://s21.q4cdn.com/736796105/files/doc_financials/Annual-Report/2011/cp-ar-2011.pdf.

Dallas, L. L., Bainbridge, S. M., & Bohinc, R. (2001). *Direktorski odbor in delničarski aktivizem v ZDA in Sloveniji.* Ljubljana: Fakulteta za družbene vede.

Dinner, J. (2023). *Who Is Virgin Galactic and What Do They Do?* Acquired from https://www.space.com/18993-virgin-galactic.html.

Downey, L. (2023). *Efficient Market Hypothesis (EMH): Definition and Critique.* Acquired from https://www.investopedia.com/terms/e/efficientmarkethypothesis.asp.

Dure, E. (2023). *Chamath Palihapitiya: Early Life, Education, Personal Life.* Acquired from https://www.investopedia.com/who-is-chamath-palihapitiya-5105271.

Greenslade, R. (2014). *Warren Buffett Says Farewell to the Washington Post in £737m Sell-off Deal.* Acquired from https://www.theguardian.com/media/greenslade/2014/mar/13/washington-post-warrenbuffett#:~:text=9%20years%20old-,Warren%20Buffett%20says%20farewell%20to%20the%20Washington,%C2%A3737m%20sell%2Doff%20deal&text=Warren%20Buffett%20is%20to%20end,Holdings%2C%20the%20.

Hagstrom, R. G. (2014). *The Warren Buffett Way* (3rd ed.). Hoboken: John Wiley & Sons.

Kenton, W. (2023). *Capital Asset Pricing Model (CAPM) and Assumptions Explained.* Acquired from https://www.investopedia.com/terms/c/capm.asp.

Klarman, S. A. (1999). Why Value Investors Are Different. Acquired from https://www.barrons.com/articles/SB918877044971819500.

NLB Skladi. (2023b). *Podskladi krovnega sklada NLB Skladi.* Acquired from https://www.nlbskladi.si/skladi/podskladi.

Peternel, E. (2023). *Naložbene strategije nekaterih najuspešnejših vlagateljev svetovnih borz in primerjava njihove donosnosti s slovenskimi skladi* [Diplomsko delo, E. Peternel]. Repozitorij samostojnih visokošolskih in višješolskih izobraževalnih organizacij. Acquired from https://revis.openscience.si/IzpisGradiva.php?lang=slv&id=9948.

Sheetz, M. (2021). *Virgin Galactic Drops 10% after Chairman Chamath Palihapitiya Dumps His $213 Million Personal Stake*. Acquired from https://www.cnbc.com/2021/03/05/chamath-palihapitiya-sells-virgin-galactic-spce-stake.html.

Tenorio, E. M. (2021). *Bill Ackman's Biography: What Is His Investment Style?* Acquired from https://www.bbva.ch/en/news/bill-ackmans-biography-what-is-his-investment-style/.

The Global Fund. (2018). *Risk Appetite Framework*. Board Approved GP/B39/DP11.

Triglav skladi. (2023a). *Triglav Evropa*. Acquired from https://www.triglavskladi.si/poskrbite-za-svoje-premozenje/nalozbeni-skladi/triglav-evropa/.

Triglav skladi. (2023b). *Vzajemni skladi in naložbene kombinacije*. Acquired from https://www.triglavskladi.si/poskrbite-za-svoje-premozenje/nalozbeni-skladi/.

United States Securities and Exchange Commission (USSEC). (2019). *Form 10-K: Annual Report Pursuant to Section 13 or 15(d) of the Securities and Exchange Act of 1934: General Instructions*. Acquired from https://www.sec.gov/files/form10-k.pdf.

Virgin Galactic. (2019). *Virgin Galactic Completes Merger with Social Capital Hedosophia, Creating the World's First and Only Publicly Traded Commercial Human Spaceflight Company*. Acquired from https://investors.virgingalactic.com/news/news-details/2019/Virgin-Galactic-Completes-Merger-with-Social-Capital-Hedosophia-Creating-the-Worlds-First-and-Only-Publicly-Traded-Commercial-Human-Spaceflight-Company/default.aspx.

Virgin Galactic. (2022a). *Virgin Galactic Announces Board Changes*. Acquired from https://investors.virgingalactic.com/news/news-details/2022/Virgin-Galactic-Announces-Board-Changes/default.aspx.

Virgin Galactic. (2022b). *Virgin Galactic Holdings Inc. (SPCE) Q4 2021 – Earnings Call Rranscript*. Acquired from https://news.alphastreet.com/virgin-galactic-holdings-inc-spce-q4-2021-earnings-call-transcript/.

Virgin Galactic. (2023). *Virgin Galactic Announces First Quarter 2023 Financial Results and Provides Business Update*. Acquired from https://investors.virgingalactic.com/news/news-details/2023/Virgin-Galactic-Announces-First-Quarter-2023-Financial-Results-And-Provides-Business-Update/default.aspx.

Yahoo Finance. (2023a). *Berkshire Hathaway Inc. (BRK-A)*. Acquired from https://finance.yahoo.com/quote/BRK-A?p=BRK-A.

Yahoo Finance. (2023b). *Pershing Square Holdings, Ltd. (PSH.AS)*. Acquired from https://finance.yahoo.com/quote/PSH.AS?p=PSH.AS&.tsrc=fin-srch.

Yahoo Finance. (2023c). *SPDR S&P 500 ETF Trust (SPY)*. Acquired from https://finance.yahoo.com/quote/SPY?p=SPY&.tsrc=fin-srch.

Luisa Anderloni and Ornella Moro

Financial Literacy, Digital Literacy and Sustainability in Small-Scale Entrepreneurship[1]

1. Introduction

Micro, small, and medium enterprises (MSMEs) in OECD countries account for 99 % of all businesses and between 50 % and 60 % of value added (OECD, 2021a). They can play an important role in sustainable, inclusive economic growth and development, provided that they have access to savings, investment, and credit and provided they can use them to improve their business. The possession of adequate financial knowledge and skills is a critic element for influence and empower their use of financial services. But MSMEs must embrace and keep pace with other important factors that influence their growth and development: on one side the digital revolution, on the other side the growing sensibility for sustainability shown by their various stakeholders.

The importance of a good level of financial literacy (FL) has long been recognized both in academia (Atkinson et al., 2007; Atkinson & Messy, 2011; Lusardi & Mitchell, 2011; Lusardi-Tufano, 2015) and by policy makers and international bodies (OECD, 2009 and various years; Xu & Zia, 2012, World bank various years, EU Commission 2012 and Eurostat, various years) with reference both, in general, to the population as a consumers, and to minor entrepreneurs.

The theme of sustainability is declined in three main domains: in the environmental one, due to the use of natural resources, pollution, and its effects; in the social one, due to the protection of individual rights and collective well-being, and in the economic one, due to the significance of corporate and institutional governance. This theme has entered vigorously among the priorities that must guide the work of people, economic organizations and non-profit and governments of countries and international communities

1 Grants and funding. This research was funded by the University of Sassari (FAR – Fondo di Ateneo per la ricerca, 2020/University Research) and partly funded by the project "APEGADRUS" under DM 737/2021 resources 2021–2022. Dm737 is one of the initiatives financed by NextGenerationEU.

Financial literacy and digital literacy are becoming critical means for fostering MSMEs' business continuity and sustainable growth (Yanto et al., 2022) and for building inclusive and resilient economies and societies. In addition, also sustainability, due to customers' and business partners' growing sensibility to these issues (resilient economies and societies), can contribute to increase MSMEs' business performance.

As for Financial literacy, alongside the studies in different age groups of the population, the research question on the level of financial literacy of entrepreneurs has emerged. Entrepreneurs, including small business owners or sole proprietors, are commonly believed to possess strong financial acumen due to their regular financial decision-making, but in the composite group of micro-entrepreneurs this belief is only partially verified. Some empirical researches show that Financial literacy of micro entrepreneurs varies according to characteristics of the business (sector, number of employees) and of the owner (gender, education level, entrepreneurial experience) (OECD, 2021b). In some countries micro entrepreneurs, compared with other individuals, show a slightly higher level of FL, mainly attributable to their income, age and education (Finaldi Russo et al., 2022) but it is difficult to believe that this is the case of very small businesses managed by entrepreneurs with low level of secondary education.

As for Digital technologies, their development and wide adoption are goals of the European Commission's policy. Digitalization has been reshaping also micro-entrepreneurs' daily instruments such as devices, networks but also use of information and communications technologies, inducing new services and supply contents. It has generated new opportunities for MSMEs by operating across greater distances and reaching to new markets and customers. It has also stimulated the birth and diffusion of a wider range of financial services for which the so called digital financial literacy has often become a critical factor to exploit opportunities for convenient financing and proper utilization of these instruments.

For MSMES one important barrier to digitalization is the fact that they lack a digital culture or literacy which encompasses more than just the ability to use new technology, learn to use new devices, or apply technology in a learning context but regards the capability of understanding the overall potential benefits of actual and future digitalization, of understanding and detecting digital risk (relative to data and to privacy issues) and of providing insurance against ICT security incidents. It means not limiting the technological uptakes to those imposed by external constraints, whether public distancing measures or consumer demand to buy online, but adopting a positive willingness towards digital technologies uptake to anticipate future evolution.

As for Sustainability, only in last decades there has been a growing awareness of environment and sustainability issues. Sustainability means meeting the needs of the present without compromising the ability of future generations to meet theirs. As above said, it is often divided into three major topics or areas: environmental, social, and governance (ESG). Environmental refers to the company's capacity to minimize its ecological footprint; social focuses on the welfare of the community, and corporate governance assesses the transparency and ethics of corporate governance practices.

For a traditional enterprise system, economic development is normally taken as its main goals and ESG goals are often omitted but in the last years they are becoming more and more important. Among them, environment issues have greater visibility and attention than social and governance issues.

The concept of sustainability has been scarcely analyzed within the context of MSMEs both in its wide spectrum of SDGs or even in the more focused greening debate: data on their environmental footprint are scarce and often unreliable. Individually, micro enterprises have insignificant impact on sustainable development, because of their size but, as they represents high percentages of business sectors in many countries, the cumulative impact of their environmental, social and economic practices is important and outweighs the one from large organizations (Wildnerova et al., 2024).

However, MSMEs have great potential in achieving many of the 17 Sustainable Development Goals (SDGs) not limiting their commitment to environment sustainability: they can contribute by creating job and alleviating in this way poverty, by enrolling female workers and reduce gender discrimination, by providing goods and services that increase wellness: a clear example is the provision of health and care services to the elder individuals (UNDESA – Report, 2020).

The heterogeneous nature of MSMs makes it difficult to generalize about their ESG impacts, as some sustainability issues may be more relevant for certain MSMEs than others. Many micro entrepreneurs have a very poor awareness and a low level of "ecoliteracy", they are focused on survival issues as well as daily operations and ignore ESG issues and they do not perceive the environment or other SDGs as their business problem due to small impacts. They also do not possess those resources, data, technical skills, expertise, and experience required to adopt sustainability management practices that are often acknowledged by larger organizations (Wildnerova et al., 2024).

But a growing number of external factors – environmental awareness and demands from customers, employees' sensibility, sustainable awareness in the B2B supply chain system, public ESG regulations, changes in the finance sector – are driving entrepreneurs to pay a greater attention to sustainability issues and to opportunities for their business. The adoption of sustainable practices, beside enhancing their environmental and social impact, can strengthen MSMEs' financial standing and give access to diverse financing resources such as loans, impact investments, and grants marked explicitly for sustainable initiatives. Conversely, a lack of action on sustainability can limit the future available financing options or can increase the cost of loans as European banks are including sustainability standards in their credit policy.

After this brief introduction to the issues relating to small businesses, the rest of the chapter is organized in the following manner: paragraph 2 outlines how the relation among the three mentioned fields of knowledge and behavior has been studied, or more frequently, as has not been investigated in literature, whereas paragraph 3 presents in an integrated way the results of surveys conducted in parallel by several European countries following a common framework proposed by OECD-INFE (OECD, 2021b), with specific reference to financial and digital literacy, but which also collect elements to assess sustainability awareness. This is a first attempt to analyze the situation in different European countries in an aggregate way and to investigate the link between the three areas. Paragraph 4 presents the conclusions of the analysis, while the Annex at the end of this work contains the tables with the description of the data sample and the regressions.

2. The Relation among Financial Literacy, Digital Experience and Sustainability Awareness in the Existing Literature

The multifaceted relation among SMEs' financial literacy, digitalization strategies-digital literacy and awareness of environmental sustainability are at present not adequately studied by Academia. Ramanathan and Indiran (2021) deals with Financial Literacy, Digital Literacy and Sustainability Literacy highlighting how they might remodel Economy through sustainable development but without considering the possible relations among these variables.

Traditionally researchers have been investigated these concepts separately, paying scarce attention to their possible connections (Isensee et al., 2020) or have been focused on relations among only two issues: generally, the growing adoption of digital technologies have strengthened the conceptual association between financial literacy and digital literacy (OECD, 2018; D'Ignazio et al., 2022; Anderloni & Moro, 2024). The conceptual framework of multifaceted relation are that of the growing diffusion and adoption of digital technologies, often induced by external stimuli such as lock down linked to the Covid pandemia (OECD, 2021b; Bhaskar et al., 2021) and the gradual acquisition of digital knowledge and skills by different age groups (OECD, 2023a), the increasing provision of financial digital products and services and, consequently, the gradual evolution of financial literacy into financial digital literacy (OECD, 2017).

As for the above mentioned growing diffusion of digital technologies, OECD report about digital technologies adoption (OECD, 2021c), gives evidence of the digital transformation of SMEs, which showed an acceleration caused by the pandemic (around 40 % of micro-firms increased their use of digital technologies during the pandemic) with differences within countries and within sectors: it is worth mentioning that countries with stringent social distancing measures experienced a higher growth rate of SMEs engaging with digital technologies (OECD, 2021a) as it is clearly shown in Figure 1[2].

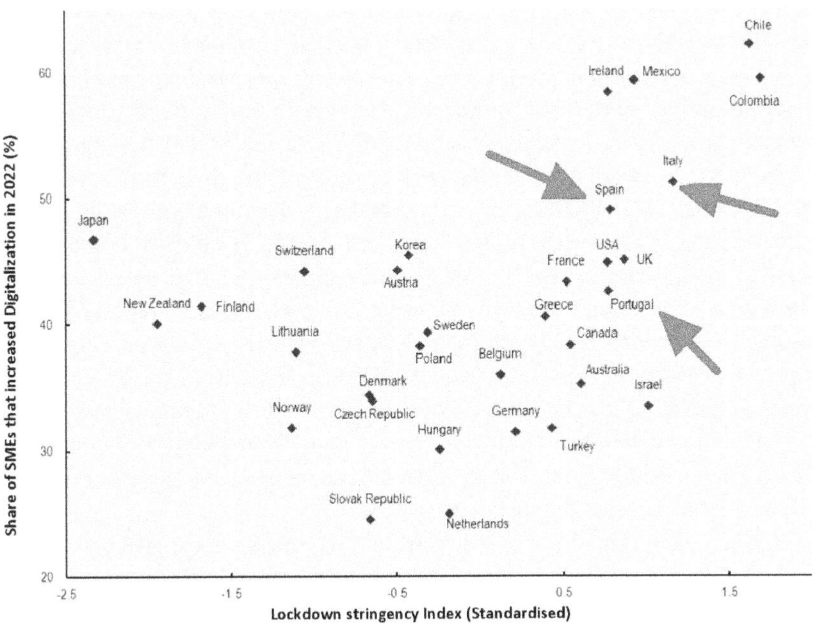

Figure 1: Where containment measures were more stringent, more SMES went digital
Source: OECD (2021a)

2 In Figure 2 we highlighted Italy Spain and Portugal to better define the external factors that contributed to shape the survey's results and data.

Differences among industries in the rate of digitalization exist and are linked to the nature of business. Businesses in industries traditionally based on proximity and contact, such as tourism and retail and food, mostly limited their digital transition to online presence on social media, online marketplaces and websites, e-commerce, click and collect, online delivery, e-banking or payments. Businesses in digitally intensive sectors have accelerated their digital transition at a faster pace than those operating in traditional sectors (Fernandez et al., 2020) and they have widened the uptake of digital technologies to a large variety of solutions – such as new software applications, cloud solutions, virtual events, videoconferences. In any case, generally MSMEs have a lower level of digitalization and of digital competences and skills than large companies in most sectors (OECD, 2021c). In industrial processes adoption and in automation, digitalization and interconnectedness among machines/products/individuals, manufacturing SMEs' steps toward Industry 4.0 are still at an early stage: technologies like data analytics, industrial internet of things (IIoT), vertical and horizontal organizational integration are scarcely present (Mittal et al., 2018; Müller & Voigt, 2017).

To better understand the mentioned diffusion of digitalization among MSMEs, small business entrepreneurs' problems and opportunities of for digital adoption have been widely analyzed (OECD, 2021d). For MSMES, important barriers to digitalization are undoubtedly the limited financial means and the limited access to experts from the IT sector, the pace of technological obsolescence, the difficulties in integrating digital systems with existing processes and legacy systems or the difficulties in changing organizational culture, workflows, and employees' roles (Bradač Hojnik & Huđek, 2023), and underdeveloped IT infrastructure or logistic infrastructure in certain geographical areas. But also the low level of digital literacy of many micro-entrepreneurs is often a great obstacle for their business's digital development.

As said before, digitalization is a multi-faceted issue covering several business activities, among which there also are the financial ones. Digital transformation enhances supply chain finance, improving MSMEs' access to financial services by offering an array of innovative services (mobile banking, digital payments, the use of alternative data for credit risk assessment, new P2P funding) and by reducing information asymmetries and transaction costs. A logical consequence is the increase of knowledge about digital financial services, product but also processes and procedures (and risks too), that is commonly referred to as digital financial literacy. If financial literature improves profitability of the firms concerned, the combination of digital literacy and financial literacy improves also growth (Fauzi et al., 2020) and influences the financial behavior of small entrepreneurs, that enhancing the impact of digital financial services (Angeles, 2022). It increases the ability to manage financial matters on digital platforms (Lyons & Kass-Hanna, 2021) and provides knowledge and tools to protect against digital fraud, thus increasing consumers' and SMEs financial well- being (Choung et al., 2023). Issues relative to digitalization, digital economy are more and more related with issues relative to financial literacy, digital financial inclusion and digital financial literacy.

Some surveys and empirical studies are giving evidence of this relation. For instance OECD surveys and reports (OECD, 2021b, 2023b) shed light on MSMEs' level of financial literacy and of digital activities, by defining a score for financial literacy components (knowledge, behavior and attitudes) and a score for digital use of financial services and by analyzing their possible support to entrepreneurs' response to covid-19 pandemic difficulties.

In Figure 2 we can see the relation between the two variables for the six European countries included in the surveys promoted by OECD-INFE in 2021 (OECD, 2021b) and the relative position of the three ones (Italy, Spain and Portugal) we analyzed in our study presented in the following pages.

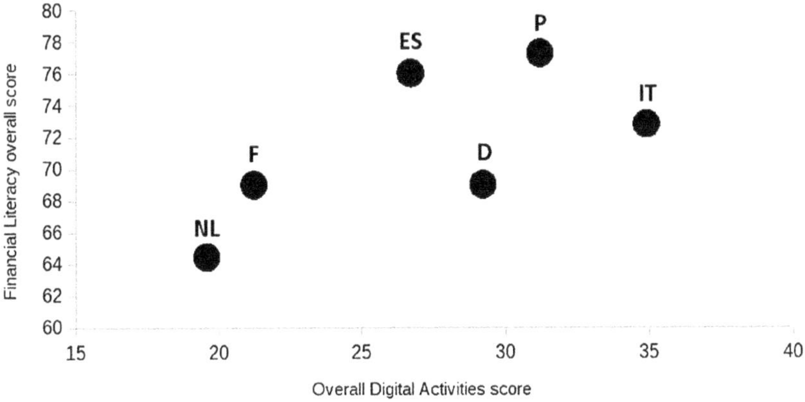

Figure 2: Overall digital activity score and financial literacy overall score
Source: our elaboration of data from OECD 2021b,

As for the sustainability, some studies focus on its relation with performance rather than with financial literacy but it is worth mentioning them to understand the meaning given to this concept. Some studies look at it as "business sustainable growth" or "business continuity" an exam of literature on this issue is provided by Jianmu & KMMCB (2019), rather than "environment or social sustainability," while others focus their analysis to ESG factors or to environmental performance

(Dechezleprêtre & Kruse, 2018; Friede et al., 2015) and financial performance (Broccardo et al., 2023) and give evidence that the financial compartment is gradually including ESG issues and goals in its analysis. Moreover it is important to note that the financial sector is broadening its supply to instruments for sustainable business growth such as green financial products (green finance, green loans and green bonds) and green insurance. This evolution implies a gradual widening, towards ESG factors, of economic and financial literacy issues, contents, and terminology. Examples are relative, for economic literature, to new concepts such as "circular economy," "climate and social risk," but also new business model which adopt "Ecological, Social and Economic practices" for obtaining sustainable growth and social and environmental profitability (together with firm's economic profitability), for financial literature, to green loans, green insurance, socially responsible investments and funds. It also implies the inclusion of ESG factors in all financial literacy components (knowledge, behavior, attitudes).

As for the relation between digitalization – term more appropriate than digital literacy – and sustainability, the former is officially considered a tool for improving sustainability considered as global well-being (European Commission, 2019; United Nations, 2015, 2020). A relation between the two has been identified but its sign is a topic of academic debate: some authors underline a positive connection, emphasizing the importance of digital technology in carrying out the sustainability agenda (i.e. it reduces the use of valuable resources, of waste and emissions, it produces economic benefits as a result of higher productivity), while others are more skeptical in terms of extraction of natural resources for digital devices' production, of energy necessary for supporting data generation in digital communication, of even in terms of social pillar (information manipulation or internet addiction). Different perspectives are well presented in Camodeca and Almici (2019) and Kuntsman and Rattle (2019).

The fragmented literature and empirical evidence mentioned above, particularly concerning micro-enterprises, support the analysis we will discuss next.

3. Our Analysis

3.1. Aims and Methodology

The aim of our analysis is to shed a light on the level of financial literacy, digital adoption and sensibility to the sustainability matters among enterprises in Europe and to investigate if there is a correlation between the three variables. Our approach is European, and we carry out a cross-country study of a small-business sample in Italy, Portugal, and Spain, which are countries where scholars can easily obtain data sets[3].

In order to create a unitary dataset, a preliminary analysis was carried out to select common questions and standardize the ranges of answers, as – even if inspired by the common metric proposed by OECD/INFE – the various national surveys present customizations and contextualization to the reality of individual countries.

For this requirement of uniformity of the variables analyzed, a sub-sample of only micro enterprises (i.e. enterprises with no more than nine full time employees) was selected from the dataset[4]. The sample consists of 4.166 non-financial micro business based in Italy (about 48 %), Portugal (about 29 %) and Spain (about 23 %). In the appendix to this chapter we present the characteristics of the sample with reference both to firm specific features (see Tables 1a–5a) and to personal characteristics of the entrepreneur/owner (see Tables 6a–12a)[5].

3.2. The Metrics

In order to study the issue of financial literacy, digital adoption and sustainability we use indexes created using the data collected by the above mentioned surveys.

As for financial literacy, according to theoretical literature and empirical studies, financial literacy is determined by three factors: financial knowledge, behavior, and attitude. Relying on the available data to assess the knowledge component, we complement the classic questions of knowledge of economic and financial concepts (dividends and inflation), understanding of relationships

---

3 We use the Italian, Portuguese and Spanish data from the Survey promoted by the International Network for Financial Education concerning "Survey instrument to measure the financial literacy of MSMEs" (OECD, 2018) and collected in early 2020, respectively, by the Bank of Italy, by a consortium of economic and financial authorities in Portugal (including the Ministry of Economy and the Sea and the National Council of Financial Supervisors) and by the Bank of Spain.

4 Indeed the survey of one of the three countries studied (Italy) includes only micro-enterprises in their sample.

5 Some information was omitted because in this sub-sample of micro enterprises there was almost no variability for them and therefore, they were not useful for multivariate analysis. The legal form (*business type*) and the financial decisions made by the owner (*owner takes financial decisions*) are both involved in this situation. In the first case, they are almost all autonomous profit-oriented business making independent financial decisions, in the latter the owner (respondent) is the person who takes financial decision.

(between equity and ownership and between risk and return and between interest payments and the duration of a loan), with questions related to "at least superficial knowledge" (having heard about…) of financial instruments and transactions that could be used in a business activity[6]. Our belief is that having knowledge of transactions in the financial markets, especially those related to entrepreneurial activity, can be a good indicator of financial literacy, along with traditional knowledge tests.

As for financial behavior, using nine questions, each financial behavior that is appropriate for good and wise business management is assessed by assigning a positive score. The questions proposed by the OECD/INFE methodology cover a wide range of situations, in line with the needs of businesses and entrepreneurs[7].

Finally, attitudes are assessed on (i) the habit of setting goals and striving to achieve them, (ii) the confidence in approaching banks and other external investors to obtain business finance and (iii) the preference to follow his/her own instinct, rather than making detailed financial plans for the business.

In order to create a financial literacy index we combined the scores of the three components (knowledge, behavior, attitudes) giving to them an equal importance. We attribute an equal weight to each component: dividing each raw score by the number of question we normalize the components, then summing up them we calculate the overall financial literacy score ranging from 0 to 3. As the aim of our study is to evaluate whether there are relations among the three domain (financial, digital and sustainability) we perform an additional standardization dividing the overall score by the number of the three components and obtain the financial literacy index, ranging from 0 to 1.

---

6 They are: *bank overdraft or credit lines, business loan from a bank, invoice discounting, corporate bonds or commercial papers, micro-credit, trade credit, venture capital, business angels. public equity, crowdfunding/peer-to-peer lending, initial coin offering, mezzanine finance, leasing or hire purchase, factoring, derivatives (such as options, futures, swaps and others), third-party liability insurance, business interruption insurance, life insurance for the owner, sustainable (social or green) bonds or loans and working loans.*

7 Questions ask whether the entrepreneur *(i) manages personal and corporate finances separate, (ii)shops around for financial products and services for the business, (iii) keeps formal track of financial records, (iv) thinks about how to finance his/her retirement, (v) has devised a plan in the event that the business equipment is stolen, (vi) securely stores business data and information; (vii) compares the cost of different sources of finance for the business, (viii) forecasts the profitability of the business regularly, and (ix) adjusts plans according to the changes in economic factors.*

As for digital literacy, literature outlined that it is too a combination of knowledge, behavior and attitude, where attitude depends largely on the frequence of use and that there a specific area of digital literacy – that is, digital financial literacy – that intersects with the two domains (Anderloni & Moro, 2024). However we can relay on six questions in the survey in order to assess the level of digitalization among micro enterprises, and it is not useful to analyze the components separately. Digital literacy is proxied by digitalization, that is the entrepreneur's engagement in six activities related both to business advertising and product/services sales and financial management of the activity[8]. We use the answer referred to the post-pandemic period, considered as the actual state of art, being aware that, as highlighted above, the lockdown promoted an acceleration in digitalization. In order to create the digital index score, we standardized the score and the index ranges from 0 to 1.

As for the sustainably, in literature and in empirical analysis it is common to refer to the ESG score based on a large number of variables available mainly for the large and/or listed companies. In our survey concerning microenterprises we have three questions that allow us to make an initial assessment of the attention paid to sustainability in environmental and social terms (while it goes without saying that governance is reflected in many aspects in good financial and digital management). The question refer to: (i) the consideration of the environmental impact of business investments, (ii) the consideration of social impact of business investments and (iii) the involvement of providers in implementing actions with low environmental impact.

We are aware of the scarcity of information available in the dataset, but this is a first attempt to analyze the sensitivity of small entrepreneurs to sustainability issues.

The sustainability score ranging from 1 to 3 was then normalized to the range 0 to 1, in order to create the index with the same scale of magnitude as the financial literacy index and the digital index.

8 In the first domain the questions include: *(i) having a dedicated website to showcase the products or services of the business and (ii) having a dedicated website to sell the products or services of the business*, while *(iii) opening a bank account completely on line, (iv) signing a financial contract (i.e. a bank loan) completely online, (v) signing an in insurance contract completely on line and (vi) using open banking services or applications to manage business finance and payments* are related to the financial domain.

3.3. A Snapshot of Financial Literacy, Digital Literacy and Sustainability Levels

On average, in the sample of three countries studied, the financial literacy has the widest diffusion with highest value (in mean) and a lower dispersion of values, as measured by standard deviation, at the second place there is the attention paid to sustainability, but with a high dispersion of values and finally there is the digital literacy with a value as mean less than one third of the maximum (Table 1).

Analyzing the elements that compose the overall financial literacy on average the behavior contributes positively to the literacy level, followed by attitude and lastly by knowledge. It is worth mentioned that our index assess the level of knowledge by means of testing few concepts and definition and considering the knowledge – even very superficial – of financial products or services or transaction. This practical approach looks specially appropriate in the case of entrepreneurs and this evidence is not surprising due to the very small scale of our sample, as highlighted also by the multivariate analysis (Table 2).

Table 1: The indexes: Main statistics

Variable	Observations	Mean	Standard deviation	Min	Max
Financial literacy index	4,166	0.6734	0.1811	0	0.974
Digital literacy index	4,166	0.2978	0.2664	0	1
Sustainability_index	4,166	0.6491	0.3901	0	1

Table 2: The components of the financial literacy index

Variable	Observations	Mean	Standard deviation	Min	Max
Financial literacy index	4,166	0.6734	0.1811	0	0.974
Knowledge score	4,166	0.5175	0.2212	0	0.923
Behavioral score	4,166	0.8234	0.1801	0	1
Attitude score	4,166	0.6793	0.3064	0	1

Considering the cross-country nature of our sample, Italy is in the last position for financial literacy (0.65), but has a higher level of digital competence in relative terms (0.42) and a high attention paid to sustainability (0.68). Spain excels financial literacy (0.73), but in relative terms, it has the lowest value for the sustainability index and a content level of digitization. Portugal has high levels of financial literacy and attention to sustainability (respectively 0.67 and 0.71), but the lowest level of digitalization (0.18). As for the contribution of the three elements that compose the financial literacy index, in all the three countries it is confirmed the ranking above highlighted. Also the dispersion of the values measured by the standard deviation follows a similar pattern (Table 3).

Table 3: The indexes and components of the financial literacy index, by country Italy

Variable	**Observations**	**Mean**	**Standard deviation**	**Min**	**Max**
Financial literacy index	1,996	0.6493	0.1814	0.0128	0.9615
Knowledge score	*1,996*	*0.4919*	*0.2152*	*0*	*0.8846*
Behavioral score	*1,996*	*0.8107*	*0.1838*	*0*	*1*
Attitude score	*1,996*	*0.6453*	*0.3109*	*0*	*1*
Digital literacy index	1,996	0.4126	0.2708	0	1
Sustainability_index	1,996	0.6755	0.3731	0	1
Portugal					
Variable	**Observations**	**Mean**	**Standard deviation**	**Min**	**Max**
Financial literacy index	1,216	0.6689	0.1644	0.0128	0.9359
Knowledge score	*1,216*	*0.4518*	*0.1929*	*0.0385*	*0.8077*
Behavioral score	*1,216*	*0.8458*	*0.1664*	*0*	*1*
Attitude score	*1,216*	*0.7092*	*0.2852*	*0*	*1*
Digital literacy index	1,216	0.1791	0.1843	0	0.8333
Sustainability_index	1,216	0.7059	0.3654	0	1
Spain					
Variable	**Observations**	**Mean**	**Standard deviation**	**Min**	**Max**
Financial literacy index	954	0.7296	0.1887	0	0.9744
Knowledge score	954	0.6552	0.2097	0	0.9231
Behavioral score	954	0.8221	0.1864	0	1
Attitude score	954	0.7124	0.3157	0	1
Digital literacy index	954	0.2091	0.2445	0	1
Sustainability_index	954	0.5217	0.426	0	1

The above presented results suggest to deepen the study with a multivariate analysis illustrated below.

3.4. The Multivariate Analysis

In order to understand how business's factors and personal factors of the entrepreneur contribute to determine the levels of literacy presented, OLS regression analyzes have been conducted.

For each domain, the index was taken as an independent variable, first the only business determinants were studied and then the personal ones of the entrepreneur were added, thus proposing two models for each regression. Results are shown in Tables 4–6.

With reference to financial literacy, several statistically significant variables have been identified that contribute to explaining the level of literacy. In the first model, variables related to the company are considered: among these we highlight the negative relationship with the micro size, both in terms of number of employees and turnover volume. The sign of the relationship is also confirmed by the evidence that, consistently, larger business (in term of turnover) have a positive impact on the level of literacy. The factor Italy, which we have seen as the country with the lowest level of financial literacy, has a negative impact, while the factor "Spain," which is the country with the highest.

As for the sectors of activity, manufacturing seems to have a negative relationship, but it is not statistically significant. However, the commercial sectors (wholesale and retail) are significantly positive, as are the information and communication services sector and business support services. This sign is easily understood by considering the nature of activities in the latter two sectors and the intensity of banking relationships, if only for payment services and working capital financing, in commercial activities. The last variable, firm specific, significant but weak, is the seniority of the entrepreneurial activity: in this case the relationship is negative. This could indicate that younger businesses are more prepared for financial management.

The relationships between the firm-specific variables and the level of financial literacy mentioned above can be confirmed by adding the owner/manager specific variables (Model II), even if the negative determinant "Italy" is weakened. All of the additional variables in model II are statistically significant: high levels of education and having studied economics in school curriculum are positively related, whereas gender and young age have negative signs, suggesting that women and young people are contributing to lower levels of financial literacy. These results are easy to understand and in line with expectations. Less explicable, if not using the experience factor, are the positive sign of the relationship for the age between 50 and 59 years and the fact that relatives also carry out or have carried out business activities.

Finally, it should be noted that the addition of owner/manager specific variables almost doubles the variability explained by the variables included in the model, even if the adjusted R-squared remains contained in absolute, but not very different from that shown by multivariate analyzes conducted in the field of financial literacy.

Common elements and differences are evident between the regression for financial literacy and that for digital literacy.

Taking the digital as a dependent variable, the statistically significant business-specific variables are – also in this case – the dimensions with negative signs for the micro sized (both for employees and turnover) and the very large ones with positive signs, while the impact of the country factor changes: Italy now has a positive impact, while Portugal has a negative impact. This is in line with the ranking of the countries according to their indexes presented in the Table 3 above.

Differences with the determinants of financial literacy are found in relation to the sectors of activity: the manufacturing sector is still not statistically significant, as does now the commercial sector. Similarly, information and communication services and business services are positive. The sector determinants include now also that of accommodation, food and beverages with a positive relationship.

Still negative, but with a greater significance is the relationship with the age of the firm's activity: it seems to be possible to deduce that more established firms have more difficulties in converting to digital.

Adding in the model the owner/manager specific variables, almost unchanged remain the determinants firm specific, while to be noted as the gender does not appear to be relevant in this domain. As in the case of financial literacy, positive and statistically significant are upper level of education, having had some elements of economics in school curriculum and to be descendent from family running a business, that may mean that he/she has acquired skills in the family. In this domain the age range of 30–39 (lower that in financial literacy) has a positive relationship with digital literacy.

As regards the explanatory force of the determinants identified, in this case the adjusted R-squared is higher, but the addition of the owner/manager-specific variables does not significantly increase the value of the explained variability.

As to the determinants of the sustainability, it is more difficult to find significant and clear results and common elements with the financial literacy and/or with the digital literacy.

Attention paid to sustainability does not appear to be related to size of the firm (the relation with a very generic range of employees is very weak), nor to the years of activity. As for countries, Italy and Portugal contribute to enhance the level of sustainability concerns (in line with the ranking shown in the Table 3 above). It is interesting to note that only two sectors now appear as determinants and these are not relevant in the previous analyzes: they are the agriculture and the construction. The first has a positive relationship, the latter a negative one: these results are not surprising given, on one hand, the widespread use of organic farming among small producers and those returning to farming after the boom in industrialization and, on the other, the specific characteristics of very small-scale construction firms.

It is more surprising to find that the personal variables specific to the entrepreneur are difficult to identify and have a weak significance. Gender is irrelevant, as is educational level, although having economic studies in the school curriculum contributes – as previously noted – positively. Being young in age seems to have a very weak negative relationship, while entrepreneurial experience at the extremes of the range seems to have a weak positive relationship.

The difficulties of interpreting these results may result from the random nature of sensitivity to sustainability issues and this seems to be confirmed by the very low level of the adjusted R-squared in both models.

Table 4: Determinants of the financial literacy index

	Model I			Model II		
Financial Literacy_index	**Coefficient**	**Std. err.**	**P>t**	**Coefficient**	**Std. err.**	**P>t**
micro_employees	–.0115	.0031	***	–.0104	.0029	***
micro_turnover	–.0511	.0062	***	–.0485	.0059	***
very_large_turnover	.0762	.0164	***	.0606	.0157	***
country_Italy	–.0419	.0066	***	–.0128	.0066	*
country_Spain	.0579	.0075	***	.0447	.0072	***
s_manufacturing	–.0133	.0123		–.0170	.0118	
s_wholesale and retail trade	.0233	.0071	***	.0224	.0068	***
s_information and communication	.0513	.0160	***	.0412	.0152	***
s_business_services	.0686	.0070	***	.0386	.0069	***
range_years_activity	–.0034	.0018	*	–.0031	.0017	*
gender (female)				–.0196	.0059	***
upper_education				.0517	.0059	***

Table 4: Continued

	Model I			Model II		
Financial Literacy_index	**Coefficient**	**Std. err.**	**P>t**	**Coefficient**	**Std. err.**	**P>t**
economic_education (elements)				.0769	.0055	***
age_50_59				.0197	.0055	***
young				−.0477	.0172	***
family of enterpreneurs				.0204	.0052	***
_cons	.7006	.0109	***	.6207	.0115	***
Observations	4,166			4,166		
Adj R-squared	0.0833			0.1698		

*** p < 0.01, p < 0.05 p < 0.1

Table 5: Determinants of the digital literacy index

	Model I					
Digital_index	**Coefficient**	**Std. err.**	**P>t**	**Coefficient**	**Std. err.**	**P>t**
micro_employees	−.0118	.0043	***	−.0116	.0042	***
micro_turnover	−.0325	.0087	***	−.0312	.0086	***
very_large_turnover	.0543	.0228	**	.0484	.0227	**
country_Italy	.1889	.0097	***	.2053	.0103	***
country_Portugal	−.0267	.0105	**	−.0242	.0105	**
s_manufacturing	−.0231	.0172		−.0248	.0171	
s_wholesale and retail trade	.0098	.0101		.0109	.0101	
s_information and communication	.0783	.0222	***	.0790	.0222	***
s_business_services	.0237	.0100	**	.0139	.0102	
s_accomodation and restaurant	.0776	.0148	***	.0803	.0148	***
range_years_activity	−.0116	.0025	***	−.0101	.0026	***
gender (female)				.0057	.0085	
upper_education				.0308	.0085	***
economic_education (elements)				.0282	.0079	***
age_30_39				.0267	.0115	**
family of enterpreneurs				.0211	.0075	***

(continued)

Table 5: Continued

	Model I					
Digital_index	**Coefficient**	**Std. err.**	**P>t**	**Coefficient**	**Std. err.**	**P>t**
_cons	.2694	.0148	***	.2122	.0166	***
Observations	4,166			4,166		
Adj R-squared	0,1874			0.1977		

*** $p < 0.01$, $p < 0.05$ $p < 0.1$

Table 6: Determinants of the sustainability index

	Model I			Model II		
Financial Literacy_index	**Coefficient**	**Std. err.**	**P>t**	**Coefficient**	**Std. err.**	**P>t**
range_empl	0.0212	0.0098	*	0.0207	0.0097	**
very_small_turnover	−0.0002	0.0019		−0.0002	0.0019	
large_turnover	0.0154	0.0171		0.0159	0.0171	
range_years_activity	−0.0065	0.0041		−0.0062	0.0042	
country_Italy	0.1257	0.0161	***	0.1326	0.0171	***
Country_Portugal	0.1745	0.0171	***	0.1553	0.0249	***
s_agricolture	0.0974	0.0299	***	0.0921	0.0303	***
s_manufactoring	0.0159	0.0271		0.0164	0.0273	
s_constructions	−0.0563	0.0191	***	−0.0516	0.0192	***
s_wholesale and retail trade	0.0211	0.0157		0.0221	0.0159	
gender (female)				0.0145	0.0138	
young_enterpreneur				0.0791	0.0368	*
very_low_education				0.0389	0.0461	
upper_education				−0.0075	0.0136	
economic_education (elements)				0.0549	0.0128	***
expert_enterpreneurs				0.0565	0.0328	*
family of enterpreneurs				0.0119	0.0121	
young				−0.0683	0.0406	*
_cons	0.5132	0.0261		0.4197	0.0421	***
Observations	4,166			4,166		
Adj R-squared	0.0385			0.0437		

*** $p < 0.01$, $p < 0.05$ $p < 0.1$

4. Conclusions

While correlation analysis has found a positive and statistically significant correlation between financial literacy, digital literacy, and sustainability – although weak[9] – it has not been possible to identify common determinants through multivariate analysis.

There are no significant determinants to interpret the variance of sensitivities for sustainability, either among firm-specific factors or among personal-specific factors.

This suggests that the sensitivity to sustainability, indeed not particularly low in absolute terms as well as relative terms, is still random and not identifiable to standard characteristics, with developments among the population somewhat leopard-like.

It is clear that more analysis on the determinants of sustainability attention is needed: in particular, it is important to carry out analyzes focused on micro-enterprises. Larger companies are already the subject of empirical studies on these issues due to the greater ease of retrieval of data and information from social balance sheets and ESG indicators developed by external analysts.

Conversely, there are still difficulties in obtaining objective evidence on behavior that may be reported in qualitative surveys and assessing its correspondence with actual behaviors in micro and small enterprises.

Furthermore, if we want to deepen the theme of sustainability, it should be done in all its aspects: not only in the most known and investigated of environmental impact, for which it is likely that there are deep differences between sector and sector (and the macro-economic sectors do not allow to give evidence of these differences), but also in those so-called social less investigated than the more "popular" ones, such as gender gap.

The management decisions made by micro-enterprises concerning their employees should be taken into account in this context, such as ensuring regular recruitment and not employing workers who are not regularly contracted.

9 The correlation matrix is as follows:

	financial_ literacy_ index	digital_index	sustainability index
financial_literacy_index	1		
digital_index	0.1307	1	
sustainability_index	0.2319	0.1234	1

Another social issue is the assumption of proper civic behavior, such as refraining from evasive or elusive behavior in tax matters.

Based on our analysis of the OECD/INFE questionnaire, we can say that the small number of questions on sustainability does not allow us to create a good index for measuring the sensibility to sustainability considered in a broad sense, with regard to social and governance issues. Consequently it is difficult to highlight the possible and multiple determinant of sustainability among micro-enterprises, nor do we have a good chance of analyzing the links with other variables.

It is undoubtedly a challenge to gather useful answers for investigating the phenomenon through a questionnaire, given the sensitivity of the investigations that may also concern behavior contrary to sustainability and even illegal (think of undeclared work or tax evasion) or even just ambiguous behavior. This type of problem, that is the sensitivity of the questions and possible ambiguity or falsity of the answers, does not arise in reference to surveys focused on financial literacy or digitization.

Green washing and the debate on regulatory instruments to deal with it can result in barriers to sustainability surveys or inaccurate answers.

The link of sustainability surveys with sets of perhaps abstract questions that refer to philosophy of conduct, rather than the specific business managed and with focus also on sustainable investment choices anchored to the theme of financial literacy could help open a window on this topic, certainly worthy of further investigation.

Annex

Table 1a: Country

	Freq.	**Percent**
Italy	1,996	47.91
Portugal	1,216	29.19
Spain	954	22.90
Total	**4,166**	**100.00**

Table 2a: Dimension (Turnover)

	Freq.	Percent
up to €10,000	199	4.96
more than €10,000 and up to €50,000	499	12.43
more than €50,000 and up to €100,000	612	15.24
more than €100,000 and up to €500,000	1,849	46.04
more than €500,000 and up to €1 million	501	12.48
more than €1million and up to €2 million	238	5.93
more than €2 milllion and up to €10 million	110	2.74
more than €10 million	8	0.20
Total	**4,016**	**100.00**
omitted	150	

Table 3a: People working in the business

	Freq.	Percent
1 (self-employed)	772	18.53
From 2 to 4 people	1,916	45.99
From 5 to 9 people	1,478	35.48
Total	**4,166**	**100.00**

Table 4a: Sector

	Freq.	Percent
Agricolture, forestry and fishing	181	4.35
Manufacturing	221	5.31
Construction and real estate	492	11.81
Wholesale and retail trade	870	20.89
Transportation, shipping, storage	116	2.79
Accomodation, food and beverage services	307	7.37
Other personal services (education, beauty, repairs, laundry)	290	6.96
Information and communication	125	3.00
Business services	858	20.60
Other	705	16.93
Total	**4,165**	**100.00**
omitted	1	

Table 5a: Years of activity

	Freq.	Percent
From 1 to 2	62	1.49
From 3 to 5	650	15.60
From 6 to 10	1,321	31.71
From 11 to 15	424	10.18
From 16 to 25	698	16.75
More than 26	1,011	24.27
Total	**4,166**	**100.00**

Table 6a: Gender

	Freq.	Percent
Male	3,093	74.35
Female	1,067	25.65
Total	**4,160**	**100.00**
omitted	6	

Table 7a: Age

	Freq.	Percent
Younger than 20	3	0.07
20–29	94	2,28
30–39	523	12.70
40–49	1,248	30.31
50–59	1,356	32.93
60–69	703	17.07
70–79	167	4.06
80 or older	24	0.58
Total	**4,118**	**100.00**
omitted	48	

Table 8a: Education

	Freq.	**Percent**
Post graduated or equivalent	631	15.34
University-level education (degree or higher-level vocational training)	1,393	33.86
Upper secondary school or high school	1,602	38.94
Lower secondary school or middle school	415	10.09
Primary school	66	1.60
No formal education	7	0.17
Total	**4,114**	**100.00**
omitted	52	

Table 9a: Economic topic in education

	Freq.	**Percent**
No	2,099	50.38
Yes	2,067	49.62
Total	**4,166**	**100.00**

Table 10a: Enterpreneurial experience

	Freq.	**Percent**
Less than 1 year	576	14.33
Between 1 and up to 2 years	688	17.11
Between 2 and up to 2 years	354	8.81
Between 5 and up to 10 years	600	14.93
More than 10 years	1,802	44.83
Total	**4,020**	**100.00**
omitted	146	

Table 11a: Parents enterpreneurs

	Freq.	**Percent**
No	2,188	52.52
Yes	1,978	47.48
Total	**4,166**	**100.00**

Table 12a: Training in money management

	Freq.	Percent
No	2,702	64.86
Yes	1,464	35.14
Total	**4,166**	**100.00**

References

Anderloni, L., & Moro, O. (2024). Financial literacy and digital literacy: Intertwined issues of increasing importance. In Gunesch & Çetin (Eds.), *International influences and inspirations in education*. Zurich, Peter Lang GmbH, Internationaler Verlag der Wissenschaften.

Angeles, I. (2022). The moderating effect of digital and financial literacy on the digital financial services and financial behavior of MSMEs. *Review of Economics and Finance*, *20*, 505–515.

Atkinson, A., & Messy, F. A. (2011). Assessing financial literacy in 12 countries: An OECD/INFE international pilot exercise. *Journal of Pension Economics & Finance*, *10*(4), 657–665.

Atkinson, A., McKay, S., Collard, S., & Kempson, E. (2007). Levels of financial capability in the UK. *Public Money and Management*, *27*(1), 29–36.

Bhaskar, C., Chaturvedi, R. S., Filipovic, C., & Brewer, G. (2021). Digital in the time of COVID: Trust in the digital economy and its evolution across 90 economies as the planet paused for a pandemic. *The Fletcher School at Tufts University*. Available at: https://sites.tufts.edu/ digitalplanet/files/2021/03/ digital-intelligence- index.pdf

Bradač Hojnik, B., & Huđek, I. (2023). Small and medium-sized enterprises in the digital age: Understanding characteristics and essential demands. *Information*, *14*, 606. Available at: https://doi.org/10.3390/info14110606

Broccardo, L., Truant, E., & Léo-Paul, D. (2023). The interlink between digitalization, sustainability, and performance: An Italian context. *Journal of Business Research*, Elsevier, *158*(C), 66–88.

Camodeca, R., & Almici, A. (2021). A digital transformation and convergence toward the 2030 agenda's sustainability development goals: Evidence from Italian listed firms. *Sustainability*, *13*, 11831. Available at: https://doi.org/ 10.3390/su132111831

Choung, Y., Chatterjee, S., & Pak, T. Y. (2023). Digital financial literacy and financial well-being. *Finance Research Letters*, *58* Part B. Available at: https:// doi.org/10.1016/j.frl.2023.104 438.

D'Ignazio, A., Finaldi Russo, P., & Stacchini, M. (2022). Micro-entrepreneurs' financial and digital competences during the pandemic in Italy. *Questioni di Economia e Finanza (Occasional Papers)*, N. 724.

Dechezleprêtre, A., & Kruse, T. (2018). A review of the empirical literature combining economic and environmental performance data at the micro-level. *OECD Economics Department Working Papers*, No. 1514. Paris: OECD Publishing. Available at: https://doi.org/10.1787/45d269b2-en.

European Commission. (2012). *Report on the results of the feasibility assessment for the development of a financial competence framework in the EU.* DG FISMA Report European Commission: Brussels, Belgium.

European Commission. (2019). *Communication from the Commission to the European Parliament, the European Council, the Council, the European Economic and Social Committee and the Committee of the Regions.* The European Green Deal; European Commission: Brussels, Belgium.

Fauzi, F., Antoni, D., & Suwarni, E. (2020). Women entrepreneurship in the developing country: The effects of financial and digital literacy on SMEs' growth. *Journal of Governance & Regulation*, *9*(4), 106–115.

Fernandez, S., Jenkins, P., & Vieira, B. (2020). Europe's digital migration during COVID-19: Getting past the broad trends and averages. *McKinsey Digital*, July 24, 2020, accessed November 30. Available at: https://www. mckinsey.com/business-functions/mckinsey-digital/our-insights/europes-digital-migration-during-covid-19-getting-past-the-broad-trends-and-averages.

Finaldi Russo, P., Galotto, L., & Rampazzi, C. (2022). The financial literacy of micro-entrepreneurs: Evidence from Italy. *Questioni di Economia e Finanza (Occasional Papers), 727*, Bank of Italy, Economic Research and International Relations Area. Available at: https://www.bancaditalia.it/pubblicazioni/qef/2022-0727/QEF_727_22.pdf

Friede, G., Busch, T., & Bassen, A. (2015). ESG and financial performance: Aggregated evidence from more than 2000 empirical studies. *Journal of Sustainable Finance & Investment*, *5*(4), 210–233. Available at: http://dx.doi.org/10.1080/20430795.2015.1118917

Isensee, C., Teuteberg, F., Griese, K. M., & Topi, C. (2020). The relationship between organizational culture, sustainability, and digitalization in SMEs: A systematic review. *Journal of Cleaner Production*, *275*. https://doi.org/10.1016/j.jclepro.2020.122944

Jianmu, Ye, & Kulathunga, K. M. M. C. B. (2019). How does financial literacy promote sustainability in SMEs? A developing country perspective. *Sustainability*, MDPI, *11*(10), 1–21, May.

Kuntsman, A., & Rattle, I. (2019). Towards a paradigmatic shift in sustainability studies: A systematic review of peer reviewed literature and future agenda setting to consider environmental (un)sustainability of digital communication. *Environmental Communications*, *13*, 567–581.

Lusardi, A., & Mitchell, O. S. (2011). Financial literacy around the world: an overview. *Journal of Pension Economics & Finance*, *10*(4), 497–508.

Lusardi, A., & Tufano, P. (2015). Debt literacy, financial experiences, and overindebtedness. *Journal of Pension Economics & Finance*, *14*(4), 332–368.

Lyons, A. C., & Kass-Hanna, J. (2021). A methodological overview to defining and measuring "digital" financial literacy. *Financial Planning Review*, *4*(2). Available at: http://dx.doi.org/ 10.2139/ ssrn.3836 330.

Mittal, S., Khan, M. A., Romero, D., & Wuest, T. (2018). A critical review of smart manufacturing & industry 4.0 maturity models: Implications for Small and Medium-Sized Enterprises (SMEs). *Journal of Manufacturing Systems, 49*, 194–214.

Müller, J. M., & Voigt, K. I. (2017). *Industry 4.0-integration strategies for small and medium-sized enterprises* (pp. 1–15). Vienna, Austria: International Association for Management of Technology (IAMOT).

OECD (2021c). *The digital transformation of SMEs, OECD studies on SMEs and entrepreneurship*. Paris: OECD Publishing. Available at: https://doi.org/10.1787/bdb9256a-en.

OECD. (2017). *G20/OECD INFE report on ensuring financial education and consumer protection for all in the digital age*. Paris: OECD Publishing. Available at: www.oecd.org/daf/fin/financial-education/G20-OECD-INFE-Report-Financial-Education-Consumer-Protection-Digital-Age.pdf

OECD. (2018). *G20/OECD-INFE policy guidance on digitalization and financial literacy*. Paris: OECD Publishing. Available at: https://doi.org/10.1787/effe2693-en.

OECD. (2021a). *SME digitalisation to "Build Back Better" digital for SMEs (D4SME)* Policy paper n° 31 2021. Paris: OECD Publishing. Available at: https://doi.org/10.1787/50193089-en

OECD. (2021b). *G20/OECD-INFE report Navigating the storm: MSMEs' financial and digital competencies in COVID-19 times*. Available at: www.oecd.org/finance/navigating-the-storm-MSMEs-financial-and digital-competencies-in-COVID-19-times.htm.

OECD. (2021d). *OECD SME and entrepreneurship outlook 2021*. Paris: OECD Publishing.

OECD. (2023a). *OECD/INFE international survey of adult financial literacy*, OECD Business and Finance Policy Papers, No. 39. Paris: OECD Publishing. Available at: https://doi.org/10.1787/56003a32-en.

OECD. (2023b). *Financial literacy and digitalisation for MSMEs in South East Europe: A tool for empowering owners and managers*. OECD Business and Finance Policy Papers, No. 29. Paris: OECD Publishing. Available at: https://doi.org/10.1787/b63091ad-en.

OECD-INFE. (2009). *Financial education and the crisis: Policy paper and guidance*. Paris: OECD Publishing.

Ramanathan, S., & Indiran, L. (2021). Remodeling economy towards sustainable society and sustainable development: The role of financial literacy, digital literacy, and sustainability literacy. *International Journal of Academic Research in Economics and Management Sciences*, *4*(3), 237–256. Aivalilable at: http://dx.doi.org/10.6007/IJAREMS/v10-i3/10602

UNDESA Report. (2020). *Micro-Small and Medium-sized Enterprises (MSMEs) and their role in achieving the Sustainable Development Goals (SDGs)*. Publisher UN-DESA. Available at: https://sustainabledevelopment.un.org/content/documents/26073MSMEs_and_SDGs.pdf

United Nations. (2015). *The 2030 agenda for sustainable development*. Paris, France: United Nations.

United Nations. (2020). *Take action for the sustainable development goals*. Paris, France: United Nations.

Wildnerova, L., Menon, C., Dehghan, R., Kinne, J., & LenzWhich, D. (2024). SMEs are greening? Cross-country evidence from one million websites. *OECD SME and Entrepreneurship Papers* No. 60.

Xu, L., & Zia, B. (2012). Financial literacy around the world: An overview of the evidence with practical suggestions for the way forward. *Policy Research Working Paper*; No. 6107. Washington, DC: World Bank. Available at: http://hdl.handle.net/10986/9322 License: CC BY 3.0 IGO.

Yanto, H., Kiswanto, Baroroh, N., Hajawiyah, A., & Rahim, N. M. (2022). The roles of entrepreneurial skills, financial literacy, and digital literacy in maintaining MSMEs during the COVID-19 pandemic. *Asian Economic and Financial Review*, *12*(7), 504–517. Available at: https://doi.org/10.55493/5002.v12i7.4535

Pedro Fernandes da Anunciação, Cátia Susana Claro Chasqueira, and Maria da Conceição dos Santos Contreiras Salema Aleixo

Information Quality: Critical Asset in a Relational Economy

1. Introduction

Since the 1950s, when the first computers were invented, an economic movement based on information. Initially, the introduction of information and communication technologies (ICT) appeared important in increasing the productivity of companies. Investment in ICT allowed, through productivity, an increase in the competitiveness of companies in the economy. However, although ICT has changed the paradigm of the functioning of companies and other institutions, reflections in organizational charts, processes, relationships, knowledge, and information have been constituted, increasingly evident, the motor of companies and the economy itself. Thus, we understand the designation of the current society as an information society.

For many years, companies focused their information systems (IS) on an internal perspective, inherent to the operation. As time has evolved, organizational IS has been transformed into inter-organizational IS, where integration and interoperability have played critical roles in the integration of companies and the agility of value chains. Similarly, architectures moved the focus on fragmented ICT or organizational areas to an integral perspective, understanding an organization as a system. This perspective of IS architecture has evolved into models of organizational urbanism in which the organizational IS is integrated into a broader and comprehensive economic system.

In all evolutions, whatever the perspective, more technological or socio-economic, there is an element that aggregates all elements of both the organizational system and the information system: the information.

Information is a vital asset for any organization, but information does not often appear in asset management definitions or descriptions. These assets, traditionally material, technological, or financial, are identified and described through information. Information is the base to support decision-making, facilitating operations, creation of products and services, as well as to demonstrate performance and obligations. We can assume information as an economic asset because it constitutes the basis of most economic operations, has economic value, and is a raw material and finished product in multiple value chains in the digital economy.

In an era of ever-increasing volumes of information and growing legal obligations supported by information, it is important that economic organizations know how to leverage their information assets, generating value and protecting them from possible risks (Esteves & Anunciação, 2022; Leming, 2015).

In a relational framework in which the information link between economic stakeholders has been intensified, companies are confronted with increased requirements for the availability and sharing of information. If previously, the requirements associated with information management assumed a predominance mainly internal, essentially focused on organizational knowledge and functioning, today the requirements associated with information are centered on the external side of companies, those stakeholders that, directly or indirectly, need information. Many of the requirements stem from external stakeholders to which companies will have to respond, due to the legal framework in force.

In this economic operating framework, the quality of information is fundamental for successful decision-making (Chang et al., 2022). The quality of information will allow differentiated effectiveness in decision-making and differentiated results in the short and long term. It is important, therefore, that managers are aware of the identification of indispensable quality dimensions that meet commercial, technical, and technological requirements (Chang et al., 2022).

2. Information Quality

The quality of information is associated with its nature. Since it is a resource that, from an organized set of data, allows a reading of a given phenomenon or situation, with a view to its understanding, this will have quality if it meets the user's needs. It will be normal that these characteristics depend on the criticality of the information, the responsibility of the decision maker, and the urgency of the decision, among other factors.

Several authors point out some relevant characteristics, namely, the precision, which expresses the coherence between the recorded values and the real (Borek et al., 2013; Woodall et al., 2015); accessibility, which highlights the possibility of access to information when necessary, as well as retrieval of existing information (Woodall et al., 2015; Broo & Schooling, 2021); the availability, which possibility of using information when necessary (Jylha & Suvanto, 2015; Broo & Schooling, 2021); the completeness, which represents the availability of all information about a given situation are presented (Borek et al., 2014; Zadeh et al., 2017); consistency, which expresses the coherence between all information related to a given situation (Woodall et al., 2015; Zadeh et al., 2017); relevance, which expresses the degree of adequacy of information to a specific situation or task (Woodall et al., 2015); the reliability, which corresponds to the credibility of the information (Cai & Zhu, 2015); the opportunity, which expresses the timeliness of information (Boreck et al., 2013; Woodall et al., 2015); and usability, achievable when all information corresponds to the needs of users (Cai & Zhu, 2015).

Although the literature indicates a set of characteristics that allow for assessment of the quality of information, it is found that some stakeholders define the requirements for the quality of information that must be sent to them by the legal power they have over economic agents. This is the case of the European Sustainability Reporting Standards (ESRS). In this case, the qualitative characteristics of the information that must be disclosed as part of the companies' sustainability reports are specified. This Directive (2013/34/EU of the European Parliament and the Council, supplemented by Commission Delegated Regulation (EU) 2023/2772 of 31 July 2023) sets out in Appendix B, the qualitative characteristics that the information presented in the sustainability declarations must satisfy (European Commission, 2023).

The first dimension, relating to relevance, is characterized, in the context of sustainability, as follows: information is relevant when it can make a difference in users' decisions within the framework of a dual materiality approach. This Directive understands this double materiality from two dimensions: the materiality of the impact and financial materiality. Materiality of impact refers to the actual or potential material impacts, positive or negative, of the company on people or the surrounding environment, in a short-, medium- or long-term time horizon. This impact may be related to their products, services, and business relationships upstream, and their operations and value chain downstream. Financial materiality concerns to the identification and management of risks or opportunities that affect or may affect the financial situation of the company, namely concerning financial performance, cash flows, access to finance, or cost of capital in the short, medium, or long term.

Information can make a difference in decision-making and condition the results obtained, depending on their relevance, quality, and timeliness. Even if some users are unable to take advantage of it, for lack of opportunity, for example, or already know about it from other sources, they should assume the possibility that these may have predictive value, confirmatory value, or both. Information has predictive value if it can be used and contribute to predicting or achieving future results. The information may also have a controlled nature, that is, it can generate confirmatory value if it confirms or alters previous assessments.

The second dimension refers to the faithful representation. In the context of sustainability, it is possible to assume the existence of a reliable representation when the information represents relevant phenomena or realities and corresponds faithfully to the substance, becoming useful in decision-making. For this representation to be true, it is necessary a complete, neutral, and accurate information. A representation can be considered complete when it includes all the material information necessary for users to understand the scope of the phenomenon under analysis. A representation is neutral when it is not biased, that is, if it is not manipulated (biased, weighted, emphasized, or de-emphasized) to increase the likelihood of influence, either forward or unfavorable, by users. They should be balanced, to cover favorable/positive and unfavorable/negative aspects.

In the field of management, neutrality presupposes prudence and prudence presupposes the ability to adopt caution in the preparation of judgments or assessments under conditions of uncertainty. The prudence means that opportunities should not be overstated, and risks should not be minimized. Similarly, this exercise of prudence should not allow the minimization of opportunities or risk exaggeration. An enterprise may present offset information if it does so in addition to absolute values and if this offsetting clarifies what is intended to be disclosed, not concealing relevant information and including a clear explanation of the effects of offsetting and the reasons for offsetting.

The accuracy of information implies completeness and completeness presupposes the adoption and implementation of appropriate internal processes and controls to avoid errors or inaccuracies. Also, in forecasts, estimates should be presented with a clear emphasis on their limitations and associated uncertainty. The precision degree required for information accuracy depends on the information nature and the related issues. For example, accuracy requires particular attention to the following dimensions: the information must be free of errors (interpretation); descriptions must be accurate (understanding); non-factual information such as estimates, approximations and forecasts shall be identified as such (nature); an appropriate process of selection and treatment according to the intended purpose should be adopted (assessment of reality or forecast estimates), identifying the contributions obtained or expected as well as stimulating the possibility of audibility (treatment); the decisions or statements are reasonable and based on information of unquestionable quality and quantity (decision). In the case of decisions regarding the future, these must accurately reflect information about assumptions, interpretations/analyzes (judgments), and expected results.

The third dimension refers to comparability. Information may be considered comparable when it can be compared with other information to which it can be related, such as information provided by the company concerning other companies, information of the company corresponding to previous periods compared with current performance, information corresponding to similar activities, etc. Comparability is related to the consistency of the "raw material," method, and instruments, among other aspects. Consistency refers to the use of the same approaches, methods, periods, nature of activity or sector. Consistency is a critical factor in the success of comparability. Comparability does not mean uniformity. For the information to be comparable, similar components must resemble each other, and different components must differentiate. As stated in the Directive, comparability of information is not improved if it makes things that are not similar look alike, nor is it improved if it makes similar things differ.

The fourth dimension refers to verifiability. Verifiability corresponds to the ability to corroborate the information itself or the data used to obtain it. This allows the various users to ensure that the information describes a faithful representation. Verifiability provides confidence to users and ensures that information is complete, neutral, and accurate. To ensure verifiability, the information must be proven by comparison with other information; shall allow the identification of data and calculation methods used to produce estimates or approximations; and must be reviewed and validated by the administrative, management, and supervisory bodies.

However, it should be borne in mind that some information may take the form of explanations or prospective information. Although there may be some difficulties related to verifiability relatively, it should be borne in mind that these disclosures must be supported by faithful representation on a factual basis (e.g., based on company strategies, plans, or risk analysis). In this context, the company must define the assumptions and methods underlying its production, as well as other factors that provide evidence that the information reflects the plans or decisions taken.

The fifth and last dimension refers to comprehensibility. We may consider that information is understandable when it is clear and concise. Understandable information allows to increase the levels of knowledge of users. Clarity should meet the specificity of needs. Information on the evolution in each period, for example in the form of reports, should be given special care, different from "permanent" or constant information, even if it remains unchanged from one period to another. Completeness, clarity, and comparability should be contextualized in a framework that facilitates the presentation of information as a coherent whole.

For example, to be consistent, in the case of disclosures, information should be presented in a way that explains the context and relationships between related information. In addition, the level of information, granularity, and technicality should be aligned with users' needs and expectations.

Regarding the above, two relevant aspects are highlighted that should be considered. The first refers to the conceptual dimension of quality. We can say that a product or service has quality when it presents a set of characteristics that meet the needs and requirements for which it is designed or produced. In this context, quality is associated with the needs and purposes of use. Considering the existence, in the management field, of three levels of management, which are associated with different needs, responsibilities, and competencies, we can assume that each of them will have different quality requirements, therefore it will require differentiated information. The different requirements of information quality result from the different scope and reach of the responsibilities of the associated management.

The second aspect refers to the information production system, known as the IS. Since information is the output of the IS, we can assume that the quality of the output will depend on the quality of the system that produces it, that is, the quality of the information depends on the quality of the processing and storage functions. In this specific case, it is interesting to note that the Commission's Delegated Regulation (EU) 2023/2772 of 31 July 2023 which complements Directive 2013/34/EU of the European Parliament and of the Council, although referring to the obligation of, within the scope of sustainability of companies, specify the information on sustainability, only refer to the term IS once.

3. Objectives and Methodology

The context for analyzing the information quality dimensions was based on Commission Delegated Regulation (EU) 2023/2772 of 31 July 2023, which supplements Directive 2013/34/EU of the European Parliament and of the Council on sustainability reporting standards. From this, based on the dimensions presented regarding the information quality in the context of sustainability reports, we tried to evaluate the overall quality of information in these companies, for a sample of companies in Portugal in the non-food retail sector.

We can hardly say that there may be information of higher or lower quality depending on the criticality of decisions, for example. Thus, the assumption adopted corresponds to the fact that the quality of information provided by IS should have the same general quality in the context of economic activities carried out by the company. Thus, regardless of the specific requirements associated with a given context, as is the case of this Directive, companies must ensure adequate levels of quality of information provided during the activities they carry out.

Based on the regulation, a questionnaire was developed from two focus areas: the quality of information and the quality of the IS. Regarding the first focus, the main points analyzed focused on the relevance of organizational information, the economic value of information, the impact of decision-making, and the provision of predictive information. Regarding the second focus, the most relevant points of analysis were the use of tools to support decision-making, the completeness of the information provided concerning decision-making, and the existence of quality evaluation practices of the information system (audit, e.g.).

A Likert scale of 5 points was adopted for the evaluation of each point, and the following classification was adopted: (1) totally disagree, (2) disagree, (3) neither agree nor disagree, (4) agree, and (5) totally agree.

The choice of the non-food retail sector resulted from some characteristics that make it challenging, particularly regarding the dynamic and competitive nature of the market. To evaluate the relevance of information quality, a sample of 15 small and medium-sized enterprises in the non-food retail sector in the region of Lisbon was selected.

4. Result Analysis

Each company was asked to answer the questionnaire of 35 questions, to evaluate how companies understand and value issues such as relevance, reliable representation, comparability, verifiability, and comprehensibility of information, as well as the relationship that they establish between this, the IS and the organization.

Regarding the quality of information, about 65 % of companies showed a strong concern with the relevance and relevance of organizational information, particularly concerning the rigorous understanding of consumers' preferences, market trends, and seasonal variations, central elements for economic success. Most companies (about 70 %) were satisfied with the added value of information for their operations, especially in contexts where detailed data on consumer behavior and purchasing patterns are needed, allowing you to personalize offers, improve customer experience, and optimize stocks.

Following the relevance 63 % consider that the information provided by their organizational IS represents, objectively, the economic and organizational reality of companies. They consider that they have quality information, which is characterized by the absence of errors, and duplication of data, and that it corresponds in a reliable way to reality. In addition, 56 % say that they access it in a timely manner when they need.

Regarding comparability, 61 % state that, by only being able to access the information provided by their IS, they can only compare internal information, and 60 % state that these comparisons are automatically made available by the system.

However, regarding predictive information, the results vary significantly. Companies that invest in advanced technologies, such as analytics and artificial intelligence, have found themselves better positioned to use predictive information to anticipate market trends, identify growth opportunities, or adapt quickly to changes in consumer preferences. Only 20 % of companies considered having a reasonable capacity to use predictive data, while about 80 % indicated difficulties in accessing effective predictive data, revealing a need to improve this dimension to increase competitiveness.

Regarding the quality of IS, approximately 60 % of companies expressed the need to improve decision support tools. The product variety and fast nature of the retail economy require robust, integrated IS that can handle large volumes of data in real time. The importance of using the same language in the different channels in which companies are present – omnichannel perspective – adds increased demands on the responses by IS, making them essential throughout the value chain.

In this context, it was possible to find that about 30 % of the companies are satisfied with current tools, and 70 % expressed the need to adopt more current IS and more innovative technologies that allow not only billing and inventory management but also, mainly, the integrated management of the whole company, the analysis of customer data and sales forecasts.

The users' confidence in IS assumed a positive highlight, to the extent that about 70 % of respondents express confidence in IS. However, they identified areas for improvement in the completeness and quality of available data, given that success in retail depends heavily on accurate and timely information. About 50 % of companies reported that the information available is not sufficiently detailed or contextual to support complex strategic decisions. In addition, only about 10 % of companies carry out regular IS quality assessment practices, such as internal and external audits, pointing to challenges in ensuring the reliability and security of their data.

In short, the results indicate that although many non-food retail companies (around 65 %) are aware of the importance of information quality and support systems for their competitiveness and growth, there is considerable scope for improvement. The need for new technologies was evident, with around 55 % of companies showing interest in investing more in predictive analysis tools and more systematic approaches to IS quality assessment and assurance.

5. Conclusions

The results show that, although there is a growing awareness of the importance of quality information and decision support systems, there are significant areas where improvements are needed to achieve optimal levels of performance and competitiveness. To prepare the future in the IS domain it is important to consider the present reality. The results obtained in this study reflect median values in most of the dimensions analyzed, which becomes insufficient when it is considered that the current context of companies' performance is information-based and that competitiveness depends on the quality of the information.

To improve their long-term competitiveness and sustainability, non-food retailers should focus efforts on three main areas. First, it highlights the investment in predictive analytics tools and advanced technologies. The study suggests that companies should increase investment in technologies that enable better predictive data analysis, such as artificial intelligence, machine learning, and big data analytics. These technologies can help companies identify consumer behavior patterns, predict market trends, anticipate changes in product demand, and adjust marketing and operations strategies more quickly and accurately. For example, using machine learning algorithms can help predict which products will have the highest demand at certain times of the year or identify more profitable customer segments for specific campaigns.

In addition, investment in advanced technologies can also optimize inventory management, reducing waste and improving operational efficiency. Predictive analytics tools can help predict stock outages, optimize inventory levels and avoiding both overstock and shortage. With the ability to predict demand, companies can make more strategic decisions about purchasing, production, and distribution, resulting in higher customer satisfaction and lower operating costs.

Secondly, it is suggested to improve information management practices and the evaluation of IS quality, namely through audits. The study reveals that many companies do not have systematic practices of quality management of their information systems, such as regular audits and continuous performance monitoring. To ensure that information is accurate, reliable and secure, companies should adopt a more proactive and structured approach in assessing the quality of data and the information systems that manage it, through the implementation of periodic audits, both internally and externally, to assess the effectiveness of information systems in terms of security, integrity, and compliance with regulations and standards. Continuous monitoring of information systems is also crucial to quickly identify problems or failures that could compromise the quality of data. In addition, companies should adopt data governance practices, setting clear policies on who has access to what data, how the data is stored and shared, and how data quality is maintained over time.

These practices ensure that business decisions are based on accurate and up-to-date data, increasing managers' confidence in the information used to guide their strategic actions. Also ensure that companies comply with legal and regulatory requirements, reducing risks associated with data protection failures or compliance.

Finally, but with equal importance, the training of human resources for effective use of information and IS is established. For companies to take full advantage of the available technologies and information, their employees must be properly trained to use these tools effectively. This requires an investment in ongoing training on how to interpret and analyze data, how to use specific analysis software and how to apply insights derived from the data in daily practice.

Empowering employees also means creating an organizational culture that values data-driven decision-making. This means promoting a collaborative approach, where different departments share relevant information, ensuring that everyone has access to the data needed to perform their functions effectively. Training should not only be technical but also include the development of analytical skills and critical thinking, so that employees can question, interpret, and extract real value from data.

In addition, encouraging innovation and the use of new technologies will help create a more agile working environment that is prepared for rapid market changes. By promoting a culture of continuous learning and innovation, companies will be better positioned to adopt new tools and practices that increase their efficiency and competitiveness.

References

Borek, A., Parlikad, A. K., Webb, J., & Woodall, P. (2013). *Total information risk management: maximizing the value of data and information assets*. Newnes.

Broo, D. G., & Schooling, J. (2021). A framework for using data as an engineering tool for sustainable cyber-physical systems. *IEEE Access*, *9*, 22876–22882.

Cai, L., & Zhu, Y. (2015). The challenges of data quality and data quality assessment in the big data era. *Data Science Journal*, *14*, 2–2.

Chang, J. Y., Garcia, J. M., Xie, X., Moretti, N., & Parlikad, A. (2022). Information quality for effective asset management: A literature review. *IFAC-PapersOnLine*, *55*(19), 235–240, ISSN 2405-8963, https://doi.org/10.1016/j.ifacol.2022.09.213.

Esteves, F. J. M., & Anunciação, P. F. (2022). Information governance: A framework proposal for enterprise managers. *Social and Economic Studies within the Framework of Emerging Global Developments, 1*, 153–167.

European commission. (2023). *Commission delegated regulation (EU) 2023/2772 of 31 July 2023 supplementing directive 2013/34/EU of the European Parliament and of the Council as regards sustainability reporting standards.* Official Journal of the EU, L 277/1, https://eur-lex.europa.eu/legal-content/PT/TXT/?uri=CELEX%3A32023R2772 (in Portuguese).

Jylhä, T., & Suvanto, M. E. (2015). Impacts of poor quality of information in the facility management field. *Facilities, 33*(5/6), 302–319.

Leming, R. (2015). Why is information the elephant asset? An answer to this question and a strategy for information asset management. *Business Information Review, 32*(4), 212–219. https://doi.org/10.1177/0266382115616301

Woodall, P., Gao, J., Parlikad, A., & Koronios, A. (2015). Classifying data quality problems in asset management. In *Engineering asset management-systems, professional practices and certification: Proceedings of the 8th World Congress on Engineering Asset Management (WCEAM 2013) & the 3rd International Conference on Utility Management & Safety (ICUMAS)* (pp. 321–334). Springer International Publishing.

Zadeh, P. A., Wang, G., Cavka, H. B., Staub-French, S., & Pottinger, R. (2017). Information quality assessment for facility management. *Advanced Engineering Informatics, 33*, 181–205.

Muharrem Umut and Enes Akkurt

Construction Completion Insurance in Türkiye

1. Introduction

The concept of insurance, with origins tracing back to ancient times, holds a significant place in today's world. In the increasingly in-demand field of insurance, there are two primary parties: the insurer and the insured. The insurer is the party that assumes the risk, while the insured is the party that transfers the risk. The market consisting of insurers is referred to as the insurance market. In this market, companies operate mainly in two categories: Life insurance and non-life insurance. Life insurance involves insuring an individual's life, while non-life insurance covers assets in which natural or legal persons have an interest. The design of insurance products is fundamentally based on the compensation provided by the insurer for the damage incurred when a specific risk materializes. As a result, a security system is established for the insured by paying compensation when the risk occurs. In Türkiye, non-life insurance types are classified under 18 general categories. Construction completion insurance (CCI) is one of the sub-categories under the general heading of surety insurance (Regulation on Insurance Branches, 2007).

Globally introduced in 1929 under construction all-risk insurance, a specific type of insurance was tailored for Türkiye as a unique insurance branch called CCI. Construction all-risk insurance is designed to cover damages that may occur during the construction phase of a structure. In contrast, CCI is a type of insurance that ensures the completion of a structure in the event that construction is halted, delayed, or cannot be finished for any reason. Essentially, CCI is a contract taken out by the insured before taking possession of the property, which terminates upon the delivery of the property. In other words, if the property cannot be delivered due to reasons specified in the coverage, the insurance company compensates the insured, thereby preventing the insured from suffering a loss. CCI was first introduced in Türkiye in 2015.

As an economy that has grown significantly through the construction sector in recent years, the importance of CCI in Türkiye is considerable. However, this type of insurance has not yet achieved sufficient development in the non-life insurance market in Türkiye. The widespread adoption of this insurance would significantly contribute to the growth of insurance companies and provide insured individuals with a greater sense of security.

In this study, the types of structures under construction in Türkiye and the developments in construction over the years are explained, followed by detailed information about CCI. The main focus of the study is to explain the importance, nature, regulatory framework, and functioning of CCI in Türkiye, supported by relevant data. Subsequently, the challenges faced in this type of insurance are addressed, and finally, some recommendations are provided.

2. Constructioncompletion Insurance

2.1. Definition and Scope of CCI

CCI covers constructions. A construction is defined as any architectural structure constructed for habitation or other purposes (Göktepe, 2019).

Globally, there is no specific product exclusively named "construction completion insurance." However, a type of insurance that encompasses the contents of CCI is offered under the category of construction all-risk insurance. This all-risk insurance product aims to cover losses and damages that may occur from the start of construction until the construction is completed, including those arising from the inability to complete the construction (Ryu, Son, & Kim, 2016).

Historically, this type of insurance was first introduced in 1929, covering the construction of the Lambeth Bridge over the Thames River in London. Its development continued with the creation of policies in Germany in 1934, marking significant progress and importance in the field (Musundire & Aigbavboa, 2015).

CCI is a relatively new type of insurance in Türkiye. Despite the absence of a specific definition, this insurance type is regulated by the CCI General Conditions published in the Official Gazette on March 16, 2015. Therefore, a definition based on these general conditions can be provided. According to the general conditions, this type of insurance applies to residential properties that are still under construction and are considered project-based (Construction Completion Insurance General Conditions, 2024).

The origin of this insurance is rooted in housing regulations, specifically based on Law No. 6502 on the Protection of Consumers, published in the Official Gazette No. 28835 on November 7, 2013. Article 42 of Chapter 4 of this law addresses this insurance type. This section deals with pre-paid housing sales and mandates that before such sales, CCI must be obtained or other forms of coverage specified by the relevant ministry must be provided (Law No. 6502 on the Protection of Consumers, Official Gazette No. 28835, 2013).

Under the scope of the Law on the Protection of Consumers (LPC), the insurance aims to cover damages arising from risks related to pre-paid housing sales contracts, pre-paid timeshare contracts, and urban transformation practices under Law No. 6306. This coverage is intended to protect against damages resulting from these risks (Karadeniz, 2021).

The subject of the CCI contract is defined under Article 12 of the Regulation on Pre-Paid Housing Sales (RPPHS), which is prepared under Article 42 of the Law on the Protection of Consumers (LPC). In this context, this type of insurance is mandatory for projects where the total number of housing units is 30 or more before the sale of the property (Regulation on Pre-Paid Housing Sales, 2014).

Like any other type of insurance, CCI involves several parties like insured and insurer (Tamer, 2021).

In CCI, which is practiced both in Türkiye and worldwide, damages are either compensated financially or through the completion and delivery of the property. Generally, it is known that financial compensation is preferred both globally and in Türkiye (Tekelioğlu, 2018). The purpose of this insurance is to address the basic need for shelter a fundamental requirement since the dawn of humanity by ensuring that individuals feel secure. The primary goal of ensuring this security is to prevent individuals from being disadvantaged when purchasing properties from models or those still under construction (Kaya, Kaya, & Yalçıner, 2016). In this context, the insurance strengthens the insured's position in terms of risk, minimizing the potential damage resulting from the risk materializing (Doğar, 2022).

The scope of coverage for CCI as outlined by the regulations is as follows (CCI General Conditions, 2024):

- **Material Damages Due to Seller's Bankruptcy:** Coverage for financial losses resulting from the seller's insolvency.
- **Material Damages Due to Seller's Death:** Coverage for financial losses resulting from the rejection of the inheritance by the heirs following the death of an individual seller.
- **Damages Due to Delayed Delivery:** Coverage for damages arising from the failure to deliver the property within 12 months after the agreed delivery date specified in the contract.

The exclusions from coverage for CCI as outlined by the regulations are as follows (CCI General Conditions, 2024):

- **Material Damages from Nuclear Sources:** Damages resulting from ionizing radiation, radioactivity, or contamination due to nuclear fuel or nuclear waste, or attributed to these causes.

- **Damages from Radioactive Materials:** Damages arising from radioactive, toxic, explosive, or other hazardous or contaminating properties of nuclear facilities, nuclear reactors, or their associated parts.
- **Damages from Nuclear Weapons:** Damages caused by atomic or nuclear fission or fusion, or other similar reactions, or from weapons or devices using radioactive power or substances.
- **Damages from Radioactive Isotopes:** Damages caused by radioactive isotopes not prepared, transported, stored, or used for industrial, commercial, agricultural, medical, scientific, or other peaceful purposes.
- **Damages from Chemical, Biological, Biochemical, or Electromagnetic Weapons:** Damages resulting from chemical, biological, biochemical, or electromagnetic weapons.
- **War-Related Damages:** Damages caused by war, warlike events, invasions, foreign enemy actions, clashes (whether declared or not), civil wars, revolutions, rebellions, uprisings, and related administrative and military actions.
- **Terrorism-Related Damages:** Damages resulting from acts of terrorism as defined by Law No. 3713 on the Fight Against Terrorism, sabotage, or biological and/or chemical contamination, pollution, or poisoning caused by interventions by authorities to prevent or mitigate such actions.
- **Damages from Project Adjustments:** Damages arising from adjustments made by public authorities to the project, provided they are not due to the seller's violations of regulations or project terms.
- **Damages from Consumer Withdrawal:** Damages arising from the consumer's withdrawal or cancellation of the contract.
- **Damages from Avoidance of Transfer or Delivery:** Damages resulting from the consumer's refusal to transfer or take delivery of the property.
- **Indirect Damages:** Indirect material damages.
- **Defective Property Elements:** Damages resulting from the use of items like tiles, faucets, flooring, door handles, or kitchen cabinets inside the property that do not meet the quality promised in the project, as long as they do not affect the habitability of the property.

In addition to these aspects, CCI offers several advantages, including (Kokkaew & Wipulanusat, 2014; Tekelioğlu, 2018; Göktepe, 2019; Doğar, 2022):

- **Motivation for Construction Firms:** It motivates the construction company to carry out its tasks with greater care and to complete the construction promptly.

- **Adherence to Contract Terms:** It ensures that both the insurance company and the construction firm adhere strictly to the terms of the contract, with everything conditioned according to plans, procedures, and operations.
- **Guarantee and Penalties:** It guarantees the timely delivery of the property by the construction firm, especially in urban transformation and mass housing projects, and allows for penalties if the contractual terms are not met.
- **Pre-Contract Inspection:** The insurance company performs necessary project inspections before the contract is finalized, preventing potential issues for the insured.
- **Contract Termination and Payment:** If the construction firm fails to meet its responsibilities, the insurance company can apply to the Ministry of Trade for contract termination as of the date of the failure. This ensures that the insured receives payment based on the maximum premium, subject to the general conditions and policy.

2.2. Importance of CCI

CCI contributes significantly to various stakeholders, including the insured, the insurance company, the construction firm, and the broader economy. The key contributions are as follows (Sigortam.net, 2024):

CCI, being a type of insurance in favor of the insured, holds significant importance in several aspects:

- **Project Continuity:** By ensuring that the construction project is under supervision and control through the insurance agreement, it guarantees the continuity of the project.
- **Financial Security:** It provides financial protection to the investor, that is, the insured, ensuring their financial security. This, in turn, minimizes the risks associated with potential issues in the project.
- **Risk Minimization:** Insurance companies conduct risk analysis to contribute to the reduction of risks associated with the project. By identifying and managing risks proactively, they help in keeping potential risks to a minimum.

In essence, this insurance not only ensures that the project is completed as planned but also safeguards the financial interests of the insured by minimizing potential risks through thorough risk analysis.

Additionally, through this type of insurance, the insurance company gains insights into construction projects, learns to identify risk situations, closely monitors the construction company's work plan, and thus develops an understanding of risk management. Furthermore, due to the experience gained from handling this type of insurance, the insurance company is better equipped to forecast and assess risks in new construction projects.

CCI is also significant for construction firms, in addition to the insured and the insurance company. This insurance helps in monitoring the construction firm, compelling the firm to act appropriately considering this oversight. The monitoring of the construction site indirectly ensures the oversight of the construction company itself, prompting the firm to improve its administrative, technical, and financial standing, thus highlighting the importance of this insurance for construction firms. Additionally, this type of insurance allows construction companies to access contract guarantees without needing to purchase bank loans or guarantee letters. Examining annual Construction permits and construction statistics according to their use underscores the importance of this insurance type for the construction sector before considering its impact on the national economy.

Table 1: Number of new and additional constructions by property ownership

	2019	**2020**	**2021**	**2022**	**2023**
Public Sector	21.687	22.089	28.343	30.854	27.480
Construction Society	509	417	506	435	202
Government Sector	1.314	1.154	1.886	1.680	1.140
Total	23.510	23.660	30.735	32.969	28.822

Source: Turkish Statistical Institute, Statistics

When examining Table 1, it is observed that the private sector has a significantly higher share compared to the other two categories over the years. In 2023, 95 % of the constructions granted construction permits belonged to the private sector, 4 % to the public sector, and 1 % to housing cooperatives. Analysis over the years reveals a noticeable increase in the number of new constructions constructed annually, with this increase occurring predominantly in the private sector. In other words, construction activities in Türkiye are quite intense and contribute significantly to the national economy. Therefore, the importance of the mentioned insurance will become even more evident in the coming years.

The distribution of Constructions granted usage permits between the years 2019 and 2023, according to their intended purposes, is provided in Table 2.

Table 2: Number of new and additional constructions completed either fully or partially, by intended use

	2019	2020	2021	2022	2023
Constructions with one flat	3.960	5.819	8.705	10.296	9.568
Constructions with two or more apartments	16.485	14.968	17.947	16.635	15.646
Public places of residence	39	31	67	42	45
Hotel etc. Constructions	138	192	177	275	233
Office (workplace) Constructions	118	426	659	702	783
Wholesale and retail trade Constructions	1.009	758	995	818	626
Traffic and communication Constructions	68	86	105	54	63
Industrial Constructions and warehouses	712	547	1.025	1.031	963
Public, entertainment, education, hospital or care facilities Constructions	437	309	300	397	371
Other non-residential Constructions	544	524	755	604	524
Total	23.510	23.660	30.735	30.854	28.822

Source: Turkish Statistical Institute, Statistics (www.tuik.gov.tr)

According to TSI data, between 2019 and 2023, the number of new and additional Constructions that were either fully or partially completed was 157,748. Table 2 shows that a large portion of these constructions were intended for residential purposes. During this period, the proportion of residential Constructions relative to the total number of Constructions exceeded 88 %. Analyzing year by year, it is evident that there has been a notable increase in the number of new Constructions constructed for residential purposes as well as for other uses.

2.3. Legal Framework of Completion Insurance

The legal framework for CCI includes relevant laws, general terms, and special terms. Firstly, the legal framework of the insurance contract consists of the General and Special Terms of CCI. Special terms are arranged optionally, provided they do not contradict the general terms of the contract. This situation is confirmed by the provision in the policy general terms stating, "The parties may determine special terms appropriate to the nature of the work in the policy" (CCI General Terms, 2015). Another legal basis for this type of insurance is the Turkish Commercial Code (TCC). The insurance law area regulated in Book 6 of the TCC includes general provisions applicable together with other insurances, organized between Articles 1453–1486 (Turkish Commercial Code, Book 6: Insurance Law,

2011). Another component of the legal framework is the Consumer Protection Law (CPL). Provisions related to this law have been addressed in previous sections. This law protects the rights of the insured. Another influential regulation, as previously mentioned, is the Regulation on Prepaid Housing Sales. Published in 2014, this regulation plays a role in implementing the CPL. The Turkish Code of Obligations also contains provisions related to insurance contracts. As explicitly stated in the Turkish Commercial Code, if there is no provision in this code, the Code of Obligations may be referred to. In this context, insurance contracts are also governed by the Code of Obligations.

3. The Current Status of Completion Insurance in Türkiye

The current production of CCI in the insurance sector and at the company level is provided in Tables 3 and 4.

Table 3: Premium production and policy numbers for CCI

Years	**2020**	**2021**	**2022**	**2023**
Premium Production	348.258 TL	336.610 TL	115.622 TL	979.579 TL
Policy Count	12	34	9	41

Source: Türkiye Insurance Association, Statistics (www.tsb.org.tr)

Table 3 provides an overview of the total policy production and the number of policies issued for CCI. It shows a decline in CCI over the years. However, due to the increase in housing construction and urban transformation projects, and the resulting construction-driven economic growth, it is anticipated that this insurance type will become significant within a few years. This view is supported by the data announced for December 2023, which shows a total premium production of 979,579 TL and a total of 41 policies issued. Although it is still relatively new, this indicates a potential increase in this type of insurance (Türkiye Insurance Association, Statistics).

Table 4: Premium production and number of policies for CCI by companies

Years	2020		2021		2022		2023	
	Premium Production	**Policy Count**	**Premium Production**	**Policy Count**	**Premium Production**	**Policy Count**	**Premium Production**	**Policy Count**
Anadolu Insurance	120.000 TL	1	60.000 TL	1	0	0	0	0
Quick Insurancce	228.258 TL	11	276.610 TL	33	115.622 TL	9	979.579 TL	41

Source: Türkiye Insurance Association, Statistics (www.tsb.org.tr)

Table 4 shows the premium production and number of policies for CCI by individual insurance companies. It is observed that while the number of policies has increased on a company basis over the years, there was a decline in 2022. Additionally, it is noteworthy that only two companies are engaged in this line of business within the insurance sector. The fact that premium production is limited to just these two companies indicates that the significance of this insurance type has not yet been fully recognized within the sector.

4. Issues Faced in Construction Completion Insurance

CCI, despite being in existence in Türkiye since 2015, is a type of insurance that faces numerous challenges within the insurance sector. As a mandatory insurance, CCI is required for construction firms to address the risks associated with incomplete or non-started construction projects. However, despite being in place for nearly nine years, the number of policies issued for this insurance type remains relatively low. In other words, insurance penetration and coverage rates are quite low, which represents a significant problem.

In addition to this, both insurance companies and construction firms, particularly contractors, face difficulties in implementing and agreeing upon the insurance contracts. A contractor is a person who specializes in various types of construction, such as residential, commercial, and infrastructure projects (Doğanoğlu & Uzukaya, 2008, p. 385). The reasons contractors avoid insurance contracts include inadequate coverage and the difficulty of the assessment process.

To elaborate, inadequate coverage refers to the situation where the risks anticipated are likely to result in a heavy financial burden, and the coverage provided by the insurance company may be insufficient to cover the anticipated damages. Another issue, the difficulty of assessment, pertains to the challenges insurance companies face in evaluating projects before finalizing the contract. This difficulty arises because the assessment process is complex and requires detailed information (Kaya, Kaya, & Yalçıner, 2016: 103). Contractors may be unwilling or find it difficult to undergo such a detailed assessment for their construction projects, which can lead to complications in this insurance type.

Another party contributing to the issues is the insurance company itself. There are three main problems faced by insurance companies in this insurance type: difficulty in finding coverage, challenges in risk forecasting, and excessive responsibilities assigned to the company. Difficulty in finding coverage refers to the challenge of obtaining the required guarantees for the parties involved in the contract, both domestically and internationally. Currently, only two insurance companies in the sector provide such coverage. Challenges in risk forecasting involve the inability of insurance companies to fully anticipate the risks associated with the projects they are insuring. Additionally, there is a lack of skilled personnel in risk assessment within the sector. Examples of this issue include the bankruptcy of a construction firm or the sudden disappearance of a firm, which can lead to financial harm for the insured parties. Furthermore, any irregularities or attempts to conceal issues during the preliminary assessment conducted by the company can place the company in a difficult situation.

Lastly, the excessive responsibilities placed on insurance companies involve the difficulty of conducting thorough assessments and research. The company must not only review the financial structure of the construction firm and its past projects, including any incomplete ones, but also examine all aspects of the construction project to be undertaken, and gather information about the insured party. All of these require additional costs. Moreover, the construction sector may not always be willing to share this information or may face challenges in maintaining regular records, complicating the information sharing process. Such issues can result in negative outcomes, such as reluctance to engage in CCI (Kaya, Kaya, & Yalçıner, 2016).

5. Conclusion and Recommendations

The purpose of CCI is to cover damages resulting from the failure to complete, start, or address other risks related to the housing units within a project as outlined in the contract. This insurance ensures that both the insured party's rights are protected and provides a safety net by compensating for damages arising from risk factors. As discussed in the study, this type of insurance is implemented both in Türkiye and globally. However, the penetration of this insurance in Türkiye remains notably low. The sector is gradually evolving and updating through legislative, policy, and legal frameworks.

In Türkiye, this insurance type, which is relatively new, has been made mandatory since 2015 for construction projects involving 30 or more residential units. It represents a significant resource for the insured parties. Nevertheless, it has not yet reached the desired level of production, as highlighted by the data provided in earlier sections of this research.

Despite its importance, the low production of this insurance type in the sector has several underlying causes, primarily attributed to the contractors from construction firms and the insurance companies themselves. Issues arising from these two elements contribute to the reluctance or avoidance of producing this insurance. As mentioned in the research, certain conditions lead to a reluctance or avoidance of production. To address these issues, measures must be taken both by the government and the private sector.

In this context, it is essential to implement policy changes or regulations promptly to increase the number of CCI policies and enhance its effectiveness within the insurance sector.

Regulations are recommended on the following aspects concerning the subject of the study:

- Reshaping the guarantees according to the wishes of the insurance company and contractors and accordingly increasing them in a reasonable manner,
- Providing government support for the cost of insurance companies' inspection of construction companies,
- Assigning and assisting experts in their fields so that insurance companies can carry out the audit quickly,
- Ensuring that the requirement for the total number of Constructions in the project to be more than 30 is reduced to a figure below 30,
- Encouraging other insurance companies to carry out production, as opposed to only 2 companies in the insurance sector,
- Raising public awareness through lower and more affordable guarantees for fewer Constructions,

Considering the above recommendations, it is crucial to introduce flexibility into the regulations. The key aspect of this necessity is that construction projects with fewer than 30 Constructions will be deprived of the opportunity to obtain this insurance. Consequently, it is of utmost importance to implement these adjustments swiftly and make the insurance more applicable for all stakeholders.

References

CCI General Terms (2015). Consumer Protection Law. 16.03.2015. https://tuketici.ticaret.gov.tr/data/5e819a8e13b876a1b04c7a4a/Bina%20Tamamlama%20Sigortas%C4%B1%20Genel%20%C5%9Eartlar%C4%B1.pdf

Construction Completion Insurance General Conditions (2024). Insurance Assocation of Türkiye. 14.06.2024. https://www.tsb.org.tr/content/Legislations/BTS%20Genel%20%C5%9Eartlar.pdf.

Doğanoğlu, A. E., & Uzunkaya, M. C. (2008). Contractor's obligation to personally create the work or have it done under his own supervision in the work contract. *Ankara University Faculty of Law Review*, 1st Edition, pp. 381–406.

Doğar, M. (2022). Impact of not obtaining CCI on prepaid residential sale agreements. *Hacettepe University Faculty of Law Journal*, Special Issue, volume number: 12, 382–414.

General Terms and Conditions of CCI, 14.06.2014. Retrieved from https://www.tsb.org.tr/content/Legislations/BTS%20Genel%20%C5%9Eartlar.pdf.

Göktepe, E. (2019). *CCI in prepaid housing sales contracts.* Master's Thesis, Institute of Social Sciences, Dokuz Eylül University, İzmir.

Karadeniz, U. (2021). *Risk in CCI contracts.* Master's Thesis, Bahçeşehir University, Institute of Social Sciences, Istanbul.

Kaya, Ö. E., Kaya, B., & Yalçıner, K. (2016). Can CCI protect purchases of properties based on models? *Journal of Financial, Political, and Economic Comments, 53*(614), 95–106.

Kokkaew, N., & Wipulanusat, W. (2014). Completion delay risk management: A dynamic risk insurance approach. *KSCE Journal of Civil Engineering, 18*(6), 1599–1608.

Law No. 6502 on Consumer Protection. (2013, November 28). Official Gazette (Issue: 28835). Access address: https://www.resmigazete.gov.tr/eskiler/2013/11/20131128-1.htm

Musundire, S., & Aigbavboa, C. (2015). Management of constructionrisk through contractor's all-risk insurance policy – a South Afrıca case study. 11. *Construction Specialty Conference, 5.* İnternational, June 8 to June 10, 2015.

Regulation on Insurance Branches (2007/1). Access Address: https://www.mevzuat.gov.tr/File/GeneratePdf?mevzuatNo=11433&mevzuatTur=Teblig&mevzuatTertip=5

Regulation on Prepaid Housing Sales. (2014, November 27). Official Gazette (Issue: 29188). Retrieved from: https://www.resmigazete.gov.tr/eskiler/2014/11/20141127-7.htm

Ryu, H., Son, K., & Kim, J. M. (2016). Loss prediction model for construction projects using insurance claim payout. *Journal of Asian Architecture and Construction Engineering, 18*(6), 507–516.

Sigortam.net. (2024). CCI. Accessed on November 14, 2024, from https://www.sigortam.net/bina-tamamlama-sigortasi-nedir

Tamer, Ş. (2021). CCI. *Journal of Istanbul Medeniyet University Faculty of Law, 6*(11), 155–199.

Tekelioğlu, N. (2018). Seller's obligation to provide security in prepaid residential sale agreements. *Journal of Ankara University Faculty of Law, 67*(1), 81–104.

Turkish Commercial Code, Book 6: Insurance Law. (2011, February 14). *Official Gazette* (Issue: 27846). Accessed at: https://tsb.org.tr/media/attachments/Turk_Ticaret_Kanunu_6.Kitap.pdf

Turkish Statistical Institute. Construction and Housing, Construction Permit Statistics. Retrieved from https://data.tuik.gov.tr/Kategori/GetKategori?p=insaat-ve-konut-116&dil=1.

Türkiye Insurance Association. Statistics. Retrieved from https://www.tsb.org.tr/.

Venelin Terziev, Marusya Lyubcheva, Marin Georgiev,
Simeon Simeonov, and Milen Dimitrov

Study of the Environment for the Development of Social Entrepreneurship in Bulgaria

1. Introduction

Social entrepreneurship is both a phenomenon and an ordinary business. Its development is determined by the attitudes of people already engaged in business groups, the young people to whom the future belongs, but also by reflections – on career development, state support, public opinion, understanding and interaction between social groups, business and educational environment. The study of young people's attitude towards social entrepreneurship, their assessment of its importance, deficits and opportunities for it to be attractive for their future, are an important part of the development of emerging perspectives on the situation of social entrepreneurship in the economy. The respondents were selected to determine the complex picture of social entrepreneurship – aged between 18–60 years, women and men from different regions, with secondary and higher education, working and unemployed.

2. What Do Social Entrepreneurs Think, Have Already Started Such a Business?

According to the respondents, the reasons for starting social entrepreneurship were mainly personal interests and interests triggered by friends. They do not believe in the power of family tradition and prioritize the presence of the following factors: a suitable economic environment, a higher degree of confidence, family support. They do not exclude start-up capital and the necessary knowledge and skills as important motivational factors for social entrepreneurship.

Respondents believe that it is very important to provide initial knowledge on the subject at the university, on social networks, on specialized sites or at narrowly profiled events. The possibilities of the non-governmental sector and the print media in terms of importance follow the logic of the respondents. School is at the bottom of their preferences.

The reluctance to start a social entrepreneurship initiative is due to the low degree of awareness of its essence and insufficient knowledge and skills. Next comes the deficit of the subject in the curricula, the fear of the new and the lack of interest that would bring a certain benefit.

Regarding the profit from starting a social entrepreneurship, the respondents are hesitant. Although they put the possibility of personal development first, they leave the possibility of profit and a great career in the background. Prestige is not only at the bottom of the ranking of preferences, but is also noted as part of the negative aspect by the respondents.

According to the respondents, teamwork is the most important skill, followed by initiative and communication. One unnecessary element for them is critical thinking, followed by empathy and creativity.

The attitude to social entrepreneurship is primarily related to the different perception of social problems and processes, the support of the local community in the efforts of this individual challenge that can develop within the framework of big business. The respondents manage to distinguish social entrepreneurship from other entrepreneurial initiatives and believe that this type of initiative is not accepted by the community and/or by the closest circle. The respondents see the directions for the development of social-entrepreneurial initiatives mainly in solving the problems of the local community and the problems of people with limited opportunities. Next, they point to environmental and local community issues.

They see the prerequisites for the development of this type of initiative in financial incentives combined with education and training and understanding of the problem. In a lower position are legislative issues, people's motivation and the development of the IT structure.

The respondents see institutional support for social entrepreneurship only at the European level, where, according to them, there is good regulation. They disagree that there is good support and regulation at the national and local level.

The figure of the social entrepreneur in the minds of the respondents is that of a "winner." In subsequent positions, they note that the social entrepreneur is a developer of new ideas and only then that he is an innovator with a high culture and sensitivity to social problems.

The capabilities of the social entrepreneur include the need for professional qualifications, a habit of continuous learning with a built-in model for maintaining competencies. Next comes the knowledge in the professional field and the necessary hard skills. Last, respondents put the need for transferable skills.

3. The Business of Social Entrepreneurship

Acting social entrepreneurs determine that the important factors that would facilitate their initiative are: the economic environment; the initial capital;

confidence and the necessary knowledge and skills. For them, support from the family is not a significant factor, while the personal problem to be solved is a negative aspect for the respondents – it is not decisive.

Awareness of social entrepreneurship is evenly distributed between school, university, public publications, internet, social media and specialized events. The role of the non-governmental sector is too small.

The reasons that determine the low level of desire to start social entrepreneurship are associated with a low level of awareness of the essence of social entrepreneurship, the lack of the topic in curricula and programs, insufficient knowledge of social entrepreneurship, fear of the new and unpreparedness to deal with difficulties, insufficient skills. Education does not provide the necessary knowledge and skills to start a social entrepreneurship.

The profit for entrepreneurs implementing initiatives in social entrepreneurship is contained in the opportunity for a good career, personal development, opportunity to create and participate in the transformation of the economy. Next is prestige.

The most important skills surveyed social entrepreneurs believe they possess are evenly distributed in importance: initiative, communication, quick decision-making, teamwork and empathy. Not so important for them are skills such as flexibility, critical thinking and creativity.

According to the respondents, their attitude towards social entrepreneurship varies from extremely positive to extremely negative. They believe that social entrepreneurship needs the support of the local community, acceptance by the close social circle, and it can develop within the framework of big business. At the other pole is the disagreement that social entrepreneurship is an individual challenge and is related to a different type of thinking about societal problems.

The opinion is unanimous about the direction of development of social entrepreneurship. Social entrepreneurship is relevant and a priority for risk groups of people and people with disabilities, but the environmental problems of the local community are also important.

Social entrepreneurs see that the development of successful initiatives depends on the development of IT infrastructure, financial mechanisms, people's motivation, social receptivity and education and training. Legislative changes are important but not a priority, according to their responses.

According to respondents, there is regulation and support at the European level for the institutional attitude. At the national and local level, it is neither well regulated nor does it exist as a support for social entrepreneurship.

Gender does not have a significant impact on starting a business initiative, but certain specific professional ones are important one feature is noticeable in women – they have a clear idea and vision of the goal. That is, they need clarity about the pursued goals and desires in order to launch an initiative. Women think that how we look from the outside is defining (a kind of competition). Because "success is measured by the opinion of others."

The main profit for a person engaged in business is the time he earns and the hobby he realizes. This is related to prioritization, a good social environment (friends) and communication in an informal setting and of an unofficial nature. A new factor appears, and that is pedantry combined with trust between partners. This condition is valid for a group with similar characteristics, such as the focus group participants.

The participants also state something very important. It is associated with the view that entrepreneurship is all about speculation. This opinion deserves attention, and the participants in this definition are motivated by the fact that it is fast-acting in the field of entrepreneurship and is likened to commerce. An important conclusion that emerges from the last finding is that social entrepreneurship needs a clear and precise definition that is consistent with the linguistic and essential characteristics of the population. Social entrepreneurship itself is more about helping a group and/or groups of people than a cause.

The group emphasizes that in the Bulgarian conditions the state is unnecessarily heavy. Extreme opinions such as "it is better that the state does not help" are expressed. Although there is consensus on the need for adequate legislation. An obstacle to the initiative is bureaucracy and the aspect of conservative bureaucracy. What the state can and should provide is the infrastructure to have a suitable business environment according to the participants. Of course, there must be competition. It is appropriate to apply the so-called good practices in business. For example: "mentoring," implies the presence of a person to help you in the process of starting an initiative. This initiative is not new and some European countries have some experience in this direction. Last but not least, the need for political will to provide certainty for the future of any initiative is unequivocal. The lack of a suitable environment for business allows the government (central or local) to fail.

Findings from the results are intriguing and can serve as a basis for different directions for different groups who will and/or are engaged in social entrepreneurship initiatives.

Obviously, provocation is the real mechanism by which the initiative is given impetus. This motivational mechanism intuitively leads to a form of independence regarding a person's life and professional path. This statement is confirmed by the result, which shows that the family as an institution has no influence on the initiative decision expressed in the answers of all the studied groups. The opposite is the opinion that the main motivating factor is self-interest. It can be perceived as a boundary between business and social entrepreneurial initiatives. When an initiative is more influenced by self-interest, then it is business in nature. In cases where the initiative has a purpose other than personal interest, it has a social entrepreneurial character.

A key element for social entrepreneurship initiatives is the right environment, which includes many factors, for example, fair competition, friendly support, trust in partners, etc. It is noted in the study, but requires further in-depth analysis.

The categorical opinion of all survey participants is that schools, universities and specially created thematic events are the main carriers of information on the topic. This determines the importance of these institutions and obliges us to take immediate measures in this directional, first-level serious academic discussion about the organization of the curriculum and deepening the interrelationships and interactions between the acquisition of knowledge and its practical transformation. The last finding is confirmed by the opinion of the respondents that the reason for the weak desire to start social entrepreneurship is due to both the low degree of awareness of the essence of social entrepreneurship and insufficient knowledge about social entrepreneurship.

The prospects for profit from starting a social entrepreneurial initiative are clearly outlined. They are mostly expressed as an opportunity for personal growth, which inevitably leads to a good career. The need for a set of certain skills to engage in social entrepreneurship is undeniable. Although there are differences in the ranking of respondents' answers, they are negligibly small and rank initiative, decision-making, teamwork and communication as the most important. Skills such as flexibility, critical thinking and creative approach are not in the view of the respondents. However, discipline, persistence, enthusiasm and creativity emerge. The development of precisely these skills has so far been underestimated. So far, they have been acquired on the basis of life and professional experience.

There is variation in respondents' responses regarding attitudes towards social entrepreneurship. They consider that social entrepreneurship is perceived by the immediate environment/family, the local community/and it is possible to develop it within the framework of big business. The difference is that those who do not engage in social entrepreneurship believe that social entrepreneurship is an individual challenge, while those who engage in this type of initiative strongly disagree. A diametrical opposite is also observed in the relationship that emerges that social entrepreneurship is related to a different type of thinking about societal problems and processes. While current social entrepreneurs disagreed with this, the other group of respondents strongly agreed with this view. However, there is unanimity between both groups – they distinguish social entrepreneurship from other types of entrepreneurial initiatives.

The framework of social entrepreneurship is more complex than a simple transfer of knowledge and skills. A transformation of approaches is required. Unanimously, as a priority in the direction of development, its positioning in risk groups, people with disabilities, without neglecting environmental problems and urgent problems of the local community is accepted. The need for support for its successful development – real financial instruments, education and training – is formed as an indisputable emphasis. For those engaged in entrepreneurial initiatives, the most important thing is to provide a good environment, know-how and idea with which to start. All are unanimous regarding the degree of influence of the legislation that defines part of the environment, but its realization through the institutions is subject to criticism. Answer "It is best that the state does not help" is an illustration of the complexity of the state-legislation-institutions relationship – weaknesses in the legislation at the national level, insufficient support at the local level.

Regarding the figure of the social entrepreneur, there are extreme assessments. Those who have not implemented social entrepreneurship associate this activity with profit. True social entrepreneurs believe that they are innovative, highly cultured and sensitive to societal issues. These differences imply not so much an intensive information campaign to reduce the social distance, but an information campaign to spread the understanding of the essence of social entrepreneurship, its specific characteristics and differences from other types of entrepreneurship. This requires specifying and determining the format of social entrepreneurship. According to V. Radulov, it is particularly important for adolescents and young people to acquire special professional skills, necessary for initial entry into the working society. The mastery of three groups of skills is important: general work skills; adaptive skills and productive skills.

Another researcher gives a detailed reading of the skills situation. According to K. Hoyt, everyone should reach several types of skills:

- Basic academic skills;
- Productive work habits;
- A sincere desire to work;
- Skills related to job search and finding;
- Skills for productive use of free time;
- Skills to humanize the workplace for oneself.

The survey results point to the need for career development specialists to supervise and support the skills-building process. In terms of skills that need to be mastered for successful implementation are most often teamwork skills and communication skills. These findings lead to an indisputable conclusion of universality in the necessary skills for professional realization. The deficit of the so-called "flexible skills" is the same for everyone and needs to be filled with appropriate forms. Expectations for a different attitude of young people towards social entrepreneurship have their reasons. But above all, they shape and give meaning to the understanding of the environment and direction for development. Surprisingly, young people are not guided by recommendations, opinions of society, other people's evaluations, and recommendations to like or not social entrepreneurship. Not even as a phenomenon but as a real economic process. Young people ask questions but do not find answers to all of them. They would engage in social entrepreneurship for personal success because it will bring them successful personal development. Approximately 52.00 % are ready to do so under certain conditions (Graph 1).

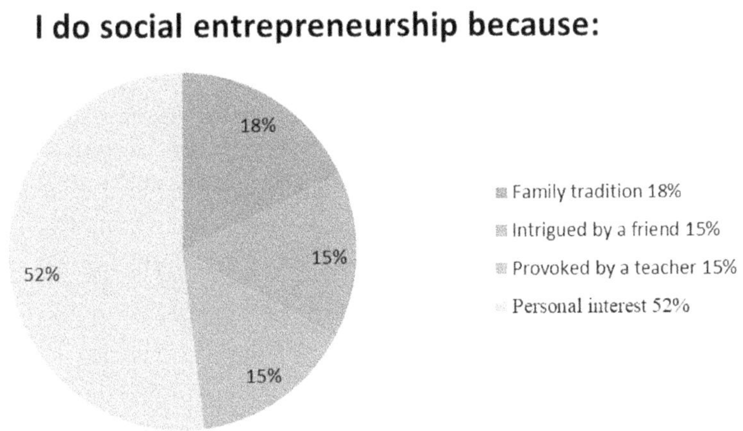

Graph 1: Social entrepreneurship
Source: Black Sea Institute, Bourgas, Bulgaria

They engage or would engage in social entrepreneurship out of personal interest, 15.00 % would follow a family tradition, and another 15.00 % – provoked by someone. The school does not give them enough information, they look for it above all from the universities, but they also rely a lot on social networks, various internet platforms, etc.

Young people hide that lack of information hinders them in their "social entrepreneurship" endeavor, but they are frank enough to admit their knowledge and skills deficits. They unequivocally talk about fear of the unknown, about fears that they will not cope, they emphasize that they are not prepared for this undertaking.

Young people have their own opinions embedded in the way they observe social processes and the immediate environment, but they are also willing to share them to seek a solution. They already know that social entrepreneurship is not ordinary entrepreneurship, it involves a different type of thinking and has a cause and a mission. They still do not dare to commit because they think that there is not enough support, and the external environment is not yet so favorable for this undertaking. There is an expectation of development, perspective and even optimism that is evident in their responses. Most of the respondents have the understanding that social entrepreneurship is different from ordinary and has a clear social need. Social entrepreneurship is a tool through which such business models can be created that are of new and different standards.

Undoubtedly, even with a favorable environment, there is fear – of the unknown, of the new, fear of themselves, whether they will succeed or fail in these new circumstances. The most frequently missed questions are related to this – what will happen to the dream career? Support is sought – in the answer to the question "Does social entrepreneurship need support" the need for personal support for young people to start this new venture is apparent. Support is needed for your different thinking and understanding of societal issues (Graph 2).

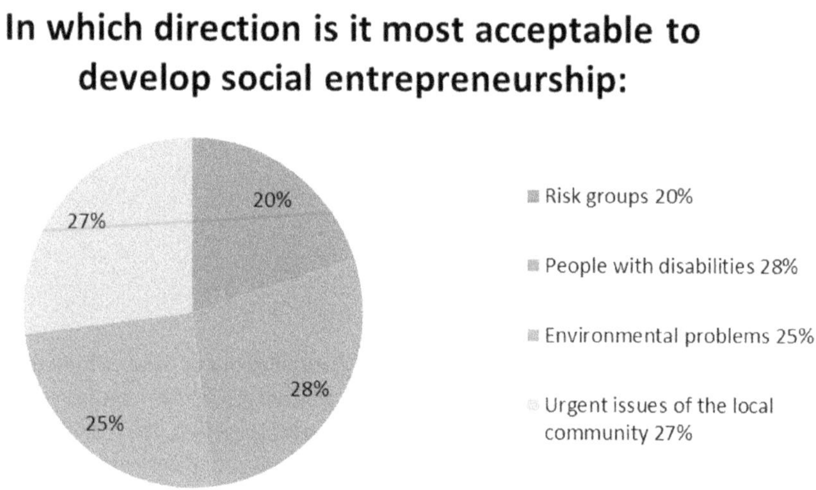

Graph 2: In which direction is it most acceptable to develop social entrepreneurship
Source: Black Sea Institute, Bourgas, Bulgaria

However, insufficient awareness does not prevent young people from considering that social entrepreneurship is not intended only for risk groups and people with disabilities, as is the understanding in society. They, by their logic, link social entrepreneurship with environmental issues, which may seem strange at first glance. Environmental protection is an issue that has an extremely social presence in people's lives, reaching security and safety, and they have realized this. It is a matter of future development that this idea of theirs finds development. Even more so, it refers to "pressing issues of the local community" – this is of high social importance, and young people appreciate this (Graph 3).

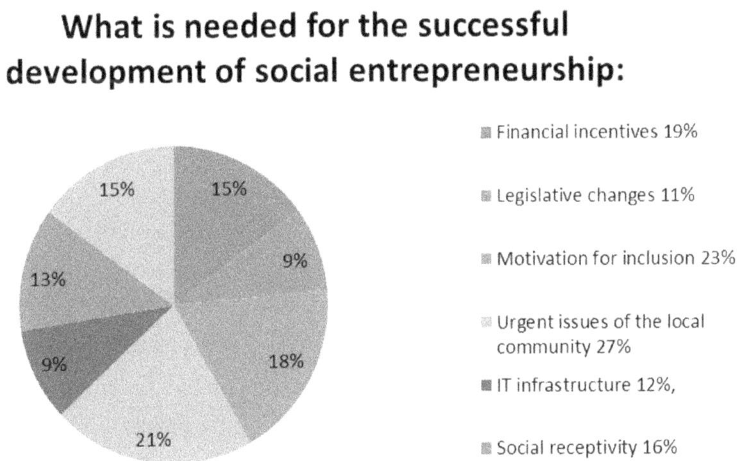

Graph 3: What is needed for the successful development of social entrepreneurship
Source: Black Sea Institute, Bourgas, Bulgaria

The environment for the development of youth social entrepreneurship includes many problems, the solution of which can also change the understanding of the social economy. Each area should be "liberated" to a level of familiarity and opportunities for inclusion. There are many factors and resources that young people value as important to support social entrepreneurs in their work and efforts to solve social problems. The provision of educational programs, courses and training in social entrepreneurship would play an important role in preparing future social entrepreneurs. It is more than clear that non-formal education and training must be relied upon. Here the ingenuity of non-formal education will connect with the non-governmental sector and the opportunities it creates.

This may include formal education at universities and informal training and workshops. Financial incentives are related to various financial resources and investments designed specifically for social entrepreneurs, which is essentially a financial investment for the future. This area, apart from being a social investment, can also be related to personal development and career investment. Two of the directions – "information resources" and "legislative changes" are an important part of the national support that young people "dream about." Without them, social entrepreneurship will move very slowly and develop with difficulty. Young people see the role of the state as particularly important – in support and in the regulations that are created. Although only 10 % of the respondents answered the question "attitude of the state towards social entrepreneurship," the reference is there – the most familiar is the national level, the second is the local level, and the third is the European Union. This is probably related to the lack of sufficient information or understanding among young people that social entrepreneurship is an issue that also has national and local understanding and receptivity.

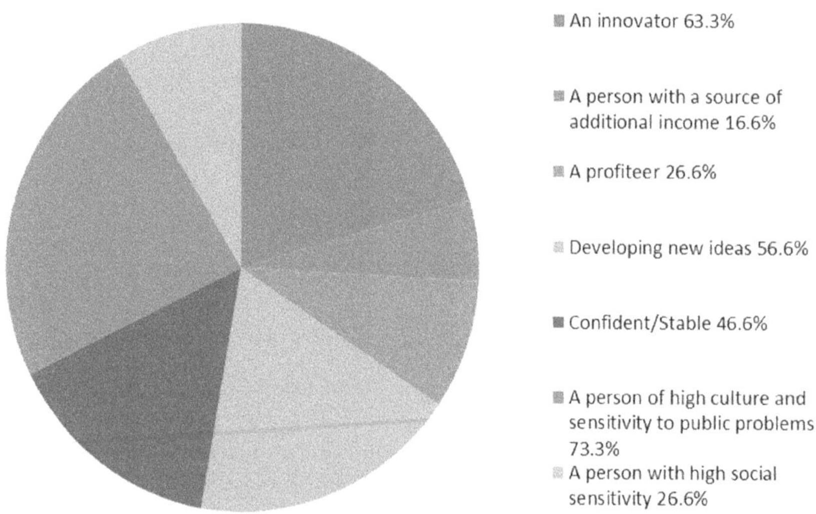

Garph 4: The social entrepreneur is
Source: Black Sea Institute, Bourgas, Bulgaria

The power of social entrepreneurship lies in the power of personal cause, empathy, and personal social sensitivity. Sometimes to the point of giving up any financial result, but with a definition that satisfies the idea or cause with which it is developed. And often, ignoring the negative energy that some social entrepreneur definitions carry, such as "profit maker." The imperative positivism towards the adoption of social entrepreneurship can concentrate much of this energy in the direction of creating new business models subject to high culture and social sensitivity (Graph 4).

4. Conclusion

All this can also be understood as a synergy between pure social entrepreneurship helping certain groups in society with big business generating social sensitivity. Therefore, many skills are needed that young people recognize, understand, and try to generate. It is no coincidence that when answering the question "The social entrepreneur has the following skills," more than 50 % of the respondents put all the mentioned skills in the first position, that is, necessary and most important.

A final emphasis in the survey, which was also answered by very few respondents, "I would easily become an entrepreneur if I had…" gives precedence to the right economic environment and personal confidence, followed by family support, the availability of start-up capital, as well as the availability of knowledge and skills.

Many opportunities for the young generation require rethinking choices and starting a career path that corresponds to intrinsic motivation based on sufficient awareness that is guided by knowledge and skills (Terziev et al., 2020a, 2020b, 2021a, 2021b; Terziev and Lyubcheva, 2022).

The present study was developed under project: 2021-2-BG01-KA210-YOU-000049806 Laboratory for Youth Social Entrepreneurship "Hot Zone," implemented under the EU program for education, training, youth and sport "Erasmus+."

References

Terziev, V., & Lyubcheva, M. (2022). Shared knowledge and changes in the higher education system in Bulgaria. In *79th International Scientific Conference on Economic and Social Development – Rabat, 25–26 March, 2022*, Economic and Social Development (Book of Proceedings), Cakovec, Croatia, 2022, pp. 228–237, ISSN 1849-7535.

Terziev, V., Lyubcheva, M., & Solovev, D. (2020a). The interaction: Business-education-investment for development. In *Proceedings of INTCESS 2020-7th International Conference on Education and Social Sciences 20–22 January, 2020 – DUBAI (UAE)*, International Organization Center of Academic Research, Istanbul, Turkey, 2020, pp. 865–869, ISBN: 978-605-82433-8-5.

Terziev, V., Lyubcheva, M., Andreeva, O., & Georgiev, M. (2020b). Revolution in industry and evolution in education or development of intelligence. In *63rd International Scientific Conference on Economic and Social Development – "Building Resilient Society" – Zagreb, 11–12 December, 2020*, Economic and Social Development (Book of Proceedings), Cakovec, Croatia, 2020, pp. 133–142, ISSN 1849-7535.

Terziev, V., Lyubcheva, M., & Georgiev, M. (2021a). Domestic and international challenges in higher education. In *7 th ITEM Conference – "Innovation, Technology, Education and Management" and 67th International Scientific Conference on Economic and Social Development – Sveti Martin na Muri, 29–30 April, 2021*, Economic and Social Development (Book of Proceedings), Cakovec, Croatia, 2021, pp. 88–97, ISSN 1849-7535.

Terziev, V., Lyubcheva, M., & Georgiev, M. (2021b). The contemporary strategic challenges facing higher education. In *Proceedings of SOCIOINT 2021 8th International Conference on Education and Education of Social Sciences 14–15 June, 2021*, International Organization Center of Academic Research, Istanbul, Turkey, 2021, pp. 134–141, ISBN: 978-605-06286-2-3.

Marin Marinov, Marin Georgiev, Teodora Petrova, and Zhivo Petrov

Unmanned Aircraft Vechicles as Digital Platforms in Agriculture

1. Introduction

In the development of society, all branches of the agro-industrial complex, including agriculture, are experiencing significant scientific and technological revolutions, each increasing the level of production organization and work efficiency. During the transition from one scientific and technical revolution to another, the organization in production is improved, which leads to an increase in crop yields, livestock productivity, an increase in labor efficiency and other significant economic and financial results in key agricultural sectors (Bezryadin, 2003; Gu et al., 2013; Terziev & Petrova, 2019a, 2019b). Predictions for the future comprise the digitization of agriculture, will allow to meet the needs of the population for agricultural products by changing the relationships in agriculture with the introduction of "smart" technologies. This will eventually transform agriculture and animal husbandry to a more efficient and production-intensive state (Saygılı & Özmen, 2022; Matkovic et al., 2005; Petrova et al., 2021). The groups of 'smart' agricultural technologies include:

- Precision agriculture – navigation systems, remote sensing and geographic information systems (GIS), differential fertilization;
- Agricultural robots – unmanned aerial vehicles, drones for monitoring the state of fields and harvesting, smart sensors;
- AIoT-platforms, AIoT-applications – control of data coming from sensors, equipment and other devices;
- Big Data – analysis of data received from sensors to make an accurate forecast and strategy.

The use of Unmanned Aerial Vehicles (UAVs) in agriculture is one of the fastest growing application areas. UAVs can be used to plan, monitor and control the stages of agricultural production. Their low cost and constantly improving UAV systems make these platforms more accessible and operational. Traditionally UAVs are used for monitoring agricultural crops, supporting land reclamation, effective herd control, land inventory, controlling the parameters of agro-technological processes, spreading fertilizers, surveillance of facilities, etc. The constant full-scale monitoring of the conditions for carrying out agricultural activities, the dynamics of changes in the condition of agricultural lands and the parameters of technological processes with the help of technical means for real-time monitoring is the most important necessary condition for the application of high-performance and efficient agricultural technologies. UAVs provide the ability to obtain effective and timely information, as well as allow this information to be accumulated for the purpose of analysis and improvement of agricultural processes. UAVs could gather enough information about crops to apply the right amount of pesticides and herbicides. This enables farmers to save on the use of chemicals, thus protecting the environment. UAVs make it possible to create a digital map base with the exact coordinates of all objects, which allows subsequent visual analysis of objects. This allows the calculation of areas of arable land, hayfields, pastures, fallows, fallows, sowing, sowing and sowing. Information about agricultural land also is used to form various maps such as soil maps, control of the dynamics of changes in the state and characteristics of the area of agricultural production, active regulation of ongoing technological processes (Terziev & Petrova, 2019a, 2019b; Petrova & Petrov, 2022, 2023).

The resulting aerial images allow the farmer:

- To establish the condition and area of plants in the field that need to be fertilized;
- To monitor the growth of seed material;
- To control the quality of work of agricultural machinery in real time;
- Use drones to protect crops;
- Protection of the product from theft.

2. Modules for Video Analysis and Computer Integration

A study of the possibilities for video surveillance automation in security systems and their applications in an agricultural holding enables the identification of new capabilities of video analysis modules and computer integration software modules. These can be used to further improve management systems concerning activities in horticulture and animal husbandry (Alanezi et al., 2022; Stewart et al., 2021; Petrova & Petrov, 2023). Figure 1 shows a general diagram of video analysis modules that are integrated into a single system for digital management of agricultural production.

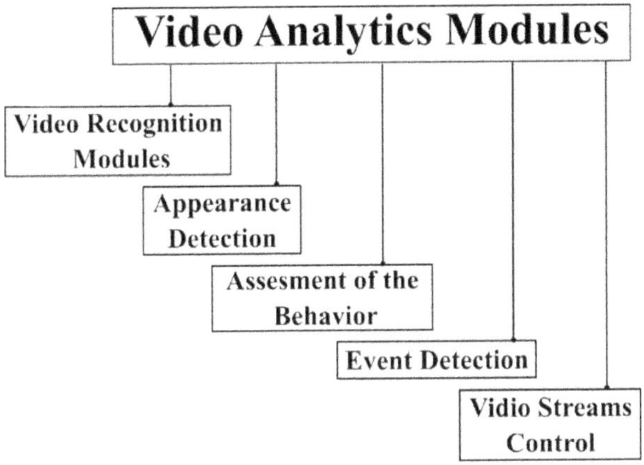

Figure 1: Diagram of video analytics modules integrated into a single control system
Source: Authors

Video Recognition Modules:

- used to manage an automated access of transport mobile vehicles to the territory of the agricultural holding;
- used to identify labels attached to the livestock; barcodes on machinery, technical facilities or on a moving object on a conveyor;
- used to recognition of the presence or absence of a numbers, labels and symbols on an object (Petrova et al., 2021; Petrova & Petrov, 2022).

Appearance Detection:

- detects and stores data of human appearance in the database;
- 3D monitoring (animal inspection, description of varietal and species characteristics of agricultural crops).

Assessment of the Behavior:

- personnel control (monitoring the presence and activity of personnel at the workplace);
- animal control (monitoring the presence and movement routes of animals in the herd);
- plant control (monitoring of growth, development and fertility).

Event Detection:

- determine the queue length to the milking machine (the number of animals in the queue, message for exceeding a specified threshold);
- detector for the accumulation of animals, people (counts the number of individuals in the crowd and notifies when a threshold is exceeded);
- smoke and fire detector (detects signs of smoke and fire in the camera's field of view);
- tamper detector (detects camera malfunctions or intentional damage);
- abandoned object detector (detects an abandoned object and the person who left it);
- loud sound detector (detects noise that exceeds a certain threshold); counting of animals in a herd or people in a group.

Video Streams Control:

- camera control (focuses, zooms in, controls the video recording settings);
- processing of audio streams (recording and transmission of sound in both directions from a video surveillance camera);
- scan (views expanded panorama image or divided into two or four frames); tracking (performs control of the perimeter of the allocated territory, borders, paths);
- creates a continuous video stream or record regardless of unexpected events; interactive search and inter-camera tracking (tracks the movement of an object between cameras, finds the target object in the archive) (Petrova et al., 2021; Petrova & Petrov, 2022).

Optical systems on a gyro-stabilized platform have gained an important place in the payload of UAVs. Their complexity and various functionalities (tracking a point in space, calculating the relative coordinates of a point in space, etc.) are constantly increasing, and the value of these devices is also growing. That is why the task of evaluating the effectiveness of the application of optical systems on gyro platforms has steadily gained more recognition. In addition, the complexity of the tasks assigned to unmanned platforms is constantly growing. Structurally, the optical systems of gyro-stabilized platforms are implemented in such a way that the lens (and the sensor system) provide relative rotation around two axes. In Figure 2, OX and OY are the two axes defining a coordinate system around which the rotation takes place with angular velocities ω_x and ω_y, respectively. The limit value of the angular rotation of the lens is usually chosen based on the purpose of the UAV on which the optical system will be mounted. A positive value of the α angle provides view and tracking of an object that is higher than the axis of the UAV.

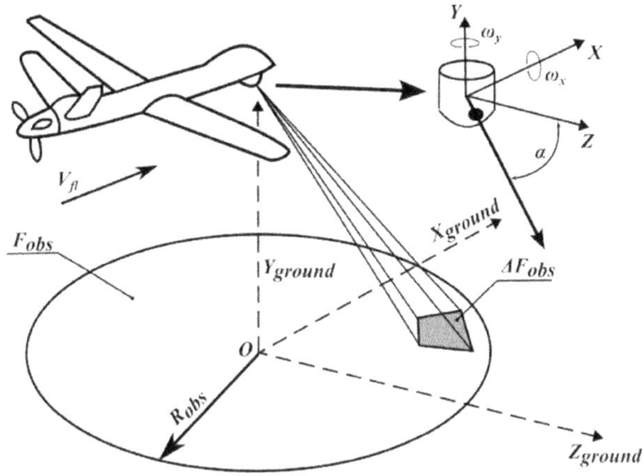

Figure 2: A reference scheme for determining the efficiency of the optical system used on a gyro platform

Source: Authors

The wide range of motion of the camera lens ensures stable tracking of an object during the maneuver and along the trajectory of the UAV equipped with the optical system.

The theoretical efficiency for the application of an optical system providing a circular overview is determined by the conditional probability that the desired object is located in the observed area F_{obs} (Figure 2). When determining this indicator, the following conditions should be taken into account (Terziev & Petrova, 2019a, 2019b; Petrova & Petrov, 2023):

- UAV to have flight speed $V_{fl} > 0$;
- The angular speed when rotating the optical axis of the lens should have a limit. In a simulation modeled system "optical device – operator" it turns out that the angular speed of rotation of the optical axis cannot be greater than *(0.06…0.07)/L* (the L-the slant distance to the center of the scan area in meters);
- The angular speed of rotation of the lens depends on the flight speed, therefore it is necessary to take into account V_{fl} and the value of the angular speed of rotation of the aircraft relative to the normal coordinate system of perfect flight trajectory. Otherwise, a blurry image with no informational value would be visualized on the screen;

- According to theoretical calculations, the observed area has the shape of a circle and it is assumed that the earth's surface is smooth and close to the surface of a sphere with a radius equal to the radius of the Earth. In fact, the Earth's surface differs significantly from an ideally smooth one;
- The sought-after object is usually found in the least expected areas. The conditional probability of detecting an object with given parameters can be determined by the expression:

$$P_{sa} = P_{oa} \cdot P_{ir} \cdot P_{no}, \tag{1}$$

where P_{oa} is the probability that, at a given moment in time, the object is within the bounds of the observed area. This parameter does not depend on the properties and characteristics of the optical system. Therefore, it is assumed to be equal to 1; P_{no} – the probability that the searched object is located in the area $F_{o\mu}$. This parameter does not appear to depend on the search pattern (i.e. on the law of changing the spatial position of the optical axis of the lens over time) for aircraft having $V_{fl} > 0$. This dependence, as will be seen later, has little relevance. Therefore, the value of can be determined from the expression:

$$P_{no} = K_{zone} \frac{\Delta F_{obs}}{F_{obs}}, \tag{2}$$

The case of $V_{fl} > 0$ needs to be considered, when the observed area has a shape other than a circle at different points in time. Then:

$$P_{no} = \frac{\Delta F_{obs}}{\pi R_{obs}^2 + 2V_{fl} R_{obs}}, \tag{3}$$

P_{ir} is the probability of instantaneous recognition of the object against the Earth's surface. This depends on the volume of information that is received for the searched object. If the volume of information is sufficient to accept the hypothesis, it can be confirmed that this is exactly the object we are looking for. Consequently, $P_{ir} = 1$.

Without losing generality, to simplify the determination of P_{ir} the following assumption is made: if the projection of the object occupies one or more pixels of the operator's screen, then $P_{\mathrm{ir}} = 1$.

The limited angular speed of rotation of the optical axis of the lens significantly limits the potential possibilities that are embedded in the optoelectronic device of the gyro-stabilized platform. Analysis shows that at a flight speed of 30 km/h, such a device is rendered useless: it cannot realize its capabilities, and the probability of finding the sought object in the area barely reaches a value of 0.05. Furthermore, increasing the observed radius sharply limits the probability of finding the desired object in the area. In this regard, the optical system as the main device that is firmly attached to the construction of the UAV (aviation cameras, TV-cameras looking down, etc.) have a significant advantage: with them P_{no} reaches values of the order of 0.95 • 0.98.

Based on the data, several conclusions can be drawn:

- when choosing an optical system for a UAV, very thorough consideration should be given to what is expected as the end result of the UAV system;
- the presence of the most technically advanced optical system on the board of the UAV does not yet guarantee its successful implementation in practice;
- the larger the size of the observed area on the earth's surface, the more difficult it is to use a small UAV and micro-UAV to solve practical tasks: their efficiency in this case is beyond reasonable consideration.

For the practical implementation of precision agricultural production, new robotic technical means are needed, especially in the conditions of geographically dispersed location of agricultural facilities and insufficient human labor. In animal husbandry, for individual animal care and effective herd management, it is promising to create a "video shepherd" based on a multifunctional mobile video surveillance unit with event signaling with self-learning and self-regulating options. In crop production, when applying the technology of differentiated agriculture, taking into account the state of each plant, it is necessary to create a "field video technologist" based on a developed multifunctional mechatrono-executive mobile unit for video surveillance with elements of self-coordination and self-organization. The management of natural resources in forestry, fishing and hunting farms, could be assisted by creating a "video inspector of territories" which is a multifunctional mobile unit for video surveillance, with self-learning and self-organization algorithms.

Other implementations of both local and integrated video surveillance systems in agriculture are possible to provide a quick visual presentation of information on the health status and behavior of animals, on the growth and development of plants, on the functional characteristics and operation of machinery and equipment, for the interaction of geographically dispersed objects. The development of video surveillance technology allows automation of the video stream management process through video analysis and computer integration modules, processing, long-term storage and analysis of video data, detection of undesirable events and visualization of predicted solutions. The joint use of video surveillance systems gives many opportunities to obtain a synergistic effect: in assessing the individual condition of the animal (identification and location of the animal in the herd, individual control and reporting of the animal's parameters, keeping a log of the animal), in the milking process (monitoring the work of the operator and the behavior of the animal), during feeding (duration of feeding, chewing of food, weight gain), in the process of insemination (identification of estrus, monitoring of animal calving), when assessing the animal's mobility (control of movement, the animal's activity, behavioral signs), when performing veterinary medical activity (checking, identification of diseases, keeping record of veterinary medical activities) (Terziev & Arabska, 2016; Kanev et al., 2017; Terziev, 2020; Terziev & Kanev, 2020; Terziev & Solovev, 2020a; Solovev et al., 2020; Kyriakopoulos et al., 2020; Terziev & Solovev, 2020b; Dolganova et al., 2020; Terziev, 2021; Solovev et al., 2021; Terziev & Solovev, 2022; Vovchenko et al., 2023; Albekov et al., 2023; Terziev, 2023; Terziev & Solovev, 2023; Vovchenko et al., 2022).

3. Conclusion

In agricultural activities, there is still an information and management resource for the development and improvement of agro-technological processes, which are about to enter the service through the wider use and integration of video surveillance equipment into a single self-organizing system. To improve agro-technological processes, increase the speed and accuracy of management, systems for managing robotic agrotechnological complexes should be developed, which use mobile remote systems for automated video surveillance, video analysis and video administration. In the design of control systems for geographically distributed agricultural production, an unprecedented improvement in the comfort and quality of labor can be achieved by using mobile and remote video surveillance, automation of unmanned video services, video robots, remote web clients – included in a single integrated system for agricultural self-management.

Acknowledgment

The research leading to these results has received funding from the Ministry of education and science under the National science program Intelligent Animal Husbandry, grant agreement №Д01-62/18.03.2021.

References

Alanezi, M. A., Salami, A. F., Sha'aban, Y. A., Bouchekara, H. R. E. H., Shahriar, M. S., Khodja, M., & Smail, M. K. (2022). UBER: UAV-based energy-efficient reconfigurable routing scheme for smart wireless livestock sensor network. *Sensors*, *22*, 6158. https://doi.org/10.3390/s22166158.

Albekov, A. U., Parkhomenko, T. V., Polubotko, A. A., & Terziev, V. K. (2023). New trends in the sustainable development of logistics systems during the impact of COVID-19. *Climate-Smart Innovation*, 319–328, https://doi.org/10.1142/9789811264252_0020.

Bezryadin, S. N. (2003). Osnovnoy nedostatok sensorov sovremennah tsifrovah kamer. 05.11.2003.

Dolganova, Y., Istomina, N., Zaborovskaya, A., & Terziev, V. (2020). State financial resources as a tool for managing sustainable development of territories. In *E3S Web Conference,* 208 (2020) 08015, (eISSN: 2267-1242), https://doi.org/10.1051/e3sconf/202020808015.

Gu K., Zhai G., et al. (2013). Subjective and objective quality assessment for images with contrast change. In *Proceedings of the IEEE International Conference on Image Processing,* Melbourne, VIC, Australia, Sep. 2013. pp. 383–387.

Kanev, D., Toncheva, S., Terziev, V., & Narleva, K. (2017). Specific aspects of motivation of seafarers. In *18 Annual General Assembly of the International Association of Maritime Universities Global perspectives in MET: Towards Sustainable, Green and Integrated Maritime Transport*, Varna, 1, 2017, ISBN 978-954-8991-96-4, pp. 392–400.

Kyriakopoulos, G. L., Solovev, D. B., Kuzora, S. S., & Terziev, V. (2020). Exploring research methods and dynamic systems toward economic development: An overview. In D. B. Solovev, V. V. Savaley, A. T. Bekker, & V. I. Petukhov (Eds.), *Proceeding of the International science and technology conference "FarEastCon 2019"* (Smart innovation, systems and technologies, vol. 172, pp. 1–29). Singapore: Springer. (Online) ISBN 978-981-15-2244-4, (Print) ISBN Online ISBN 978-981-15-2243-7. https://doi.org/10.1007/978-981-15-2244-4_1.

Matkovic, K., et al. (2005). Global Contrast Factor – a New Approach to Image Contrast, Computational Aesthetics, 2005, pp. 159–168.

Petrova, T., & Petrov, Zh. (2022). Linear images coprocessing in environmental monitoring. In *Proceedings of the 23rd International Conference on Computer Systems and Technologies (CompSysTech'22)* (pp. 91–94). New York, NY, USA: Association for Computing Machinery. https://doi.org/10.1145/3546118.3546144.

Petrova, T., & Petrov, Zh. (2023). Contrast Enhancing by Applying Histogram Analysis in Image Processing. In *2023, 22nd International Symposium INFOTEH-JAHORINA (INFOTEH)*, East Sarajevo, Bosnia and Herzegovina, 2023, pp. 1–4, https://doi.org/10.1109/INFOTEH57020.2023.10094055.

Petrova, T., Petkova-Georgieva, St., & Petrov, Zh. (2021). Improving the environmental monitoring process through the application of unmanned aerial vehicles. *Journal of Environmental Protection and Ecology*, 22(3), 1144–1150, ISSN 1311-5065.

Saygılı, Z., & Özmen, G. (2022). İnsansız Hava Araçlarında Gömülü Sistem Üzerinden Derin Öğrenme ile Nesne Tespiti, Avrupa Bilim ve Teknoloji Dergisi, No. 34, pp. 292–298, Mar. 2022, https://doi.org/10.31590/ejosat.1081713.

Solovev, D. B., Kuzora, S. S., & Terziev, V. (2021). Simulation-based methodical approach to applying managerial decisions in innovation. In D. B. Solovev, V. V. Savaley, A. T. Bekker, & V. I. Petukhov (Eds.), *Proceeding of the International science and technology conference "FarEastCon 2020"* (Smart innovation, systems and technologies, vol. 227, pp. 1–11). Singapore: Springer. Online ISBN978-981-16-0953-4, Print ISBN978-981-16-0952-7. https://doi.org/10.1007/978-981-16-0953-4_1.

Solovev, D. B., Kuzora, S. S., Kyriakopoulos, G. L., & Terziev, V. (2020). Algorithmic approach to the assessment of innovation. In D. B. Solovev, V. V. Savaley, A. T. Bekker, & V. I. Petukhov (Eds.), *Proceeding of the International science and technology conference* "FarEastCon 2019" (Smart innovation, systems and technologies, vol. 172, pp. 31–50). Singapore: Springer, (Online) ISBN978-981-15-2244-4, (Print) ISBN ISBN978-981-15-2243-7 (Online). https://doi.org/10.1007/978-981-15-2244-4_2.

Stewart, A., Faraj, F., You, H., Plante, J., Lim, M., Kasa, K., Beauchamp, A., Webster, A., Martin-Boyd, L., Wong, K., Braun, A., & Macdonald, A. J. (2021). A modular system for behaviour analytics from airborne full-motion video. In *Proceedings of the SPIE 11746, Artificial Intelligence and Machine Learning for Multi-domain Operations Applications III*, 117460I (12 April 2021); https://doi.org/10.1117/12.2584816.

Terziev, V. (2020). Provision of integrated employment and social assistance services in Bulgaria. In D. Solovev (Ed.), *Smart technologies and innovations in design for control of technological processes and objects: Economy and production. FarEastCon 2018* (Smart innovation, systems and technologies, vol. 138, pp. 24–39). Cham: Springer. (Print) ISBN978-3-030-15576-6, (Online) ISBN978-3-030-15577-3, https://doi.org/10.1007/978-3-030-15577-3_3.

Terziev, V. (2021). Management control as an effective instrument in implementation of the social program. In *30th Eurasia business and economics society conference, Eurasian business and economics perspectives, Eurasian studies in business and economics 17*, 2021, pp. 87–100, ISSN 2364-5067, ISSN 2364-5075 (electronic), ISBN 978-3-030-65146-6, ISBN 978-3-030-65147-3 (eBook), https://doi.org/10.1007/978-3-030-65147-3.

Terziev, V. K. (2023). Innovation development of industrial business organizations. In M. Okur Dinçsoy & H. Can (Eds.), *Optimizing energy efficiency during a global energy crisis* (pp. 282–306). IGI Global. https://doi.org/10.4018/979-8-3693-0400-6.ch016.

Terziev, V., & Arabska E. (2016). Sustainable rural development through organic production and community-supported agriculture in Bulgaria. *Bulgarian Journal of Agricultural Science (BJAS), 22*, (4), 527–535. ISSN 1310-0351.

Terziev, V., & Kanev, D. (2020). Modern developments in behavioral economics. In D. Solovev (Ed.), *Smart technologies and innovations in design for control of technological processes and objects: Economy and production. FarEastCon 2018* (Smart innovation, systems and technologies, vol. 138, pp. 10–23). Cham: Springer. Print ISBN 978-3-030-15576-6, Online ISBN978-3-030-15577-3. https://doi.org/10.1007/978-3-030-15577-3_2.

Terziev, V., & Petrova, T. (2019a). Analysis and evaluation of effectiveness of the use of unmanned aircrafts for environment monitoring. In *Proceedings of ADVED 2019-5th International Conference on Advances in Education and Social Sciences*, 21–23 October 2019- Istanbul, Turkey, pp. 419–425, ISBN: 978-605-82433-7-8.

Terziev, V., & Petrova, T. (2019b). Analysis of the methods for registration of images received from the information systems of non-motorized aircrafts. In *Proceedings of ADVED 2019-5th International Conference on Advances in Education and Social Sciences*, 21–23 October 2019, Istanbul, Turkey, pp. 485–492, ISBN: 978-605-82433-7-8.

Terziev, V., & Solovev, D. B. (2020a). The education of cadets and psychological aspect of the reasons for their drop-out of the National Military University. In D. B. Solovev, V. V. Savaley, A. T. Bekker, & V. I. Petukhov (Eds.), *Proceeding of the International science and technology conference "FarEastCon 2019"* (Smart innovation, systems and technologies, vol. 172, pp. 1013–1023). Singapore: Springer. Print ISBN 978-981-15-2243-7, Online ISBN 978-981-15-2244-4. https://doi.org/10.1007/978-981-15-2244-4_98.

Terziev, V., & Solovev, D. B. (2020b). Psychological characteristics of cadets from the military schools as subjects of educational activity. In D. B. Solovev, V. V. Savaley, A. T. Bekker, & V. I. Petukhov (Eds.), *Proceeding of the International science and technology conference "FarEastCon 2019"* (Smart innovation, systems and technologies, vol. 172, pp. 1025–1038). Singapore: Springer. Print ISBN 978-981-15-2243-7, Online ISBN 978-981-15-2244-4, https://doi.org/10.1007/978-981-15-2244-4_99.

Terziev, V., & Solovev, D. B. (2022). Analysis of the management of sector "Security" as part of the strategic management of Bulgaria. In D. B. Solovev, V. V. Savaley, A. T. Bekker, & V. I. Petukhov (Eds.), *Proceeding of the International science and technology conference "FarEastCon 2021"* (Smart innovation, systems and technologies, vol. 275, pp. 95–111). Singapore: Springer. Online ISBN 978-981-16-8829-4, Print ISBN 978-981-16-8828-7. https://doi.org/10.1007/978-981-16-8829-4_9.

Terziev, V., & Solovev, D. B. (2023). Development of the education system in Bulgaria in a period of economic transformations. In *AIP Conf. Proc.* 2910, 020064 (2023), (Online ISSN 1551-7616, Print ISSN 0094-243X), https://doi.org/10.1063/5.0167861.

Vovchenko, N. G., Andreeva, O. V., Dmitrieva, V. D., Galazova, S. S., & Krstev, T. V. (2022). Modelling of economic clusters in the Russian regions in the context of formation of the industry 4.0. In P. V. Trifonov & M. V. Charaeva (Eds.), *Strategies and trends in organizational and project management. DITEM 2021* (Lecture notes in networks and systems, vol. 380). Cham: Springer. https://doi.org/10.1007/978-3-030-94245-8_91.

Vovchenko, N. G., Andreeva, O. V., Dmitrieva, V. D., Kaptsova, V. S., & Terziev, V. K. (2023). Technological, economic, and social changes: The role of end-to-end technologies. In E. N. Makarenko, N. G. Vovchenko, & E. N. Tishchenko (Eds.), *Technological trends in the AI economy* (Smart innovation, systems and technologies, vol. 625, pp. 13–20). Singapore: Springer. Print ISBN978-981-19-7410-6, Online ISBN978-981-19-7411-3), https://doi.org/10.1007/978-981-19-7411-3_2.

Dijana Vuković, Tanja Grmuša, and Tanja Unterwegs

Communication about the Sustainability of Fashion Brands – True Desire for Change in Fashion Industry or a Good PR?

1. Introduction

Advocacy of sustainability in the fashion industry is present almost every day, but theory is one thing, and practice is something completely different: there is a lack of examples of real application, there is uncertainty about the structure of business models, and research so far has mainly focused on individual cases of brand behavior or a national approach (Villa Todeschini et al., 2020: 2), as well as differences between consumers. The fashion industry employs a large number of people, leaving a significant impact on the economy and society. The data highlight the fashion industry's share of 2 % in GDP (Fashion United, 2023 according to Grazzini et al., 2023: 2), and in the next five years (2024–2029) growth is expected by 8.94 % (Statista, 2024). However, recently it has been talked about negatively, especially in the context of the devastating consequences of climate change and environmental pollution (Berg et al., 2020), and fast fashion, which the world's leading brands have turned to (Subhasis & Lipsa, 2023: 3). The Covid-19 virus pandemic has brought into focus all the challenges facing the fashion industry, such as the need to look for new business models, but also the change in individual consumer habits that insist on sustainability and reducing the carbon footprint. On the other hand, consumers also want fashion manufacturers to take their share of responsibility for the environment and for the people who work for them (Granskog et al., 2020). Labeled as one of the biggest polluters, the fashion industry opens up to the public, offering insight into the production process and thereby advocating business transparency. Predictions show that GHG emissions in the fashion industry will reach 2.7 trillion tons by 2030, which is an annual growth rate of 2.7 % (Berg et al., 2020). Aware of the negative image that exists about them in the public due to environmental pollution, but also the growing demands of consumers for greater transparency, clothing manufacturers strive to defend their positions by strengthening corporate values and communication tactics centered on sustainability (Perrini & Vurro, 2010 according to Arriga, 2015: 9). Positive emotions and a sense of altruism in consumers encourage sustainable behavior, which also affects marketing messages that rely on positive psychological principles such as empathy to motivate sustainable consumer practices (Strübel et al., 2023: 18, 19) and personal involvement of consumers in life product cycle (McGarth, 2012). The concept of sustainability must be integrated into business models from research, development to design. It is a complex and long-term process that seeks to extend the life of the product through "reselling, repairing or recycling" (Daukantienė, 2023: 999).

2. Sustainability in the Fashion Industry and Corporate Social Responsibility from the Perspective of Consumers

The application of CSR in the fashion industry came to the fore in the late 80s and 90s through numerous campaigns directed against the wearing of fur or the omission of animals from testing clothing products. Fashion leaders of global fashion brands are abandoning the previously dominant reactive approach and taking a proactive one (BSR, 2012: 1), shifting the focus to organizational goals and strategies and following sustainability indices (Nike Inc's Materials Sustainability Index and Outdoor Association Eco-index) to prove application of ethical and responsible practices. "The concept of sustainable development was mentioned in 1987 in the Brundtland Report" (WCED, 1987: 43 according to Arriga, 2015: 10; Sengupta & Sengupta, 2020: 76) when "three pillars of sustainability were defined: 'people, profit and planet,'" which is In 2012, it was replaced by "people, planet and prosperity" (Arriga, 2015: 10). Integrating the concept of sustainability strongly affects the business of the fashion industry in the context of the approach to change: pragmatic or radical (Mukendi et al., 2020), as well as supply chains seeking the allocation of resources to other areas with the aim of achieving sustainability. Attention is also drawn against numerous synonymous terms with the terms sustainable fashion, such as "eco-fashion," "green-fashion," "ethical" or "slow fashion" (Khandual & Pradhan, 2019 according to Sengupta & Sengupta, 2020: 76; Grazzini et al., 2023: 6). At the same time, some authors (Griskevicius et al., 2010; Widloeher, 2010 according to Grazzini et al., 2023: 3) call the concept of sustainable fashion an oxymoron (Subhasis & Lipsa, 2023: 3) and question it (Harris et al., 2011: 1) due to the complexity of clothing as a phenomenon and cultural differences, the study of consumer motivation, ethical dilemmas. Tryphena and Aram further warn that the term sustainability should not and cannot be observed only in the context of the materials used, but also encompasses the production method as well as consumption patterns (2023: 2). This requires greater care for waste and its recycling, as well as more creativity and courage in cooperation between all stakeholders in the industry (Niinimäki, 2018: 30–32).

Anish et al. warn of the lack of qualitative research on consumer behavior and on sustainable fashion accessories and a deeper insight into the aforementioned (Anish et al. 2024: 533). It is also warned that earlier studies focused on millennials (Motwani et al., 2024) or Generation Z (Eitelwein & Paquet, 2020), as well as on the influence of age (Karlsson & Karlsson, 2023) and gender (Mandarić et al., 2021) on shopping habits, while this paper provides a comparative analysis of different groups and generations with the aim of determining differences in shopping behavior. A review of the literature shows a complex process of interconnectedness of values (Hong et al., 2024), price sensitivity, quality expectations, social influences, brand perception, and sociodemographic and psychographic characteristics (2024: 537) in the study of consumer behavior.

3. Communication Strategies of Fashion Brands

Each brand has its own strategy for different consumers, and in order to leave a mark it is important to highlight the qualities of your brand. Choosing the appropriate communication tactic depends on the choice of media, but also on the location of our audience. Building a brand is a complex task, and it all starts with building an identity. The meaning behind the name strongly influences the market position (Tungate, 2005 according to Scheide & Marques, 2018), but also the consumer's understanding of the brand. At the same time, brands are faced with the challenges of providing as much information as possible about their work through numerous channels and positively framed messages (Grappi et al., 2024: 2), which often results in accusations of greenwashing (Vuković et al., 2023) and at the same time find an information balance (Foroozeesh, 2021).

Bringé (2023) points out that the issue of sustainability is highly present in public discourse, and this can be an incentive for brands to create an image. It is a big challenge to achieve sustainable practices if we take into account the fact that the fashion industry has been facing numerous criticisms for years due to the way it works and its impact on the environment. The research mentioned earlier shows that consumers are now more willing to buy sustainable products and motivate brands to include the concept of sustainability in their operations, and it is also shown that this has a positive effect on local communities. Gárgoles Saes and Sabado (2018), states the importance of brand reputation, and adds that there is a direct connection between brand reputation and sustainability. The issue of corporate sustainability requires a clear organizational strategy, but also includes other stakeholders – internal and external (Dillick & Hockerts, 2002 according to Arriga, 2015: 10) on all aspects of the production process, and environmental impacts (Gárgoles Saes and Sabado, 2018: 20). The concept of sustainability should not only be viewed through a financial prism, but also through an environmental and moral one (2015: 11). Achieving sustainability in the fashion industry is challenging for several reasons: (1) understanding sustainability at the operational level, (2) the fragmentation of the fashion industry into many sub-segments, and (3) achieving mass-market sustainability (Kozlowski et al., 2015 according to Arriga, 2015: 12).

Sengupta and Sengupta bring several strategies to include sustainability in the business agenda: relying on digital marketing campaigns (influencer marketing), using alternative marketing strategies that will include various groups in society (minorities and marginalized), promoting inclusion and freedom, returning the debt to society through donations, by creating a more transparent information system, as well as payment of workers, as well as cooperation with local artists (2020: 82–84).

4. Research Results

Many brands claim to be committed to ecological and ethical practices, but the question that arises is: is sustainable fashion a trend that leads to real change or is it just a well-designed PR stunt? This essay explores both sides of this debate by analyzing consumer perceptions, actual brand investments, and their impact on purchasing decisions. Consumer perception plays a key role in the success of sustainable fashion. Consumers are becoming increasingly aware of environmental issues, and many want to support brands that share their values. However, there is a significant amount of scepticism regarding the sincerity of brands' sustainability claims. Research shows that many consumers believe sustainability claims are often exaggerated and used as a marketing tool, commonly known as greenwashing. For example, surveys show that a significant number of consumers doubt the actual implementation of sustainable practices by fashion brands and believe that these claims are mainly motivated by a desire to improve their image. One of the key indicators of whether sustainable fashion is a trend or a PR trick lies in the actual investment of brands in sustainable practices. The real trend would be manifested through significant financial investments in research and development of environmentally friendly technologies and materials. Following what was stated in this research, the following research objectives were set:

- Investigate how consumers perceive the claims of fashion brands about sustainability and whether they believe that these claims are sincere or just a marketing ploy;
- Examine the level and type of investment of fashion brands in sustainable practices, such as environmentally friendly materials, recycling and ethical production;

- Understand how sustainability claims influence consumer behavior and decisions when purchasing fashion products.

  H1: Fashion brands that implement sustainable practices and communicate them to the public do so out of a genuine desire to reduce their environmental footprint and improve social responsibility and prove it through investments in sustainable practices.
  H2: Communication of the sustainability of fashion brands is mainly aimed at improving the image of the company (greenwashing), without a significant impact on actual environmental and social practices.

Table 1: Socio-demographic structure of respondents

	Number of respondents	%
Sex:	509	60.12 %
Female	327	39.88 %
Male		
Age:	112	17.18 %
<25	225	34.51 %
26–35	194	29.75 %
36–45	213	32.67 %
46–55	92	14.11 %
>55		
Education degree:	65	7.78 %
high school education	311	37.20 %
College	448	53.59 %
College	12	1.44 %
Doctorate		
Number of persons in the household:	58	6.94 %
1 person	218	26.08 %
2 persons	291	34.81 %
3 people	200	23.92 %
4 people	11	1.32 %
>4 people		
Amount of monthly income in euros:	92	11.00 %
Up to 1,000 euros	309	36.96 %
From 1,001 to 1,500 euros	300	35.88 %
From 1,501 to 2,000 euros	82	9.81 %
From 2,001–2,500 euros	53	6.34 %
>from 2,500 euros		
In working relationship:	639	76.44 %
That	53	23.56 %
Not		

Source: Author's work.

Eight hundred thirty-six respondents participated in the research, of which 60.12 % were women, which represents one of the key limitations of this research, or the demographic profile of the respondents. The results obtained in this research do not represent the views of the entire population. Men as a demographic segment may have different attitudes and perceptions about sustainable fashion that are not adequately represented in these surveys. This limitation may affect the generalization of the results and the interpretation of the trend of sustainable fashion as an overall social phenomenon. Future research must include a more diverse population of respondents to gain more comprehensive insights into this complex phenomenon. Women as the main respondents provide valuable insights, but broadening the demographic representation can provide a broader perspective and better understanding of sustainable fashion. There are 112 respondents under the age of 25 or 17.18 %, 34.51 % of respondents or the largest number of respondents are between the ages of 26 and 35. From 36 to 45 years of age, there are 194 respondents or 29.75 %. While also a significant group consists of respondents between 46 and 55 years of age or 32.67 % of respondents. When it comes to education, 37.20 % of the respondents have a university degree, 53.59 % of the respondents have a university degree and only 1.44 % of the respondents have a doctorate. The largest number of respondents have monthly incomes between 1,001 and 1,500 euros 36.96 %. The second significant group consists of 1,501 respondents – 2,000 euros. Most of the respondents are employed – 639 respondents or 76.44 % of respondents.

The analysis of the standardized regression values shows that all of them are greater than 0.5, which is considered the limit when it comes to exploratory research (Hair et al., 2010: 722), and they are all statistically significant, and from this it can be concluded that the reliability of the construct is ensured.

Table 2: Crombach Alpha and item-to-total correlations for the three factors of sustainable fashion in the main study

	Crombach Alpha	Item to-total correlation
Consumer Perception of Sustainable Fashion Brands' Honesty	**0.875**	0.724
I believe that brands that claim to be sustainable actually implement sustainable practices		0.592
I am skeptical of sustainability claims coming from fashion brands.		0.761

Table 2: Continued

	Crombach Alpha	Item to-total correlation
I believe that fashion brands are transparent about their sustainable practices.		0.517
I believe that fashion brands are really reducing their environmental footprint as part of their sustainable initiatives.		0.728
I believe that fashion brands exaggerate their sustainability claims to improve their image.		0.762
Investments in Sustainable Practices	**0.834**	0.670
Brands that claim to be sustainable use recycled or environmentally friendly materials in their products		0.614
I believe that fashion brands invest enough in research and development of sustainable technologies.		0.597
Fashion brands are transparent about their business practices and supply chain.		0.659
I believe that fashion brands work to reduce waste through recycling and reuse of materials.		
Fashion brands transparently report on their investments in sustainability.		
Influence on Buying Decisions	**0.849**	
I am willing to pay more for products from fashion brands that practice sustainability.		0.719
Sustainability claims significantly influence my brand loyalty.		0.768
I only buy products from fashion brands that are transparent about their sustainable practices.		0.616
Sustainability is more important than price, quality and design when choosing a fashion product.		0.599

Source: Author's work.

To fully verify the model according to the recommendations of Churchill (1979), it is necessary to check the convergent and discriminant validity. Convergent validity (Table 2) is ensured to the extent that the factors are highly correlated with each other because they measure the same construct together. In the refined model, consumer perception of brand sincerity correlates with involvement (0.602), perception of sincerity with investments in sustainable practices (0.736), and investments with sustainable practices (0.727). In addition to high correlations, they are also statistically significant, on the basis of which it can be concluded that convergent validity is insured.

Discriminant validity refers to the extent to which a measurement construct is truly unique and not a reflection of some other variable. Comparing the average extracted variance (AVE) root and correlation coefficients with other factors – where the AVE root needs to be larger – is how discriminant validity is demonstrated. Upon examining Table 3, it is evident that the discriminant validity is satisfied for the factors pertaining to consumer perception of nrands' honesty in implementing sustainable strategies and investment in sustainable practices. However, the factor of investment in sustainable practices exhibits a deviation of 0.01. The authors of the paper admit that, in spite of the statistical constraint, the assumed model is a useful instrument for quantifying the notion of sustainable fashion, considering the tiny deviation observed in one component of the construct.

Table 3: Discriminant validity

AVE		Sincerity	Investments	Shopping
.513	Sincerity	**0.717**		
.553	Investments	0.602	**0.743**	
.581	Shopping	0.727	0.736	**0.762**

Source: Author's work.

After the measuring instrument for the construct of sustainable fashion as a trend or as a public relation trick has been purified and proved to be a suitable measuring instrument, it is possible to continue with the data analysis with the aim of making judgments about the connection between the variables of the initially proposed model of consumer perception of the sincerity of the sustainable fashion brand on the impact of the purchase decision on a sustainable fashion product. The model will be tested using the multivariate PLS-SEM method, which is adequate for the exploratory nature of research in the form of testing new theories and in cases of small number of observations (Henseler et al., 2016), which is why it is considered an adequate method of data processing.

Structural theory shows how latent variables are related to each other, and the PLS approach to structural models is based on variance with an emphasis on not doing PLS regression, which is also a popular multivariate analysis method, but unlike PLS, it is based on regression that observes linear relationships between variables (Hair et al., 2014: 15). On the other hand, PLS-SEM is based on a specified network of connections between selected constructs as well as between constructs and their measuring instruments.

Structural theory shows how latent variables are related to each other, and the PLS approach to structural models is based on variance with an emphasis on not doing PLS regression, which is also a popular multivariate analysis method, but unlike PLS, it is based on regression that observes linear relationships between variables (Hair et al., 2014: 15). On the other hand, PLS-SEM is based on a specified network of connections between selected constructs as well as between constructs and their measuring instruments.

The structural model aims to check the strength, direction and statistical significance of:

- The influence of the perception of the sincerity of the sustainable fashion brand on the decision to purchase a sustainable fashion clothing product,
- The impact of consumer attitudes, subjective norms, and perceived sincerity on the sincerity of brands, such as sustainable fashion producers, arises from the growing ecological consciousness of modern consumers and their inclination to endorse brands that align with their principles.
- The impact of perceived investments in sustainable practices on the purchase of environmentally friendly goods.

Table 4: Indicators of validity and reliability of reflective variables in the sustainable fashion purchase model

Construct and indicators	Factor loads	Average variance extracted (AVE)	Composite reliability (CR)	Cronbach Alpha
Customer attitudes		0.653	0.849	0.759
Paragraph I	0.788			
Paragraph II	0.766			
Paragraph III	0.866			
Subjective norms		0.678	0.891	0.835
Norms I	0.865			
Norms II	0.591			
Norms III	0.891			
Norms IV	0.906			
Health awareness		0.756	0.925	0.894
Awareness I	0.891			
Awareness II Awareness	0.825			
II Awareness IV	0.909			
	0.851			

(*continued*)

Table 4: Continued

Construct and indicators	Factor loads	Average variance extracted (AVE)	Composite reliability (CR)	Cronbach Alpha
Concern for the environment		0.628	0.834	0.721
Concern I Concern II Concern III	0.858 0.690 0.820			
Perception of knowledge about investments in sustainable fashion		0.691	0.870	0.783
Knowledge Knowledge II Knowledge III	0.823 0.823 0.776			
Cosmopolitanism		0.691	0.870	0.783
K towards plants K towards animals K to the environment	0.823 0.823 0.776			
Deep understanding and knowledge		0.697	0.873	0.784
Carbon footprint Ethics and CSR Protection of resources	0.818 0.895 0.787			
Purchase intent		0.813	0.928	0.885
Awareness of sustainability Ecological attitudes and values Quality and aesthetics	0.838 0.923 0.939			

Source: Author's work.

The first step in the analysis of convergent validity is the analysis of the loading of particles according to the variable they measure. It is recommended that the loading be greater than 0.7 (Hair et al., 2014: 103), which in the case of this research is true for all particles, except for the second statement that measures the subjective norms of consumers. Hair et al. (2011) suggest that a loading of 0.4–.7 should be tested before dropping a particle, that is, it is dropped only if it improves the average variance extracted (AVE) and composite validity (CR).

The model was repeated for both claims, and there were no significant improvements in the mentioned indicators, which is why the claims were left in the model. The average extracted variance (AVE), as a measure of convergent validity, for each reflective variable must be greater than 0.5 (Hair et al., 2014: 103), which is satisfied for all variables in the model. Composite reliability (CR) takes into account the difference in the loadings of statements, or particles, and is interpreted in the same way as Chronbach's Alpha. It must be above 0.7, the same as the traditional reliability indicator, Cronbach Alpha (Hensller et al., 2016). Both indicators, for all observed variables, amount to more than the given norm, so it can be concluded that they are reliable.

Furthermore, to ensure that all constructs are sufficiently unique – that is, that they differ from one another – it is imperative to verify the discriminant validity. The size of the average extracted variance and squared correlations between variables – also referred to as Fornell and Larcker's criterion of discriminant adequacy – are compared in PLS to demonstrate this. As can be seen in Table 5, every extracted variance of the reflecting variables is higher than the squared correlations, indicating that this requirement is likewise satisfied.

Table 5: Discriminant validity of reflective variables in the model

	Attitudes	**Subjective norms**	**Health awareness**	**Concern for the environment**	**Knowledge of investments**	**Cosmopolitanism**	**Deep understanding**
Customer attitudes	**0.808**						
Subjective norms	0.551	**0.823**					
Health awareness	0.389	0.605	**0.870**				
Concern for the environment	.0231	0.464	0.381	**0.793**			
Knowledge of investments	0.222	0.162	0.167	0.439	**0.831**		
Cosmopolitanism	0.287	0.306	0.202	0.546	0.526	**0.835**	
Deep understanding	0.123	0.390	0.340	0.333	0.133	0.254	**0.901**

Source: Author's work.

There is one formative variable in the model, which is the consumer's perception of brand sincerity, and it is viewed differently, because, according to Diamantopulous (2006: 11), due to the assumption that the formative variables are error-free, it is not founded on investigating the reliability quality of indicators. Nomological validity is ensured based on the theoretical assumptions on which the model was built. The significance of the weights of all three factors of the sustainable marketing construct is ensured with a statistical significance of 10 % for integration (p = 0.004), involvement (0.085), and ability (0.001). The VIF indicator, which suggests possible multicollinearity among the model variables, was also analyzed. VIF values must be below 5 (Hair et al., 2016, 212: 430), which is satisfied for all indicators in the model. Subjective norms have the highest VIF value of 2, which is still considered acceptable. Because of the above, it is concluded that all variables in the model are valid and reliable.

The theory of socially responsible business informs three sub-hypotheses that determine the first hypothesis. Following previous research in the model, it was assumed that attitudes, subjective norms and concern for the environment are good predictors of investment intentions and the turn of business towards sustainable fashion, and then of responsible and ethical behavior in the marketing-communication department, so investment intentions are and investment as a result of those three variables.

Table 6: Statistical significance of the structural coefficient between attitudes, subjective norms, concern for the environment and investments in sustainable fashion

Hypothesis	The direction of the relationship	Appraisal Beta coefficient	Standard error	t value	p-value	
H1						YES
H1a	Attitudes → Investment in sustainable fashion	0.145	0.088	1.666	0.000**	YES
H1b	Subjective Norms →investment in sustainable fashion	0.387	0.108	3.567	0.000**	YES
H1c	Concern for the environment → Investment in sustainable fashion	0.348	0.081	4.283	0.000**	YES
Remark **p<0.001						

Source: Author's work.

Table 7: Statistical significance of the structural coefficient between the communication of sustainability of fashion brands and the improvement of the company's image (greenwashing) without a significant impact on actual environmental and social practices

Hypothesis	The direction of the relationship	Appraisal Beta coefficient	Standard error	t value	p-value	
H2	Communication→ Image improvement					YES
		0.356	0.096	3.723	0.000**	YES

Source: Author's work.

The research carried out, to conclude the role and importance of transparent communication and adequate marketing strategies that are credible, confirmed the assumed hypotheses in the model of consumer sincerity perceptions in sustainable fashion, that is, in producers of sustainable fashion→investment in sustainable fashion→purchasing in sustainable fashion product, are research phases that have met the methodological and statistical prerequisites. However, given that it is a relatively new field within marketing communication, there was no possibility of a significant comparison with similar research, without referring to only one of the three assumed dimensions of sustainable fashion. Limitation of the research, conducted with the purpose of exploratory factor analysis, despite the methodological adequacy, has a limitation in the form of a sample, mostly women are represented as respondents in the research. Accordingly, due to the rigorous statistical and methodological procedure of designing the measuring instrument, it is possible that there was an excessive number of ejected particles, which theoretically corresponded to the described construct. Given that sustainable fashion is a concept based on a long-term perspective, and the model was observed in a situational context, that is, it does not have an element of time tracking of changes in results, the consequence of the relationships identified in the model, especially the one between the sustainable perception of the sincerity of consumers and manufacturers of fashion products and purchase intent, must be viewed contextually.

5. Conclusion

Whether sustainable fashion is a trend or a public relations trick depends on consumer perception, actual brand investments and influence on purchasing decisions. Although there is considerable scepticism among consumers, having a genuine effort and investment in sustainable practices can transform this industry and lead to real change. Sustainable fashion has the potential to become a permanent trend that not only meets the needs of environmentally conscious consumers but also contributes to the preservation of our planet. The key is transparency and honesty – only in this way can fashion brands win and keep the trust of their customers. However, future research must include a more diverse population of respondents to gain more comprehensive insights into this complex phenomenon.

References

Anish, A. G., Roopa, V. K. (2024). *Research Paper on Sustainable Fashion and Consumer Buying Behaviour, 11*(1), 531–558.

Arriga, E. (2015). Corporate Sustainability in Fashion and Luxury Companies. *SYMPHONYA Emerging Issues in Management, 4*, 9–23.

Berg, A., Magnus, K. H., Kappelmark, S., Granskog, A., Lee, L., Sawers, C., Lehman, M., Syrett, H., & Arici, G. (2020). *Fashion on Climate: How the Fashion Industry Can Urgently Act to Reduce Its Greenhouse Gas Emissions.* New York, McKinsey & Company Global FashionAgenda.

Bringé, A. (2023). The State of Sustainability in the Fashion Industry (And What It Means for Brands). *Forbes.* January 2, 2023, Available at: https://www.forbes.com/sites/forbescommunicationscouncil/2023/01/02/the-state-of-sustainability-in-the-fashion-industry-and-what-it-means-for-brands/, access date 25 July 2024.

BSR. (2012). *Sustainable Fashion Design: Oxymomorn No More*? Available at: https://www.bsr.org/reports/BSR_Sustainable_Fashion_Design.pdf, access date 27 July 2024.

Daukantienė, V. (2023). Analysis of the Sustainability Aspects of Fashion: A Literature Review. *Textile Research Journal, 93*(3–4), 991–1002.

Diamantopoulos, A. (2006). The Error Term in Formative Measurement Models: Interpretation and Modeling Implications. *Journal of Modelling in Management, 1*(1), 7–17.

Eitelwein, O., & Paquet, S. (2020). *Greenwashing Won't Eash – The New Sustainability Imperative.* London, EY.

Foroozesh, S. (2021). Sustainability in the Fashion Industry: Avoiding Communication Landmines. *Forbes.* July 13, 2021, Available at: https://www.forbes.com/sites/forbesbusinesscouncil/2021/07/13/sustainability-in-the-fashion-industry-avoiding-communication-landmines/, access date 25 July 2024.

Gárgoles Saes, P., & Sabado, T. (2018). *How to Improve Fashion Reputation: The Role of Sustainability*, New York, US: Global Fashion.

Granskog, A., Lee, L., Magnus, K. H., & Sawers, C. (2020). *Survey, Consumer Sentiment on Sustainablitiy in Fashion*. July 17, 2020. Available at: https://www.mckinsey.com/industries/retail/our-insights/survey-consumer-sentiment-on-sustainability-in-fashion access date 25 July 2024.

Grappi, S., Bergianti, F., Gabrielli, V., & Baghi, I. (2024). The Effect of Message Framing on Young Adult Consumers' Sustainable Fashion Consumption: The Role of Anticipated Emotions and Perceived Ethicality. *Journal of Business Research, 170* https://doi.org/10.1016/j.jbusres.2023.114341

Grazzini, L., Acuti, D., & Ailello, G. (2023). Solving the Puzzle of Sustainable Fahsion Consumption: The Role of Consumers' Implicit Attitudes and Perceived Warmth. *Journal of Cleaner Production, 287*(2). https://doi.org/10.1016/j.jclepro.2020.125579

Griskevicius, V., Tybur J. M. & Van den Bergh, B. (2010). Going green to be seen: status, reputation, and conspicuous conservation. *J Pers Soc Psychol.* 98(3), 392–404. doi: 10.1037/a0017346.

Hair, J. F., Tatham, R. L., Anderson, R. E., & Black, W. (2010). *Multivariate Data Analysis*. 7. izd. Upper Saddle River, NJ: Pearson Prentice Hall.

Hair, J.F., Ringle, C.M. and Sarstedt, M. (2011), "PLS-SEM: indeed a silver bullet", *Journal of Marketing Theory and Practice*, 19(2), 139–151.

Hair, J. F., Sarstedt, M., Hopkins, L. and Kuppelwieser, V.G. (2014), "Partial least squares structural equation modeling (PLS-SEM): an emerging tool in business research", *European Business Review*, 26(2), 106–121.

Harris, F., Roby, Hair, J. F., Ringle, C. M., & Sarstedt, M. (2011). PLS-SEM: Indeed a Silver Bullet. *The Journal of Marketing Theory and Practice, 19*(2), 139–152.

Hong, Y., Al Mamun, A., Yang, Q., & Masukujjaman, M. (2024). Predicting Sustainable Fashion Consumption Intentions and Practices. *Sci Rep., 14*(1), 1706. https://doi.org./10.1038/s41598-024-52215-z

Karlsson, A., & Karlsson, O. (2023). *Swedish Consumers' Attitudes toward Sustainable Products within the Fast Fashion Industry.* Sweden: University Sweden. Master Thesis.

Kozlowski, A., Searcy, C., & Bardecki, M. (2015). Corporate sustainability reporting in the apparel industry: an analysis of indicators disclosed. *International Journal of Productivity and Performance Management*, 64(3), 377–397. http://dx.doi.org/10.1108/IJPPM-10-2014-0152

Mandarić, D., Hunjet, A., & Kozina, G. (2021). Perception of Consumers' Awareness about Sustainability of Fashion Brands. *Journal of Risk and Financial Management, 12*(14), 1–14. https://doi.org./10.3390/jrfm14120594

McGarth, S. A. (2012). Fashioning Sustainability: How the Clothes We Wear Can Support Environmental and Human Well-Being? *Sustainable Fashion, 3*(8), 18-26..

Motwani, B., Haryani, S., & Matharu, S. (2024). The Influence of Generation X, Y and Z on Sustainable Fashion Products. *Academy of Marketing Studies Journal, 28*(55), 1–10.

Mukendi, A., Davies, I., McDonagh, P., & Glozer, S. (2020). Sustainable Fashion: Current and Future Research Directions. *European Journal of Marketing*. https://doi.org./10.1108/EJM-02-2019-0132

Niinimäki, K. (2018). Sustainable Fashion in a Circular Economy, pp. 12–42. In Kirsi Niinimäki (Ed.), *Sustainable Fashion in a Circular Economy*. Helsinki: Aalto University.

Perrini, F. & Vurro, C. (2010). Corporate sustainability, intangible assets accumulation and competitive advantage constraints, *Symphonya. Emerging Issues in Management* (symphonya.unimib.it), 2: 25–38. http://dx.doi.org/10.4468/2010.2.03perrini.vurro

Roby, H., & Dibb, S. (2016). Sustainable Clothing: Challenges, Barriers and Interventions for Encouraging More Sustainable Consumer Behaviour. *International Jorunal of Consumer Studies, 40*(3), 309–318.

Sengupta, M., & Sengupta, N. (2020). Sustainable Fashion: The Isuess, Challenges and Prospects. *MANHATAN: Journal of Commerce and Management, 7*(2), 74–94.

Statista. (2024). Fashion – Worldwide. Available at: https://www.statista.com/outlook/emo/fashion/worldwide, access date 25 July 2024.

Strübel, J., Goswami, S., Kang, J. H., & Leger, R. (2023). Improving Society and the Planet: Sustainability and Fashion Post-Pandemic. *Sustainability, 15*(17), 36–44.

Subhasis, R., & Lipsa, N. (2023). Marketing Sustainable Fashion: Trends and Future Directions. *Sustainability, 15*(7), 6202, https://doi.org/10.3390/su15076202

Tryphena, R., & Aram, A. I. (2023). Consumer Perception of Sustainable Clothing among Urban Indians. *Journal of Engineered Fibers and Fabrics, 18*(1), 1–11. https://doi.org.10.1177/15589250231168964

Tungate, M. (2005). *Fashion Brands: Branding style from Armani to Zara*. London: Kogan Page.

Villa Todeschini, B., Nogueira Cortimiglia, M., Callegaro-de-Menzes, D., & Ghezzi, A. (2020). Innovative and Sustainable Business Models in the Fashion Industry: Entreprenuiral Drivers and Opportunities and Challenges. *Business Horizons*, 2017, *60*(6), 759–770.

Vuković, D., Grmuša, T., & Borić Radić, D. (2023). Greenwashing Technique – An (Un)Acceptable Tool of Marketing Communication? Experiences and Attitudes of Marketing Experts and Consumers. In *9th International Scientific-Business Conference LIMEN 2023 – Selected Papers*, https://doi.org/10.31410/LIMEN.S.P.2023.123

Widloecher, P. (2010). *Luxe et développement durable: Je t'aime, moi non plus. In Luxefrancais Environmental and Social Sustainability in Fashion: A Case Study Analysis of Luxury*. Springer: Cham, Switzerland.

Tatiana Dănescu, Roxana Maria Stejerean, and Elena Linca

Empirical Study on the Relationship between Digitization and Financial Performance

1. Introduction

As far as the banking sector is concerned, digitization is in a phase of consolidation and diversification. Banks are already offering their customers mobile apps, mobile wallets and a plethora of financial products and services, which brings with it several challenges. To remain competitive, banking entities must embrace the latest innovations and fully integrate them into their operations. In a sector where consumer trust and awareness are high, digital success relies on experiences that simplify rather than overwhelm. The goal of digital transformation is to improve efficiency, productivity and experience, but also to change the way these entities operate, serve customers and empower employees. Tasks that were previously manual and time-consuming can now be automated, which improves customer relationships.

This is a complex process, and digitization is essential for financial institutions that want to succeed in the future. Therefore, choosing the best strategy and the right technological tools are steps towards the digital transformation of the banking sector.

2. Literature Review

The year 2020 has become a decisive year for the economic situation worldwide, with the COVID-19 pandemic affecting all sectors of the global economy, whose activity has been strongly affected by the new type of coronavirus. Despite the significant impact in bringing the entire banking system to a standstill, the responsibility of banks remains to their customers and potential customers. The pandemic has also triggered a new era in the banking sector by expanding services and products, and digitization has been a key element in this. Remote and mobile banking played a key role during the pandemic, allowing accounts to be managed from anywhere. Customers benefited from new tools, increasing convenience and security. Innovative services have reduced physical presence in branches and simplified procedures. Consequently, customers now have diverse options for financial management through banking services (Postolache, 2022).

The concept of digital banking is also often confused with the term internet banking or mobile banking. So, we can say that online banking or internet banking means banking using a desktop, laptop, tablet, smart phone, and digital banking means automating every step of banking, making a visit to the bank's premises unnecessary. Thus, if the existence of internet banking or mobile banking applications requires a prior visit to the bank, the existence of digital banking implies the beginning of the customer's relationship with the bank in the virtual environment (Sbarcea Ioana Raluca Ioana, 2019).

Digitization significantly improves operational efficiency by automating routine tasks, integrating data systems and improving process flows. Technologies such as artificial intelligence (AI) and machine learning (ML) optimize decision-making processes, reduce operational costs, and improve productivity (Chen et al., 2020). The shift to digital banking has had a profound impact on the customer experience by offering personalized services and improving accessibility through multiple digital channels. Digital platforms allow customers to conduct transactions anytime and anywhere, significantly improving convenience (Khan et al., 2021). The use of data analytics enables banks to offer personalized services, increasing customer satisfaction and loyalty (Capgemini, 2021). However, addressing digital literacy and ensuring inclusive access to digital banking services remain critical challenges (OECD, 2021).

Digitization can decrease human error and thus increase customer reliability. A new wave of technology is revolutionizing the way customers interact with their finances. From social to mobile capabilities, banks need to rethink the way they do business to deliver a better customer experience and stay competitive. It is part of our not-so-distant future when we expect driverless cars and robots, thus, it should be just as easy for us to envision a future banking system with its own form of artificial intelligence (AI) (Jyoti Suraj Harcherkar, 2018). AI-enabled tools such as chatbots have already been deployed by banks to interact with customers. AI has the potential to change organizations on an extraordinary scale, from virtual financial assistants to computerized credit scoring and predictive analytics (Jyoti Suraj Harcherkar, 2018).

Eisenbach, Konver, and Lee (2022) model how cyberattacks can be amplified in the financial system, focusing on the wholesale payment network. The reverse stress test shows that attacks on clusters of small banks can also affect a large part of the network. Xu, Saunders, Xiao, and Li (2020) studied the impact on an entity when it changes its relationship with a bank.

Liao, Chen, and Lu (2009) analyze the impact of agency issues and information asymmetry embedded in structural credit models on bank credit risk assessment.

Ozlem Dursun de Neef and Schandlbauer (2022) argue that, during the pandemic, households accumulated savings in their deposit accounts due to cost savings from limited mobility. This led to a significant increase in deposits.

Chen, Lee, and Shen (2022) argue that a bank with high income diversity and high liquidity has a high probability of having problems in the next period.

Corbisiero (2022) shows that liquidity infused into banks in the affected country may lead to risk financing rather than stimulating lending. Digital banking has meaning for both customers and the bank itself. Digitization in the banking sector does not only mean offering DBS (digital banking services) to customers, but also the total digital transformation of internal processes within the banks themselves (Mansurovna, 2023).

The concept of trust in DBS adoption has also been questioned by another research. In their study, Martínez-Navalón et al. (2023.) analyzed the significance of variables such as trust, privacy and ease of use when examining digital banking. These researchers stated in their study that trust in digital banking services would be higher if customers felt more privacy and security when using digital platforms. Consequently, if customers feel more trust, they will use DBS more. These aspects are also essential in financial reporting on social media, where transparency and accessibility are key elements (Danescu, 2022). One of the main services that customers use, given financial services, is payment. Researcher Ponsree et al. (2023) investigated what are the determinants of digital payments among the younger generation. He found that "performance expectancy, effort expectancy, and social influence expectancy positively influence young people's behavioral intention" (Ponsree et al., 2023). Behavioral intention itself, along with facilitating conditions have a positive effect on young people's usage behavior.

The research that has been conducted on the awareness and usage of e-banking services among the youth revealed that they use banking services through traditional channels (Jain, 2023), concluding that they are still not making much use of mobile, SMS and phone banking services but are focusing on ATM.

3. Research Methodology

In order to explore in depth, the impact of digitalization on the financial performance of Banca Transilvania and to understand how recent events have influenced this process, we formulated the following research questions:

1. ***Has there been a significant increase in the level of digitization within Banca Transilvania during the Covid-19 pandemic?***

The Covid-19 pandemic has had a profound impact on economies and consumer behaviors globally, forcing many organizations to rethink their strategies and adopt digital technologies to remain operational and competitive. In the banking sector, this period was marked by a rapid transition to digital services, driven by the need for social distancing and the closure of physical branches.

2. ***Is there a correlation between the level of digitization and the bank's financial performance?***

The first step in this research journey is to construct the digitalization index. To achieve this objective, seven core indicators have been selected that capture various dimensions of digital transformation in the banking sector: Digital Transactions, IT Investment, Adoption of Advanced Technologies, Digital Customer Engagement, Number of Digital Products, Operational Automation and Cybersecurity Measures. Each indicator was normalized on a scale from 0 to 1, weighted according to its importance, and aggregated to calculate the overall digitization index for each year. To obtain the digitization score, each indicator was normalized using the standard normalization formula, allowing the indicators to be compared on a common scale and eliminating differences in magnitude between them:

$$\text{normalized\_value} = \frac{\text{value} - \text{min\_value}}{\text{max\_value} - \text{min\_value}}$$

where:

- *value* is the value of the indicator for a given year,
- *min_value* is the minimum value of the indicator in the period analyzed,
- *max_value* is the maximum value of the indicator in the same period.

After normalization, each indicator was weighted according to its relative importance, as assigned in the previous section. The final digitization score for each year was calculated using the following calculation formula:

$$\text{score} = \sum(\text{normalized\_value} \times \text{weight})$$

where:

- normalized_value is the normalized value of the indicator,
- weight is the weight assigned to that indicator.

3.1. Selection and Normalization of Indicators

Each indicator has been assigned a weight based on its perceived importance. The weights reflect the relative contribution of each indicator to the overall success of digitization efforts:

- *Digital Transactions: 20 %;*
- *IT Investments: 15 %;*
- *Adoption of Advanced Technologies: 15 %;*
- *Digital Customer Engagement: 20 %;*
- *Number of Digital Products: 10 %;*
- *Operational Automation: 10 %;*
- *Cyber Security: 10 %.*

The high share attributed to Digital Transactions reflects the critical importance of the use of digital channels for banking transactions as a major indicator of customer technology adoption and operational efficiency. Frequent use of digital channels indicates a high level of customer convenience and trust, which directly contributes to the success of bank digitization. According to the literature, digital transactions are a leading indicator of a bank's digital maturity.

Investments in IT infrastructure and Adoption of Digital Technologies are fundamental to implementing and sustaining digitization initiatives. The 15 % weighting emphasizes the critical role of IT investments in modernizing systems and facilitating the adoption of new technologies. High IT investments are often correlated with better digital capabilities and increased efficiency (Srinivasan & Venkatraman, 2018).

The adoption of Advanced Technologies such as AI, blockchain and machine learning is essential to remain competitive in an increasingly digitized banking environment, enabling banks to improve service delivery, optimize processes and constantly innovate. The 15 % share reflects the importance of these technologies in the overall digitalization strategy. This binary indicator has been assigned a value of 1 if the bank has adopted advanced technologies and 0 otherwise and is based on a similar methodology to that used by Chen et al. (2020).

Digital Customer Engagement is a direct indicator of the success of digitization initiatives, as Furst et al. (2020) point out. A high percentage of customers who are active in using digital services indicates effective technology adoption and a positive user experience. Allocating a 20 % share reflects the major importance of customer engagement in the bank's digital ecosystem as a key determinant of long-term success.

Diversity and Number of Digital Financial Products offered by the bank are essential to attract and retain customers in the digital era. A diverse range of digital products indicates the bank's ability to respond to different customer needs and constantly innovate. The 10 % share reflects the importance of this indicator in the digital transformation, without overstating its relative contribution.

Through Digital Automation, banks can improve the speed and accuracy of internal processes, reducing errors and increasing efficiency. The 10 % share underscores the importance of operational automation as part of digitization, while recognizing that other factors can have a more direct impact on customer interactions.

With an exponential increase in digital transactions and activities, Cybersecurity has become crucial. Protecting customer data and transactions is vital to maintaining the trust and integrity of the banking system. Allocating a weight of 10 % reflects the major importance of cybersecurity measures in the digitization strategy, without neglecting the impact of other factors.

After selecting the criteria considered for the construction of the index, we proceeded with the data collection, resulting in the following panel of data, presented in Table 1:

Table 1: Digitization indicators

Indicators	2019	2020	2021	2022	2023
Tdigital transactions	50	64	68	73	78
IT Investments	2.8	3.1	3.5	3.9	4.2
Embracing advanced technologies	–	AI, ML	AI, ML	AI, ML	AI, ML, BLOCKCHAIN
Digital customer engagement	50	75	80	85	89
Number of digital products	5	8	10	12	15
Operational automation	20	30	40	50	60
Cyber security	Moderated	High	High	Very high	Very high

Source: Authors' projections, administrators' annual reports (2019–2023)

The digitization path of Banca Transilvania, as shown in Table 2, is in line with the global trends observed in the banking industry. The upward trajectory of the digitalization index indicates a strategic focus on improving digital capabilities and customer engagement. The bank's increased IT investments reflect a commitment to building a robust digital infrastructure, which is essential to sustain long-term growth in the digital era (Bharadwaj et al., 2013). Analyzing the evolution of Banca Transilvania's digitalization score over the period 2019–2023, a significant increase in digitalization levels is observed, especially during the Covid-19 pandemic, thus positively answering the first research question posed.

Table 2: Digitization index results

Year	2019	2020	2021	2022	2023
Index value	0.434	0.574	0.648	0.725	0.782

Source: Authors' calculations

In 2019, Banca Transilvania's digitalization score reflected an early stage of digital transformation. Digital transactions and the number of digital products started to increase, but IT investments and the adoption of advanced technologies were still in preliminary stages. Customer digital engagement was moderate, and operational automation and cybersecurity measures were emerging priorities.

The 2020 digitization score showed significant growth, fueled by an acceleration in digital transactions and a notable increase in customer digital engagement. The COVID-19 pandemic played a crucial role in driving digital channel adoption. IT investments increased considerably, reflecting a greater commitment to digital infrastructure and cybersecurity.

In 2021, the digitalization score continued to rise, marked by the widespread adoption of advanced technologies such as AI and machine learning. Digital customer engagement reached new heights and operational automation was stepped up to improve efficiency and reduce costs. IT investments were strengthened and the number of digital products on offer increased significantly.

The 2022 digitization score reflected a mature level of digital transformation. Digital transactions and customer engagement continued to increase, and the bank deployed new advanced technologies to improve user experience and operational efficiency. IT investments and cybersecurity measures remained key priorities, ensuring a secure and robust digital environment.

In 2023, Banca Transilvania's digitalization score reached a new high, indicating a fully integrated digital transformation. All indicators showed significant improvements, with a particular focus on cybersecurity and the adoption of advanced technologies. Digital customer engagement was at its highest level ever, reflecting growing trust and satisfaction in the digital services offered by the bank. Operational automation and the number of digital products continued to expand, reinforcing Banca Transilvania's position as a leader in digital innovation in the banking sector.

3.1.1. *Multiple Regression Analysis*

To understand the impact of digitalization on the financial performance of Banca Transilvania, that is, to obtain an answer to the second research question, we conducted a multiple regression analysis using a comprehensive set of financial indicators. In this study, we aim to understand how digitization, as measured by the Digitization Index, influences various financial indicators of Banca Transilvania. We also include return on assets (ROA) as a control variable to account for its influence on financial performance.

3.1.2. *Selection of Dependent Variables*

We used the following financial indicators as dependent variables:

- ROE (return on equity);
- Cost-to-income ratio;
- Total net income;
- Provisions for credit risk;
- Gross profit; – Risk-weighted assets;
- Total assets; – Total equity.

For each financial parameter, we specified a multiple regression model using the following formula:

$$\textbf{Financial Metric}=\beta 0+\beta 1{*}\textbf{Digitalization Index}+\beta 2{*}\textbf{ROA}+\epsilon$$

We used Ordinary Least Squares (OLS) regression to estimate the model coefficients. The OLS method minimizes the sum of squared differences between observed and predicted values.

4. Results and Discussions

In order to apply multiple regression, the following financial indicators were processed using the annual reports published by the bank during the analyzed period. Thus, Table 3 shows the centralization of the financial indicators used as dependent variables.

Table 3: Financial indicators

Financial Information of the Group	**2023**	**2022**	**2021**	**2020**	**2019**
ROE	25.54 %	24.93 %	18.45 %	14.73 %	21.10 %
Cost/income	45.38 %	47.51 %	48.28 %	45.15 %	47.47 %
Total net income, RON thousand	7,724,962	6,279,956	4,934,037	4,536,165	4,614,986
Provisions for credit risk, RON thousand	(513,088)	(495,155)	(256,616)	(865,840)	(292,646)
Gross profit, RON thousand	3,705,963	2,801,053	2,302,798	1,622,428	2,131,583
Net profit, RON thousand	2,984,230	2,488,417	2,024,533	1,424,078	1,847,893
Risk Weighted Assets, RON million	69,393	60,552	51,729	57,544	51,581
Total Assets, RON million	169,169	140,511	132,501	107,492	91,722
Total equity, RON million	13,897	9,472	10,564	10,414	9,214

Source: Authors' calculations

Multiple regression analysis, the results of which are centralized in Table 4 and Appendix 1, respectively, show that the digitalization index has, in general, a positive impact on most of the financial parameters of Banca Transilvania, with statistically significant results for net profit and gross profit, taking ROA as a control variable. The results suggest that increased digitalization is associated with improved financial performance, although the small sample size and possible multicollinearity should be considered when interpreting these findings.

Table 4: Multiple regression results

Dependent Variable	**R-squared**	**Adj. R-squared**	**F-statistic**	**P>|t| (Digitalization Index)**	**P>|t| (ROA)**
Net Profit	0.994	0.989	176.3	0.003	0.007
Total Net Income	0.91	0.82	10.12	0.049	0.169
Cost/Income	0.14	−0.719	0.1634	0.854	0.682
Provisions for Credit Risk	0.486	−0.028	0.9449	0.972	0.31
Gross Profit	0.961	0.921	24.39	0.024	0.049
Risk Weighted Assets	0.644	0.287	1.807	0.198	0.73
Total Assets	0.97	0.941	32.73	0.015	0.255
Total Equity	0.455	−0.09	0.834	0.326	0.825

Source: Authors' calculations

For Net Profit, the model explains 99.4 % of the variance (R-squared = 0.994) with an adjusted R-squared of 0.989. The F-statistic is 176.3 with a p-value of 0.00564 indicating that the model is statistically significant. The digitization index has a significant positive coefficient (p-value = 0.003), and ROA also shows a significant positive effect (p-value = 0.007). These results highlight that higher levels of digitization are strongly associated with higher net profits, even after accounting for the impact of ROA. The regression model for Gross Profits shows an R-squared value of 0.961 and an adjusted R-squared of 0.921. The F-statistic is 24.39, with a p-value of 0.0394, indicating a significant model. The digitization index has a significant positive effect on gross profit with a p-value of 0.024, while ROA also shows a significant positive impact with a p-value of 0.049.

5. Conclusions

Our analysis revealed that the digitization index has a positive and significant impact on certain financial metrics of Banca Transilvania, in particular on the net and gross profit. These results are consistent with the existing literature highlighting the benefits of digitalization in the banking sector.

Multiple regression results showed that digitalization positively influences the net and gross profit of Banca Transilvania, with statistically significant coefficients for the digitalization index. This suggests that investments in technology and adoption of digital channels lead to an increase in financial performance. These findings are supported by studies such as Chuang and Hu (2015), which find that digitization can increase operational efficiency and improve profitability by reducing costs and attracting more digital customers.

For other financial metrics, such as Cost/Income and Provisions for Credit Risk, the results were not statistically significant. This may indicate that while digitization has an overall positive impact, its effects on certain operational and risk aspects are more complex and require more detailed analysis. The literature, such as the study by Gomber et al. (2018), suggests that the impact of digitization on risk and cost may vary depending on the specific implementation and organizational context.

Our study was limited by the small sample size and potential multicollinearity issues. These limitations suggest caution in interpreting the results and emphasize the need for further research to confirm and extend our findings.

Annex 1: Multiple Regression Results

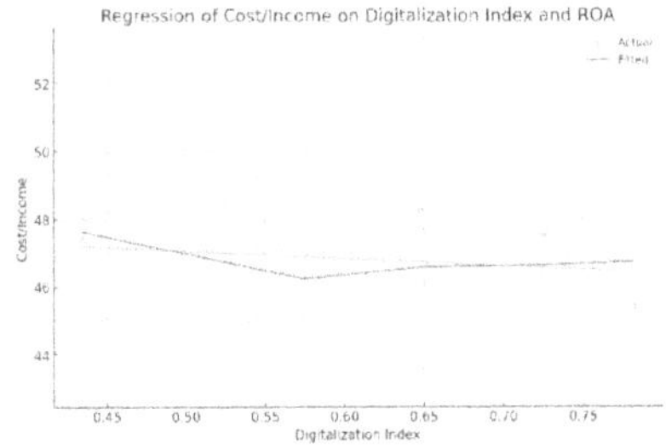

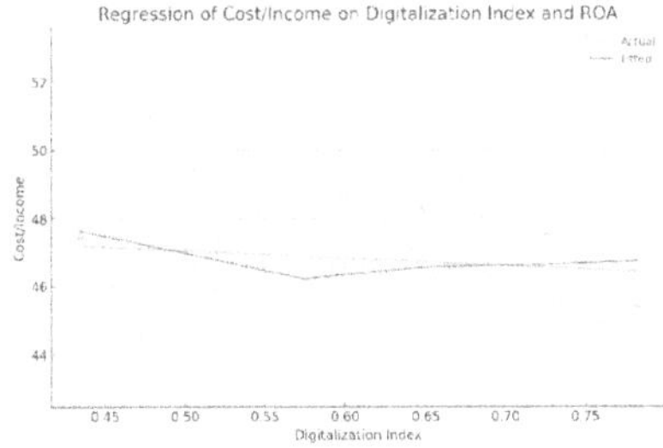

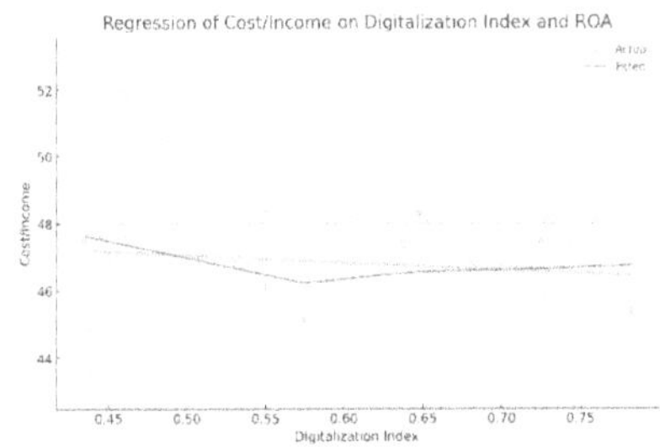

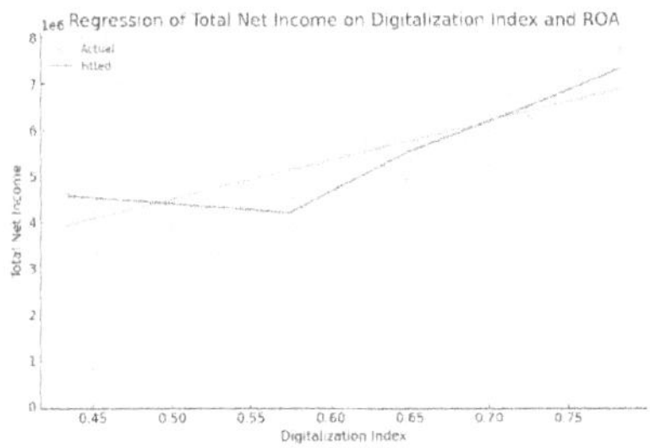

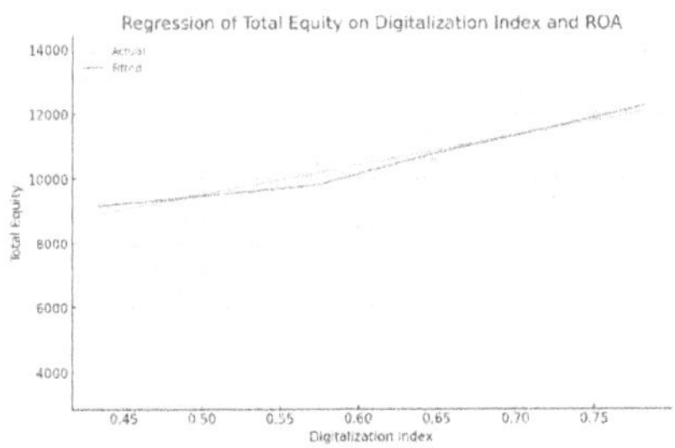

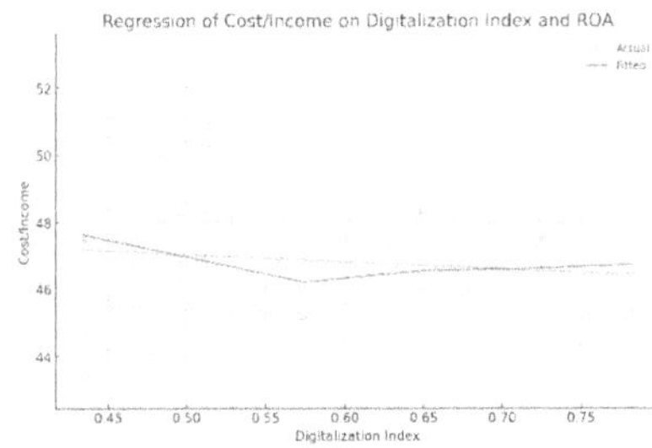

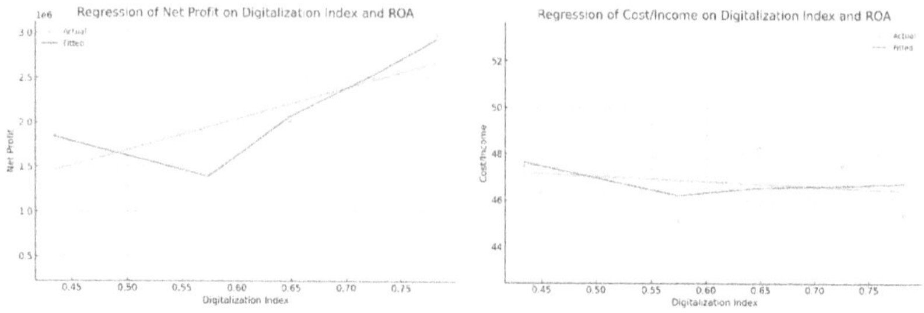

References

Bharadwaj, A., El Sawy, O. A., Pavlou, P. A., & Venkatraman, N. (2013). Digital business strategy: Toward a next generation of insights. *MIS Quarterly, 37*(2), 471–482.

Capgemini. (2021). World retail banking report 2021. Retrieved from https://www.capgemini.com.

Chen, M. J., et al. (2020). The implications of digitalization for productivity, employment, and inequality. *The Future of Work in the Digital Economy*, *12*, 113–135.

Chen, T.-H., Lee, C.-C., & Shen, C.-H. (2022). Liquidity indicators, early warning signals in banks, and financial crises. *The North American Journal of Economics and Finance*, 62.

Chuang, S. H., & Hu, F. (2015). The impact of digitalization on business performance: A case study of high-tech companies in Taiwan. *Technology in Society, 43*, 143–150. https://doi.org/10.1016/j.techsoc.2015.10.003.

Corbisiero, G. (2022). Bank lending, collateral, and credit traps in a monetary union. *European Economic Review*, *144*, 3–42.

Dănescu, T., & Stejerean, R. M. (2022). Financial reporting on social media: Empirical study on the European medical sector. *ACTA Marisiensis, Oeconomics Series*, 15–24. https://doi.org/10.2478/amso-2022-0002.

Eisenbach, T. M., Kovner, A., & Lee, M. J. (2022). Cyber risk and the U.S. financial system: A pre-mortem analysis. *Journal of Financial Economics, 145*(3) 802–826.

Furst, K., Lang, W. W., & Nolle, D. E. (2020). Internet banking: Developments and prospects. *Journal of Financial Services Research, 22*(1), 95–117.

Gomber, P., Koch, J. A., & Siering, M. (2018). *Digital Finance and FinTech: Current research and future research directions*. *Journal of Business Economics, 88*(5), 537–580. https://doi.org/10.1007/s11573-018-0910-8.

Interim Condensed Consolidated and Separate Financial Statements of Banca Transilvania, 2019–2023.

Jain, M. (2023). A study of financial literacy level towards electronic banking amongst youth. *Journal of Corporate Finance Management and Banking System (JCFMBS)*, *3*(03), 39–55. ISSN: 2799-1059.

Khan, B. K., et al. (2021). Digital customer experience in E-banking: Emerging mobile Web 2.0-based business models. *VINE Journal of Information and Knowledge*, *7*(3), 1–19.

Liao, H. H., Chen, T. K., & Lu, C. W. (2009). Bank credit risk and structural credit models: Agency and information asymmetry perspectives. *Journal of Banking & Finance*, *33*(8), 1520–1530.

Mansurovna, M. L. (2023). Digital bankıng, its advantages and disadvantages. *BioGecko*, *12*(3), 5189–5193.

Martínez-Navalón, J. G., Fernández-Fernández, M., & Alberto, F. P. (2023), Does privacy and ease of use influence user trust in digital banking applications in Spain and Portugal?. *International Entrepreneurship and Management Journal*, *19*, 781–803.

Mrs Jyoti Suraj Harchekar. (2018). Digitalization in banking sector. *International Journal of Trend in Scientific Research and Development*, 103–109.

OECD. (2021). Digital financial literacy. Retrieved from https://www.oecd.org/finance/digital-financial-literacy.htm

Özlem Dursun-de Neef, H., & Schandlbauer, A. (2022). COVID-19, bank deposits, and lending. *Journal of Empirical Finance*, *68*, 20–33.

Ponsree, K., Phongpaew, T., & Naruetharadhol, P. (2023). Study of Thai youths in the northeastern region of Thailand on the effectiveness of digital payment behavior. *Journal of Promotion Management*, *29*(4), 569–605, https://doi.org/10.1080/10496491.2022.2163035.

Postolache, D. (2022). The impact of digitalization and mobile banking on Romanian banking sector performance in the COVID-19 context. *Journal of Financial Studies and Research*, 2022, 1–11.

Sbarcea Ioana Raluca. (2019). BANKS DIGITALIZATION – a challenge for the Romanian banking sector. *Studies in Business and Economics*, *14*(1), 221–230.

Srinivasan, R., & Venkatraman, N. (2018). Digital transformation: Strategies and implementation. *Harvard Business Review*, *96*(3), 94–104.

Xu, Y., Saunders, A., Xiao, B., & Li, X. (2020). Bank relationship loss: The moderating effect of information opacity. *Journal of Banking & Finance*, *118*, 1–25.

Norbert Laurisz and Katarzyna Sanak-Kosmowska

Entrepreneurial Skills Development in a Non-Skills-Focused Education System

1. Introduction

The modern business environment is characterized by uncertainty, complexity and a rapid pace of change. In today's globalized, technology-driven and evolving labor market, individuals must demonstrate adaptability and innovative thinking to succeed. In this context, fostering and developing entrepreneurial attitudes and intentions, as well as vocational skills, is a crucial element in preparing students for future professional and societal challenges. As the OECD (2018) highlights, the modern labor market demands not only specialized skills but also entrepreneurial thinking, adaptability and innovation. In the contemporary labor market, entrepreneurial skills are becoming an indispensable asset for young people (Laurisz, 2022).

It is imperative that the education system adapts to the demands of the labor market by equipping pupils and students with the professional competencies and skills they require to thrive. The traditional education system, which does not prioritize skills development, has been the dominant model of education in many countries since the 19th century. The education system is unable to meet today's challenges because it is based on outdated assumptions about knowledge development rather than skills development. The system primarily focuses on imparting theoretical knowledge to students, with verification through various forms of assessment such as tests, examinations or oral questions (Laurisz et al., 2022). The teacher is the main source of knowledge, while students are largely passive recipients of information.

A review of the research literature enables us to identify the key features of a system that is not focused on skills development:

- A strong focus on theoretical knowledge: Traditional educational systems are often dominated by the so-called "classroom" or "bench" model of education (Freire, 1970). In this model, the teacher is responsible for transferring knowledge to the students, who are expected to simply receive, memorize and reproduce it. This approach fails to recognize the active role of the student in the learning process and fails to facilitate the development of practical skills and critical thinking. Furthermore, this approach significantly constrains the

growth of creative abilities, the development of autonomy, decisiveness, and self-assurance, which is counterproductive to the cultivation of entrepreneurial capabilities.
- The use of examinations and tests as a primary assessment tool: Examinations and tests, which are a fundamental component of the traditional educational system, reflect an assessment model based on behavioral theory. The behavioral theory posits that learning is a function of conditioning and that knowledge can be gauged through tests that assess students' ability to reproduce information (Zimbardo et al., 2016). Contemporary research indicates that these types of assessments can diminish students' motivation to engage in learning and may not reflect their abilities (Walters et al., 2017).
- Limited development of practical skills: Education should facilitate the development of practical skills through experience and interaction with real-world problems (Dewey, 1997). However, the traditional educational system often fails to address these aspects by focusing on abstract knowledge, which results in a lack of practical preparation for students to navigate life beyond the school walls. Dewey's observations are supported by research on contemporary education systems (Rogacheva, 2016).
- Lack of incentives for innovative teaching methods: research shows that the lack of support for innovative teaching methods is a key obstacle to the modernization of education. A number of studies have indicated that teachers are discouraged from adopting new methods due to a lack of adequate support and resources, which in turn leads to the maintenance of traditional, less effective educational practices (Hargreaves & Fullan, 2012).

A system structured in this way has a number of adverse effects, the most important of which are: poor preparation of students for entry into the labor market; a lowering of the prestige of education and the education system; a halt to the development of innovation in teaching; and a strong increase in inequality in student development and access to education.

In the literature on the incompatibility between education and the labor market, the theory of 'mismatch skills' is frequently referenced (Leuven & Oosterbeek, 2011; Salas-Velasco, 2021). These studies demonstrate that education systems that do not prioritize the development of practical skills result in graduates who possess a formal education but lack the key competencies required by the labor market, including the ability to work in a team, think critically and adapt to new technologies.

The concept of education as a process of 'knowledge production' that has no direct or practical application may result in a decline in its perceived value by society. Bourdieu (1984) highlights the importance of aligning education with the real needs of students and the labor market to maintain its value as a form of social capital. A decline in the perceived value of education may also result in an increased demand for alternative forms of learning.

A 2018 OECD study on innovation in education highlighted that education systems that fail to adapt to changing social and technological realities can impede the development of innovation. The failure to introduce modern teaching tools and methods results in a lack of progress, limiting opportunities for both students and teachers to develop. Consequently, the systems suffer from the crowding out effect of good practice and good teachers.

Cultural capital theory is frequently employed to elucidate the manner in which educational systems that espouse traditional pedagogical approaches can engender the exacerbation of existing inequalities (Bourdieu, 1984). Students from lower-status families may encounter difficulties in learning within the traditional system, which can result in disparities in educational outcomes and restrict their access to further education and the labor market. A second issue is the necessity to obtain knowledge through the non-formal system, which is fee-paying and geographically limited.

2. The Development of Entrepreneurial Attitudes and Intentions in Education

It is evident that the integration of entrepreneurial skills into the educational curriculum is a relatively recent phenomenon. The concept of entrepreneurship was introduced into the education system in the 1970s, coinciding with the recognition of the need to prepare students for the evolving economic landscape and a changing labor market. Peter Drucker was one of the first researchers to emphasize the crucial role of entrepreneurship in adapting to economic change (Drucker, 1985). Since that time, teaching methods for entrepreneurship have evolved to include a variety of didactic techniques, such as group projects and business simulations. Furthermore, this education is no longer solely focused on running a business. Its main focus has shifted to developing skills that facilitate professional growth in both career and business contexts. Research indicates that educational programs that integrate entrepreneurial elements have a positive impact on students' competencies and skills, which is crucial for career development in today's labor market (Oosterbeek et al., 2010; Sánchez, 2011).

Developing entrepreneurial skills is a direct response to the challenges of the labor market. The modern labor market is characterized by rapid change, necessitating not only specialized skills but also entrepreneurial thinking, adaptability and innovation. The term "entrepreneurship" is not simply defined as the ability to start one's own business. It is, in fact, a proactive, independent, responsible, creative and innovative attitude that is necessary to function effectively in a complex and changing professional environment (Gibb, 2002; Gibb & Haskins, 2014). It is vital that entrepreneurship is defined in a broad sense, primarily as the capacity to think innovatively, solve problems in a critical manner and manage resources. In this context, entrepreneurial education is a vital tool for aligning students' skills with the demands of the labor market.

Education has a significant impact on students' development by fostering and reinforcing attitudes and intentions (Fayolle & Redford, 2014). Entrepreneurship contributes to enhancing self-confidence, decision-making skills and adaptability. Research shows that education that stimulates entrepreneurial attitudes and intentions develops students' sense of agency – a key element that translates into their later success both professionally and personally. Entrepreneurial attitudes also promote the development of critical thinking, creativity and self-reliance (Liñán & Fayolle, 2015).

Such education, prepares students for future career challenges by developing basic management, planning and risk-taking skills. Research findings suggest that graduates of entrepreneurial education programs are more likely to achieve career success (Laurisz et al., 2022). These skills are becoming increasingly sought after by employers who are looking for employees who can solve problems independently and adapt to new conditions. In this context, an education that fosters entrepreneurial attitudes and intentions positively influences students' ability to adapt to the changing demands of the labor market.

Furthermore, educating students in this way has a considerable impact on their social development. Students who develop entrepreneurial skills are more likely to engage in social innovation, create jobs and support the economic development of their communities (Fayolle & Redford, 2014). As a result, entrepreneurial education becomes a tool for social change, promoting attitudes of social.

3. Factors Determining the Development of Entrepreneurial Attitudes and Intentions among Students in a Non-Skills-Focused System

A review of the literature and research in the field of education provides insight into the various factors that shape the development of entrepreneurial attitudes and intentions. A review of the literature reveals that studies conducted among Polish students indicate the importance of school climate, family support, quality of education and involvement in extracurricular initiatives (Laurisz & Sanak-Kosmowska, 2022, 2024). These studies demonstrate that successful entrepreneurial education programs require a holistic approach that integrates a variety of educational experiences and supports the development of entrepreneurship at multiple levels.

Entrepreneurship in education, defined as the process of developing students' abilities to identify and seize opportunities, take risks and create value, is becoming an increasingly crucial element in preparing young people for a rapidly changing labor market and societal challenges. The Theory of Planned Behavior (Ajzen, 1991), the Self-Determination Theory (Deci & Ryan, 2013) and the Entrepreneurial Learning Model (Cope, 2005) provide a theoretical framework for understanding how different elements of the educational environment influence the development of entrepreneurial intentions and attitudes among students. Empirical research has confirmed and expanded upon these theories, identifying additional factors that are especially crucial in the context of inefficient educational systems that focus primarily on building theoretical knowledge rather than developing practical skills.

3.1. The Influence of Family and Environment

The Theory of Planned Behavior (Ajzen, 1991) suggests that behavioral intentions, which are the primary predictor of actual actions, are influenced by three main factors: attitudes towards behavior, subjective norms and perceived behavioral control. In the context of developing students' entrepreneurial intentions, family support is a crucial factor in shaping subjective norms and perceived behavioral control. Families that promote values such as initiative, entrepreneurship and risk-taking foster an environment that is conducive to the development of entrepreneurial attitudes (Laspita et al., 2012). Similarly, the local environment in which students are raised also plays an important role. Other research indicates that communities with a robust entrepreneurial culture and access to resources that facilitate business development are conducive to the formation of entrepreneurial intentions (Aldrich & Jennings, 2003). However, when the education system does not provide adequate support for skill development, external factors such as family and local environment become even more crucial. The cited research shows that in educational systems that focus only on theoretical knowledge transfer, family and local community support can bridge the gap by offering students the resources and motivation to develop entrepreneurial attitudes outside the formal education system.

3.2. School Climate

The school climate, defined as the emotional and social environment within the educational setting, has been identified as a key factor influencing the development of students' entrepreneurial attitudes. The Self-Determination Theory (Deci & Ryan, 2013) posits that the fulfillment of three fundamental psychological needs – autonomy, competence and relationships – is pivotal to an individual's intrinsic motivation and overall well-being. Schools that support these needs foster an entrepreneurial climate. Research indicates that teachers who encourage creativity, innovation and risk-taking can significantly influence the development of students' entrepreneurial attitudes by fostering positive perceptions of entrepreneurship (Blumenfeld et al., 2004).

However, the need for autonomy and relational support may be overlooked in traditional educational systems that prioritize the transmission of theoretical knowledge and assessment through examinations. Furthermore, research indicates that students may not fully realize their entrepreneurial potential unless they receive additional emotional and motivational support from teachers or peers (Deci & Ryan, 2013). In such cases, the school climate can act as both a catalyst and an inhibitor for the development of entrepreneurial attitudes, depending on the extent to which it meets students' psychological needs.

3.3. Perceptions of Educational Quality

The perception of educational quality, defined as the evaluation of the quality and effectiveness of the educational experience, is a significant factor influencing the development of entrepreneurial intentions. The Theory of Planned Behavior posits that positive attitudes towards entrepreneurial behavior are strongly correlated with how students value their education. Students who perceive that their school offers a high-quality education demonstrate greater confidence and self-assurance, which translates into their willingness to pursue entrepreneurial initiatives (Fayolle & Gailly, 2004).

However, in educational systems that are not focused on developing skills but only on imparting knowledge, these perceptions can be negative, which can limit students' motivation to develop entrepreneurial attitudes. Research on self-esteem and self-efficacy indicates that students who lack confidence in the quality of their education tend to perceive a lower sense of control over their own actions, which in turn reduces their propensity to engage in entrepreneurial activities (Bandura, 1993).

3.4. Out-of-School Initiatives

Out-of-school initiatives, including soft skills programs, apprenticeships and entrepreneurial projects, are instrumental in addressing the shortcomings of an education system that inadequately develops practical competencies. The Entrepreneurial Learning Model (Cope, 2005) emphasizes that the acquisition of practical experience and subsequent reflection on it is a key driver of the development of deep entrepreneurial knowledge and skills. Research indicates that involvement in such programs enhances students' sense of competence and autonomy, which is vital for their intrinsic motivation and willingness to take risks (Gibb, 2002).

In the context of an education system that lacks the necessary resources to adequately develop practical competencies, out-of-school initiatives can bridge this gap by offering students hands-on experiences that are absent from traditional teaching methods. Research indicates that such programs can significantly influence the development of entrepreneurial attitudes, particularly when combined with reflection on lessons learned (Kolb, 1984).

3.5. Mentoring

Mentoring plays a pivotal role in fostering entrepreneurial attitudes, particularly in educational systems that lack adequate support. The Self-Determination Theory emphasizes the role of relationships in intrinsic motivation. Further research demonstrates that mentoring programs in which students have access to experienced mentors can significantly influence the development of entrepreneurial attitudes (St-Jean & Audet, 2009). Mentors provide more than just emotional support; they also help students develop a sense of competence by offering practical advice and feedback on their entrepreneurial initiatives (Kubberoed & Hagen, 2015).

In an educational context where support for skills development is lacking, mentors can act as guides, helping students navigate the complex world of entrepreneurship (St-Jean & Mitrano-Méda, 2016). By acting as role models, mentors can boost students' motivation to take risks and pursue their entrepreneurial goals.

3.6. Media and Technology

Modern technology and social media are playing an increasingly important role in developing students' entrepreneurial attitudes (Ćwiek et al., 2021; Laurisz,

2022). In the Entrepreneurial Learning Model (Cope, 2005), these technologies are seen as tools for gaining knowledge, testing ideas and reflecting on lessons learned. Research shows that social media offers access to educational resources, inspirational success stories and business networks, which foster entrepreneurial intentions.

In the context of suboptimal education systems that lack sufficient support for skills development, educational technologies can bridge the gap by offering online courses, workshops and business simulations. These tools provide students with the flexibility to learn at their own pace, which is particularly beneficial for those who lack access to high-quality formal education (Kubikova et al., 2024). Furthermore, the reflection on progress enabled by online tools allows students to analyze their actions on an ongoing basis and plan for the further development of entrepreneurial skills.

4. Conclusions

Entrepreneurship education is widely recognized as an important component of the curriculum in many countries, but its implementation is often constrained. Research indicates that in educational systems focused on developing practical skills, entrepreneurship is a key area of emphasis, with an emphasis on group projects, business simulations and practical experiences (Cedefop, 2022; OECD, 2018; WEF, 2023). Nevertheless, in many education systems, entrepreneurship remains marginalized due to traditional curricula, lack of resources and resistance to change. An example of best practice can be found in Scandinavian countries, where entrepreneurship is an integral part of education, enabling students to develop key skills such as project management and problem solving.

In the context of global competition and evolving economic conditions, the value of entrepreneurial education is poised to grow. An increasing number of countries are acknowledging the necessity to incorporate entrepreneurship into the curriculum at all levels of education. Going forward, there will be a greater focus on differentiated and practical forms of teaching, including the increased use of educational technology and collaboration with the private sector. However, the development of entrepreneurial education will depend on the ability of education systems to adapt and innovate. The growth of non-formal education, including online courses and mentoring programs, indicates that students will increasingly pursue avenues to develop entrepreneurial abilities beyond the conventional school structure.

The traditional education system, which prioritizes theoretical knowledge, is becoming increasingly ill-equipped to meet the demands of a dynamic labor market and society. The focus on knowledge to the detriment of practical skills has a number of adverse effects, including mismatches in competence, a decline in innovation and an increase in social inequalities. While there is a clear need for education outside the formal system, this approach is often costly and can lead to stress and exclusion of students from less affluent families. Research by Cedefop (2015) indicates that traditional education systems contribute to the phenomenon of skills mismatch, resulting in higher graduate unemployment and lower economic productivity as workers are not fully utilized according to their potential. In light of these challenges, it is imperative that we reform the education system to integrate the development of practical skills aligned with the demands of the labor market.

References

Ajzen, I. (1991). The Theory of Planned Behavior. *Organizational Behavior and Human Decision Processes*, *50*(2), 179–211. https://doi.org/10.1016/0749-5978(91)90020-T

Aldrich, H., & Jennings, J. (2003). The Pervasive Effects of Family on Entrepreneurship: Toward a Family Embeddedness Perspective. *Journal of Business Venturing*, *18*, 573–596. https://doi.org/10.1016/S0883-9026(03)00011-9

Bandura, A. (1993). Perceived Self-Efficacy in Cognitive Development and Functioning. *Educational Psychologist*, *28*(2), 117–148. https://doi.org/10.1207/s15326985ep2802_3

Blumenfeld, P., Paris, A., & Fredricks, J. A. (2004). School Engagement: Potential of the Concept, State of the Evidence. *Review of Educational Research – REV EDUC RES*, *74*, 59–109. https://doi.org/10.3102/00346543074001059

Bourdieu, P. (1984). *Distinction: A Social Critique of the Judgement of Taste*. Boston, US: Harvard University Press.

Cedefop. (2015). *Skills, Qualifications and Jobs in the EU: The Making of a Perfect Match?* https://www.cedefop.europa.eu/en/publications/3072

Cedefop. (2022). *Challenging Digital Myths: First Findings from Cedefop's Second European Skills and Jobs Survey*. Publications Office of the European Union. https://data.europa.eu/doi/10.2801/818285

Cope, J. (2005). Toward a Dynamic Learning Perspective of Entrepreneurship. *Entrepreneurship Theory and Practice*, *29*, 373–397. https://doi.org/10.1111/j.1540-6520.2005.00090.x

Ćwiek, M., Ćwiklicki, M., Firszt, D., Jabłoński, M., Laurisz, N., Pacut, A., & Sołtysik, M. (2021). *Cyfryzacja i rynek pracy/Digitalisation and the labour market*. Krakow, Poland: Wydawnictwo MSAP UEK.

Deci, E. L., & Ryan, R. M. (2013). *Intrinsic Motivation and Self-Determination in Human Behavior*. New York, US: Springer Science & Business Media.

Dewey, J. (1997). *Democracy and Education*. New York, US: Simon and Schuster.

Drucker, P.F. (1985). *Innovation and Entrepreneurship*. Harper & Row.

Fayolle, A., & Gailly, B. (2004). *Using the Theory of Planned Behaviour to Assess Entrepreneurship Teaching Programs: A First Experimentation*.

Fayolle, A., & Redford, Da. (2014). *Handbook on the Entrepreneurial University*. Cheltenham, UK: Edward Elgar Publishing Limited.

Freire, P. (1970). *Pedagogy of the Oppressed*. New York, US: Seabury Press.

Gibb, A. (2002). Creating Conducive Environments for Learning and Entrepreneurship. *Industry and Higher Education, 16*, 135–148. https://doi.org/10.5367/000000002101296234

Gibb, A., & Haskins, G. (2014). *The University of the Future: An Entrepreneurial Stakeholder Learning Organization?* (pp. 25–63). https://doi.org/10.4337/9781781007020.00008

Hargreaves, A., & Fullan, M. (2012). *Professional Capital: Transforming Teaching in Every School*. New York, US: Teachers College Press.

Kolb, D. (1984). Experiential Learning: Experience as the Source of Learning and Development. *Journal of Business Ethics, 1*. New Jersey, US: Prentice-Hall.

Kubberoed, E., & Hagen, S. T. (2015). Mentoring Models in Entrepreneurship Education. EDULEARN15 Proceedings, 4059–4069.

Kubikova, K., Bohacova, A., Slowik, J., & Pavelkova, I. (2024). Student Adaptation to Distance Learning. *Social Sciences & Humanities Open, 9*, 1–12. 100875. https://doi.org/10.1016/j.ssaho.2024.100875

Laspita, S., Breugst, N., Heblich, S., & Patzelt, H. (2012). Intergenerational Transmission of Entrepreneurial Intentions. *Journal of Business Venturing, 27*, 414–435. https://doi.org/10.1016/j.jbusvent.2011.11.006

Laurisz, N. (2022). Cyfrowa praca i cyfrowy rynek pracy – Wyzwania stojące przed edukacją / Digital work and the digital labour market – Challenges for education. *Uniwersytet i edukacja wobec wyzwań współczesności*. Krakow, Poland: Wydawnictwo MSAP UEK.

Laurisz, N., & Sanak-Kosmowska, K. (2022). Differences in Perceptions of the Quality of Education and Employment Effectiveness of Schools in a Non-Skills-Focused Education System. *Journal of Public Governance, 61*(3), Article 3. https://doi.org/10.15678/PG.2022.61.3.04

Laurisz, N., & Sanak-Kosmowska, K. (2024). Fostering Entrepreneurial Intentions in a Non-Skills-Focused Education System. *Educational Studies Review, 1*(44), 34–52. https://doi.org/Doi:10.12775/PBE.2024.005

Laurisz, N., Mazur, S., & Sanak_Kosmowska, K. (Eds.). (2022). *Uniwersytet i edukacja wobec wyzwań współczesności / University and education in the face of contemporary challenges*. Wydawnictwo MSAP UEK.

Leuven, E., & Oosterbeek, H. (2011). Overeducation and Mismatch in the Labor Market. In *Handbook of the Economics of Education* (Vol. 4, pp. 283–326). Elsevier. https://doi.org/10.1016/B978-0-444-53444-6.00003-1

Liñán, F., & Fayolle, A. (2015). A Systematic Literature Review on Entrepreneurial Intentions: Citation, Thematic Analyses, and Research Agenda. *International Entrepreneurship and Management Journal, 11*(4), 907–933. https://doi.org/10.1007/s11365-015-0356-5

OECD. (2018). *Teaching for the Future: Effective Classroom Practices to Transform Education*. Paris, France: Organisation for Economic Co-operation and Development.

Oosterbeek, H., van Praag, M., & Ijsselstein, A. (2010). The Impact of Entrepreneurship Education on Entrepreneurship Skills and Motivation. *European Economic Review, 54*(3), 442–454. https://doi.org/10.1016/j.euroecorev.2009.08.002

Rogacheva, Y. (2016). The Reception of John Dewey's Democratic Concept of School in Different Countries of the World. *Espacio, Tiempo y Educación, 3*(2), 65–87. https://doi.org/10.14516/ete.2016.003.002.003

Salas-Velasco, M. (2021). Mapping the (Mis)match of University Degrees in the Graduate Labor Market. *Journal for Labour Market Research, 55*(1), 14. https://doi.org/10.1186/s12651-021-00297-x

Sánchez, J. C. (2011). University Training for Entrepreneurial Competencies: Its Impact on Intention of Venture Creation. *International Entrepreneurship and Management Journal, 7*(2), 239–254. https://doi.org/10.1007/s11365-010-0156-x

St-Jean, E., & Audet, J. (2009). The Role of Mentoring in the Learning Development of the Novice Entrepreneur. *International Entrepreneurship and Management Journal, 8*, 119–140. https://doi.org/10.1007/s11365-009-0130-7

St-Jean, E., & Mitrano-Méda, S. (2016). *Should Mentors of Entrepreneurs be Trained or Their Experience Is Enough?* InTech. https://doi.org/10.5772/65625

Walters, S., Silva, P., & Nikolai, J. (2017). Teaching, Learning, and Assessment: Insights into Students' Motivation to Learn. *The Qualitative Report, 22*(4), 1151–1168. https://doi.org/10.46743/2160-3715/2017.2777

WEF. (2023). *Future of Jobs Report 2023*. World Economic Forum. Holtzbrinczk Publishing, Stuttgart, German.

Zimbardo, P. G., Johnson, R. L., & McCann, V. (2016). *Psychology: Core Concepts*. New York, US: Pearson.

Aliya Akhmedieva, Abdurashid Kadirov, Bahtiyor Mamurov, Zulkhumor Fazliddinova, Sirojiddin Abrorov, and Roman Pantin

Development of the Export Potential of the Fruit and Vegetable Sector of the Republic of Uzbekistan

1. Introduction

The climatic conditions of Uzbekistan allow us to grow fresh fruits, vegetables and berries in large quantities and a wide assortment. On this basis, the agricultural processing industry is developing in the country, which includes enterprises for the production of canned fruits and vegetables, vegetable and fruit juices, wine products, soft drinks, fruit and vegetable purees, pastes and syrups, dried and frozen fruits and vegetables. According to some of these items (tomato paste, dried fruits and dried vegetables) Uzbekistan is one of the world's largest producers.

Meanwhile, Uzbekistan has a huge potential to increase the production of fruit and vegetable products both to ensure the domestic market and to increase exports. More than 19 million tons of fruit and vegetable products are produced annually in Uzbekistan, the volume of production is provided by farmers and dehkan (personal subsidiary farms) farms that provide domestic and foreign markets with high-quality fruits and vegetables. The total volume of storage facilities in the republic is growing, including modern refrigerating chambers. This contributes to the uninterrupted supply of the main types of agricultural products to the population, the expansion of its exports. The transport infrastructure is developing dynamically, at the same time work is underway to provide interconnected logistics networks, foreign trade relations are expanding, ensuring the growth of the export potential of the sector.

2. Literature Review and Development Hypothesis

The Concept of Agricultural Development adopted by the government until 2030 defined the main directions for continuing structural transformations in agricultural production, the introduction of innovative agricultural technologies, integrated mechanization of agriculture and deepening the processing of raw materials, etc.[1]. It provides for the gradual optimization of areas for cotton due to the withdrawal of low-yielding lands, followed by the placement of fruit and vegetable crops, potatoes and other crops on the released area, as well as the organization of intensive gardens, the further development of breeding and seed production. Theoretical and methodological aspects of the growth of competitiveness of national economies and strategies for the development of foreign economic relations have been studied in the works of such foreign scientists as R. Dornbush, J. Stiglitz, M. Porter, P. Krugman, K. Ohmae, R. Kaplinsky, Y. Handayati, P. Dannenberg, V. Leontiev, T. Akhmedov, U. Umurzakov, A. Abdurazakov, A. Alimov, A. Isadzhanov, N. Sirazhiddinov, S. Eshmatov, O. Zhumaev, etc.[2].

In addition to the theoretical foundations, empirical studies have demonstrated that the diversification of agricultural exports, especially in the fruit and vegetable sector, contributes significantly to economic growth and stability. Research findings indicate that countries with well-developed value chains and export-oriented agricultural policies are more resilient to global market fluctuations and external shocks. Strengthening logistical infrastructure, improving access to international quality certification, and fostering cooperation between producers and exporters are key factors in enhancing the competitiveness of Uzbekistan's fruit and vegetable sector in the global market. The integration of digital technologies in supply chain management and the implementation of precision agriculture techniques further support sustainable growth and increased export potential. Moreover, the adoption of sustainable farming practices and environmentally friendly production methods plays a crucial role in ensuring long-term agricultural productivity and meeting the growing demand for organic and high-quality food products in international markets.

---

1 Decree of the President of the Republic of Uzbekistan "On approval of the strategy for the development of agriculture of the Republic of Uzbekistan 2020–2030", 23 October 2019, PF-5853.

2 Kaplinsky, R. (2000). *Spreading the gains from globalization: What can be learned from value chain analysis.* Institute of Development Studies Working Paper 110. Brighton. Porter, M. E. (1985). *Competitive advantage: Creating and sustaining superior performance.* London: Friedland. Dannenberg, P., & Kulke, E. (2014). Editorial: Dynamics in agricultural value chains. *Journal of the Geographical Society of Berlin,* 145(3). Handayati, Y. et al. (2015). Value co-creation in agri-chains network: An agent-based simulation. *Procedia Manufacturing, 4* (2015), 419–428. Umurzakov, A., & Eshmatov, S. (2017). The importance of vertical and horizontal integration in the fruit and vegetable value chain. *Journal of Financier Reference.* №8(68).

3. Research Methodology

In the course of the study, a systematic approach was used in the study of economic analysis, a comparative method, logical thinking. Predictive studies and empirical estimates are based on multivariate econometric analysis.

4. Findings and Discussion

Foreign economic relations continue to develop under the influence of the consequences of the coronavirus pandemic. In a joint statement, the Food and Agriculture Organization of the United Nations, the World Health Organization and the World Trade Organization warned of the dangers of measures aimed at combating the pandemic, which could jeopardize global trade and food security. As it is emphasized, uncertainty about sufficient food supply can generate a wave of export restrictions, creating a shortage in the global market.

World experience in the development of economic systems shows that strong competitive advantages in the global economy are based largely on factors of a regional nature. Factors of geographical and spatial concentration as competitive advantages play a significant role in the framework of the international division of labor. It can be defined as the specialization of individual countries or regions within the world economy on certain types of products and services, which determines and assumes the exchange of these goods and services on the world market. Thus, the international division of labor is a spatial form of organization of production and consumption of goods and services, characterized by the effective use of competitive advantages of territories. The natural and climatic conditions of the country are favorable for growing a variety of vegetables and fruits with excellent taste qualities. A significant part of agricultural land in almost all regions of the republic is suitable for the production of fruit and vegetable products. There is a steady growth trend in the production of almost all types of fruit and vegetable products, which is mainly due to the growth of acreage (Table 1).

Thus, the sown area of vegetables for 2016–2022 increased by 33.6 %, melons – by 10.8 % of fruits and berries (at the fruiting age) – by 69.3 %, and grapes (at the fruiting age) increased by 6.8 %. The growth of sown areas of fruit and vegetable crops occurred primarily due to a reduction in sown areas under cotton (due to reducing the production of raw cotton by 350 thousand tons, about 170.5 thousand hectares of irrigated land are released).

In 2016–2022, the per capita production of fruits and berries remained unchanged, vegetables decreased – from 319.8 kg to 313.6 kg, grapes – from

50.7 kg to 49.8 kg, and melons increased – from 64.2 kg to 68.6 kg. Since 2015, Uzbekistan has created new intensive gardens on an area of 9.7 thousand hectares and vineyards on 9.2 thousand hectares. Greenhouses have been created on 444 hectares, as well as the reconstruction of gardens on an area of 12.3 thousand hectares and vineyards – 7.5 thousand hectares.

Table 1: Dynamics of fruit and vegetable production in the Republic of Uzbekistan

Indicators	2016	2017	2018	2019	2020	2021	2022	Changes 2022 to 2016	
								%	(+), (-)
Acreage (thousand hectares):									
vegetables	206.0	189.7	219.0	220.0	222.8	233.7	239.6	116.3	+33.6
melons	58.8	52.3	52.6	53.4	61.1	67.3	68.9	117.2	+10.1
fruits and berries	279.6	271.6	319.2	336.6	336.3	342.5	348.9	124.8	+69.3
grape	131.2	114.5	113.3	120.2	128.2	133.7	138.0	105.2	+6.8
Yield (hundred weight hectare):									
vegetables	271.1	253.6	237.1	235.6	234.4	236.0	242.8	89.6	−28.3
melons	209.4	197.9	189.8	180.4	168.3	176.2	186.6	89.1	−22.8
fruits and berries	134.1	118.3	121.6	118.5	116.7	122.1	127.7	95.2	−6.4
grape	141.9	157.0	157.5	153.5	152.0	154.7	160.7	113.3	18.8
Production per capita (kg):									
vegetables	319.8	315.5	296.2	304.2	301.8	310.8	313.6	98.1	−6.2
melons	64.2	62.7	55.7	61.6	61.8	65.5	68.6	106.8	+4.3
fruits and berries	82.0	80.7	82.1	82.0	81.4	81.7	82.0	100.0	0.0
grape	50.7	50.2	48.2	47.7	46.5	48.6	49.8	98.2	−0.9

Source: Compiled by the authors

In our study, we have developed an econometric model of a multidimensional time series. According to these econometric equations, the resulting indicators are the practice of fruit and vegetable production in our country for 2009–2022. The initial data for the analysis of samples from the database of Statistics agency under the President of the Republic of Uzbekistan.

In this regard, the analysis was carried out and econometric models of the equation were developed using multifactorial time series: vegetable consumption per capita, income per capita, acreage and vegetable yield in the national economy for 2009–2022. According to the hypothesis, vegetable consumption per capita depends on these factors (Table 2).

Table 2: Initial data

Years	Consumption of Vegetables Per Capita, kg	Per Capita Income, Million Soums	The Area of Vegetable Crops, Thousand Hectares	Vegetable Yield, Hundred Weight
	Y	X1	X2	X3
2009	210.9	1385.4	165.4	253.6
2010	224.8	1668.1	173.0	252.5
2011	239.5	2133.3	175.4	264.0
2012	262.8	2601.9	183.8	265.6
2013	284.0	3166.5	189.4	270.9
2014	304.6	3577.1	192.0	268.3
2015	326.5	3930.4	194.0	271.0
2016	351.0	4565.2	206.0	271.1
2017	315.5	5750.2	189.7	253.6
2018	296.2	8580.0	219.0	237.1
2019	304.2	10891.3	220.0	235.6
2020	301.8	12279.1	222.8	234.4
2021	310.8	14869.8	233.7	236.0
2022	313.6	17807.3	23.6	242.8

Source: Compiled by the authors

The following conditions of cointegration in multidimensional time series were tested:

time series were checked for stationarity;
the correlation relationship of the initial data has been verified;
a regression model is constructed (Table 3).

Table 3: Regression equation and variance analysis indicators for vegetable consumption per capita and vegetable acreage

Regression Statistics						
Multiple R			0.678240801			
R-square			0.460010584			
Normalized R-square			0.415011466			
Standard error			30.82035568			
Observations			14			
			Analysis of variance			
	df	SS	MS	F	Significance of F	
Regression	1	9710.444598	9710.444598	10.22265777	0.007671035	
Remains	12	11398.73189	949.8943242			
Total	13	21109.17649				
	Coefficients	Standard error	t-statistics	P-Value	Lower 95 %	Upper 95 %
Y-intersection	55.30504754	73.55967886	0.751839165	0.466638772	-104.9677245	215.5778196
X2	1.166986371	0.364992443	3.197289129	0.007671035	0.371736153	1.962236589

Source: Compiled by the authors

Interpretation of regression coefficients. The constant evaluates the aggregated influence of other factors (other than those taken into account in the model X_i) on the result Y and means that Y in the absence of xi would be 55.3050. The coefficient b_1 indicates that with an increase of X2 by 1, Y increases by 1.1669.

As a result of calculations, the multiple regression equation was obtained:

$$Y = 55.3050 + 1.1669X2$$

An economic interpretation of the model parameters is possible: an increase in the area of vegetable crops (X2) by 1 unit, it leads to an increase in the consumption of vegetables per capita (Y) by an average of 1,167 units.

According to the maximum coefficient of elasticity E1 = 1.073 we conclude that the area of vegetable crops (X2) has the greatest impact on the result of vegetable consumption per capita (Y).

At the same time, in the face of increasing global challenges, it is important not to stop there and continue working on the development of the agro-industrial complex and strengthening the country's food security.

Today, serious support is provided to exporters in our country for the implementation of these tasks. In particular, the application of penalties against economic entities for overdue accounts receivable on foreign trade operations is suspended at the expense of funds allocated to the Export Promotion Agency under the Ministry of Investment and Foreign Trade, it is envisaged to reimburse exporters of fruit and vegetable products 50 % of their transportation costs[3].

As a result of the ongoing reforms in the agricultural sector of the economy, the share of dehkan farms in all indicators of fruit and vegetable production retains a significant share from year to year (Figure 1).

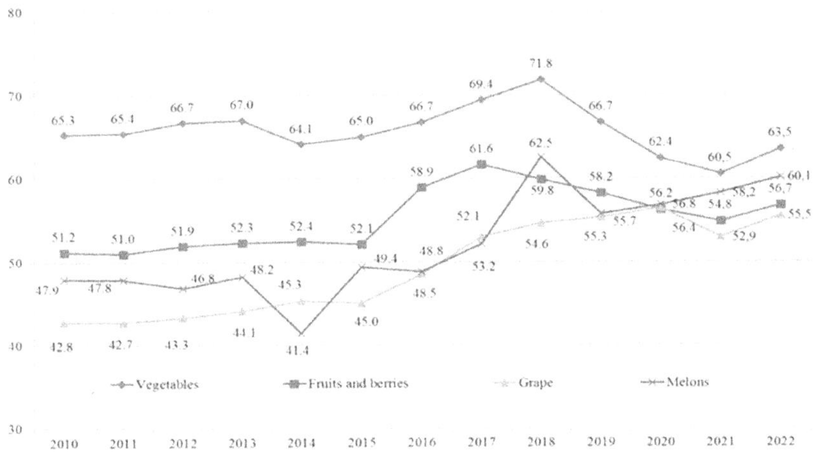

Figure 1: Change in the share of Dehkan farms in the production of fruit and vegetable products in the Republic of Uzbekistan

Source: Compiled by the authors

As the analysis shows, the share of dehkan farms in the production of vegetables decreased from 65.3 % in 2010 to 63.5 % by 2022, fruits and berries increased from 51.2 % to 56.7 %, grapes from 47.9 % to 55.5 % and melons from 47.9 % to 60.1 %.

There is a steady growth trend in the production of fruit and vegetable products per capita. The production of fruits and vegetables per capita by region indicates that these indicators are close to the consumption standards recommended by the Ministry of Health of the Republic of Uzbekistan (Figure 2).

3 Resolution of the President of the Republic of Uzbekistan "On measures to further support export activities" dated May 7, 2020, PP-4707.

The per capita production of fruits and berries in the Republic of Uzbekistan in 2010 amounted to 60.1 kg in 2022 amounted to 84.5 kg, grapes in 2010 amounted to 34.7 kg in 2022 50.9 kg, melons in 2010 41.5 kg in 2022 67.6 kg, vegetables in 2010 amounted to 222.9 kg in 2022 amounted to 326.2 kg.

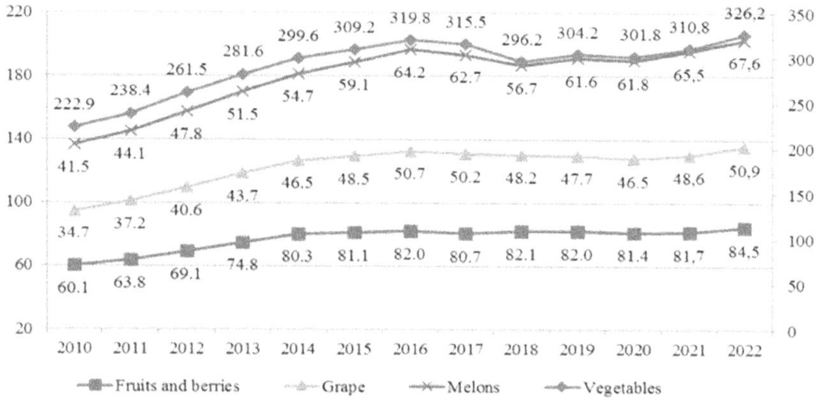

Figure 2: Dynamics of fruit and vegetable production per capita in the Republic of Uzbekistan, kg

Source: Compiled by the authors

Such a significant increase in the production of fruit and vegetable products per capita is due to both the growth of domestic demand for these products, associated with an increase in household incomes, and a significant increase in its exports in fresh and processed form. Taking into account the geographical location and climatic conditions, there are areas of specialization in the production of fruits and vegetables, such as Samarkand (in 2021, the share in the production of vegetables is 16.1 %, fruits and berries-12.6 % of the total production in the republic), Tashkent (vegetables-9.7 % and pilaf and berries-3.8 %), Andijan (vegetables-15.1 % and fruits and berries-23.0 %), Ferghana (vegetables-10.9 %, fruits and berries-13 %), Namangan (vegetables-8.2 %, fruits and berries-10.4 %) and Bukhara (vegetables-7.3 %, fruits and berries-9.2 %) regions (Table 4).

Table 4: The share of regions in the production of the main types of fruit and vegetable products, %

Regions	2017		2018		2019		2020		2021		Changes 2021 to 2017 (+), (−)	
	A*	B**	A*	B**	A*	B**	A*	B**	A*	B**	A*	B**
Republic of Uzbekistan	100.0	100.0	100.0	100.0	100.0	100.0	100.0	100.0	100.0	100.0	-	-
Republic of Karakalpakstan	2.4	1.8	2.6	1.8	2.7	2.1	2.7	2.1	2.8	2.2	+0.4	+0.4
regions:												
Andijan	14.5	21.8	16.1	22.4	15.6	23.0	15.4	22.5	15.1	23.0	+0.6	+1.2
Bukhara	6.8	10.3	7.1	10.4	7.1	10.5	7.4	10.8	7.3	9.2	+0.5	−1.1
Jizzakh	3.9	3.3	4.0	3.0	4.2	3.2	4.1	3.1	4.0	3.2	+0.1	−0.1
Kashkadarya	5.1	6.2	5.1	6.7	4.8	6.2	4.7	5.8	4.6	6.0	−0.5	−0.2
Navoi	2.6	3.8	2.9	3.6	2.8	3.6	2.8	3.7	2.8	3.7	+0.2	−0.1
Namangan	7.5	9.2	8.1	9.9	8.0	9.7	8.0	10.1	8.2	10.4	+0.7	+1.2
Samarkand	17.5	14.7	14.7	12.3	15.5	12.2	15.7	12.3	16.1	12.6	−1.4	−2.1
Surkhandarya	9.9	5.3	9.4	5.7	9.5	5.7	9.7	5.8	9.8	6.0	−0.1	+0.7
Syrdarya	3.0	1.7	2.8	1.4	3.0	1.4	3.0	1.4	3.0	1.5	0	−0.2
Tashkent	12.1	3.9	11.1	5.3	10.4	4.8	10.0	4.1	9.7	3.8	−2.4	−0.1
Ferghana	8.5	12.4	10.3	12.0	10.7	12.1	10.8	13.0	10.9	13.0	+2.4	+0.6
Khorezm	6.2	5.6	5.8	5.5	5.7	5.5	5.7	5.3	5.7	5.4	−0.5	−0.2

* A – vegetables, ** B – fruits and berries
Source: Compiled by the authors

Development of regional strategies (for the medium and long term.) export-oriented fruit and vegetable products and their promotion to the world market (taking into account Uzbekistan's intention to join the World Trade Organization) is becoming an important tool for increasing the competitiveness of the industry.

In general, the state of the fruit and vegetable industry of the Republic of Uzbekistan can be characterized as dynamically developing, thanks to state support and the growing demand of the population and foreign markets for grapes, fruits and vegetables. As the domestic market becomes saturated, export supplies may become the main driving force (incentive) of this industry (Table 5).

Table 5: Dynamics of changes in the structure of exports of fruits and vegetables of the Republic of Uzbekistan

Products	2016	2017	2018	2019	2020	2021	Changes (+), (–)				
							2021 to 2016	2021 to 2017	2021 to 2018	2021 to 2019	2021 to 2020
Fruits and berries, USD million	217.4	254.4	357.7	406.8	353.9	280.6	+63.2	+26.2	−77.1	−126.2	−73.3
share in, %	39.9	40.1	42.0	34.1	36.2	30.0	−9.9	−10.1	−12.0	−4.1	−6.2
Vegetables, USD million	187.6	217.7	307.7	471.3	400.0	422.0	+234.4	+204.3	+ 114.3	−49.3	+22.0
share in, %	34.2	34.3	36.1	39.5	40.9	45.2	+11.0	+10.9	+9.1	+5.7	+4.3
Grapes million US dollars	142.1	159.5	179.7	223.7	188.3	208.5	+66.4	+49	+28.8	−15.2	+20.2
share in, %	25.9	25.1	21.1	18.7	19.3	22.3	−3.6	−2.8	+1.2	+3.6	+3.0
Melons, million US dollars	2.0	3.3	6.5	13.1	35.6	22.7	+20.7	+19.4	+16.2	+9.6	−12.9
share in, %	0.4	0.5	0.8	1.1	3.6	2.4	+2.0	+1.9	+1.6	+1.3	−1.2
Total, millions of US dollars	549.1	634.9	851.6	1114.9	977.8	933.4	+384.3	+298.5	+81.8	−181.5	−44.4
share in total exports in, %	4.6	5.1	6.3	6.9	9.6	5.8	+1.2	+0.7	−0.5	−1.1	−3.8

Source: Compiled by the authors

From 2016 to 2021, the share of the fruit and vegetable industry in total exports increased from 4.6 % to 5.8 %, while a significant increase was noted in the export of fruits and berries by 129.1 %, vegetables 224.9 %, grapes 146.7 % and melons 11.4 times.

This was facilitated by state support for the development of export-oriented production of the fruit and vegetable industry, for example, a decision was made:

- exporters will be refunded 50 % of transport costs for the supply of products by road and air transport. Prior to that, only export shipments by rail were subsidized, but this was not very effective, since deliveries by this type of transport were carried out rarely and in small volumes;
- the Export Promotion Agency under the Ministry of Investment and Foreign Trade will compensate the insurance premium of exporters if the insurance is used as collateral. It is also a very effective tool to guarantee the financial security of supplies;

- by the end of 2021, during the customs clearance of goods for export, the verification of the presence of debts on mandatory payments and executive documents, both for legal entities and individuals, will be canceled, which will speed up and simplify export procedures[4].

As the geography of fruit and vegetable exports in the Republic of Uzbekistan (2022) shows, the main partners are the CIS countries, Kyrgyzstan 18.5 %, Kazakhstan 25.7 % and the Russian Federation 26.1 % (Figure 3).

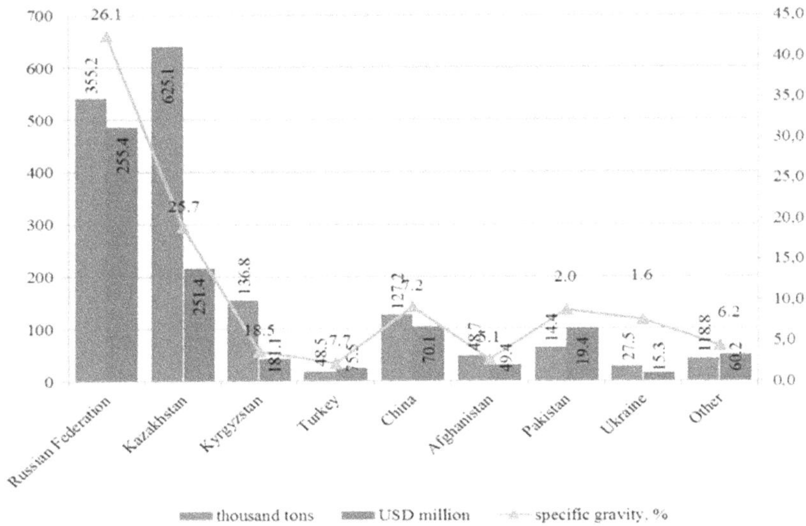

Figure 3: Geography of fruit and vegetable exports in the Republic of Uzbekistan (2022)
Source: Compiled by the authors

These countries account for 63.2 % of total exports of fruit and vegetable products, which is due to geographical location, administrative, legal and infrastructural conditions, knowledge of consumer psychology, language, etc. Further integration into the markets of the CIS countries requires the development of a

4 Resolution of the President of the Republic of Uzbekistan "On measures to implement the project "Modernization of agriculture of the Republic of Uzbekistan" with the participation of the International Bank for Reconstruction and Development and the International Development Association" dated August 11, 2020, No. PP-4803.

large industrial greenhouse complex with an export orientation to the markets of the Russian Federation and Kazakhstan (taking into account the growth of competition in these markets due to the development of own greenhouses in these countries) using modern technologies (including energy-saving and the use of alternative energy sources):

expansion of exports of fresh and processed fruit and vegetable products, implementation of targeted programs to modernize existing and create new processing enterprises;
creation of specialized territories in the mountain-foothill zone for the production of fruits and vegetables, viticulture, fruits and berries;[5]
have good climatic conditions, environmental characteristics, historical skills and culture of agriculture and entrepreneurship, with the formation of brand territories, etc.;
implementation of targeted programs for the development of viticulture and its processed products;
the mechanism for implementing the target program can be the use of a public-private partnership mechanism, with a clear distribution of responsibility between partners.;
one of the main directions of fruit and vegetable growing development should be the solution of problems related to the insufficient development of the storage and refrigerator network, logistics and travel costs;
strengthening and deepening the specialization of the above-listed areas in production, as well as in the processing of fruits and vegetables, ensuring full utilization of existing capacities, increasing the volume of production of fruit and vegetable products with high added value, increasing the level of certification of fruit and vegetable products according to world standards;
the insufficiency of the marketing approach to the organization of production, the unsuitability of existing production and export mechanisms to changing economic conditions;
for the promotion of fruit and vegetable products, a marketing approach with a differentiated study of the product sales markets (EU and CIS markets, China, Turkey, Iran, etc.) is needed;

5 Jomaev, A. (2004). *Organizational and economic basis for the development of cooperation in the fruit and vegetable complex in the conditions of a multi-ukled economy.* diss. the avt. i.f.n., Tashkent. Uzbekistan.

given the high level of demand for fresh fruits and vegetables on the domestic and foreign food market (according to FAO experts, most fruits and vegetables are consumed fresh), comprehensive development and large-scale modernization of the storage and processing of fruits and vegetables should be an important priority;

creation of large mechanized commodity fruit and vegetable farms, on the basis of which it is possible to develop storage and processing, all-round development and expansion of large-scale production (clustering and cooperation) of fruits and vegetables.

Taking into account the current trends in the development of the fruit and vegetable sector and demand in foreign markets, the main scenarios of strategic development have been developed: a pessimistic scenario (from the point of view of methodology, this scenario has significant limitations, the main of which is binding to the average industry trends), an inertial scenario (the scenario provides for an increase in the agrotechnological level of production) and an optimistic scenario (assumes an increase in export opportunities by creating and implementing innovative technologies, strengthening existing and creating new competitive advantages).

The figure below shows fruit and vegetable production in the Republic of Uzbekistan by mapping (Figure 4).

Among the agricultural products grown in all economic categories of the republic, vegetables have the largest share (101.9 %) in the Andijan region, and the smallest share (90.9 %) in the Syrdarya region. The largest (108.1 %) contribution to the production of fruits and berries corresponds to Bukhara, and the smallest (102.5 %) to Navoi region. Also, Andijan region took the last place in the cultivation of grapes and melons (100.1 %). Bukhara is the leader in grape cultivation (106.4 %). In Tashkent region, in 2022, the largest share of melons is more (119.2 %), and in the republic, melons are grown more than vegetables, fruits and berries, and grapes. The volume of agricultural products (fruits and vegetables) by region is represented by the map diagram. The largest volume of agricultural products corresponds to Andijan and Samarkand regions, and the smallest volume corresponds to the share of Navoi and the Republic of Karakalpakstan.

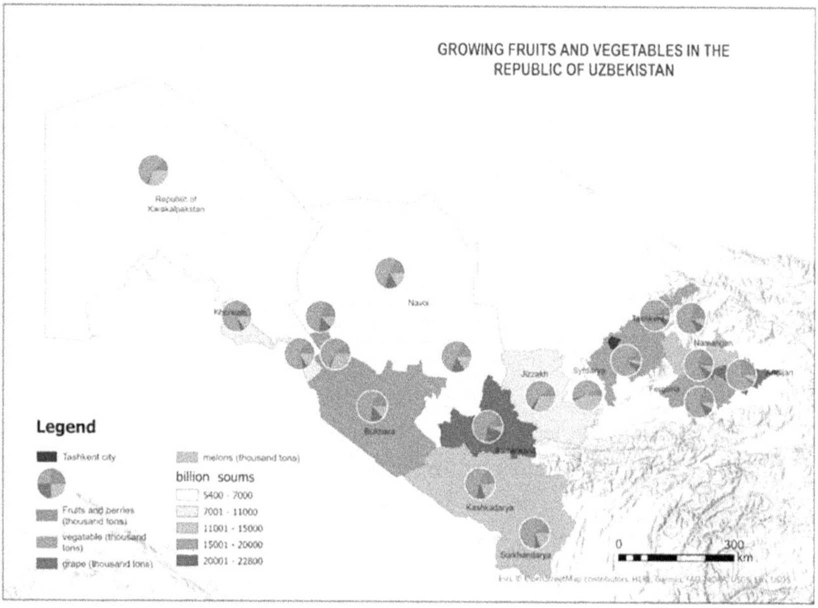

Figure 4: Map of fruit and vegetable production in the Republic of Uzbekistan (2022)
Source: Compiled by the authors

5. Conclusion

The results of the research allow us to draw the following conclusions:

1. The export potential of the fruit and vegetable sector is quite high, which is due to the presence of its own raw material base (fruits, vegetables, grapes, etc.), certain climatic conditions and historical experience accumulated by local producers, and the already existing resource and material base for the production of these types of products. These circumstances suggest that Uzbekistan has comparative advantages and should deepen its specialization in these positions. Along with this, it is necessary to expand the range of cultivated fruit and vegetable products, paying special attention to products with high profitability (broccoli, arugula, iceberg, new varieties of large-caliber cherries, melons, etc.);
2. Insufficient marketing approach to the organization and sale of fruit and vegetable products, many potential foreign consumers do not know about the unique taste qualities of Uzbek fruits, melons and vegetables, and small

producers are unable to conduct an active advertising campaign, there are practically no trademarks and brand names of Uzbek fruit and vegetable products (brand) in the markets of European countries. For example, most of the fresh fruit and vegetable products are produced by small dehkan and farms, for which the organization of production based on the study of the needs of foreign and local consumers, the selection and updating of varieties depending on consumer preferences and expected market conditions present certain difficulties. For this reason, all the activities of producers of fruit and vegetable products are reduced to offering the sale of those products that are produced (insufficient consideration of real demand, with the practical absence of market research in developed countries, etc.);

3. Exports are carried out most often by individuals who offer products to foreign buyers without appropriate sorting labeling and packaging;
4. Deficiencies in quality management (HASP ISO food safety standards, laboratories, harmonization of phytosanitary standards, certification, etc.) and control of the process and compliance with the rules of sanitary and hygienic standards at all stages of production and sale of fruit and vegetable products make it difficult to promote products to European markets (importers from these countries are interested in companies that are engaged in growing fresh produce and its processing);
5. There are a number of problems for small businesses and private entrepreneurship: lack of information about the price parameters of the products grown; lack of experience in finding, establishing contact, negotiating with potential partners in the value chain; lack of experience in the correct drafting of contracts (it usually takes about two to three months and significant expenses to work out one export contract); to ensure the quality of products in accordance with international standards imposed by foreign buyers, arising from the lack of control of shipment on the ground; the problem of timely registration and shipment of products due to the lack of small businesses, the necessary knowledge, skills and experience in exporting, etc.;
6. Exporters do not have actual information about transportation services. It is necessary to unify all transport companies and provide price information on routes;
7. Agro information Network (AIN Exports). Creation of a specialized information and analytical portal, formation of an information system and dissemination of information on market conditions, consultations on the promotion of products for export, the state and change of the business environment in importing countries, etc. Based on digital technologies aimed at automating the processes of data collection, storage, analysis, and transmission (Big

Data) in the market of fruit and vegetable products, which will allow the use of business intelligence (BI) methods[6].

References

Abrorov, S., & Ahmadjonov, A. (2023). Prospects for the development of the fund market through Islamic securities in the digital economy. In *Proceedings of the 6th International Conference on Future Networks & Distributed Systems (ICFNDS '22)* (pp. 74–80). New York, NY: Association for Computing Machinery. https://doi.org/10.1145/3584202.3584214

Dannenberg, P., & Kulke, E. (2014). Editorial: Dynamics in agricultural value chains. *Journal of the Geographical Society of Berlin, 145*(3), pp. 121–126.

Decree of the President of the Republic of Uzbekistan "On approval of the strategy for the development of agriculture of the Republic of Uzbekistan 2020–2030" 2019 23 October PF-5853.

Ergashev, A. (2017). *Analysis of fruit and vegetable supply, demand, diet quality and nutrition in Uzbekistan.* Dissertation. Rheinische Friedrich-Wilhelms-Universität Bonn.

Handayati, Y. et al. (2015). Value co-creation in agri-chains network: An agent-based simulation. *Procedia Manufacturing, 4* (2015), 419–428.

Iminova, N., Abdimuminova, S., & Mamurov, B. (2019). Risk management and insurance. *International Journal of Innovative Technology and Exploring Engineering, 8*(12), 5429–5432. https://doi.org/10.35940/ijitee.G5722.1081219.

Jomaev, A. (2004). *Organizational and economic basis for the development of cooperation in the fruit and vegetable complex in the conditions of a multi-ukled economy.* diss. the avt. i.f.n., Tashkent. Uzbekistan.

Kadyrov, A, Akhmedieva, A, Bazarov, F., & Mamurov, B. (2021). Formation of information society and its influence on competitiveness of national economies in the context of world economy globalization. In *The 5th International Conference on Future Networks & Distributed Systems (ICFNDS 2021)* (pp. 672–684). New York, NY: Association for Computing Machinery. https://doi.org/10.1145/3508072.3508205

---

6 Kadyrov, A., Akhmedieva, A., Bazarov, F., & Mamurov, B. (2021). Formation of Information Society and Its Influence on Competitiveness of National Economies in the Context of World Economy Globalization. In *The 5th International Conference on Future Networks & Distributed Systems (ICFNDS 2021).* New York, NY: Association for Computing Machinery, pp. 672–684. https://doi.org/10.1145/3508072.3508205

Kaplinsky, R. (2000). *Spreading the gains from globalization: What can be learned from value chain analysis*. Institute of Development Studies Working Paper 110, Brighton.

Larson, D., Khidirov, D., & Ramniceanu, I. (2015). Uzbekistan – Strengthening the horticulture value chain (English). *Uzbekistan vision 2030 background paper series*. Washington, DC.

Murodov, Sh. M. (2020). *Fruit and vegetable products of the cooperative for the formation of*: auth. diss. i.f.n. – T. -51 p.

Porter, M. E. (1985). *Competitive advantage: Creating and sustaining superior performance*. London: Friedland.

Resolution of the President of the Republic of Uzbekistan "On measures to further support export activities" dated May 7, 2020, PP-4707.

Resolution of the President of the Republic of Uzbekistan "On measures to implement the project "Modernization of agriculture of the Republic of Uzbekistan" with the participation of the International Bank for Reconstruction and Development and the International Development Association" dated August 11, 2020, No. PP-4803.

Shoh-Jakhon Khamdamov. (2022). Calculating share of factors of intensive economic growth in Uzbekistan. In *The 5th International Conference on Future Networks & Distributed Systems (ICFNDS 2021)*. New York, NY: Association for Computing Machinery, 393–397. https://doi.org/10.1145/3508072.3508144.

Shoh-Jakhon Khamdamov. (2023). Theoretical and methodological aspects of intensive economic growth in ensuring sustainable economic development. In *Social and economic studies within the framework of emerging global developments* (vol. 3, pp. 283–293). Zurich: Peter Lang.

Umurzakov, A., & Eshmatov, S. (2017). The importance of vertical and horizontal integration in the fruit and vegetable value chain. *Journal of Financier Reference*. №8(68), pp. 51–55.

Aliya Akhmedieva, Abdurashid Kadirov, Bahtiyor Mamurov, Dilobar Ruzieva, Rimma Yunusova, and Sitora Khaydarova

Macroeconomic Aspects of Improving the Mechanism of Leasing Investment in the Republic of Uzbekistan

1. Introduction

The peculiarities of the functioning of leasing investment mechanisms in the world are determined by the dual nature of ownership of property in which it belongs to all subjects participating in leasing relations. Given the recent objective economic situation in the world, the decline in the inflow of international investment has led to a slowdown in the implementation of investment projects. The total flow of direct investments in the European Union decreased by 80 % and amounted to 73 billion US dollars. This figure has decreased to 57 % in the UK, 47 % in France and 34 % in Germany. The flow of investments to the United States decreased by 40 % due to a decrease in reinvested income and amounted to 156 billion US dollars[1].

Today, despite the fact that the macroeconomic aspects of improving the leasing mechanism of investment have been studied in developed countries, nevertheless, the development of new investment mechanisms by leasing companies remains an urgent issue. When studying the macroeconomic aspects of improving the leasing mechanism of investment in the world, attention is drawn to the importance of directing financial flows in the form of fixed capital investments to the real sector of the economy and establishing stable economic relations between the subjects of the leasing market.

2. Literature Review

Scientific research of the fundamental and theoretical foundations of the effective use of investments can be observed in the scientific works of foreign and domestic authors, such as M. Moore, H. Schmitz, G. Burman, Z. Bodi, J. Gitman, S. V. Gubanov, D. M. Keynes, V. Sharp, V. V. Bocharov, B. T. Baykhonov,

---

1 World Investment Report-2021: Investing in sustainable recover. UNCTAD/WIR/2021. https://unctad.org/system/files/official-document/wir2021_en.pdf

R. Zainiddinov, U. Otazhonov, I. Karimov, I. Tukhtakhonov, O. S. Sobirov, S. I. Mustafakulov.

Of particular importance for the conducted research are the special works of the following domestic and foreign authors devoted to leasing. In particular, T. A. Penchukova, V. M. Jukha, V. D. Gazman, V. A. Goremykina dealt with some aspects of the financial situation of leasing companies (risks of leasing companies, problems of financial stability, features of attracting debt financing, etc.). In Uzbekistan, the problems of leasing relations were studied by A. Kadirov, A. Akhmedieva, B. Mamurov, D. G. Gazibekov, H. A. Tukhsanov, O. S. Sabirov, I. A. Sattorov, V. V. Golyshev, G. M. Davlyatov, S. S. Gulyamov, etc.

3. Data and Methodology

The research uses methods of a systematic approach, methods of statistical, structural and comparative analysis, SWOT analysis, expert and predictive assessment, stress test, sociological survey, econometric modeling methods.

4. Results and Discussion

Despite the significant contribution of domestic and foreign economists to the development of mechanisms of leasing relations, there are a number of problems that have not been fully studied. Such problems include the limited public funds allocated to finance reproduction processes in entrepreneurship, insufficient knowledge of the mechanism of leasing investment and its regulatory framework, the formation of alternative sources of financing leasing transactions in the real sector of the economy.

The leasing mechanism is an important element of the investment activity of economic entities; measures to stimulate and support leasing activity are included in the investment policy of many foreign countries. According to the European Federation of Equipment Leasing Company Association (www.leaseurope.org), the prevalence and nature of leasing activity is one of the indicators of the level of economic development of the country[2].

The limited financial resources arising in the conditions of growing market competition motivates entrepreneurs to improve technological processes through attracting investments from alternative sources. Thus, a new macroeconomic environment is emerging that regulates economic relations in the field of leasing, through mechanisms of state support, taxation, financial and credit

2 Rapport sur le contract de credit-bail (leasing). UNIDROIT. 1975. EtudeLIX – Doc. 17p.

policy, development of institutions and infrastructure, insurance and others (Figure 1).

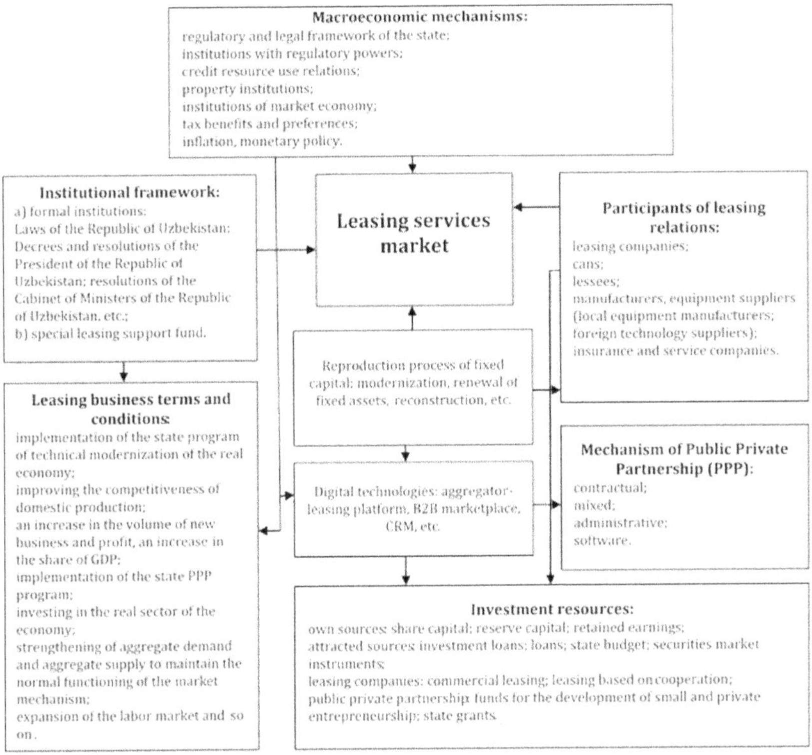

Figure 1: Macroeconomic environment of the leasing services market in the Republic of Uzbekistan

Source: Compiled by the authors

As the analysis showed, the existing regulatory legal acts of the Republic of Uzbekistan have created the necessary institutional framework for the development of leasing companies. At the same time, certain provisions of the existing legislation limit the possibilities of using leasing relations for investment support of updating fixed assets, as well as modernization of the real sector of the national economy (Table 1).

Table 1: Proposed amendments to the Law of the Republic of Uzbekistan "On Leasing"

Current Situation	**Offer**
Article 8. Leasing activity	
Leasing activity is a type of investment activity for the acquisition by the lessor of a leasing object at the expense of its own and (or) attracted funds and its transfer to the lessee	Leasing is a type of investment activity involving the acquisition by the lessor of a leasing object at the expense of its own and (or) attracted funds and transfer to individuals and legal entities (lessee) under a leasing agreement
Article 2. The concept of leasing	
Leasing is a special type of financial lease in which one party (the lessor), on behalf of the other party (the lessee), acquires from a third party (the seller) the property stipulated by the leasing agreement (the leasing object) and provides it to the lessee for a fee on the terms defined by such an agreement for possession and use for a period exceeding twelve months	Leasing is a special type of financial lease in which one party (the lessor), on behalf of the other party (the lessee), acquires from a third party (the seller) the property stipulated by the leasing agreement (the leasing object) and provides it to the lessee for a fee on the terms defined by such an agreement for possession and use for a period exceeding twelve months
Article 9. The Law of the Republic of Uzbekistan "On Leasing"	
Restricts the acquisition of a leasing object by a purchase and sale agreement	Restricts the acquisition of a leasing object by a purchase and sale agreement
Article 3. The Law of the Republic of Uzbekistan "On Leasing"	
"objects of leasing can be any non-consumable things used for entrepreneurial activity" (limits the composition of lessees, for example, individuals, innovative and social projects, startups, individual entrepreneurship, etc.)	"objects of leasing can be any non-consumable things used for entrepreneurial activity" (limits the composition of lessees, for example, individuals, innovative and social projects, startups, individual entrepreneurship, etc.)

Source: Compiled by the authors

The need to improve the legal framework of leasing relations is associated with the implementation of the following provisions:

- creating conditions for increasing the share of the leasing mechanism in the reproduction of fixed capital;
- expanding sources of investment in technological modernization of production, including for entrepreneurs with limited financial capabilities;
- promotes the development of competition among financial institutions, expanding the sources of investment for the subjects of the real sector of the economy;

- does not require additional collateral, provides equipment in accordance with the requirements of the lessee, and also provides service support for investment projects;

The participation of the Republic of Uzbekistan in the Convention "On the International Lease of Equipment" (Ottawa, May 28, 1988) will provide access to the international market of equipment suppliers under the leasing scheme.

The introduction of state regulation will positively affect the organization of the leasing relations market, in this regard, the study justifies the following:

- in the implementation of investment programs, the functions of leasing regulation can be transferred to the Ministry of Economic Development and Poverty Reduction of the Republic of Uzbekistan, and control and supervisory functions can be retained by the Ministry of Finance of the Republic of Uzbekistan;
- The concept of self-regulation of leasing activities (SRO) is put forward. A self-regulating organization should develop standards and rules for leasing operations and ensure their compliance by all its members, as well as create and maintain a system for protecting the rights and interests of consumers of leasing services (Association of Lessors of Uzbekistan);
- the necessity of introducing a register of leasing companies according to the criterion of equity sufficiency is proposed, which will raise the question of the amount of own funds of leasing companies. The introduction of capital adequacy standards for leasing companies will increase the openness and transparency of leasing companies for creditors and investors.

In general, as the analysis of macroeconomic indicators of the development of the Republic of Uzbekistan shows, the growth of investment and consumption contributed to the growth of gross domestic product from 5.4 % in 2019 to 5.8 % in 2020, in 2022, GDP growth accelerated to 7.4 % against 1.9 % in 2021.

According to the results of a survey of leasing companies' specialists, factors of sustainable economic growth are of priority importance for the development of the leasing services market (38.5 % of respondents). The next most important conditions for the development of the market, according to respondents, should be a reduction in the cost of borrowed funds for leasing companies (21.3 %) and easier access to financial resources (15.6 %).

The study defines the functions of leasing as a form of financing investments that contribute to an increase in economic potential, both at the level of the business entity and at the macro and meso levels; the basis of the methodological approach is the developed macroeconomic indicators of the development of the leasing market.

At the same time, it is advisable to use the following macroeconomic indicators of leasing intensity of investments: the share of leasing in GDP; the share of leasing in investments in fixed assets; the share of leasing of equipment, vehicles in investments in equipment and vehicles. In the study, taking into account the place and importance of leasing in investment processes, a comparative analysis of leasing payment methods is proposed, including depreciation of leasing property for the entire term of the lease agreement, compensation of the lessor's fee for the borrowed funds used by him, commission to the lessor, payment for additional services of the lessor according to the lease agreement, the cost of redeemable property, if it is provided for by the contract and the procedure for its payments, the amount of tax on leasing property.

Companies, the following results of the priority of risk reduction were obtained: 32.1 % of market respondents believe that the current requirements applied to the amount of collateral in the risk management of companies should be mitigated, 24.2 % of survey participants believe that it is possible to reduce the minimum level of advance payment, 10.4 % of respondents believe that it is possible to weaken the requirements for the sufficiency of own funds and 14.0 % believe that it is possible to lower the requirements for the financial stability of the lessee.

To assess risks, the following method of economic analysis is proposed (Table 2). Based on expert methods[3], which uses a certain composition of financial and economic indicators differentiated by the following groups: general characteristics of the lessee, financial stability, the quality of the lessee's investment project, the quality of the leasing transaction and the overall assessment of the risk level of the transaction.

Table 2: Method of determining the risk level of a transaction with a lessee

#	Name	Criteria	Norm (points)	Received (points)	Weight Coefficients	Rating Number
1			I. Characteristics of the lessee			
1.	Transaction history	Successful	100	100	0,05	5,0
		Not	0			
2.	Enterprise management	The manager has high qualifications and experience	60	60	0,05	3,0
		The management has no experience	0			

3 This approach was tested on the example of JSC "Uzselkhozmashleasing".

Table 2: Continued

#	Name	Criteria	Norm (points)	Received (points)	Weight Coefficients	Rating Number
3.	The level of organization of production	High	100	60	0,2	12,0
		Average	60			
		Low	0			
4.	The place of the enterprise in the market	Monopolist	100	60	0,4	24,0
		A significant market segment	60			
		Market share is insignificant	0			
5.	Characteristics of the industry	Dynamic development	100	60	0,3	18,0
		Stability	60			
		Decline	0			
	Total	-	-	-	**1,0**	**62,0**
2		**II. Financial stability**				
2.1.	Profitability	High	60	60	0,2	12,0
		Low	0			
2.2	Liquidity	High	100	100	0,5	50,0
		Low	0			
2.3	Turnover	High	100	100	0,3	30,0
		Low	0			
	Total				**1,0**	**92,0**
3		**III. The quality of the lessee's investment project**				
		Economic efficiency of the project				
3.1	NPV	<0	0	100	0,3	30,0
		>0	100			
3.2	Internal rate of return	Acceptable	100	100	0,1	10,0
		Unacceptable	0			
3.3	Payback period (discounted)	< lease term	100	100	0,3	30,0
		> lease term	0			
3.4	Solvency	Solvent	100	60	0,3	18
		Insolvent	0			
	Total	-	-	-	**1,0**	**88,0**

(continued)

Table 2: Continued

#	Name	Criteria	Norm (points)	Received (points)	Weight Coefficients	Rating Number
4	**IV. The quality of the leasing transaction**					
4.1	Liquidity of the leasing object	High	100	60	0,3	18,0
		Average	60			
		Low	0			
4.2	Security scheme	Absent	0	60	0,3	18,0
		Reliable	60			
4.3	The effectiveness of the transaction for the lessor	Acceptable	100	100	0,4	40,0
		Unacceptable	0			
	Total				**1,0**	**76,0**
5	**V. General assessment of the transaction risk level**					
5.1	Characteristics of the lessee		100,0	62,0	0,2	12,4
5.2	Financial stability		100,0	92,0	0,3	27,6
5.3	The quality of the lessee's investment project		100,0	88,0	0,2	17,6
5.4	The quality of the leasing transaction		100,0	76,0	0,3	22,8
	Total		**100,0**		**1,0**	**80,4**
6	**VI. Risk category assessment and decision-making**					
6.1	Participation is possible		100 and higher			
6.2	Participation is possible, but additional justification is required		70–100		**80,4**	
6.3	Participation is not possible		less than 50			

Source: Compiled by the authors

Thus, the proposed risk assessment system formalizes the risk management process in a leasing company, while methodically ensuring the required ratio of profitability, liquidity and risk, both within the project and across the entire portfolio as a whole, as well as the measurability of initial data, analysis methods and management results.

As the results of factor analysis have shown, its share in the gross domestic product depends on the quality of the investment climate and the level of development of leasing institutions.

A comparative analysis of trends and factor aspects of the current state of development of leasing investment in the country has revealed the following limitations, in particular: the level of capitalization of leasing companies remains insufficient (this leads to a lack of confidence in them on the part of commercial banks and other international investment and credit institutions), which limits the access of leasing companies to financial resources, inconsistency with the principles of corporate governance and IFRS (international requirements for tax accounting, statistical and accounting reporting); restriction of the participation of leasing companies in the securities market due to the underdevelopment of economic mechanisms for the acquisition of assets, as well as stimulating the investment of free funds of investors in the sphere of leasing services, which is associated with the quality of certain legislative and regulatory norms; restriction in the use of the leasing instrument only for business purposes, the absence of consumer leasing, which is widespread in international practice due to the presence of restrictions in legislation, according to which leasing cannot be used for consumer purposes; the existing regional imbalances in the functioning of the leasing market, where about 40 % of the leasing services market falls on the city of Tashkent, which limits the active use of leasing investment in technological modernization.

Based on the above, the priorities of the strategy for the development of leasing investment in Uzbekistan are substantiated, including:

- the transition from the mechanism of traditional leasing for the supply of single equipment to the concept of technological leasing by organizing complete deliveries of new equipment and the introduction of high-tech modules (for example, for processing enterprises of the agro-industrial complex), implementation of cluster leasing technologies, when equipment will be provided along the value chain, which gives a synergistic and multiplicative effect, turnkey leasing from the preparation of a business plan to staff training;
- introduction of the innovative leasing mechanism as a flexible instrument for financing innovations (at the present stage, innovative leasing is becoming one of the main forms of promoting high-tech equipment required for R&D to the market). The use of innovative leasing leads not only to an improvement in the innovative attractiveness of enterprises in the real sector of the economy, but will also contribute to the possibility of implementing such innovative types of leasing services as leasing with a full set of services (full-service leasing); the introduction of digital technologies and platform solutions aimed at automating the processes of data collection, storage, processing and transmission in all areas of leasing companies' activities, which will allow

- the use of business intelligence (BI) methods based on big data (Big Data). This will require the creation of technological and software infrastructure for data collection, storage, processing and transmission (digital "Aggregator," virtual B2B marketplace "Showroom"), including participation in data center construction projects (Figure 2).

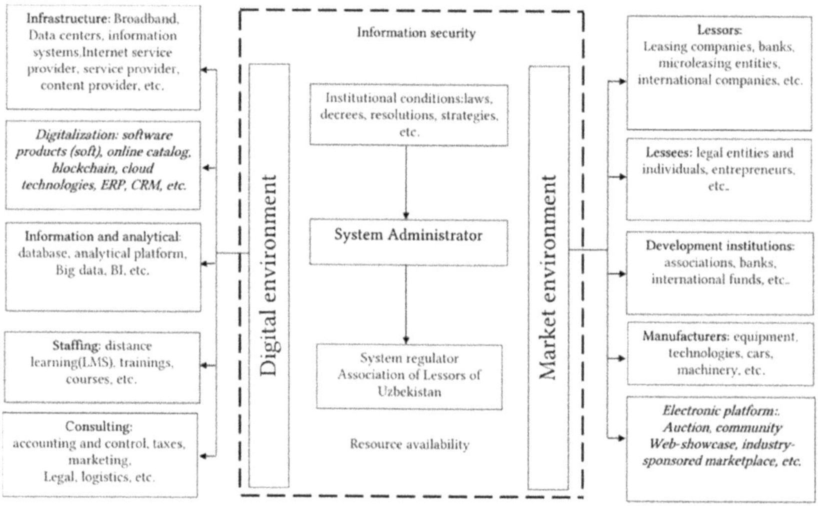

Figure 2: Digital "Aggregator" for the development of the leasing services market in the Republic of Uzbekistan

Source: Compiled by the authors

It is necessary to automate processes in all areas of companies' activities, transfer them to electronic document management, implement integrated company management systems, which will make all business processes as transparent as possible, eliminate subjectivity associated with the human factor, and use a digital "Aggregator" as a tool for the development of the leasing services market; creation of specialized (captive) leasing companies (e.g., in the automotive industry) in order to increase sales of products by increasing the purchasing power of the population in the purchase of housing, cars, household appliances, furniture and other expensive household items, as well as the institute of micro leasing (support for private and small firms, family entrepreneurship and home improvement, in particular, leasing of small equipment for processing vegetables and fruits, food, animal husbandry, sewing equipment, etc.); introduction of a mechanism for issuing and circulating securities of leasing companies, which allows to increase their resource base, as well as reduce the final cost of leasing, the use of a mechanism for accelerated depreciation of property, the development of secondary leasing of machinery and equipment, as well as improving the methodology for determining the residual value of fixed assets.

The study aims to study, analyze and evaluate the factors that affect the volume of leasing services. For this purpose, the following factors were selected: the volume of leasing services (billion soums) – Y; investments in fixed assets (billion soums) – X1; annual inflation rate (%) – X2; income of the population in monetary terms (billion soums) – X3; industrial production index, (%) – X4; volume of foreign investments, (USD million) – X5.

To build a multifactorial empirical model, all of the above factors affecting the volume of leasing services are taken and checked how they behave in the model. To predict the development of the leasing services sector, we use a linear and power law multifactorial econometric model based on the evaluation of criteria. At the same time, the least squares method is used to construct and analyze econometric models of the relationship between the development of leasing services and the factors affecting them.

Evaluating the existing model by criteria, you can see the following results, where usually the coefficient of determination takes values in the range from 0 to 1.

In this case, the coefficient of determination is 0.992, which means that the model has a fairly strong relationship between these economic indicators. Based on the EViews nine program, the following empirical model has been created:

$$y = e^{-33,855} * X_1^{0,412} * X_2^{0,744} * X_3^{0,41} * X_4^{6,153} * X_5^{0,124}$$
$$t(-3,698)\,(2,151)(3,767)(2,071)(3,219)(2,043)$$

F – the actual value of the criterion is found in the table value.
F – criteria. The value of the tabular F-criterion depends on the degree of significance of α and the degree of freedom is equal to Fcalc = 249,4738 and Ftab = 4,9646.

If the actual value is greater than the value in the table, then the constructed multivariate econometric model is called statistically significant or adequate to the studied process.

Fcalc > Ftab satisfies the condition, which is statistically significant, since the calculated value of the F-criterion is greater than its value in the table, it can be used to predict the development of the leasing services sector in future periods. This indicates the absence of autocorrelation of the residues of the effective feature of the factor. Analyzing the result of the empirical model built to predict the development of leasing services, we obtained the following result: with an increase in fixed capital investment (X1) by 1 %, the volume of leasing services (Y) increased by 0.412 %; with an increase in household income by 1 %, the volume of leasing services (Y) increased by 6.153 %; the volume of foreign investments (X5) increased by 1 %, then the volume of leasing services (Y) increased by 0.124 %.

In this direction, the remaining trend models of factors were considered, their adequacy was also constructed and verified using evaluation criteria and the most optimal models were selected, adequate regression equations were also formed, but currently, given the high demand for leasing services, as well as taking into account the changing socio-economic situation, the author offers trend models of regression equations of the third of the order (Table 3).

Table 3: Trend models of factors affecting the volume of leasing services

#	Factors	Trending Models	R^2
1.	Volume of leasing services,	$Y=2{,}4703t^3-46{,}304t^2+309{,}73t-333{,}29$	0.961
2.	Investments in fixed assets	$X1=30{,}162t^4-836{,}86t^3+7897{,}9t^2-25249t+24812$	0.992
3.	Monetary income of the population	$X3=1848{,}6t^2-10859t+26558$	0.992
4.	Industrial Production Index	$X4=0{,}0102t^3-0{,}2709t^2+1{,}7145t+107{,}28$	0.805
5.	Volume of foreign investments	$X5=2{,}2521t^3-59{,}205t^2+524{,}16t-553{,}29$	0.827

Source: Compiled by the authors

Having analyzed the multifactorial level empirical model and the dynamics of changes in influencing factors, trend models of significant factors were constructed for the implementation of forecast options for the medium-term period (2021–2027). Analysis of the results of the constructed trend model shows that $R^2 = 0{,}9606$, Fcalc = 3234,0.

Tcalc = 54,12 ($\alpha = 0.05$ that is, ttab = 2,1314, Ftab=2,4034), y = 2,4703t3 – 46,304t2 + 309,73t – 333,29.

The volume of investments in fixed assets increased by 1,458 times in 2021 compared to 2020, while in 2027 it will increase by 9,598 times.

At the same time, the volume of foreign investments is projected to increase by 1,003 times in 2021 compared to 2020, and by 3,277 times in 2027 (Figure 3).

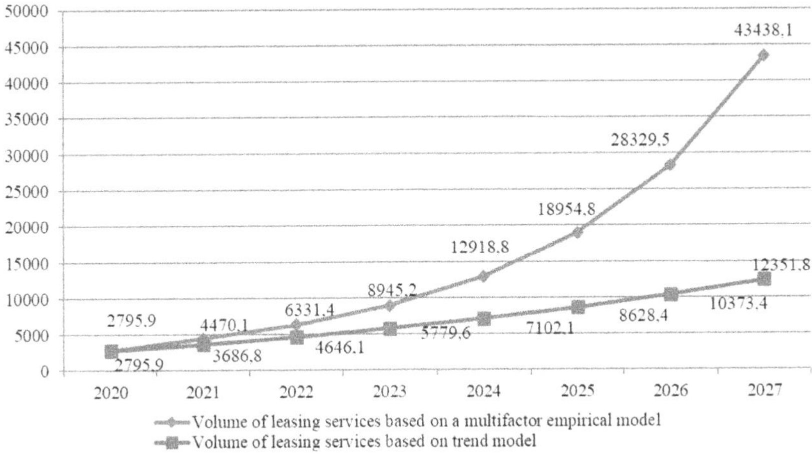

Figure 3: Forecast of the volume of leasing services, billion sum (multifactorial empirical trend model)

Source: Compiled by the authors

Based on the author's research, it can be concluded that an increase in the volume of investment in fixed assets will most of all affect the volume of leasing services, and this in turn affects the growth of the economy as a whole.

Thus, the measures taken for the development of leasing in the Republic of Uzbekistan, in our strategy, are designed to encourage all participants in leasing activities to use additional benefits and advantages more profitably for the implementation of the strategy for the development of the leasing services market.

5. Conclusion

The results of the research allow us to draw the following conclusions:

1. Based on global trends, it has been revealed that leasing is an effective tool of investment policy, plays an important role in the development of production. Due to its special economic nature, combining elements of credit, investment and financial transactions, this type of activity is able to make a real contribution to economic growth.
2. The economic category of leasing investment as an institution of development is disclosed and a comparative analysis of the concepts of leasing-lease,

leasing-loan, leasing-installment is carried out with the definition of the functions of leasing as an investment financing mechanism.

3. The factors contributing to the development of leasing relations have been identified and methodological approaches to assessing the investment attractiveness of the national economy have been studied. The methodological approach is based on factors affecting macro-, meso- and micro-levels consisting of similar indicators.
4. Approaches have been developed and improved as institutional mechanisms for regulating the development of leasing relations based on securitization of leasing assets.
5. The criteria for classification of leasing risks are recommended and the systematization of methods for ensuring the financial stability of leasing companies is carried out. The proposals on stress testing of the financial stability of the company based on the analysis of sensitivity, autonomy coefficients, liquidity, financial leverage, provision of own working capital, investment coverage, short-term debt and others are given.
6. Proposals have been prepared for the "Creation of a special fund to support leasing activities" in order to develop leasing investment in Uzbekistan;
7. The analysis of the current state of the use of leasing mechanisms in the investment process is carried out and their relationship with economic growth is revealed. As the results of the analysis of leasing activity in Uzbekistan have shown, it is most effectively implemented in the agricultural sector (25.5 %), in the light and food industries (25.1 %). Among the market segments, supplies of equipment for the engineering industries are "undervalued" (4.2 %).
8. A strategy for the development of leasing and mechanisms for stimulating leasing investment in Uzbekistan has been developed with the definition of priorities for its development directly related to the long-term socio-economic goals of the country. The ways of improving the regulatory mechanisms of state institutions in the development of the leasing services market, including macroeconomic and institutional aspects, are recommended.

References

Baikhanov, B. T. (2016). Uzbekistan is an economic republic investing in stock analysis. *"Economics and Technological Innovations" Electronic Journal of Science*. #5(5), 18–26. September-October.

Bocharov, V. V. (2018). *Investments*. St. Petersburg: Peter I-lib, 276 p.

Body, Z. (2002). *Principles of investment*. M.: Williams, 994 p.

Burman, G. (2003). *Economic analysis of investment projects*. Moscow: Banks and Exchanges, UNITY, 631 p.

Clark, T. (2005). *Leasing finance* (2nd ed.). Publisher: London, Euromoney. http://economy-lib.com/gosudarstvennoe-regulirovanie-lizingovoy-deyatelnosti#ixzz6sPPgsAI5

Contino, M. Richard (2002). *Complete equipment-leasing handbook: A deal maker's guide with forms, checklists and worksheets*. Saranac Lake, NY: AMACOM.

Davlyatova, G. M. (2011). *Improving the system of leasing relations at textile industry enterprises autoref dissertation for the degree of candidate of economics*. Tashkent: Institute of Economics of the Academy of Sciences.RUz, 24 p.

Gazibekov, D. G. (2004). *Leasing relations: Theory and practice*. Tashkent: Science and Technology, 308 p.

Gazman, V. D. (2020). *Leasing: Statistics of development*. Moscow: Higher School of Economics, 592 p.

Gitman, L. J. (1997). *Fundamentals of investing*. Moscow: Delo, 1008 p.

Golyshev, V. V. (2011). Leasing as a factor of activation of the investment policy of the Republic of Uzbekistan autoref. Disser. for the degree of Candidate of Economics – F. 24 p.

Goremykin, V. V., Marushchak, I. I., & Yakovleva, I. N. (2017). *Financial and economic mechanism of leasing relations* (vol. 2: Monograph). Moscow: Rusains.

Gubanov, S. V. (2019). Deep problems of investment processes. *Economist* (8), 60–62.

Gulyamov, S. S., Shermukhammedov, A. T., & Shermukhamedov, U. A. (2010). Leasing as a type of investment, entrepreneurial and innovative activity. In the materials of the International scientific and practical Conference "Milliy iktisodietni modernizationalash sharoitida innovation faoliyatni investyalash." November 19. Tashkent: Republican Banking and Finance Academy, pp. 347–351.

Iminova, N., Abdimuminova, S., & Mamurov, B. (2019). Risk management and insurance. *International Journal of Innovative Technology and Exploring Engineering*, 8(12), 5429–5432. https://doi.org/10.35940/ijitee.G5722.1081219.

Juha, V. M. (2021). *Leasing*. New York: Phoenix, 320 p.

Kadyrov, A., Akhmedieva, A., Bazarov, F., & Holmatjanovich Mamurov, B. (2022). Formation of information society and its influence on competitiveness of national economies in the context of world economy globalization. In *The 5th International Conference on Future Networks & Distributed Systems (ICFNDS 2021)*. New York, NY: Association for Computing Machinery, pp. 672–684. https://doi.org/10.1145/3508072.3508205

Karimov, I. (2020). Modern investment policy in the Republic of Uzbekistan. *Young Scientist. # 5* (295). January.

Keynes, J. M. (1978). *General theory of employment, interest and money.* Moscow: Progress, 444 p.

Moore, M., & Schmitz, H. (2016). *Idealism, realismand the investment climatein developing countries.* Sussex: Institute of Development Studies, p. 22.

Mustafakulov, G. I. (2017). Investment environment of the josibadorliga: Theory, medicine and operations. *Monograph. – Tashkent: Iqtisod-moliya.* – 328 b.

Otazhonov, U. (2020). Improvement of methods of assessing the investment climate of the regions of the Republic of Uzbekistan. *Tashkent State Economic University Journal* (March–April), 5489–5499. ISSN: 0193-4120.

Penchukova, T. A. (2013). Development of the system of state regulation of leasing services in Russia. *Russian Economic Online Magazine* (3), 36..

Rapport sur le contract de credit-bail (leasing). (1975). UNIDROIT. EtudeLIX – Doc. 17p.

Ruzieva, D. I. (2024). The fusion of digital technologies in small business for ensuring the socio-economic development: Panel data analysis. https://doi.org/10.54216/FPA.150106

Sabirov, O. Sh. (2020). Povishenie investisionnoy privlekatelnosti i sozdanie blagopriyatnogo investisionnogo klimata. *Scientific electron magazine "Economics and innovative technologies"* Issue # 5, September–October.

Sattarov, I. O. (2007). Formation of the leasing system in the agro-industrial complex and its improvement. T.: Research Institute of Market Reforms. *Economic Review*, (4), 70–73.

Sharp, W. (2001). *Investments*. Moscow: Infra-M, 1028 p.

Shoh-Jakhon Khamdamov, Anvar Saidmakhmudovich Usmanov, Ogiloy Abdulazizova, Fakhriddin Isaev, Nodirbek Kholbaev, Samariddin Makhmudov, & Sabina Kholbaeva. (2023). Econometric modeling of Central Bank refinancing rate in Uzbekistan. In *Proceedings of the 6th International Conference on Future Networks & Distributed Systems (ICFNDS '22).* New York, NY: Association for Computing Machinery, pp. 253–257. https://doi.org/10.1145/3584202.3584239

Shoh-Jakhon Khamdamov. (2023). *Theoretical and methodological aspects of intensive economic growth in ensuring sustainable economic development* (Social and economic studies within the framework of emerging global developments, vol. 3, pp. 283–293). Peter Lang.

Sirojiddin Abrorov & Abdulloh Ahmadjonov. (2023). Prospects for the development of the fund market through Islamic securities in the digital economy. In *Proceedings of the 6th International Conference on Future Networks &*

Distributed Systems (ICFNDS '22). New York, NY: Association for Computing Machinery, pp. 74–80. https://doi.org/10.1145/3584202.3584214

Tukhsanov, H. A. (2006). *Leasing: Recognition, evaluation and accounting* (p. 240). Tashkent: Norm.

Tykhtakhonov, I. (2020). Investment faoliyatini noananaviy moliyalashtirish manbalari ni shakllantirishning nazari asoslari. *Bank-moliya akademiyasi journal*. #4, 166 p.

World Investment Report-2021: Investing in sustainable recover. (2021). UNCTAD/WIR/2021. https://unctad.org/system/files/official-document/wir 2021_en.pdf

Zainiddinov, R. (2020). Ways to take advantage of advanced foreign experience in Uzbekistan in increasing the attractiveness of the investment environment. *Scientific Electronic Journal "Economics and innovative technologies"* (5), 9.

Dawood Ahmad, Laila Mohebi, and Fatma AlMaghribi

Effects of Social Media Usage with Academic Performance of University Students: A Comparative Study of UAE and Pakistan

1. Introduction

It has been observed that the effect of smartphones on the academic performance of students in universities is radically increasing. This research study is an effort to determine the association between social media usage (SMU) and AP of university students in the United Arab Emirates (UAE) and Pakistan from a comparative perspective. In this case, the significance of the undertaken study is more directly related to the academic achievement (AA) of students at UAE and Pakistani universities. Therefore, the researchers examine various consequences of the use of smartphones on young people in the UAE and Pakistan. This is due to the fact that Arabs generally regard Emiratis to be early adopters and trendsetters. Concerns about the effects of excessive smartphone usage among UAE youth are among the many issues raised by the rising number of smartphone users among Emiratis.

Focusing on the demographic of university students, the onset of 2023 saw the UAE boasting 19.05 million mobile connections, as reported by Groupe Special Mobile Association (GSMA) Intelligence. The same source indicated that mobile connections in the UAE surpassed the population count by 200.9 % in January 2023. Meanwhile, Pakistan recorded 191.8 million active mobile connections early in the year, covering 80.5 % of its populace. A study by Ahmed et al. (2019) revealed that a significant 60 % of Pakistani youths are categorized as intensive smartphone users.

The COVID-19 pandemic has profoundly impacted the educational landscape worldwide, with issues such as student dropouts, diminished retention, compromised educational performance, and increased academic procrastination becoming increasingly prevalent. This scenario persists despite the flexible and beneficial learning modes introduced (Baccal & Ormilla, 2021; Cerezo et al., 2017), which seemingly absolve students from taking full responsibility for their educational progress. The digital era compels students towards internet dependence for information gathering, although distractions, notably social media, often lead to neglect of academic duties. The allure of social media, if unchecked, adversely affects students' time management skills – crucial for maintaining academic focus. Amidst the educational adjustments during the pandemic, unchecked social media engagement has the potential to significantly delay academic tasks, paving the way for academic procrastination, as observed by Anierobi et al. (2021).

Numerous investigations have established a connection between procrastination and negative emotions, including anxiety, inability to self-regulate, and diminished self-confidence. A significant body of this research highlights the detrimental effects of academic procrastination on students' scholastic performance, particularly among adolescents (Alih & Alvarez, 2021). Academic procrastination is characterized by delaying or avoiding schoolwork without valid reasons, leading students away from their educational responsibilities. Ipem and Okwara-Kalu (2020) suggest that an overindulgence in social media is a major factor contributing to students neglecting their academic duties, as it occupies time that could be spent on school assignments.

1.1. Social Media Addiction (SMA)

The issue of social media addiction (SMA) is increasingly affecting students, as highlighted in recent findings (Marengo et al., 2022). Social media, while offering significant advantages such as facilitating the easy dissemination of knowledge and promoting collaborative study among college attendees (Adjin-Tettey et al., 2022), also accelerates the distribution of educational content, potentially enhancing learning efficiency when utilized correctly (Adjin-Tettey et al., 2022; Uzochukwu & Anierobi, 2020). Earlier investigations have underscored the positive influence of social media and internet usage on students' academic results and their social well-being.

Conversely, an overuse of social media among students has been identified to negatively affect various aspects of their life (Brailovskaia et al., 2021). Research indicates that excessive social media usage (SMU) adversely affects students' academic performance (AP), health, social interactions, and overall well-being (Alaika et al., 2020). Furthermore, Haand and Shuwang (2020) noted that SMU could contribute to unhealthy eating patterns, sleep disturbances, cognitive fatigue, depression, and a decline in AP. Students also reported struggling to manage their time effectively between social media and academic commitments.

Moreover, internet addiction has been associated with a tendency among students to procrastinate on academic tasks (Nwosu et al., 2020). Research conducted by Hayat et al. (2020) revealed a strong link between internet addiction and academic procrastination in medical students at Shiraz University. Üztemur

(2020) found that while there is a positive relationship between SMU and academic procrastination, there exists a negative correlation between SMU and academic success.

1.2. Academic Achievement (AA)

An excellent education leads to academic success, which is still essential for the growth of both learners and society. According to Crede et al. (2015), academic achievement (AA) is determined by the General Average (GA) that is shown on students' most recent report cards. Using the grades earned in each course during that quarter as a basis, the grades were totaled and averaged as indicators of academic proficiency. According to earlier research, academic procrastination is typically linked to poor AA (Karataş, 2015). Previous studies have found a strong negative correlation between students' reports of procrastination and their AA. Students that delay more often receive poorer grades and are less motivated to succeed (Karataş, 2015).

Additionally, a number of studies have shown a connection between students' use of social media and their AA (Yildiz Durak et al., 2022). According to a study by Cao and Tian (2020), educational institutions may use social media to improve communication create a love of learning, and motivate students to learn. Additionally, it has a favorable correlation with students' academic progress (Al-Rahmi et al., 2018). However, research conducted by Rashid and Asghar (2016) contends that SMA is unrelated to AA. Thus, the study's main focus is on how academic procrastination affects the relationship between SMA and academic accomplishment. This insight could serve as a valuable foundation for both students and educators to devise effective strategies for optimizing social media usage within university settings, ultimately enhancing student learning and boosting academic outcomes.

2. Literature Review

2.1. Time Students Spend on Social Media

Multiple studies have repeatedly focused on how much time students spend on social media to understand how this affects their AP and overall well-being. The length of time students spend using mobile social media platforms is discussed in the study by Giunchiglia et al. (2018), offering a useful lens on how these temporal engagements may be related to academic outcomes. The results imply this connection between time and AA, pointing to a complex relationship in which spending more time on social media may be equivalent to less academic involvement or the opposite. In addition, Alwagait et al. (2015) study, which concentrated on students in Saudi Arabia, also addressed this aspect. Their research sheds light on students' SMU patterns in frequency and length, as well as potential effects on AA.

The Saudi Arabian environment gives the discussion of time spent on these platforms a special cultural perspective. Lau (2017) also offered a unique viewpoint by highlighting the quantity of time spent on social media and its nature, specifically, multitasking. Balancing social media contacts with academic work can reveal more about how students spend their time and the possible effects of such multitasking activities. The different social media platforms and the variable amounts of time children might spend on each are other aspects to consider.

Maqableh et al. (2015) examined various social media networks and their individual effects to address this. Even though the study's primary focus was on how these platforms affected students' academic results, the underlying subject of time allocation across numerous platforms is still relevant. In their study, Boahene et al. (2019) discussed academic self-efficacy in social media use.

Social media time is compared to students' self-confidence in completing academic tasks. Such a viewpoint can provide insightful information into how extended use of social media may be associated with decreased academic efficacy or confidence. In their study of students in Terengganu, Malaysia, Othman et al. (2017) provided insight into SMU habits. The temporal characteristics of how students used social media platforms remain an integral feature of the study even though its direct impact on AP is being measured.

2.2. Social Media Usage and Academic Performance

SMU and AA research have revealed potential interactions between these variables. Giunchiglia et al. (2018) investigated the relationship between mobile social media use and academic results. Their findings imply that there may be a potential link between students' frequent use of mobile social media and their AA. These results align with those of Hasnain et al. (2015), who examined the effects of social media on university students' AP in a study presented at the 2nd International Research Management and Innovation Conference. Their findings emphasized the worries about the potential negative impact of excessive social media use on academic results.

Furthermore, the geographical setting doesn't lessen the significance of this association. For instance, a study by Alwagait et al. (2015) that looked specifically at Saudi Arabian students revealed that social media use affected students' academic results.

These conclusions are consistent with those made by Al-Rahmi and Othman (2013), who raised comparable issues about university students' AP and SMU in their pilot study. The study by Mingle et al. (2016) evaluated the SMU and AA of students in senior high schools that were both public and private, bringing another layer to the discussion by raising the possibility that there might be differences depending on the type of institution.

Another factor that has been considered is gender. An informative examination of gender differences in SMU and AP among University of Sharjah students was offered by Alnjadat et al. (2019). Their research focused on the subtle gender inequalities that might exist, which is important for understanding the broader effects of social media on academic outcomes. In addition, the study by Lau (2017) focused on the impact of social media multitasking and SMU on AP. Such multitasking tendencies might worsen social media's detrimental effects on AA. Maqableh et al. (2015) provided a thorough analysis of various platforms and their potential repercussions in their discussion of the impact of social media networks on students' AP.

The narrative was supported by Bhandarkar et al. (2021), who focused on the effects of social media on AP in specialized educational domains in their research of undergraduate medical students.

2.3. Time Spent on Social Media by UAE Students

Several studies have shed light on UAE students' time spent on social media. In their research, Alnjadat et al. (2019) specifically addressed gender variations in SMU among students at the University of Sharjah. While the primary focus was on understanding gender differences, their findings can be instrumental in quantifying the average time students in the UAE allocate to various social media platforms. Additionally, Cao and Tian (2020) conducted a comprehensive analysis of social media use and its repercussions on university students in the UAE. Their work can be pivotal in offering nuanced data about the temporal aspects of SMU among the Emirati student population.

2.4. Academic Performance (AP) of UAE Students

The AP of UAE students in the context of SMU has been a topic of interest in recent years. Badri et al. (2017) explored the relationship between social networking effects and school performance. Their research, conducted in Abu Dhabi, provides a deep understanding of the academic outcomes of school children about their online habits. Furthermore, the study by Azizur Rahman et al. (2020), presented at the 2020 IEEE 44th Annual Computers, Software, and

Applications Conference, evaluated the effects of SMU on health and AP among students at the University of Sharjah. By drawing correlations between health and academic metrics, this research can be crucial in gauging the AP of UAE students in a broader context.

2.5. Correlation between Social Media Usage (SMU) and the Academic Performance (AP) of UAE Students

Several studies provide insights into the interplay between SMU and AP among UAE students. In their research, Cao and Tian (2020) delved into how social media use might influence the academic outcomes of university students in the UAE. Their findings can offer a foundational understanding of the correlation between these two variables.

Similarly, Alghizzawi et al. (2019) concentrated on the impact of SMU on students' e-learning acceptance in higher education (HE), specifically in the UAE. Their work touches upon the indirect effects of social media on AP, especially in an e-learning environment. This research adds another layer to the discourse, emphasizing the evolving educational dynamics in the UAE and how they intersect with students' online habits.

2.6. Time Spent on Social Media Usage (SMU) by Pakistani Students

Several research endeavors provide insights into Pakistani students' frequency and duration of SMU. For instance, Waqas et al. (2016) explored the impact of social networking sites on the academic outcomes of university students in Lahore. While their primary emphasis might be on outcomes, the nature of their investigation could also offer data regarding the amount of time students dedicate to such platforms. Similarly, Arif and Kanwal (2016) assessed the adoption of social media technologies and their subsequent influence on students' AA. Their study could provide an insight into the digital habits of distance education students in Pakistan, including the time they spend online.

2.7. Academic Performance (AP) of Pakistani Students

The AP of Pakistani students vis-à-vis their social media habits has garnered attention from various researchers. (Hasnain et al., 2015), in their study presented at the IRMIC, specifically scrutinized the repercussions of social media use on the academic results of university students. Their findings can be instrumental in gauging the academic metrics of Pakistani students. Another study by Kausar and Awan (2019) delved into the ramifications of social media use on the AA of graduate students in Pakistan. Their research can add another dimension to understanding the academic landscape of Pakistani tertiary education institutions.

2.8. Correlation between Social Media Usage (SMU) and the Academic Performance (AP) of Pakistani Students

Several studies provide evidence regarding the relationship between SMU and AP among Pakistani students. For instance, Waqas et al. (2016) analyzed the potential impacts of social networking sites on university students' AP in Lahore, illuminating possible correlations. Similarly, Shakoor et al. (2021) examined the influence of smartphone usage on learning behavior and academic outcomes. Their findings can highlight the nuances of how technology, especially smartphones, interplays with the AA of students in Pakistan.

2.9. Correlation between Social Media Usage (SMU) and the Academic Performance (AP) of UAE and Pakistani Students

While the mentioned studies provide insights into SMU and AP within their respective countries, drawing correlations between UAE and Pakistani students would require a comparative analysis of findings from the studies conducted in both regions. One is to analyze datasets from studies like those by Cao and Tian (2020) (for UAE students) and Waqas et al. (2016) (for Pakistani students) to discern overarching trends or disparities. This could then formulate an informed understanding of the relationship between SMU and AP in the two distinct populations.

3. Theoretical Framework

The research model for this study (Figure 1), which is based on the aforementioned literature analysis, examines a number of variables, including SMU, AP, and university students (US). These elements are thought to have an impact on how well college students succeed academically. This model also takes into account all facets of students' AP, as well as their SMU.

Figure 1: Conceptual model including social media usage and academic performance of students was added as a result of the review of literature

The current study intends to investigate how students use social media (SM), taking into account contextual elements related to SMU. The primary drivers of time spent and related specific activities on social media are retained by social media use, along with information and usage of mobile phones and related applications.

In contrast, the connection between SMU and AP among students is significant because of its significance for assessing students' AP. It was interesting to see that students actually used social media for learning and teaching purposes. Therefore, sharing of resources, expertise, and information is crucial for SMU and students' academic success and pleasure in HE.

This study investigates how social media affects students' perceptions of using social media and their satisfaction with their education. The results of the study would help HE institutions' educators and policy makers improve and create more effective plans. In the future, social networks will be used as tools for education. In order to answer the question of how users accept and use social media, specifically students' intentions towards SMU and their AP, SMU and AP were adopted as the fundamental study framework.

The results of the current study should also provide complementary and comparative data for studies on the views of social networking platform adoption in emerging nations. Students believed that their teachers may encourage Facebook usage in which both teachers and students became socialized, according to research on the effect of social media on student achievement (Chakraborty, 2020). The development of positive interactions between students and teachers/lecturers also helped students' AP (Al-Maatouk, 2020).

3.1. Social Cognitive Theory

Social cognitive theory is known as a systematic theory that involves perceiving people's interaction and reaction toward the environment or other people around them. It helps to understand the social environment dynamic more accurately, and how widely a person can learn and behave accordingly. Social cognitive theory has frequently been employed recently by various researchers to explore the outcomes and results of any cognitive processes.

Santrock (2009) explained Bandura's social cognitive theory which emphasizes the symbiotic relationship in Figure 2 between the three factors: behavior, environment, and person or the cognitive aspect. In the current research paper, the researchers, we focus and discuss the impact of social media on the behavior, cognition, and academic self-efficacy of the students from the perspective of the social cognitive framework.

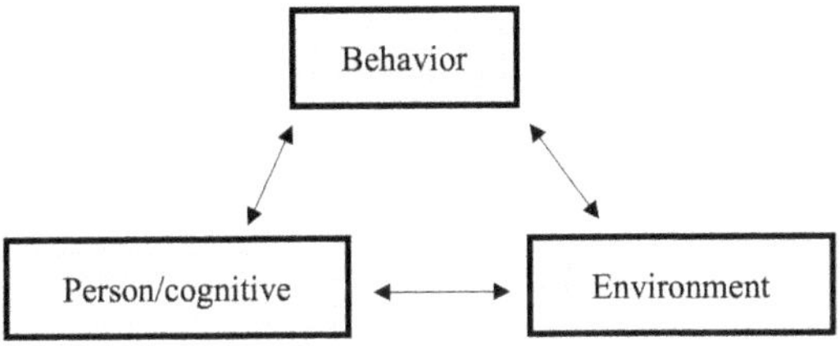

Figure 2: Symbiotic relationship

Currently, social media plays a massive role in the daily routine of people, as well as the academic aspect. It connects the students with the social system and networking that requires distinctive driving forces and importantly continues the necessitated change in any person, whether this is his behavior, skills or self-efficacy. In the figure, it shows the perceptions on the achievement of the students while using social media, whether it's affected negatively or positively. Unidirectional causality is a term that is commonly used to define human behavior, where behavior is formed and regulated by inner or external factors.

Based on Fonagy's (2018) description, personal aspects such as mental, social, and natural occurrences, private behavior standards, and environmental changes are shaping variables that are mutually influencing one another. Therefore, if the students were to get influenced positively by the SMU, a positive environment will lead to a positive outcome in the academic self-efficacy and the behavior, and vice versa if the influence were to be negative.

Although social media offers a variety of benefits for students to gain different knowledge and foster collaborative learning as mentioned in the introduction of this paper, however, the increasing issue of SMA was revealed as notably prevalent among students. Consequently, several earlier studies revealed that social media and internet usage can have both positive and negative impact on students' learning outcomes and social well-being.

As this has been the topic of interest in recent years, it could also be seen from the social cognitive aspect in order to connect all the related factors together, such as the relationship between the social and AP, or cognition and skills abilities. For instance, in research that was conducted in Abu Dhabi by Badri et al. (2017), where the relationship between social networking effects and school performance was investigated, the outcomes of this research provide a deep understanding about the online habits of school children.

With regard to the above, the behavior which is categorized under the social cognitive theory has a tendency to distinguish the relative causality between different elements in the factors that determine students' self-efficacy, skills, and performance. Social cognitive theory believes that it is possible for social media to play a significant role in the formation of self-efficacy and the perception of social norms. A recent study showed that students themselves get engaged with other people on social media to widen their social interaction and communication to help in their assignment and resources or other educational materials (Oguguo et al., 2020). In addition, the performance of students at universities can be influenced by their self-efficacy and perceived social norms as they spend an average of two to four hours daily on social media.

Students often grasp the nuances of reality by engaging in interactions within their surroundings, achieving their objectives through the use of social media to connect with peers, instructors, or access learning materials. Unlike the traditional model of computer-based learning, which is perceived as somewhat limited to imparting knowledge, skills, and abilities, the contemporary digital era has seen a shift towards valuing social interactions, thereby enriching the learning experience. Vygotsky (1987) posited that learning is inherently a social endeavor, with academic self-efficacy and development being fostered through diverse interactive activities, even those extending beyond the immediate educational circle through social media platforms.

The importance of social interaction in the learning and developmental process has been echoed by psychologists like Bandura, Piaget, and Vygotsky, highlighting it as a pivotal aspect of educational psychology. The desire for knowledge in today's digitally inclined students is fueled by the potential for social engagement, suggesting that computer-based learning environments could benefit from integrating features that facilitate meaningful social interactions (Kim & Baylor, 2006).

Perkins (2001) emphasized the dynamic nature of academic engagement, where students interact with each other, as well as with various tools and contexts, thereby enhancing their performance and influencing cognitive patterns. Thus, overlooking the social-cognitive aspects of learning could hinder the effectiveness of educational interventions; hence, the design of computer-based learning environments should support social-cognitive interactions.

This paper adopts a social cognitive framework to explore the dual impact of social media on students' academic performance (AP), advocating for a nuanced perspective that recognizes both its challenges and benefits. By promoting a positive outlook towards social media use among university students and guiding them in leveraging social interactions and educational content, this approach aims to positively affect their cognitive and emotional development. The findings underscore the value of social cognitive theories not only as an analytical lens but also as a practical guide for enhancing students' academic self-efficacy.

3.2. Research Objectives

1. To calculate the time spent on social media usage by different age group students
2. To know the students activities while using social media
3. To find out social media usage trends among students
4. To explore the role of social media in academic performance of students
5. To calculate social media usage by students of UAE and Pakistan

4. Methodology

4.1. Research Design

The survey approach was employed with the aim of providing answers to the objectives posed above and to gather data regarding the impact of university students' use of social media on their AP. The survey method was chosen because it provides the best opportunity to compile more detailed responses (Creswell, 1994). The poll was simultaneously conducted in two institutions in the UAE and Pakistan. A Google Docs questionnaire was created online. Every survey was carried out in October of the year it was reported. Via the WhatsApp groups at their university, the students received a link to the questionnaire. Students who did not engage in the poll received reminders through their WhatsApp groups. There was no sampling of the staff or professors at any university.

4.2. Population

Students from Zayed University in the UAE and The University of Faisalabad in Pakistan participated in the research in 2023. All enrolled students were encouraged to take part in the study over a three-week period by personal visits to the classes and through student-run WhatsApp groups. The researchers received 273 replies to the survey. Gender-wise, there were 115 male respondents, 157 female respondents, and 1 participant who preferred not to reveal their gender. There were 127 Pakistani respondents and 146 UAE respondents.

4.3. Data Collection Instrument

To better measure how students use SMU, the researchers designed the Social Media Usage Questionnaire, a data gathering tool based on professional experiences and literature reviews. In addition to content validity, the questionnaire's construct validity was improved by having two subject-matter experts evaluate each item. The questionnaire asks demographic details like gender and age. Additionally, it includes metrics about SMU usage, like time spent on social media. To determine if the questions raised the same answers at the two periods in time, the questionnaire about the thoughts of the students was given again a month later.

The pilot testing included 33 items and a Cronbach Alpha of 0.959 gave confidence that the questionnaire was dependable despite its repeated administration. The main purpose of the survey questions was to ascertain why university students were using social media. There are 33 survey questions, some of which are selected response questions. The questionnaire is divided into three main sections: (1) student time spent on social media; (2) student activities related to SMU; (3) student search trends related to SMU and (4) the impact of SMU on students' AA as well as SMU by students from each competing nation.

4.4. Data Analysis

The demographic features of the sample were illustrated using descriptive and inferential statistics, and regression analyzes were carried out to answer the study objectives.

5. Results

5.1. Demographic Information

Descriptive statistics and demographic information are used to report the findings. A total of 273 people in all responded to the study, with 146 responders from the UAE and 127 from Pakistan. However, 115 male and 157 female students took part in the study. Table 1 shows the student population's percentages by gender, age, education, nationality and SMU respectively.

Table 1: Demographic and other information

Variable	Frequency	Percentage
Gender		
Male	115	42.1
Female	157	57.5
Prefer not to say	1	0.4

Table 1: Continued

Variable	Frequency	Percentage
Age		
Below 20	95	34.8
Between 20 and 25	89	32.6
Between 25 and 30	49	17.9
Between 35 and 40	26	9.5
Above 41	14	5.1
Education		
High school diploma or equivalent	65	23.8
Diploma degree	10	3.7
Bachelor's degree	117	42.9
Master's degree	71	26
Doctoral degree (PhD or equivalent)	10	3.7
Nationality		
Pakistan	127	46.5
UAE	146	53.5
SMU Daily Usage		
Less than 1 hour	15	5.5
1–2 hours	59	21.6
3–4 hours	102	37.4
5–6 hours	58	21.2
More than 6 hours	39	

Table 1 shows that 57.5 % of the study participants were female students and 42.1 % were male students. A total of 32.6 % of the students were between 20 and 25 years old and the highest percentage (42.9 %) of students reported having a bachelor's degree.

It is also evident that 46.5 % of the students were from Pakistan and 53.5 % of the students were from the UAE. It was also reported that 37.4 % of the students were using social media between 3 and 4 hours daily which was observed as the maximum time with 5.5 % reporting a minimum time of under one hour spent on social media.

Table 2 shows a significant relationship between SMU and the age of the respondents. The R square value is 0.123 whereas the adjusted R square is 0.119. It shows significant association between SMU and age.

Table 2: Association of SMU with age

Model Summary				
Model	**R Square**	**Adjusted R Square**	**Std. Error of the Estimate**	
1	0.123	0.119	1.363	
Model Significance ANOVA*				
Model	**Sum of Squares**	**df**	**Mean Square**	**Sig.**
1	70.316	1	70.316	.000**
	503.317	271	1.857	
	573.634	272		

Predictors: (Constant), SMU age *Dependent Variable: SMU daily **Predictors: (Constant), age.

Table 3 reflects a significant relationship between students' activities and SMU. The R square value is 0.042 whereas the adjusted R square is 0.038. It shows significant association between students' activities and SMU.

Table 3: Students' activities and SMU

Model Summary				
Model	**R Square**	**Adjusted R Square**	**Std. Error of the Estimate**	
1	0.042	0.038	1.072	
Model Significance ANOVA*				
Model	**Sum of Squares**	**df**	**Mean Square**	**Sig.**
1	13.597	1	13.597	.001**
	311.312	271	1.149	
	324.908	272		

Predictors: (Constant), Students activities. *Dependent Variable: SMU daily **Predictors: (Constant), students' activities.

Table 4 reflects a significant relationship between social media trends and daily usage of social media by the students. The R square value is 0.029 whereas the adjusted R square is 0.026. It shows significant association between social media trends and daily usage of social media by the students.

Table 4: SMU search trends among students

		Model Summary		
Model	**R Square**	**Adjusted R Square**	**Std. Error of the Estimate**	
1	0.029	0.026	1.079	
		Model Significance ANOVA*		
Model	**Sum of Squares**	**df**	**Mean Square**	**Sig.**
1	9.503	1	9.503	.005**
	315.406	271	1.164	
	324.908	272		

Predictors: (Constant), SMU search trends among students. *Dependent Variable: SMU daily **Predictors: (Constant), SMU search trends among students.

Table 5 reflects a significant relationship between social media trends and academic performance of students. The R square value is 0.016 whereas the adjusted R square is 0.012. It shows significant association between "Role of SMU towards AP of Students."

Table 5: Role of SMU towards AP of students

		Model Summary		
Model	**R Square**	**Adjusted R Square**	**Std. Error of the Estimate**	
1	0.016	0.012	1.086	
		Model Significance ANOVA*		
Model	**Sum of Squares**	**df**	**Mean Square**	**Sig.**
1	5.126	1	5.126	.038**
	319.782	271	1.18	
	324.908	272		

Predictors: (Constant), role of SMU. *Dependent Variable: AP of students **Predictors: (Constant), role of SMU.

Table 6 shows a significant relationship between Association of Nationality with SMU. It shows significant association between Nationality with SMU.

Table 6: Association of nationality with SMU

		Model Summary			
Model	**R**	**R Square**	**Adjusted R Square**		**Std. Error of the Estimate**
1	0.188[a]	0.035	0.032		0.492
		Model Significance ANOVA*			
Model	**Sum of Squares**	**df**	**Mean Square**		**Sig.**
Regression	2.390	1	2.390	9.883	0.002**
Residual	65.530	271	0.242		
Total	67.919	272			

Predictors: (Constant), SMU daily. *Dependent Variable: Nationality **Predictors: (Constant), SMU daily.

6. Discussion

This study investigated whether social media use in the classroom has evolved over time. The study's overall findings showed that there have been substantial, beneficial changes in the way that social media has been used throughout time. The results align with the research conducted by Archambault and Grudin (2012), which indicates that there are variations in the rise of Facebook usage depending on factors such as gender, age, purpose of use, and educational attainment. It was observed that students' usage of social media has varied throughout time; for example, they tended to use it more when they were by themselves.

Since the majority of students in the 2013 survey accessed social media via smartphones, the location from where they previously connected to social media has also changed dramatically (Arteaga Sánchez et al., 2014). This has allowed the students to access social media more frequently. For instance, academic procrastination often manifests when students become engrossed in social media, leading to delays in fulfilling their academic responsibilities. Ipem and Okwara-Kalu (2020) argue that the substantial time students dedicate to social media platforms detracts from their focus on academic work.

According to Elsayed (2015), Karakose et al. (2022), López-Carril et al. (2021), Rasheed et al. (2020), and others, students in educational settings may utilize social media for a range of reasons, including knowledge discovery, collaboration, and social engagement. The usage of social media and undergraduate university students' academic performance and accomplishment have been linked in a number of researches (Al-Maatouk, 2020; Alnjadat et al., 2019; Al-Rahmi et al., 2020). According to studies (Al-Qaysi et al., 2019; Vandeyar, 2020), social media tools enhance learning by promoting social and collaborative learning.

Therefore, in order to support their research training and educational projects, graduate research students are using a range of social networking platforms (such as Facebook, Twitter, LinkedIn, and TikTok). In addition, the use of social media has the potential to increase cross-user information sharing (Ahmed et al., 2019; Almaiah & Al Mulhem, 2018).

According to Al Mansoori et al. (2023), using VR goggles in the LMS helps students visualize their creativity, have powerful experiences, and enjoy arenas that visualize abstract ideas. These benefits even extend to improving students' critical thinking skills and morale in a formal learning environment. Usability, perceived simplicity of use, and usefulness are the main criteria that encourage students to utilize the Microsoft Teams application. According to Habes et al. (2023) they are able to complete their education through digital methods since they rely so much on the Microsoft Teams tool.

According to Salloum et al. (2021) perceived ease of use (PEOU) and perceived usefulness (PU) are positively impacted by information sharing, motivation and uses, and social media elements. As Salloum et al. (2019) concludes that social media behaviors including knowledge sharing, social media features, motivation, and usage have a major beneficial influence on perceived utility (PU) and perceived ease of use (PEOU). According to Habes et al. (2019), social media use, perceived usefulness, social bookmarking, and YouTube features are significant predictors of students' academic achievement when it comes to utilizing social media for e-learning in Jordan.

6.1. Limitations of the Study and Future Work

As the study was conducted in Pakistan and UAE, therefore the responses were from these two countries' residents. To get a broader scope of similar research should be conducted involving other Middle Eastern countries in future so that we may know more about the authenticity of this research.

7. Conclusion and Policy Recommendations

This study is among the first to be recorded that looked at SMU changes in terms of education. Overall, the findings demonstrated how SMU has evolved in a more favorable and consistent manner throughout time. Between 2009 and 2013, there was a steady increase in the use of social media for education among university students. In other words, SMU can serve as a hub for HE by fostering relationships between teachers and students outside of the traditional classroom setting. It is possible that the rapid and extensive use of SMU in other disciplines was influenced by its growing acceptance and popularity in the education sector.

When social media first came about, the community thought of it as a platform for socializing, meeting people, and passing the time. Most institutions now have distinct social media offices in order to gain a competitive edge and attract more students. In the past, certain nations, organizations, and universities barred or restricted access during academic working hours.

Since social media is currently the most effective tool for commerce, education, advertising, and mass communication at free cost, users have explicitly learned to respect it as society has come to understand its true potential. Seeing SMU's potential in educational settings is insufficient. Developing understanding of how to harness its true power purposefully in order to reap its true benefits should be the true mission. It is concluded that social media can be a valuable tool to support university students' learning and for their academic success. However, it is important for students to be mindful of their social media usage and to avoid excessive use for non-educational purposes.

Another important policy implication according the findings of this study is that the usage of social media according to age and gender varies. We need to bring awareness among the youth about the positive usage of social media so that they may gain maximum benefit of it. As students age is very crucial for the usage of social media to get advantage of it, in this regard counseling and proper guidance sessions should be arranged in the universities.

7.1. Funding

This research study did not receive any funding.

7.2. Ethical Approval

The research project obtained ethical approval from Zayed University with reference ZU23_056_F OCT23 and from The University of Faisalabad with reference Tuf/gRB/252/23. the researchers deeply appreciate the support extended by various departments throughout the data collection process. Furthermore, the researchers secured clearance as indicated by the reference letter.

7.3. Declarations Conflict of Interest

There were no disclosed potential conflicts of interest.

References

Adjin-Tettey, T. D., Selormey, D., & Nkansah, H. A. (2022). Ubiquitous Technologies and Learning. *International Journal of Information and Communication Technology Education, 18*(1), 1–16. https://doi.org/10.4018/ijicte.286758

Ahmed, R. R., Streimikiene, D., Berchtold, G., Vveinhardt, J., Channar, Z. A., & Soomro, R. H. (2019). Effectiveness of Online Digital Media Advertising as a Strategic Tool for Building Brand Sustainability: Evidence from FMCGs and Services Sectors of Pakistan. *Sustainability, 11*(12), 3436. https://doi.org/10.3390/su11123436

Al Mansoori, A., Ali, S., Pasha, S. A., Alghizzawi, M., Elareshi, M., Ziani, A., & Alsridi, H. (2023). Technology Enhanced Learning through Learning Management System and Virtual Reality Googles: A Critical Review. *Studies in Systems, Decision and Control*, 557–564. https://doi.org/10.1007/978-3-031-28314-7_48

Alaika, O., Doghmi, N., & Cherti, M. (2020). Social Media Addiction among Moroccan University Students: A Cross Sectional Survey. *PAMJ – One Health, 1*. https://doi.org/10.11604/pamj-oh.2020.1.4.21930

Alghizzawi, M., Habes, M., Salloum, S. A., Ghani, M. A., Mhamdi, C., & Shaalan, K. (2019). The Effect of Social Media Usage on Students' E-Learning Acceptance in Higher Education: A Case Study from the United Arab Emirates. *International Journal of Information Technology and Language Studies, 3*(3), Article 3.

Alih, N.-I. I., & Alvarez, A. L. (2021). Academic Procrastination: Its Effect on The Learning Productivity of Senior High School Students in Mindanao State University-Sulu. *Indonesian Community Empowerment Journal, 1*(2), 77–89. https://doi.org/10.37275/icejournal.v1i2.10

Al-Maatouk, Q. (2020). Applying Communication Theory to Structure and Evaluate the Social Media Platforms in Academia. *International Journal of Advanced Trends in Computer Science and Engineering, 9*(2), 1505–1517. https://doi.org/10.30534/ijatcse/2020/92922020

Almaiah, M. A., & Al Mulhem, A. (2018). Analysis of the Essential Factors Affecting of Intention to Use of Mobile Learning Applications: A Comparison between Universities Adopters and Non-adopters. *Education and Information Technologies, 24*(2), 1433–1468. https://doi.org/10.1007/s10639-018-9840-1

Alnjadat, R., Hmaidi, M. M., Samha, T. E., Kilani, M. M., & Hasswan, A. M. (2019). Gender Variations in Social Media Usage and Academic Performance Among the Students of University of Sharjah. *Journal of Taibah University Medical Sciences, 14*(4), 390–394. PubMed. https://doi.org/10.1016/j.jtumed.2019.05.002

Al-Qaysi, N., Mohamad-Nordin, N., Al-Emran, M., & Al-Sharafi, M. A. (2019). Understanding the Differences in Students' Attitudes Towards Social Media Use: A Case Study from Oman. *2019 IEEE Student Conference on Research and Development (SCOReD)*, 176–179. https://doi.org/10.1109/SCORED.2019.8896251

Al-Rahmi, A. M., Shamsuddin, A., & Alismaiel, O. A. (2020). Task-Technology Fit Model: The Factors Affecting Students' Academic Performance in Higher Education. *Universal Journal of Educational Research*, *8*(12), 6831–6843. https://doi.org/10.13189/ujer.2020.081249

Al-Rahmi, W. M., Alias, N., Othman, M. S., Marin, V. I., & Tur, G. (2018). A Model of Factors Affecting Learning Performance through the Use of Social Media in Malaysian Higher Education. *Computers & Education*, *121*, 59–72. https://doi.org/10.1016/j.compedu.2018.02.010

Al-Rahmi, W., & Othman, M. (2013). The Impact of Social Media Use on Academic Performance among University Students: A Pilot Study. *Journal of Information Systems Research and Innovation*, *4*(12), 1–10.

Alwagait, E., Shahzad, B., & Alim, S. (2015). Impact of Social Media Usage on Students Academic Performance in Saudi Arabia. *Computers in Human Behavior*, *51*, 1092–1097. https://doi.org/10.1016/j.chb.2014.09.028

Anierobi, E. I., Etodike, C. E., Okeke, N. U., & Ezennaka, A. O. (2021). Social Media Addiction as Correlates of Academic Procrastination and Achievement among Undergraduates of Nnamdi Azikiwe University Awka, Nigeria. *International Journal of Academic Research in Progressive Education and Development*, *10*(3). https://doi.org/10.6007/ijarped/v10-i3/10709

Archambault, A., & Grudin, J. (2012). A Longitudinal Study of Facebook, LinkedIn, & Twitter Use. *Proceedings of the SIGCHI Conference on Human Factors in Computing Systems*, 2741–2750. https://doi.org/10.1145/2207676.2208671

Arif, M., & Kanwal, S. (2016). Adoption of Social Media Technologies and Their Impact on Students' Academic Performance: The only Way for Future Survival of Distance Education Students in Pakistan. *Pakistan Journal of Information Management and Libraries*, *18*(1), 25–36. https://doi.org/10.47657/2016181947

Arteaga Sánchez, R., Cortijo, V., & Javed, U. (2014). Students' Perceptions of Facebook for Academic Purposes. *Computers & Education*, *70*, 138–149. https://doi.org/10.1016/j.compedu.2013.08.012

Azizur Rahman, S., Al Marzouqi, A., Variyath, S., Rahman, S., Rabbani, M., & Iqbal Ahamed, S. (2020). *Effects of Social Media Use on Health and Academic Performance Among Students at the University of Sharjah*. 711–716. https://doi.org/10.1109/compsac48688.2020.0-176

Baccal, V. S., & Ormilla, R. C. G. (2021). The Implementation of Alternative Learning System in Public Schools in Isabela, Philippines. *EDUCATUM Journal of Social Sciences*, *7*(1), 19–29. https://doi.org/10.37134/ejoss.vol7.1.3.2021

Badri, M., Nuaimi, A. A., Guang, Y., & Rashedi, A. A. (2017). School Performance, Social Networking Effects, and Learning of School Children: Evidence of Reciprocal Relationships in Abu Dhabi. *Telematics and Informatics*, *34*(8), 1433–1444. https://doi.org/10.1016/j.tele.2017.06.006

Bhandarkar, A. M., Pandey, A. K., Nayak, R., Pujary, K., & Kumar, A. (2021). Impact of Social Media on the Academic Performance of Undergraduate Medical Students. *Medical Journal, Armed Forces India*, *77*(Suppl 1), S37–S41. PubMed. https://doi.org/10.1016/j.mjafi.2020.10.021

Boahene, K. O., Fang, J., & Sampong, F. (2019). Social Media Usage and Tertiary Students' Academic Performance: Examining the Influences of Academic Self-Efficacy and Innovation Characteristics. *Sustainability*, *11*(8), 2431. https://doi.org/10.3390/su11082431

Brailovskaia, J., Margraf, J., & Schneider, S. (2021). Social Media as Source of Information, Stress Symptoms, and Burden Caused by Coronavirus (COVID-19). *European Psychologist*, *26*(4), 373–386. https://doi.org/10.1027/1016-9040/a000452

Cao, G., & Tian, Q. (2020). Social Media Use and Its Effect on University Student's Learning and Academic Performance in the UAE. *Journal of Research on Technology in Education*, *54*(1), 18–33. https://doi.org/10.1080/15391523.2020.1801538

Cerezo, R., Esteban, M., Sánchez-Santillán, M., & Núñez, J. C. (2017). Procrastinating Behavior in Computer-Based Learning Environments to Predict Performance: A Case Study in Moodle. *Frontiers in Psychology*, *8*, 1403–1403. PubMed. https://doi.org/10.3389/fpsyg.2017.01403

Chakraborty, P. (2020). Effects of Using Facebook on Academic Performance of Students: A Review. In *2020 IEEE 5th International Conference on Computing Communication and Automation (ICCCA)*, pp. 763–767. https://doi.org/10.1109/ICCCA49541.2020.9250881

Crede, J., Wirthwein, L., McElvany, N., & Steinmayr, R. (2015). Adolescents' Academic Achievement and Life Satisfaction: The Role of Parents' Education. *Frontiers in Psychology*, *6*, 52–52. PubMed. https://doi.org/10.3389/fpsyg.2015.00052

Creswell, J. W. (1994). *Research Design: Qualitative and Quantitative Approaches.* Thousand Oaks: SAGE Publications.

Elsayed, A. M. (2015). The Use of Academic Social Networks Among Arab Researchers. *Social Science Computer Review, 34*(3), 378–391. https://doi.org/10.1177/0894439315589146

Fonagy, P. (2018). *Attachment Theory and Psychoanalysis*. New York, NY: Routledge.

Giunchiglia, F., Zeni, M., Gobbi, E., Bignotti, E., & Bison, I. (2018). Mobile Social Media Usage and Academic Performance. *Computers in Human Behavior, 82*, 177–185. https://doi.org/10.1016/j.chb.2017.12.041

Haand, R., & Shuwang, Z. (2020). The Relationship between Social Media Addiction and Depression: A Quantitative Study among University Students in Khost, Afghanistan. *International Journal of Adolescence and Youth, 25*(1), 780–786. https://doi.org/10.1080/02673843.2020.1741407

Habes, M., Alghizzawi, M., Ahmad, A. K., & Almuhaisen, O. (2023). The Impact of Digital Media Learning Apps on Students' Behaviors in Distance Learning During COVID-19 at the University of Jordan. *Studies in Media and Communication, 11*(3), 47. https://doi.org/10.11114/smc.v11i3.5982

Habes, M., Salloum, S. A., Alghizzawi, M., & Mhamdi, C. (2019). The Relation between Social Media and Students' Academic Performance in Jordan: YouTube Perspective. *Advances in Intelligent Systems and Computing*, 382–392. https://doi.org/10.1007/978-3-030-31129-2_35

Hasnain, H., Nasreen, A., & Ijaz, H. (2015). Impact of Social Media Usage on Academic Performance of University Students. In *2nd International Research Management & Innovation Conference (IRMIC)*, pp. 26–27.

Hayat, A. A., Kojuri, J., & Amini, M. (2020). Academic Procrastination of Medical Students: The Role of Internet Addiction. *Journal of Advances in Medical Education & Professionalism, 8*(2), 83–89. https://doi.org/10.30476/JAMP.2020.85000.1159

Ipem, J. N., & Okwara-Kalu, C. E. (2020). Internet Addiction and Academic Performance of Undergraduate Students of Alvan Ikoku Federal College of Education (Aifce) Owerri. *Journal of the Nigerian Academy of Education, 16*(2), Article 2.

Karakose, T., Ozdemir, T. Y., Papadakis, S., Yirci, R., Ozkayran, S. E., & Polat, H. (2022). Investigating the Relationships between COVID-19 Quality of Life, Loneliness, Happiness, and Internet Addiction among K-12 Teachers and School Administrators-A Structural Equation Modeling Approach. *International Journal of Environmental Research and Public Health, 19*(3), 1052. PubMed. https://doi.org/10.3390/ijerph19031052

Karataş, H. (2015). Correlation among Academic Procrastination, Personality Traits, and Academic Achievement. *Anthropologist, 20*(1), 243–255.

Kausar, S., & Awan, A. G. (2019). Impact of Using Social Media on Academic Performance of Students at Graduate Level: Evidence from Pakistan. *Glob J Manag Soc Sci Humanities*, *5*(1), 116–142.

Kim, Y., & Baylor, A. L. (2006). A Social-Cognitive Framework for Pedagogical Agents as Learning Companions. *Educational Technology Research and Development*, *54*(6), 569–596. https://doi.org/10.1007/s11423-006-0637-3

Lau, W. W. F. (2017). Effects of Social Media Usage and Social Media Multitasking on the Academic Performance of University Students. *Computers in Human Behavior*, *68*, 286–291. https://doi.org/10.1016/j.chb.2016.11.043

López-Carril, S., González-Serrano, M. H., Calabuig-Moreno, F., Añó, V., & Anagnostopoulos, C. (2021). Development and Preliminary Validation of Social Media as an Educational and Professional Tool Student Perceptions Scale (SMEPT-SPS). *Sustainability*, *13*(4), 1814. https://doi.org/10.3390/su13041814

Maqableh, M., Rajab, L., Quteshat, W., Masa'deh, R. M. T., Khatib, T., & Karajeh, H. (2015). The Impact of Social Media Networks Websites Usage on Students' Academic Performance. *Communications and Network*, *07*(04), 159–171. https://doi.org/10.4236/cn.2015.74015

Marengo, D., Angelo Fabris, M., Longobardi, C., & Settanni, M. (2022). Smartphone and Social Media Use Contributed to Individual Tendencies Towards Social Media Addiction in Italian Adolescents During the Covid-19 Pandemic. *Addictive Behaviors*, *126*, 107204. https://doi.org/10.1016/j.addbeh.2021.107204

Mingle, J., Adams, D. M., & Adjei, D. E. A. (2016). A Comparative Analysis of Social Media Usage and Academic Performance in Public and Private Senior High Schools. *Journal of Education and Practice* *7*(7), 12–18.

Nwosu, K. C., Ikwuka, O. I., Ugorji, O. M., & Unachukwu, G. C. (2020). Does the Association of Social Media Use with Problematic Internet Behaviours Predict Undergraduate Students Academic Procrastination? *Canadian Journal of Learning and Technology*, *46*(1). https://doi.org/10.21432/cjlt27890

Oguguo, B. C., Ajuonuma, J. O., Azubuike, R., Ene, C. U., Atta, F. O., & Oko, C. J. (2020). Influence of Social Media on Students' Academic Achievement. *International Journal of Evaluation and Research in Education (IJERE)*, *9*(4), 1000. https://doi.org/10.11591/ijere.v9i4.20638

Othman, W., Fariha, Z., & Ngah, N. (2017). Impact of Social Media Usage on Students Academic Performance in Terengganu, Malaysia. *Journal of Applied Environmental and Biological Sciences*, *7*(5), 140–144.

Perkins, D. N. (2001). Person-Plus: A Distributed View of Thinking and Learning. In G. Salomon (Ed.), *Distributed Cognition: Psychological and Educational Considerations* (pp. 88–110). Cambridge, UK: Cambridge University Press.

Rasheed, M. I., Malik, M. J., Pitafi, A. H., Iqbal, J., Anser, M. K., & Abbas, M. (2020). Usage of Social Media, Student Engagement, and Creativity: The Role of Knowledge Sharing Behavior and Cyberbullying. *Computers & Education, 159*, 104002. https://doi.org/10.1016/j.compedu.2020.104002

Rashid, T., & Asghar, H. M. (2016). Technology Use, Self-Directed Learning, Student Engagement and Academic Performance: Examining the Interrelations. *Computers in Human Behavior, 63*, 604–612. https://doi.org/10.1016/j.chb.2016.05.084

Salloum, S. A., Al-Emran, M., Habes, M., Alghizzawi, M., Ghani, M. Abd., & Shaalan, K. (2019). Understanding the Impact of Social Media Practices on E-Learning Systems Acceptance. *Advances in Intelligent Systems and Computing*, 360–369. https://doi.org/10.1007/978-3-030-31129-2_33

Salloum, S. A., Al-Emran, M., Habes, M., Alghizzawi, M., Ghani, M. Abd., & Shaalan, K. (2021). What Impacts the Acceptance of E-learning Through Social Media? An Empirical Study. *Studies in Systems, Decision and Control*, 419–431. https://doi.org/10.1007/978-3-030-64987-6_24

Santrock, J. W. (2009). *Educational Psychology*. New York, NY: McGraw-Hill.

Shakoor, F., Fakhar, A., & Abbas, J. (2021). Impact of Smartphones Usage on the Learning Behaviour and Academic Performance of Students: Empirical Evidence from Pakistan. *International Journal of Academic Research in Business and Social Sciences, 11*(2), 862–881. https://doi.org/10.6007/ijarbss/v11-i2/8902

Uzochukwu, O., & Anierobi, E. (2020). The Influence of Social Media on Aggressive Behaviours of In-School Adolescents in Anambra State. *Journal of the Nigerian Academy of Education, 16*(1), 279–292.

Üztemur, S. (2020). The Mediating Role of Academic Procrastination Behaviours in the Relationship Be. *International Journal of Education Technology and Scientific Researches, 5*(11), 63–101. https://doi.org/10.35826/ijetsar.112

Vandeyar, T. (2020). The Academic Turn: Social Media in Higher Education. *Education and Information Technologies, 25*(6), 5617–5635. PubMed. https://doi.org/10.1007/s10639-020-10240-1

Vygotsky, L. S. (1987). *Mind in Society: The Development of Higher Psychological Processes*. Harvard University Press. http://dx.doi.org/10.2307/j.ctvjf9vz4.5

Waqas, A., Afzal, M., Zaman, F., & Sabir, M. (2016). The Impact of Social Networking Sites' Usage on the Academic Performance of University Students of Lahore, Pakistan. *International Journal of Social Sciences and Management*, *3*(4), 267–276. https://doi.org/10.3126/ijssm.v3i4.15962

Yildiz Durak, H., Kidiman Demirhan, E., & Citil, M. (2022). Examining Various Risk Factors as the Predictors of Gifted and Non-gifted High School Students' Online Game Addiction. *Computers & Education*, *177*, 104378. https://doi.org/10.1016/j.compedu.2021.104378

Fatima AlMohsen, Laila Mohebi, Alanood Alshamsi, and Mariam AlHammadi

Exploring the Dual Facets of Online Teacher Training in Ghana: Benefits, Challenges, and Implications for Future Development

1. Introduction

In the wake of the COVID-19 pandemic, the education landscape has undergone a dramatic shift, with online training modules becoming the lifeline for sustaining teaching and learning. This sudden transition has significantly increased the enrolment of pre-service and in-service teachers into online training programs (Almahasees et al., 2021). Africa, like the rest of the world, had to adapt to this "new normal" to keep its education system afloat amidst the crisis (Bekele et al., 2021). Ghana, among many other countries, suspended face-to-face learning, embracing the remote learning model (Ceesay, 2021). Interestingly, even after the return of face-to-face instruction post-COVID-19, the popularity of online training modules persisted (Tartavulea et al., 2020). This has led to a blend of synchronous and asynchronous online teaching alongside traditional classroom instruction in many academic institutions, marking a new era of coexistence. The growing interest in online instruction has attracted significant scholarly attention, with numerous studies exploring its effectiveness compared to face-to-face teaching (Bekele et al., 2021; Ceesay, 2021; Tartavulea et al., 2020). However, while quantitative analyzes have been abundant, there is a notable lack of rigorous qualitative research, particularly in the context of online education in Ghana (Tartavulea et al., 2020). This is especially crucial considering the reported shortcomings of online learning in various African countries (Adarkwah, 2021; Sarpong et al., 2022).

This study aims to address this research gap by conducting an in-depth qualitative exploration of the factors driving teachers' interest in online training modules in Ghana. By understanding the motivations and experiences of pre-service and in-service teachers, this study seeks to provide valuable insights for improving the content, delivery methods, and overall effectiveness of online training programs (Tilley, 2019). As online teaching and learning are expected to become a permanent fixture in education, it is imperative to comprehend the factors influencing teachers' uptake and satisfaction with online training modules (Yeigh

& Lynch, 2020). This knowledge will enable stakeholders to take necessary measures to ensure that educators can make the most of this evolving landscape. The purpose of this study is to assess the effectiveness of online training modules for pre-service and in-service teachers in Ghana through a comparative qualitative analysis. By exploring the perceptions, experiences, and satisfaction levels of these two groups, the study aims to provide valuable insights for enhancing the quality and impact of online teacher training programs in the country.

2. Background and Objective of the Study

2.1. In-Service and Pre-service Training in the "New Normal"

The COVID-19 pandemic necessitated abrupt changes in the routine of pre-service and in-service teacher training (Nketsia et al., 2021). In Ghana, teacher training is guided by the ministerial vision to prepare and enable teachers to function effectively in primary and second-cycle schools. This vision aims to develop reflective and proficient practitioners capable of delivering quality education to Ghanaian children (Ministry of Education, 2012). To achieve this goal, teachers must be equipped with the requisite skills and knowledge to be both reflective and proficient in their practice. The traditional path of preservice and in-service training, as outlined by the Colleges Act 847, was upended by the pandemic, necessitating a rapid shift towards online instruction to ensure the continuity of teacher preparation.

Ghana's teacher education landscape has undergone significant transformations in recent years. The Colleges Act 847 upgraded Colleges of Education into tertiary institutions, paving the way for the introduction of four-year Bachelor's degree programs (Buabeng et al., 2020). These programs encompass both content and methodologies, along with practical teaching experiences through on-campus peer teaching and off-campus practicum in real school settings. The objective is to produce three categories of teachers: generalists (grades 1–6), early childhood educators, and specialists (Buabeng et al., 2020). The on-campus peer teaching phase is designed to boost preservice teachers' confidence by allowing them to teach in a familiar environment. In contrast, the off-campus phase exposes prospective teachers to the challenges and realities of teaching in actual school contexts.

However, the COVID-19 pandemic disrupted this established system, forcing the suspension of face-to-face instruction. Teacher education in Ghana had to swiftly adapt to online instruction to remain relevant and competitive in the face of this unprecedented crisis. In-service teachers also found themselves navigating the challenges of balancing their professional development needs with the demands of the new reality. Consequently, online training became a crucial aspect of professional development for teachers in Ghana (Adarkwah, 2021; Nketsia et al., 2021; Sarpong et al., 2022). This shift has highlighted the importance of understanding the factors that influence teachers' satisfaction with and uptake of online training modules to ensure that these programs effectively meet their professional development needs in the "new normal."

2.2. Uptake of Online Training Modules in Africa

Online instruction was not considered an option modality in many African countries before the COVID-19 pandemic. The reluctance was there despite continual calls for the adoption of information and communication technology and online instructions from researchers (Ferdig & Kennedy, 2014). However, the onset of the pandemic compelled Africa, like the rest of the world, to swiftly embrace online instruction to avoid falling behind (Bekele et al., 2021; Gumede & Badriparsad, 2022). This transition necessitated dramatic changes to the learning environment as countries sought to maintain educational continuity through online means (Gumede & Badriparsad, 2022). Thus, the COVID-19 pandemic opened the prospect of successful integration of online instruction in teaching and learning processes in Africa, presenting both opportunities and challenges.

In-service and pre-service teachers in training also quickly warmed up to online training modules in the background of the COVID-19 pandemic. Online learning is focused on learning experiences that can be synchronous or asynchronous, utilizing different devices, such as mobile phones and laptops that have internet access (Dhawan, 2020). Synchronous and asynchronous teaching modules were adopted to remain relevant. Synchronous means that the students and the faculty meet at a prescheduled time for interactive learning (Almahasees et al., 2021; Dhawan, 2020). Asynchronous is more of the opposite in which there is no interaction; the faculty gives the course, and students enjoy the flexibility of taking the course at convenient times. In several cases, institutions combine both synchronous and asynchronous methods.

The adoption of online training brought several advantages. In Jordan, for example, students appreciated the time flexibility and comfort afforded by the ability to schedule their learning (Almahasees et al., 2021). This learner-centered approach shifts the responsibility for learning to the student, fostering autonomy and the ability to learn anytime, anywhere (Dhawan, 2020). Consequently, the student can take charge of their learning schedules, bringing in a level of autonomy. This self-paced nature of online instruction aligns with constructivist principles, as it allows for personalized learning experiences. Additionally, online platforms can significantly reduce institutional costs associated with transportation and accommodation (Dhawan, 2020).

Despite its advantages, online instruction also faces significant challenges and criticisms. One major criticism is the lack of peer interaction, which can impact the learner's personality (Almahasees et al., 2021). Instruction becomes more individualized, leaving no room for interaction. Additionally, online instruction heavily relies on internet availability. Not all African countries have easy access to the internet, leading to disparities in education opportunities. Equity becomes a concern as some students are digitally illiterate and lack access to the internet (Gumede & Badriparsad, 2022). In countries like South Africa, the digital literacy divide was exposed, as some individuals who expected to take online instruction were unable to due to their lack of digital literacy (Gumede & Badriparsad, 2022). This disruption affects the learning progress of vulnerable and digitally illiterate students who are unable to access the material (Gumede & Badriparsad, 2022; Kalloo et al., 2020). Furthermore, online training is criticized for being theoretical and not allowing students to practice and learn effectively, thus creating a gap in the learning process (Mahyoob, 2020; Mukhtar et al., 2020).

2.3. The Accelerated Interest in Online Instruction and Professional Development

Online training modules are not a recent invention but have been an available option for many academic institutions the world over. However, the interest and uptake were generally lower before the COVID-19 pandemic (Pokhrel & Chhetri, 2021; Tadesse & Muluye, 2020). Just a year preceding the COVID-19 pandemic in 2018, only 15 % of the share went to online instruction (Burquel & Busch, 2020). That situation has drastically changed due to the COVID-19 pandemic, which curtailed face-to-face instruction. The closure of schools to facilitate social distancing prompted the adjustment to online instruction. Ideally, the accelerated interest in online instruction was meant to face a natural demise following the return to face-to-face instruction. However, this has not been the case as the interest continues to accelerate in the COVID-19 pandemic era (Bashir et al., 2021). In light of this observation, it is considered prudent to interrogate this interest to ensure that it is not only driven by convenience but also should assist in meeting the global goals of teaching and learning. The goals of education, in general, also need to be the driving force behind the accelerated interest.

Since the factors contributing to the satisfaction and uptake of online training modules are largely unknown in the context of Ghana, the current study sought to answer two broad questions given below to explain the satisfaction of pre-service and in-service teachers with the online training modules:

1. How do pre-service and in-service teachers perceive the online training module?
2. What factors explain the uptake and satisfaction with the online training module among pre-service and in-service teachers?

The objective of this study is to explore the factors that contribute to satisfaction with online training modules among pre-service and in-service teachers in Ghana. By comparing the insights gathered from these two groups of teachers, the study aims to provide a comprehensive understanding of their experiences and perspectives.

3. Methodology

This study employed a phenomenological research approach to deeply explore the lived experiences and perceptions of pre-service and in-service teachers regarding the online training module. Phenomenology is well-suited for this research as it allows for a rich, contextualized understanding of the participants' subjective experiences with the phenomenon of interest (Adarkwah, 2021). By eliciting detailed accounts from the teachers, this approach enables the researchers to uncover the essential structures and meanings underlying their satisfaction, or lack thereof, with the online training.

3.1. Study Participants

The participants were purposefully selected from the pool of pre-service and in-service teachers who had completed the online training module in Ghana. Purposive sampling ensures the inclusion of information-rich cases that can provide valuable insights into the research questions (Yeigh & Lynch, 2020). The sample consisted of 49 teachers, with 27 females (55 %) and 22 males (45 %). Of these, 19 were in-service teachers (39 %) and 30 were pre-service teachers (61 %), representing a range of age groups, with the majority (55 %) being 25–34 years old. This diverse sample allowed for a comprehensive exploration of the phenomenon from multiple perspectives.

3.2. Videos Used in the Training Module

The training module is mainly comprised of instructional videos. The videos contain an animated script about learning environments covering various topics such as the importance of play in early childhood education, Piaget's theory of cognitive development, strategies to motivate students and Social and Emotional Learning. Each video was carefully designed to align with the training objectives and learning outcomes. They are designed not only to impart knowledge but also to engage learners in an immersive and interactive educational journey.

Below are the links to the videos:

Video 1: Demonstrate knowledge of play as part of the learning environment
https://www.youtube.com/watch?v=0QcK4BL1SL4&list=PL7IK2zH0NXnyty4BbNf3kWdMv1jyGkJw4&index=8&t=47s
Video 2: Understand how to identify and integrate strategies that motivate students
https://www.youtube.com/watch?v=ZxU64nmrYuM&list=PL7IK2zH0NXnyty4BbNf3kWdMv1jyGkJw4&index=3
Video 3: Identify the various ways students process information (multiple intelligences)
https://www.youtube.com/watch?v=Cj4S-5t4LBI&list=PL7IK2zH0NXnyty4BbNf3kWdMv1jyGkJw4&index=13
Video 4: Demonstrate knowledge of Piaget's theory of cognitive development
https://www.youtube.com/watch?v=dd_JhPb7ah8&list=PL7IK2zH0NXnyty4BbNf3kWdMv1jyGkJw4&index=14&t=15s
Video 5: Demonstrate knowledge of the importance of Social and Emotional Learning
https://www.youtube.com/watch?v=0tFzEvlBotQ&list=PL7IK2zH0NXnyty4BbNf3kWdMv1jyGkJw4&index=17&t=23s
Video 6: Understand the basics of differentiated learning
https://www.youtube.com/watch?v=Bzibzic0Evw&list=PL7IK2zH0NXnyty4BbNf3kWdMv1jyGkJw4&index=23&t=5s
Video 7: Flexible Classrooms
https://www.youtube.com/watch?v=WDp7HyI0yl0&list=PL7IK2zH0NXnyty4BbNf3kWdMv1jyGkJw4&index=29&t=45s

3.3. Data Collection

The primary data collection method was an anonymous survey questionnaire. The survey included both demographic items and open-ended questions designed to elicit rich, detailed responses from the participants. The open-ended questions probed the teachers' perceptions, experiences, and factors underlying their satisfaction with the online training module. This approach enabled the researchers to gather in-depth, contextual data that could be analyzed thematically (Braun & Clarke, 2012).

3.4. Data Analyzes

In the analysis process, a detailed thematic analysis was employed, adhering to the guidelines proposed by Braun and Clarke (2012). Initially, a subset of the data was independently reviewed to familiarize with the content, noting initial ideas and patterns. Subsequent discussions were conducted to discuss and refine these initial codes, ensuring consistency in interpretation. Through iterative discussions, a coding framework was developed and applied across the entire dataset. Codes were grouped into potential themes, with constant comparison against the data to ensure accurate representation. This phase also involved identifying and mapping relationships between themes. Investigator triangulation was utilized, with multiple researchers independently coding and analyzing the data, followed by discussions to reach consensus on the final themes. The process was meticulously documented, including the development of the codebook, to allow for replicability and provide transparency in the analytical procedure. By outlining these steps, the aim is to enable other researchers to understand and potentially replicate the study, thereby contributing to the body of knowledge with methodological rigor.

The thematic analysis of the qualitative data identified several key themes that reflect the experiences and perceptions of pre-service and in-service teachers regarding the online training modules. Several factors underlying the uptake and satisfaction with the online training module were unraveled. These factors are reported below in terms of the themes identified, which are presented with illustrative quotes from participants and a discussion of their relevance to the study's objectives.

3.5. Accessibility and Convenience

Many participants highlighted the ease of accessing the training modules and the convenience of being able to complete them at their own pace. For instance, one in-service teacher noted, "The flexibility to access the modules anytime made it seamlessly fit into my busy schedule." This theme underscores the importance of flexible learning opportunities for educators. The quality of video and audio recordings was noted as important in determining satisfaction with online instruction. When the video recordings are of quality and clearly visible, students easily follow the online lessons. This is also dependent on not having downloading errors and login problems. If the video is quickly accessible at the desired time, then the teachers can proceed with the lesson without hassle.

3.6. Relevance and Significance

The relevance of the course was also noted as a driving factor for satisfaction. Most of the participants who saw the course module as relevant were satisfied with the course. Participant A1 stated, "It will help me as a teacher to know how to deliver in the classroom." Similarly, Participant A13 expressed their satisfaction, saying, "I learned to incorporate technology and practicals in our teaching and learning field." It was found that satisfaction is primarily dependent on the relevance of the module in terms of teaching and learning. The teacher, in this case, is equipped with ways to incorporate technology in teaching. The incorporation of technology is essential, considering the challenges posed by the COVID-19 pandemic.

Participant A3, who was satisfied with the course, saw it as relevant because it allowed him to understand individual differences among the learners. He stated: "I learned that each individual is unique." The understanding of individual differences was appreciated because it allowed the teacher to arrange the content and teaching approaches to suit the individual needs of the learners. Besides being relevant in teaching and learning, some of the prospective teachers appreciated the relevance of the module in terms of classroom management. Participant A7 remarked, "The ability to resolve conflicts within the kids goes a long way to help them express their feelings." Professional development, in this case, gave the teacher the capacity to resolve conflicts among the learners, thereby creating a conducive learning environment.

The participants saw the course module as less satisfying; it was mainly because they did not see the relevance and significance of the course. Participant A15 was not satisfied, and he noted that there was "nothing new" and that he did not "gain much." Similarly, A24 said, "Nothing interests me" in the course. This outcome may have been driven by the fact that the student was already equipped with the contents of the course or failed to appreciate its application in his teaching context. As noted from participant A18, who felt less satisfied, remarked, "I am familiar with all the material." Thus, dissatisfaction with the course was caused by the fact that the course could not give the students new information.

3.7. Learning with Fun

Besides the relevance of the course, participants also appreciated the fun that came with online instruction. Participants appreciated the video and audio components, which were considered fun. Participant A13 shared, "It is fun and educative," in response to the probing question on why they found the module satisfying. Similarly, A8 remarked, "Playing is relevant to the teaching and growth of the child…." The fun component was revealed as one of the motivating factors in teaching and learning. In turn, the online module elicited satisfaction. The combination of fun and education was found to be a driving factor towards satisfaction. The video recordings need to be entertaining so that they are both educative and fun. The play should, however, be meaningful, "Meaningful play should help a child to make his/her own decision" (Participant A23). This implies that there should be a balance between the educative and fun components of the video recordings.

3.8. Content Structure

Notably, the content structure of the course also drives satisfaction. Participants who were satisfied with the course generally appreciated its contents. Participant A4 summed up her assessment by saying, "I have learnt everything in the various courses I have read." In the same vein, participant A19 referred to the course as "a good teaching approach making it possible for children to use their bodies to solve environmental problems."

These themes align with existing literature on online teacher training and professional development. Studies have consistently emphasized the importance of accessibility, flexibility, and relevance in online learning (Tilley, 2019; Yeigh & Lynch, 2020). The findings also resonate with research highlighting the role of interactive and engaging content in promoting learner motivation and satisfaction (Almahasees et al., 2021; Tartavulea et al., 2020). However, the study also reveals some unique insights specific to the Ghanaian context. The emphasis on play-based learning and the use of technology in teaching, as highlighted by participants, reflects the growing recognition of these pedagogical approaches in Ghana's education system (Adarkwah, 2021; Sarpong et al., 2022). Additionally, the varying levels of satisfaction based on participants' prior knowledge and experience underscore the need for differentiated and personalized learning opportunities in online teacher training programs (Nketsia et al., 2021).

These findings have important implications for the design and implementation of online training modules for teachers in Ghana. They suggest that online training programs should prioritize accessibility, relevance, interactivity, and comprehensive content to maximize teacher engagement and satisfaction. Moreover, the study highlights the need for tailored training opportunities that cater to the diverse needs and backgrounds of teachers, ensuring that the content is appropriately challenging and relevant for all participants. Finally, this qualitative analysis provides valuable insights into the factors that contribute to pre-service and in-service teachers' uptake and satisfaction with online training modules in Ghana. By understanding and addressing these factors, educational stakeholders can design more effective and engaging online professional development programs that meet the needs of teachers and ultimately enhance the quality of education in the country.

4. Discussion

This study sought to explore the factors motivating satisfaction with the online training module among preservice and in-service teachers in Ghana. The findings uncovered various themes that directly address the research questions, providing a comprehensive understanding of teachers' perspectives on online education. These themes include accessibility and convenience, relevance and significance, learning with fun, and content structure. The easy accessibility to the learning material emerged as the most significantly highlighted factor contributing to teachers' satisfaction with the online training module. Accessibility refers to the ease with which participant teachers can obtain, interact with, and benefit from the educational content provided through digital platforms. As one in-service teacher noted, "The flexibility to access the modules anytime made it seamlessly fit into my busy schedule." This aligns with the findings of Rice and Ortiz (2020), who emphasized the critical role of accessibility in the success of online learning and training in developing countries.

Creating an inclusive learning environment that accommodates the diverse needs of all learners is crucial in online training. Participant A11 remarked, "I love that it does not let me get bored or lose interest," highlighting the importance of engaging content and flexibility in maintaining learners' motivation. This resonates with the idea that accessibility in online training is about removing barriers and ensuring equal opportunities for all learners to participate and benefit from the educational experience (Adarkwah, 2021; Sarpong et al., 2022). Relevance of the online module was also identified as a critical factor driving its uptake. Participants assessed the relevance of the course in terms of their needs as teachers. Participant A1 stated, "It will help me as a teacher knowing how to deliver in the classroom," indicating the value placed on content that assists in classroom delivery. Similarly, Participant A13 expressed satisfaction, saying, "I learned to incorporate technology and practicals in our teaching and learning field." These findings suggest that teachers appreciate modules that equip them with the requisite skills for teaching and classroom management.

Conversely, participants who found the module less useful, possibly because they were already familiar with the content, expressed lower satisfaction. Participant A15 noted, "Nothing new," while A24 said, "Nothing interests me."

This highlights the importance of tailoring online training to the specific needs and prior knowledge of teachers. As Dhawan (2020) pointed out, some online courses may be too theoretical and fail to provide opportunities for practice and practical learning. Ensuring that learners have the chance to apply what they have learned is crucial for a complete learning process. The content structure of the online training module also influences satisfaction. Participants who found the module fun and entertaining expressed higher satisfaction. The quality of video and audio components was noted as an important determinant. Participant A13 described the module as "fun and educative," while A8 remarked, "Playing is relevant to the teaching and growth of the child." These findings underscore the significance of incorporating engaging and interactive elements in online training to maintain learners' interest and motivation (Almahasees et al., 2021; Tartavulea et al., 2020).

However, striking a balance between education and entertainment is crucial. Participant A23 noted, "Meaningful play should help a child to make his/her own decision," suggesting that the fun components should be purposefully designed to support learning objectives. The content structure should also focus on imparting valuable skills. Participants appreciated the module for providing skills in using information and communication technologies, which are considered significant for improving lesson delivery (Fu, 2013; Umar & Yusoff, 2014). The findings of this study are deeply rooted in the Ghanaian educational context, reflecting the unique cultural, educational, and socio-economic dynamics of the country. Ghana's recent educational reforms and rapid digitalization efforts provide a distinctive backdrop against which the adoption of online training must be understood (Adarkwah, 2021; Nketsia et al., 2021). This focus on Ghana allows for a more nuanced interpretation of the data, ensuring that the conclusions drawn are directly relevant and applicable to the teachers, policymakers, and stakeholders within the Ghanaian educational ecosystem.

While the study highlights the positive aspects of online training modules, it is equally important to acknowledge the challenges and limitations associated with this mode of delivery. Participants occasionally reported issues related to internet connectivity and access to appropriate technology, which can significantly hinder the effectiveness of online learning. Additionally, some teachers expressed concerns over the lack of direct peer interaction and hands-on experiences, which are crucial for fostering a collaborative learning environment and practical skills development. Concerns were also raised about the potential for digital divide issues, where teachers in more remote or under-resourced areas may find it difficult to participate fully in online training opportunities. Acknowledging these challenges is essential for developing comprehensive strategies that address both the opportunities and barriers presented by online training modules. By considering these limitations, stakeholders can better tailor online training programs to meet the diverse needs of all teachers, ensuring equitable access to professional development resources.

The insights gained from this study have important implications for the design and implementation of online training modules for teachers in Ghana. Prioritizing accessibility, relevance, interactivity, and comprehensive content is essential to maximize teacher engagement and satisfaction (Tilley, 2019; Yeigh & Lynch, 2020). Moreover, the findings highlight the need for differentiated and personalized learning opportunities that cater to the diverse needs and backgrounds of teachers, ensuring that the content is appropriately challenging and relevant for all participants (Nketsia et al., 2021). To sum up, this study provides valuable insights into the factors that contribute to pre-service and in-service teachers' uptake and satisfaction with online training modules in Ghana. By understanding and addressing these factors, educational stakeholders can design more effective and engaging online professional development programs that meet the needs of teachers and ultimately enhance the quality of education in the country. The findings emphasize the importance of accessibility, relevance, engaging content, and tailored learning experiences in driving satisfaction and uptake of online training modules among Ghanaian teachers.

5. Conclusion

This qualitative study aimed to explore the perceptions and experiences of pre-service and in-service teachers in Ghana regarding online training modules. The findings revealed that teachers generally held positive views about the online training module, with several key factors contributing to their satisfaction and uptake. The accessibility and convenience of the online platform, the relevance and significance of the course content, the engaging and interactive learning experience, and the well-structured curriculum emerged as the main drivers of satisfaction among the participants. The insights gained from this study have important implications for the design and implementation of online teacher professional development programs in Ghana. Educational stakeholders should prioritize the factors identified as influencing satisfaction and uptake to create more effective and engaging online training modules. This involves ensuring easy access to learning platforms, developing practical and relevant content, incorporating interactive elements, and providing a comprehensive curriculum that addresses the specific needs of Ghanaian teachers. By doing so, online training modules can empower educators with the skills and knowledge necessary to effectively utilize online teaching models in their classrooms, thus enhancing the quality of education in the country. While the primary focus of this study was on the Ghanaian context, the findings may have broader relevance for other countries facing similar challenges in teacher professional development, particularly in Africa. However, it is crucial to consider the unique socio-cultural, educational, and technological contexts of each setting when applying these insights. Future research could explore the long-term impact of online training modules on teacher practice and student learning outcomes, as well as investigate the perspectives of other stakeholders to gain a more comprehensive understanding of the ecosystem surrounding online teacher professional development in Ghana. As the education sector continues to evolve, investing in high-quality online teacher training will be essential in equipping educators with the competencies needed to navigate the challenges and opportunities of the 21st-century classroom.

In addition, this study provides valuable insights into the perceptions and experiences of pre-service and in-service teachers regarding online training modules in Ghana. However, it is crucial to acknowledge certain limitations that may affect the generalizability of the findings. First, the qualitative nature of this study, while providing depth and nuance, limits the ability to generalize the results across all educational contexts in Ghana or other countries. The sample size, although diverse, represents a specific subset of the teaching population, and the findings may not fully encapsulate the experiences of all teachers in different regions or educational settings. Additionally, the study focuses on self-reported data, which could introduce bias related to personal perceptions and experiences. Future research could address these limitations by incorporating quantitative measures, expanding the sample size, and including participants from a wider range of educational contexts. Recognizing these limitations is essential for placing the study's findings within the appropriate scope and for guiding future research efforts aimed at exploring the complex dynamics of online teacher training.

References

Adarkwah, M. A. (2021). "I'm Not Against Online Teaching, but What About Us?": Ict in Ghana Post Covid-19. *Education and Information Technologies*, *26*(2), 1665–1685. https://doi.org/10.1007/s10639-020-10331-z

Almahasees, Z., Mohsen, K., & Amin, M. O. (2021). Faculty's and Students' Perceptions of Online Learning During COVID-19. *Frontiers in Education*, 6. https://doi.org/10.3389/feduc.2021.638470

Bashir, A., Bashir, S., Rana, K., Lambert, P., & Vernallis, A. (2021). Post-COVID-19 Adaptations; the Shifts Towards Online Learning, Hybrid Course Delivery and the Implications for Biosciences Courses in the Higher Education Setting. *Frontiers in Education*, 6, 711619. https://doi.org/10.3389/feduc.2021.711619

Bekele, D., Tolossa, T., Tsegaye, R., & Teshome, W. (2021). The Knowledge and Practice Towards Covid-19 Pandemic Prevention Among Residents of Ethiopia: An Online Cross-Sectional Study. *PloS One*, *16*(1), e0234585. PubMed. https://doi.org/10.1371/journal.pone.0234585

Braun, V., & Clarke, V. (2012). Thematic Analysis. In H. Cooper, P. M. Camic, D. L. Long, A. T. Panter, D. Rindskopf, & K. J. Sher (Eds.), *Apa Handbook of Research Methods in Psychology, Vol 2: Research Designs: Quantitative, Qualitative, Neuropsychological, and Biological* (pp. 57–71). American Psychological Association. https://doi.org/10.1037/13620-004

Buabeng, I., Ntow, F. D., & Otami, C. D. (2020). Teacher Education in Ghana: Policies and Practices. *Journal of Curriculum and Teaching*, *9*(1), 86. https://doi.org/10.5430/jct.v9n1p86

Burquel, N., & Busch, A. (2020). Lessons for International Higher Education Post Covid-19. *University World News*. https://www.universityworldnews.com/post.php?story=2020042408501836

Ceesay, E. K. (2021). Potential Impact of COVID-19 Outbreak on Education, Staff Development and Training in Africa. *Research in Globalization*, *3*, 100049. https://doi.org/10.1016/j.resglo.2021.100049

Dhawan, S. (2020). Online Learning: A Panacea in the Time of COVID-19 Crisis. *Journal of Educational Technology Systems*, *49*(1), 5–22. https://doi.org/10.1177/0047239520934018

Ferdig, Ri. E., & Kennedy, K. (Eds.). (2014). *Handbook of Research on K-12 Online and Blended Learning*. Pittsburgh, PA: ETC Press.

Fu, J. S. (2013). Ict in Education: A Critical Literature Review and Its Implications. *International Journal of Education and Development Using Information and Communication Technology (IJEDICT)*, *9*(1), 112–125.

Gumede, L., & Badriparsad, N. (2022). Online Teaching and Learning Through the Students' Eyes – Uncertainty Through the Covid-19 Lockdown: A Qualitative Case Study in Gauteng Province, South Africa. *Radiography (London, England : 1995)*, *28*(1), 193–198. PubMed. https://doi.org/10.1016/j.radi.2021.10.018

Kalloo, R. C., Mitchell, B., & Kamalodeen, V. J. (2020). Responding to the Covid-19 Pandemic in Trinidad and Tobago: Challenges and Opportunities for Teacher Education. *Journal of Education for Teaching*, *46*(4), 452–462. https://doi.org/10.1080/02607476.2020.1800407

Mahyoob, M. (2020). Challenges of e-Learning during the COVID-19 Pandemic Experienced by EFL Learners. *Arab World English Journal, 11*(4), 351–362. https://doi.org/10.24093/awej/vol11no4.23

Ministry of Education. (2012). *Pre-Tertiary Teacher Professional Development and Management in Ghana: A Policy Framework*. Accra: Ghana Education Service.

Mukhtar, K., Javed, K., Arooj, M., & Sethi, A. (2020). Advantages, Limitations and Recommendations for Online Learning during Covid-19 Pandemic Era. *Pakistan Journal of Medical Sciences, 36*(COVID19-S4), S27–S31. PubMed. https://doi.org/10.12669/pjms.36.COVID19-S4.2785

Nketsia, W., Opoku, M. P., Mohamed, A. H., Kumi, E. O., Twum, R., & Kyere, E. A. (2021). Preservice Training Amid a Pandemic in Ghana: Predictors of Online Learning Success among Teachers. *Frontiers in Education, 6*, 745623. https://doi.org/10.3389/feduc.2021.745623

Pokhrel, S., & Chhetri, R. (2021). A Literature Review on Impact of COVID-19 Pandemic on Teaching and Learning. *Higher Education for the Future, 8*(1), 133–141. https://doi.org/10.1177/2347631120983481

Rice, M., & Ortiz, K. (2020). Perceptions of Accessibility in Online Course Materials: A Survey of Teachers from Six Virtual Schools. *Journal of Online Learning Research, 6*(3), 245–264.

Sarpong, S. A., Dwomoh, G., Boakye, E. K., & Ofosua-Adjei, I. (2022). Online Teaching and Learning Under COVID-19 Pandemic; Perception of University Students in Ghana. *European Journal of Interactive Multimedia and Education, 3*(1), e02203. https://doi.org/10.30935/ejimed/11438

Tadesse, S., & Muluye, W. (2020). The Impact of COVID-19 Pandemic on Education System in Developing Countries: A Review. *Open Journal of Social Sciences, 08*(10), 159–170. https://doi.org/10.4236/jss.2020.810011

Tartavulea, C. V., Albu, C. N., Albu, N., Dieaconescu, R. I., & Petre, S. (2020). Online Teaching Practices and the Effectiveness of the Educational Process in the Wake of the COVID-19 Pandemic. *Amfiteatru Economic, 22*(55), 920–936. https://doi.org/10.24818/ea/2020/55/920

Tilley, S. (2019). The Role of Critical Qualitative Research in Educational Contexts: A Canadian Perspective. *Educar Em Revista, 35*(75), 155–180. https://doi.org/10.1590/0104-4060.66806

Umar, I. N., & Yusoff, M. T. M. (2014). A Study on Malaysian Teachers' Level of Ict Skills and Practices, and Its Impact on Teaching and Learning. *Procedia – Social and Behavioral Sciences, 116*, 979–984. https://doi.org/10.1016/j.sbspro.2014.01.331

Yeigh, T., & Lynch, D. (2020). Is Online Teaching and Learning Here to Stay? *Academia Letters*. https://doi.org/10.20935/al24

Suha Karaki, Areej El Sayary, Laila Mohebi, and Lawrence Meda

Examining the Impact of a Professional Development Program in Preparing Teachers for Inclusive Education

1. Introduction

Right-based education and the inclusion of students with special educational needs and disabilities (SEND) was stipulated by numerous universal legislations: United Nations Convention on the Rights of the Child (UNCRC) in 1980, Individuals with Disabilities Education Act (IDEA) in 1990, Salamanca Statement in 1994, the reauthorization of IDEA in 2004 and the United Nations Convention on the Rights of Persons with Disabilities (UNCRPD) in 2006. These regulations called for equal educational opportunities for students with SEND, so they become active and supported members in the classroom (Florian, 2019). However, for inclusion to be fair and appropriate, the learner should not only be provided with the right services but also valued and given the chance to belong in a meaningful, positive and non-restrictive environment (Merry, 2020).

The integration of students with SEND in the general classroom creates several challenges, especially since teachers are to create classroom environments that are highly supportive (Mcallister & Maguire, 2012). Inclusion entails several challenges for educators as they need to focus on: the right individualized educational program (IEP), identification, monitoring, interventions, strategies, differentiation, goals, scaffolding, assessment and support system (Grigorenko et al., 2018). When the school has far-sighted leaders that accentuate acceptance, cooperation, professional development, multidisciplinary support, parental engagement and curricular differentiation (Lipsky & Gartner, 1997), inclusion will lead to the attainment of the child with social and academic goals (Lindsay et al., 2013).

This is where the importance of professional development lies, as it makes teachers more aware, knowledgeable, and capable of ensuring suitable planning for the exceptional learner (Jenkins & Yoshimura, 2010). When educators take part in training programs, they are coached by other professionals in the field who provide them with guidance on how to support students with SEND. There is a need for inclusive education professional development programs (PDP) as the numbers of vulnerable students including those with special needs has increased because of the COVID-19 global pandemic (Smith-Spark, 2021). Teacher professional development programs (PDP) enable teachers to learn new ways of providing quality and equitable education to all students. This helps teachers become more experienced and increases their self-efficacy as they implement inclusive strategies in their classrooms (Hollins-Alexander, 2013; Stadler-Heer, 2019). Consequently, the learning environment is enhanced and the student experience, in addition to their performance and sense of belonging, is elevated (Hills & Sessoms-Penny, 2021; Roberts & Simpson, 2016).

The purpose of this study was to examine the impact of a PDP in preparing teachers for inclusive education. The study was guided by one critical question, to what extent has the program prepared teachers to teach and manage students with learning difficulties and disabilities at a school? The paper begins with this first section of introduction and background to the study. This is followed by a literature review which focuses on what research presents about inclusive education and its prerequisites, one of which is the adequate professional development of teachers so they become more competent, accepting and aware of the pillars and schemes of inclusion in the classroom and beyond. Theoretical framework and context of the study are presented thereafter. This is followed by methodology, results, and discussion sections. The paper ends with a succinct conclusion along with some implications for further future research.

2. Literature Review

2.1. Inclusion and What It Entails

Inclusive education is defined as a system of instruction wherein all students, including those with serious disabilities, have equal access to conventional classrooms with appropriate support, this principle flipped traditional thinking on its head (Amor et al., 2018). The change meant that, unlike before where the problem was handled in terms of "integrated education," children's preparedness was no longer regarded the most important factor in their admittance into mainstream schools. Adaptation requirements were now directed at schools, which were supposed to become even more accepting of youngsters with varying abilities (Saloviita, 2020). When educational institutions excluded school children, who were seen as distinct (such as those with learning difficulties or who were members of a poor class or came from disadvantaged backgrounds), the inclusive education concept was launched as a reaction. Such structures of distinction are extremely important because they have influenced pupil inclusion and participation in educational institutions over time (Waitoller & Artiles, 2013).

The Salamanca Statement (UNESCO, 1994) has been hailed as a watershed moment for inclusive education on a global level. Differentiated instruction was to be substituted with inclusive education which meant that separate education alternatives would be abandoned and the regular classroom would be more accessible to diversity (Nilholm, 2021). Inclusive education understands that students come from a variety of cultures and have had a diversity of experiences within the same school. It's a way of thinking about education that emphasizes being progressive in detecting and removing hurdles that limit access to high-quality education, as well as reducing those barriers and impediments that contribute to discrimination and inequities (Juang & Chitewere, 2020). For bulk of the teaching day, children with impairments as well as other challenges are taught alongside their classmates in a standard classroom. While most experts talk about "mainstream schools," they don't mean segregated units or schools, or integrating students with special needs in inclusive settings as long as they can adjust (integration). The concept behind inclusive education is that all students have the opportunity of being in the same school and classroom (Cobley, 2018).

2.2. Inclusion and Teacher Attitudes

The significance of teacher attitudes in these inclusive settings may appear to be self-evident. If a school teacher does not want a certain student in her school, it is tough to comprehend how more resources, materials or experience could prevent the placement from failing. The sheer presence of resources, such as knowledge or support, does not guarantee a positive result. It's also important for the teacher to put these materials to good use in order to achieve a specific aim (Saloviita, 2020). Several studies have been conducted to know teachers' attitudes and self-efficacy toward inclusive education in different cultures and countries, researchers show that teachers' viewpoint differ depending on social and cultural context (Yada & Savolainen, 2017). The teacher has a significant impact on inclusive classrooms and the creation of inclusive schools; their expertise, attitudes, and ideals are undertaken in formulating an efficient learning environment for the students. The way educators conduct themselves in the classroom will significantly impact how well their students comprehend the attitudes and beliefs connected with inclusion, and this is where the significance of teacher training lies (Reynolds, 2001).

If teaching staff want to be good inclusive practitioners, they must learn and sustain not only skills and experience, but also favorable attitudes regarding the educational system (Yada et al., 2018). Having taken a pragmatic approach to a proficient activity in the context of incorporation of these students enables us to concentrate our attractions on how insights serve as the instantaneous conceptual components to practice, the jumping-off points for special needs student's classroom teachers, service providers, and others who act in the daily life of children with disabilities. And also look at how professional development can help the process (Vasianovych et al., 2020). According to literature on inclusive education, one of the most significant hurdles to implementing inclusion is that several instructors believe they are undertrained to provide appropriate services to kids with special education. As a result of the drive toward inclusive education, teacher preparation programs have been pushed to adequately train teachers to work with children of determination and other students in the classroom. Several school institutions now demand teacher training programs to generate teachers who can respond to varied school students in their regular classes (Kurniawati et al., 2014).

2.3. Teacher Training and Inclusion

In order to encourage inclusive education, teacher development programs are critical. Among the most critical problems that countries are experiencing is ensuring that teachers are adequately prepared to execute inclusive education initiatives in their classrooms. Teachers must obtain necessary training on inclusive education if they are to become effective, inclusion professionals who comprehend and satisfy the needs of individual learners (Siddik & Kawai, 2020). Numerous professional issues persist, posing a threat to the most effective provision of Inclusive education. Despite the fact that teachers are well conscious of the importance of a fully inclusive classroom, there are still gaps among what teaching staff perceive to be required of them in regard to student acceptance of what they take into account to be virtuously worthy – and what seems to be feasible or even worth considering in the classroom setting (Perrin et al., 2021).

To encourage inclusive practice, it's crucial to understand the elements that influence instructors' competence and readiness to integrate children with varying needs in their classes. Although studies have also shown that both instructors' competency and dispositions have an influence on inclusive teaching, few studies have looked into the relationship that exists (Pit-ten Cate et al., 2018). Countries all across the world deserve an accessible, balanced, and high-quality inclusive class environment (Siddik & Kawai, 2020).

Quality education for those students with exceptionalities is currently a challenge. It necessitates ongoing activity planning in order to provide efficient and effective psychological and educational support to those pupils and their families. As a result, the teacher believes that pragmatism is a valid viewpoint to use when researching the topic (Vasianovych et al., 2020). Rather than focusing just on teachers' ideas and attitudes, it is necessary to evaluate educators' competence for inclusive classrooms, particularly their expertise and training. This is because teachers' awareness of inclusive education may vary from existing views (Zagona et al., 2017).

Nilholm and Göransson (2017) argue that there are challenges in inclusion practices in schools, such as problems in policies and procedural, facilities and infrastructure, skilled personnel, trained teachers, instructional methodologies, adaptable curricula, managerial support, and societal values are all known hurdles to inclusive education. However, instead of concentrating on flaws, it could be more valuable to consider how established and recognized inclusive classroom strategies might be recognized and implemented successfully (Schuelka, 2018). In addition, while teacher training programs are developed and implemented in various ways, it's vital to analyze what these programs entail and how they might be regarded as successful (Kurniawati et al., 2014).

2.4. Inclusive PDPs around the World

Right-based education has been a common trend in different countries, and to make inclusion a reality, nations are working closely with educators by training them and providing them with adequate guidance (Jenkins & Yoshimura, 2010). According to Sharma et al. (2013), the Asia-Pacific has witnessed a spur of teacher training in inclusion, and this has even become a mandate in some places like Vietnam. This not only requires acceptance from those teachers, but it relies heavily on knowledgeable experts who are willing and capable of providing such professional development. Additionally, countries like India and Pakistan are aware of the fact that such a program cannot be successful without including school leaders who, in turn, need to understand the concept of inclusion before adapting it as an educational scheme within the school community (Caceres et al., 2010). In Greece, studies show that teachers are asking for more courses in inclusion and that those who receive inclusive training feel more at ease implementing the right strategies in their classrooms, and they do it with an open mind and with high levels of self-efficacy (Avramidis & Kalyva, 2007; Martínez, 2003). Yet another country that is highlighting the importance of PDP is Brazil, where research around inclusion is underlining the positive impact of training on inclusive awareness and implementation. Haegele et al. (2016) state that such programs not only promote acceptance but also enhance competence when it comes to teachers and their inclusive practices within mainstream classrooms.

3. Theoretical Framework

This paper investigates the impact of a PDP on teacher preparation in inclusive settings as it endows them with necessary skills, knowledge and competency. Studies state that evaluating training can be done by utilizing the Kirkpatrick model which looks at four aspects: (1) how participants in a PDP feel about the program – which includes their attitudes towards the facilitator, content and delivery; (2) participants' knowledge after the PDP, the learning they received and if outcomes were met; (3) change in participants' attitudes towards the training topic and how well they are able to apply their learning into their workplace; and (4) participants' ability to instill change in their working environment post training (Rafiq, 2015; Smidt et al., 2009). This model is important when looking at inclusion PDPs and their impact on participants, especially with the fact that training in this realm aims at promoting inclusion and encouraging acceptance, implementation and community change.

Students learn in environments that support them and help them construct knowledge in socially engaging environments (Vygotsky, 1987), and this is essential for students with SEND. For teachers to be ready for inclusion, they are required to engage learners, to differentiate instruction and learning and be able to understand the nature of adaptations for learners with SEND. Tomlinson (1999) proposed an instruction framework that aims to ensure that all students' needs are responded to in an environment that respects differences and supports student-based learning, autonomy, success, flexible classrooms, well-planned curricula and student-teacher partnerships. This model embodies the four aforementioned theories in a class that involves: enjoyable instruction, positive collaborations, monitoring (Reis et al., 2011), ongoing and opportunity-maximizing assessment (Tomlinson, 2003), in addition to awareness of variations in students' "readiness, interest and learning profile" (Tomlinson, 1999: 18). In this philosophical approach, a pre-set plan is determined with the following fundamentals: students, how knowledge-ready they are, what they are interested in and how they would like to learn (Gregory & Chapman, 2002). The implementation of such an educational scheme can only be done if teachers receive adequate inclusive education training, and this is where the importance of investigating PDPs and their impact lies (Mcallister & Maguire, 2012).

3.1. Context of the Study

The United Arab Emirates (UAE) began recognizing these rights of students with SEND in 1979, and the Ministry of Education (MOE) reinstated this acknowledgment in 2006 by stipulating Federal Law no. 29 that came after the country ratified UNCRPD and ensured equal academic opportunities for students with SEND (AlGhawi, 2007; Gaad, 2019; Ministry of Education, 2019; Ministry of Social Affairs, 2006; Suliman, 2000). In 2010, the School for All initiative was launched to discuss inclusion requirements in schools: staff professional development, equity, support teams, awareness, in addition to curriculum, environment and assessment adaptations (Alborno & Gaad, 2014; Ministry of Education, 2010). And since inclusion cannot be effective without clear regulations and legislations (Anati & Ain, 2012), the emirate of Dubai and its Knowledge and Human Development Authority (KHDA) presented schools with an inclusive education policy (Knowledge and Human Development Authority, 2017) and a supplementary guide (Knowledge and Human Development Authority, 2019). These documents required educators to attain inclusive education professional development sessions. With this vision of inclusive education, one of the initiatives that the country put forth in 2013 is the Ta'alouf Inclusion Special Education Teacher Training Programme, a project led by the non-profit Al Jalila Foundation (AJF) in collaboration with a federal university in the UAE. The aim of this initiative revolves around training of teachers, promoting inclusion and consequently providing adequate support to children with SEND and their caregivers. Fifteen schools across the UAE took part in this endeavor, and the 63 participants included teachers, department heads, principals, social workers and learning support assistants. Six online training sessions (total of 24 hours) were provided to the program participants, and topics were all related to inclusive education and special educational needs and disabilities such as: inclusion laws, the gifted and talented, learning difficulties, physical disabilities, intellectual disabilities, attention deficit hyperactivity disorder (ADHD), hearing/sight impairment, and Autism Spectrum Disorder (ASD). Furthermore, 13 faculty members from the federal university that AJF partnered with provided three hours of online mentoring to each participant, with the aim of assisting them in project assignments, building confidence, setting goals and understanding inclusion and its pertaining strategies and requirements. Mentors were to subsequently submit weekly tracking sheets which included their discussions with the mentees, their insights and any related feedback about the sessions. Attaining the program certificate depended on participant assignments that included questions related to the training sessions. In their answers, participants were asked to reflect, apply and discuss what they learned in the professional development training program, and their work was then evaluated by the involved university faculty. Also, participants attended three online Professional Learning Community meetings which were designed to shed light on previous research on inclusion and how to implement the results of those studies within the inclusive environment.

Additionally, participants set up their own PLCs, where they discussed their beliefs about inclusion and students with SEND and then transformed them into realistic goals and a consequent work plan that could be applied into their schools under the umbrella of inclusion.

4. Methods

The study was conducted using a qualitative approach and its paradigmatic position was interpretivism. A qualitative approach was selected as it enabled researchers to collect rich textual data (Creswell & Creswell, 2017) about their experiences of participating in the PDP. A qualitative approach was ideal as it enabled participants to share their views about the phenomenon. This is consistent with Cohen et al. (2017) who contend that a qualitative approach is suitable for a study that seeks to understand people's views about something. Interpretive paradigm was selected as it is compatible with a qualitative approach. The interpretive paradigm has greater focus on more detailed aspects and characteristics related to a situation, as it digs deeper into what is beyond individuals' physical processes. It produces greater depth in interpretations, predicated on the idea that humans and their experiences cannot be studied in quantitative processes (Pham, 2018).

The researchers used a phenomenological research design. The phenomenological model is part of the qualitative research approach. Phenomenology focuses on real-life situations with which we are familiar but lack in-depth and precise understanding (Creswell & Creswell, 2017). The phenomenology approach was used since the objective was to extensively investigate subjective views about the extent to which an inclusive education PDP impacted on teachers. Following this research design, certain steps were followed for selecting a sample, data collection, and analysis.

4.1. Sample and Data Collection

A study population is a group of individuals in which the researcher is interested in exploring the phenomenon under study. Population in the current study comprised of teachers and school administrators who were taking part in an inclusive education PDP. Purpose of the PDP was to work on the improvement of teachers and school administrators' performance in their school with regard to inclusive education. The study comprised of 20 participants who were selected using purposive sampling. The approach of purposive sampling is one important type of a non-probability sampling frameworks. It is sometimes referred to as judgmental, discriminating or subjective sampling, refers to a collection of sampling procedures that are centered on the researchers' selection of a group to participate in the individuals being researched. Purposive sampling frameworks include non-probabilistic sampling and homogeneous sampling, to name a couple of examples (Sharma, 2017). After selecting the sample of the study, data was collected using one-on-one semi-structured interviews. After recording interviews, they were transcribed and analyzed using thematic data analysis technique. Semi-structured interviews were used as they enabled researchers to interact extensively with participants to understand the phenomenon.

4.2. Ethical Consideration

In qualitative research studies, the main role of ethics is to regulate the situation between the interviewer and the interviewee. Experts point out that the contact between the interviewer and the interviewee while data gathering can develop moral ramifications in typical phenomenological research. Consequently, it is necessary to define criteria and follow in order to avoid ethical repercussions. The key considerations that produce ethical difficulties in qualitative research as a whole include anonymity of the respondents, as well as written informed consent (Adhabi & Anozie, 2017). In this study, participants were ensured that their identity would not be shown to anyone at any cost, and the data collected for this research would be used for study purposes only. In addition, ethical issues were observed by obtaining ethical clearance for the research project. The purpose of the study was explained to all participants and they were informed that their participation was voluntary. All participants were accorded the freedom to withdraw from the study at any point. Pseudonyms were used and confidentiality was maintained throughout the study. Consent forms were signed by all participants prior to data collection.

5. Results

This section presents findings of the study, and they are categorized according to three themes which emerged. The themes are, comprehensive knowledge about inclusion, application of knowledge, and ability to help others.

5.1. Comprehensive Knowledge about Inclusion

All participants reiterated that the program helped them gain comprehensive knowledge about inclusive education. They learnt information which they did not know. A participant said,

The course instructor gave us a lot of knowledge about children with different special needs and how to identify them. To be very honest with you, I had no clue about it. All that I used to get was an IEP [Individual Education Plan] from the Special Education Needs department at the school which was just a paper which had no sense to me. All that I knew was, this kid has dysgraphia, this kid is autistic, this kid has dyscalculia, but I did not know what those meant. But, this particular AJF program that I attended with Dr. X gave me vast knowledge about how to deal with a kid who has dysgraphia, what are the kind of manipulatives that you can use for these kids, what are the kind of recommendations that you can use during your school time with the school as your great support.

Some participants heard the term inclusive education before, but they did not know what it meant let alone knowing how to support SEND students. A participant said,

I did not know what inclusive education was. I heard that term, but I never realized this is the meaning of that. I only knew what inclusive education meant when I was collecting data for my portfolio for the AJF program.

Similarly, another participant echoed the same sentiment about knowing about inclusion after joining the AJF program: "I did not know about inclusion, but now it is totally opposite. I am ready to experience what I have learnt. Unfortunately, our school do not have students with special needs at the moment." All teachers felt that the program has enabled them to gain a lot of knowledge about inclusion. They learnt about different learning difficulties and disabilities and they feel prepared to implement what they learnt.

Participants reported that they learnt how to categorize children's behavior and deal with it accordingly, and to differentiate gifted from talented students. This is supported by a participant who said,

The program gave me good knowledge about special need students. I learnt how to identify and categorize some types of students' behaviors and deal with them accordingly. I am now able to recognize the type of learning difficulty that a student may be having. In addition, I did not know the difference between a gifted and talented child. I thought they meant the same thing. I thought students who achieve good marks in class are talented and gifted. I was thinking like that. But, after completing this program, I can differentiate gifted from talented students.

Similarly, another participant reported that she learnt from the program that gifted and talented are not the same. The participant said,

I learnt how to deal with gifted and talented students in my class. I learnt how to develop their talents. I used to say that gifted students and hardworking students are the same. I could not tell the difference between gifted, talented, and

hardworking. After joining this course, I learnt how to differentiate between gifted students and hard workers.

Very few teachers who participated in the program had prior experience of working with SEND children. One of the participants who had experience of working with SEND students acknowledged that the program added more value in terms of knowledge and approaches to inclusion. The participant said,

To be honest with you, the program increased the level of information and awareness that I had. I am actually dealing with people of determination [SEND student] from all over. However, there are some cases that I have never delt with before like, down syndrome for example. I have never delt with a student with this condition. Through the program, I learnt how to teach children with down syndrome and how I can keep in mind that this kid is not completely different than the rest of the kids.

Teachers who did not have prior knowledge of special education or experience of dealing with SEND students benefitted from the program more. One participant said,

I did not have prior knowledge about special needs education in depth like the way I have now. I knew that there are kids with special needs, but, I did not know how to handle them. I knew that there are children who throw tantrums, but I did not know how to handle them. After having an opportunity of studying the AJF program, I am well equipped with all kinds of strategies of handling children with diverse needs. I know I am ready to go.

Similarly, another participant who did not have prior knowledge and experience of working with SEND students attested that the program benefitted her:

Before taking this course, I had an autistic child in my class. I did not have kids with ADHD but, I remember that I had a child like two years ago and I was not very sure that he was autistic. He was presenting all the signs but, still I had that doubt you know. I did not know he had autism. But, after taking the course, I know how to identify a child with autism, how to teach and modify the curriculum for him or her.

The program equipped teachers with comprehensive knowledge which enabled them to cater for the needs of SEND students in their classes. The program also enabled school officials to open doors for SEND students to enroll in their schools. The schools were not enrolling SEND students all along as teachers were not trained to support them. Teachers from such schools reported that they feel prepared to teach and support children with disabilities because of the knowledge they gained from the PDP. A participant said,

Our school was not ready to accept students with special needs and disabilities because we, the teachers did not know how to teach them. But, after we got these

AJF certificates, the school management is thinking about making the school inclusive which is really great. The school management got excited that we got trained and they are ready to enroll special education and disabled children as they now have trained teachers. I feel that I am adequately prepared to work with special need and disabled children as I now have a good understanding of different learning difficulties and disabilities.

Another participant from the same school who attended the program echoed the same sentiment saying,

The school management is happy that I got a certificate of inclusion. They are saying that starting from next year they are going to provide facilities and resources for SEND students. They are having some interviews with some SEND students now. This is fascinating. The school did not have any special need child because there were no inclusion teachers. But, it now has five teachers who got certificates from AJF. That is why they are planning to enroll special need children from next year. I just had a meeting with the principal about this, we were talking about that.

The program has helped participants develop confidence in dealing with SEND students and improve inclusive practices. It helped them develop confidence that they can teach the children even if they did not have experience of working with special needs before. A participant said,

Because I had a class with more than one special need kid in the classroom, and each one was different. So, yes, the program has a positive impact to be honest. I had no experience of teaching SEND students. I now feel more confident to deal with SEND students whom I am having right now and those that I will have in the future inshallah (God willing).

Another participant supported the view that the program added more knowledge on inclusion and boosted all teachers' confidence when dealing with SEND students:

The program made us feel so comfortable when dealing with SEND students. The AJF instructor made us understand this inclusion and believe that it is not a big thing as we thought. I used to say, oh my God, inclusion is something which is tough, whenever a SEND student was in my class, I would say, oh my God, this year it is going to be tough as I must plan more and work harder. It is very difficult to manage them. But, thankfully, I must say we are confident enough. We now know a lot. We can say, yeah, this strategy will work on this child, this does not work, and we have plan b in place. So, the program taught us everything and it made us confident. The assignment and project work which we completed made us more confident as we gained knowledge and how to Google many things.

The confidence in dealing with SEND students which participants gained from the program made them realize that they can provide quality inclusive pedagogical approaches in their classes. They felt that the program has given them a green light to implement inclusion fully compared to old ways they used to do. Some participants attended some PDP different from the AJF. However, they singled the AJF as the one that gave them a good foundation to identify children's special needs and provide adequate support. A participant supported this view saying,

Previously, I took other courses related to special education, but, I could say that this AJF course clarified many things for me. It clarified very specific things, for instance how you can recognize an autist child or a child with ADHD. The course was well structured. I think that now I can identify and assess a child with a special need. Everything is clearer to me.

The quantitative data which was collected supports the view that all participants found the AJF program helpful as it helped them gain more knowledge about inclusive education. Figure 1 shows what participants said. All participants affirmed that the program helped them gain comprehensive knowledge about inclusion. None of the participants neither disagreed not strongly disagreed with the statement that the AJF program helped them.

5.2. Application of Knowledge

Participants reiterated that the knowledge they gained from the AJF program will go a long way in helping them when dealing with children with diverse learning needs in their classrooms. Some of the participants have already started applying the knowledge they gained into their classrooms while others are envisioning to start implementing soon.

We just finished the program about a month and half ago, so I have not implemented what we have learnt. But I am planning to do so next year. If students of determination are still in my physical classes, I will be implementing what I learnt from the program. For sure, next year if students are with us and hopefully life return back to normal I will be teaching using strategies which I learnt. As a matter of fact, I did not give away my portfolio. All the information that I got whether from Dr X or my mentor, I have it on record and I will be using it when helping special need students.

Another participant who will be applying the knowledge said,

I have a student whose name is Mildred and she has autism. I will be using the information I gained from AJF to assist that student. I will apply the same strategies of teaching students with autism as I learnt them from the AJF program. That will help me a lot.

One participant reported that her approach to teaching in the classroom has changed. She said,

I was a general teacher all along. But, after completing this AJF program, I feel that I am ready to implement a completely different teaching approach now. My teaching has already changed as I am very inclusive. I am catering for the diverse needs of all my students regardless of their special needs and behaviors. I was unable to do that before.

Another participant reported that she feels adequately trained to teach inclusively. She is ready to teach, but it was hard to do so online because of students' absenteeism.

The thing that prevented me to apply all the strategies was the absence of the students. Some special need students who were in my class were not attending online classes. That is the biggest challenge that prevented me from applying strategies that I learnt from AJF

Another participant said, *"some of the things I applied with my students and some, I will apply through the coming years and through my experiences with new students. Hopefully they will benefit from me."*

5.3. Ability to Help Others

Teachers who participated in this study mentioned that the knowledge they gained from the AJF program will not only benefit them and students in their classes, but the school and parents as well. One participant said, "I can give advice to other people on how to deal with SEND students." Other people referred to in this case are some teachers at the school who did not attend the program. The program empowered teachers and made them feel obligated to share their knowledge and expertise with other teachers. One participant supported this view saying,

Before I joined the Al Jalila, I would probably run to my HOD [Head of Department] and say, Aha the kid is making a lot of throwing tantrums and he is disturbing my class. But now, since I know how to deal with these kids, I would probably share that knowledge with my co-teachers so that they know how to help them to deal with those kids.

The teacher felt empowered so much that she will be able to deal with SEND students without reporting to the HoD and also to help other teachers deal with inclusive related matters. The essence of the AJF is to train a few teachers from each school so that they train all other teachers at the same institution. That is why AJF selected only a few teachers to attend the training so that they can help their colleagues.

Another participant echoed the same sentiment about empowering other teachers with knowledge which she gained. She said,

I can help my colleagues who did not participate in the program. I have few colleagues who have cases of special need children, but they did not join the program. So, I might help them with the information I learn from this program. So, the knowledge I gained from the AJF program is useful not only to me, but the whole school.

Another participant reported that she did not have SEND students in her class, but felt that the knowledge she gained can be used to assist other teachers deal with inclusive cases they were having. She said,

I was having a SEND student last year. But this year, I am not having any. Other teachers are having SEND students in their classes this year and I will be giving ideas to them when they come to me and say, see what is happening in my classes, what shall I do. So, since I am a bit trained of all these things, I will be able to offer some assistance by telling them how to deal with specific cases related to inclusion. I have also given some sessions at my school about how to handle a SEND child online. I was a bit confident to give some few suggestions and advice since I learnt the information from AJF program.

Teachers who attended the AJF program felt that they became resourceful in their respective schools as they were helping others who did not attend the course. Some felt that knowledge gained from AJF can be used to assist parents as well. A participant said who was a social worker at the school said,

The knowledge I gained from AJF can also help me to assist parents and advise them about the specific learning difficulties that their children may be having. I will be able to advise parents in terms of where to take the child for professional assistance. I can also give some advice to the HOD or teachers and I can give the advice to the principle and I can give an advice to the parents. So, now I can help any student, just by giving an advance. Even if I haven't practiced anything.

Based on the evidence provided by all participants, the program had a positive impact on them as it enabled them to gain comprehensive knowledge about inclusion, learn how to apply some inclusive pedagogical practices, and have the ability to help parents and other teachers. The program was like a game changer to teachers as it provided knowledge and skills which helped change their attitudes towards inclusion.

6. Discussion

Inclusive schools work to provide a high-quality education to all students while also contributing to the development of a fully integrated society by responding to individual needs, combating attitudes, and creating supportive communities. In this light, inclusive schools accept and incorporate all children, irrespective of their special educational needs, into regular classrooms (Perrin et al., 2021). Various researchers pointed out that there is always a dearth of research over whether academic institutions have become much more inclusive, and teachers and parents have differing viewpoints about the applicability of inclusive education (Nilholm, 2021). The benefits of inclusion include methodically raising knowledge of disability concerns and educational demands (Siddik & Kawai, 2020).

In such right-based inclusive settings, teachers are "crafting escalators of learning" and hence have many responsibilities that require adequate professional development (Tomlinson, 1999: 91). They know their students well, help them create meanings and are aware of the fact that instruction, the curriculum and the environment are tightly connected (Salhyyieh, 2016). They are conscious of the need to proactively respond to student needs in a manner that reflects teacher positivity, time, eagerness, energy and potential-realizing efforts. They formulate their instruction and the curriculum considering relevance to students and their inclinations, routine, organization, clear direction and constant feedback (Tomlinson, 1999). Moreover, teachers use learning contracts, involve students in the planning process, listen to them and encourage them to also organize, regulate and assess the learning process. They use positive classroom management, constantly evaluate learner progress in different ways (Parsons et al., 2013), consider student strengths (Tomlinson, 2003) and are assertive on the teaching and learning process being a joint effort and cannot be made possible with the students' role (Senturk & Sari, 2018). These inclusion requirements cannot be successful without proper training and readiness (Mcallister & Maguire, 2012).

In fact, many factors may influence the degree to which inclusive practice can be adopted successfully. However, research suggests that in order to function efficiently in inclusive classrooms, teaching staff must possess not only the necessary awareness, skills, expertise, and comprehension, and also specified beliefs and ideals, with teaching staff' professionalism being linked to their behaviors toward learners with disabilities (Pit-ten Cate et al., 2018).

Additionally, it is evident from the literature that after getting skills and knowledge, teachers perform at their best. They are matchless after receiving knowledge and perform better than teachers with less knowledge (Nilholm & Göransson, 2017). Zagona et al. (2017) believe that improving the capabilities of teachers' development programs and professional learning measures to ensure teachers have the knowledge and experience to incorporate effective practices for teaching and learning in inclusive classes is one way of supporting pupils with severe disabilities to have significantly larger access to school setting and coursework.

7. Conclusion

The purpose of this study was to examine the impact of a PDP in preparing teachers for inclusive education. As evidenced in the results, teachers have different levels of understanding inclusion. Prior to joining the AJF PDP, some teachers had no idea about learning difficulties and disabilities. Some knew what they were, for example ADHD, dyslexia, and autism, but did not know what they meant let alone how to support children with those conditions in their classrooms. It is in that backdrop that this study concludes that it is a fallacy of composition to think that since teachers know about some learning difficulties and disabilities, they know what they mean and how to support a child with the conditions in a classroom. Results of this study illuminated that teachers may have heard about the learning difficulty or disability, but will not have any idea about including the child in a class. This necessitates an inclusive education PDP to fill the gap. Since we are in the 21st century where many countries have ratified numerous inclusive education policies, guidelines and frameworks, there is a need to ensure that teachers are adequately trained about different types of learning difficulties and disabilities. The best way to do it for in-service teachers is by offering PDP related to inclusion and afford them opportunities to study different learning difficulties and disabilities. The AJF program provided a milestone of achievement in terms of making teachers realize a paradigm shift from teaching exclusively to inclusively. It has enabled teachers to gain comprehensive knowledge about inclusion, change their mindsets and subsequently transform their attitudes and approaches to teaching SEND students. The teachers felt adequately prepared to promulgate inclusion at school level and implement inclusive pedagogical practices in their classes.

Acknowledgment

The authors wish to acknowledge the unwavering support they received from the Al Jalila Foundation (AJF). Without the AJF, the authors would not have been able to conduct this research.

References

Adhabi, E. A. R., & Anozie, C. B. L. (2017). Literature Review for the Type of Interview in Qualitative Research. *International Journal of Education*, *9*(3), 86. https://doi.org/10.5296/ije.v9i3.11483

Alborno, N. E., & Gaad, E. (2014). "Index for Inclusion": A Framework for School Review in the United Arab Emirates. *British Journal of Special Education*, *41*(3), 231–248. https://doi.org/10.1111/1467-8578.12073

AlGhawi, M. A. (2007). *Bridging the Gap between Theory and Practice of Inclusion in the United Arab Emirates* [M.Ed. Dissertation]. The British University in Dubai.

Amor, A. M., Hagiwara, M., Shogren, K. A., Thompson, J. R., Verdugo, M. Á., Burke, K. M., & Aguayo, V. (2018). International Perspectives and Trends in Research on Inclusive Education: A Systematic Review. *International Journal of Inclusive Education*, *23*(12), 1277–1295. https://doi.org/10.1080/13603116.2018.1445304

Anati, N. M., & Ain, A. (2012). Including Students with Disabilities in UAE Schools: A Descriptive Study. *International Journal of Special Education*, *27*(2), 75–85.

Avramidis, E., & Kalyva, E. (2007). The Influence of Teaching Experience and Professional Development on Greek Teachers' Attitudes towards Inclusion. *European Journal of Special Needs Education*, *22*(4), 367–389. https://doi.org/10.1080/08856250701649989

Caceres, S., Awan, M., Nabeel, T., Majeed, Z., & Mindes, J. (2010). *Inclusive Education in Pakistan: Experiences and Lessons Learned from the ENGAGE Project: (537642012-001)* [dataset]. https://doi.org/10.1037/e537642012-001

Cobley, D. (2018). *Disability and International Development: A Guide for Students and Practitioners* (1st ed.). Routledge. http://dx.doi.org/10.4324/9781315208558

Cohen, L., Manion, L., & Morrison, K. (2017). *Research Methods in Education* (8th ed.). Routledge. https://doi.org/10.4324/9781315456539

Creswell, J. W., & Creswell, J. D. (2017). *Research Design: Qualitative, Quantitative, and Mixed Methods Approaches*. SAGE Publications.

Florian, L. (2019). On the Necessary Co-existence of Special and Inclusive Education. *International Journal of Inclusive Education*, *23*(7–8), 691–704. https://doi.org/10.1080/13603116.2019.1622801

Gaad, E. (2019). Educating Learners with Special Needs and Disabilities in the UAE: Reform and Innovation. In K. Gallagher (Ed.), *Education in the United Arab Emirates: Innovation and Transformation* (pp. 147–159). Springer. https://doi.org/10.1007/978-981-13-7736-5_9

Gregory, G. H., & Chapman, C. (2002). *Differentiated Instructional Strategies: One Size Doesn't Fit All*. SAGE Publications.

Grigorenko, E. L., Stephanie, T., Lebedeva, E. L., & Bondar, Y. A. (2018). Evidence-Based Interventions for ASD: A Focus on Applied Behavior Analysis (ABA) Interventions. *Journal of the Higher School of Economics*, *15*(4), 711–727. https://doi.org/10.17323/1813-8918-2018-4-711-727

Haegele, J. A., Hodge, S., Filho, P. J. B. G., & de Rezende, A. L. G. (2016). Brazilian Physical Education Teachers' Attitudes toward Inclusion Before and After Participation in a Professional Development Workshop. *European Physical Education Review*, *24*(1), 21–38. https://doi.org/10.1177/1356336x16662898

Hills, D. C., & Sessoms-Penny, S. (2021). Pre-service Professional Development for Inclusion Teachers. *Research in Higher Education Journal*, *40*, 1–17.

Hollins-Alexander, S. (2013). *Online Professional Development Through Virtual Learning Communities*. Corwin.

Jenkins, A. A., & Yoshimura, J. (2010). Not Another Inservice!: Meeting the Special Education Professional Development Needs of Elementary General Educators. *Teaching Exceptional Children*, *42*(5), 36–43. https://doi.org/10.1177/004005991004200504

Juang, L. P., & Chitewere, T. (2020). Teachers of Migrant Background and Inclusive Education. In I. A. Wojciechowicz, D. N. Kayser, & M. Vock (Eds.), *Teacher Education in the Context of Current Refugee Migration: Perspectives, Ideas, and Inquiries* (pp. 58–70). Beltz Juventa Verlag.

Knowledge and Human Development Authority. (2017). *Dubai Inclusive Education Policy Framework*. https://www.khda.gov.ae/cms/webparts/texteditor/documents/Education_Policy_En.pdf

Knowledge and Human Development Authority. (2019). *Implementing Inclusive Education: A Guide for Schools*. https://www.khda.gov.ae/Areas/Administration/Content/FileUploads/Publication/Documents/English/20190123084554_SENDPOLICYSCHOOLS_EN.pdf

Kurniawati, F., De Boer, A. A., Minnaert, A. E. M. G., & Mangunsong, F. (2014). Characteristics of Primary Teacher Training Programmes on Inclusion: A Literature Focus. *Educational Research*, *56*(3), 310–326. https://doi.org/10.1080/00131881.2014.934555

Lindsay, S., Proulx, M., Thomson, N., & Scott, H. (2013). Educators' Challenges of Including Children with Autism Spectrum Disorder in Mainstream Classrooms. *International Journal of Disability, Development and Education*, *60*(4), 347–362. https://doi.org/10.1080/1034912x.2013.846470

Lipsky, D. K., & Gartner, A. (1997). *Inclusion and School Reform: Transforming America's Classrooms*. P.H. Brookes Publishing Company.

Martínez, R. (2003). Impact of a Graduate Class on Attitudes toward Inclusion, Perceived Teaching Efficacy and Knowledge about Adapting Instruction for Children with Disabilities in Inclusive Settings. *Teacher Development*, *7*(3), 473–494. https://doi.org/10.1080/13664530300200215

Mcallister, K., & Maguire, B. (2012). Design Considerations for the Autism Spectrum Disorder-Friendly Key Stage 1 Classroom. *Support for Learning*, *27*(3), 103–112. https://doi.org/10.1111/j.1467-9604.2012.01525.x

Merry, M. S. (2020). Do Inclusion Policies Deliver Educational Justice for Children with Autism? An Ethical Analysis. *Journal of School Choice*, *14*(1), 9–25. https://doi.org/10.1080/15582159.2019.1644126

Ministry of Education. (2010). *School for All: General Rules for the Provision of Special Education Programs and Services (Public & Private Schools)*. https://www.moe.gov.ae/English/SiteDocuments/Rules/SNrulesEn.pdf

Ministry of Education. (2019). *Education for People of Determination*. https://u.ae/en/information-and-services/education/education-for-people-with-special-needs

Ministry of Social Affairs. (2006). *UAE Federal Law 29/2006*. https://www.mocd.gov.ae/en/about-mocd/laws-and-legislations.aspx

Nilholm, C. (2021). Research about Inclusive Education in 2020 – How Can We Improve Our Theories in Order to Change Practice? *European Journal of Special Needs Education*, *36*(3), 358–370. https://doi.org/10.1080/08856257.2020.1754547

Nilholm, C., & Göransson, K. (2017). What Is Meant by Inclusion? An Analysis of European and North American Journal Articles with High Impact. *European Journal of Special Needs Education*, *32*(3), 437–451. https://doi.org/10.1080/08856257.2017.1295638

Parsons, S. A., Dodman, S. L., & Burrowbridge, S. C. (2013). Broadening the View of Differentiated Instruction. *Phi Delta Kappan*, *95*(1), 38–42. https://doi.org/10.1177/003172171309500107

Perrin, A.-L., Jury, M., & Desombre, C. (2021). Are Teachers' Personal Values Related to Their Attitudes toward Inclusive Education? A Correlational Study. *Social Psychology of Education*, *24*(4), 1085–1104. https://doi.org/10.1007/s11218-021-09646-7

Pham, L. (2018). *A Review of Key Paradigms: Positivism, Interpretivism and Critical Inquiry*. University of Adelaide. https://doi.org/10.13140/RG.2.2.13995.54569

Pit-ten Cate, I. M., Markova, M., Krischler, M., & Krolak-Schwerdt, S. (2018). Promoting Inclusive Education: The Role of Teachers' Competence and Attitudes. *Insights into Learning Disabilities*, *15*(1), 49–63.

Rafiq, M. (2015). Training Evaluation in an Organization Using Kirkpatrick Model: A Case Study of PIA. *Journal of Entrepreneurship & Organization Management*, *04*(03). https://doi.org/10.4172/2169-026x.1000151

Reis, S. M., McCoach, D. B., Little, C. A., Muller, L. M., & Kaniskan, R. B. (2011). The Effects of Differentiated Instruction and Enrichment Pedagogy on Reading Achievement in Five Elementary Schools. *American Educational Research Journal*, *48*(2), 462–501. https://doi.org/10.3102/0002831210382891

Reynolds, M. (2001). Education for Inclusion, Teacher Education and the Teacher Training Agency Standards. *Journal of In-Service Education*, *27*(3), 465–476. https://doi.org/10.1080/13674580100200164

Roberts, J., & Simpson, K. (2016). A Review of Research into Stakeholder Perspectives on Inclusion of Students with Autism in Mainstream Schools. *International Journal of Inclusive Education*, *20*(10), 1084–1096. https://doi.org/10.1080/13603116.2016.1145267

Salhyyieh, R. M. K. (2016). *English Teachers' Perceptions Toward Differentiated Assessment in Cycle Two at Al Ain Public Schools* [M.Ed. Dissertation]. United Arab Emirates University.

Saloviita, T. (2020). Attitudes of Teachers Towards Inclusive Education in Finland. *Scandinavian Journal of Educational Research*, *64*(2), 270–282. https://doi.org/10.1080/00313831.2018.1541819

Schuelka, M. (2018). The Cultural Production of the "Disabled" Person: Constructing Difference in Bhutanese Schools. *Anthropology & Education Quarterly*, *49*(2), 183–200. https://doi.org/10.1111/aeq.12244

Senturk, C., & Sari, H. (2018). Investigation of Impacts of Differentiated Instruction Applied in a Primary School in Attitudes of Students Towards the Course. *Cypriot Journal of Educational Sciences*, *13*(2), 240–248. https://doi.org/10.18844/cjes.v13i2.3359

Sharma, G. (2017). Pros and Cons of Different Sampling Techniques. *International Journal of Applied Research*, *3*(7), 749–752.

Sharma, U., Forlin, C., & Deppeler, J. (2013). Reforming Teacher Education for Inclusion in Developing Countries in the Asia-Pacific Region. *Asian Journal of Inclusive Education*, *01*(1), 03–16. https://doi.org/10.59595/ajie.01.1.2

Siddik, M. A. B., & Kawai, N. (2020). Government Primary School Teacher Training Needs for Inclusive Education in Bangladesh. *International Journal of Whole Schooling*, *16*(2), 35–69.

Smidt, A., Balandin, S., Sigafoos, J., & Reed, V. A. (2009). The Kirkpatrick Model: A Useful Tool for Evaluating Training Outcomes. *Journal of Intellectual & Developmental Disability*, *34*(3), 266–274. https://doi.org/10.1080/13668250903093125

Smith-Spark, L. (2021, January 15). *How Will School Closures Affect Children in the Long Run? Wars, Disease and Natural Disasters Offer Clues*. CNN. https://www.cnn.com/2021/01/15/world/schools-closures-impact-children-history-intl/index.html

Stadler-Heer, S. (2019). Inclusion. *ELT Journal*, *73*(2), 219–222. https://doi.org/10.1093/elt/ccz004

Suliman, O. M. (2000). *A Descriptive Study of the Educational System of the United Arab Emirates* [Ed.D. Dissertation]. University of Southern California.

Tomlinson, C. A. (1999). *The Differentiated Classroom: Responding to the Needs of All Learners*. Association for Supervision and Curriculum Development.

Tomlinson, C. A. (2003). Deciding to Teach Them All. *Educational Leadership, 61*(2), 6–11.

UNESCO. (1994). *The Salamanca Statement and Framework for Action on Special Needs Education*. https://unesdoc.unesco.org/ark:/48223/pf0000139394

Vasianovych, H., Budnyk, O., Klepar, M., Beshok, T., Blyznyuk, T., & Latyshevska, K. (2020). Pragmatism in Philosophy of Inclusive Education Studies and Problems of Teacher Training. *Revista Inclusiones, 7*, 59–73.

Vygotsky, L. S. (1987). Mind in Society: The Development of Higher Psychological Processes. Harvard University Press. http://dx.doi.org/10.2307/j.ctvjf9vz4.5

Waitoller, F. R., & Artiles, A. J. (2013). A Decade of Professional Development Research for Inclusive Education. *Review of Educational Research, 83*(3), 319–356. https://doi.org/10.3102/0034654313483905

Yada, A., & Savolainen, H. (2017). Japanese In-Service Teachers' Attitudes Toward Inclusive Education and Self-Efficacy for Inclusive Practices. *Teaching and Teacher Education, 64*, 222–229. https://doi.org/10.1016/j.tate.2017.02.005

Yada, A., Tolvanen, A., & Savolainen, H. (2018). Teachers' Attitudes and Self-Efficacy on Implementing Inclusive Education in Japan and Finland: A Comparative Study Using Multi-Group Structural Equation Modelling. *Teaching and Teacher Education, 75*, 343–355. https://doi.org/10.1016/j.tate.2018.07.011

Zagona, A. L., Kurth, J. A., & MacFarland, S. Z. C. (2017). Teachers' Views of Their Preparation for Inclusive Education and Collaboration. *Teacher Education and Special Education: The Journal of the Teacher Education Division of the Council for Exceptional Children, 40*(3), 163–178. https://doi.org/10.1177/0888406417692969

Hena Oak

Has the World Become Truly Sustainable? Evidence from the Top Carbon Emitters of 2022

1. Introduction

United Nations has defined sustainable development as development that meets the needs of the present without compromising the ability of future generations to meet their own needs. The importance of pursuing sustainable development goals has become even more important due to the rising problems associated with global warming. In this regard, numerous international agreements have been suggested, debated, and ratified. The UN Framework Convention on Climate Change, 1992 was the first global treaty on climate change. UNFCCC was the architect of legally binding climate treaties like the Kyoto Protocol and the Paris Agreement. But has the increased environmental cognizance of the countries translated into concrete policies?

One of the important indicators of a country's commitment towards sustainable development can be gauged by analyzing its carbon dioxide (CO_2) emissions generated per annum. This is directly correlated with the consumption of non-renewable energy. As per the 2023 Statistical Review of World Energy, primary energy consumption rose from 155.91 Exajoules (EJ) in 1965 to 604.04 EJ in 2022, with a CAGR of 2.36 %. World Development Indicators data indicates 94 % of the energy comprised of fossil fuels in 1965. It fell to 79 % in 2015, and data extrapolation shows that its likely to have fallen to approximately 75 % in 2022, thereby hinting at a move away from emission-intensive energy sources towards greener sources. However, the global trend may not be emulated by all countries homogeneously. As per the 2022 data, the top four emitters of CO_2 were China, USA, India, and Russia in that order. The total fossil fuel energy consumption in these four countries together increased from 130.31 EJ in 1990[1] to 285.69 EJ, with a CAGR of 2.41 %. The rise in fossil fuel energy has been the highest for China, resulting in the concomitant increase in its emissions.

The purpose of this paper is to analyze a set of sustainability energy indicators, to test if the top four emitters have become more environmentally conscious in

1 The period has been taken from 1990 because of disintegration of USSR.

their energy use overtime. The paper then tests for cointegration between a set of sustainability indicators, viz., per capita energy consumption, per capita emissions, and per capita GDP to check for the existence of a long-run relationship between the variables. A vector autoregressive model (VAR) and a vector error correction model (VECM) is estimated accordingly.

Empirical results show that for India per capita energy consumption, per capita emissions, and per capita GDP are not cointegrated, and so there does not exist a long-term causal relationship between the variables. For China, Russia, and USA long run elasticities have been computed for the variables, and the results are statistically significant for per unit energy consumption and emissions. There does not exist short run relationship between most variables.

2. Analysis of Sustainable Development Indicators

The world has seen numerous international agreements on climate change, some of them binding, being signed, and supported by nations. This section analyzes some of the sustainability indicators to see if trends have become positive over the sample period of 1990–2022 for the top four emitters of 2022. China, USA, India, and Russia have accounted for more than 54 % of the global CO_2 emissions. But within these four nations, the trends are quite heterogeneous. As Figure 1 shows, India and Russia have always been at the bottom of the chain for the period 1990–2022, India because it is an emerging economy and Russia because of its disintegration that greatly reduced its energy consumption.

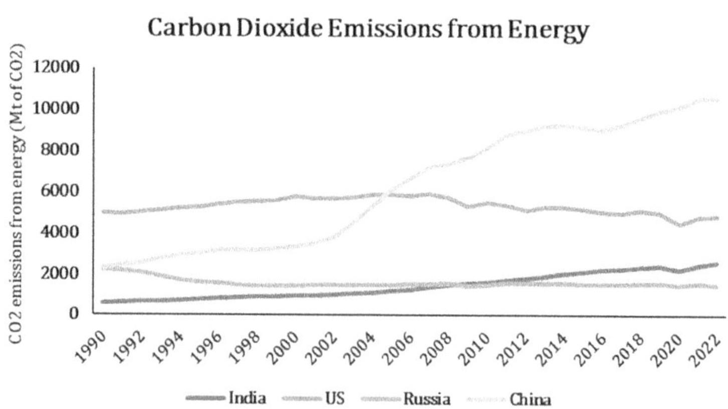

Figure 1: Carbon dioxide emissions from energy

Estimates given in Table 1 shows the huge gaps in the CO_2 emissions between the top four nations. In 1990, compared with India, USA's CO_2 emissions from energy were 826 %, China's were 384 % and Russia's were 371 %. India's share in overall global emissions in 1990 was the lowest at only 2.82 %, while USA's share was the highest at 23.3 %. In 2022, USA's emissions were 186 % of India's, while China's share rose to 406 %. Russia's share declined substantially to 56 % of India's emissions from energy. India's share in global emissions rose in 2022 to 8 %, while China recorded a significant increase from 11 % in 1990 to 31 % in 2022. The global shares of both USA and Russia declined from their 1990 levels.

Table 1: Emissions of county *i* w.r.t country *j* in 1990 and 2022 ($i \neq j$)

	Emissions of Country *i* w.r.t *j* in 1990				**Emissions of Country *i* w.r.t *j* in 2022**			
	Country i				***Country i***			
Country j	**India**	**US**	**Russia**	**China**	**India**	**US**	**Russia**	**China**
India	100.00 %	825.58 %	371.04 %	383.48 %	100.00 %	185.90 %	56.15 %	406.43 %
US	12.11 %	100.00 %	44.94 %	46.45 %	53.79 %	100.00 %	30.20 %	218.62 %
Russia	26.95 %	222.50 %	100.00 %	103.35 %	178.10 %	331.10 %	100.00 %	723.86 %
China	26.08 %	215.29 %	96.76 %	100.00 %	24.60 %	45.74 %	13.81 %	100.00 %
World	2.82 %	23.30 %	10.47 %	10.83 %	7.55 %	14.04 %	4.24 %	30.69 %

CO_2 emissions are directly correlated with consumption of fossil fuels. The paper uses data from Statistical Review of World Energy, 2023 and WDI to construct the series on fossil fuel energy consumption for the period 1990–2022.

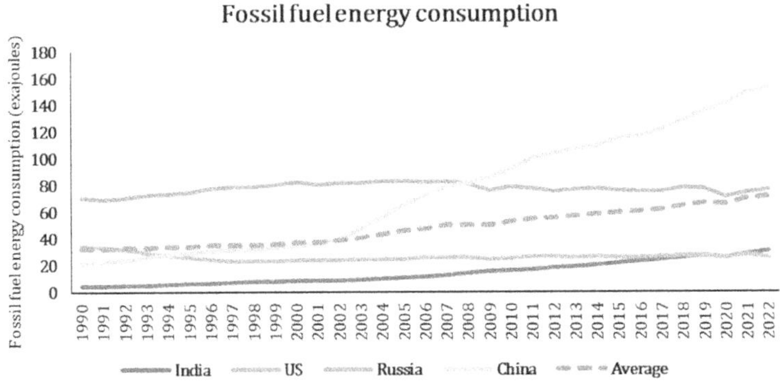

Figure 2: Fossil fuel energy consumption (exajoules)

Figure 2 shows India and Russia's average fossil fuel energy consumption were consistently below average. China's fossil fuel consumption was also below average till 2001–02, after which there was a steady upward trend. The dynamics related to energy consumption changed in the 2000s as compared to the 1990s, as shown in the map below.

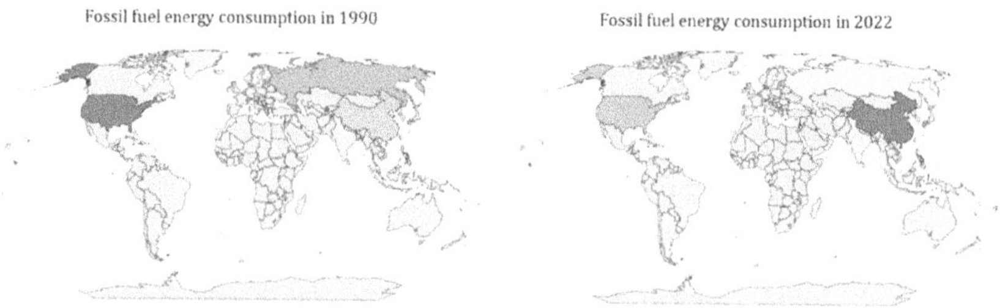

Figure 3: Changing pattern of fossil fuel energy consumption (exajoules) in 1990 and 2022

Data source for Fig. 3 is World Development Indicators, World Bank. Fig. 4 is own calculations Data source for Fig. 6 is World Development Indicators, World Bank. Data has been taken for Fossil fuel energy consumption and Population. Per capita calculations are own calculations.

USA has historically recorded values above average, but now the values are converging towards average, while the values for China shows a clear divergence. However, for USA, this trend may not necessarily reflect actual movement away from fossil fuel consumption, but simply a fall in industrial activity due to the economic crisis. Fossil fuel consumption declined between 2005 and 2012 due to the bursting of the housing bubble. Consumption picked up again after 2012, but declined once again with the COVID-19 pandemic.

Starting from 1990 to 2022, fossil fuels worth 12142 EJ of energy have been consumed globally, out of which more than 52 % has been consumed by the top four emitters alone. Within this, more than 40 % of the fossil fuel has been consumed by USA and China. India's share is relatively minuscule at 3.87 %, followed by Russia at 7.13 %.

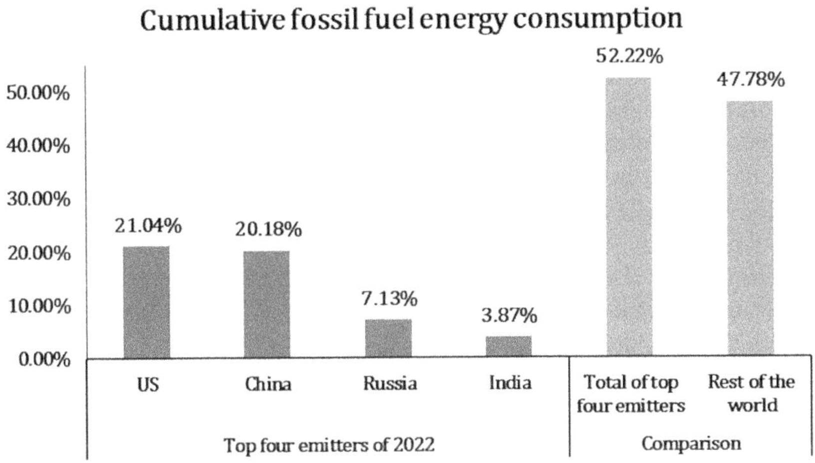

Figure 4: Cumulative fossil fuel energy consumption (exajoules)

These values will have a direct bearing on the reserve-to-production ratio or RPR, defined as the number of years a natural resource will last. Figure 5 below shows the RPR for coal, oil and natural gas[2].

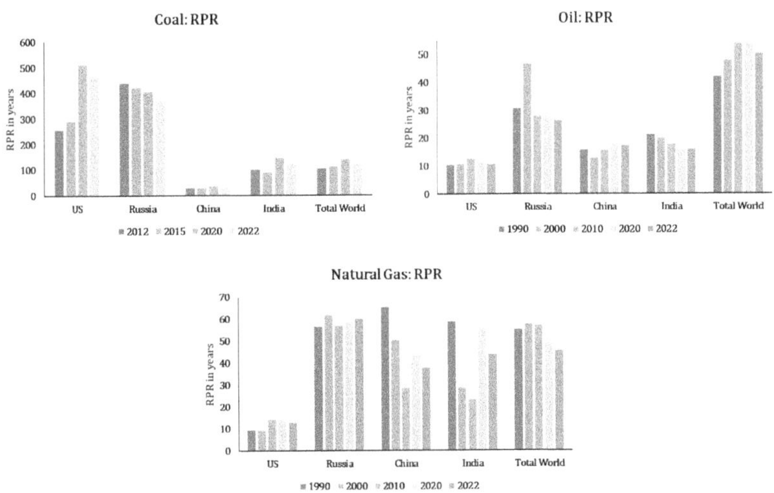

Figure 5: Reserve-to-production in years for coal, oil and natural gas (select years)

2 Data for coal reserves was available from 2012.

USA has the largest deposit of coal in the world. The RPR between 2012 and 2015 increased from 257 years to 292 years because of the fall in fossil fuel consumption in USA. It increased further in 2020, mainly because of the adverse effect on economic activity due to the COVID-19 pandemic. This trend in increase in RPR is true for the rest of the world as well. But after industrial activity picked up pace once again, the RPR for coal began to decline globally. Calculations show that the RPR in years for coal is approximately 122 years as of 2022. The RPR for oil and natural gas is found to be 50.4 years and 45.42 years respectively.

Besides absolute consumption of fossil fuel, per capita consumption of fossil fuel is also an important indicator of sustainable development because it will help to assess the shares of individuals in the overall aggregates.

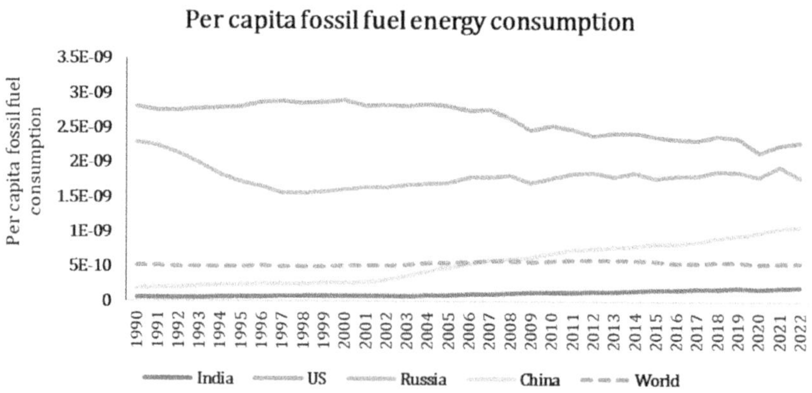

Figure 6: Per capita fossil fuel energy consumption (exajoules)

Between 1990 and 2022, per capita fossil fuel energy consumption is the highest for USA, followed by Russia, while both these countries are the least populated out of the four. India's per capita consumption has been the lowest, even lower than global values. China's values were close to India, but after 2001–2002 there was a rapid increase. On an average, USA's per capita energy consumption has been more than 2725 % higher than that of India for the period 1990–2022. These values reflect uneven distribution and uneven access to fossil fuels across nations.

Several international agreements have addressed the issue of climate change resulting from emissions. The first legally binding treaty on climate change was the Kyoto Protocol, that was adopted in December 1997 and came into force on

16 February 2005, to be continued till 31 December 2012. Emission reduction targets were imposed on Annex I countries, that included USA and Russia. These two countries were requited to reduce their emissions by 7 % and 0 % respectively by 2012 as compared to the base year emissions. The base year was set to be the year 1990. However, USA declared that it would not ratify the Kyoto Protocol. Figure 7 below shows the emission level in the target year for USA had it ratified the Kyoto Protocol, and for Russia.

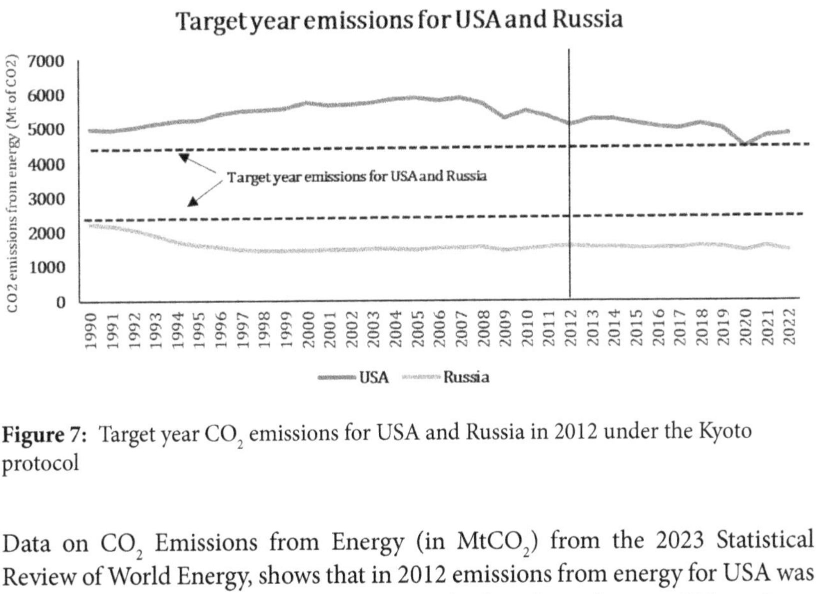

Figure 7: Target year CO_2 emissions for USA and Russia in 2012 under the Kyoto protocol

Data on CO_2 Emissions from Energy (in $MtCO_2$) from the 2023 Statistical Review of World Energy, shows that in 2012 emissions from energy for USA was 5089.15 $MtCO_2$, which was 466.59 $MtCO_2$ higher than what would have been if USA had ratified the Kyoto Protocol. Russia had to maintain the emissions at its 1990 level, but it achieved a reduction in CO_2 emissions by 653.28 $MtCO_2$ in 2012 compared to its 1990 level.

An important positive indicator of sustainable economic growth is rising share of renewable energy. Figure 8 below shows the share of renewable energy in total energy consumption, and the trends in CO_2 intensity, defined as CO_2 emissions per unit of GDP.

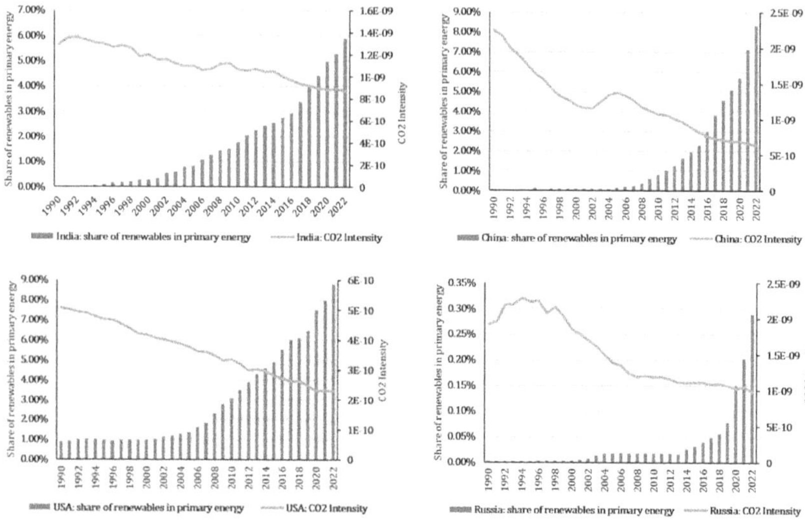

Figure 8: Share of renewables in total primary energy consumption and CO_2 intensity for 1990–2022

For all the countries, the share of renewables as a percentage of total primary energy consumption was less than 1 % in 1990. It rose to approximately 6 % for India, 8 % for China, 9 % for USA, and 0.3 % for Russia. The CAGR of renewable energy between 1990 and 2004 was 41 % for India, 35 % for China, 4 % for USA, and 13 % for Russia. The period 2005–2012 which was the implementation period for the Kyoto Protocol saw a 19 %, 38 %, 13 % and 1 % rise in renewable energy consumption for India, China, USA, and Russia respectively. Even though USA had not ratified the Kyoto Protocol, there was a substantial rise in the share of renewables during the implementation period. The last sub-period of the sample from 2013 to 2022, which includes the implementation period for Paris Agreement, saw a rate of growth of 13 %, 21 %, 8 % and 33 % for the four countries. Countries seem to be on the right path before the 2030 compliance period for the Paris Agreement.

3. Econometric Methodology

The paper uses cointegration, VAR and VECM to estimate the short run and long run relationship between three variables, viz., per unit energy consumption $(lnenergy)$, per unit CO_2 emissions $(lnemissions)$ and per unit GDP $(lngdp)$, all taken in logs. Energy consumption is defined as fossil fuel energy consumption in Mtoe. CO_2 emissions are emissions from energy in MtCO2. GDP refers to gross domestic product in constant 2015 US$. Data is taken from Statistical Review of World Energy, 2023 and WDI, World Bank data.

The paper first checks for stationarity of the variables through a unit root test, using the Levin-Lin-Chu unit root test, which is a common unit root process. For panel data, LLC test considers the null hypothesis that each individual time series in the panel contains a unit root against the alternative hypothesis that all individual series are stationary. Since the series is found to be non-stationary, the first difference terms are taken for all the series, after which the series become stationary. Therefore, they are found to be integrated of order 1 or $I(1)$.

Since all the variables are $I(1)$, Johansen test for cointegration is applied to check for the existence of a long run relationship between the variables. Both the trace test and maximum eigenvalue test statistics are applied (λ_{trace} and λ_{max}). But in case of any discrepancy, λ_{max} test is used as it has a sharper alternative hypothesis (Enders, 2004). The null hypothesis of the λ_{max} test states that the number of cointegrating vectors is r against the alternative hypothesis that it is $r + 1$.

In case the variables are not found to be cointegrated, a VAR model is estimated to get the short-term relationship between variables, as follows with a lag length of 1:

$$lnemissions_t = \alpha_1 + \beta_1 lnemissions_{t-1} + \gamma_1 lnenergy_{t-1} + \delta_1 lngdp_{t-1} + \mu_{1t}$$

$$lnenergy_t = \alpha_2 + \beta_2 lnemissions_{t-1} + \gamma_2 lnenergy_{t-1} + \delta_2 lngdp_{t-1} + \mu_{2t}$$

$$lngdp_t = \alpha_3 + \beta_3 lnemissions_{t-1} + \gamma_3 lnenergy_{t-1} + \delta_3 lngdp_{t-1} + \mu_{3t}$$

In case variables are found to be cointegrated, a VECM model is estimated to get the short-term and long-term relationship between variables.

- First, the cointegrating equation and long-run model is given as:

$$ECT_{t-1} = lnemissions_{t-1} - \varphi_1 lnenergy_{t-1} - \phi_1 lngdp_{t-1}$$

where ECT is the error correction term. The equation is normalized w.r.t. $lnemissions$.

- Second, VECM is estimated as

$$\Delta lnemission_t = a_1 + b_1 \Delta lnemissions_{t-1} + c_1 \Delta lnenergy_{t-1} + d_1 \Delta lngdp_{t-1} + \lambda_1 ECT_{t-1}$$

$$\Delta lnenergy_t = a_2 + b_2 \Delta lnemissions_{t-1} + c_2 \Delta lnenergy_{t-1} + d_2 \Delta lngdp_{t-1} + \lambda_2 ECT_{t-1}$$

$$\Delta lngdp_t = a_3 + b_3 \Delta lnemissions_{t-1} + c_3 \Delta lnenergy_{t-1} + d_3 \Delta lngdp_{t-1} + \lambda_3 ECT_{t-1}$$

4. Results and Discussion

Table 2 below gives the results from the unit root test. All the three variables are found to be non-stationary in levels, but they are stationary in first difference. Therefore, all the variables are found to be $I(1)$ at 5 % level of significance.

Table 2: Levin-Lin-Chu Unit root test

Variable	t-statistic	t-statistic after 1st difference
lnemissions	−0.941 (0.174)	−2.496 (0.006)*
lnenergy	−1.239 (0.108)	−2.463 (0.007)*
lngdp	0.987 (0.838)	−1.736 (0.041)*

* Null hypothesis of presence of unit root is rejected at 5 % level of significance.

Table 3 below gives the results from the Johansen test for cointegration. For all the four countries, only the λ_{max} statistic is reported due to brevity.

Table 3: Johansen test for cointegration

Rank	Max Statistic	5 % Critical value	1 % Critical value
India			
0	19.1625	23.78	28.83
1	7.2169	16.87	21.47
2	3.6154	3.74	6.40
USA			
0	23.9091	23.78*	28.83
1	16.4343	16.87	21.47
2	2.9262	3.74	6.40

Table 3: Continued

Rank	Max Statistic	5 % Critical value	1 % Critical value
Russia			
0	27.2053	23.78*	28.83
1	9.6209	16.87	21.47
2	6.2710	3.74	6.40
China			
0	30.7091	23.78*	28.83*
1	9.6543	16.87	21.47
2	0.0127	3.74	6.40

* Indicates significance at the given level.

Results show that for India variables are not cointegrated using the λ_{max} test statistic, while the other three countries have one cointegrating equation each. Therefore, a short-run VAR model can be estimated to study the interdependencies between the three variables for India. For the other three countries, VECM can be estimated to study both short-run and long-run dynamics between variables.

4.1. India

Table 4 gives the short-run VAR model, with the lag length of 1 as per the Akaike information criterion.

Table 4: Short run dynamics using VAR Model for India

Variables	$lnemissions_t$	$lnenergy_t$	$lngdp_t$
$lnemissions_{t-1}$	0.969** (0.172)	0.261 (0.191)	−0.024 (0.159)
$lnenergy_{t-1}$	−0.183 (0.163)	0.529** (0.181)	0.213 (0.151)
$lngdp_{t-1}$	0.208* (0.113)	0.281** (0.126)	0.825** (0.105)
Constant	−4.604* (2.584)	−5.463* (2.869)	4.169* (2.389)

* and ** Null hypothesis rejected at 10 % and 5 % levels of significance.
Robust standard errors in parenthesis

Results show that $lngdp$ has a positive and statistically significant impact on both $lnemissions$ and $lnenergy$. Increase in GDP in period $t-1$ causes energy consumption and emissions to rise in the next period. An increase in $lnenergy$ in period $t-1$ also causes a rise in $lngdp$, but the relationship is weakly significant at 15 % level of significance.

Table 5 below gives the results of the granger casualty test to understand if one variable helps to forecast the other variable.

Table 5: Granger casualty test

Equation	Excluded	χ^2 value	p-value
$lnemissions$	$lnenergy$	1.2578	0.262
$lnemissions$	$lngdp$	3.3744	0.066
$lnenergy$	$lnemissions$	1.8732	0.171
$lnenergy$	$lngdp$	4.9771	0.026
$lngdp$	$lnemissions$	0.02215	0.882
$lngdp$	$lnenergy$	1.9966	0.158

Results show that $lngdp$ granger causes $lnemissions$ and $lnenergy$. Therefore, there is evidence of unidirectional causality from $lngdp$ to $lnemissions$ and from $lngdp$ to $lnenergy$, and the lagged values of $lngdp$ causes both $lnemissions$ and $lnenergy$. Therefore, in the Indian case it is important to formulate policies that will persuade sectors to undertake energy efficiency policies. Since industry is the highest consumer of energy, it is important to coerce the industrial sector to undertake efficient use of energy. In this regard, a positive development has been the implementation of the Perform-Achieve-Trade policy that was started in the year 2012. This scheme has set energy intensity targets for certain high energy consuming industries of the country. The targets must be met within a specified period. Achieving of the targets results in granting of energy saving certificates, and failure to meet the targets results in a penalty in the form of purchase of the energy saving certificates to undertake further production.

The impulse response function from the VAR model in Figure 9 traces the response of variables in case of a shock or impulse on one of the endogenous variables.

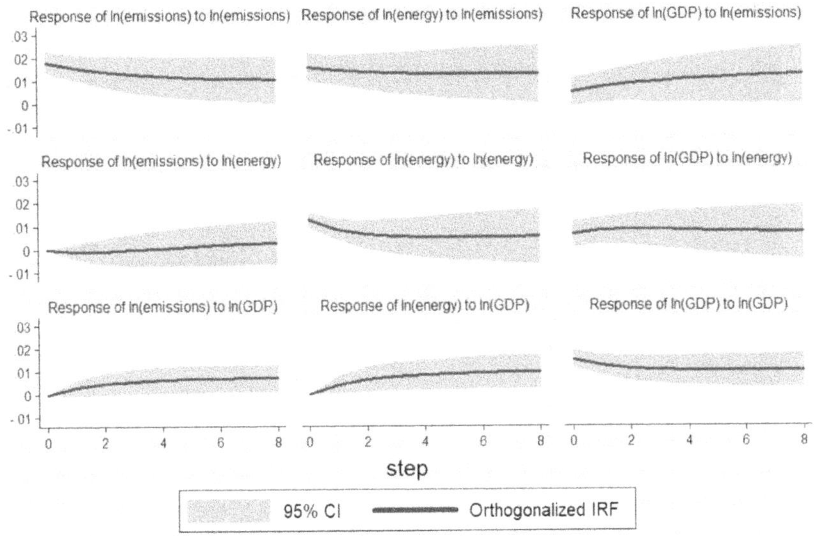

Figure 9: Impulse response functions

The figure shows that when there is a one unit rise in *lnenergy*, its impact on *lnemissions* is not felt in the first period. Its only after the second period that *lnemissions* begin to rise, and continues to do so for the next eight periods, although the rate of increase is quite slow. On the contrary, the effect of *lnGDP* is felt immediately and there is a continuous rise in *lnGDP* due to a rise in *lnenergy*. A one unit or one standard deviation rise in *lnGDP* has an impact on *lnemissions* and *lnenergy*. For both the variables, the immediate effect is zero. But between periods 0–2, there is a continuous rise, with the rise being greater for *lnenergy*. After that, for both variables, it stabilizes at a higher level. Finally, a one standard deviation shock to *lnemissions* will cause a very slight decline to *lnenergy* in the short run. Over the long run, the effect becomes stable. The effect on *lnGDP* is positive, with a rise in the short run that continues over the long run, but at a slow rate.

4.2. USA, Russia, and China

USA, Russia and China exhibit a long run relationship as they are $I(1)$. Table 6 gives the cointegrating vector for the three countries. Since the variables are in logs, the estimates can be interpreted as long run elasticities.

Table 6: Cointegrating equation with dependent variable $lnemissions_t$

Cointegrating Equations	USA	Russia	China
$lnenergy_t$	4.873* (2.448)	0.606** (0.364)	1.561* (0.408)
$lngdp_t$	2.535* (1.99E-10)	0.016 (0.095)	−2.066* (0.336)

Normalized w.r.t lnemissions
* and ** Null hypothesis rejected at 10 % and 5 % levels of significance.
Robust standard errors in parenthesis.

Results show that a 1 % rise in $lnenergy$ causes $lnemissions$ to rise by 4.87 %, and a 1 % rise in $lnGDP$ causes $lnemissions$ to rise by 2.54 % for USA. A similar positive and statistically significant relationship exists between $lnenergy$ and $lnemissions$ for Russia and China, but the effect is the highest for USA. The relationship between $lnGDP$ and $lnemissions$ is found to be negative for China, implying that over the long run a rise in GDP causes more investment in emission reduction policies. The next table displays the short run relationships between variables for the three countries.

Table 7: Short run dynamics using VECM

Variables	$\Delta(lnemissions)_t$	$\Delta(lnenergy)_t$	$\Delta(lngdp)_t$
USA			
ECT_{t-1}	−0.021 (.020)	−0.029 (0.016)	−0.008 (0.011)
$\Delta(lnemissions)_{t-1}$	0.464 (0.942)	0.635 (0.735)	−0.133 (0.499)
$\Delta(lnenergy)_{t-1}$	−0.737 (1.187)	−0.833 (0.925)	0.153 (0.629)
$\Delta(lngdp)_{t-1}$	0.038 (0.619)	0.072 (0.483)	0.047 (0.328)

Table 7: Continued

Variables	$\Delta(\boldsymbol{lnemissions})_t$	$\Delta(\boldsymbol{lnenergy})_t$	$\Delta(\boldsymbol{lngdp})_t$
Constant	−0.006 (0.014)	−0.0002 (0.011)	0.016 (0.007)
Russia			
ECT_{t-1}	−0.142** (0.057)	−0.143** (0.056)	−0.341** (0.062)
$\Delta(lnemissions)_{t-1}$	−1.258** (0.584)	−0.828 (0.577)	0.054 (0.639)
$\Delta(lnenergy)_{t-1}$	1.213* (0.627)	0.661 (0.619)	0.519 (0.686)
$\Delta(lngdp)_{t-1}$	0.1667 (0.185)	0.184 (0.183)	−0.059 (0.203)
Constant	−0.019** (0.008)	−0.014* (0.008)	0.014* (0.008)
China			
ECT_{t-1}	−0.019 (0.033)	−0.023 (0.031)	0.064** (0.014)
$\Delta(Inemissions)_{t-1}\cdot$	0.964 (0.609)	0.780 (0.565)	0.070 (0.263)
$\Delta(lnenergy)_{t-1}$	−0.161 (0.639)	−0.004 (0.593)	0.070 (0.276)
$\Delta(lngdp)_{t-1}$	−0.055 (0.462)	−0.104 (0.429)	−0.177 (0.199)
Constant	0.032 (0.026)	0.052** (0.025)	0.029** (0.011)

ll variables are in logs and represent per capita values, except the error correction term ECT
* and ** Null hypothesis rejected at 10 % and 5 % levels of significance.
Robust standard errors in parenthesis

For USA, the coefficient of the error correction term that gives the speed of adjustment, is negative and statistically significant for *lnenergy*. This gives evidence of a long-term causal relationship from *lnemissions* and *lnGDP* to *lnenergy*. But there is no evidence of a long-term causal relationship for the other combinations. Similarly, there is absence of short-term causality in all three cases.

Russia demonstrates a long-run causal relationship between various sets of variables because the error correction term is negative and statistically significant for all the three combinations. In the short-run, there is a statistically significant relationship only between energy consumption and emissions. A 1 % rise in *lnenergy* causes *lnemissions* to rise by 1.21 %.

China does not show the presence of any long run causal or short run causal relationship between various variables.

5. Conclusion

Growing concerns about climate change has made the world more environmental conscious. Multiple international agreements have been signed to address the issue, some of them being legally binding as well. The paper analyzes the sustainability indicators for the top four emitters of the world. Simple data analysis shows considerable gap in fossil fuel energy consumption and CO_2 emissions for China and USA on one hand and Russia and India on the other hand, with the latter category being quite low as compared to the former. Empirical results show the existence of a long run causal relationship only between a few variables. India shows the existence of short run dynamics between variables.

Though international agreements like the Kyoto Protocol, or the Paris Agreement have set targets for member nations, these need to be supplemented by domestic policies that will impose binding restrictions w.r.t. emissions or energy intensity on the economic participants. Adherence to the same is the only way targets can be met by member nations. For example, India launched the Perform-Achieve-Trade scheme in 2012 to reduce energy intensity in high energy consuming industries. Several countries in Europe have implemented white certificates, that show that a certain reduction of energy consumption has been achieved. Such policies help to achieve both energy efficiency and emission reduction through energy efficacy, without compromising on the growth objective.

References

Enders, W. (2004). *Applied Econometric Time Series* (2nd ed.). New York: Wiley.

Statistical Review of World Energy. (2023).

The World Bank Data. https://data.worldbank.org/indicator.

Ileana Hamburg

Remote Work and Cybersecurity Risks

1. Introduction

Remote work has become a norm for companies. It is a type of flexible work arrangement; these have the advantage of not just attracting and retaining top talent but also ensuring more engaged and productive employees.

Some used forms of flexible working environments are (https://www.hrleader.com.au/learning/25002-5-types-of-flexible-working-arrangements-for-smes-in-2024):

- Hybrid work which allows employees to split their time between working in the office and working remotely. It offers flexibility to employees with varying work preferences and responsibilities but poses challenges for team integration and requires effective communication strategies to prevent gaps in collaboration.
- Remote work allows employees to work from almost any location, such as their home, a co-working space, a telecenter, or other worksites, such as a client's office. It increases employee productivity due to reduced commute time and fewer workplace distractions but requires vigilant monitoring of remote employee wellbeing and performance. Other challenges will be presented in this paper-
- Flexitim involves removing the traditional schedule and instead offering employees more flexibility in their work week. It's suitable for employees with personal commitments outside of work but requires that is, coordination challenges for meetings and team interactions.
- Compressed workweek means an arrangement in which employees can work their contracted hours over fewer workdays. It reduces office overhead costs. However, potential workload issues for other team members appear.
- Job sharing is a working arrangement in which two part-time employees complete the same job on different days – effectively sharing the role one full-time worker might fill.

In 2020, companies had to find working and communication solutions to adapt quickly to a global pandemic. The best solution was shifting from office-based work to a remote one, particularly from home. This shift required new approaches and much research about the different challenges of remote work like used technologies, and problems with data security (Peiris & Jayathilake, 2022). Remote work is the most used form of flexible working. The development of new information and communication technology (ICT) was a key enabler for the success of remote working (Mariana et al., 2023) facilitating working from home (Bloom et al., 2021) and within new remote learning and communication environments. Flexible working and social relations between employees and employers in a virtual environment using information and communication technologies (Gorokhova et al., 2021) are characteristics of remote work. However, remote employees should be connected through secure servers, and this requires a remote work cyber security infrastructure to be installed in companies and corresponding employee training to avoid cyber threats. Employees had to install work devices through their home networks in cooperation with employers, and the company IT departments had to work on a new concept of cyber security. Data should be moved into the cloud and secured through virtual private networks so that companies can maintain the continuity of operations. However, when company data processing is based on networking and cloud services, vulnerabilities must be identified and corresponding measures developed. In this context, according to a study by IBM, the average cost of preventing a data breach increased by 10 % between 2020 and 2021. It was the highest one in the last seven years. The average cost was $1.07 million higher for breaches where people were working remotely (https://securityintelligence.com/posts/whats-new-2021-cost-of-a-data-breach-report/). So, to have employees connected to secure servers and avoid cyber threats, a remote work cyber security infrastructure, and corresponding training should be developed within the companies.

In the following parts, the shift to remote work is briefly described including the used technology, some cybersecurity risks remote workers face, and how to mitigate such risks to utilize the benefits of remote work fully that is, through the development and use of corresponding frameworks and cybersecurity awareness employee training. Future author's work in this context is also shortly described.

2. The Shift to Remote Work and Corresponding Technology

It is known that for some years, due to the pandemic, employers had to make decisions about how to organize remote work in their companies, which technology and how virtual communication platforms will be used, and familiarize teams with digital tools for common work (https://gxait.com/business-technology/leveraging-technology-for-remote-work-a-guide-for-smes/).

HR departments had to discuss a distance workplace culture. Project leaders searched for new methods to ensure productivity within their teams. Employees have to find corresponding workplaces for their remote work.

After several months of experimenting with future workplaces, and methods, many companies decided to use long-term remote working, due to its benefits (Angelucci et al., 2020).

So, remote work has many benefits for both employees and employers, facilitating higher job performance and worker retention. Remote work supports flexibility and autonomy within the job, and this contributes to increased work-life balance, individual performance, and satisfaction for employees. Also, employers benefit from improved productivity and employee satisfaction (Felstead & Henseke, 2017). If remote work is well organized, it can lead to higher organizational commitment and job-related well-being for employees, which are beneficial also for employers (Lang et al., 2022). Employers have access to a global talent pool, so they can use a diverse range of expertise and skills (Appelgren, 2021). But employers should facilitate effective team performance of remote workers which can enhance overall productivity and individual well-being, benefiting both employees and employers (Lang et al., 2022). If well organized, remote work can ensure employees higher employment security and faster promotions, which are advantageous for both employers and employees (Appelgren, 2021).

Remote work can support the development of good relations between employees, effective communication, and work efficiency, increasing employee commitment and job satisfaction. Remote work can reduce work-related stress. Employees who can work remotely have more opportunities for part-time jobs, secondary employment, and working via the Internet and this offers them flexibility and better income options.

The use of suitable technology supporting remote work that is, digital tools and platforms that facilitate employees working remotely outside the offices is important for remote work. Successful working remotely needs technology supporting flexibility, business scalability, and resilience to survive disruptions such as global health crises or natural disasters.

Remote work technology can simulate a traditional office. By using virtual communication tools, cloud-based services, and project management software, a virtual office accessible to employees anytime and anywhere (Singh et al., 2022) can be simulated. This virtual space improves productivity where remote teams can collaborate, share ideas, and manage workflows without the need for physical presence within office environments https://gxait.com/business-technology/leveraging-technology-for-remote-work-a-guide-for-smes/).

Remote work technology should be a catalyst for innovation within companies, encouraging a culture of digital transformation, supporting them to rethink their business processes and adopt more efficient, technology-driven methodologies (https://www.rightworks.com/blog/5-essential-work-from-home-technologies-maximizing-remote-productivity/).

Cloud computing is a technology used within remote work to support access to computing resources and data storage. Cloud services enable companies to host and manage applications and data on remote servers, ensuring employees' access to necessary information and tools from any location with internet connectivity. This flexibility supports a mobile and responsive workforce.

One important problem in connection with remote work remains the number and increasing complexity of cyber threats. New practical solutions are necessary so that cyber risks can be detected in a short time and measures taken to make them less aggressive/mitigate or avoid them (https://medium.com/@gupta.brij/the-impact-of-remote-work-on-cybersecurity-challenges-and-solutions-1e7aa5db9927)

Artificial intelligence (AI) is a tool to improve cybersecurity measures. Integrating AI and cloud infrastructure from Amazon Web Services AWS can address such challenges (Singh, 2021).

Besides such solutions, virtual private networks (VPNs) have a big role in remote work infrastructure. A secure tunnel between remote devices and company networks is created and transit data are encrypted. So, sensitive information is protected from cyber threats.

Another challenge within remote work is to improve/adapt the education and training of employees and employers to the new requirements so that they have the necessary skills and competencies for remote work, corresponding technology, and avoiding cyber threats (Hiji & Alam, 2022).

Some ideas in this context are the following:

> "Educators have to catch up with commercial organizations, who are way ahead when it comes to delivering experiential learning and recognizing its value," (https://www.extern.com/post/a-paradigm-shift-to-remote-work)
>
> "Our top advice to universities in a post-COVID world? Break your business model. There is still value you can offer, but not in the way you have traditionally done so. The four-year degree where you have historically made your money is not going to be sustainable, but offers an agile, micro degree and there is significant value and opportunity in the market for you. Schools need to invest in virtual technology, rather than continue to brand their campuses." (https://www.quora.com/Why-should-schools-invest-in-digital-devices-and-infrastructure).

Skills necessary in the workplace, particularly in connection with remote work, technology, and cyber-attacks are constantly changing and 53 % of organizations expect that half of their workforce will need to be reskilled in the next three years to be prepared for such challenges.
Companies recognize the need of prepared employees and started to recruit people who can demonstrate resilience, creativity, innovativeness, and critical thinking, important within remote work. So, also education and training shall develop and apply innovative approaches to develop such skills within the programs they offer, to create employable students.

3. Security Risks for Remote Workers

The use of remote work increased the potential for cyber-attacks also due to the intensive use of information and communication technologies. Cyber attackers can exploit new vulnerabilities and possibilities created by networking, cloud services, and private devices. It was difficult for IT departments to ensure security technology to a workforce distributed remotely with conventional methods and tools in a short time. So, the number of remote work cyber security threats has increased during the past few years. Some of the most common risks for cybersecurity within remote working are the following (https://www.rocket.chat/blog/remote-work-cybersecurity):

- Networks of companies have security features, such as encryption, firewalls, filtering, etc., but employees do not have the same level of security at home by wireless networks. Hackers can easily spy on connections and get access to confidential information if employees do not follow strong security practices working on their home's Wi-Fi to connect computers, tablets, smartphones, and other devices to the internet.
- By using malware and phishing attacks, cybercriminals block or lock employees' access to their data. Having control over the system or data, they delete/alter/sell it until their ransom demand. Attackers send malware through emails with malicious attachments and infect data or a device. Recovering data is difficult and expensive for the organization.
- File-sharing solutions to share documents with their colleagues hosted on corporate networks are safe, but not the same level of security exists during remote work on other devices. Vulnerable data are used by hackers' data and fraud, ransomware attacks, etc. take place.
- Many employees use their devices to access or transfer work-related files and these personal devices do not have always sufficient security measures. Employees also use their devices, such as phones, to work and communicate,

and this poses a threat to remote work cyber security. If an employee uses a not secure device to log into their business accounts, hackers can breach through it.

- Sometimes when employees quit the organization, they may continue holding confidential data stored on their devices knowingly or unknowingly. When an employee starts using the company's devices for non-work-related activities like shopping online or accessing own social media accounts, a severe data threat can happen.
- Another remote work cybersecurity threat is the use of weak passwords for protecting corporate accounts if employees use firewalls, VPNs, etc. Often people use passwords that are easy to remember. Cybercriminals know different methods to crack such passwords by using simple strategies.

4. Some Measures to Ensure Cybersecurity in a Remote Working Framework

Some measures to mitigate cybersecurity risks within remote work are the following (https://www.rocket.chat/blog/remote-work-cybersecurity):

1. A VPN – Virtual Private Network – should be developed to ensure that an unauthorized person, including hackers and internet providers, cannot have access. In order not to have a slowdown internet speed and affect the quality of bandwidth-intensive tasks, VPN services known for their speed and stability, should be used.
2. Security protocols for the company which should be followed by employees to minimize potential risks must be developed, that is, for each new device antivirus software and a firewall, should be installed.
3. The secure regulations must be respected as well as protocols that help employees to adhere to data sovereignty.
4. Encryption of sensitive data and cloud-based file sharing should be done.
5. Using existing on the market available secure, user-friendly communication tools, that is, with features like open source, ISO certification, data encryption, minimal use of metadata, etc. is a big advantage.
6. Antivirus software should be installed to save company data from breaches. The employees should have this antivirus software also on their devices.
7. Security audits are periodically necessary to verify the security of the organization's systems, involving the security of a system's physical configuration, software, information handling processes, user practices, etc.
8. Multifactor authentication and strong passwords on all used devices and apps are necessary to protect from malware attacks during remote work. Passwords

should be long, strong, and unique – at least twelve characters with a mix of numbers, symbols, capital and lowercase letters.
Additional passwords that will be difficult for hackers to access can be used while working with sensitive data. Password manager tools can be used to keep difficult passwords.
9. Zero trust network access is necessary providing secure and remote access to the organization's applications to ensure that only authorized people will have access.

5. Cybersecurity Awareness Frameworks and Corresponding Training

Despite the importance of cybersecurity issues, not much research has been conducted on the capacity to support cybersecurity skills, and awareness training for remote working employees after the COVID-19 pandemic. Organizations need to implement cybersecurity frameworks to define requirements for avoiding cyber threats within remote work, and to provide awareness as well as train their employees regarding the recent social-engineering-based cyber-attacks and threats. The frameworks could help organizations identify the cybersecurity-relevant weaknesses in their systems and measure their employees' capability toward cyber threats, attacks, and incidence management. Moreover, implementing practices described in the framework will improve the organization's cybersecurity infrastructure.

The existing frameworks/models refer mainly to software and hardware, not to methods to organize cybersecurity awareness training but 82 % of data attacks involve human errors (Hiji and Alam, 2022; Sabillon et al., 2019). Continuing cybersecurity awareness training sessions are necessary to help employees recognize phishing attacks, share data securely, lock devices, etc.

One of the main goals of the future research work of the authors is to propose a framework for cybersecurity awareness and training that will help companies, particularly small and medium-sized companies (SMEs), to evaluate employees' capability for remote work in the cybersecurity domain, managing security-related issues and challenges to protect company critical information and how to train employees to assure security for data and information they us as well as for the data system of the organization. Empirical studies and existing frameworks/models, including NIST (National Institute of Standards and Technology) "Building an Information Technology Security Awareness and Training Program" (Hash & Wilson, 2012), have been consulted and cybersecurity experts, consultants, testers, and developers will be interviewed. The basis for the development of the planned framework is the NIST as well as the framework and the cyber security training program (Hamburg & Sommer, 2022; Hamburg, 2022) developed within the European project InCyT, with the participation of the author. Efficient and up-to-date cybersecurity training is important for closing cybersecurity employee skill gaps and preparing remote employees who can detect and avoid cybersecurity threats.

AI methods, that is, natural language processing, machine learning, and simulations can be used during the training and could help IT experts as well as employees to understand and avoid cybersecurity threats they can meet (Hamburg & Sommer, 2024).

AI together with Amazon Webservice (AWS) can support the development of virtual training environments where employees can test and improve their skills and competencies in real similar environment (Villegas et al., 2024). The training platform to be used should make possible continuous updating and adaptation of training content as well as the creation of scenarios and simulations to explain cybersecurity threats. The learning platform and the digital training modules developed within InCyT will be improved by using AI and cloud services and new ones will be developed.

A methodology for the competence framework has been developed and discussed with SME remote workers and representatives and consultants. The main topics of the training modules have been proposed. Cooperation with VET representatives has been established in order to make the training modules accessible also for VET; many VET students work in companies remotely and suffer cybersecurity threats.

6. Conclusions

The future landscape of remote work presents both challenges for employers and employees and promises for efficient work. Remote work offers opportunities for increased flexibility, productivity, and talent retention but requires challenges related, that is,, used technology, cybersecurity, and team cooperation/cohesion. The rapid advancement of suitable remote technology, development of corresponding changes within organizational practices, security practices, and assuring skills and training make remote work a sustainable and inclusive model for companies.

But to ensure successful remote work, robust cybersecurity measures should be developed and applied, as well as comprehensive training programs for remote workers, using emerging technologies such as virtual reality and artificial intelligence to enhance remote collaboration and communication. Numerous cyber-attacks during remote work due to cybersecurity vulnerabilities in working environments require technological solutions, like secure connections, multi-factor authentication, and fostering a culture of cybersecurity awareness, corresponding policy development, and employee and employer training.

Companies should build resilient infrastructures that can support long-term remote work, diversity, and inclusion to use remote work opportunities.

Future research is necessary for understanding the long-term impacts of remote work on productivity, and organizational culture, for managing remote teams and fostering inclusion in virtual environments. The author engages in such research work.

References

Angelucci, M., Angrisani, D., Bennett, A., Kapteyn, A. & Schaner, S. (2020). Remote work and the heterogeneous impact of COVID-19 on employment and health. *SSRN Electronic Journal.*

Appelgren, E. (2021). Media management during covid-19: Behaviour of Swedish media leaders in times of crisis. *Journalism Studies*, *23*, 5–6, 722–739.

Bloom, N., Davis, S., & Zhestkova, Y. (2021). Covid-19 shifted patent applications toward technologies that support working from home. *Aea Papers and Proceedings*, *111*, 263–266.

Felstead, A., & Henseke, G. (2017). Assessing the growth of remote working and its consequences for effort, well-being and work-life balance. *New Technology Work and Employment*, *32*(39), 195–212.

Gorokhova, A., Akhyadov, E., & Shishkin, A. (2021). The effect of remote work on the successful development of engineering companies. *Revista Gestão Inovação E Tecnologias*, *11*(4), 4345–4356.

Hamburg, I. (2022). Using interdisciplinary problem-based learning and critical thinking in cyber training (Abstract). In European Association of Erasmus Coordinators (eds.), *Abstract Booklet 2022 of the Eracon & Career EU on 27th June – 1st July* 2022 (7). Thessaloniki.

Hamburg, I., & Sommer, D. (2022). Cyber-Sicherheitstraining für kleine und mittelständische Unternehmen – Das Erasmus+-Projekt InCyT. Forschung Aktuell, 2022 (12). Gelsenkirchen: Institut Arbeit und Technik, Westfälische Hochschule Gelsenkirchen Bocholt Recklinghausen.

Hamburg, I., & Sommer, D. (2024). AI & Cyber Security Awareness. In K. Cebeci & M.V. Kaye (Eds.), *Social & Economic Studies within the Framework of Emerging Global Developments* (pp. 61–68). Berlin, Bruxelles, Chennai, Lausanne, New York, Oxford: Peter Lang.

Hash, J., & Wilson, M. (2012). Building an Information Technology Security Awareness and Training Program NIST 2012, pp. 800–850.

Hijji, M., & Alam, G. (2022). Cybersecurity Awareness and Training (CAT) Framework for Remote Working Employees. *Sensor 2022*, *22*, 8663.

Lang, C., Dony, J., & Roberts, D. (2022). The Future of Teamwork: Facilitating Effective Team Performance in Virtual and Hybrid Work Environments in a Post-Pandemic World. *Proceedings of the Human Factors and Ergonomics Society Annual Meeting*, *66*(1), 1085–1089.

Mariana, Y., Wijaya, F., & Dwinandana, D. (2023). Design of Workstation for Remote Workers with Work Environment Consideration. *Iop Conference Series Earth and Environmental Science*, *1169*(1), 012061.

Peiris, K., & Jayathilake, P. (2022). Factors Influencing the Effective Implementation of the Remote Working Teams in Insurance Companies in Sri Lanka. *Journal of Management Matters*, *9*(2), 23–37.

Sabillon, R., Serra-Ruiz, J., & Cavaller, V. (2019). An Effective Cybersecurity Training Model to Support an Organizational Awareness Program: The Cybersecurity Awareness Training Model (CATRAM). A Case Study in Canada. *J. Cases Inf. Technol. JCIT* 2019, *21*, 26–395.

Singh, T. (2021). The Effect of Amazon Web Services (AWS) on Cloud-Computing. *Int. J. Eng. Res. Technol. 10*, 1–31.

Singh, P., Bala, H., Dey, Dr. & Filieri, R. (2022). Enforced Remote Working: The Impact of Digital Platform-Induced Stress and Remote Working Experience on Technology Exhaustion and Subjective Wellbeing. *Journal of Business Research*, *6*(3), 55–68. 2022 – Elsevier.

Villegas-Ch, W., Govea, J., & Ortiz-Garces, I. (2024). Developing a Cybersecurity Training Environment through the Integration of OpenAI and AWS. *Applied Sciences*, *14*, 679.

Dora Naletina, Ivana Štulec, and Nikolina Filipović

Pioneering Sustainable Transport: A Case Study on the Adoption of Electric Trucks

1. Introduction

Road transport plays an important role in many aspects of human lives. The development of transport enabled better connectivity. Numerous studies show that there is a positive correlation between the development of road infrastructure and the economic growth of a country, since the development of road infrastructure allows better access to markets and affects employment, while also reducing the costs and time required for transporting people and goods (Ng et al., 2019). Along with all the positive effects of the transport development, there are also negative ones, with environmental pollution being the biggest one. According to data from 2015, the transport sector accounts for 19 % of the global demand for energy, the majority of which are fossil fuels that lead to the emission of greenhouse gases (Khalili et al., 2019). In 2020, road transport accounted for 78 % of total transport greenhouse gas emissions making it evident to be the biggest polluter among carriers. Among road transporting vehicles, automobiles account for the largest share of gas emissions (59.4 %), followed by heavy-duty vehicles and buses (28.3 %) (EC, 2022).

In addition to harmful gas emissions, another side effect of traffic systems is noise pollution. It is estimated that around 135 million people in OECD countries suffer from traffic noise levels higher than 65 db. Heavy-duty vehicles significantly contribute to the emission of harmful gases, and the age of said vehicles is also a decisive factor in their efficiency and sustainability (de Armiño et al., 2022). In 2019, the EU adopted the first CO_2 standards for new heavy vehicles. The regulation sets average fleet reduction targets of 15 % by 2025 and 30 % by 2030 compared to the 2019/2020 baseline. This will reduce CO_2 emissions from new trucks and allow hauliers to save on fuel costs. The 90 % CO_2 reduction target may seem close enough to full decarbonization at first glance, but due to a number of shortcomings, the proposal would only reduce heavy vehicle emissions by 56 % by 2050 (compared to 1990 levels). The current definition of a Zero Emission Vehicle under CO_2 standards for heavy duty vehicles includes internal combustion trucks powered solely by hydrogen.

Social and economic changes encouraged the mandatory reorganization of road transport in the last decade, so the development of new technologies is an attempt to reduce the harmful impact of trucks on the environment. The most obvious course of action is the application of new technologies in combination with a decisive energy policy. Other complementary lines of action are focused on the dedication and adaptation of the infrastructure and promotion of intermodality in the efficient management of supply chains (de Armiño et al., 2022). Proper implementation of technical solutions in the production of heavy-duty road vehicles can lead to a reduction in annual fuel consumption by more than 11 billion liters in a period of 10 years, which is associated with a reduction of 8.3 million tons of emissions of greenhouse gases only in the United States of America (Lowell & Balon, 2009). Such insights led to the need for the development of EU emission standards with stricter consumption and transport emission requirements for carbon monoxide, nitrogen oxides and harmful particles.

The objective of the chapter is to provide insights into how electric trucks can serve to achieve sustainability in road transport and thus enable understanding of its positive and negative aspects needed to compare their profitability to classic trucks. A case study of two large European automobile and truck manufacturers was conducted with primary focus on the process of development and adoption of electric trucks. In our study we address following research questions:

RQ1: What are advantages and disadvantages of electric trucks compared to classic trucks?

RQ2: What is realistically achievable in adoption of sustainable road transport in the near future?

RQ3: What should viable strategies for sustainable transport incorporate?

The analysis and discussion offer valuable recommendations for manufacturers and policy makers on designing and implementing sustainable road transport strategies that have the power to achieve all three goals of sustainability: economic development, society well-being and minimal ecological footprint.

2. The Role of Electric Trucks in Achieving Road Transport Sustainability

Political and practical reasons have produced an environment that is increasingly conducive to the growing presence of electric truck (EVs). The popularization of EVs started first with electric cars, and later many delivery companies have decided to introduce EVs into their fleet. This has become possible due to advances in the development of technology, which enables the production of sufficiently powerful batteries that can power delivery vehicles with a gross weight of 4,500–9,000 kg and a range of 130–160 km (Davis & Figliozzi, 2013).

According to many studies, strong ecological efficiency of electric trucks has been confirmed, which serves as a strong motive for the adoption of their use and stronger commercialization. However, when analyzing the role of EVs in achieving transport sustainability, all three pillars of sustainability should be taken into account.

Focusing firstly on the environmental footprint, we present the study of Laberteaux and Hamza (2018) who conducted a comparative study of equivalent greenhouse gas (GHG) emissions of conventional versus electrified trucks. Authors revealed several policy choices that facilitate the adoption of electric trucks to achieve greater GHG reductions. Providing vehicle-to-grid regulation for electric trucks can significantly reduce greenhouse gas emissions compared to conventional trucks. Lee et al. (2013) present that electric trucks emit 42–61 % less GHGs and consume 32–54 % less energy than diesel trucks, depending upon vehicle efficiency cases. With increasing renewable energy, battery EVs can outperform diesel and fuel cell with green hydrogen decreases environmental impact (Wolff et al., 2021). Electric heavy-duty trucks can achieve an annual reduction of 115.8 tons of NOx emissions, 0.7 tons of PM emissions, and 18,000 tons of CO_2 emissions (Dou et al., 2023). Furthermore, Onat et al. (2019) studied the source-to-wheel water footprint of an EV compared to conventional vehicles in the US. That research showed that, in the worst case, a Battery EV (BEV) can consume up to 70 times more water than a traditional vehicle, while a BEV with electricity generated from a solar charger has the lowest level of water consumption and can reduce its water footprint by up to 97 %.

Decarbonization of road freight transport using battery-powered heavy-duty electric trucks is generally considered difficult, that is, limited in performance as a means of combating climate change, with the high costs and low gravimetric specific energy of batteries most often seen as a limiting factor. Although some recent studies have been optimistic about this matter, the most common opinion is that the possibility of electric cargo vehicles with a battery for light-duty vehicles is more likely. Nykvist & Olsson (2021) conclude that there is a possibility of performance for heavy-duty vehicles, although the cost competitiveness of heavy-duty battery electric trucks, compared to traditional diesel trucks, is very sensitive to the underlying assumptions, especially in terms of battery costs and performance. Under the mentioned conditions, fast charging enables a smaller battery and thereby improves competitiveness in the segment of heavy-duty vehicles. Sensitivity analysis confirms that heavier trucks can lighten the weight load. Furthermore, the life cycle of the battery may be more important than the cost per kWh, and if fast charging is available the additional weight of the battery becomes less of a limiting factor for heavy-duty EVs (Nykvist & Olsson, 2021).

Taking into account the social perspective of sustainability, Zhou et al. (2019) investigated how psychological determinants can influence drivers' intention to drive electric trucks. Technology anxiety is considered a negative determinant of the behavior of urban delivery drivers to adopt electric trucks. Expected performance, effort, expectancy, social influence, and facilitating conditions are considered positive determinants of behavioral intention, and facilitating conditions and behavioral intention are considered positive determinants of usage behavior. Behavioral intention is a partial mediator between facilitating conditions and usage behavior. Technology anxiety is often caused by a mismatch between the use of technology and the availability of resources. This can lead to customer reluctance to adopt new technology. There is also a difference in the level of acceptance of new technology with regard to the driver's age, education level and financial situation.

In order to encourage the acceptance of new technologies, it is necessary to adequately educate drivers and show them the positive effects that new technologies have in order to reduce the level of anxiety. According to an interview conducted in 2022 with drivers who test drove an electric truck, drivers said that reduced noise is one of the key positive aspects of electric trucks. Their working environment is improved and, according to the conducted research, it is less stressful for them to do their work (Werner & Onufrey, 2022). Hovi et al. (2019) analyzed the experience of electric truck users, focusing on purchasing processes, technology, vehicle selection, user experience and various aspects of performance. Respondents reported positive experiences of using EVs, but at the same time technological limitations were identified as barriers to adoption. The research highlights the importance of financial support from the government. In general, both managers and drivers are satisfied with electric trucks, and several operators commented that they contribute to a good working environment. They cited trust in new technology and overcoming fear of range as the main challenges. It was also concluded that the main obstacles to electrification in the short term stem from limited driving range, limited engine power and, as a result, limitations in the ability to drive with a trailer.

From a socio-economic perspective, the widespread adoption of EVs is expected to cause structural change in the energy industry, from changes related to employment in supply chains in various sectors to tax balance and profitability (Onat et al. 2019). Regarding the social aspect of sustainability, taking into account a penetration of 10 %, BEVs cause a loss of employment, benefits and taxes of up to 8 %, 7 % and 9 %, respectively. However, in the same scenario, they can reduce the negative impact on human health by up to 8 % (Onat et al. 2019).

3. Case Study

A study of development and adoption of electric trucks was carried out on the case of two large automobile and truck companies: Reanult and Volvo Trucks. In its offer of EVs, Renault has smaller delivery vehicles and electric trucks for city deliveries, while Volvo is the first serial manufacturer of electric trucks and offers both smaller electric trucks for city deliveries and larger models suitable for larger distances and between city deliveries.

A long-time employee of 19 years, currently at the position of regional manager, provided insight into electric truck development at Renault. In 2019, the manufacturer delivered the first electric trucks. That delivery consisted of 20 trucks that were delivered in Switzerland, and since then the number of electric trucks in their production has been increasing. Hydrogen-powered vehicles are also an option, but the manufacturer is currently mostly based on EVs for short distances, while they expect that in the future, hydrogen-powered engines will be used more for trucks that drive long distances, because the first disadvantage of battery electric trucks is their short range.

The company goal is that by 2030, 50 % of the trucks that participate in the road transport of goods in Europe are electric trucks, and by 2040, the goal is for that share to be 100 % in order to reduce environmental pollution by classic trucks. The respondent states that government stimulation and interference is an extremely important factor in the development of electric trucks, due to their higher price compared to a classic truck, and he encourages the governments of the EU countries to develop charging infrastructure. In addition to providing infrastructure, the role of the government is to provide financial incentives to carriers for the purchase of electric trucks. The respondent names Switzerland as an example of a country with a good policy. In Switzerland, the government has been the main driver of the shift to electric trucks by abolishing the tax on EVs, thus increasing their popularity. If, for example, we take a 40-ton truck that exceeds 80,000 km in a year, that tax amounts to 80,000 euros, so 1 euro per km, and owners of EVs are completely exempt from paying that tax.

The interest of customers is constantly increasing, especially for trucks that are used within the city, for example, waste collection trucks. In order to encourage customers to buy an electric truck, the manufacturer provides a warranty for the batteries. The duration of the warranty is determined by estimating the battery's lifetime with respect to the route planned for that truck. If the customer wants to use the truck longer than the estimated lifetime of the battery, the option of contracting a favorable service package is offered, which includes the replacement of the battery after the time estimated as the battery's lifetime has expired. Battery life is not only affected by the route of the vehicle, but also by some other external and internal factors. The duration of the battery also depends on the type of upgrade of the truck. For example, if the truck has an upgrade for waste removal, then the electricity from the batteries is also used to start the upgrade, and not only to start the vehicle itself, thus reducing the range of the truck. Electric trucks with classic batteries have a range of 300–400 km, depending on the driving conditions. A waste collection truck is an ideal indicator of the profitability of replacing a classic truck with an electric one. Since such trucks are used within the city and have a short range during their working hours, charging the battery is not a problem, and their use reduces the emission of harmful gases and reduces the noise level in cities. Batteries are also affected by outside temperature; batteries work better at lower temperatures than at higher temperatures. In order to keep the external influence as low as possible, a system was developed that cools the batteries at extremely high temperatures, and heats them when the temperatures are too low. Just as every classic truck has its own chassis number, batteries also have a number that allows them traceability. Batteries are disposed in a way to apply the principles of circular economy. The idea is to use old batteries to store new energy, which is produced by, for example, solar panels.

The innovations and environment director with work experience of 27 years offered insights into electric truck development at Volvo Trucks. Volvo started development in the mid-90s with the concept of ecological trucks and buses. These were hybrid vehicles with a focus on improving energy efficiency. The next step was parallel hybrid diesel vehicles that reduced fuel consumption and had the ability to drive in emission-free mode for short distances. The company saw the greatest potential in the urban environment and the battery-powered electric bus went into production in 2010. Initially, for urban uses, the focus was on air quality and noise. A quieter truck could be used during the evening to help reduce congestion and improve productivity. However, with replacing the diesel engine with a quieter electric motor, new sources of noise became visible that needed to be dealed with. Moreover, with electric trucks used in construction and long haulage, the benefits for the climate are even more in focus. The company's own climate targets are a CO_2 reduction of 50 % by 2030 and 100 % by 2040 for new trucks (source to wheel). Table 1 provides the comparison of the environmental footprint of a classic Volvo FH truck and an electric Volvo FH truck, where it can be seen that in the production of an electric truck there is a higher CO_2 emission than in the production of a classic one.

Table 1: Comparison of environmental footprint of a classic and electric truck

		Volvo FH Electric	Volvo FH Classic
CO_2 EQ	Production:	4,970 kg	1,590 kg
	Usage:	903 kg	59,200 kg
	End-of-Life:	−1,370 kg	−554 kg
	Net:	4,510 kg	60,300 kg
Energy	Production:	22 MWh	8 MWh
	Usage:	107 MWh	234 MWh
	End-of-Life:	−3 MWh	−2 MWh
	Net:	126 MWh	240 MWh
Water	Production:	64 m^3	575 m^3
	Usage:	84 m^3	52 m^3
	End-of-Life:	−2 m^3	−1 m^3
	Net:	146 m^3	626 m^3
NOx	Production:	11 kg	3 kg
	Usage:	1 kg	38 kg
	End-of-Life:	−2 kg	−1 kg
	Net:	10 kg	40 kg
Material	Production:	846 kg	614 kg
	Usage:	137 kg	178 kg
	End-of-Life:	−591 kg	−500 kg
	Net:	391 kg	292 kg

Source: Internal company data

Electric trucks tend to offset their disadvantages with their benefits, resulting thus with a better net footprint compared to classic trucks. Batteries have a significant impact on the climate during production, but must be mentioned that the truck will break even in just one year when using renewable electricity. When the batteries run out in the first truck, they will undergo a remanufacturing process and become reusable. After secondary use, they can be repurposed and used as energy storage. Then in the last stage they will go through recycling and the valuable materials can be reused in new batteries. Furthermore, electric trucks have fewer moving parts and therefore maintenance costs should be lower up to 30 % compared to classic trucks.

Regarding the interest of transport companies in electric trucks, the respondent points out that transport companies have their own environmental goals, just like many of their clients. In many cases, they see electric trucks as a way to retain and gain new business. Profitability is determined by many factors such as total cost of ownership and revenue. The best business practice exists in countries with investment support and toll exemptions plus low electricity prices.

The comany's beliefs are that EVs will not completely replace classic ones. They firmly believe that there is a need for battery electric trucks, fuel cell electric trucks and trucks with combustion engines (using biofuels). The technologies complement each other and will be used in different ways depending on the application, infrastructure availability and business practice. Already today, it is possible to cover 45 % of freight transport in the EU with a battery electric truck with a range of 300 km. A quick charge during a lunch break can provide a range of 500 km. Volvo's goals in Europe are that 70 % of sales by 2030 should be electric.

The first 5,000 electric trucks that Volvo has sold so far will primarily be charged at the base facility during the night. But in the future there will be a need for "destination charging" in warehouses and distribution centers. There is a possibility to drive long distances with a battery electric truck, but it requires battery improvements, charging infrastructure and many fast charging stations. In many cases, a fuel cell electric truck that uses hydrogen will be an important supplement for long and heavy hauls. Volvo Trucks has begun testing fuel cell EVs (FCEVs) that would be used for long-distance driving, and such trucks are expected to be available in the second half of this decade. Fuel cells use hydrogen as a source that generates electricity for an electric motor. FCEVs are considered suitable for long-haul and heavy-duty, energy-intensive tasks, complementing BEVs. They are also considered a suitable option in situations where there is not enough time to charge, as well as in countries where there are limited opportunities to develop infrastructure for charging classic batteries. FCEVs will have a range of up to 1,000 km, which is similar to classic diesel trucks, and their charging time will be less than 15 minutes. Volvo Trucks' plan is to start selling FCEVs in Europe and in North America. The detailed plan will take into account the expansion of charging stations, policy and the price of hydrogen. After the start of sales in Europe, pilot tests in Asia and South America are planned.

The use of trucks with fuel cells would have an extremely favorable impact on the environment, since such trucks emit only water and heat, no pollutants or greenhouse gases. The main disadvantages of using hydrogen are the high costs of building the necessary infrastructure, hydrogen fuel cells are also expensive to produce, as is the hydrogen tank. In addition, the cost of hydrogen fuel will be higher than the cost of diesel fuel. Volvo currently has three main technology paths they consider best for achieving decarbonization of heavy haulage, namely battery electric trucks, hydrogen fuel cell electric trucks and internal combustion engines using biofuels, the best solution varying by region and type of transport. Battery electric trucks are a solution that already exists and such trucks can perform numerous tasks related to the transport of goods, and for Volvo Trucks it is currently the main path towards achieving complete decarbonization of road transport of goods.

4. Discussion on the Viable Strategies for the Adoption of Greater Sustainability in Transport

To achieve greater sustainability in the road transport of goods, several strategies can be implemented. Route optimization and consolidation centers can reduce fuel consumption and emissions by improving logistics efficiency. Transitioning to electric, hybrid, and alternative fuel vehicles will lower carbon footprints. Implementing emissions standards and offering incentives for clean technology will encourage the adoption of sustainable practices. Developing charging infrastructure for electric trucks is essential. Promoting collaborative freight transport and using freight exchange platforms can minimize empty runs. Encouraging local sourcing and production can reduce the distance goods need to be transported. Finally, corporate partnerships and sustainability reporting will drive broader adoption of sustainable transport practices.

Government plays a vital role in achieving greater transport sustainability, and one solution that is gaining more and more importance lately is green public procurement (GPP). GPP refers to the process by which public authorities procure goods and services with a reduced environmental impact throughout their life cycle. It can help accelerate the adoption of zero emission vehicles in freight transport, but success depends on prioritizing such tasks, prioritizing political decisions, and addressing financial barriers (Karlsson et al., 2022). Public transport authorities have the potential to support more environmentally sustainable solutions through public procurement, with stricter environmental requirements in larger areas and within cities (Aldenius et al., 2021). The competitive dialog procedure can facilitate sustainable public procurement by incorporating environmental and social considerations in the bid evaluation process (Uttam et al., 2015). Karlsson et al. (2022) identified following success factors in GPP implementation: consistent operational goals and policies, national campaigns, ethics, professionalism, capability and knowledge among employers, and systems for checks and balances between participants in the entire procurement process.

Chatti (2020) advocates the role of ICT in reducing the environmental footprint of transport. The study uses data from the World Bank and the OECD from 2002 to 2014 and covers 43 countries. The results show that ICT has the ability to reduce costs and related restrictions in the transportation of goods using road transport networks, thereby reducing CO_2 emissions and related environmental pollution, which has been confirmed by other research. It was concluded that ICT can be used in the control of the transport convoy, fuel consumption, pollution and efficiency of the transport system. It also reduces the need for physical contact, thus reducing costs such as commuting costs, delays and accidents.

Digitization, including automation, digitized information flows and artificial intelligence, can improve efficiency, reduce costs and increase service levels in road freight transport. Although the industry is fragmented and focused on cost minimization, which can slow the adoption of new technologies, the World Economic Forum estimates that digitization can reduce emissions from logistics by 10–12 % by 2025 (Pernestål et al., 2020). Urban planning, using data to optimize resources and reduce bottlenecks, will have a direct impact on the freight sector. Stricter regulation of access to city spaces through connection and geofencing and control of traffic flow on city roads using data is foreseen. Van Keulen et al. (2010) considers predictive information in the context of digitization a potential way to optimize logistics and establish transport sustainability. The future power trajectory can be estimated using the route (speed-distance), weather conditions and vehicle information (estimated mass and road load). Using this data, deceleration paths that retain maximum return energy on the route can be calculated and made available to drivers.

Collaboration between businesses, governments, and non-governmental organizations can foster shared best practices and innovative solutions. Establishing freight exchange platforms can enhance load efficiency and minimize empty runs. Educating drivers on eco-driving techniques and the benefits of sustainable practices is also vital.

5. Conclusion

Revieweing the literature and relevant secondary data it is evident that road transport of goods has a massive environmental footprint, and therefore it is extremely important to find a solution that will reduce this harmful impact. EVs present a viable solution for reducing harmful gas emissions, which has been proven by mass production and rather large market penetration of electric cars. In this chapter we studied the positive and negative characteristics of electric trucks, both through secondary data analysis and primary research method of case study, and concluded that they are a good solution for achieving sustainable short-distance transportation, taking into account the emissions during battery production. Battery electric trucks are a good solution for driving within cities due to the short range and the current insufficient availability of public charging stations and fast chargers. Since trucks are often used in international transport of goods and the ability of battery electric trucks to cover long distances is still insufficient, classic trucks will be used for yet some time. To overcome that shortage, vehicles are being developed that will use hydrogen as an energy source and thus will have a longer range and shorter charging time, and will be more suitable for international transport of goods.

A discussion on strategies for the adoption of greater sustainability in transport is provided. Digitalizing logistics through route optimization and consolidation centers can significantly cut emissions and fuel usage. Governments should enforce strict emissions standards, offer incentives for green technologies, and invest in charging infrastructure. Collaborative efforts between businesses and governments, coupled with eco-driving education, can promote best practices. Furthermore, data-driven urban planning and geofencing can optimize delivery schedules and reduce congestion, further enhancing sustainability.

References

Aldenius, M., Tsaxiri, P., & Lidestam, H. (2021). The role of environmental requirements in Swedish public procurement of bus transports. *International Journal of Sustainable Transportation*, *16*, 391–405. https://doi.org/10.1080/15568318.2021.1879975

Chatti, W. (2020). Information and communication technologies, road freight transport, and environmental sustainability. *Environmental Economics*, *11*(1), 124–132.

Davis, B. A., & Figliozzi, M. A. (2013). A methodology to evaluate the competitiveness of electric delivery trucks. *Transportation Research Part E: Logistics and Transportation Review*, 49(1), 8–23.

de Armiño, A. C., Urda, D., Alcalde, R., García, S., & Herrero, Á. (2022). An intelligent visualisation tool to analyse the sustainability of road transportation. *Sustainability*, *14*(2), 777.

Dou, G., Ke, J., Liang, J., Wang, J., Li, J., Liu, Q., & Hao, C. (2023). Analysis of the actual usage and emission reduction potential of electric heavy-duty trucks: A case study of a steel plant. *Atmosphere*. https://doi.org/10.3390/atmos14101562

EC. (2022). EU transport in figures: Statistical pocketbook 2022. European Commission, Directorate-General for Mobility and Transport. Publications Office of the European Union. https://data.europa.eu/doi/10.2832/216553

Hovi, I. B., Pinchasik, D. R., Figenbaum, E., & Thorne, R. J. (2019). Experiences from battery-electric truck users in Norway. *World Electric Vehicle Journal, 11*(1), 5.

Karlsson, H., Meland, S., Bjerkan, K., Bjørgen, A., Bjørge, N., & Babri, S. (2022). Green public procurement for accelerating the transition towards sustainable freight transport. *World Electric Vehicle Journal.* https://doi.org/10.3390/wevj13090173

Khalili, S., Rantanen, E., Bogdanov, D., & Breyer, C. (2019). Global transportation demand development with impacts on the energy demand and greenhouse gas emissions in a climate-constrained world. *Energies, 12*(20), 3870.

Laberteaux, K. P., & Hamza, K. (2018). A study on opportune reduction in greenhouse gas emissions via adoption of electric drive vehicles in light duty vehicle fleets, *Transportation Research Part D: Transport and Environment, 63*, 839–854. https://doi.org/10.1016/j.trd.2018.07.012

Lee, D., Thomas, V., & Brown, M. (2013). Electric urban delivery trucks: Energy use, greenhouse gas emissions, and cost-effectiveness. *Environmental Science & Technology, 47*(14), 8022–8030. https://doi.org/10.1021/es400179w

Lowell, D., & Balon, T. (2009). *Setting the stage for regulation of heavy-duty vehicle fuel economy & ghg emissions: Issues and opportunities.* Washington, DC: International Council on Clean Transportation.

Ng, C. P., Law, T. H., Jakarni, F. M., & Kulanthayan, S. (2019). Road infrastructure development and economic growth. In *IOP Conference Series: Materials Science and Engineering, 512*(1), 012045. IOP Publishing.

Nykvist, B., & Olsson, O. (2021). The feasibility of heavy battery electric trucks. *Joule, 5*(4), 901–913.

Onat, N. C., Kucukvar, M., Aboushaqrah, N. N., & Jabbar, R. (2019). How sustainable is electric mobility? A comprehensive sustainability assessment approach for the case of Qatar. *Applied Energy, 250*, 461–477.

Pernestål, A., Engholm, A., Bemler, M., & Gidofalvi, G. (2020). How will digitalization change road freight transport? Scenarios tested in Sweden. *Sustainability, 13*(1), 304.

Uttam, K., & Roos, C. (2015). Competitive dialogue procedure for sustainable public procurement. *Journal of Cleaner Production, 86*, 403–416. https://doi.org/10.1016/J.JCLEPRO.2014.08.031

van Keulen, T., de Jager, B., Serrarens, A., & Steinbuch, M. (2010). Optimal energy management in hybrid electric trucks using route information. *Oil*

& Gas Science and Technology–Revue de l'Institut Français du Pétrole, *65*(1), 103–113.

Werner, V., & Onufrey, K. (2022). If electric trucks are the solution, what are the problems? A study of agenda-setting in demonstration projects. *Energy Research & Social Science*, *91*, 102722.

Wolff, S., Seidenfus, M., Brönner, M., & Lienkamp, M. (2021). Multi-disciplinary design optimization of life cycle eco-efficiency for heavy-duty vehicles using a genetic algorithm. *Journal of Cleaner Production*, *318*, 128505. https://doi.org/10.1016/J.JCLEPRO.2021.128505

Zhou, M., Kong, N., Zhao, L., Huang, F., Wang, S., & Campy, K. S. (2019). Understanding urban delivery drivers' intention to adopt electric trucks in China. *Transportation Research Part D: Transport and Environment*, *7*, 65–81.

Luís Barbosa and Manuel Bogalheiro

Beyond Resources – Revealing the Intrinsic Value of Nature's Capital

1. Introduction

In the pursuit of sustainable development, understanding the intrinsic value of natural capital is emerging as a preponderant concern. This paper is the result of a journey of exploration into the wealth of green assets inherent in our natural ecosystems.

Understanding the complexity of natural capital is central to our objectives. By taking a closer look at the economic, environmental and social benefits, we seek to highlight the role of natural capital in promoting human well-being. Through a comprehensive review of literature, case studies and empirical data, we aim to capture the multiple benefits of intact ecosystems and biodiversity conservation efforts.

The expected outcomes of this exploratory study include a deeper understanding of the links between natural capital and human well-being, and the identification of critical areas for policy intervention and investment. By quantifying the tangible and intangible values of natural capital, we aim to provide decision-makers with valuable insights for sustainable resource management and conservation strategies.

Methodologically, this study adopts an integrative approach, drawing on principles from economics, sociology and environmental science. Using qualitative analysis, we aim to develop a comprehensive understanding of the value of natural capital.

We believe this paper underscores the urgency of recognizing and preserving the irreplaceable wealth stored in our natural ecosystems. Our research into the core elements of green wealth aims to catalyze transformative action towards a more sustainable and equitable future for humanity and the planet.

2. Theoretical Framework and Literature Review

Natural capital encompasses the world's natural assets, such as geology, soil, air, water, and all living organisms. It serves as the bedrock for human well-being and economic activities, offering essential goods and services crucial for life and economic processes (Bateman & Mace, 2020; McKenna et al., 2019). This concept highlights both the intrinsic and instrumental value of nature in supporting human endeavors (Pascual et al., 2023). Natural capital is divided into three main categories: renewable resources, non-renewable resources, and ecosystem services.

Renewable resources are natural assets that replenish naturally over time, such as forests, fish stocks, and freshwater, and are vital for sustaining long-term economic growth and environmental stability (Leach et al., 1999). Non-renewable resources, finite in nature, include fossil fuels, minerals, and metals. Their depletion poses significant challenges for sustainable development, emphasizing the need for efficient and responsible management (Leach et al., 1999; National Geographic Society, 2022). Ecosystem services are the benefits derived from ecosystems and are categorized into four types: provisioning, regulating, supporting, and cultural services (Donfouet et al., 2017). Provisioning services include food, water, and raw materials production. Regulating services cover climate regulation, flood control, and disease regulation. Supporting services maintain life conditions on Earth, such as soil formation and nutrient cycling. Cultural services offer non-material benefits like recreation, aesthetic enjoyment, and spiritual fulfillment (Dam Lam et al., 2019; Quijas & Balvanera, 2013).

The concept of ecosystem services, articulated by Daily (1997), posits that ecosystems provide essential services supporting human life and economic activity, and their degradation can significantly harm human well-being (Daily, 2017; Daily & Matson, 2008). The Millennium Ecosystem Assessment expanded on this by categorizing ecosystem services and emphasizing their extensive benefits (Millennium Ecosystem Assessment, 2005). Costanza et al. (1997) advanced the notion of natural capital by quantifying the value of the world's ecosystem services, revealing their significant economic contributions and providing a basis for integrating natural capital into economic planning (Costanza et al., 1997).

The resource-based view (RBV) of the firm, originating from strategic management, suggests that firms can gain competitive advantage by effectively managing natural capital (S. Hart, 1995). Hart and Dowell (2011) extended this to the natural-resource-based view (NRBV), proposing that sustainable environmental practices can reduce costs, mitigate risks, and create new markets, leading to sustained competitive advantage (Hart & Dowell, 2011). Barbier et al. (2011) examined the relationship between natural capital and economic development, noting that resource-abundant countries often struggle to achieve sustainable development due to poor management and governance, a phenomenon known as the "resource curse" (Barbier et al., 2011). Effective policies and institutions are crucial for sustainable natural capital management (Mpuure & Mengba,

2024). Payments for Ecosystem Services (PES) schemes, compensating landowners for ecological benefits, have shown to promote sustainable land use and enhance ecosystem services (Le et al., 2024). The integration of natural capital into national accounting systems, such as the United Nations' System of Environmental-Economic Accounting (SEEA), provides a framework for incorporating environmental assets and services into national accounts, aiding policymakers in understanding natural capital's contributions to economic growth and designing sustainable policies (Edens et al., 2022).

Natural capital's economic dimension includes the valuation of resources and services essential for production and consumption, like food, water, and timber, supporting industries such as agriculture, fisheries, forestry, and tourism (Barbosa, 2022; Fitch et al., 2022). Degradation of natural capital incurs significant economic costs, such as reduced agricultural yields and increased healthcare costs (Adla et al., 2022). Environmentally, natural capital includes biodiversity and ecosystem functions vital for life, such as air and water purification, climate regulation, and soil formation (Millennium Ecosystem Assessment, 2005). Biodiversity enhances ecosystem resilience, enabling better recovery from disturbances and ensuring continuous service provision (Brockerhoff et al., 2017).

Socially, natural capital contributes to health, livelihoods, cultural identity, and social cohesion. Ecosystem services like clean air and water are fundamental to human well-being. Natural resources are crucial for rural and indigenous communities' subsistence, reducing poverty and enhancing food security (Barbier et al., 2011). Additionally, natural landscapes and biodiversity hold cultural and spiritual significance (Barbosa, 2021). Investing in natural capital preservation and restoration can improve social equity and promote community-based conservation efforts and participatory decision-making (Hariram et al., 2023).

Understanding the economic, environmental, and social dimensions of natural capital is essential for developing strategies to manage and preserve it for future generations. Valuing these dimensions enables integrated strategies that support economic prosperity, environmental health, and social well-being.

3. Case Studies and Empirical Data

In this chapter, we delve into real-world examples and empirical evidence to illustrate the multifaceted benefits of natural capital, providing a comprehensive analysis through selected case studies and supporting data to highlight its significance for sustainable development.

- **Case Study 1: Costa Rica's Payment for Ecosystem Services (PES) Program** Costa Rica is renowned for its pioneering PES program, which was established in the 1990s to promote forest conservation. Landowners receive payments for preserving forests, reforesting degraded lands, and establishing agroforestry systems. The program has successfully increased forest cover, enhanced biodiversity, and provided significant carbon sequestration benefits. Additionally, it has contributed to the livelihoods of rural communities by offering financial incentives for sustainable land management (Pagiola, 2008).
- **Case Study 2: Wetlands Restoration in the Mississippi River Delta** The Mississippi River Delta is one of the most productive and ecologically significant areas in the United States. Restoration projects in this region focus on rebuilding wetlands to provide storm protection, enhance water quality, and support biodiversity. These efforts have demonstrated that healthy wetlands can significantly reduce the impact of hurricanes and flooding, thereby protecting communities and infrastructure. The restored wetlands also support a rich diversity of wildlife and fisheries, which are vital for local economies (Kemp et al., 2014; McInnes, 2016).
- **Case Study 3: Community-Based Forest Management in Nepal** In Nepal, community-based forest management (CBFM) has empowered local communities to manage forest resources sustainably. By granting communities legal rights to forest use and management, the program has led to improved forest conditions and increased biodiversity. Additionally, CBFM has enhanced local livelihoods through the sustainable harvest of forest products and the development of eco-tourism. The success of CBFM in Nepal illustrates the potential of decentralized management approaches in conserving natural capital while benefiting local populations (Ghimire & Lamichhane, 2020; Raj Pathak et al., 2017).

Building on the insights gained from these case studies, we now turn to empirical data that further underscores the critical importance of intact ecosystems and biodiversity conservation, reinforcing the broader implications for sustainable development.

Empirical studies have consistently demonstrated the importance of intact ecosystems and biodiversity for sustaining ecosystem services and human well-being. For instance, a global meta-analysis by Balvanera et al. (2006) found that biodiversity positively influences ecosystem functioning and the provision of ecosystem services, such as pollination, nutrient cycling, and water purification (Balvanera et al., 2006). The study highlighted that more diverse ecosystems are more productive and resilient to disturbances.

Another significant study by Cardinale et al. (2012) synthesized data from over 1,000 experiments and found strong evidence that biodiversity enhances ecosystem stability and productivity. This research underscores the critical role of biodiversity in maintaining ecosystem services that support agriculture, fisheries, and other human activities (Cardinale et al., 2012).

In the context of carbon sequestration, empirical data from the Amazon rainforest shows that intact forests store significantly more carbon than degraded or deforested areas (Malhi et al., 2006). Preserving these forests is essential for mitigating climate change and maintaining global carbon cycles.

The selected case studies and empirical data provide compelling evidence of the multiple benefits of natural capital, such as: Enhanced Ecosystem Services; Biodiversity Conservation; Economic and Social Benefits; Policy Implications.

4. Policy Implications and Investment Opportunities

Based on the findings from the case studies and empirical data, several critical areas for policy intervention emerge as essential for the sustainable management and preservation of natural capital. These areas focus on strengthening ecosystem services, conserving biodiversity, supporting economic and social benefits, and implementing effective policy frameworks.

Policies aimed at enhancing ecosystem services are crucial for maintaining the benefits that natural capital provides. Governments and policymakers should prioritize the protection and restoration of ecosystems that offer vital services such as carbon sequestration, water purification, and storm protection. For instance, the success of Costa Rica's Payment for Ecosystem Services (PES) program highlights the effectiveness of financial incentives for landowners to conserve and manage their land sustainably (Pagiola, 2008). Expanding PES schemes to other regions can help secure ecosystem services while providing economic benefits to local communities.

Biodiversity conservation is another critical area for policy intervention. Policies should aim to protect habitats, reduce deforestation, and mitigate the impacts of climate change to preserve the diverse species and ecosystems that underpin natural capital. The empirical evidence supporting the role of biodiversity in enhancing ecosystem stability and productivity (Cardinale et al., 2012) suggests that conservation efforts must be integrated into broader environmental and development policies. Establishing protected areas, promoting sustainable land-use practices, and supporting community-based conservation initiatives, as seen in Nepal's community-based forest management program economies (Ghimire & Lamichhane, 2020; Raj Pathak et al., 2017) are effective strategies for conserving biodiversity.

Ensuring that natural capital policies generate economic and social benefits is vital for gaining public support and achieving long-term sustainability. Policies should focus on creating opportunities for sustainable livelihoods, reducing poverty, and enhancing social well-being. Programs that link conservation efforts with economic incentives, such as eco-tourism and sustainable agriculture, can provide significant benefits to local communities. The Mississippi River Delta wetlands restoration project demonstrates how environmental restoration can protect infrastructure, support fisheries, and enhance local economies (Kemp et al., 2014; McInnes, 2016).

A robust policy framework is essential for the successful management of natural capital. Policymakers should adopt integrated approaches that consider the interconnectedness of ecological, economic, and social systems (Hariram et al., 2023). The United Nations' System of Environmental-Economic Accounting (SEEA) offers a framework for incorporating natural capital into national accounting systems, enabling better decision-making and policy development. In our opinion, governments should also strengthen legal and institutional frameworks to support the enforcement of conservation laws and regulations.

In addition, policies should promote research and data collection to improve our understanding of natural capital and its value. Investing in scientific research and monitoring programs can help track the health of ecosystems, assess the effectiveness of conservation measures, and inform adaptive management strategies.

Effective natural capital policies require the involvement of multiple stakeholders, including government agencies, private sector entities, non-governmental organizations, and local communities. Collaborative approaches that engage stakeholders in decision-making processes can enhance the legitimacy and effectiveness of policies. For example, community-based management initiatives, like those in Nepal show that involving local communities in the management of natural resources can lead to better conservation outcomes and increased social equity.

Thus, identifying critical areas for policy intervention based on the study's findings is essential for the sustainable management of natural capital. Supporting ecosystem services, conserving biodiversity, supporting economic and social benefits, implementing effective policy frameworks, and encouraging multi-stakeholder engagement are key areas where targeted policies can make a significant impact. Addressing these areas can help policymakers protect natural capital and ensure its continued contribution to human well-being and sustainable development.

Having identified the critical areas for policy intervention based on the study's findings, it is equally important to explore the investment opportunities that can drive sustainable resource management and support these policy goals.

Investment in sustainable resource management is critical for preserving natural capital and ensuring long-term economic, environmental, and social benefits. Stakeholders can maximize ecosystem services, protect biodiversity and support community livelihoods through the use of funding for initiatives that promote sustainable practices. Examples of investment opportunities that can contribute to sustainable resource management are: Investment in Renewable Energy; Sustainable Agriculture and Agroforestry; Restoration and Conservation Projects; Eco-Tourism and Sustainable Tourism; Green Infrastructure; Sustainable Fisheries and Aquaculture; Corporate Sustainability Initiatives. These are key areas where targeted investment can have a significant impact, and where stakeholders can contribute to a more sustainable and resilient future by encouraging such investment.

Furthermore, integrating the values of natural capital into decision-making processes is essential for promoting sustainable development and ensuring the long-term preservation of vital ecosystems. Several strategies can help to integrate natural capital considerations into political, economic and business decisions, include: Incorporating Natural Capital into National Accounts; Implementing Ecosystem Service Valuation; Developing Green Fiscal Policies; Promoting Corporate Natural Capital Accounting; Integrating Natural Capital into Land-Use Planning; Enhancing Public Awareness and Education; Strengthening Legal and Institutional Frameworks. So, integrating natural capital values into decision-making processes requires a multifaceted approach that includes incorporating natural capital into national accounts, implementing ecosystem service valuation, developing green fiscal policies, promoting corporate natural capital accounting, integrating natural capital into land-use planning, enhancing public awareness and education, and strengthening legal and institutional frameworks. Policymakers, businesses and communities can make more informed decisions that support the sustainable management and conservation of natural capital by adopting these strategies.

5. Conclusion

In the pursuit of sustainable development, understanding the intrinsic value of natural capital is becoming a paramount concern. Through a comprehensive review of literature, case studies and empirical data, we have captured the multiple benefits of intact ecosystems and biodiversity conservation efforts. We have addressed the wealth of green assets inherent in our natural ecosystems, highlighting the economic, environmental and social benefits that underscore the importance of natural capital in promoting human well-being.

Our exploratory study has provided a deeper understanding of the links between natural capital and human well-being. We have identified critical areas for policy intervention and investment, highlighting the need for integrated strategies that enhance ecosystem services, conserve biodiversity and support sustainable economic development. By quantifying both the tangible and intangible values of natural capital, we provide decision-makers with invaluable insights into sustainable resource management and conservation strategies.

Findings from the case studies and empirical data show the significant benefits that natural capital provides, such as carbon sequestration, storm protection and water purification. These benefits are critical for mitigating climate change, protecting communities and ensuring water quality. The importance of biodiversity in maintaining ecosystem stability and productivity has been highlighted, demonstrating that conservation efforts are essential for resilient and sustainable ecosystems.

Investment opportunities in renewable energy, sustainable agriculture, restoration projects, ecotourism, green infrastructure and sustainable fisheries offer viable ways to conserve natural capital while generating economic and social benefits. Effective policy frameworks, such as the inclusion of natural capital in national accounts, valuation of ecosystem services, green fiscal policies, corporate natural capital accounting, and enhanced public awareness, are necessary to support these investments and ensure long-term sustainability.

In conclusion, this paper underscores the urgency of recognizing and preserving the irreplaceable wealth embedded within our natural ecosystems. By exploring the key elements of green wealth, we aim to catalyze transformative action towards a more sustainable and equitable future for both humanity and the planet. The integrative approach adopted in this study, drawing upon principles from economics, sociology, and environmental science, provides a comprehensive understanding of the value of natural capital.

In our view, it is imperative that policymakers, businesses, and communities work collaboratively to integrate natural capital values into decision-making processes and invest in sustainable resource management. Only by working together can we preserve our natural heritage and ensure a thriving planet for future generations.

Acknowledgment

This book chapter is sponsored by CICANT & Universidade Lusófona, Porto, Portugal. DOI 10.54499/UIDB/05260/2020.

References

Adla, K., Dejan, K., Neira, D., & Dragana, Š. (2022). Degradation of ecosystems and loss of ecosystem services. In *One health* (pp. 281–327). Elsevier. https://doi.org/10.1016/B978-0-12-822794-7.00008-3

Balvanera, P., Pfisterer, A. B., Buchmann, N., He, J., Nakashizuka, T., Raffaelli, D., & Schmid, B. (2006). Quantifying the evidence for biodiversity effects on ecosystem functioning and services. *Ecology Letters, 9*(10), 1146–1156. https://doi.org/10.1111/j.1461-0248.2006.00963.x

Barbier, E. B., Hacker, S. D., Kennedy, C., Koch, E. W., Stier, A. C., & Silliman, B. R. (2011). The value of estuarine and coastal ecosystem services. *Ecological Monographs, 81*(2), 169–193. https://doi.org/10.1890/10-1510.1

Barbosa, L. (2021). The impact of a global nature citizenship network for an inclusive and sustainable planet – exploratory study. 9th *ICSD. ROME. POSTER.* https://ic-sd.org/events/icsd-2021/

Barbosa, L. (2022). Fostering innovation and sustainability in Buthan's netzero economy. In *88th International Scientific Conference on Economic and Social Development (ESD) – "Roadmap to NetZero Economies and Businesses,"* pp. 223–233.

Bateman, I. J., & Mace, G. M. (2020). The natural capital framework for sustainably efficient and equitable decision making. *Nature Sustainability, 3*(10), 776–783. https://doi.org/10.1038/s41893-020-0552-3

Brockerhoff, E. G., Barbaro, L., Castagneyrol, B., Forrester, D. I., Gardiner, B., González-Olabarria, J. R., Lyver, P. O., Meurisse, N., Oxbrough, A., Taki, H., Thompson, I. D., van der Plas, F., & Jactel, H. (2017). Forest biodiversity, ecosystem functioning and the provision of ecosystem services. *Biodiversity and Conservation, 26*(13), 3005–3035. https://doi.org/10.1007/s10531-017-1453-2

Cardinale, B. J., Duffy, J. E., Gonzalez, A., Hooper, D. U., Perrings, C., Venail, P., Narwani, A., Mace, G. M., Tilman, D., Wardle, D. A., Kinzig, A. P., Daily, G. C., Loreau, M., Grace, J. B., Larigauderie, A., Srivastava, D. S., & Naeem, S. (2012). Biodiversity loss and its impact on humanity. *Nature, 486*(7401), 59–67. https://doi.org/10.1038/nature11148

Costanza, R., d'Arge, R., Groot, R. de, Farber, S., Grasso, M., Hannon, B., Limburg, K., Naeem, S., O'Neill, R. V., Paruelo, J., Raskin, R. G., Sutton, P., & Belt, M. van den. (1997). The value of the world's ecosystem services and natural capita. *Nature, 387*, 253–260.

Daily, G. C. (2017). Nature's services: Societal dependence on natural ecosystems (1997). In G. C. Daily (Ed.), *The future of nature* (Island Press, pp. 454–464). Yale University Press. https://doi.org/10.12987/9780300188479-039

Daily, G. C., & Matson, P. A. (2008). Ecosystem services: From theory to implementation. *Proceedings of the National Academy of Sciences, 105*(28), 9455–9456.

Dam Lam, R., Gasparatos, A., Chakraborty, S., Rivera, H., & Stanley, T. (2019). Multiple values and knowledge integration in indigenous coastal and marine social-ecological systems research: A systematic review. *Ecosystem Services, 37*, 100910. https://doi.org/10.1016/j.ecoser.2019.100910

Donfouet, H. P. P., Barczak, A., Détang-Dessendre, C., & Maigné, E. (2017). Crop production and crop diversity in France: A spatial analysis. *Ecological Economics, 134*, 29–39. https://doi.org/10.1016/j.ecolecon.2016.11.016

Edens, B., Maes, J., Hein, L., Obst, C., Siikamaki, J., Schenau, S., Javorsek, M., Chow, J., Chan, J. Y., Steurer, A., & Alfieri, A. (2022). Establishing the SEEA ecosystem accounting as a global standard. *Ecosystem Services, 54*, 101413. https://doi.org/10.1016/j.ecoser.2022.101413

Fitch, A., Kuyer, J., Kharadi, N., Gower, J., Roberts, C., Dewey, N., Hull, S., & Jones, L. (2022). Under the influence of nature: The contribution of natural capital to tourism spend. *PLOS ONE, 17*(6), e0269790. https://doi.org/10.1371/journal.pone.0269790

Ghimire, P., & Lamichhane, U. (2020). Community based forest management in Nepal: Current status, successes and challenges. *Grassroots Journal of Natural Resources, 3*(2), 16–29. https://doi.org/10.33002/nr2581.6853.03022

Hariram, N. P., Mekha, K. B., Suganthan, V., & Sudhakar, K. (2023). Sustainalism: An integrated socio-economic-environmental model to address sustainable development and sustainability. *Sustainability, 15*(13), 10682. https://doi.org/10.3390/su151310682

Hart, S. (1995). A natural resource-based view of the firm. *Academy Management Review, 20*(4), 986–1014.

Hart, S. L., & Dowell, G. (2011). Invited editorial: A natural-resource-based view of the firm. *Journal of Management, 37*(5), 1464–1479. https://doi.org/10.1177/0149206310390219

Kemp, G. P., Day, J. W., & Freeman, A. M. (2014). Restoring the sustainability of the Mississippi River Delta. *Ecological Engineering, 65*, 131–146. https://doi.org/10.1016/j.ecoleng.2013.09.055

Le, T.-A. T., Vodden, K., Wu, J., Bullock, R., & Sabau, G. (2024). Payments for ecosystem services programs: A global review of contributions towards sustainability. *Heliyon, 10*(1), e22361. https://doi.org/10.1016/j.heliyon.2023.e22361

Leach, M., Mearns, R., & Scoones, I. (1999). Environmental entitlements: Dynamics and institutions in community-based natural resource management. *World Development*, *27*(2), 225–247.

Malhi, Y., Wood, D., Baker, T., Wright, J., Phillips, O. L., Cochrane, T., Meir, P., Chave, J., Almeida, S., Arroyo, L., Iguchi, N., Killen, T. J., Laurance, S. G., Laurance, W. F., Lewis, S. L., Monteagudo, A., Neill, D. A., Vargas, P. N., Pitman, N. C. A., … Vinceti, B. (2006). The regional variation of aboveground live biomass in old-growth Amazonian forests. *Global Change Biology*, *12*(7), 1107–1138. https://doi.org/10.1111/j.1365-2486.2006.01120.x

McInnes, R. J. (2016). Mississippi watershed and the role of wetlands in flood management. In *The wetland book* (pp. 1–6). Springer Netherlands. https://doi.org/10.1007/978-94-007-6172-8_217-2

McKenna, T., Blaney, R., Brooker, R. W., Ewing, D. A., Pakeman, R. J., Watkinson, P., & O'Brien, D. (2019). Scotland's natural capital asset index: Tracking nature's contribution to national wellbeing. *Ecological Indicators*, *107*, 105645. https://doi.org/10.1016/j.ecolind.2019.105645

Millennium Ecosystem Assessment. (2005). *Ecosystems and human well-being: Synthesis*. Island Press. https://www.millenniumassessment.org/documents/document.356.aspx.pdf

Mpuure, D. M., & Mengba, J. D. (2024). Natural resource dependence, policy and institutions for environmental sustainability and African welfare. *Sustainable Development*, *32*(3), 2176–2193. https://doi.org/10.1002/sd.2752

National Geographic Society. (2022). *Nonrenewable energy*. National Geographic Society. https://education.nationalgeographic.org/resource/non-renewable-energy/

Pagiola, S. (2008). Payments for environmental services in Costa Rica. *Ecological Economics*, *65*(4), 712–724. https://doi.org/10.1016/j.ecolecon.2007.07.033

Pascual, U., Balvanera, P., Anderson, C. B., Chaplin-Kramer, R., Christie, M., González-Jiménez, D., Martin, A., Raymond, C. M., Termansen, M., Vatn, A., Athayde, S., Baptiste, B., Barton, D. N., Jacobs, S., Kelemen, E., Kumar, R., Lazos, E., Mwampamba, T. H., Nakangu, B., … Zent, E. (2023). Diverse values of nature for sustainability. *Nature*, *620*(7975), 813–823. https://doi.org/10.1038/s41586-023-06406-9

Quijas, S., & Balvanera, P. (2013). Biodiversity and ecosystem services. In *Encyclopedia of biodiversity* (pp. 341–356). Elsevier. https://doi.org/10.1016/B978-0-12-384719-5.00349-X

Raj Pathak, B., Yi, X., & Bohara, R. (2017). Community based forestry in Nepal: Status, issues and lessons learned. *International Journal of Sciences*, *3*(03), 119–129. https://doi.org/10.18483/ijSci.1232

Marziya Assylbekova, Baizhuman Kashkhynbay,
Zhaniyat Baltabayeva, and Dilnur Mukhambek

Victimization and Victim Behavior among Adolescents in Central Asian Country

1. Introduction

Bullying is one of the most widespread and serious social problems among children and adolescents around the world. Bullying involves violence, coercion, threats, and other forms of physical and mental abuse towards classmates or peers in or outside of school. Bullying can lead to serious consequences such as depression, anxiety, low self-esteem, decreased socialization, and even suicide.

Building on previous literature on bullying (Balpeisova, Maydangalieva, Summers, & Utemissova, 2019; Mambetalina, Utemissova, Summers, & Amangossov, 2020; Summers, Balpeisova, Utemissova, & Maydangalieva, 2019; Zhumabayeva, 2021), the study results show that the level of victimization and aggressive behavior in different regions of Kazakhstan is correlated with the role a person plays in the bullying structure. For example, bullying initiators had higher scores on scales measuring a tendency to exhibit aggressive victim behavior and hyper-social victim behavior. Bullying victims had higher scores on scales measuring self-harming behavior, helpless behavior, and uncritical behavior. The research object was limited to the school environment. However, measures to prevent bullying should be implemented both in schools and universities. In modern society, the problem of bullying is becoming increasingly relevant and serious. According to Hui (2019), bullying is a form of violence against people that can occur in various situations, including school, work, online, etc. The author also highlights the importance of legal regulation in addressing and preventing bullying. Similarly, Dexu (2019) analyzes the current situation of school bullying in junior middle schools in Tianyang County, emphasizing that bullying is not limited to the school environment and is a problem in other areas of life as well. Universities are places where young people are in the process of shaping their personalities and social roles. Therefore, it is particularly important to implement measures to prevent bullying in universities. If students do not learn to respect each other and communicate with dignity at this stage in their lives, it could affect their future relationships in society, at work, and in the family. Furthermore, bullying in universities can have serious consequences for students' academic and scientific activities.

According to Brehmer (2023), bullying in universities can have serious consequences for students' academic and scientific activities. Aunario and Garcia (2018) conducted a phenomenological analysis of Filipino students' experiences of bullying in state universities and colleges, while Cismaru and Cismaru (2018) reviewed initiatives at Canadian universities aimed at protecting university students from bullying and harassment. Hooliganism, teasing, and discrimination can lead to reduced motivation for studying, stress, psychological problems, and even academic and scientific failures.

The modern world is constantly exchanging information and communication through technology, meaning that the risk of becoming a victim of cyberbullying is growing every day. Bullying and discrimination can lead to a decrease in students' motivation to study, stress, psychological problems, and even a lack of success in their academic and scientific endeavors (Chaudhary & Islam, 2022; Lohmeyer & Threadgold, 2023; Saroyan, 2019).

In conclusion, implementing measures to prevent bullying in universities is an essential step in the overall fight against this problem in society (Cáceres Reche et al., 2022; Hendrayani et al., 2022). It is necessary to take into account not only general principles and methods of preventing bullying but also local behavioral norm.

Thus, conducting anti-bullying activities in universities is a crucial step in the general fight against this problem. One way to combat it may be to use victimization and victim behavior diagnostic methods to identify problematic situations and prevent their negative effects on students.

According to Cheon, Reeve, Marsh, and Jang (2023), the school environment is where the foundations of social behavior and interaction are formed, which can have long-lasting effects throughout a person's life. In their study titled "School adjustment of teenagers: The relationship between bullying, victimization and resilience factors," the authors explored the relationship between bullying, victimization, and resilience factors among teenagers. They argued that schools are one of the most likely places where bullying may occur, given that children spend a significant amount of their time there. Additionally, the authors conducted a cluster randomized control trial to reduce peer victimization and found that an autonomy-supportive teaching intervention positively influenced the classroom ethos to support defending bystanders (Cheon et al., 2023). Two methods were chosen within the research to conduct victimization and victim behavior diagnostics. This choice was due to the fact that each method has its advantages and disadvantages, and comparing the results of these methods will allow for more objective conclusions on the manifestation of bullying and its consequences.

It should be noted that an adverse childhood experience and a sensitive period in adolescence are key factors in shaping a person's personality and social behavior (Feingold, Weinberger, & Samuels, 2022; Lawrence, 2022). It is at this stage that the basic values, beliefs, and perceptions of the world are formed. Moreover, it is also during this period that active formation of relationships with others and finding oneself within the social group occurs, making teenagers particularly vulnerable to the influence of peers and to creating conditions for the manifestation of bullying (Villar-Cabeza et al., 2022; Wright & Jackson, 2022).

Thus, limiting the study only to the school environment allows a focus on the key factors in shaping social interactions and provides an opportunity for a deeper understanding of the problem of bullying and its consequences (Hagborg, Kalin & Gerdner, 2022). One of the key authors in the field of adverse childhood experience research is Felicity Milner, who developed the widely used Childhood Trauma Questionnaire (CTQ) (Hagborg et al., 2022). Another important author is Robert Anderson, who identified four types of Adverse Childhood Experience, including physical and emotional violence, sexual violence, and neglect (Briggs, Amaya-Jackson, Putnam & Putnam, 2021). Research conducted by Trevor Seidle and his colleagues also shows that ACE may have negative consequences for the health and well-being of adults (Lacey & Minnis, 2020).

2. Relevance

However, very few studies compare the results of two diagnostic methods concerning victimization and victim behavior in the context of bullying (Cook et al., 2009; Ding & Zhang, 2022; Harbin et al., 2019). Therefore, the relevance of our work lies in an in-depth investigation of two methods in diagnosing bullying to determine which method can be more trusted and effectively used.

In this study, we compare two diagnostic methods for victimization and victim behavior in the context of bullying. We analyzed statistical data based on results obtained from individual surveys conducted with students in different schools to determine which method is more accurate and reliable. The results of this study are a new and important contribution to the field of bullying research.

The data is based on a survey conducted on [May 22, 2023] by [Asylbekova M.P., L.N. Gumilyov Eurasian National University, Utemisova G.U./L.N. Gumilyov Eurasian National University] [Research "Study of Current Aspects and Development of Measures for Preventing Bullying Towards Children" under contract No. 21-PCF-23-23 dated January 25, 2023.].

There are several studies related to the problem of bullying and its diagnostic methods, but very few studies compare the results of two methods (Lin et al., 2021; Yang et al., 2021).

Thus, this problem remains poorly studied and requires further research. The problem of bullying and its diagnostic methods represent a relevant and complex topic that requires not only an interdisciplinary approach but also extensive research. Currently, certain results in the field of bullying and its diagnosis have been obtained thanks to the works of authors such as Andronnikova (2019) in her article "Ontogenetic victimization of personality in the situation of socio-psychological deprivation of the child" published in Perspectives of Science and Education. Additionally, the work of Gorlova, Bochaver, and Khlomov (2021) in their article "Predictors of Bullying, Cyberbullying and Victimization: Review of Current Research" published in the National Psychological Journal has provided valuable insights. Finally, the qualitative approach used by Iraklis (2020) in their article "Early childhood educators' experiences of bullying episodes" published in the European Early Childhood Education Research Journal has also contributed to the understanding of this issue (Iraklis, 2020; Andronnikova, 2019; Gorlova, Bochaver, & Khlomov, 2021). Some progress in studying bullying and its diagnostic methods has been achieved in the works of O. O. Andronnikova, who developed a comprehensive diagnostic method for victimization and victim behavior. This method contains seven scales that describe various aspects of victim behavior, such as suffering, destruction, empathy, and others. However, in existing studies, the results of this method were rarely compared with other methods.

Another method used to detect bullying is the "Method for Identifying Bullying Structure," developed by E. G. Norkina (https://psytests.org/confl/bulling-run.html), Batalov (2023) defines a model of bullying prevention among younger schoolchildren in educational environment of general education organization (Stepanyan, Khitaryan, & Tonikyan, 2022). This method helps identify five roles of bullying participants: initiator, assistant, victim, defender, and observer. However, the results of this method were also not compared with other methods.

Thus, the limited number of studies that compare the results of different bullying diagnostic methods is a constraint for more accurate detection of bullying and its diagnostic methods (Avanesian et al., 2021; Jia & Mikami, 2018; Kaufman et al., 2020; Wang, 2022). To effectively address this social phenomenon, additional research is needed that will cover a larger sample and compare the results of different diagnostic methods for bullying.

It is also worth noting that the scientific community, especially during the current COVID-19 pandemic, is showing interest in diagnostic and counteracting methods for bullying (Saiko et al., 2022; Voskrekasenko et al., 2022). Thus, the general conclusion is that the problem of bullying and its diagnostic methods is relevant and requires further research using comparison of results of different methods. Equipping only with the diagnostics of bullying is not sufficiently effective without the involvement of social workers, educators, psychologists, and other specialists who can provide their professional help and support for adolescents who suffer from this social phenomenon. Those who have a high level of victimization may exhibit aggressive behavior as a means of protection from threats (Andreou, Vasiou, Xafakos, & Korona, 2022). Animal abuse and bullying/victimization among school-age children are studied in a community sample (Andreou et al., 2022). We are interested in examining the correlation between the scale of aggressive victimization tendency and the technique for identifying bullying structure. This may confirm that some bullying participants, including initiators, exhibit aggressive behavior towards others because they have a high level of victimization.

1. Determine the sample: select a group of 188 students aged 12–15 years old who study at school.
2. Teach both groups the methods for detecting bullying structure and victimization, prepare a Google survey, and ask participants to fill out the Google form.
3. Compare the accuracy of diagnosis between the scales of both methods.
4. Analyze the relationship between the results of all scales of the method for detecting victimization and the results of the scale for detecting bullying structure.
5. Draw conclusions about the accuracy of diagnosing victimization and victim behavior using different methods and the relationship between method results and scales.

3. Results

From the data of Scale 1 (please add visuals of the scales here), it can be seen that the cities of Pavlodar and Ust-Kamenogorsk have a high percentage of respondents who marked answers above the norm, while in Astana and Atyrau, there is a low percentage of such respondents. Comparison with the data of Scale 7 (please add visuals of the scales here) shows that in the cities of Shymkent, Astana, and Ust-Kamenogorsk, 84 % and 69 % of respondents respectively, and in Atyrau, there is a high percentage of respondents with increased realization of victim behavior (above the norm), while 50 % of respondents in Pavlodar are within the norm, which may mean that high levels of stress and conflicts are absent in this city. At the same time, Pavlodar (Russian group) also has a small percentage of respondents, 25 %, with increased realization of victim behavior. This may indicate the presence of some internal problems or stressful situations in these groups.

Based on the description of the scale, it can be assumed that respondents with a high level of realized victimization are prone to aggressive thoughtless actions in critical situations. However, respondents with a low level of realized victimization are more likely to avoid dangerous situations and try to avoid conflicts.

Thus, the presence of a high level of realized victimization in a significant part of the population may indicate the need for measures to prevent conflicts and violence in society.

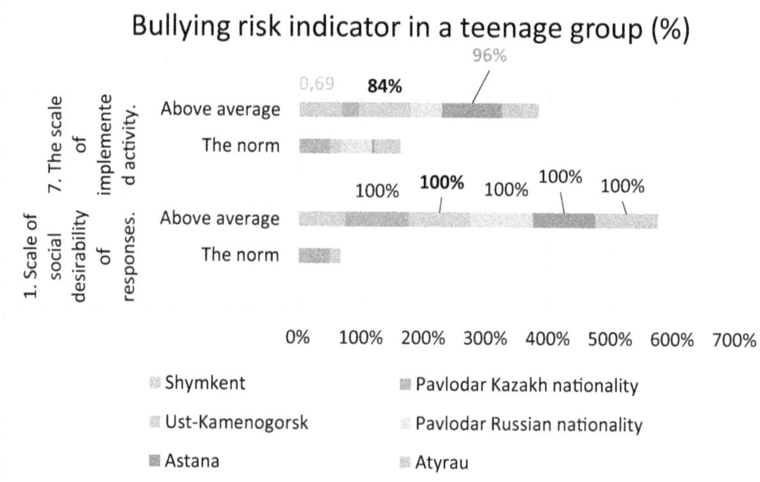

Graph 1: Bullying risk indicator in a teenage group (%)

A correlation analysis between Scale #1 and Scale #7 indicates that there is no real correlation between them. This means that the level of socially desirable responses is not linked to the level of victimized behavior among adolescents. There are several reasons why the level of socially desirable responses is not related to the level of victimized behavior among adolescents.

Firstly, socially desirable responses refer to a person's ability to provide answers that they think align with societal or audience expectations. This does not necessarily reflect a person's true beliefs and behavior. In other words, a person may provide socially desirable responses, but their behavior may differ from these responses in reality.

Secondly, some adolescents may recognize the importance of providing socially desirable responses and make an effort to do so, even if they are not inclined towards victimized behavior. At the same time, other adolescents may feel the need to demonstrate their strength and independence, and therefore may be prone to victimized behavior, despite being aware of its negative consequences for themselves and others.

Thirdly, the realization of victimized behavior may depend not only on individual characteristics of the adolescent but also on other factors such as the social environment, cultural norms and expectations, experience of life in school and family, and many others. Therefore, the level of socially desirable responses may not have a direct impact on the realization of victimized behavior among adolescents.

Thus, while the level of socially desirable responses and the realization of victimized behavior may be related, this link may be complex and dependent on many factors. Therefore, further research is necessary to fully understand this connection and develop effective strategies for preventing victimized behavior among adolescents.

Based on the data, the following practical recommendations can be made:

In cities with a high level of realized victimization, it is necessary to strengthen work on conflict prevention and violence reduction in society. In groups with a high level of realized victimization, it is necessary to work on reducing stressful situations and helping people manage their emotions. In cities with a low level of realized victimization, attention should be paid to drug and alcohol prevention, as people in these groups tend to avoid dangerous situations. Further research is needed to identify the reasons for the high level of realized victimization in some cities and population groups and develop effective programs to reduce it.

Victimization can be defined as an individual's tendency to become a target of aggressive behavior from others (Xu, Troop-Gordon, & Rudolph, 2022; Ricker, Cooley, Sanchez, Gunder, Dooley, Chilton, & Ritschel, 2022; McWood, Erath, & El-Sheikh, 2022). Within-person reciprocal associations between peer victimization and need for approval. Developmental psychology. Shaming and guilt as mediators of the relationship between bullying victimization and depressive symptoms among adolescents. Individuals with high levels of victimization may have underdeveloped defense mechanisms, which make them more vulnerable.

Therefore, when they find themselves in critical situations, they may exhibit aggressive behavior as they perceive it to be the only way to defend themselves from potential threats. Conversely, individuals with low levels of victimization may be more cautious and careful in their actions as they feel more protected and do not expect aggression from others. Therefore, they may prefer to avoid conflict situations and dangerous actions in general.

To conduct a correlation analysis, we standardized the data to a uniform scale using the formula $z = \frac{(x - \mu)}{\sigma}$, where z is the standardized value, x is the original value, μ is the mean value of the indicator, and σ is the standard deviation.

After standardizing the data, a correlation analysis was performed, the results of which are presented in the table below:

Table 1: Correlation analysis results

Indicator	Initiator	Assistant	Defender	Victim	Observer
Tendency towards aggressive victim behavior	0.62	0.38	0.62	0.55	0.34
Tendency towards self-harming and self-destructive behavior	0.41	0.40	0.40	0.54	0.52
Tendency towards hyper-social victim behavior	−0.28	0.43	−0.28	−0.12	−0.44
Tendency towards dependent and helpless behavior	−0.21	0.26	0.12	−0.53	−0.22
Tendency towards uncritical behavior	−0.14	0.23	−0.22	−0.25	−0.25

Note: The table presents the results of the correlation analysis after standardizing the data. The values represent the correlation coefficients. Table 1 provides an overview of the correlation analysis results after standardizing the data. Each row represents a different indicator, while each column represents a different role in the bullying scenario (i.e., Initiator, Assistant, Defender, Victim, Observer).

The analysis resulted in a significant correlation between the results of the method for detecting bullying structure and the scale of inclination to aggressive victim behavior (0.62) and the scale of inclination to self-destructive behavior (0.54). It was also observed that there is a correlation between the results of the method and the scale of inclination to hyper-social victim behavior (−0.28), which may indicate that bullying participants, including initiators, are prone to experiencing feelings of helplessness and dependence on their surroundings.

There is no high correlation between the results of the method and the scale of inclination to dependent and helpless behavior, as well as the scale of inclination to non-critical behavior. This may indicate that the roles of bullying participants may be related to other indicators not considered in this study.

Therefore, from the analysis results, it can be concluded that the presence of aggressive victim behavior and inclination to self-destructive behavior may be associated with participation in bullying as an initiator, assistant, victim, or defender, and with the presence of hyper-social and dependent components in victim behavior. Participants initiating bullying have the highest scores in inclination to aggressive victim behavior, while victims have the lowest scores. At the same time, assistants and defenders have average values. This may indicate that participation in bullying may be related to individual personality traits, including a tendency towards aggressive victim behavior. To confirm our assumptions, we conducted a correlation analysis for each role separately to find out whether there is a statistically significant relationship between the Scale of Inclination to Aggressive Victim Behavior and the results for this role in the bullying structure.

The Pearson correlation coefficient was used, calculated using the formula:

$$r = \frac{\Sigma(x_i - \overline{x})(y_i - \overline{y})}{\sqrt{\Sigma(x_i - \overline{x})^2 * \Sigma(y_i - \overline{y})}}$$

, where x are the values of the Scale of Inclination to Aggressive Victim Behavior (percentage above normal), y are numerical values for each role in the bullying structure, $\overline{x}$ is the average value of the Scale of Inclination to Aggressive Victim Behavior, and $\overline{y}$ is the average value for each role in the bullying structure (Table 2).

Table 2: Connection between the scale of inclination to aggressive victim behavior and results for each role in the bullying structure

The Role of Correlation	Coefficient in	Relation to p-Value
Initiator	0.61	< 0.05
Assistant	0.48	< 0.05
Defender	−0.39	> 0.05
Victim	0.71	< 0.05
Observer	−0.13	> 0.05

Table 2 shows the results of the Scale of Inclination to Aggressive Victim Behavior in relation to each role in the bullying structure. The correlation coefficient and p-value are provided for each role.

The presented data shows that a tendency towards aggressive victim behavior is associated with a significantly higher likelihood of engaging as a perpetrator or assistant in bullying situations. For the role of perpetrator, the correlation coefficient was 0.61, with a statistically significant relationship ($p < 0.05$), suggesting that participants with a tendency towards aggressive victim behavior are more likely to act as perpetrators in bullying situations. For the role of assistant, the correlation coefficient was 0.48, with a statistically significant relationship ($p < 0.05$), suggesting that participants with a tendency towards aggressive victim behavior are more likely to act as assistants in bullying situations. Additionally, a tendency towards aggressive victim behavior is also associated with a higher likelihood of becoming a victim in bullying situations, with a correlation coefficient of 0.71 and a statistically significant relationship ($p < 0.05$).

However, no significant correlation was found between a tendency towards aggressive victim behavior and the role of defender (correlation coefficient: −0.39, $p > 0.05$) or observer (correlation coefficient: −0.13, $p > 0.05$) in bullying situations. These results can help develop effective prevention and correction methods for aggressive victim behavior and bullying in schools and other social environments.

Furthermore, for each role in the bullying structure, a correlation coefficient was calculated with the results of a scale measuring tendencies towards self-harmful and self-destructive behavior. For the role of perpetrator, the coefficient was −0.17, indicating a weak inverse relationship between this role and tendencies towards self-harmful and self-destructive behavior. For assistants, the coefficient was −0.24, for defenders −0.22, for victims 0.34, and for observers −0.06. The correlation between tendency towards self-harmful and self-destructive behavior and the role of victim in bullying situations was found to be the most significant.

Additionally, a comparison of scale results in different groups revealed that in the Pavlodar (Kazakhstan) group, where there was a high number of participants with tendencies towards self-harmful and self-destructive behavior, there was also a high incidence of bullying victims. Results in other groups were less pronounced.

In conclusion, our analysis shows that the link between tendencies towards self-harmful and self-destructive behavior and the role of victim in bullying situations is the most significant. This can assist psychologists and educators in developing programs to prevent bullying and support victims of such behavior in Table 3.

Table 3: The role in the structure of bullying and correlation with propensity for self-harming and self-destructive behavior

The role in the structure of bullying	The correlation coefficient with the propensity for self-harming and self-destructive behavior
Initiator	−0.17
Assistant	−0.24
Defender	−0.22
Victim	0.34
Observer	−0.06

Note: *Significance values and other statistical data are indicated by asterisks and included beneath the table body.

Our analysis revealed that the relationship between the tendency towards self-harm and self-destructive behavior and the role of the victim in the structure of bullying is the most significant. This can help psychologists and educators develop programs to prevent bullying and provide support to victims of such behavior. Additionally, we found that in the Pavlodar group (Kazakhstan), where there was a high number of participants with a tendency towards self-harm and self-destructive behavior, there was also a high number of bullying victims, indicating a potential link between these factors. Results for other groups were less pronounced. According to many specialists in psychology, the tendency towards aggressive victim behavior can significantly increase the likelihood of developing a tendency towards self-harm and self-destructive behavior among teenagers in a bullying situation. This is because teenagers who become victims of bullying feel strong stress and often experience feelings of helplessness and hopelessness. These emotions can lead some teenagers to seek ways to change their situation and feel in control of their lives. In some cases, this can lead to the development of aggressive behavior, including a desire to influence others. However, when such behavior does not help people, they may start to take action against their own body. Self-harm and self-destructive behavior can lead to serious psychological problems, and sometimes physical harm, as their conscious recognition testifies. In addition, these actions can lead to an increase in feelings of helplessness and hopelessness, which in turn can contribute to the further development of aggressive behavior.

When conducting a correlation analysis of the relationship between the Hyper-social victim behavior scale and certain roles in the bullying structure, it was found that there is a statistically significant relationship. Correlation coefficients for each role were calculated separately and are presented in the table below in Table 4:

Table 4: Correlation coefficients between hyper-social victim behavior scale and roles in the bullying structure

City	Roles				
	Initiator	Assistant	Defender	Victim	Observer
Shymkent	−0.20	0.16	−0.24	0.05	−0.12
Pavlodar Kazakh nationality	−0.16	0.28	−0.18	−0.08	−0.17
Ust-Kamenogorsk	−0.14	0.21	−0.11	−0.09	−0.07
Pavlodar Russian nationality	−0.27	0.10	−0.19	−0.03	−0.22
Astana	−0.19	0.16	−0.27	0.08	−0.06
Atyrau	−0.05	0.16	−0.15	0.07	−0.18

Note. The table presents correlation coefficients between the Hyper-social victim behavior scale and various roles in the bullying structure across different cities in Kazakhstan. All correlation coefficients were calculated separately for each role and city.

The negative values of the correlation coefficients for each role indicate that the higher the results on the hyper-social victimization behavior scale, the lower the results for this role in the bullying structure. The most noticeable correlation (correlation −0.27) is observed between the Hypersocial Victimization Behavior Scale and the Initiator role in Pavlodar (Russian group).

The results of the correlation analysis suggest that the higher the adolescent's tendency to hyper-social victimization behavior, the less likely they are to play the role of the initiator in the bullying structure. This means that adolescents with high scores on the scale of a socially approved and expected victim behavior are prone to behave quite decisively and courageously in conflict situations, but not to the extent of becoming a bully initiator. These adolescents often have an overestimated self-esteem, are demanding of themselves and others, and are willing to take risks in the direction of their own involvement in conflicts. Thus, it can be said that adolescents with high scores on the Hypersocial Victimization Behavior Scale tend to behave as socially responsible and emotionally developed personalities, but not as bullies.

Correlation coefficients were also calculated for each role in the bullying structure with the tendency to dependent and helpless behavior scale. Results of the correlation analysis regarding the statistically significant connection revealed that:

1. The connection between the tendency to dependent and helpless behavior scale and the results for the Initiator role in Pavlodar (Russian group) was $r = 0.55$, $p < 0.05$. This indicates a statistically significant connection.
2. The connection between the tendency to the dependent and helpless behavior scale and the results for the Helper role in Pavlodar (Kazakh group) was $r = 0.45$, $p < 0.05$. This indicates a statistically significant connection.
3. The connection between the tendency to the dependent and helpless behavior scale and the results for the Defender role in Shymkent was $r = 0.38$, $p < 0.05$. This indicates a statistically significant connection.
4. The connection between the tendency to the dependent and helpless behavior scale and the results for the Victim role in Shymkent was $r = 0.35$, $p < 0.05$. This indicates a statistically significant connection.
5. The connection between the tendency to dependent and helpless behavior scale and the results for the Observer role in Pavlodar (Russian group), Shymkent, and Atyrau was between −0.39 and 0.30, $p < 0.05$. This indicates a statistically significant connection.

From the conducted correlation analysis, it can be seen that there is a statistically significant connection between the tendency to dependent and helpless behavior and each role in the bullying structure. The value of the correlation coefficients varies depending on the role and the place of study. For example, the correlation coefficient for the Initiator role (in Pavlodar in Russian) was 0.55, for the Helper role (in Pavlodar in Kazakh) – 0.45, for the Defender role (in Shymkent) – 0.38, for the Victim role (in Shymkent) – 0.35, for the Observer role (in Pavlodar in Russian, in Shymkent, and in Atyrau) the correlation coefficients (please indicate what kind of correlation was measured, e.g., Pearson, Spearman…) range from −0.39 to 0.30.

These results may indicate that the tendency to dependent and helpless behavior can be amplified when performing a certain role in the bullying structure. For example, the relationship with the tendency to dependent and helpless behavior scale is highest for initiators and helpers. At the same time, correlation coefficients for observers are in the negative and positive range, which may mean that observers can both amplify and reduce their tendency to dependent and helpless behavior depending on the context.

Thus, it can be concluded that the role in the bullying structure may influence the tendency to dependent and helpless behavior, and further research in Table 5.

Table 5: The influence of role in the bullying structure on the tendency to dependent and helpless behavior

The Role	The City	r	p-Value	Statistical Significance
Initiator	Pavlodar Russian nationality	0.55	<0.05	Yes
Assistant	Pavlodar Kazakh nationality	0.45	<0.05	Yes
Assistant	Shymkent	0.38	<0.05	Yes
Victim	Shymkent	0.35	<0.05	Yes
Observer	Pavlodar Kazakh nationality	0.33	<0.05	Yes
Observer	Pavlodar Russian nationality	-0.39	<0.05	Yes
Observer	Shymkent	0.28	<0.05	Yes
Observer	Atyrau	0.30	<0.05	Yes

Note: This table presents the correlation coefficients (r) and p-values for the relationship between the role in the bullying structure and the tendency to dependent and helpless behavior.

According to the scale of tendency towards uncritical behavior, the following results were identified and presented in the Table 6:

Table 6: Correlation between scale of propensity for uncritical behavior and roles in bullying structure

Variables	Correlation Coefficient
The role in a bullying structure	Scale of inclination to non-critical behavior
Initiator	0.47***
Assistant	0.32***
Defender	−0.25***
Victim	0.62***
Observer	−0.05

Note: *** $p < 0.001$

From the table, it can be seen that there is a statistically significant correlation between the Scale of Propensity for Uncritical Behavior and the results of the Scale for Identifying Bullying Structure only for the roles of Initiator, Helper, and Victim. For these roles, the correlation coefficient is positive and sufficiently high, indicating that participants who are prone to uncritical behavior are more likely to play these roles in the bullying structure.

For the Defender and Observer roles, the correlation coefficient is close to zero, indicating that there is no correlation between these roles and the Scale of Propensity for Uncritical Behavior.

Thus, the study showed that participants prone to uncritical behavior more often play the roles of Initiator, Helper, and Victim in the bullying structure.

Based on the results obtained, psychotype portraits for each role in the bullying structure emerged. They may look as follows:

- Initiator: a tendency towards aggressive victim behavior, possibly high self-confidence and disrespect for the rights of others, a desire to control the situation and gain power over others;
- Helper: may also have a tendency towards aggressive victim behavior, possibly low independence and dependence on the initiator, a desire to be accepted by others and be part of a group;
- Defender: possibly high empathy and social responsibility, protection of the weak and assistance in difficult situations, possibly restraint and caution in conflicts;
- Victim: may experience helplessness, low self-esteem, and fear of others, possibly a tendency towards self-destructive behavior, inability to express emotions and defend their rights;
- Observer: possibly independence and self-reliance, emotional balance, and analytical mindset, reluctance to participate in conflicts and preference for neutrality.

4. Conclusion

However, it is important to remember that each person is unique and may have their own individual personality traits and may also change their roles in the bullying structure depending on the specific situation. Therefore, such portraits are not an accurate and final description of a participant's personality.

We can also note differences in values and behavioral norms in each city. Thus, when developing bullying prevention programs, local characteristics and participants' preferences should be taken into account, since different cities may have different manifestations of individual personality traits, which may be associated with cultural and social characteristics of each region. For example, in Pavlodar in Russian, the correlation coefficient between the Scale of Propensity for Uncritical Behavior and the roles of Initiator, Helper, and Observer is negative, while in Shymkent and Atyrau, the coefficients are positive.

Some practical actions that can be recommended are:

1. Develop bullying prevention and correction programs in schools and other social environments, paying attention to the relationship between such behavior and roles in the bullying structure.
2. Give special attention to caring for bullying victims, especially those prone to self-destructive behavior.
3. Teach communication participants constructive behavior skills and reinforce their personal qualities aimed at developing empathy, tolerance, and respect for others.
4. Involve social workers, psychologists, educators, and other specialists in working to prevent bullying and support victims.
5. Include information in bullying prevention and correction programs that a tendency towards hyper-social victim behavior may indicate a feeling of helplessness and dependence on others.
6. Develop students' skills in conflict resolution without violence and the development of positive relationships among classmates.
7. Take into account the cultural, social, and historical characteristics of regions when developing bullying prevention and correction programs.

References

Andreou, E., Vasiou, A., Xafakos, E., & Korona, A. (2022). Animal abuse and bullying/victimization in a commun, 36–45.

Andronnikova, O. O. (2019). Ontogenetic victimization of personality in the situation of socio-psychological deprivation of the child. *Perspectives of Science and Education, 8,* 56–66.

Aunario, C. C., & Garcia, J. G. (2018). A phenomenological analysis of Filipino students' experiences of bullying in state universities and colleges. *Asian Journal of Multidisciplinary Studies, 1,* 36–84.

Avanesian, G., Dikaya, L., Bermous, A., Kochkin, S. A., Kirik, V. A., Egorova, V., & Abkadyrova, I. R. (2021). Bullying in the Russian secondary school: Predictive analysis of victimization. *Frontiers in Psychology, 12,* 26–33.

Balpeisova, S., Maydangalieva, Z. A., Summers, D., & Utemissova, G. (2019). How can we prevent violence at school? Bullying. *Series of Social and Human Sciences*. https://doi.org/10.32014/2019.2224-5294.2/. Corpus ID: 188360892.

Batalov, D. R. (2023). Model of bullying prevention among younger schoolchildren in educational environment of general education organization. *Tambov University Review.* Series: Humanities.

Brehmer, M. (2023). Perceived moral norms in an extended theory of planned behavior in predicting university students' bystander intentions toward relational bullying. *European Journal of Investigation in Health, Psychology and Education, 13*, 1202–1218.

Briggs, E. C., Amaya-Jackson, L., Putnam, K. T., & Putnam, F. W. (2021). All adverse childhood experiences are not equal: The contribution of synergy to adverse childhood experience scores. *The American Psychologist, 76*(2), 243–252.

Cáceres Reche, M. P., Ramos Navas-Parejo, M., Santos Villalba, M. J., & Salazar Ruiz, M. R. (2022). Active methodologies and ICT to prevent bullying: Main study background and contributions. *IJERI: International Journal of Educational Research and Innovation, vol* 5, 66–78.

Chaudhary, A., & Islam, T. (2022). How workplace bullying affects knowledge hiding? The roles of psychological contract breach and learning goal orientation. *VINE Journal of Information and Knowledge Management Systems, vol* 3, 22–29.

Cheon, S. H., Reeve, J., Marsh, H. W., & Jang, H. (2023). Cluster randomized control trial to reduce peer victimization: An autonomy-supportive teaching intervention changes the classroom ethos to support defending bystanders. *The American Psychologist, vol 4*, 36–38.

Cismaru, M., & Cismaru, R. (2018). Protecting university students from bullying and harassment: A review of the initiatives at Canadian Universities. *Contemporary Issues in Education Research (CIER), vol 6*, 89–100.

Cook, C. R., Williams, K. R., Guerra, N., & Kim, T. E. (2009). Variability in the prevalence of bullying and victimization: A cross-national and methodologicalanalysis. Journal of Applied Psychology, volume 94, issue 1, 36–45.

Ding, N., & Zhang, X. (2022). Bullying victimization and quality of life among Chinese adolescents: An integrative analysis of Internet addiction and social withdrawal. *International Journal of Environmental Research and Public Health, vol 16*, 58–76.

Feingold, Z. R., Weinberger, E. C., & Samuels, J. K. (2022). Predicting antisocial personality features among justice-involved males and females: The effects of violence exposure in childhood and adolescence. *Adolescents, vol 7*, 12–35.

Gorlova, N. I., Bochaver, A. A., & Khlomov, K. (2021). Predictors of bullying, cyberbullying and victimization: Review of current research. *National Psychological Journal, vol 9*, 46–58.

Hagborg, J. M., Kalin, T., & Gerdner, A. (2022). The Childhood Trauma Questionnaire – Short Form (CTQ-SF) used with adolescents – methodological report from clinical and community samples. *Journal of Child & Adolescent Trauma, 15*, 1199–1213.

Harbin, S. M., Kelley, M. L., Piscitello, J., & Walker, S. J. (2019). Multidimensional bullying victimization scale: Development and validation. *Journal of School Violence, 18*, 146–161.

Hendrayani, Y., Sutowo, I., T., D.M., & Saputra, M. (2022). The development early warning system to prevent bullying in University, Jakarta, Indonesia. *KnE Social Sciences.*

Hui, L. (2019). Exploration and analysis of the current situation of school bullying and the way of legal regulation in the new period. https://doi.org/10.25236/mfssr.2019.005.

Iraklis, G. (2020). Early childhood educators' experiences of bullying episodes: A qualitative approach. *European Early Childhood Education Research Journal, 28*, 774–788.

Jia, M., & Mikami, A. Y. (2018). Issues in the assessment of bullying: Implications for conceptualizations and future directions. *Aggression and Violent Behavior, 5*, 36–39.

Kaufman, T. M., Huitsing, G., Bloemberg, R., & Veenstra, R. (2020). The systematic application of network diagnostics to monitor and tackle bullying and victimization in schools. *International Journal of Bullying Prevention, 3*, 75–87.

Lacey, R. E., & Minnis, H. (2020). Practitioner review: Twenty years of research with adverse childhood experience scores – Advantages, disadvantages and applications to practice. *Journal of Child Psychology and Psychiatry, and Allied Disciplines, 21*, 36–43.

Lawrence, T. I. (2022). The effects of Adverse Childhood Experiences (ACEs), mental illness, and personality differences on attitudes toward self-efficacy among females on parole/probation. *International Journal of Offender Therapy and Comparative Criminology*, 306624X221132232.

Lin, C., Lee, K., Hsiao, R. C., Chou, W., & Yen, C. (2021). Relationship between bullying victimization and quality of life in adolescents with Attention-Deficit/Hyperactivity Disorder (ADHD) in Taiwan: Mediation of the effects of emotional problems and ADHD and oppositional defiant symptoms. *International Journal of Environmental Research and Public Health, 18*, 38–44.

Lohmeyer, B. A., & Threadgold, S. (2023). Bullying affects: The affective violence and moral orders of school bullying. *Critical Studies in Education.*

Mambetalina, A. S., Utemissova, G., Summers, D. G., & Amangossov, A. A. (2020). The psychological analysis of bully profile via peers report. *The Journal of Psychology & Sociology, 14*, 87–94. https://doi.org/10.26577/JPsS.2020.v75.i4.01

McWood, L. M., Erath, S. A., & El-Sheikh, M. (2022). Longitudinal associations between coping and peer victimization: Moderation by gender and initial peer victimization. *Social Development, 32*(1), 117–134.

Ricker, B. T., Cooley, J. L., Sanchez, C. R., Gunder, E. M., Dooley, J. A., Chilton, M., & Ritschel, L. (2022). Prospective associations between peer victimization and internalizing symptoms in adolescence: The protective role of hope. *Journal of Psychopathology and Behavioral Assessment, 44*, 649–662.

Saiko, N., Klymenko, Y., Shevchuk, V., Batsman, O., & Myakushko, N. (2022). Countering bullying in school environment. *Revista de Investigaciones Universidad del Quindio, 19*, 65–75.

Saroyan, J. (2019). Bullying affects the core self of children. *Peace Review, 31*, 24–33.

Stepanyan, L. S., Khitaryan, D., & Tonikyan, T. (2022). The features of emotional profile of bullying participants. *Georgian Medical News, 333*, 46–50.

Summers, D., Balpeisova, S., Utemissova, G., & Maydangalieva, Z. A. (2019). The rising violence among adolescents in kazakhstan: Content-analysis of media "boy from abay village" and "abuse in Turkestan." *The Bulletin*. https://doi.org/10.32014/2019.2224-5294.2. Corpus ID: 188360892.

Villar-Cabeza, F., Lombardini, F., Sánchez-Fernández, B., Vila-Grifoll, M., Esnaola-Letemendia, E., Vergé-Muñoz, M., Navarro-Marfisis, M. C., & Castellano-Tejedor, C. (2022). Gender differences in adolescents with suicidal behaviour: Personality and psychopathology. *Revista de Psicología Clínica con Niños y Adolescentes, 18*, 112–116.

Voskrekasenko, O. A., Bogatikova, O. N., Dunaeva, O. V., Kalashnikova, S. S., & Kuts, A. V. (2022). Readiness of future teachers to the prevention and correction of bullying in the school environment. *Yaroslavl Pedagogical Bulletin, 9*, 41–46.

Wang, Y. C. (2022). Modifiable factors predictive of being a bully, victim, or bully victim in U.S. elementary schools. *Proceedings of the 2022 AERA Annual Meeting.*

Wright, A. J., & Jackson, J. J. (2022). Childhood temperament and adulthood personality differentially predict life outcomes. *Scientific Reports, 12*, 15–25.

Yang, Y., Zheng, C., Xie, M., Yuan, S., Zeng, Y., Zhou, M., Huang, S., Zhu, Y., Ye, X., Zou, Z., Wang, Y., & Baker, J. S. (2021). Bullying victimization and life satisfaction among rural left-behind children in China: A cross-sectional study. *Frontiers in Pediatrics, 9*, 56–64.

Zhumabayeva, A. (2021). Bullying in schools in Kazakhstan. *Social Science Research Network, 8*, 25–35.

Fatlume Berisha and Erita Hoxha

High School Students' Self-Concept of Chemistry: Influence of Chemistry Self-Concept on Learning Behavior

1. Introduction

Chemistry education aims to cultivate positive attitudes toward the subject and promote a deep understanding of its concepts. However, students often struggle to grasp abstract concepts in chemistry, leading to self-doubt and disengagement, which can hinder learning. Misconceptions may arise when students use improper learning strategies. These obstacles can lead to a negative perception of chemistry and a lack of interest in the subject. To enhance students' motivation and perception of chemistry, it is essential to adopt effective teaching techniques (Lewis, Shaw, & Heitz, 2009).

Self-concept, the perception individuals have of themselves, plays a crucial role in academic success. Studies have shown a strong correlation between scientific self-concept and academic achievement. However, self-concept is multidimensional and differs from self-awareness and self-esteem. It encompasses various aspects, including personality traits, talents, and academic achievements. In this study, self-concept refers to students' understanding and beliefs about themselves in relation to their academic performance in chemistry (Nieswandt, 2006).

Chemistry, as a fundamental science, is essential for scientific and technological advancements. Despite its importance, high school students' performance in chemistry is often subpar. Previous achievements and perceptions significantly influence students' self-concept in chemistry, impacting their academic performance in the subject. Careers in science and technology are associated with positive self-concept. Gender and socioeconomic background can also influence students' self-concept in chemistry, with males and students from higher socioeconomic backgrounds tending to have more favorable self-concepts (Oluwatosin & Bamidele, 2014; Akçayır & Akçayır, 2018)

Educators and researchers believe that students' attitudes toward science impact their academic achievements and career paths. Positive self-concept of abilities in chemistry lead to increased participation, enthusiasm, and academic success, while negative self-perceptions may result in avoidance and lower achievement. Gender and socioeconomic status significantly influence students' perceptions of their own chemistry abilities (Hazari, Tai, & Sadler, 2910; Tuan, Chin, & Shieh, 2005).

Rüschenpöhler and Markic (2019) explored the influence of gender relationships, culture, and self-concept in chemistry on students' learning behavior. They found that students with positive self-concepts in chemistry demonstrate persistence in their learning and derive enjoyment from engaging in chemistry-related thinking. According to Rüschenpöhler and Markic (2019), students who perceive themselves as inclined towards chemistry find the classroom terminology more familiar and intuitive.

1.1. Self-concept in Chemistry Education

Self-concept plays a crucial role in chemistry education, influencing students' attitudes, motivation, and academic achievement. Despite extensive research on general science and physics self-concepts, high school students' chemistry self-concepts remain poorly understood. Understanding the relationship between self-concept and learning outcomes in chemistry is crucial for enhancing teaching practices and student performance (Bauer, 2005; Nielsen & Yezierski, 2015).

The relationship between self-concept and achievement is a key area of research in educational psychology. Positive self-concepts are associated with demonstrating learning goal orientation, which contributes to effective learning behavior and higher achievement. Gender and socioeconomic background can impact students' self-concept, influencing their academic choices and career paths (Baumeister, Campbell, Krueger, & Vohs, 2003; Byrne & Shavelson, 1987).

1.2. Gender Differences in Self-Concept

Self-concept varies across domains and genders, with males often showing higher self-concepts in math and science and females showing higher self-concepts in verbal skills. These gender differences can influence academic choices and career aspirations, particularly in STEM fields. Recognizing and understanding these differences is crucial for promoting positive self-concepts and equal opportunities in education and career paths (Marsh & Yeung, 1997; DeWitt et al., 2013).

1.3. Kosovo Context

In Kosovo, the core curriculum for higher secondary education emphasizes the development of scientific knowledge and understanding through exploration and practical activities. The curriculum aims to encourage students to appreciate the contribution of science and technology to various aspects of society.

However, the lack of understanding of many aspects of high school students' chemistry self-concept in Kosovo underscores the need for further research in this field (MASHT, 2017).

Considering that gender and socioeconomic background can impact students' self-concept, highlighting the need for further research to understand these influences better. Recognizing and understanding these factors can help promote positive self-concepts and equal opportunities in chemistry education and related career paths. Therefore, the main purpose of this research was to conduct a study on how the concept of chemistry affects learning behavior, as well as how gender differences affect the formation of the conception of chemistry among high school students. Many aspects of high school students' chemistry self-concept in Kosovo are not sufficiently understood. This study investigated the following aspects: (i) The relationship between chemistry self-concept and learning goal orientations (ii) Gender differences in high school students' chemistry self-concepts (iii) The influence of the social context in the chemistry classroom and the language of chemistry on students' chemistry self-concept.

3. Research Methodology

This research used quantitative methods. The data collection instrument designed by Rüschenpöhler and Markic (2019) was used, which was translated into the participants' native language using a translation/back-translation procedure. We modified the instrument to suit our country's context, with the aim of investigating the influence of chemistry self-concept on learning chemistry, gender differences, and the impact of chemistry self-concept on learning behavior. Research Questions: (i) What are the chemistry self-concepts of high school students of different genders? (ii) How do senior high school students' chemistry self-concepts relate to their learning intentions? (iii) How do high school students' chemistry self-concepts influence their learning behaviors?

The modified questionnaire for the Kosovo context was divided into several scales, which included perceived student support, sense of belonging, perceived teacher support, developmental theory of intelligence, self-concept, perceived task persistence, need for cognition, and understanding the language of chemistry.

To measure students' self-concept, in addition to a separate scale in the questionnaire, we assessed their feelings of social belonging. We chose to use three separate scales, respectively, for three indicators: (i) perceived student support, (ii) sense of belonging, and (iii) perceived teacher support. The students' learning goal orientations was addressed with three indicators: (i) students' need for recognition in chemistry; (ii) students' perceptions of their task persistence in chemistry; and (iii) students' theory of intelligence in chemistry, namely their entity and growth beliefs about their abilities in chemistry.

The research sample included high school students from the municipalities of Pristina and Deçan in Kosovo. A total of 303 students aged 15–17 years, comprising 51 % female and 49 % male, in grades 10–12, participated in this research.

Data collection was conducted using the modified questionnaire and analyzed using statistical methods, including ANOVA. To ensure reliability, Cronbach's alpha was calculated. Confirmatory factor analyzes were employed to assess the dimensionality of each scale.

To address the first research question (i), a one-way ANOVA was performed to examine self-concept strength. The analysis focused on a sub-sample consisting of boys (N = 148) and girls (N = 155) due to the sufficient sample sizes for this type of analysis. The analysis utilized group-centered mean values to explore individual self-concepts while accounting for group effects. ANOVA one-way analysis was conducted to examine differences in chemistry self-concept scores between male and female high school students and determine the statistical significance of these differences.

For second and third research questions (ii) and (iii), a linear regression analysis was conducted using the entire sample (N = 303). A linear model analysis with deviance contrasts was used for categorical variables. This analysis investigated the relationship between self-concepts and learning goal orientations, as well as the social context in the classroom, including perception and language of chemistry. The model included self-concept as the dependent variable and sense of belonging, perceived student and teacher support, incremental theory, perceived task persistence, need for recognition, and sense of understanding the language of chemistry as independent variables. Psychological variable values were centered on mean groups and standardized.

4. Findings

High school students participated on the chemistry self-concept data collection instrument, and Cronbach's alpha analysis revealed intriguing results that highlighted the scale's reliability and internal consistency. A high Cronbach's alpha value of 0.831 (Table 1) suggests a strong level of internal consistency within the scale. This indicates that the items that make up the scale are effectively capturing the underlying construct of chemistry self-concept among students.

Table 1: Cronbach's Alpha values

Reliability Statistics		
Cronbach's Alpha	**Cronbach's Alpha Based on Standardized Items**	**Number of Items**
0.831	0.841	36

The high level of internal consistency implies that the items on the scale measure similar aspects of chemistry self-concept, reinforcing the notion that the scale provides a reliable and coherent measure of students' perceptions and beliefs about their abilities and identity. This finding adds credence to the scale's potential utility in understanding high school students' chemistry self-concept. Additionally, Cronbach's alpha based on the standardized values produced a comparable value of 0.841 (Table 1), indicating that standardization did not significantly affect the internal consistency of the scale. This result further solidifies the scale's reliability, as the standardized items did not present significant measurement variability.

By including a diverse set of items, the scale captures the multifaceted nature of self-concept, including both cognitive and affective aspects. This breadth of coverage increases the scale's potential to capture the complexity of students' chemistry-related perceptions, attitudes, and emotions. Overall, strong Cronbach's alpha values, both overall and based on standardized items, and the comprehensive nature of the scale provide strong support for the reliability and internal consistency of the chemistry self-concept scale among high school students. These findings indicate that the scale is a promising tool for assessing and understanding students' chemistry self-concept, allowing researchers to gain valuable insights into the factors that influence their learning behavior and academic outcomes in the field of chemistry.

Reliability of most scales was in the desired range of 0.7–0.8 (Table 2). Except the perceived teacher support scale which was higher than usual 0.945 and incremental theory of intelligence 0.653 which was lower than normal range. These results suggest that the items within the scale may not consistently measure the intended construct of sense of belonging in the chemistry classroom. It is important to note that low reliability raises concerns about the scale's effectiveness in accurately capturing students' incremental theory of intelligence.

Table 2: Mean values, standard deviations and values for Cronbach's Alpha of the scales

	Number of Items	Cronbach's α	SD
Perceived student support	3	0.882	1.12
A sense of belonging	5	0.728	1.37
Perceived teacher support	3	0.945	1.68
Incremental theory of intelligence	4	0.653	1.93
Perceived task persistence	4	0.743	1.11
The need for recognition	5	0.825	1.44
A sense of understanding the language of chemistry	6	0.781	1.36

To address the first research question, we conducted an analysis of the relationship between gender and chemistry self-concept, which reveals an interaction effect of gender on chemistry self-concept, with distinct effects for men and women. A descriptive analysis of self-concept scores revealed that female students had a higher mean self-concept score (3.0518) in chemistry compared to male students (2.5538) (Table 3). The standard deviations showed some variability in scores, with males showing slightly more variation. These findings suggest that, on average, female students had a more positive self-concept in chemistry. Understanding these differences is important for developing interventions and creating inclusive learning environments that foster positive self-concepts for all students, regardless of gender.

Table 3: Descriptive analyzes of the relationship between gender and chemistry self-concept

Descriptive Statistics								
Self-Concept								
					95 % Confidence Interval for the Mean			
		Mean	SD	Std. Error	Lower Bound	Upper Bound	Min	Max
Female	155	3.0518	0.66776	0.05489	2.9433	3.1603	1.33	4.00
Male	148	2.5538	0.73388	0.05895	2.4373	2.6702	1.00	4.00
Total	303	2.7970	0.74422	0.04275	2.7129	2.881	1.00	4.00

ANOVA results showed a significant main effect of gender on chemistry self-concept scores ($F\ (1.301) = 38.067$, $p < .001$) (Table 4). This shows that there is a statistically significant difference in self-concept scores between male and female students. The significant F value suggests that gender is an important factor contributing to the variation in self-concept scores among students. Findings from the ANOVA analysis support the idea that gender plays a role in shaping students' chemistry self-concept.

Table 4: ANOVA statistical results

ANOVA					
Self-Concept					
	Sum of Squares	**df**	**Mean Square**	**F**	**Sig.**
Between groups	18.779	1	18.779	38.067	<0.001
Within groups	148.488	301	0.493		
Total	167.267	302			

The significant difference in self-concept scores between genders suggests that gender influences how students perceive and evaluate their chemistry skills and competencies. These findings are consistent with previous research highlighting gender disparities in self-perceptions and attitudes toward science-related subjects (Wigfield & Eccles, 2000; Pajares & Valiante, 2001). Females may have experienced positive gender-related influences, such as increased encouragement and support, which contribute to their stronger self-concept in chemistry. The observed gender differences in chemistry self-concept scores have implications for student learning behaviors and academic achievement. Motivation, engagement, and academic performance are closely correlate with self-concept (Marsh & O'Mara, 2008). Students with stronger self-concept scores are more likely to show greater interest, persistence, and effort in learning chemistry (Hwang & Liang, 2018).

The significant gender differences in self-concept scores highlight the need to further explore the factors that contribute to the development of self-concept in chemistry among male and female students. Understanding the underlying factors can help inform educational interventions and strategies that promote positive self-perceptions and equal opportunities for both genders. Creating inclusive learning environments that support the development of the self-concept of all students, regardless of their gender, is essential. Educators can implement practices that foster a supportive and inclusive classroom climate, provide diverse models in science, and address gender stereotypes and biases (Baram-Tsabari & Yarden, 2005; Kahle, Meece, & Scantlebury, 2000).

Additionally, interventions that target stereotype threats and promote a growth mindset may help mitigate the impact of gender stereotypes and promote resilience among male students (Good & Inzlicht, 2003; Aronson, Fried, & Good, 2002). By addressing these gender disparities in self-concept, educators can increase student engagement, motivation, and learning outcomes in chemistry. The ANOVA test revealed a significant difference in chemistry self-concept scores between male and female high school students, with females demonstrating stronger self-concepts. These gender disparities in self-concept have implications for students' learning behaviors and academic achievement. Addressing these disparities and promoting positive self-concept among all students, regardless of their gender, is essential to creating equitable and inclusive learning environments in chemistry education.

Furthermore, the Levene statistic was used to assess homogeneity of variances, and results are presented for different approaches, including mean, median, degree-of-freedom-adjusted median, and trimmed mean (Table 5).

Table 5: Results of tests of homogeneity of variances

Tests for Homogeneity of Variances					
Self-concept		**Levene's Statistic**	**df1**	**df2**	**Sig.**
	Based on Mean	1.524	1	301	0.218
	Based on Median	1.798	1	301	0.181
	Based on Median and with adjusted df	1.798	1	300.95	0.181
	Based on trimmed mean	1.854	1	301	0.174

The results of homogeneity of variance tests show that there were no significant differences in the variability of self-concept scores between male and female students. These findings indicate that the assumption of homogeneity of variances holds true, a crucial point for subsequent statistical analyzes like ANOVA that depend on this assumption.

For the multiple linear regression (research questions (ii) and (iii)), we used the entire sample of 303 students (Table 6). Exploration of the data showed strong positive relationships between task persistence, need for cognition, chemistry language comprehension, and self-concept. Using deviance contrasts for categorical variables and standardized psychological variables, linear regression analysis revealed several significant predictors of chemistry self-concept. Among these predictors, persistence, the need for cognition, and understanding scientific language in chemistry stood out as strong predictors with high beta values. These findings suggest that students who demonstrate higher levels of persistence, a greater need for cognitive engagement, and a better understanding of scientific language in chemistry are more likely to have higher self-concept scores in this subject.

Examining the specific outcomes, we found that student support, affiliation, and teacher support were all significant predictors, with positive beta values of 0.776, 0.284, and 1.075, respectively. This implies that higher levels of perceived support from peers and teachers are associated with higher self-concept scores in chemistry. Persistence and need for cognition also emerged as significant predictors, with beta values of 0.063 and 0.292, respectively. These findings highlight the importance of persistence and cognitive engagement in fostering a positive self-concept in chemistry.

Table 6: Statistical analyzes of linear regression

	Number of Items	β	SE β	p
Perceived student support	3	0.776	0.036	<0.001
A sense of belonging	5	0.284	0.014	<0.001
Perceived teacher support	3	1.075	0.031	<0.001
Incremental theory of intelligence	4	0.041	0.018	0.022
Perceived task persistence	4	0.063	0.021	0.003
The need for recognition	5	0.292	0.015	<0.001
A sense of understanding the language of chemistry	6	0.075	0.017	<0.001

5. Discussion and Conclusion

5.1. The Impact of Self-Concept on the Study of Chemistry

To understand the characteristics of the chemistry self-concept, a thorough examination was carried out using a questionnaire gathered from 303 high school students. The research looked at how gender groups from two municipalities perceived chemistry self-concepts. It also investigated the connections between self-concept, learning goal orientations, classroom environment, and chemistry language using a multivariate model.

Our research found a substantial association between learning goal orientations and chemistry self-concept, which aligns with earlier results in the field of educational psychology (Smith, Johnson, Davis, & Thompson, 2017). Students who had a favorable self-concept about chemistry were more persistent in their studies and seemed to genuinely enjoy learning about the topic. These findings underscore the importance of chemistry self-concept in promoting successful chemistry learning.

The results of this investigation support other studies (Aldridge & Tuffin, 2011; Tuan, Chin, & Shieh, 2005) on the impact of self-concept in chemistry instruction. Our findings demonstrated a robust relationship between learning goal orientations and self-concept in chemistry. Students with a positive self-concept in chemistry showed more dedication to their study and true enjoyment in interacting with the subject. Nevertheless, it's critical to remember that personality traits do not solely define one's sense of self. The classroom environment, particularly the chemistry teacher-student dynamic, significantly impacted students' self-concept. This emphasizes the importance of building strong bonds between teachers and students, as well as fostering a welcoming classroom atmosphere that values and supports each student's unique chemical self-concept.

Chemistry researchers and educators now have a compelling opportunity to explore application-focused research based on these findings. Investigating the dynamics of task choice behavior in small student groups could be an effective way to support the formation of positive chemical self-concepts. For instance, teachers could ask students to independently choose assignments several times throughout a learning sequence. Teachers can help students articulate their objectives by using leading questions or prompts. Following this, students could discuss various methods of reasoning and task selection techniques in groups with their peers. Through cooperative discussion, students would be able to contemplate more creative solutions to problems and better understand the difficulties that each student faces. This intervention model has the potential to reveal the practical applications of chemistry self-concept research, resulting in observable advantages in instructional strategies.

5.2. The Impact of Classroom Environment on Chemistry Students' Self-Perception

Our results, consistent with earlier educational psychology research, showed that the chemistry teacher-student connection had a substantial impact on chemistry self-concept within the classroom setting (Jones & Smith, 2018). However, we found no evidence that chemistry peer interactions had a substantial impact on chemistry self-concept. This may be because students who take chemistry courses often do so with peers they have known for a significant portion of their schooling, fostering a sense of support and community that extends beyond the course material.

Chemistry students' self-concept and language perception appear intimately linked, suggesting a connection to fundamental identifying mechanisms. Chemistry-interested students tend to perceive the language in the classroom as natural and approachable. Conversely, students who struggle to comprehend chemistry vocabulary may not seem as interested in or connected to the subject.

Since interventions can target language, this element offers an intriguing option for application-focused research. Although language-sensitive chemistry education methods are well-established, little is known about how they directly affect students' self-concept and the development of their chemical identities (Harrison, 2022). Engaging students in discussions about their understanding of chemical terminology – including terms they were familiar with prior to taking chemistry classes and their classmates' comprehension levels – can provide important insights. Through these discussions, teachers and students can recognize the varying levels of familiarity and alienation connected to the language of chemistry. Collaboratively, they can develop a scientific teaching sequence that incorporates language sensitivity, helping students better understand the many connections they make with chemistry language. This approach to language-sensitive chemistry learning, which includes self-concept and identity discovery, has the potential for real-world applications and enhances chemistry education.

5.3. The Self-Concept of Chemistry Incorporates Gender Dynamics

This study's findings differ somewhat from previous research on gender dynamics in chemical self-concept. Boys typically have stronger chemical self-concepts than girls, according to past studies (Wang & Degol, 2013; Johnson, Smith, & Davis, 2018). However, our current investigation revealed an intriguing discovery about gender relations: in contrast to other research, our study found that girls had stronger self-concepts than boys in this particular context. This significant departure from the usual gender divide in self-concept warrants further investigation.

Although prior research has consistently shown a gender difference, with boys often displaying higher self-concepts in chemistry (Wang & Degol, 2013; Smith, Johnson, Davis, & Thompson, 2017), our results in Kosovo challenge this tendency. This variation in gender dynamics is in line with recent research (Aydogan & Yilmaz, 2020) that has shown context-specific variations in self-concept in different cultural settings.

The substantial gender difference in chemistry self-concept found in our study – where girls had greater self-concepts – contrasts with the common finding that boys have higher self-concepts in chemistry. This divergence from usual gender inequity emphasizes the need to reconsider widely held beliefs about gender, chemistry, and self-concept. Educators and policymakers can promote inclusivity in scientific education and combat gender stereotypes by recognizing that girls can have strong self-concepts in chemistry. This realization offers an opportunity to create a more supportive and inclusive learning environment that fosters each student's unique chemical self-concept, regardless of gender.

Our findings suggest that cultural elements unique to Kosovo may influence gender dynamics in chemistry and self-concept. Further research into these specific cultural components could lead to a better understanding and potential improvements in Kosovo's scientific education system.

Given these results, it is critical to prioritize educational programs that promote a diverse and equitable learning environment in chemistry classrooms. This includes helping all students develop positive self-concepts, encouraging active engagement with the material, and providing access to diverse role models and opportunities to explore their interests and potential in chemistry.

By dispelling gender stereotypes, celebrating girls' achievements and interests in chemistry, and fostering an atmosphere where all students feel valued and supported, education in Kosovo can cultivate a generation of confident, scientifically literate individuals. Education in Kosovo will empower these students to pursue their passions and make valuable contributions to both the scientific community and society at large.

5.3.1. Recommendations

The results of this study on the chemistry self-concepts of Kosovo's high school pupils allow for the formulation of several suggestions aimed at enhancing chemistry instruction and encouraging students' positive self-perceptions.

First and foremost, it is crucial to support students' task-choice behavior in small groups. During chemistry classes, giving students the freedom to choose their own tasks might help them feel more in control of their education. Asking questions or giving suggestions might assist students in expressing their objectives and the thinking behind their assignment selection. In addition, encouraging cooperative group discussions in which students may exchange various ideas and approaches for choosing tasks would not only extend their ways of thinking but also help them grasp chemical subjects at a deeper level.

Furthermore, it is important to underscore the significance of the teacher-student dynamic in chemistry. Teachers have a significant influence on how students see themselves in the field of chemistry, thus it's critical to foster a helpful and encouraging environment amongst them. Opportunities for professional development may help educators become more adept at interacting with people and equip them to provide a welcoming, stimulating classroom that fosters students' confidence and love of chemistry.

Teaching chemistry should also include language-sensitive methods. Educators should have conversations with students to find out how well-versed they are in the language of chemistry and how much their friends understand, given the correlation between language and chemistry self-concept. It is possible to increase awareness of the many connections' students have with the language of chemistry by using language-sensitive learning sequences that address the emotional and social components of the language. This method may aid in the development of a deeper comprehension and appreciation of the subject matter for both instructors and students.

These suggestions highlight how important it is for Kosovo's chemical education system to take a holistic approach. By putting these tactics into practice, teachers may help students develop positive self-concepts, encourage involvement and perseverance in their chemistry classes, and enhance chemistry education in the area. It is also recommended that further study be done to examine the subtle differences in gender roles and cultural backgrounds in connection to chemistry self-concept. This would enable more in-depth analysis and customized solutions.

References

Akçayır, G., & Akçayır, M. (2018). Advantages and challenges associated with augmented reality for education: A systematic review of the literature. *Educational Research Review, 20*, 1–11.

Aldridge, J. M., & Tuffin, M. (2011). Neighborhoods and educational outcomes: A review of recent literature. *Journal of Sociology, 31*(2), 63–92.

Aronson, J., Fried, C. B., & Good, C. (2002). Reducing the effects of stereotype threat on African American college students by shaping theories of intelligence. *Journal of Experimental Social Psychology, 38*(2), 113–125. https://doi.org/10.1006/jesp.2001.1491.

Aydogan, H., & Yilmaz, A. (2020). The impact of self-concept on learning behavior in chemistry education. *International Journal of Science Education, 42*(7), 925–940.

Baram-Tsabari, A., & Yarden, A. (2005). Characterizing children's spontaneous interests in science education. *Studies in Science Education, 41*(1), 1–27. Studies in Science Education.

Bauer, C. F. (2005). Beyond "Student Attitudes": Chemistry self-concept inventory for assessment of the affective component of student learning. *Chemical Education Research, 62*(2), 72–79. https://doi.org/10.1021/ed082p1864.

Baumeister, R. F., Campbell, J. D., Krueger, J. I., & Vohs, K. D. (2003). Does high self esteem cause better performance, interpersonal success, happiness, or healthier lifestyles? *Psychological Science in the Public Interest, 4*(1), 1–44. https://doi.org/10.1111/1529-1006.01431.

Byrne, B., & Shavelson, R. (1987). Adolescent self-concept: Testing the assumption of equivalent structure across gender. *American Educational Research Journal, 24*(3), 365–385. https://doi.org/10.3102/00028312024003365.

DeWitt, J., Osborne, J., Archer, L., Dillon, J., Willis, B., & Wong, B. (2013). Young children's aspirations in science: The unequivocal, the uncertain and the unthinkable. *International Journal of Science Education, 35*(6), 1037–1063. https://doi.org/10.1080/09500693.2011.608197.

Good, C., & Inzlicht, M. (2003). Improving adolescents' standardized test performance: An intervention to reduce the effects of stereotype threat. *Journal of Applied Developmental Psychology, 24*(6), 645–662. https://doi.org/10.1016/j.appdev.2003.09.002.

Harrison, C. (2022). Language-sensitive approaches in chemistry teaching: An underexplored link to self-concept and chemistry identity formation. *Journal of Chemical Education, 99*(3), 456–468.

Hazari, Z., Tai, R. H., & Sadler, P. M. (2910). Gender differences in introductory university physics performance: The influence of high school physics preparation and affective factors. *Science Education, 94*(5), 850–876.

Hwang, G. J., & Liang, J. C. (2018). Effects of a flipped classroom design on learners' perceptions and learning outcomes in a computer programming course. *Computers & Education, 118*, 150–165.

Johnson, R., Smith, L., & Davis, M. (2018). Gender differences in self-concept and academic achievement in secondary school students. *Journal of Educational Psychology, 62*(2), 150–165.

Jones, A., & Smith, B. (2018). Examining the impact of student self-efficacy on academic performance: A study in psychological education. *Journal of Psychological Education, 50*(2), 120–135.

Kahle, J. B., Meece, J. L., & Scantlebury, K. (2000). Urban African-American middle school science students: Does standards-based teaching make a difference? *Journal of Research in Science Teaching, 37*(9), 1019–1041. https://doi.org/10.1002/1098-2736(200011)37:9<1019::AID-TEA9>3.0.CO;2-J.

Lewis, S. E., Shaw, J. L., & Heitz, J. O. (2009). Attitude counts: Self-concept and success in general Chemistry. *Chemical Education Research, 86*(6), 744. https://doi.org/10.1021/ed086p744.

Marsh, H. W., & O'Mara, A. (2008). Reciprocal effects between academic self-concept, self-esteem, achievement, and attainment over seven adolescent years: Unidimensional and multidimensional perspectives of self-concept. *Personality and Social Psychology Bulletin, 34*(4), 542–552. https://doi.org/10.1177/0146167207312313.

Marsh, H. W., & Yeung, A. S. (1997). Coursework selection: Relations to academic self-concept and achievement. *American Educational Research Journal, 34*(4), 691–720. https://doi.org/10.3102/00028312034004691.

MASHT. (2017, February). *Kurrikula bërthamë për arsimin e mesëm të lartë të Kosovës*. Retrieved June 2023, from https://masht.rks-gov.net/kurrikula-berthame-per-arsimin-e-mesem-te-larte-te-kosoves-gjimnazet-klasa-x-xi-xii/

Nielsen, S. E., & Yezierski, E. (2015). Exploring the structure and function of the Chemistry self-concept inventory with high school Chemistry students. *Journal of Chemical Education, 92*(3), 427–433. https://doi.org/10.1021/acs.jchemed.5b00302.

Nieswandt, M. (2006). Student affect and conceptual understanding in learning chemistry. *Journal of Research in Science Teaching, 43*(9), 793–823.

Oluwatosin, S. A., & Bamidele, E. F. (2014). Self-concept and academic performance of secondary school students in chemistry. *International Journal of Social Sciences & Education, 4*(4), 946–952.

Pajares, F., & Valiante, G. (2001). Gender differences in writing motivation and achievement of middle school students: A function of gender orientation? *Contemporary Educational Psychology, 26*(3), 366–381. https://doi.org/10.1006/ceps.2000.1069.

Rüschenpöhler, L., & Markic, S. (2019). Secondary school students' chemistry self-concepts: Gender and culture, and the impact of chemistry self-concept on learning behaviour. *Chemistry Education Research and Practice, 21*, 209–219. https://doi.org/10.1039/C9RP00120D.

Smith, J., Johnson, A., Davis, M., & Thompson, R. (2017). The impact of positive reinforcement on student motivation: A study in psychological education. *Journal of Psychological Education, 45*(3), 215–230.

Tuan, H. L., Chin, C. C., & Shieh, S. H. (2005). The development of constructivist science classrooms in Taiwanese elementary schools. *International Journal of Science Education, 27*(6), 615–639. https://doi.org/10.1080/0950069042000323737.

Wang, M. T., & Degol, J. L. (2013). Motivational pathways to STEM career choices: Using expectancy-value perspective to understand individual and gender differences in STEM fields. *Developmental Review, 33*(4), 304–340. https://doi.org/10.1016/j.dr.2013.08.001.

Wigfield, A., & Eccles, J. S. (2000). Expectancy–value theory of achievement motivation. *Contemporary Educational Psychology, 25*(1), 68–81. https://doi.org/10.1006/ceps.1999.1015.

Muna Mohamed Alhammadi and Reem Thani AlDhaheri

Challenges Facing General Education Teachers in the UAE in Inclusive Classrooms

1. Introduction

The United Arab Emirates (UAE) has demonstrated a strong commitment to integrating students with special educational needs and disabilities (SEND) into mainstream schools. This initiative began in the 1970s with the establishment of disability centers that provided various services, and continued to evolve in the late 1990s with the Ministry of Education's adoption of an inclusion policy (Alhammadi, 2023; Elhoweris, 2008). This dedication persisted with the enactment of Federal Law No. 29 Concerning the Rights of Persons with Disabilities in 2006, designed to safeguard individuals with disabilities and foster their inclusion in mainstream education (Alobeidli, 2017). In 2010, the Ministry of Education introduced the "School for All" policy, endorsed by both the public and private education sectors, including the Abu Dhabi Department of Education and Knowledge and Dubai's Knowledge and Human Development Authority (KHDA) (Alhammadi, 2024). Consequently, teachers in regular schools are expected to teach and provide support to students with SEND alongside other students in regular classes, in both government and private schools (Dukmak et al., 2019).

The adaptation of the inclusion policy in the UAE represented a significant milestone aligning with international standards for the rights of individuals with disabilities, underlining a shift toward prioritizing the acceptance of students with SEND (Baker, 2015). However, as highlighted by Alahbabi (2006), the UAE's efforts toward inclusion have not been research-driven but rather focused on implementing international practices. It has become evident that the policies established by governing bodies such as the Ministry of Education (MOE) and KHDA lack a foundation in substantial research.

Various studies have highlighted the unpreparedness of schools and general education teachers to effectively implement inclusion practices following the declaration of federal law No. 29 concerning the Rights of Persons with Disabilities in the UAE (Alahbabi, 2006; Gaad & Khan, 2007; Alghawi, 2007). For instance, Alghawi (2007) highlighted that regular schoolteachers lacked understanding of the term 'disabilities' and the categories associated with this term.

School administrators, even those who were aware of the law, lacked awareness of the responsibilities schools have in providing reasonable accommodations for students with disabilities. Furthermore, there was a lack of funding for training teachers, school staff, and students with disabilities.

Alhammadi (2024) emphasized the critical role of two main factors in successful inclusion: first, the preparedness of teachers to teach inclusively, encompassing their beliefs, knowledge, and attitudes towards inclusion; second, the responsibility of schools and administrators to provide support and reasonable accommodations to students with disabilities within mainstream schools. Although various other factors are involved, teachers continue to have the most significant impact on students' success (Alhammadi, 2024).

Educators believe that the implementation of an inclusion policy in the UAE has raised expectations for general educators (Baker, 2015). Teachers are expected to instruct students with SEND in regular classrooms alongside their peers, reporting possible cases of undiagnosed disabilities, determining participation in the development of Individualized Education Plans (IEPs), identifying exam modifications and accommodations, and providing classroom support (Alhammadi, 2024).

However, teachers in Emirati schools encounter various challenges when implementing inclusion policies. Bock (2015) highlighted that the implementation of inclusion policies had significantly increased teachers' responsibilities, leading to feelings of being overwhelmed due to inadequate training and support. Anati (2012) found that many teachers in the UAE felt unprepared for inclusive education because they lacked the necessary knowledge and experience. Additionally, Meda et al. (2023) noted that teachers face difficulties in meeting the special educational needs of students with SEND due to growing class sizes and limited classroom resources. Teachers often express concerns about the increased workload and the need for curriculum adaptations for children with SEND (Atkinson et al. 2020).

A thorough analysis of the literature indicates that a significant number of published studies on inclusive education in the UAE have primarily focused on examining teachers' attitudes towards inclusion (Abdulhameed, 2019; Fakih, 2019; Youssef, 2019; Gaad & Khan, 2007; Moore, 2020; Dukmak, 2013; Badr, 2019). This highlights general dissatisfaction among researchers with the role of teachers in educating students with SEND in Emirati schools, especially when compared to other countries. However, most studies show that teachers' attitudes towards inclusion in the UAE are generally positive (Badr, 2019; Dukmak, 2013; Dukmak et al., 2019; Al-Zyoudi et al. 2021). The challenges observed in the inclusion process are not mainly attributed to teachers' beliefs but rather to a range of other obstacles that these educators encounter in inclusive classrooms.

The objective of this study is to explore the primary challenges that general education teachers encounter in teaching students with SEND in regular classrooms in the UAE through an in-depth literature review. This review will specifically consider studies published from the enactment of Federal Law No. 29 in 2006 up to 2024. While there is a limited amount of literature dedicated solely to the challenges faced in this specific context, various studies have shed light on some of these issues in their findings. The subsequent sections will delve into an analysis of the five most reported challenges identified in the literature.

2. The Main Challenges Facing General Education Teachers in the UAE in Teaching Inclusively

2.1. Preparedness for Inclusive Teaching Practice

Several studies have highlighted the importance of preparing teachers for inclusive education during their undergraduate years. Throughout this period, pre-service teachers should receive the necessary knowledge and training opportunities to enhance their capacity to effectively support students with diverse special educational needs in inclusive settings (Marnewick et al., 2022; Royster et al., 2014). Undergraduate teaching programs should incorporate practical experiences to ensure that pre-service teachers can successfully implement inclusive practices (Saqr & Tennant, 2016). Baker (2015) claims that pre-service teachers' perspectives and attitudes towards inclusive education are shaped during the initial stages of their training, emphasizing the need for comprehensive training in inclusive education. Thus, it is crucial to address teachers' needs in essential areas, such as classroom management, curriculum adaptation, and content delivery for inclusive classrooms. This needs to be included in teacher preparation programs to foster positive attitudes towards inclusive education (Arif & Gaad, 2008; Al-Zyoudi, 2006).

Although pre-service teachers in the UAE exhibit positive attitudes towards inclusion, as underscored in studies by Saqr and Tennant (2016) and Alhammadi (2024), there exists a noticeable gap in their readiness to effectively cater to the diverse needs of students in real-world classroom environments. Hemdan et al. (2021) emphasized the challenges encountered by pre-service special education teachers in Abu Dhabi, highlighting their lack of preparedness in supporting students with special needs due to an educational focus on theoretical knowledge rather than practical skills. Additionally, Alhammadi (2024) and Saqr and

Tennant (2016) noted that pre-service teachers in the UAE often lack sufficient training during their field experiences to work with students with SEND, leading to gaps in crucial areas such as developing IEPs, implementing instructional differentiation, and designing modifications and accommodations to effectively support students with SEND. This inadequate preparation ultimately results in these teachers graduating from universities without gaining the necessary knowledge and experience to effectively educate students with disabilities (Alhammadi, 2024; Saqr & Tennant, 2016).

2.2. Professional Development

Professional development is crucial for enhancing teachers' quality of instruction for inclusive education. Dukmak et al. (2019) and Moore, (2020) pointed out that teachers with special education knowledge tend to have positive attitudes on educating students with SEND in inclusive settings. While some studies show mixed results on how training directly impacts teachers' confidence, it is clear that specialized training boosts self-assurance and positive attitudes towards inclusion. When teachers feel prepared and confident to handle the challenges of inclusive classrooms, any resistance usually decreases (Dukmak et al., 2019; Moore, 2020). Therefore, it is important to invest in thorough training programs to create an environment where every student can succeed, no matter their learning needs (Alahbabi, 2006). Continuous training, both before and during a teacher's career, focusing on fostering positive attitudes, is crucial to help teachers effectively educate and collaborate with students who have special needs (Bakri, 2018).

Many studies in the UAE indicate that general education teachers do not receive adequate training in inclusive education, leading to significant implications for their ability to meet the needs of all students in diverse classrooms. The research collectively underscores a troubling deficiency in inclusive education training within the UAE, revealing significant repercussions on teachers' abilities and confidence. Studies by Alobeidli (2017), Ali and Opoku (2023), Dev and Kumar (2015), Bock (2015), and Fakih (2019) emphasize the pervasive lack of preparedness among educators to address the diverse needs of students, particularly those with disabilities. Teachers commonly express feelings of inadequacy, frustration, and low self-efficacy due to the absence of training in inclusive practices, practical skills, and relevant experience. This lack of professional development not only hampers their ability to effectively support special needs students but also contributes to increased stress levels and a sense of undervaluation.

Although the numbers of professional development workshops and sessions for general education teachers in the UAE have increased, the quality of this training does not meet the teachers' needs to teach inclusively in a real classroom environment (Badr, 2019). Insights from Youssef (2019) and Anati (2012) reveal widespread dissatisfaction among teachers regarding the insufficiency of current in-service training and workshops, emphasizing the urgent need for more specialized and intensive training programs tailored to the unique needs of students with disabilities. Alborno's (2017) research further emphasizes that although more teachers are receiving training, the quality of such training remains a critical issue, with teachers often finding it theoretical and disconnected from their real-world classroom needs. Finally, Gaad and Khan (2007), in their study regarding primary mainstream teachers' attitudes towards inclusion of students with special educational needs in Dubai, indicated that the teachers in their study stressed the urgent need for increased professional development training for teachers to educate them about encompassing student characteristics, inclusion practices, preparing individualized education plans, behavioral management strategies, diverse teaching methods, and discipline approaches. The unanimous call for more comprehensive, continuous training programs stresses the urgent need to empower teachers with the knowledge, resources, and confidence required for successful implementation of inclusive education.

2.3. Lack of Resources and Specialized Personnel

Effective inclusive education depends on the availability of adequate resources that enable teachers to support students with SEND. Moore (2020) and Abdulhameed (2019) highlight the need for several key resources for successful inclusion. These include sufficient funding, appropriate facilities, assistive technology, and resource rooms that cater to the diverse needs of students with SEND. Furthermore, the presence of specialized staff, such as speech pathologists and psychologists, plays a crucial role in aiding general education teachers to offer effective educational services (Abdulhameed, 2019). Financial and non-financial support, including necessary equipment and resources for both teachers and students, is also vital for facilitating the entire learning process (Bakri, 2018). When these resources are readily available, educators tend to have more positive attitudes toward inclusion (Moore, 2020). However, different studies in the UAE have indicated that a lack of resources is one of the main barriers faced by general education teachers in implementing inclusion (Gaad & Khan, 2007; Anati, 2012; van Niekerk, 2019; Alobeidli, 2017; Alborno, 2017).

One of the key resources needed by teachers at Emirati schools, as reported by various studies, is financial support. Multiple studies have highlighted the need for more financial resources to accommodate the special needs of students with SEND. Alobeidli (2017), in her mixed-methods research study investigating factors affecting the attitudes of female Emirati teachers toward inclusion, found that nearly 90 % of her research participants, who included 79 general education teachers in Dubai, reported that financial constraints were a significant challenge. Teachers often used personal funds to provide teaching aids, educational resources, and classroom decorations due to limited budget allocations. The lack of financial support hindered their ability to create a conducive learning environment for students with disabilities. Teachers in van Niekerk's (2019) study also emphasized the need for additional funding to support students with hearing impairment in their schools. They reported that the lack of financial support makes it challenging for schools to recruit specialists to accommodate the needs of students with hearing loss and to offer training for general education teachers.

Moreover, various studies highlight the absence of appropriate disability specialists in Emirati schools to support students with SEND, posing challenges for general teachers in providing adequate support (Alhammadi, 2023; van Niekerk, 2019; Alborno, 2017; Dev & Kumar, 2015). For example, Alhammadi (2023) emphasizes the critical need for specialized teachers to support students who are visually impaired and deaf or hard of hearing, as general educators lack the expertise to support these groups. Furthermore, the lack of behavioral therapists and speech therapists presents additional obstacles for general teachers, especially in catering to students with emotional and behavioral disorders and speech delays (Alborno, 2017). The scarcity of assistant or shadow teachers further complicates the accommodation of students with severe disabilities in regular classrooms (Meda et al., 2023). This shortage of specialized staff places a considerable burden on teachers, negatively affecting the inclusion and progress of students with disabilities (Fakih, 2019).

Finally, several studies have highlighted the significant challenge that the lack of assistive technology poses for general education teachers in inclusive classrooms in the UAE (Meda et al., 2023; Anati, 2012; Fakih, 2019; van Niekerk, 2019). Alobeidli (2017) emphasized that insufficient teaching aids, assistive technology devices, and adapted materials contribute to the inadequacy of accommodations, often due to limited funds for inclusion programs. Conversely, Alhammadi (2023) argues that the Ministry of Education does provide students with SEN various assistive technologies in public schools. However, the primary challenge lies in the lack of adequate training. The shortage of assistive technology specialists results in teachers and students with SEN not receiving sufficient training on utilizing the technology they require. Alborno's (2017) study further supports these findings, highlighting that inadequate training hinders the proper utilization of assistive technology devices, leading to underutilization from fear of damaging the equipment.

2.4. Managing Inclusive Classrooms

One of the most important challenges facing teachers in inclusive classrooms is classroom management. The increased workload associated with teaching students with disabilities is one of the perceived barriers to successful inclusion (Atkinson et al., 2020). The heavy workload and administrative responsibilities of teachers, along with large class sizes, the number of students, and the nature of disabilities, can significantly impact teachers' willingness to work with students with disabilities in inclusive classrooms (Alobeidli, 2017). A significant struggle that adds to general education teachers' responsibilities in inclusive classroom is managing behavioral disorders of students with disabilities. Minor behavioral problems such as inattention in class, excessive talking, or more serious issues like fighting and bullying pose a challenge for teachers responsible for inclusion in their classes (Opoku et al., 2023).

Various studies in the UAE have highlighted the ongoing struggle for general education teachers in managing inclusive classrooms. Gaad and Khan (2007) noted that teachers face difficulties due to large class sizes, with reports of up to 30 students per class. Balancing the needs of special education students with those of the rest of the class becomes a challenge in such settings. Teachers emphasize the importance of reduced class sizes and additional time to provide personalized instruction for students with special needs. Meda et al. (2023) argue that some teachers in the UAE believe that having just one student with SEND in the class can make it difficult to balance instruction between this one student and all other students when the class is too big.

Moreover, Bock (2015) stated that the incorporation of SEN students into mainstream classrooms has been perceived as substantially increasing teachers' responsibilities, leading to feelings of being overworked and stressed due to the demands of adapting teaching methods without adequate preparation or support. Teachers have expressed a need for professional development and managerial support to manage these pressures effectively. Additionally, unrealistic expectations from school leadership, coupled with a lack of necessary support and resources, have further exacerbated these issues, leading to teacher exhaustion and increased pressure (Bock, 2015). Fakih (2019) investigated attitudes of teachers in private schools in Dubai towards inclusion. Teachers in her study reported being overwhelmed by the dual responsibility of maintaining classroom order and attending to the needs of students with SEND. One of the challenges cited by teachers in the study was their unpreparedness to manage challenging behaviors due to lack of training. The lack of knowledge and skills to manage difficult behaviors in inclusive classrooms adds to the stress mainstream teachers experience in creating inclusive classes for students with SEND.

2.5. Challenges in Collaboration

Collaboration is essential for the success of inclusive education, as highlighted by various studies. Moore (2020) notes that supportive and involved parents contribute to more favorable attitudes among teachers, facilitating better understanding and collaboration between home and school environments. When parents actively engage in their child's education and support their educational needs, teachers are more likely to adopt inclusive practices. Furthermore, Bock (2015) emphasizes that teachers need opportunities to collaborate and share ideas to enhance their teaching practices. Creating a collaborative culture among teachers when implementing an inclusive model is vital for fostering confidence and support. Additionally, Bakri (2018) points out that a positive working environment, teacher appreciation, and support from parents, fellow students, and the community are crucial factors in encouraging teachers to embrace inclusive teaching. Together, these studies underscore the importance of collaboration in making inclusion successful.

Nevertheless, teachers in the UAE encounter various challenges when cooperating with diverse stakeholders. Several studies have identified obstacles in collaborating with parents of special needs children. Meda et al. (2023) highlighted that teachers in their study faced difficulties in partnering with parents of students with special needs. Some of the challenges they mentioned concerned a lack of support, parents' reluctance to acknowledge their child's disability, and excessive dependence on teachers and the school to address their child's special needs. In a similar vein, Ali and Opoku (2023) pinpointed communication gaps and inconsistent cooperation from parents. These hindrances in parent-teacher collaboration can significantly impact the efficacy of inclusive education. Moreover, cultural sensitivities and negative attitudes toward disabilities in the UAE introduce further hurdles for productive collaboration with parents (Bock, 2015).

Gaad and Khan (2007) identified other challenges related to teacher collaboration with school administration. Teachers in their study highlighted the lack of administrative understanding and support as a barrier to effective inclusion. While some teachers did report motivation from administrators, many emphasized the need for greater administrative involvement in scheduling and a shift in focus from 'grade level goals' to 'individual goals for all students' (p. 104).

Another barrier to collaboration highlighted by some studies is the relationship between general education teachers and special education teachers. In particular, research has shown a lack of coordination and partnership in the development and implementation of IEPs among teachers across different schools. The absence of discussions among teachers regarding goal-setting and plan execution further exacerbates this issue. Additionally, the insufficient collaboration between schools in the context of transferring students with special educational needs compounds the challenge (Ali & Opoku, 2023). Similarly, Fakih (2019) argues that there is a notable deficiency in teachers' understanding of IEP development, with some teachers expressing a sense of isolation and burden in creating these plans without adequate support from the special needs department. This lack of collaboration and shared responsibility in creating IEPs for students with SEND may hinder effective support and inclusion practices in schools,

3. Conclusion

This study of challenges facing general education teachers in the UAE in inclusive classrooms sheds light on significant obstacles hindering the effective implementation of inclusion policies. The primary challenges identified include lack of preparedness for inclusive teaching practice, inadequate professional development opportunities, scarcity of resources and specialized personnel, difficulties in managing inclusive classrooms, and challenges in collaboration with various stakeholders. These challenges impact the ability of teachers to provide appropriate support to students with SEND in mainstream classrooms.

The study emphasizes the crucial need for comprehensive training programs for pre-service and in-service teachers to equip them with the knowledge, skills, and confidence necessary for successful inclusive education. Professional development should be tailored to address the specific needs of teachers in managing diverse classrooms effectively. Adequate resources, including financial support, assistive technology, and specialized personnel, are essential to support teachers in meeting the diverse needs of students with SEND. Additionally, fostering collaboration among teachers, parents, school administrators, and special education professionals is vital for creating a supportive and inclusive learning environment.

Addressing these challenges requires a multi-faceted approach that involves policy changes, increased investments in teacher training and resources, and fostering a collaborative culture within schools. By overcoming these obstacles, educators in the UAE can better support the inclusion of students with special needs and disabilities, ultimately promoting a more inclusive and equitable education system for all learners.

References

Abdulhameed, T. N. (2019). *An investigative study to explore teachers attitude towards the inclusion of learners on the autism spectrum disorder and learners with meares Irlen syndrome in private schools in the UAE.* [Master's thesis, The British University in Dubai]. Dissertations for Special and Inclusive Education (SIE). https://bspace.buid.ac.ae/buid_server/api/core/bitstreams/afb29cb9-afc4-4d51-8ac8-5562a99ac3fc/content

Alahbabi, A. (2006). *K-12 special and general education teachers' attitudes toward the inclusion of students with special needs in general education classes in the United Arab Emirates (UAE).* [Doctoral dissertation, George Washington University]. https://www.researchgate.net/publication/288688320_K-12_special_and_general_education_teachers'_attitudes_toward_the_inclusion_of_students_with_special_needs_in_general_education_classes_in_the_united_arab_emirates_UAE

Alborno, N. E. (2017). The 'yes … but' dilemma: Implementing inclusive education in Emirati primary schools. *British Journal of Special Education, 44*(1), 26–45. https://doi.org/10.1111/1467-8578.12157

Alghawi, M. (2007). *Bridging the gap between theory and practice of inclusion in the United Arab Emirates.* [Master's Thesis.] The British University, UAE. Retrieved from https://bspace.buid.ac.ae/buid_server/api/core/bitstreams/09d74707-b6c5-46c4-99aa-c1b52cdec1f9/content

Alhammadi, M. M. (2023). Availability of disability specialists for students with vision or hearing impairment in the United Arab Emirates: Current status and future needs. *Disability and Rehabilitation: Assistive Technology*. https://doi.org/10.1080/17483107.2023.2228827

Alhammadi, M. M. (2024). Assessing the efficiency of teacher education program in Emirati university for preparing pre-service teachers for inclusive education. *Cogent Education, 11*(1). https://doi.org/10.1080/2331186X.2024.2369966

Ali, M. S. H., & Opoku, M. P. (2023). "One child, two schools": Teachers' perspectives on the dual enrolment of students with disabilities in private special and inclusive schools in the United Arab Emirates. *Journal of Research in Special Educational Needs*. https://doi.org/10.1111/1471-3802.12635

Alobeidli, A. (2017). *An investigative study of the factors affecting the attitudes of female Emirati teachers toward the inclusion of students with intellectual disabilities in the government primary schools in Dubai, the United Arab Emirates.* [Doctoral dissertation, The British University in Dubai]. https://bspace.buid.ac.ae/buid_server/api/core/bitstreams/0a93a1be-6507-4ebc-938a-e39034b2de85/content

Al-Zyoudi, M. (2006). Teachers' attitudes towards inclusive education in Jordanian schools. *International Journal of Special Education, 21*(2), 55–63. https://files.eric.ed.gov/fulltext/EJ843606.pdf

Anati, N. (2012). Including students with disabilities in UAE schools: A descriptive study. *International Journal of Special Education, 27*, 75–85. https://www.researchgate.net/publication/285994640_Including_students_with_disabilities_in_UAE_schools_A_descriptive_study#fullTextFileContent

Arif, M., & Gaad, E. (2008). Special needs education in the UAE: A system perspective. *Journal of Research in Special Education Needs, 8*(2), 111–117. https://doi.org/10.1111/j.1471-3802.2008.00108.x

Atkinson, S. J., Takriti, R. A., & Elhoweris, H. (2020). Teachers' perceptions of successful transition to school for children with and without Downs Syndrome in the UAE and England. *Education 3–13, 49*(7), 860–871. https://doi.org/10.1080/03004279.2020.1809489

Badr, H. M. (2019). Exploring UAE teachers' attitude towards the successful implementation of the general rules in the "School for All" Initiative. *Journal of Language Teaching and Research, 10*(1), 92–102. https://doi.org/10.17507/jltr.1001.11

Baker, F. S. (2015). Developing teachers and children for inclusive educational practices in Abu Dhabi, United Arab Emirates. *Childhood Education, 91*(4), 283–291. https://doi.org/10.1080/00094056.2015.1069159

Bakri, H. (2018). *Dubai private schools readiness to adopt successful inclusion of students with Special Needs & Disability (SEND): An investigative study.* [Master's dissertation, The British University in Dubai]. Dissertations for Special and Inclusive Education (SIE). https://bspace.buid.ac.ae/buid_server/api/core/bitstreams/507e7bc3-396c-4185-9daf-a5d8f6bdb774/content

Bock, S. M. (2015). *The inclusion of Special Educational Needs (SEN) students in United Arab Emirates (UAE) mainstream schools: An exploratory study.* [Masters' dissertation, University of South Africa]. https://portal.qader.org/cached_uploads/download/2018/12/05/the-inclusion-of-special-educational-needs-in-united-arab-emirates-in-mainstream-schools-1544009520.pdf

Dev, S., & Kumar, J. (2015). Teacher's perception towards integration of learning disabled students into regular classroom – a study in Dubai & Abu Dhabi schools. *Procedia-Social and Behavioral Sciences, 211*, 605–611. https://doi.org/10.1016/j.sbspro.2015.11.079

Dukmak, S. (2013). Regular classroom teachers' attitudes towards including students with disabilities in the regular classroom in the United Arab Emirates. *The Journal of Human Resource and Adult Learning*, 9(1), 26–39. https://www.researchgate.net/publication/272748089

Dukmak, S., Aburezeq, I. M., & Khaled, A. (2019). Public school teachers' perceived sense of self-efficacy in teaching students with disabilities in the United Arab Emirates. *International Journal of Economics and Business Research, 17*(1), 34–52. https://doi.org/10.1504/IJEBR.2019.09658

Elhoweris, H. (2008). The effect of the child's disability on United Arab Emirates in service teachers' educational decisions regarding gifted and talented children. *Educational Studies, 34*(5), 557–564. https://doi.org/10.1080/03055690802288536

Fakih, M. K. (2019). *Teachers' attitudes towards inclusion of learners with disabilities at American private early childhood education in Dubai: An investigative study.* [Master's dissertation, The British University in Dubai]. https://bspace.buid.ac.ae/handle/1234/1477

Gaad, E., & Khan, L. (2007). Primary mainstream teachers' attitudes towards inclusion of students with special educational needs in the private sector: A perspective from Dubai. *International Journal of Special Education, 22*(2), 95. Retrieved from https://files.eric.ed.gov/fulltext/EJ814493.pdf

Hemdan, A., Efstratopoulou, M., & Moustafa, A. (2021). Special education and teacher training in Abu Dhabi: Reality and prospects. In N. Bakali & N. A. Memon (Eds.), *Teacher training and education in the GCC: Unpacking the complexities and challenges of internationalizing educational contexts* (pp. 75–92). ProQuest Ebook Central. https://gces.ae/announcements/book-release-teacher-training-and-education-in-the-gcc

Marnewick, C., Meda, L., Condy, J., & Phillips, H. (2022). Using an intervention programme to empower intellectually disabled learners to use WhatsApp in a special needs unit in Cape Town, South Africa. *Cogent Education, 9*(1). https://doi.org/10.1080/2331186X.2022.2142447

Meda, L., ElSayary, A., & Mohebi, L. (2023). Exploration of in-service teachers' preparedness and perceived challenges about inclusive education in the United Arab Emirates. *Journal of Educational and Social Research, 13*(1), 22. https://doi.org/10.36941/jesr-2023-0003

Moore, K. M. (2020). *Private education teachers in Abu Dhabi, UAE and their acceptance of the inclusion of students with disabilities.* [Doctoral dissertation, Northcentral University, School of Education]. Retrieved from https://www.researchgate.net/publication/285994640_Including_students_with_disabilities_in_UAE_schools_A_descriptive_study

Opoku, M. P., Elhoweris, H., Moustafa, A., Miezah, D., Shah, H., & Oppong, A. (2023). Perceived competence of teachers in the implementation of trauma-informed practices for students with disabilities in classrooms in the United Arab Emirates. *Journal of Child & Adolescent Trauma,* 1–15. https://doi.org/10.1007/s40653-023-00591-5

Royster, O., Reglin, G. L., & Losike-Sedimo, N. (2014). Inclusion professional development model and regular middle school educators. *Journal of At-Risk Issues, 18*(1), 1–10. https://api.semanticscholar.org/CorpusID:153567499

Saqr, S., & Tennant, L. J. (2016). Emirati general education pre-service teachers' preparedness for diversity in inclusive classrooms. *International Journal of Education, 8*(2), 105–121. http://dx.doi.org/10.5296/ije.v8i2.9396

Van Niekerk, A. C. (2019). *"School for all": Teachers' perspective of inclusive education for hearing-impaired learners in Dubai, UAE.* [Master's thesis, University of the Witwatersrand]. Electronic Theses and Dissertations (ETD) Collection. https://hdl.handle.net/10539/30598

Youssef, Z. (2019). *Assessing teachers' attitude toward adopting KHDA framework for Special Education Needs in UAE.* [Doctoral dissertation, The British University in Dubai (BUiD)]. BUiD Space. https://bspace.buid.ac.ae/buid_server/api/core/bitstreams/28430a0c-0978-418d-91f3-12a728c2a399/content

Edona Berisha Kida, Ali Rakipi, and Anita Zenuni

Enhancing Educational Sustainability: The Role of Artificial Intelligence and Augmented Reality

1. Introduction

1.1. Theoretical Framework of Sustainable Education

To ensure the prosperity of both the present and future generations, sustainable education refers to educational methods and institutions created to support social responsibility, environmental trusteeship, and economic equality. The concept incorporates sustainability principles into the curriculum, instructional strategies, and school administration to cultivate a student-centered approach that achieves sustainable understanding and dedication to lifelong best perspectives. The objective is to provide students with the values, knowledge, and abilities needed to confront and resolve the 21st century's social, economic, and environmental problems (Wals, 2014; Tilbury, 2011).

Sustainable education covers the below written principles:

- *Interdisciplinary Approach* (Holistic understanding, real-world relevance),
- *Systems Thinking* (Understanding interconnections, complex problem-solving),
- *Critical Thinking and Problem Solving* (Encouraging inquiry, innovative solutions),
- *Ethical and Values-Based Learning* (Environmental ethics, social responsibility),
- *Active Participation and Empowerment* (Student engagement, empowerment), and
- *Long-term perspective* (Future orientation, legacy building, collaborative learning) (Sachs, 2015; Wals, 2014; Tilbury, 2011).

The use of technology, artificial intelligence, and augmented realities in education is proven to be a tool that ignites and supports sustainable education principles.

1.2. Contextualizing Artificial Intelligence and Augmented Realities in Education

Conceptually Artificial Intelligence (AI) and Augmented Reality (AR) started their development in the 50s, respectively 60s (Turing, 1950; McCarthy, Minsky,

Rochester & Shannon, 1956; Heilig, 1962) achieving their functional peaks recently and having great impact almost everywhere let alone in the field of education (Smith 2022; Bae & Hwang, 2020; Dorner, Schmalstieg & Billinghurst, 2020). AI has the potential to revolutionize education by personalizing instruction and simplifying administrative tasks for teachers (Holmes, Bialik & Fadel, 2019). On the other hand, offering more tailored, contextually relevant, and interactive learning, Augmented Reality (AR) has great promise for improving educational experiences. AR offers interactive learning environments that enhance comprehension and encourage a closer bond with the subject matter (Dieck& Jung, 2017). This way through different mechanisms such as enhanced understanding of complex concepts through visualization, interactive stimulation, contextual learning, engagement and motivation, increased enjoyment and interest, collaborative work, etc., AI and AR directly support students' cognitive and emotional processes in education settings (Cai, Lin & Zhang, 2020; Bodily &Verbert, 2017; Jou, Huang & Hsu, 2016).

1.3. Objectives and Scope of the Chapter

This chapter offers a thorough analysis of the principles of sustainable education as well as the use and effects that Augmented Reality (AR) and Artificial Intelligence (AI) have on sustainability in education. To investigate how these technologies complement different learning theories, theoretical views are reviewed. The chapter also looks at how AI and AR are currently used in educational contexts, highlighting their advantages as well as their challenges. Starting this theoretical summary was reinforced by an ongoing project that shows how technology and AI influence English language learning by Kosovar students. Notably, the still unpublished survey shows that more than 60 % of kids starting first grade are almost fluent in English, a result linked to kids using electronics and AI technologies informally, inevitably influencing education policies and teachers' work (Berisha Kida, 2024 unpublished). Even the inevitable use of such contemporary technologies including AI is reflected in the development of the actual chapter, indicating their support is becoming a valuable experience to be properly used by new researchers and scholars.

2. Theoretical Foundations

2.1. Constructivist Theories and Experiential Learning

Principles of both Constructivist and Experiential theories are supported by AI and AR technologies as enhancing learning abilities and reinforcing education sustainability. For example, constructivist pedagogy places a strong emphasis on *active learning*, in which students build their knowledge and understanding by direct experiences and reflection (Piaget, 1950) while AI and AR create immersive, interactive environments that support active learning. With AR, students can actively interact with content by superimposing digital information onto real-world environments. For instance, real-time AR applications in science can help students visualize intricate processes, like the inner workings of the human body.

Constructivism emphasizes *inquiry-based learning* and *problem-solving*, where students investigate real-world issues to create knowledge (Vygotsky, 1978). Through the creation of scenarios that call for judgment and critical thought, AI and AR aid in problem-solving. For example, while AI can evaluate students' approaches to problem-solving and offer help or alternate answers, augmented reality simulations can pose challenges for students to solve. This compatibility with inquiry-based learning promotes greater comprehension for students.

Another core concept in the constructivist approach is *scaffolding* where learners are supported through gradual steps until they can independently apply new knowledge (Wood, Bruner, & Ross, 1976). AI-driven educational tools and Augmented Realities can offer scaffolding by providing step-by-step guidance, hints, and adaptive challenges based on students' performance.

AI has the potential to accelerate active learning by providing students with scaffolding, allowing for customization of learning paths, and encouraging a deeper comprehension (Shah, 2023). Further, as David Kolb in his theory of experiential learning points out learning occurs through experience, reflection, and application (Kolb, 1984), AI and AR support the learning process to be built upon these principles as well.

2.2. The Behaviorist Approach

According to behaviorist theory, actions can be modified by reward and feedback, and it places an emphasis on learning as a reaction to environmental stimuli. AI can offer individualized, real-time feedback and reinforcement, improving learning efficiency and opening the door for the large-scale use of behaviorist techniques (Shah, 2023).

Here are a few applications of AI for feedback and reinforcement:

- Instant feedback: AI-powered systems can deliver individualized, real-time student performance feedback, dispelling myths and encouraging positive behaviour.
- Adaptive learning: AI-powered learning platforms may customize practice exercises and information to meet the needs of specific students, strengthening the acquisition of desirable behaviours and competencies.

- Gamification: To encourage and strengthen students' learning and engagement, AI systems might include gamification components like badges and awards.
- Progress tracking: By tracking students' performance and progress, AI systems enable teachers to give tailored feedback and encouragement.

(Holmes et al., 2019; Wu, Lee, Chang & Liang, 2013)

2.3. Cognitive Load Theory and Learning Efficiency

AI and AR improve learning and productivity by regulating the way information is processed and presented and this way they have a revolutionary impact on cognitive load management. AI supports the cognitive load theory principles through personalized learning experiences, adaptive learning platforms, automated feedback and assistance (Chen, Haung & Liu, 2021; Zou, Xie & Zheng, 2020). At the same time AR contribution to the theory's principles is through enhanced contextualization, interactive learning environments, visualization and guidelines (Zhu, Lin & Liu, 2023; Zhang, Zhang & Xu, 2022; Bacca, Bandiris & Fabregat, 2014).

AI and AR offer interactive and contextually rich educational experiences that greatly improve learning efficiency and retention. Through the use of interactive features and simulations of real-world settings, they develop engaging learning environments. This draws students' attention and encourages deeper engagement with the material, which enhances learning effectiveness and retention (Bacca et al., 2014; Mikropoulos & Natsis, 2011).

2.4. Socio-cultural Theories

AI and AR through their ability to facilitate interactions, enable the building of shared knowledge, and bridge socio-cultural learning gaps, play important roles in improving collaborative education and social learning. These responsibilities are consistent with sociocultural theories, which highlight the significance of cultural environments and social interactions in the learning process. Concepts like zone of proximal development (ZPD) (Vygotsky, 1978) and social constructivism are very well supported by AI and AR technologies. ZPD is supported by providing step-by-step help for students who cannot perform a task independently. Social constructivism happens when these technologies facilitate collaborative learning and shared knowledge creation (Paavola, Lipponen, & Hakkarainen, 2004). The impact of AI and AR in social learning dynamics is essential when taking in consideration cultural inclusivity and diversity as well. Educators may create more engaging and fair learning experiences that respect and reflect a variety of cultural backgrounds and learning requirements by using these tools.

3. Applications of Artificial Intelligence and Augmented Realities in Education

3.1. K-12 Education: Engagement and Motivation in Younger Learners with Practical Learning Experiences

Recently, the generation of educational content has increasingly involved AI technologies. A fundamental shift in the way students receive personalized, adaptive, and interactive learning is represented by intelligent tutoring systems. These systems nowadays make use of machine learning and artificial intelligence algorithms to comprehend each student's distinct learning preferences, styles, and talents (Young, 2024).

AR technology as elaborated above in this chapter, can be utilized to improve educational content as an instructional medium, in which users can interact with the virtual content by combining virtual knowledge with their real environment (Arif, 2023). When students can interact with and visually see the various occurrences and concepts they are studying, they learn and perceive information more effectively. Applications of AR have shown to be highly successful, particularly in the field of education. These apps help students learn more effectively by enhancing their learning, and motivation and by facilitating interactive study that makes complex concepts easier to understand (Arif, 2023; Garzon, 2019). AR gives students easy access to unobservable phenomena that have been identified by teachers and prior research as problematic for students' easy comprehension. Examples of these phenomena include the behavior of magnetic fields or the movement of the sun which would be easily understood in AI-AR stimulated classroom environments (Garzon, 2019). AR is also useful for educating about historical sites-events and astronomy (Arif, 2023).

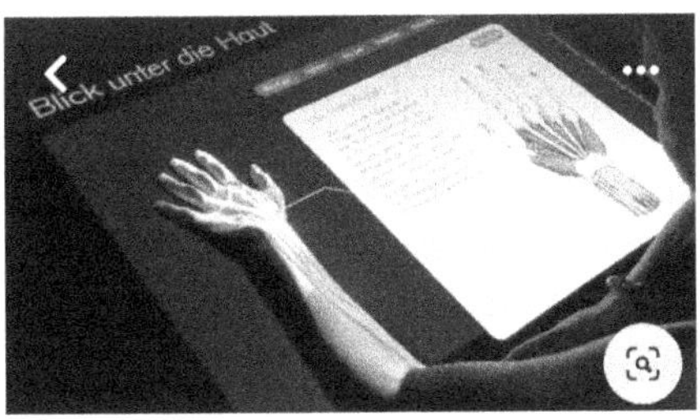

Figure 1: AR interactive digital human anatomy

(Photo by Pinterest)

Figure 2: Relieve augmented box

(Photo by Pinterest)

Figure 1: ART+COM Studios. (2009) Discover what moves us...Science Center Medical Technology. Pinterest. https://pin.it/1FWvjhzKq
Figure 2: Interactive Sandbox (n.d) Relieve augmented box. Pinterest. https://pin.it/1XO2NpHCs

3.2. The Use of AI-AR in Higher Education

Finally, AI can be used in colleges and universities. It is largely used especially after the break of the COVID-19 pandemic (Daugherty & Wilson, 2020). In addition to recommending, or automatically delivering, particular course sections or supplementary materials for students to review, educational software based on AI algorithms evaluates the progress of each student (Netragaonkar, 2024).

Instead of using traditional learning methods, students can visualize and fully comprehend a variety of challenging topics by interacting with augmented virtual objects. This allows for collaborative learning that exceeds the need for physical presence (Arif, 2023). AI/AR technologies have the potential to engage students in remote learning and virtual campuses. Students from many nations can collaborate and self-organize to accomplish their objectives thanks to intelligent systems. This is made possible with an internet connection and a variety of programs and applications.

4. Sustainability and Equity in Artificial Intelligence and Augmented Education

An attractive area of sustainable education involves lowering the carbon footprint of educational needs through the use of AI and AR, as well as virtual field excursions and labs. These technologies help create a greener future with the ability to create virtual learning environments that require fewer physical resources and transportation. By superimposing digital data on tangible objects, AR can reduce the need for paper handouts and printed textbooks. By adapting to each student's unique learning demands, these tools increase efficiency in the classroom and reduce waste.

Students can perform experiments and engage in scientific inquiry using virtual labs without requiring real lab supplies and equipment. This decreases the waste associated with traditional lab experiments and eliminates the need for resource-intensive lab setups. Also, students' awareness of environmental issues is aided by using AI-AR technologies in education thus contributing to educational sustainability: For example, a virtual lab may model the implications of different environmental policies, or a virtual field trip could investigate how climate change affects various ecosystems.

Equity, accessibility and ethical issues are very important when using AI-AR in educational settings. Inclusivity should always be considered while designing AI apps for use in education. To guarantee that all students can benefit from AI-enhanced education, considerations for a range of learning styles, preferences, and accessibility requirements should be taken into account (Young, 2024). Maintaining student privacy, being transparent, and holding people accountable are all part of using AI ethically in education. Upon the potential for integrating AI into educational technology, some issues must be resolved, including data protection, ethical concerns, and ensuring that all students have equal access to AI-driven resources (Young, 2024). Different issues linked with the ethical use of AI-AR technologies are considered to be challenging and will be addressed in the below section.

5. Challenges and Limitations

5.1. Technical and Financial Barriers

A potential challenge for the use of these recent technologies is the cost associated with them. Since the 1992 introduction of the ARtoolkit, the AR Software Development Kits (SDK) have been fast expanding. With even inexpensive smartphones supporting the presentation of augmented reality content, AR-based applications aimed at the education sector are becoming more and more accessible. Anyway, longitudinal research on how AR influences learning outcomes compared to other technologies is still missed (Kljun, Geroimenko & Čopič Pucihar, 2020). Despite the applications that work through smartphones, for more professional use such as in various fields of healthcare learners with immersive simulation-based training in interactive digital human anatomy, or astronomy with educational applications about the cosmos, there are developed head-mounted AR displays such as Microsoft HoloLens 10 and MagicLeap.11 which costs are not reachable for everyone (Kljun et al., 2020).

Another potential challenge in linked to infrastructure requirements given that AI-AR learning necessitates studio-based simulations and methodology, which differs greatly from traditional teacher-centered techniques. (Young, 2024).

5.2. Pedagogical Challenges

- **Adapting curriculum and teaching strategies for AI/AR integration**
  Including AI-AR in curriculum frameworks presents both advantages and challenges. Academics emphasize how important it is to match curricular objectives and learning objectives with AI-AR experiences. The creation of

frameworks and rules that make it easier to incorporate AI-AR into current educational systems while preserving pedagogical coherence is very important (Arif, 2023).

It is very crucial to have an integrated, multidisciplinary strategy when integrating AI- AR into the education system. Taking in consideration that ensuring basic educational abilities is a difficulty on a global scale, it is obvious that developing successful AI-AR systems in schools require significant work, challenges and efforts. But there's a big payoff: Once created, AI-AR are useful tools for teaching and learning environments that may be reused again and again (Kljun et al., 2020).

- **Teacher training and professional development needs**
  Concerns over teacher job displacement may arise from the use of AI-AR in education. Among the ethical factors is the idea of teachers' professional development that need to adjust to new responsibilities and make sure AI-AR technologies enhance rather than replace human abilities (Young, 2024). As teachers may have difficulty implementing technology, adoption of AI-AR technologies should rely on training educators to use them. The research community should intervene and support educators in their familiarization with technologies and discovery of the best opportunities for enhancing their teaching capacities (Young, 2024; Garzon, 2019).

5.3. Psychological and Social Concerns

Long-term use of AI and AR has a variety of psychological and emotional repercussions on students, making it a complex issue. An outline of several possible effects, both favorable and unfavorable, is provided below:

- Positive impacts related to (1) Enhanced Engagement and Motivation (Through immersive learning and immediate feedback), (2) Personalized Learning Experiences (Through tailored instructions), and (3) Improved Cognitive Skills (Through improving critical thinking and problem-solving abilities) are all elaborated above in this chapter.
- Negative impacts may be related to (1) Screen Time and Digital Overload (impacting mental fatigue, eye strain, and other physical health issues), (2) Dependency and Reduced Social Interaction, (3) Anxiety, and Stress (Performance pressure and privacy data concern). There are hypothetical risks of negative long-term effects on cognitive, emotional, and social development to be further researched. This includes the risk that over-reliance on these technologies might impact the development of cognitive skills like attention span, memory, and critical thinking, students' capacity to form

interpersonal relationships and participate in meaningful social interactions outside of virtual environments may be impacted by a prolonged dependence on digital tools and so on (Cullen, Muntz, Marsh, Simmonds, Mayes, O'Neill & Duncan, 2024; Muppalla, Vuppalapati, Reddy Pulliahgaru & Sreenivasulu, 2023; Ricci, Paulo, Freitas, Ribeiro, Pires, Facina, Cabral, Parduci, Spegiorin, Bogado, Chociay Junior, Carachesti & Larroque, 2022).

AR and AI in education are designed to provide ongoing support and enhance learning but run the risk of overly recording mistakes or failures of students in the programed tasks. In the psycho-pedagogical aspect, there should be carefulness as it may happen that instead of focusing on learning and improvement, students might become discouraged or anxious if they are constantly reminded of their mistakes. At the same time being always supported by AI could lead to a stressful atmosphere if educators believe AI is watching and grading them all the time. They may feel more watched than helped, which could have an impact on their efficacy as teachers and general job happiness (Luckin & Hennessy, 2016). So, the ethical concern revolves around the privacy of both learners and teachers. For students, the worry that every mistake would be documented could undermine their well-being and motivation. Being watched over could make teachers more stressed and harm their performance. So, there should be a balance between using these educational supporting technologies and the need to maintain trust and respect for personal privacy in the classroom.

6. Conclusions: Future Directions and Implications

This chapter explores the intersection of sustainable education, artificial intelligence (AI), and augmented reality (AR), emphasizing their theoretical underpinnings and practical applications. Insights into how AI and AR might transform education are presented through discussion of present uses, obstacles, and future possibilities. The introductory section outlines the theoretical framework of sustainable education and situates AI and AR within this context. Further explaining the theoretical foundations of using AI-AR for sustainable education are rooted in various learning theories such as *Constructivist Theories and Experiential Learning* (focusing on how learners build knowledge through experiences given by AI-AR), *The Behaviorist Approach* (emphasizing reinforcement and repetition in learning through AI-AR), *Cognitive Load Theory and Learning Efficiency* (addressing the optimization of cognitive resources for effective learning stimulated by AI-AR) and *Socio-Cultural Theories* (exploring the impact of social interactions and cultural contexts given through AI-AR on the learning processes).

Applications of AI and AR in education are examined across different educational levels such as *K-12 Education* (demonstrating how AI and AR can enhance engagement and motivation through interactive and practical learning experiences) and *Higher Education* (exploring the role of advanced applications, including personalized learning and data-driven insights).

The chapter further addresses *Sustainability and Equity* in AI and AR applications, advocating for their responsible and equitable implementation to benefit diverse learner populations. However, several *Challenges and Limitations* are acknowledged: *Technical and Financial Barriers* (highlight the infrastructure and cost issues associated with implementing these technologies), *Pedagogical Challenges* (examine the difficulties in integrating AI and AR effectively into existing curricula), *Psychological and Social Concerns* (discuss the impact on learners' mental health and social interactions).

In conclusion, the future directions for integrating AI and AR into education involve overcoming these challenges while maximizing their potential to enhance learning outcomes. Future research should focus on developing sustainable practices, addressing equity, psychological, and ethical concerns, and ensuring that technological advancements align with educational goals. The implications for educators, policymakers, and technology developers include a call for collaborative efforts to create inclusive and effective educational environments as the traditional teaching approaches have no place in our current world when children are exposed to advanced communication tools and engaged with sophisticated video games. The entire process of teaching and learning, which involves listening to lectures, taking notes, reading information from books, and taking tests, has become unattractive and disincentive to Generation Z students (Kumar, 2014). AI algorithms assess each student's learning style and modify the curriculum to meet their needs thus, addressing the challenges of diverse learning. Serious collaboration between educators, policymakers, and technology developers is needed these customized tools have the power to transform traditional teaching strategies and improve the effectiveness, accessibility, and sustainability of education (Young, 2024; Netragaonkar, 2024).

References

Alzyoudi, M., Al Nuaimi, S., & Almazroui, K. (2021). Inclusive education practices for children with disabilities in the United Arab Emirates. Africa Education Review, 18(1–2), 1–15. https://doi.org/10.1080/18146627.2022.2105727

Arif, M. T. A. (2023, November). *Augmented reality and its applications in* [Open access publication].

Bacca, J., Baldiris, S., & Fabregat, R. (2014). Augmented reality for the evaluation of educational content in technology education: A case study. *Journal of Educational Technology & Society, 17*(4), 273–284.

Bae, S., & Hwang, J. (2020). Augmented reality in education: A review of current trends and future prospects. *Journal of Educational Technology, 25*(3), 45–67.

Berisha Kida, E. (2024). *The impact of Artificial Intelligence technologies in Acquiring English Language by Kosovar Children* (Unpublished manuscript). Faculty of Education, University of Prishtina, Kosovo.

Bodily, R., & Verbert, K. (2017). Augmented reality in education: An overview of recent research. In *Proceedings of the 2017 International Conference on Augmented Reality and Virtual Reality* (pp. 53–60). Association for Computing Machinery.

Cai, S., Lin, X., & Zhang, X. (2020). The impact of augmented reality on learning: A systematic review. *Journal of Educational Technology Research and Development, 68*(3), 1481–1506.

Chen, C. M., Huang, Y. M., & Liu, T. C. (2021). The effect of adaptive learning system on students' cognitive load and learning performance. *Educational Technology Research and Development, 69*(3), 1407–1428.

Cullen, J., Muntz, A., Marsh, S., Simmonds, L., Mayes, J., O'Neill, K., & Duncan, S. (2024). Impacts of digital technologies on child and adolescent health: Recommendations for safer screen use in educational settings. *New Zealand Medical Journal, 137*(1598), 9–13.

Daugherty, P. R., & Wilson, H. J. (2020). *The age of AI: And our human future.* Hachette Books.

Dieck, M. C., & Jung, T. (2017). Augmented reality applications in educational settings: A review of current research. *Educational Technology & Society, 20*(1), 25–39.

Dorner, J., Schmalstieg, D., & Billinghurst, M. (2020). Augmented reality in education: The future of interactive learning. In *Advances in augmented reality research* (pp. 101–120). Springer.

Garzon, J. P. (2019). Systematic review and meta-analysis of augmented reality in education. *Virtual Reality, 23*(4), 567–589.

Garzon, J. P. (2019, December). Systematic review and meta-analysis of augmented reality in education. *Virtual Reality.*

Heilig, M. (1962). *Sensorama simulator.* US Patent No. 3,050,870.

Holmes, W., Bialik, M., & Fadel, C. (2019). Artificial intelligence in education: Promises and implications for teaching and learning. Center for Curriculum Redesign.

Jou, M., Huang, H., & Hsu, H. (2016). The role of augmented reality in enhancing students' learning experiences. *Interactive Learning Environments, 24*(2), 244–263.

Kljun, M., Geroimenko, V., & Čopič Pucihar, K. (2020). Augmented reality in education: Current status and advancement of the field. In V. Geroimenko (Ed.), *Augmented reality in education* (pp. xx–xx). Springer Series on Cultural Computing. Springer. https://doi.org/10.1007/978-3-030-42156-4_1

Kolb, D. A. (1984). Experiential learning: Experience as the source of learning and development. Prentice-Hall.

Kumar, A. D. (2014). *Augmented reality in education*. Paper presented at the National Conference on Inspired Learning. https://www.researchgate.net/publication/316279910_Augmented_Reality_in_Education

Luckin, R., & Hennessy, S. (2016). *Intelligence unleashed: An argument for AI in education*. Pearson.

McCarthy, J., Minsky, M., Rochester, N., & Shannon, C. E. (1956). A proposal for the Dartmouth summer research project on artificial intelligence. *AI Magazine*, 27(4), 12–14.

Mikropoulos, T. A., & Natsis, A. (2011). Augmented reality in education: A review of the literature. *Educational Technology & Society, 14*(1), 42–53.

Muppalla, S. K., Vuppalapati, S., Reddy Pulliahgaru, A., & Sreenivasulu, H. (2023). Effects of excessive screen time on child development: An updated review and strategies for management. *Cureus, 15*(6), e40608. https://doi.org/10.7759/cureus.40608

Netragaonkar, D. Y. (2024). Role of artificial intelligence (AI) and augmented reality. *Scholarly Research Journal for Interdisciplinary Studies, 11*(65), 8–10.

Paavola, S., Lipponen, L., & Hakkarainen, K. (2004). The role of the teacher in supporting the collaborative construction of knowledge. *The Journal of the Learning Sciences, 13*(3), 307–341.

Piaget, J. (1950). *The psychology of intelligence*. London, UK, Routledge.

Ricci, R. C., Paulo, A. S. C., Freitas, A. K. P. B., Ribeiro, I. C., Pires, L. S. A., Facina, M. E. L., Cabral, M. B., Parduci, N. V., Spegiorin, R. C., Bogado, S. S. G., Chociay Junior, S., Carachesti, T. N., & Larroque, M. M. (2022). Impacts of technology on children's health: A systematic review. *Revista Paulista de Pediatria, 41*, e2020504. https://doi.org/10.1590/1984-0462/2023/41/2020504

Sachs, J. D. (2015). *The age of sustainable development*. Columbia University Press.

Shah, P. (2023). *AI and the future of education*. John Wiley & Sons. Inc.

Smith, J. (2022). *The impact of artificial intelligence and augmented reality in modern education*. Educational Technology Press.

Tilbury, D. (2011). *Education for sustainable development: An expert review of processes and learning*. UNESCO.

Turing, A. M. (1950). Computing machinery and intelligence. *Mind*, 59(236), 433–460. https://doi.org/10.1093/mind/LIX.236.433

Vygotsky, L. S. (1978). *Mind in society: The development of higher psychological processes*. Harvard University Press.

Wals, A. E. J. (2014). *Learning for sustainability in times of accelerating change*. Wageningen Academic Publishers.

Wood, D., Bruner, J. S., & Ross, G. (1976). The role of tutoring in problem solving. *Journal of Child Psychology and Psychiatry, 17*(2), 89–100. https://doi.org/10.1111/j.1469-7610.1976.tb00381.x

Wu, M., Lee, J., Chang, H., & Liang, J. (2013). *Augmented reality in education: Current trends and future directions. Educational Technology & Society, 16*(1), 71–80.

Young, J. A. P. (2024, February). The rise of artificial intelligence in education. *International Journal of Innovative Research and Development, 13*(2), 74–82.

Zhang, X., Zhang, D., & Xu, Y. (2022). Augmented reality in education: A systematic review and meta-analysis. *Educational Technology Research and Development, 70*(2), 621–643. https://doi.org/10.1007/s11423-021-09955-4

Zhu, M., Lin, Y., & Liu, J. (2023). Visualization techniques in augmented reality for enhancing learning efficiency and reducing cognitive load. *Interactive Learning Environments, 31*(1), 67–80. https://doi.org/10.1080/10494820.2022.2147365.

Zou, D., Xie, H., & Zheng, L. (2020). Impact of adaptive learning on cognitive load and learning outcomes: A meta-analysis. *Educational Technology & Society, 23*(3), 112–125. https://www.jstor.org/stable/26959114

Georg Ikoro and Eneken Titov

The Concept of Test City from a Modern Smart City Perspective

1. Introduction

Literature and research highlight the need to create an environment that facilitates integration, optimization, and collaboration within an innovative ecosystem that enables all components to interact, adapt, and evolve (Svítek et al, 2020). Experimentation has become a crucial element in the governance of sustainability transitions. This comes into effect through the collaboration of different urban actors within the ecosystem (von Wirth, et al., 2019). According to Linde et al. (2021), innovation is rooted in the dynamism of a Smart City's capability and emerges primarily through knowledge-based management (Bloem and Salimi, 2022).

Innovation is often analyzed as being diversely technological, which has prompted Smart Cities to adopt the concept of integrating testbeds within urban spaces. This approach allows cities to explore and implement innovations by selecting solutions from organizations that are already validated in their market (McKinsey & Company, 2018). In this study, the authors will analyze the application of Test City, and self-assessment tools, such as horizon models as strategic instruments for evaluating and selecting organizations that align with the diverse requirements of Smart Cities.

The Test City, often referred to as Urban Living Labs, is a concept rooted in experimentation and pre-validation (e-Estonia, 2023). It provides a solid approach to managing the influx of innovative companies by leveraging conceptual models such as the horizon model. These tools offer a dynamic approach to evaluating organizations according to their developmental processes and innovation potential, ensuring their alignment with the evolving capabilities of Smart Cities (McKinsey & Company, 2018). These initiatives ultimately enhance cities' attractiveness, fostering economic growth through increased investments from innovative companies (Marchesani et al., 2023).

However, despite the theoretical alignment between initiatives such as Urban Living Labs and testbeds, and their influence on promoting sustainable innovation, the existing research leaves a gap in understanding their practical effectiveness (Popescu, 2020; Gupta et al., 2023). This gap will be discussed by analyzing relevant use cases in the study providing insight into how the Test City and the Horizon model contribute to sustainable long-term growth, investment attractions, and innovation adoption in Smart Cities. The case of Ülemiste Test City is used in this article to demonstrate how a structured approach can enhance the adoption and integration of innovative technologies into the urban environment. Ülemiste City, located in Tallinn has evolved into one of the leading tech hubs in the Baltic region, where Startups and globally renowned companies converge to drive innovation forward. Originally founded as a real estate company, Ülemiste City has since transformed into a multifaceted urban innovation ecosystem. Often referred to as a "city within a city," Ülemiste City has developed from the brand as a city to an ecosystemic urban environment that serves as a testing ground for green urban solutions and technological advancement in Smart City development. The environment provided by Ülemiste City encompasses a wide range of resources including infrastructure such as flexible office spaces, a campus with business parks, road networks, an environmentally conscious urban setting, and a tech-savvy community.

2. Theoretical Background

The concept of "Smart Cities" is not universally defined and is interpreted differently across various literature, as it has been used to describe specific objectives and perspectives (Marchesani et al., 2023). In this article, the definition of Lara et al. (2016) is taken as one suitable approach in describing smart city initiative and content – a Smart City is a community that systematically promotes the overall well-being of all its members, and is flexible enough to proactively and sustainably become an increasingly better place to live, work, and play. Smart City initiatives such as innovation projects or Urban Living Labs typically focus on advancing urban sustainability, transitioning to low-carbon economies, and creating an appealing digital urban environment. Over the decades, these initiatives have gained significant momentum, reflecting a strategic shift towards the use of high-tech services as a means to drive sustained economic growth while simultaneously reducing environmental footprint (Noori et al., 2020).

However, becoming a Smart City is not an ultimate goal. It is a continuous and iterative process designed to address urban challenges and enhance the quality of life (McKinsey & Company, 2018). Innovations within Smart Cities are not just about technology. It extends to urban governance, citizen involvement, and infrastructural improvements aimed at enhancing sustainability across all urban development initiatives (Von Wirth et al., 2019). Even the world's most advanced Smart Cities are only at the beginning stages of their transformation journey, suggesting that there is still a long road ahead to fully realizing the potential of these urban ecosystems (McKinsey & Company, 2018). Successful innovation adoption in Smart Cities requires a systematic evaluation of the city's existing technological and organizational capabilities (Linde et al. 2021). This evaluation process is crucial, as it allows the city to determine what external innovations and solutions can be effectively integrated into existing infrastructure.

In many instances, city governments do not need to independently develop each Smart City solution. Instead, they often rely on partnerships with other companies that possess specialized expertise and capabilities in providing innovative technologies and services (Woetzel & Remes, 2018). This approach allows cities to adopt cutting-edge technologies more efficiently without overstretching their internal resources. Additionally, the systematic interaction between the public, private sector, academia, and citizens is crucial for bridging the gap between technological innovation and practical urban application, accelerating the deployment of sustainable and scalable solutions (Noori et al., 2020). It is necessary to build up the system to continuously attract, pilot, and implement new solutions. Figure 1 explains how the integration of technological and sustainable innovation relies on continuous engagement and value exchange among stakeholders, creating a dynamic ecosystem for urban transformation.

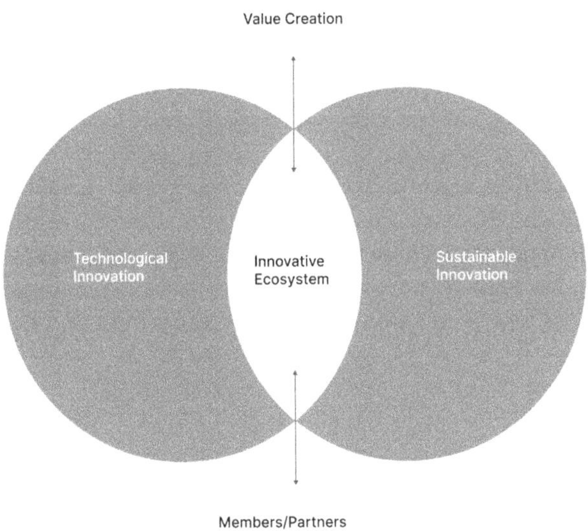

Figure 1: Innovative system

Technological Innovation involves using modern-day digitalization to introduce new and advanced technologies into urban infrastructure, community, and environment as an interconnected means to enhance efficiency, sustainability, and quality of life (Bibri et al., 2019). This is a crucial component of Smart Cities, significantly contributing to the attraction of skilled talents and innovative businesses (Marchesani et al., 2023). This includes installing high-sensor cameras, big data analytics, AI-driven technologies, and incorporating smart grids into different spheres of smart city initiatives such as mobility, health, energy, etc.

Sustainable Innovations are adopted to prioritize environmental sustainability aimed at promoting green urban spaces, enhancing resource efficiency, and reducing carbon footprint in compliance with several (7, 8, 9, 11, 12, 13, & 17) sustainable development goals (United Nations, 2024). This includes waste management systems, energy-efficient buildings, and a green environment. According to Gupta et al. (2023), innovation within Smart Cities is increasingly tied to ecosystem orchestration. Creating an innovative ecosystem is directly linked to the joint creation of value among members of private companies, government-owned entities, institutions of higher education, and citizens (Ricardo et al., 2023).

The drastic change and disruption of technology in the 21st century have diversified the role of innovation in business models (Van Balen, n.d.). With this shift in era, Smart City has a major role in dictating which technology or urban solution is best fit to adopt on a large scale. With the significant reliance on external companies to provide Smart City solutions (Woetzel & Remes, 2018), it is essential to assess the developmental stage of organizations to identify their potential to drive innovation. The three-horizon model serves as a strategic framework that helps organizations evaluate their growth, potential, and long-term opportunities over time (Mittal, 2024). In the context of Smart Cities, this model can be applied to manage the integration and scaling of innovative technologies and solutions. This framework helps balance the immediate needs of the city with the long-term vision of innovation and growth (Popescu, 2020).

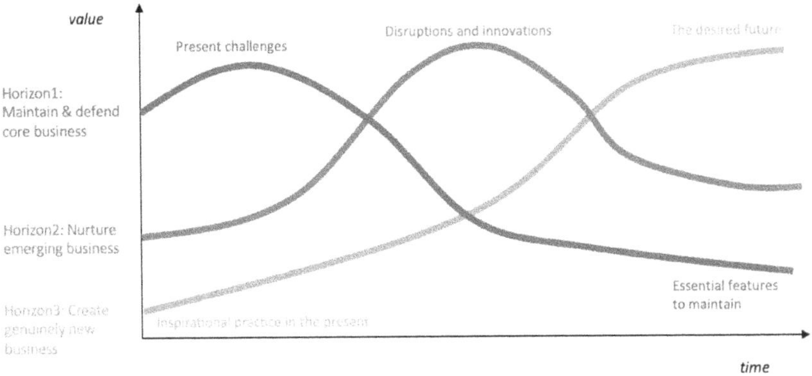

Figure 2: McKinsey's three-horizon model, adapted from Markapoulus et al. (2020), Mittel (2024), and McKinsey & Company (2018)

Figure 2 shows the trajectory of the horizon models, highlighting their suitability for addressing challenges across different timeframes. Horizon 1 focuses on initiatives that can optimize and extend the existing core business (McKinsey & Company, 2018; Mittal, 2024). It serves as a tool for assessing the short-term core capabilities of an organization, the duration depends on the nature of the organization (Blank, 2019). Horizon 2 focuses on explorations and developing emerging opportunities that can become the core business in the future for organizations. It is usually an experimental phase that takes longer than Horizon 1 to manifest (McKinsey & Company, 2018; Mittal, 2024). They are more innovative than Horizon 1 activities but still require validation and experimentation. Horizon 3 focuses on next-generation innovations that potentially disrupt the industry or create new markets. They are in the experimental phases and may not generate immediate returns. They are usually long-term investments focused on future capabilities (McKinsey & Company, 2018; Mittal, 2024). Such might include AI-driven city planning using digital twins.

In general, the horizon model opens for the Smart City a new path in enabling the exploration of industry compatibility with Smart Cities and long-term sustainability trajectory. Horizon 1 innovations provide a stable foundation for Smart Cities, offering immediate benefits during the initial stages of implementation. However, their limited flexibility presents a challenge for future development particularly as the urban environment evolves in 5–10 years. In contrast, Horizon 2 and Horizon 3, which are experimental and disruptive, may exhibit minimal impact at the onset but hold considerable potential for advancing the

Smart City ecosystem over the long term. Smart Cities committed to improving their long-term capabilities should focus on integrating Horizon 2 and Horizon 3. They align with the evolution of urban spaces prompting the creation of semi-controlled environments such as sandboxes and Test City which play a crucial role in addressing challenges such as innovation adoption in this study.

The concept of Test City offers an essential platform that facilitates the validation of innovative ideas and technologies within a controlled real-world environment. This model leverages Smart City's components such as infrastructure for companies to test their solutions, including office spaces, streets, and road networks on campuses, thereby allowing for the simulation of real urban conditions (e-Estonia, 2023). In most literature, it is often referred to as Urban Living Labs (Von Wirth, et al., 2019). Test City's concept extends beyond offering mere infrastructure provision to include technical services like consultation and mentorship programs for emerging entrepreneurs and cities alike. This concept not only aids in product development but also strengthens the ecosystem by connecting various stakeholders in Smart City development such as Private/Public institutions, educational institutions, and citizens (Ricardo et al., 2023).

Moreover, studies from Linde et al. (2021) and Popescu (2020) emphasize that urban transformation initiatives, in this case, Test City, are key to ensuring that urban innovations are not only tested in a semi-controlled environment but also refined and adapted for broader deployment, increasing their sustainability and potential for long-term growth. Thus, this approach spans various Smart City development domains, integrating technology, policy, and urban design to deliver comprehensive solutions for modern urban challenges. By providing these real-world validation environments, Smart Cities can effectively support the development of innovations that align with their evolving technological and infrastructural needs, enhancing the city's attractiveness and fostering economic growth through increased investments.

3. Methodology

In this research, grounded theory was employed as the primary methodological approach to systematically explore and develop a theoretical understanding of the complex process involved in innovation adoption and integration within Smart Cities, particularly in the context of Ülemiste City. Grounded theory was chosen due to its suitability for existing phenomena where existing theories are either insufficient or require further elaboration (Birks & Mills, 2019). This research aimed to generate a theoretical framework that explains how the Horizon model, Test City concept, and innovative ecosystems interact and contribute to the sustainable development of Smart Cities. To gain additional insight into this study the following research questions were derived:

- How can Smart Cities design and implement innovations that are scalable and sustainable over time?
- What factors are inhibiting the systematic adoption of innovation in Smart Cities?
- What considerations should Smart Cities prioritize when adopting and integrating new technologies into urban environments?

This research relies on secondary data obtained from multiple documented sources, including strategic planning documents, performance evaluations, and policy reports from Ülemiste City, as well as relevant municipal and governmental bodies in Estonia. In addition to these documents, unstructured interviews with experts at Ülemiste City were conducted to capture qualitative insights and practical perspectives on the implementation and challenges of their Smart City strategies.

4. Results and Discussion

Based on the interviews with experts and an analysis of documented reports, six distinctive themes organized into three main categories were identified through the research (Table 1). According to the experts, urban infrastructure was consistently highlighted as a foundational element necessary for supporting the integration of innovations. For mobility-focused innovations, the road networks and campus areas within Ülemiste City were noted as key environments for testing and deployment. Innovations that required physical space, such as hardware installations, could use office spaces and other semi-controlled environments.

Table 1: Themes and categories identified from interviews

S/N	Themes	Category A	Category B	Category C
1	**Urban Infrastructure**	Physical Spaces, Office Spaces,	Digital and Technological Infrastructure	Road Network, Business Parks, Campus
2	**Collaboration and Stakeholder Engagement**	Public-Private Partnerships	Academic-Industry Collaboration	Startup, Corporate and Citizens Synergy
3	**Business and Service Models**	Horizon 1, 2 and 3 Innovations	Test City concepts	Urban Ecosytems
4	**Innovation Adoption Challenges**	Scalability Issues	Barriers and Risk Management	Policy and Legal frameworks
5	**Sustainability and Urban Growth**	Environmental Considerations	Semi-controlled environment	Economic Growth through innovation
6	**Public Recognition**	Pre-validation and Pilot Programs	Iterative testing by involving Citizens	Feedback loops

The experts further emphasized that successful innovation implementation relies heavily on the effective collaboration of diverse stakeholders including public institutions, private companies, academia, and citizens. Each stakeholder group was seen as essential in contributing knowledge and sharing resources such as data and expertise that collectively drive innovation forward.

Experts also stressed the importance of aligning innovation with their stage of development and understanding how these innovations can influence future transitions. The introduction of the Test City concept at Ülemiste City was cited as a forward-thinking approach that strategically incorporated Horizon 2 and Horizon 3 innovations, with an emphasis on long-term growth. While Horizon 1 innovations had already been established within the City, the primary focus of development was on more experimental and transformative technologies associated with Horizon 2 and Horizon 3.

Challenges in scaling and fully realizing the potential of these innovations were frequently mentioned by the experts. Specifically, concerns were raised about the scalability of solutions, the barrier of entry, and the complexities of risk management, particularly for Horizon 2 and Horizon 3 companies. Legal and policy validation were highlighted as significant obstacles, often needing additional verification, which the Test City concept was designed to address. Experts further identified the need to evaluate impacts and address environmental considerations as a critical component of successful innovation integration. Pilot tests and feedback loops, generated through the active engagement of citizens, were seen as a crucial mechanism for refining solutions and ensuring their readiness for large-scale implementation.

The new model of theory as mapped from the analysis and interviews is used to describe and validate the case of the Ülemiste Test City.

Ülemiste City introduced its Test City in 2023 to utilize its environment and community as a catalyst for supporting the growth ambitions of innovative companies. This initiative leverages the concept of testing urban solutions within a controlled environment, where projects are classified and executed according to innovation criteria. These criteria are described using the Horizon Model as shown in Figure 4. By integrating projects across all horizons, Ülemiste Test City has contributed to broadening the scope of Smart City innovation, allowing for the validation of theoretical frameworks while providing practical, and real-world results.

For example, Bikeep, classified as a Horizon 1 company, introduced smart bike parking stations throughout the city, which were successfully integrated and validated through the Test City framework. Such projects illustrate how Horizon 1 innovations contribute to enhancing urban functionality with minimal disruption. Ülemiste City also incorporates Horizon 2 and Horizon 3 companies into its ecosystem, reflecting a shift towards long-term transformative innovations that require extensive testing and iterative refinement.

When Horizon 2 and Horizon 3 companies bring their products and services to Ülemiste City, some of these innovations are not immediately accessible to the public due to legal restrictions or public reasons. Another example is Grab2go, a company characterized as a Horizon 2 company

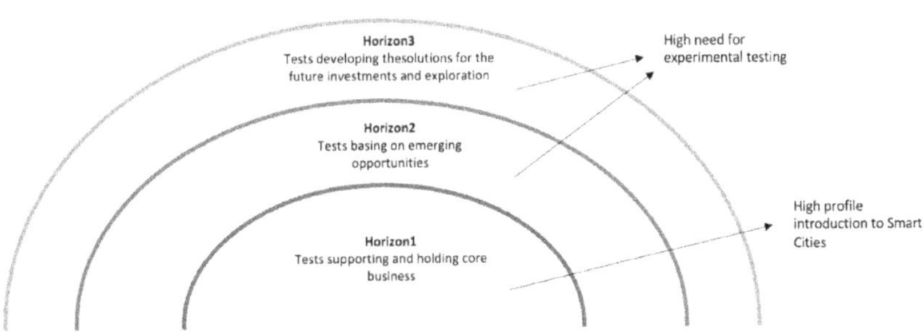

Figure 3: Ülemiste city three-horizon model

The Test City concept in Ülemiste City initially started with companies at the Horizon 1 innovation level. When companies operating within Horizon 2 & 3 come to test their products and services, these innovations are not immediately available to the public. Instead, collaboration occurs in preparation for five years and beyond. The nature of these innovations differs significantly from those already validated in the market and requires iterative testing. For example, Bikeep, a company categorized under Horizon 1, strategically installed smart bike parking stations throughout the city. This innovation was successfully integrated and validated through the Test City concept. Clevon in collaboration with DPD introduced robotic self-driving vehicles into the Ülemiste City environment, a pilot test program that helps to understand how such logistics solutions can be integrated into a green urban environment. Similarly, Grab2go installed automated store systems where people could buy things such as pharmaceuticals, and grocery items. According to the Three horizon model (Figure 3), the applying companies and their innovative solutions they want to test are classified and support system is enabled based on the horizon, test city concept and strategy (describing the testing process and its support system, Figure 4).

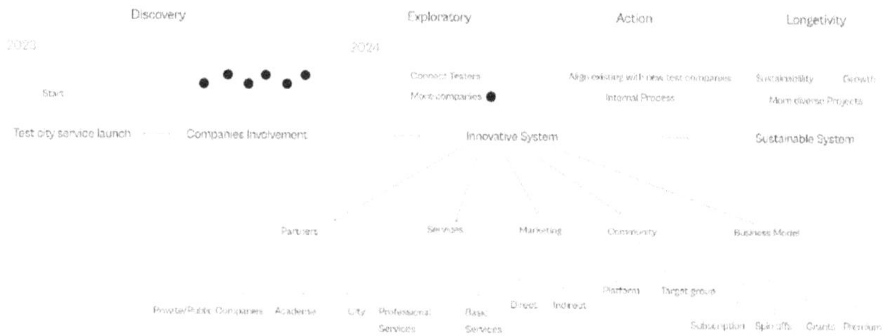

Figure 4: Ülemiste Test City strategy

The Three Horizon Model provides a framework for Smart Cities to systematically manage innovation across different stages of maturity, from well-established solutions (Horizon 1) to emerging and experimental technologies (Horizon 2 & 3). With the practical application of the Test City concept, Smart Cities can manage resources more effectively by ensuring that their infrastructure and services evolve gradually through experimentation and pre-validation.

Test City offers a semi-controlled environment where companies, particularly those in Horizon 2 & 3 can test their solutions. This provides a safety net for both the City and the innovators, allowing them to explore new technologies reducing risks associated with integrating untested solutions, such as operational failures, public dissatisfaction, financial losses, and large-scale implementation failure.

The Integration of Horizon 2 and 3 innovation through Test City allows cities to plan the future more effectively. As these solutions are validated and tested, they can be gradually incorporated into the city's long-term strategic planning, ensuring that the environment evolves sustainably. This approach helps cities to future-proof their infrastructure by adopting flexible and scalable solutions that can grow as new technologies emerge. This proactive approach helps cities meet the UN Sustainable Development Goals (SDGs) by ensuring innovations align with the long-term environmental objectives.

The adoption of these green urban innovations especially within the frameworks of Smart Cities, requires directive guidance to establish a working framework for evaluating and integrating new technologies. Such a framework is essential for the successful alignment of these innovations with the City's goals for sustainability, economic growth, and technological advancement. However, the implementation of these innovations poses several challenges and opportunities, particularly when applied through Smart City initiatives such as the Test City concept.

Companies that operate in Horizon 2 and 3 face significant risk due to the untested nature of their innovation (McKinsey & Company, 2018; Mittal, 2024). These innovations require extensive pilot testing, pre-commercialization efforts, and multiple iteration cycles before they can reach market maturity (Von Wirth et al., 2019). From the case study above, these innovations are quite resource-intensive and may not always achieve the desired outcome, leading to extra delays and scalability issues.

The integration of new technologies within established urban areas can be challenging. Cities often favor Horizon 1 innovations because they carry fewer risks, are easier to integrate, and require minimal adjustments to existing systems. However, the reliance on Horizon 1 solutions limits the transformative potential of Smart Cities, as they rely on incremental improvement rather than disruptive changes (McKinsey & Company, 2018).

The success of Horizon 2 and 3 innovation relies heavily on collaboration between multiple stakeholders including Startups, government entities, established businesses, and everyday citizens (Ricardo et al., 2023). This can prove difficult to manage priorities, expectations, and risk among all parties involved which could create delays and potential conflicts in project executions.

Horizon 3 innovations, being at the early stage, are often unfamiliar to the public and may face challenges related to adoption and acceptance (McKinsey &

Company, 2018). Ensuring that citizens are comfortable with and accepting new technologies is a key challenge that was observed in the use cases, and public resistance can hinder the broader deployment of the innovations (Kohtamäki, et al., 2020).

The Test City concept employed by Ülemiste City exposes opportunities for both companies and Smart Cities to exploit (e-Estonia, 2023). It provides an ideal platform for companies at different stages of development to test and refine their innovation in a real-world environment (Büch & Esch, 2023). This allows companies, particularly those in Horizon 2 and 3 to gather valuable feedback, refine their solutions, and ensure they are market-ready. In the examples Bikeep's Horizon 1 innovation was able to rapidly achieve validation through the Test City service, demonstrating the potential for other companies to achieve similar success through effective testing and iteration

The collaboration between Smart Cities such as Ülemiste City and companies in Horizon 2 and 3 presents opportunities for long-term partnerships that drive urban innovation. By providing access to real-world infrastructure and a collaborative ecosystem, The Test City enables Startups, established businesses, government officials, and citizens to work together on ambitious projects that contribute to sustainable urban development (Ricardo et al., 2023). Clevon's collaboration with DPD for autonomous logistics solutions is an example of how these partnerships can create new opportunities for growth and innovation.

5. Conclusion

The application of the horizon models in Smart Cities serves as an important component in the strategic advancement of the urban environment. These horizon models extend beyond the mere creation of value by addressing immediate societal challenges but go further to prepare Smart Cities for future solutions. Through the integration of concepts such as Test City, there is a need for a collaborative effort from diverse stakeholders where these horizon innovations can be incorporated effectively into the ecosystem.

It is essential to recognize that each of the three horizons holds equal importance in the overall success and progress of Smart Cities. The horizons models should be appreciated as they hold unique attributes in addressing the present and future urban challenges. It is also notable that most innovations that come into Smart Cities can start from Horizon 3 and develop into a Horizon 1 innovation which creates more basis to further understand the evolution process of innovation across the three horizons in a Smart City context.

Once innovations are validated in the Test City environment, they hold significant potential for scaling and replication in other urban contexts. The successful implementation of these innovations can set a precedent for other cities looking to adopt similar technologies. This can help Cities create solutions that address local challenges and have broader applicability across different urban environments globally.

References

Bibri, S. E., & Krogstie, J. (2019). Generating a vision for smart sustainable cities of the future: A scholarly backcasting approach. *European Journal of Futures Research, 7*(5). https://doi.org/10.1186/s40309-019-0157-0

Birks, M., & Mills, J. (2019). *Grounded theory: A practical guide* (2nd ed.). SAGE Publications. https://books.google.ee/books?hl=en&lr=&id=YsGICwAAQBAJ

Blank, S. (2019). McKinsey's three horizons model defined innovation for years: Here's why it no longer applies. *Harvard Business Review*. https://hbr.org/2019/02/mckinseys-three-horizons-model-defined-innovation-for-years-heres-why-it-no-longer-applies

Bloem, V., & Salimi, N. (2022). Role of knowledge management processes within different stages of technological innovation: evidence from biotechnology SMEs. *Knowledge Management Research & Practice, 21*(4), 822–836. https://doi.org/10.1080/14778238.2022.2064352

Büch, D., & Esch, M. (2023). CiTe: A testbed for smart city applications and architectures. In *2023 IEEE International Conference on Omni-layer Intelligent Systems (COINS)*, pp. 1–6. https://doi.org/10.1109/COINS57856.2023.10189229

e-Estonia. (2023). Ülemiste City launched Test City – a unique testing environment for new technologies in the Nordics. *e-Estonia*. https://e-estonia.com/ulemiste-city-introduced-test-city-a-unique-testing-environment-for-new-technologies-in-the-nordics/

Gupta, A., Panagiotopoulos, P., & Bowen, F. (2023). Developing capabilities in smart city ecosystems: A multi-level approach. *Organization Studies, 44*(10), 1703–1724. https://doi.org/10.1177/01708406231164114

Kohtamäki, M., Parida, V., Patel, P. C., & Gebauer, H. (2020). The relationship between digitalization and servitization: The role of servitization in capturing the financial potential of digitalization. *Technological Forecasting and Social Change, 151*, 119804. https://doi.org/10.1016/j.techfore.2019.119804

Lara, A. P., Moreira Da Costa, E., Zilinscki Furlani, T., & Yigitcanlar, T. (2016). Smartness that matters: Towards a comprehensive and human-centered characterization of smart cities. *Journal of Open Innovation: Technology, Market, and Complexity, 2*(2), 1–13. https://doi.org/10.1186/s40852-016-0034-z

Linde, L., Sjödin, D., Parida, V., & Wincent, J. (2021). Dynamic capabilities for ecosystem orchestration: A capability-based framework for smart city innovation initiatives. *Technological Forecasting and Social Change, 166*, 120614. https://doi.org/10.1016/j.techfore.2021.120614

Marchesani, F., Masciarelli, F., & Bikfalvi, A. (2023). Smart city as a hub for talent and innovative companies: Exploring the (dis)advantages of digital technology implementation in cities. *Technological Forecasting and Social Change, 193*, 122636. https://doi.org/10.1016/j.techfore.2023.122636

Markopoulus, E., Aggarawal, V., & Vanharanta, H. (2020). Democratization of intrapreneurship and corporate entrepreneurship within the McKinsey's three horizons innovation space in human systems engineering and design II, http://dx.doi.org/10.1007/978-3-030-27928-8_150

McKinsey & Company. (2018). Smart cities: Digital solutions for a more livable future. Retrieved from https://www.mckinsey.com/business-functions/sustainability/our-insights/smart-cities-digital-solutions-for-a-more-livable-future

Mittal, S. (2024). Strategic foresight in action: Leveraging McKinsey's 3 horizon model for balanced financial and strategic planning. *International Journal of Science and Research (IJSR), 13*(4). https://dx.doi.org/10.21275/SR24401010207

Noori, N., de Jong, M., Janssen, M., Schraven, D., & Hoppe, T. (2020). Input-output modeling for smart city development. *Journal of Urban Technology, 28*(1–2), 71–92. https://doi.org/10.1080/10630732.2020.1794728

Popescu, A. I. (2020). Long-term city innovation trajectories and quality of urban life. *Sustainability, 12*(24), 10587. https://doi.org/10.3390/su122410587

Ricardo, A. J., Vallejo, M. A., & Aedo, J. E. (2023). Co-creating products and services for smart cities. In *2023 IEEE Colombian Conference on Communications and Computing (COLCOM)*, Bogota, Colombia, pp. 1–5. https://doi.org/10.1109/COLCOM59909.2023.10334247

Svítek, M., Dostál, R., Kozhevnikov, S., & Janča, T. (2020). Smart city 5.0 testbed in Prague. In *2020 Smart City Symposium Prague (SCSP)*, Prague, Czech Republic, pp. 1–6. https://doi.org/10.1109/SCSP49987.2020.9133997

United Nations. (2024). *The sustainable development goals report 2024: Advance unedited version.* https://unstats.un.org/sdgs/files/report/2024/SG-SDG-Progress-Report-2024-advanced-unedited-version.pdf

Von Wirth, T., Fuenfschilling, L., Frantzeskaki, N., & Coenen, L. (2019). Impacts of urban living labs on sustainability transitions: Mechanisms and strategies for systemic change through experimentation. *European Planning Studies, 27*(2), 229–257. https://doi.org/10.1080/09654313.2018.1504895

Woetzel, L., & Remes, J. (2018). *Is your company ready for the rise of smart cities?* McKinsey & Company. https://www.mckinsey.com/capabilities/operations/our-insights/smarter-cities-are-resilient-cities

Vjollca Ahmedi and Arta Morina

The Impact of Personal and Professional Factors on Teachers' Perceptions of Student Assessment: An Empirical Analysis

1. Introduction

In the educational context of Kosovo, an important transformation in the student assessment methodology is underway. This change reflects the transition from a traditional approach, which focused on testing content knowledge and using a limited number of instruments to measure how well the student has remembered facts, to a more contemporary competency-based assessment approach. This new approach focuses on assessing different aspects of students' development, including their skills, attitudes and values, and not just the knowledge gained from learning (Saeed, Tahir, & Latif, 2018).

In teaching, the assessment is complex and requires the teacher to consider not only the acquisition of knowledge by the students, but also the overall development of their competencies. This makes assessment a delicate process, which can affect students' emotions and their willingness to learn (Tosuncuoglu, 2018) Furthermore, assessment should provide valuable information on students' awareness, understanding and attitudes towards learning, and help plan and improve the learning process (Pllana-Breznica, 2016).

A key aspect of this change is the impact of teachers' perceptions on fostering a culture of student assessment and monitoring. The assessment should contribute to raising student scores and help tailor teaching methods to meet their needs (Saeed, Tahir, & Latif, 2018). In this context, the use of different assessment methods – such as worksheets, quizzes, homework and tests, as well as evaluation of progress and efforts – is essential to ensure a fair and comprehensive assessment of students (Woolfolk, 2011; Musai, 2003).

This change in approach aims to create a learning environment more focused on developing the full potential of students, integrating a wider palette of assessment methods that reflect the reality and day-to-day needs of the educational process.

2. Literature Review and Development Hypothesis

Obtaining information about student learning is essential for effective teaching. As noted by Udofia and Michael, assessment helps the teacher to modify teaching methods to meet the individual needs of students, making it an important process for all participants in education (Udofia, & Michael, 2017). Bani-Hamad et al. describe assessment as a process used to gather information about students' performance in assessment tasks and to determine whether the intended learning outcomes have been achieved (Bani-Hamad, Elmetwaly, & Hassan, 2022).

In a broader context, Pinkus (2009) quoted in Cheema et al. (2022) emphasize that assessments are the cornerstone of any education system, as they measure whether learning objectives have been achieved and collect feedback to compare student performance (Cheema, Siddiqui, & Massod, 2022). Formative assessment, according to (Ahmed, 2019), helps to identify students' level of knowledge and promotes their learning. Oli and Olkaba (2020) consider assessment as a key component in the teaching process, providing teachers with important information for classroom decision-making and for understanding the ideas built by students (Oli & Olkaba, 2020).

According to Linn and Gronlund (2005), cited in Gemechu (2022), assessment is a systematic process that begins with the identification of learning goals and ends with a judgment about the progress of these goals (Gemechu, 2022). This process is essential for effective teaching and helps to improve educational and learning practices. Students can be assessed in different ways. There are a variety of assessment techniques which enable teachers to carry out their assessment in different forms, always adapting to the age of the students.

1.2. Impact of Teachers' Perceptions on Students' Assessment

While it is important to know how teachers implemented assessment activities in the classroom, it is equally important to understand the rationale and perceptions of teachers who used assessment strategies (Yao, 2015). As Greenstein (2010) and Stiggins (2010) suggested, quoted in Yao, teachers need to develop a solid understanding of classroom assessment so that they can develop a balanced approach to assessment for learning and assessment of learning (Yao, 2015).

It is believed that the effectiveness of assessment is influenced by many factors, such as: lack of time, storage spaces, knowledge of assessment techniques, large number of students, workload for teachers, etc. However, according to Okyere and Larbi, the ineffectiveness of classroom assessment goes beyond these to include the kind of perception teachers have of classroom assessment. The use of assessment by teachers in the classroom is believed to be heavily influenced by their perception. Teachers who see assessment as a tool to improve student performance are likely to use it quite often in the classroom (Okyere & Larbi, 2019). So, the way students are assessed depends very much on the perception that the teachers have. Teachers should develop classroom assessment that aligns with the practices recommended by educational assessment experts. Unfortunately, the findings from classroom assessment practice studies have consistently expressed a concern about the appropriateness of teacher assessment practices. These studies have shown that there are some contradictions between the practices of teachers and the recommendations of evaluation experts related to evaluation issues in the classroom. This lack of agreement between teacher practices and expert suggestions has been attributed to teachers' knowledge and attitudes about assessment (Volante & Fazio, 2007).

According to Susuwele-Banda, teachers' perceptions of classroom assessment had an impact on their classroom assessment practices. There has been very little effort to understand how students were learning, for example, one teacher said that it is not possible to assess students on a daily basis while they are learning mathematics (Susuwele-Banda, 2005). In a study conducted by Chester and Quitler (1998), as quoted in Susuwele-Banda, to investigate teachers' perception of classroom assessment, standardized testing, and alternative methods, the conclusion drawn was that teachers' classroom practices were influenced by their perception. They found that teachers who often used the standardized test were those who paid less attention to classroom assessment. Such teachers were less likely to see the value of assessment for classroom use. Among their recommendations was a focus on in-house training to enable teachers to see the value of assessment methods instead of 'how' to rate students for points (Susuwele-Banda, 2005).

A study conducted by Green (1992), as quoted in Susuwele-Banda, on pre-service teachers with instrument training found that the first 30 teachers tended to believe that standardized tests addressed important educational outcomes and believed that classroom tests are less useful. In the same study, service teachers believed that standardized tests are important, but not to the degree that pre-service teachers did (Susuwele-Banda, 2005).

According to Keller (1979), as quoted in Alkharusi, Kazem & Al-Musawai, theoretically, levels of knowledge improve when learned materials are seen as useful and appropriate to one's needs and the individual perceives himself as adept at performing relevant tasks (Alkharusi, Kazem, & Al-Musawai, 2011). Therefore, teachers will apply the assessment based on their individual perception of the assessment. Research on teacher attitudes and self-perception of skills in relation to educational measurement has shown that the perceived usefulness and importance of educational measurement correlates positively with perceived ability in assessment (Alkharusi, 2009). Findings from studies about attitudes and perception suggest that teachers who judge their skills in performing educational measurement tasks as low are likely to develop negative attitudes toward educational measurement, which, in turn, can translate into either poor assessment practices or avoiding the use of contemporary assessment techniques (Alkharusi, Kazem, & Al-Musawai, 2011).

Based on many studies, as noted, it was found that the perceptions and attitudes of teachers play an important role in the assessment of students. Therefore, it would be good for teachers to draw from the guidance of education experts, specifically evaluation experts, since experts make their recommendations based on scientific expertise.

1.3. Research Hypotheses

Alternative Hypothesis (HA): Teachers have different perceptions regarding students' assessment.

Auxiliary hypotheses:

Hypothesis 1.1: There are differences in the perception of teachers of different ages to encourage students to improve their assignments.
Hypothesis 1.2: There are statistically significant differences between female and male teachers for discussing test questions with each student.
Hypothesis 1.3: There are differences in teachers' perception based on their age for identifying students' strengths.
Hypothesis 1.4: There are differences in the perception of teachers based on the number of assessment trainings, regarding the commitment of teachers to improving students' weaknesses.
Hypothesis 1.5: There are differences in the perception of teachers based on their gender to inform students about the evaluation criteria.

3. Research Methodology

3.1. Sample Selection and Data Collection

In this study, a quantitative approach was used to analyze the perceptions of primary school teachers in Kosovo on student assessment.

The study was conducted with teachers in primary schools in Kosovo. The study population consists of all primary school teachers, who in the school year 2022–2023 were about 17,099 according to education statistics in Kosovo (MEST

& ASK, 2023). Considering that the number of teachers in primary schools cannot exceed 10,000, it was decided to select a sample of 370 teachers based on the tables of Cohen et al. (2007).

Table 1. Teacher demographics (N = 378)

Variable	Category	Frequency	Percentage (%)
Teachers' Residence	Village	52	13.8 %
	City	326	86.2 %
Teachers' Gender	Female	284	75.1 %
	Male	94	24.9 %
Number of trainings/workshops on assessment	No training	37	9.8 %
	Up to 3 trainings	136	36.0 %
	4–6 trainings	85	22.5 %
	7–9 trainings	56	14.8 %
	More than 9 trainings	64	16.9 %

3.2. Measurement Tools

For measuring variables, questionnaires designed to measure teachers' different feelings and perceptions were used. The questionnaires contain Likert scales to measure the frequency of different trainings and experiences, on the use and efficiency of evaluation methods. The instrument for teachers is a questionnaire of the Likert scale, which was used to identify the perception of primary school teachers for the assessment of students. This instrument has been found ready and is standardized. The questionnaire was used by Ron Jonathan Pat-El and his collaborators in the paper Validation of Assessment for Learning Questionnaires for teachers and students (Pat-El et al., 2013).

3.3. Data Analysis

The data was analyzed using SPSS software. The questionnaires were coded with the five-level Likert scale for measuring perceptions (5. Totally agree, 4. Agree, 3. Neither agree nor disagree, 2. Disagree, 1. Totally disagree).

In order to test the internal stability of the instrument, the Alpha Cronbach coefficient was used, where values higher than 0.7 are considered reliable. The Alpha Cronbach coefficient for the instrument was 0.913, indicating a very high reliability.

3.4. The Reliability of the Instrument

Based on empirical results, it was found that the mean of the instrument is M = 130.22 and the standard deviation, DS = 8.502. The overall average is 4.65, the mean variance is 0.310, the mean interval is 0.516, and the variance interval is 0.449, the total mean of the correlations between the queries (inter-item correlations) is 0.285, the minimal correlation is 0.022, while the maximum correlation is 0.536.

From the results, it is noted that the question – total correlations, are between 0.365 and 0.600.

The total Alpha coefficient of instrument reliability, calculated in the table, is 0.913, while the predicted value is 0.918. This is a very high value and shows that the instrument used is very reliable and can be used for research. The reliability value of the queries ranges from 0.908 to 0.914, which are values approximating the value of Cronbach's Alpha coefficient, 0.913.

The Hotelling's T^2 test, which tests the equality of question averages, is calculated as $p = 0.000$. This result shows that there is a statistically significant difference at least between the two averages of the questions.

Table 2: Scale statistics

Scale Statistics			
Mean	Variance	Std. Deviation	N of Items
130.22	72.276	8.502	28

Table 3: The reliability of the instrument

Reliability Statistics		
Cronbach's Alpha	Cronbach's Alpha Based on Standardized Items	N of Items
913.	918.	28

Table 4: ANOVA test

ANOVA						
		Sum of Squares	df	Mean Square	F	Sig
Between People		973.139	377	2.581		
Within People	Between Items	145.569	27	5.391	23.920	000.
	Residual	2294.324	10179	225.		
	Total	2439.893	10206	239.		
Total		3413.032	10583	323.		
Grand Mean = 4.65						

Table 5: Hotelling's test T2

Hotelling's T-Squared Test				
Hotelling's T-Squared	F	df1	df2	Sig
319.623	11.021	27	351	000.

4. Hypothesis Testing

In this part, the hypotheses will be tested, from which the results can be deduced if the alternative hypothesis is supported.

Alternative Hypothesis (HA): Teachers have different perceptions regarding students' assessment.

4.1. Hypothesis 1.1

Alternative Hypothesis (HA): There are differences in the perception of teachers of different ages, related to encouraging students to improve their assignments.

The testing of this hypothesis was carried out through the parametric test ANOVA One Way, through which the averages of the results of teachers of different ages were compared.

Table 6: Average teachers' results, based on age

Descriptives								
	N	Mean	Std. Deviation	Std. Error	95 % Confidence Interval for Mean		Minimum	Maximum
					Lower Bound	Upper Bound		
Up to 30	35	4.60	651.	110.	4.38	4.82	3	5
31–40	110	4.86	370.	035.	4.79	4.93	3	5
41–50	118	4.81	439.	040.	4.73	4.89	3	5
51–60	85	4.73	447.	048.	4.63	4.83	4	5
Over 60	30	4.70	535.	098.	4.50	4.90	3	5
Total	378	4.78	459.	024.	4.73	4.82	3	5

Table 7: Variance homogeneity test, for the hypothesis: There are differences in the perception of teachers of different ages, related to encouraging students to improve their tasks

Tests of Homogeneity of Variances					
		Levene Statistic	df1	df2	Sig.
I encourage students to think about how they can improve their skills.	Based on Mean	10.481	4	373	000.
	Based on Median	2.891	4	373	022.
	Based on Median and with adjusted df	2.891	4	325.148	022.
	Based on trimmed mean	9.543	4	373	000.

Table 8: ANOVA hypothesis test: There are differences in the perception of teachers of different ages, related to encouraging students to improve their assignments

ANOVA					
I encourage students to think about how they can improve their skills.					
	Sum of Squares	df	Mean Square	F	Sig.
Between Groups	2.385	4	596.	2.891	022.
Within Groups	76.948	373	206.		
Total	79.333	377			

4.2. Hypothesis 1.2

Alternative Hypothesis (HA): There are statistically significant differences based on the gender of the teachers, related to the discussion with each student about the test answers

Table 9: Descriptive hypothesis results: There are statistically significant differences based on the gender of the teachers, related to the discussion with each student on the test answers

Group Statistics					
	Gender	N	Mean	Std. Deviation	Std. Error Mean
After checking the results of a test, I discuss the answers given with each student.	Female	284	4.65	547.	032.
	Male	94	4.73	490.	051.

Table 10: Homogeneity test and hypothesis test: There are statistically significant differences based on the gender of the teachers, related to the discussion with each student of the test answers

Independent Samples Test									
After checking the results of a test, I discuss the answers given with each student.	Levene's Test for Equality of Variances		t-test for Equality of Means						
	F	Sig.	t	df	Sig. (2-tailed)	Mean Difference	Std. Error Difference	95 % Confidence Interval of the Difference	
								Lower	Upper
Equal variances assumed	4.851	028.	-1.356	376	176.	-.086	064.	-.211	039.
Equal variances not assumed			-1.434	175.747	153.	-.086	060.	-.205	032.

4.3. Hypothesis 1.3

Alternative Hypothesis (HA): There are differences in teachers' perception based on their age for identifying student strengths related to the learning process

Table 11: Descriptive hypothesis results: There are differences in teachers' perception based on their age for identifying students' strengths related to the learning process

Descriptives						
	N	Mean	Std. Deviation	Std. Error	95 % Confidence Interval for Mean	
					Lower Bound	Upper Bound
Up to 30	35	4.63	598.	101.	4.42	4.83
31–40	110	4.68	523.	050.	4.58	4.78
41–50	118	4.74	479.	044.	4.65	4.82
51–60	85	4.66	524.	057.	4.55	4.77
Over 60	30	4.40	563.	103.	4.19	4.61
Total	378	4.67	525.	027.	4.61	4.72

Table 12: Hypothesis homogeneity test: There are differences in the perception of teachers based on their age to identify the students' strengths, related to the learning process

Tests of Homogeneity of Variances					
		Levene Statistic	df1	df2	Sig.
Identify students' strengths related to the learning process	Based on Mean	2.385	4	373	051.
	Based on Median	1.088	4	373	362.
	Based on Median and with adjusted df	1.088	4	366.654	362.
	Based on trimmed mean	2.276	4	373	061.

Table 13: ANOVA hypothesis test: There are differences in the perception of teachers based on their age to identify students' strengths, related to the learning process

ANOVA					
	Identify students' strengths related to the learning process				
	Sum of Squares	df	Mean Square	F	Sig.
Between Groups	2.803	4	701.	2.583	037.
Within Groups	101.197	373	271.		
Total	104.000	377			

4.4. Hypothesis 1.4

Alternative Hypothesis (HA): There are differences in the perception of teachers based on the number of trainings or workshops attended for assessment, regarding the commitment of teachers to improving students' weaknesses

Table 14: Descriptive results for hypothesis: There are differences in teachers' perception based on the number of assessment trainings, related to teachers' commitment to improving students' weaknesses

Descriptives						
	N	Mean	Std. Deviation	Std. Error	95 % Confidence Interval for Mean	
					Lower Bound	Upper Bound
I have not participated in any training	37	4.41	644.	106.	4.19	4.62
I have participated in up to 3 trainings or workshops for assessment	136	4.64	540.	046.	4.55	4.73
I have participated in up to 4–6 trainings or workshops for assessment	85	4.64	553.	060.	4.52	4.75
I have participated in up to 7–9 trainings or workshops for assessment	56	4.57	568.	076.	4.42	4.72
More than 9 trainings or workshops	64	4.77	427.	053.	4.66	4.87
Total	378	4.63	546.	028.	4.57	4.68

Table 15: Homogeneity of variances for the hypothesis: There are differences in teachers' perception based on the number of assessment trainings, related to teachers' commitment to improving weaknesses

Tests of Homogeneity of Variances					
		Levene Statistic	df1	df2	Sig.
Together with the students, I explore ways to improve their weak points.	Based on Mean	6.078	4	373	000.
	Based on Median	2.553	4	373	039.
	Based on Median and with adjusted df	2.553	4	362.892	039.
	Based on trimmed mean	5.347	4	373	000.

Table 16: ANOVA test for hypothesis: There are differences in teachers' perception based on the number of assessment trainings, related to teachers' commitment to improving weaknesses

ANOVA					
Together with the students, I explore ways to improve their weak points.					
	Sum of Squares	df	Mean Square	F	Sig.
Between Groups	3.247	4	812.	2.774	027.
Within Groups	109.157	373	293.		
Total	112.405	377			

4.5. Hypothesis 1.5

Alternative Hypothesis (HA): There are differences in teachers' perceptions based on their gender, related to informing their students about assessment criteria.

Table 17: Descriptive hypothesis results: There are differences in teachers' perceptions based on their gender, related to informing their students about assessment criteria

Group Statistics					
	Gender	N	Mean	Std. Deviation	Std. Error Mean
My students know what the assessment criteria are for their work.	Female	284	4.49	659.	039.
	Male	94	4.69	529.	055.

Table 18: Homogeneity test and hypothesis test: There are differences in the perception of teachers based on their gender, related to informing their students about the evaluation criteria

Independent Samples Test									
My students know what the assessment criteria are for their work.	Levene's Test for Equality of Variances		t-test for Equality of Means						
	F	Sig.	t	df	Sig. (2-tailed)	Mean Difference	Std. Error Difference	95 % Confidence Interval of the Difference	
								Lower	Upper
Equal variances assumed	12.158	001.	−2.697	376	007.	−0.202	075.	−0.349	−0.055
Equal variances not assumed			−3.009	196.022	003.	−0.202	067.	−0.334	−0.070

5. Conclusion

In summary, research results suggest that teachers with more training and experience in education have more positive perceptions on students' assessment practices. Moreover, perceptions are influenced by the geographic region, with notable differences between teachers in urban and rural areas. This part of the study summarizes the empirical results of primary school teachers' perceptions regarding student assessment. The results show that the vast majority of teachers (96.4 %) have a positive perception of their students' assessment, with a high average perception of M = 4.36. In addition, statistical analyzes have revealed that there are statistically significant differences in teachers' perceptions based on age, training, and gender. For example, teachers aged 31–40 encourage more students to improve their assignments, while those over the age of 60 have a lower perception to identify students' strengths. Also, teachers who have attended more than nine trainings for students' assessment are more engaged in improving students' weaknesses. As per gender, male teachers have a higher perception of their correctness in informing students about assessment criteria. The results support alternative hypotheses of the study, suggesting that there are significant differences in teachers' perceptions regarding student assessment.

Empirical results showed that, despite having a high perception, not all teachers perceive assessment equally. Some of them believe that they assess their students more accurately than their peers. Teachers should use clear criteria and be objective in assessing students. To assess their students correctly, teachers need to be well prepared for this, by participating in various trainings and workshops. This study shows the perception (self-reporting) of teachers and differences based on specific characteristics (gender, age, participation in training, etc.), for which efforts should be made to overcome these differences.

References

Ahmedi, V. (2019). Teachers' Attitudes and Practices towards Formative Assessment in Primary Schools. *Journal of Social Studies Education Research, 10*(3), 161–175.

Alkharusi, H. (2009). Correlates of Teacher Education Students' Academic Performance in an Educational Measurement Course. *International Journal of Learning, 16*, 1–15.

Alkharusi, H., Kazem, A. M., & Al-Musawai, A. (2011). Knowledge, Skills, and Attitudes of Preservice and Inservice Teachers in Educational Measurement. *Asia-Pacific Journal of Teacher Education, 39*(2), 113–123.

Amua-Sekyi, E. (2016). Assessment, Student Learning and Classroom Practice: A Review. *Journal of Education and Practice, 7*, 1–6.

Andrade, H., & Valtcheva, A. (2009). Promoting Learning and Achievement through Self-Assessment. *Theory Into Practice, 48*(1), 12–19.

Angelo, Th. A., & Cross, K. P. (1993). *Classroom Assessment Techniques: A Handbook for College Teachers* (2nd ed.). San Francisco: Jossey-Bass Publishers.

Bani-Hamad, I. M. H., Elmetwaly, A. A., & Hassan, J. (2022). Assessment of Jordanian Science Teachers Perceived Skill in Classroom Assessment. *Res Militaris, 12*(6), 1581–1589.

Black, P., & Wiliam, D. (1998). Assessment and Classroom Learning, Assessment in Education: Principles, Policy & Practice. *Assessment in Education, 5*(1), 7–74.

Brown, H. D., & Abeywickrama, P. (2019). *Language Assessment: Principles and Classroom Practices* (3rd ed.). New York: Pearson.

Capraro, R. M. (2012). Research Summary: Assessment. *Association for Middle Level Education*, 1–6.

Chappuis, J., Chappuis, S., & Stiggins, R. (2009). Formative Assessment and Assessment for Learning. In L. M. Pinkus (Ed.), *Meaningful Measurement: The Role of Assessments in Improving High School Education in the Twenty-First Century* (pp. 55–76). Washington, DC: Alliance for Excellent Education.

Cheema, S., Siddiqui, M., & Massod, S. (2022). Perceptions of Teachers about Assessment Practices at Primary Level in Private Schools of Lahore. *Global Educational Studies Review, VII*(II), 263–274.

Chin, P. (2016). Peer Assessment. *New Directions in the Teaching of Physical Sciences*, (3), 13–18.

Claire Selltiz et al. in Kothar. (2004). *Research Methodology: Methods and Teqniques.* New Delhi: New Age International.

Cohen, L., Lawrence, M., & Marrison K. (2007). *Research Methods in Education* (6th ed.) London and New York: Routledge/Falmer.

Creswell, J., & Plano, C. V. (2007). *Designing and Conducting Mixed Methods Research.* Thousand Oaks, CA: Sage.

Gemechu, D. T. (2022). Information and Knowledge Management. *An Assessment of the Impact of Instructors' Knowledge and Attitude Toward the Implementation of Continuous Assessment, 12*(3), 1–7.

Ministry of Education, Science, and Technology (MEST) & Agency of Statistics of Kosovo (ASK). (2023). Education statistics in Kosovo 2022–2023. Ministry of Education, Science, and Technology (MEST).

Musai, B. (2003). *Metodologji e Mësimdhënies.* Tiranë: Pegi.

Musai, B. (2014). *Metodologji e mësimdhënies: Arti dhe shkenca për të përgatitur nxënës të suksesshëm (botimi i dytë).* Tiranë: CDE.

Nasri, N. et al. (2010). Teachers' Perception on Alternative Assessment. *Procedia Social and Behavioral Sciences 7*(C), 37–42.

Okyere, M., & Larbi, E. (2019). Senior High School Mathematics Teachers' Perception and Use of Assessment in the Classroom. *African Journal of Educational Studies in Mathematics and Sciences, 15*(2), 43–54.

Oli, G., & Olkaba, T. T. (2020). Practices and Challenges of Continuous Assessment in Colleges of Teachers' Education in the West Oromia Region, Ethiopia. *Journal «ScienceRise: Pedagogical Education», nr. 36*, 4–15.

Pat-El, R. J., et al. (2013). Validation of Assessment for Learning Questionnaires for Teachers and Students. *British Journal of Educational Psychology, 83*, 98–113.

Pllana-Breznica, A. (2016). Vlerësimi në arsimin e mesëm të lartë-shkolla profesionale. *Buletini shkencor, Revista shkencore ndërkombëtare*, 113–120.

Popham, W. J. (2017). *Classroom Assessment: What Teachers Need to Know* (8th ed.). Boston: Pearson.

Price, J. K., Pierson, E., & Light, D. (2011). Using Classroom Assessment to Promote 21st Century Learning in Emerging Market Countries. *Global Learn*, 419–429.

Price, J., Pierson, E., & Light, D. (2011). Using Classroom Assessment to Promote 21st Century Learning in Emerging Market Countries. In S. Barton, J. Hedberg, & K. Suzuki (Eds.), *Proceedings of Global Learn Asia Pacific 2011 – Global Conference on Learning and Technology* (pp. 419–429). Melbourne, Australia: Association for the Advancement of Computing in Education (AACE).

Quilter, S. M., & Chester, C. (1998). Inservice Teachers' Perceptions of Educational Assessment. Paper presented at the Annual Meeting of the Mid-Western Educational Research Association, Chicago, IL, October 14–17, 1998.

Rennie, L. J., Goodrum, D., & Hackling, M. W. (2001). Science Teaching and Learning in Australian Schools: Results of a National Study. *Research in Science Education 31*, 455–498.

Saeed, M., Tahir, H., & Latif, I. (2018). Teachers' Perceptions about the Use of Classroom Assessment Techniques in Elementary and Secondary Schools. *Bulletin of Education and Research, 40*(1), 115–130.

Settiawana, D., & Hilmawan, R. (2015). Increasing Transparency in Assessment to Improve Students' Learning at Language Development Centre of UIN Suska Riau. *ICTTE FKIP UNS, vol 3*, 364–368.

Susuwele-Banda, W. J. (2005). *Classroom Assessment in Malawi: Teachers' Perceptions and Practices in Mathematics: A Dissertation Submitted to the Virginia Polytechnic Institute and State University*. Blacksburg, Virginia.

Topping, K. J. (2005). Trends in Peer Learning. *Educational Psychology, 25*(6), 631–645.

Topping, K. J. (2009). Peer Assessment. *Theory Into Practice, 48*(1), 20–27.

Topping, K. J. (2017). Peer Assessment: Learning by Judging and Discussing the Work of Other Learners. *Interdisciplinary Education and Psychology*, 1(1), 1–17.

Tosuncuoglu, I. (2018). Importance of Assessment in ELT. *Journal of Education and Training Studies, 6*(9), 163–167.

Udofia, N., & Michael, A. A. (2017). Impact of Classroom Assessment, Management and Control on the Academic Performance of Secondary School Students in Akwa Ibom State. *Journal of Education and Practice, 8*(18), 30–36.

Vitello, S., & Williamson, J. (2017). Internal versus External Assessment in Vocational Qualifications: A Commentary on the Government's Reforms in England. *London Review of Education, 15*(3), 536–548.

Volante, L., & Fazio, X. (2007). Exploring Teacher Candidates' Assessment Literacy: Implications for Teacher Education Reform and Professional Development. Canadian Journal of Education, 30(3), 749–770.

Woolfolk, A. (2011). *Psikologji Edukimi (botimi i njëmbëdhjetë)*. Tiranë: CDE.

Yao, Y. (2015). Teacher Perceptions of Classroom Assessment: A Focus Group Interview. *SRATE Journal, 24*, 51–58.

Yigzaw, A., & Bishaw, A. (2015). Primary School Teachers' Knowledge, Attitude and Perceived Practice of Continuous Assessment. *Ethiop. J. Educ. & Sc, 11*(1), 49–60.

Zhang, G., et al. (2011). Using the Context, Input, Process, and Product Evaluation Model (CIPP) as a Comprehensive Framework to Guide the Planning, Implementation, and Assessment of Service-learning Programs. *Journal of Higher Education Outreach and Engagement, 15*(4), 57–84.

Zimmerman, B., & Schunk, D. (2004). Self-regulating Intellectual Processes and Outcomes: A Social Cognitive Perspective. In D. Y. Dai & R. J. Sternberg (Eds.), Motivation, Emotion, and Cognition: Integrative Perspectives on Intellectual Functioning and Development (pp. 323–349). Mahwah, NJ: Lawrence Erlbaum Associates.

Rozafa Ferizi Shala and Violeta Buza

Professional Support for Educators through Training and Follow-Up of Changes in Practices of Working with Children of Ages Up to 3 Years Old

1. Introduction

It is becoming increasingly evident that early childhood education is the basis for overall child development. The first five years of a child's life are decisive for their growth and quality development (Schleicher, 2019), being described as a critical period for developing the foundations of thinking, behaving and emotional well-being of a child (Bakken et al., 2017). Despite global attempts, early childhood education continues to represent a challenge for undeveloped and developing countries, such as the Republic of Kosovo. Apart from the lack of approach, the quality of services provided for children in early childhood is very challenging, especially for the age group up to 3 years old. The longitudinal study by Bakken et al. (2017) concludes that quality programs in early childhood can improve children's academic performance, develop their social skills, and enhance their positive attitude towards school, compared to other children who attended regular education programs during early childhood. These data confirm the fact that a higher quality in children's early education and quality early intervention can create a better future for all children.

The meta-analysis carried out by Fukkink et al. (2017) on the quality of early childhood education considered from a scientific production, among main categories, apart from the organizational aspect, staff qualification, and infrastructure, defined the quality of direct interaction between educators and children, as well as the improvements of initial and continuous training systems and professional development of educators during their career (González-Alfaya, et al., 2024). It means that the way the professional development of educators takes place impacts how they can advance the practices of working with children and beyond.

The work of an educator is quite dynamic, and it always requires maximum engagement in interacting with children, preparing the environment, observation, working with parents, colleagues, etc. Based on a study carried out by Cole-Albäck (2020), the work of an educator goes beyond curriculum implementation;

she/he must interact with the child since interaction has a great impact on the development and experience the child is having. Another crucial component is that for the children to be ready to learn, they must initially feel comfortable, welcomed, and safe; only this way, children are ready to develop their potential (Cole-Albäck et al., 2024).

Findings from the study OECD also indicate that in-service training that includes early childhood education and care-specific content is associated with better staff-child interactions and better child development and learning outcomes, especially literacy skills, for all groups of children (Schleicher, 2019).

However, according to Schleicher (2019), the staff working in childcare centers have fewer opportunities for professional development than those working in pre-primary education. Also, the number of studies at a global level, including the ages of zero to 3, is more limited (OECD, 2018) compared to the ones for higher levels of education. Also, in Kosovo, lack of attention for ages 0–3 is more emphasized in terms of the approach towards professional development and the study aspect as well.

According to UNICEF (2022) in Kosovo, responsible childcare and a stimulating environment for children up to 3 years old at home are lacking, and in addition, the possibilities for early childhood education are low – compared to other countries in the region (p. 23). In Kosovo, only 15 % of children aged 3–4 attend an early education program (UNICEF, 2022), whereas, for children aged 0–2, inclusion remains very low, with a total of 3.9 % of children included in early childhood education institutions (MESTI, 2022; Demas et al., 2021). According to the Ministry of Education, Science, Technology and Innovation (MESTI, 2022), difficulties faced by early childhood education in Kosovo include inadequate distribution of preschool institutions in the country, low number of public preschool institutions, lack of sufficient infrastructure for children inclusion, lack of human resources to provide integrated services of well-being, health and education for overall children development (p. 32). In addition, based on the data reported regarding teacher inclusion in training according to MESTI (2022), the level of teacher inclusion in professional development has decreased constantly during the last years due to lack of financing, but also due to teacher licensing system not being implemented (MESTI, 2022).

As seen, Early Childhood Education is facing challenges in many aspects since there is a lack of services provided and a lack of preschool institutions in several cities in Kosovo. In some cities, the number of institutions is insufficient for the number of children, whereas in rural areas the services are not provided at all for children of age 0–3, resulting in an unequal approach to education. In cases where there are early childhood education institutions, improving the quality of services provided by these institutions remains a challenge. The need to develop this education stage is urgent, both in terms of the level of inclusion of children 0–3 and the quality of services provided for children in early childhood. Research indicates that quality early education has a compensating effect for the development gap in children who are part of vulnerable social groups (UNICEF, 2022); therefore, the faster the interventions and the higher their quality for the age group 0–3, the greater the possibilities for the development of child potential and long-term benefits.

Educators' professional development activities can be provided in several ways, such as workshops, national and local conferences, different courses, coaching, training, community of practice, etc. (Sheridan et al., 2009; Desimone, 2011). Moreover, "best practices in professional development are integrated into early childhood intervention studies and methods for enhancing outcomes through professional support are implemented and documented" (Sheridan et al., 2009: 397) Therefore, it is crucial to provide scientific evidence to improve professional support practices, which directly affect in increasing the quality in early childhood education.

In the study carried out by Bicaj and Buza (2020) with 113 educators working in both the public and private sectors in Kosovo, results show that training has a significant impact on increasing educators' perceived self-esteem and self-evaluated performance when working with children. In addition, in the study report drafted by Gjelaj (2023) on the importance of investment in early childhood education in Kosovo, over 90 % of educators included in this program have evaluated the training as a suitable form for their professional education and advancement of working practices to be applied with children of ages 0–3 and 3–6.

Taking this into consideration, the training program *"Organization of educational work with children aged 0–3 in preschool institutions"* has been drafted; the training program aims to advance the current working practice with children up to 3 years old and offer new perspectives on how to address work with children of this age group.

This study aims to provide initial scientific evidence on the professional support this training program offers for the participants, considering that the number of trainings for early childhood education is very limited, specifically the work with children of age 0–3.

2. Methodology

The study is based on a quantitative and quality approach (Fraenkel et al., 2012), using an initial questionnaire before the start of the training to analyze the expectations of participants from the training and to check for their availability. Whereas to observe whether the training has met participants' expectations, the questionnaire with the same indicators was distributed once more at the end of the training. On the other hand, the content analysis based on portfolio review and notes taken during discussions and reflections of educators (Matthews & Ross, 2010) were used to see whether educators participating in the training had managed to change their practices working directly with children.

The study is based on the following research questions:

Does the training program enhance educators' knowledge on the topics covered during the training?

What were the changes implemented by educators in their direct work with children after a two-day training period?

3. Training Program Structure

The training program *"Organization of educational work with children of 0–3 in preschool institutions"* was designed based on the characteristics of the Participatory Adult Learning Strategy (Dunst & Trivette, 2009) so that the work with the in-service educators is aligned with their predisposition to implement the knowledge received in practice and to advance their current practice. The State Council on Teacher Licensing approved the program pursuant to decision No.106/2024 from 26.02.2024 to 26.02.2025 (MESTI, 2024). The training program is basic and focuses on working with children up to 3 years old; it is a 3-day program divided into 10 sessions, as presented in Table 1.

Table 1: Training program design

Training Day	Session
Training Day One	SESSION 1: Understanding the work with children of age up to 3 years old – interaction educators–children SESSION 2: The adjustment and transition period for the child from a family to a preschool institution – the role and duties of educators and parents SESSION 3: Arranging and adapting the environment SESSION 4: Adapting the environment and enriching it with materials

Table 1: Continued

Training Day	Session
Training Day Two	SESSION 5: Organizing daily routines SESSION 6: Observation and planning activities SESSION 7: Toys, playing and activities for children up to 1 year old SESSION 8: Toys, playing and activities for children 1 to 3 years old
Practical implementation in early education institutions	Participants will build a portfolio, presenting through reflections, images, and other evidence the changes they have implemented in advancing their work based on the training attended
Training Day Three Follow-up day training	SESSION 9: Reflection on the work done – sharing experiences SESSION 10: Portfolio presentation, discussion and further steps

Training sessions were drafted to align with adult learning methods (Figure 1) as per Dunst and Trivette (2009). Trainers also considered other issues in implementing professional development, such as time between meetings and time needed for practice, internet access – meetings online consultation and supervision to ensure changes are implemented (Dickinson & Brady, 2006).

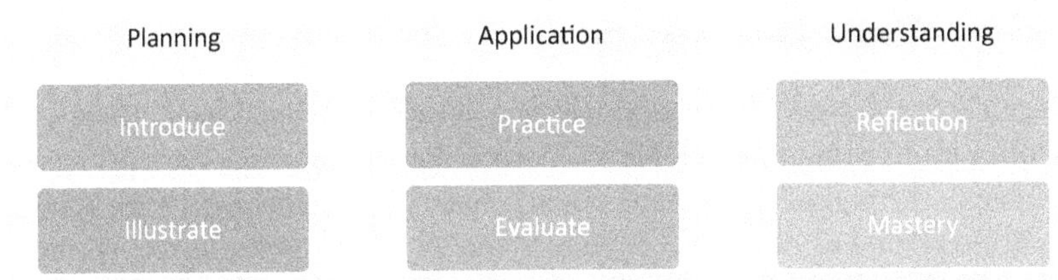

Figure 1: Characteristics of the adult learning methods based on Dunst and Trivette
Source: Dunst and Trivette (2009)

With every session offering possibilities for the participants to disclose their previous knowledge, attain new information, reflect on current practices, and, based on that practice, build a more quality practice, offering strategies that could facilitate and increase the quality of services provided but also research on how a certain practice could be tailored to their working practice. From the beginning of the training process, the participants were given the ethical criteria and considerations, and all agreed with them.

4. Research Instruments

The questionnaire consists of two parts. The first part contains the demographic questions, and the second includes ten questions covering all training sessions. Two open questions were included at the end of the second part of the questionnaire, aiming to understand which was the most necessary session for them and their recommendations for future trainings. A scale of 1 strongly disagree to 5 strongly agree was used to determine pre- and post-test mean scores. The significance level was set to the value of 0.05. The quantitative data analysis was made by SPSS version 23.

After the first two days of training, a period of more than two weeks was allocated to enable participants to implement newly received knowledge in their daily work, documenting them in their portfolio at the same time. For content analysis purposes, participants were asked to send their portfolios by email. In addition, another protocol was built for portfolio evaluation (Cambridge et al., 2001). In the follow-up day training, the participants presented their portfolios, discussed and reflected together on their work, notes were taken during the discussions and comments on each other's work.

5. Data Collection and Analysis

The research involved 23 educators working in early childhood institutions with children up to 3 years old (Table 2). As per the demographic data presented in Table 2, the highest percentage of participants (65 %) belong to age groups 31–40 (30 %) and 41–50 (35 %). 91 % of them hold a bachelor's degree. Whereas regarding their work experience, around 52 % of participants have up to three years of work experience. If we compare these data to the age of respondents, we notice that they entered the job market several years after completing their studies. Only 40 % of participants attended training programs dedicated to age groups up to 3 years old. The most frequent trainings included nutrition in early childhood and the childcare and well-being program.

Table 2: Demographic characteristics of the sample (N = 23)

Demographic		Frequency	Valid %
Age	up to 25 years	2	8.7
	26–30 years	3	13.0
	31–40 years	7	30.4
	41–50 years	8	34.8
	up to 51 years	3	13.0
Qualification	Higher secondary education	0	0
	Bachelor level	21	91.3
	Master level	2	8.7
Work experience	Up to 3 years	12	52.2
	4–10 years	7	30.4
	11–15 years	3	13.0
	16–20 years	1	4.3
Training for working with children up to 3 years old	Yes	9	39.1
	No	14	60.9

In order to comprehend if the training had an effect, measurements were taken before and after the training. The questionnaire distributed at the beginning of the training aimed to understand how the participants were knowledgeable about each training session. The questionnaire distributed at the end of the training aimed to understand if this level of knowledge had increased. As to measuring the reliability of the questionnaire, the Cronbach Alpha analysis was performed first (Table 3), which resulted in excellent internal consistency for both questionnaires.

Table 3: Cronbach's Alpha for pre- and post-training questionnaires

	Item	*Cronbach's Alpha*
Pre-training questionnaire	10	0.921
Post-training questionnaire	10	0.912

To evaluate the impact of the intervention measured by a questionnaire, paired samples t-tests were conducted (Table 4) for each item on the questionnaire to compare pre-training and post-training results. In evaluating the overall impact of the intervention, Cohen's d was calculated for the total scores of the questionnaire (Table 5).

Table 4: Paired sample T-test for each item of the questionnaire

		Pre-mean	SD	Post mean	SD	df	t	p
1	Interaction	4.57	0.507	4.83	0.388	22	−2.787	0.011
2	Transition characteristics from family to ECE	4.39	0.656	4.87	0.344	22	−3.140	0.005
3	Characteristics of the learning environment	4.30	0.703	4.74	0.619	22	−2.472	0.022
4	Organization of daily routine	4.43	0.662	4.87	0.344	22	−4.114	0.000
5	Organization of play according to age groups	4.39	0.656	4.78	0.422	22	−3.219	0.004
6	Observation of children	4.48	0.593	4.83	0.388	22	−2.577	0.017
7	Creating materials for play and exploration	4.43	0.590	4.83	0.491	22	−3.219	0.004
8	Development of ideas for creating new games and toys	4.48	0.593	4.78	0.518	22	−2.612	0.016
9	Evaluating a child's achievements	4.13	0.869	4.78	0.422	22	−3.761	0.001
10	Adaptation of the child in ECE	4.04	0.767	4.74	0.541	22	−4.362	0.000

Table 5: Measuring the effect size of the training

	Items	Mean	SD	Cohen's d
Pre-training questionnaire	10	4.364	0.164398	3.6422
Post-training questionnaire	10	4.805	0.0479	

The results of a paired samples t-test comparing the pre-and post-training scores across all questionnaire items indicated a significant improvement in scores after the training (Table 4) compared to the scores before the training. These findings suggest that the training positively affected the measured training sessions. The mean score for pre-trained participants was ($M = 4.364$) ($SD = 0.164$), while the mean score for post-trained participants was ($M = 4.805$) ($SD = 0.047$). The effect size (Table 5), as measured by Cohen's d, was ($d = 3.64$). According to

Cohen (Cohen, 1988), these results represent a very large effect size, indicating that the post-training scores were significantly higher than pre-training scores. This large effect size suggests that the intervention substantially impacted the participant's scores.

A content analysis of the documentation was conducted to understand changes made by the participants during training by analyzing the portfolios submitted and presented on the third day of the training. This was also the follow-up session on the changes undertaken in practice after two days of training. The protocol built for reviewing portfolios was divided into 7 parts (Table 6), each part corresponding to a training session. Only sessions 7–8 of the training were set as a single session because the educators developed the game for 0–1 and 2–3 age groups, depending on their working age group. Three of the participating educators did not submit their portfolios, while the rest of them did (n=20). A measuring scale from 0–3 (0-no evidence, 1- minimal, 2- moderate, 3- high) in the form of a rubric was constructed to evaluate the portfolios.

Table 6: Content analysis of portfolios based on criteria

	Sessions	**Minimum (1)**	**Moderate (2)**	**High (3)**	**No evidence (0)**
1	*Interaction*	3	*2*	*1*	*14*
2	*Transition*	3	*0*	*0*	*17*
3	*Learning environment*	13	*2*	*1*	*4*
4	*Daily routine*	*15*	*3*	*2*	*0*
5	*Children's play*	14	*3*	*3*	*0*
6	*Observation of children*	13	*2*	*0*	*5*
7	*Evaluating*	8	*1*	*1*	*10*

After a qualitative analysis of the portfolios, most educators could present the changes made in their work environments. Although most of them stand at a minimum level of presentation, there is evidence that change may be possible. Table 7 gives some examples of educators' portfolios and the evaluation carried out according to evaluation criteria.

Table 7: Content analysis of portfolios based on criteria description

<table>
<tr><th>Example from Portfolio</th><th>Description</th></tr>
<tr><td>

Description:
Topic: Playing together
In this activity, children socialized even more by sharing toys and creating different imaginary toys.
Social-emotional competence</td><td>Minimal criteria
Interaction between children
No record has been made of which children are playing. The textual description of the photographs is very general, and it does not allow for further observation or evaluation of the children's interaction.
t</td></tr>
<tr><td>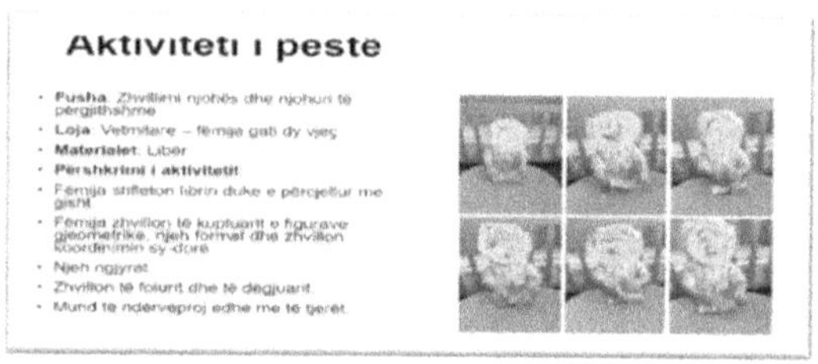

Description:
Developmental Area: Cognitive development and general knowledge
Game: Alone – almost two-year-old child
Materials: Book
Description of the activity:
The child flips through the book, following it with a finger. The child develops an understanding of geometric figures, recognizes shapes, and develops hand-eye coordination.
Recognizes colors.
Develops speaking and listening.
Also, can interact with others.</td><td>Moderate criteria
Children's play
The educator provided information about the age and the type of play; presented photos show the learning process. Some of the descriptions of the child's actions in the play are rather general (shapes, figures, and colors are general).</td></tr>
</table>

Table 7: Continued

Example from Portfolio	Description
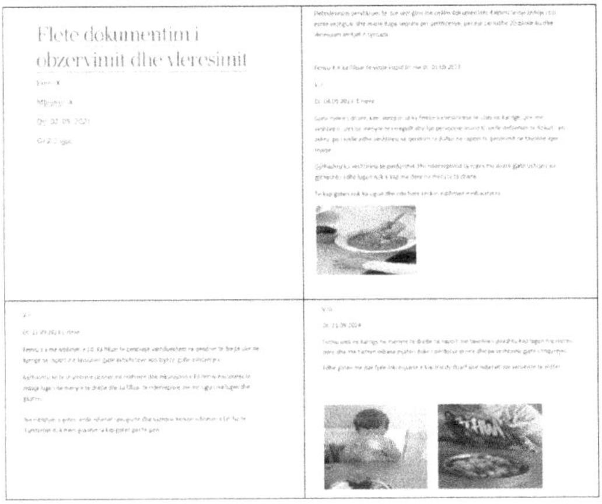 Flete dokumentimi i obzervimit dhe vleresimit Description: A document describes the systematic observation of the child during 3 weeks in forming skills such as sitting on a chair, holding a spoon, and holding a glass. The document presents evidence for each observation.	***High criteria*** ***Evaluating*** *Data such as the child's name, surname, and exact age are presented and described in a paragraph, which is the starting point for this assessment. The process is given from the moment a difficulty is identified: continuous work and continuous observation. After three weeks, it is evaluated whether the child has achieved the skill in focus.*

Based on the data and the quantitative analysis, the impact of the training measured by pre- and post-questionnaire was significant from a statistical point of view and highly effective. Therefore, it was expected to have a greater impact on the practice of working with children aged 0–3 years. The qualitative analysis verified that the change has occurred, but this documented change is generally within the minimum criteria. In most cases, more complete and meaningful documentation is missing. The greatest difficulties are observed in evidencing children's interaction with other children, with the environment and adults, registering the transition process, which may also be related to the child's ability to move from one activity to another in a natural setting. Another noted difficulty was the evaluation of children, which is, in fact, related to the entire process of the educator's work from the moment of planning activities, their implementation, observation, and finally, documenting the process for the purpose of evaluation. There are cases where children's play is presented. However, no developmental or cognitive momentum is documented, only showing what the child is currently doing and describing the expected processes for the child.

In the follow-up session during which the participants presented their work and experience during this period, trainers and researchers took brief notes. Only the notes kept by both parties were used for the analysis. The notes were compared, and the challenges and improvements to be made were grouped into two groups. It must be emphasized that the data were collected during the presentation and discussion of the portfolios phase.

For the preparation of portfolios and documenting the work, the educators stated that they cooperated with each other, but mainly at the level of the institution where they work or at the level of the age group they work. What was noticed during the presentation of the portfolios was the lack of constructive feedback from the participants. Comments were mostly positive and encouraging, but there was a lack of perspective for the future. (How can we do things better? What can we do differently?) The trainers continuously encouraged the discussion in this direction with their questions.

During the joint discussion and reflection, the educators highlighted some challenges they faced. For example, there were too many children to reorganize the space in the room, the creation of a culture that the children had already created and the impossibility of intervening now, challenges in cooperation with parents, and a significant lack of materials, as well as their professional development, since the university studies were oriented towards working with children in the 3–6 year age group.

While as to what could be done better in the future, during the discussion, the educators emphasized that there should be better work planning from the beginning of the new year when the new groups of children arrive, reorganize the learning environment, supply with materials which can be reused, a better, healthier routine, a more gradual transition of the child from the family to the institution is necessary, better cooperation with the parents. Also, cooperation between them can help to improve the continuous work with children.

6. Discussion

This study aimed to bring initial scientific evidence on how professional support through training and follow-up training can improve the practice of working with children when it is known that the number of training for the age group 0–3 years is exceptionally low. The study by Rogers et al. (2020), later supported by González-Alfaya et al. (2024), provides scientific evidence that the form of professional development, being a combination of training with new knowledge and reflective practice, affects the improvement of results in early childhood education.

The time of holding the training in two consecutive days, followed by a more than two-week break and the follow-up joint meeting for the presentation of portfolios, discussion, and joint reflection, enabled educators to practice the innovations elaborated during the two initial days of training. According to Desimone (2011), professional development can be more effective when opportunities for contacts between professional development specialists and practitioners are provided over a longer period. Also, the optimal number of participants in the group has created opportunities for continuous interaction and discussion, creating authentic opportunities for participants. Dunst (2015) also emphasizes that the effects of professional development are higher when opportunities are created for authentic learning by the participants.

The data from the quantitative analysis proved that there are significant differences between the data before and after the training. The training also had one exceptionally large effect size ($d = 3.64$), proving that the training had an impact on the educators' knowledge before and after the training regarding the covered contents. The findings are also supported by study by Bicaj and Buza (2020) with educators who work in early childhood education institutions, which concluded that training should be offered continuously. The training organized in the last 12 months positively impacted the general professional preparation and self-confidence of educators. However, the training organized in previous periods had little impact on their work.

While analyzing the content and reviewing the educators' portfolios, it was evident that the knowledge attained during the training was applied for two weeks and documented in the educators' portfolios. Document data from training sessions such as the learning environment, daily routine, children's play, and observing children, although, at minimum criteria, there was sufficient evidence. As for the evaluation documentation, there was evidence, but not to a great extent (Table 6). The areas of training for which it was impossible to collect sufficient evidence in the educators' portfolios were interaction, children's transitions and evaluation.

According to Beka and Kulinxha (2021), portfolios help teachers clearly present the goals for their work and the path they will follow to document the work done. Therefore, this approach will help educators raise awareness concerning professional development. Although in Kosovo, there is a legal framework for teacher licensing and professional advancement, as documented by Perolli-Shehu et al. (2023), the current level of implementation does not ensure career advancement. Therefore, teachers' professional development and performance evaluation continues to be challenging. For the educators who work with the age groups 0–3 years and 3–5 years, there is no system that supports their professional development and performance evaluation as per the nature of the work when it is known that working in early childhood institutions is in many aspects different from the teachers' work in schools.

A continuous critical reflection would help the educator understand the weight he/she has in the child's life. This is a critical moment that will push forward formal and informal professional development in all its forms. Therefore, reflection is not said to be used only for the purpose of documentation but also as a tool to learn (Shala et al., 2023) and to improve the practice of working with children aged 0–3 years.

Early childhood institutions, working conditions and how much and what is invested in early childhood education in general have a crucial role. Educators emphasize a series of challenges, which, in certain cases, can also affect the quality of their work. According to Saqipi et al. (2014), the context in which school teachers practice their profession and the conditions and circumstances in which their work takes place shape their professionalism. The same can be said for educators. Although early childhood education has been treated as a priority by the Government of Kosovo, the challenges in this sector, including the professional development of educators, are high.

7. Conclusions

Based on the research questions in the study, professional development-based training is an acceptable form of professional development, but it must always be followed by follow-up training days to ensure that the intended change is implemented.

For the training to be more effective, it should be spread over several working days, creating opportunities for deepening the sessions and increasing the time for group discussions and sharing experiences, creating guiding instruments for the development of critical reflections, and giving constructive comments. Even though the training planning was based on all forms of adult learning, according to Dunst and Trivette (2009), participants should be more dedicated and oriented towards reflective practices and mastery of the skills required in working with children in Early Childhood Education.

The small number of participants (N = 23) may have influenced the production of a higher intervention effect, a systematic follow-up of the group after 3 or 6 months could provide data on whether this intervention has been sustainable. Also, it would be interesting to see if other training groups could achieve these results even later.

References

Bakken, L., Brown, N., & Downing, B. (2017). Early childhood education: The long-term benefits. *Journal of Research in Childhood Education, 31*(2), 255–269. https://doi.org/10.1080/02568543.2016.1273285

Beka, A., & Kulinxha, G. (2021). Portfolio as a tool for self-reflection and professional development for pre-service teachers. *International Journal of Learning, Teaching and Educational Research, 20*(2), 22–35. https://doi.org/10.26803/ijlter.20.2.2

Bicaj, A., & Buza, V. (2020). Professional development experiences and expectations for early childhood teachers in Kosovo. *Issues in Educational Research, 30*(4), 1221–1244. https://search.informit.org/doi/10.3316/informit.606093307713182

Cambridge, B. L., Kahn, S., Tompkins, D. P., & Yancey, K.B. (Eds.). (2001). *Electronic portfolios: Emerging practices in student, faculty, and institutional learning*. Washington, DC: American Association for Higher Education.

Cohen, J. (1988). *Statistical power analysis for the behavioral sciences* (2nd ed.). New Jersey, US: Lawrence Erlbaum Associates.

Cole-Albäck, A. (2020). Children's rights in early childhood: An exploration of child rights pedagogy in England and Finland. PhD thesis, Birmingham City University in collaboration with the Centre for Research in Early Childhood (CREC). https://www.open-access.bcu.ac.uk/13325/

Cole-Albäck, A., Pascal, C., & Bertram, T. (2024). A *Significant Events Approach to Children's Rights* with children under three in early childhood education and care. *European Early Childhood Education Research Journal*, 1–15. https://doi.org/10.1080/1350293X.2024.2334873

Demas, A., Aliu, M., Coll-Black, S., Zafeirakou, A., Hankey, A., & Gotcheva, B. (2021). A situational analysis of Early Childhood Development (ECD) services in Kosovo. Accessed: August, 2024. https://documents1.worldbank.org/curated/en/896121631867828915/pdf/A-Situational-Analysis-of-Early-Childhood-Development-ECD-Services-in-Kosovo.pdf

Desimone, L. M. (2011). A primer on effective professional development. *Phi Delta Kappan, 92*(6), 68–71. https://doi.org/10.1177/003172171109200616

Dickinson, D. K., & Brady, J. P. (2006). Toward effective support for language and literacy through professional development: A decade of experience and data. In M. Zaslow & I. Martinez-Beck (Eds.), *Critical issues in early childhood professional development*. Baltimore: Brookes Publishing.

Dunst, C. J. (2015). Improving the design and implementation of in-service professional development in early childhood intervention. *Infants & Young Children, 28*(3), 210–219. https://doi.org/10.1097/IYC.0000000000000042.

Dunst, C. J., & Trivette, C. M. (2009). Let's be PALS: An evidence-based approach to professional development. *Infants & Young Children, 22*(3), 164–176. https://doi.org/10.1097/IYC.0b013e3181abe169.

Fraenkel, J. R., Wallen, N. E., & Hyun, H. H. (2012). *How to design and evaluate research in education.* New York: McGraw Hill Companies.

Fukkink, R., Jilink, L., & Oostdam, R. (2017). A meta-analysis of the impact of early childhood interventions on the development of children in the Netherlands: An inconvenient truth?. *European Early Childhood Education Research Journal, 25*(5), 656–666. https://doi.org/10. 1080/1350293X.2017.1356579

González-Alfaya, M. E., Mérida-Serrano, R., Olivares-García, M. D. L. Á., & Rodríguez-Carrillo, J. (2024). Democratic spaces for ECEC teachers' professional development: The case of the RIECU Network in Spain. *European Early Childhood Education Research Journal*, 1–15. https://doi.org/10.1080/1350293X.2024.2387566

Gjelaj, M. (2023). The importance of investigation in early childhood; study report. Evaluation of the integrated community-based ECCD model in Kosovo. *Save the Children.* https://resourcecentre.savethechildren.net/document/the-importance-of-investing-in-early-childhood/

MASHTI. (2022). Strategjia e Arsimit 2022–2026. [Education Strategy 2022–2026] Prishtinë. Accessed: August 2024. https://masht.rks-gov.net/wp-content/uploads/2022/10/03-Strategja-e-Arsimit-2022-2026-Alb-Web.pdf

MASHTI. (2024). Katalogu i programeve të aprovuara për zhvillim profesional të mësimdhënësve dhe punonjësve arsimor. Edicioni i shtatë. [Catalog of approved programs for the professional development of teachers and teachers education] 7th edition. Prishtinë. https://masht.rks-gov.net/wp-content/uploads/2024/08/Katalogu-2024-compressed.pdf

Matthews, B., & Ross, L. (2010). *Research methods, a practical guide for the social sciences.* London, UK: Pearson Education Limited.

OECD. (2018). *Engaging young children: Lessons from research about quality in early childhood education and care.* Paris: Starting Strong, OECD Publishing. https://dx.doi.org/10.1787/9789264085145-en

Perolli-Shehu, B., Eisenschmidt, E., & Kaçaniku, F. (2023). Current practices of teacher education in Kosovo in light of the intended teacher professionalism. In K. Vanari, F. Kaçaniku, E. Eisenschmidt, & B. Saqipi (Eds.). *Innovative practices and quality assurance in initial teacher education* (pp. 17–49). Kosova, Albas.

Rogers, S., Brown, C., & Poblete, X. (2020). A systematic review of the evidence base for professional learning in early years education (The PLEYE Review). *Review of Education, 8*(1), 156–188. https://doi.org/10.1002/rev3.3178

Saqipi, B., Asunta, T., & Korpinen, E. (2014). Understanding the context of teacher professionalism in education systems undergoing transition–Kosovo case. *Procedia-Social and Behavioral Sciences*, *112*, 635–646. https://doi.org/10.1016/j.sbspro.2014.01.1211

Schleicher, A. (2019). *Helping our youngest to learn and grow: Policies for early learning, international summit on the teaching profession*. Paris: OECD Publishing. http://dx.doi.org/10.1787/9789264313873-en

Shala, R. F., Gjelaj, M., Rozman-Krivec, L., & Bercnik, S. (2023). Mentor teachers' perspective of qualities of student teachers' skills and attitudes for the profession of early childhood educator: Kosovo and Slovenia context. In K. Vanari, F. Kaçaniku, E. Eisenschmidt, & B. Saqipi (Eds.). *Innovative practices and quality assurance in initial teacher education* (pp. 133–165). Kosova, Albas.

Sheridan, S. M., Edwards, C. P., Marvin, C. A., & Knoche, L. L. (2009). Professional development in early childhood programs: Process issues and research needs. *Early Education and Development*, *20*(3), 377–401. https://doi.org/10.1080/10409280802582795

UNICEF. (2022). *Një fillim më i mirë në jetë për të gjithë fëmijët në Kosovë: Raport i politikave i bazuar në gjetjet e MICS 2019/ 2020*. [A better start in life for all children in Kosovo: Policy report based on MICS findings 2019/2020] UNICEF Kosovo. Retrieved September 2024, from https://www.unicef.org/kosovoprogramme/media/3716/file/English-2022.pdf

Donghui Zhao, Sue Lin Ngan, Ainul Huda Jamil, Mohd Fairuz Md Salleh, and Wan Sallha Yusoff

The Evolution of ESG Integration in Finance: A Two-Decade Bibliometric Analysis

1. Introduction

Environmental, Social, and Governance (ESG) factors have become essential in finance, reflecting a shift towards sustainable investment. Integrating ESG into financial decisions meets ethical expectations and supports long-term value creation and risk management, evolving from a peripheral concern to a strategic priority (Dmuchowski et al., 2023; Tsang et al., 2023). This bibliometric review uses data from the Web of Science to examine the progress and growing significance of ESG considerations in finance from 2004 to 2024. The substantial increase in ESG-centric academic work, particularly after 2017, demonstrates a worldwide commitment to sustainability, aligning with the United Nations' Sustainable Development Goals (Fund, 2015). This underscores ESG's vital role in enhancing corporate resilience, reducing risks, and fostering long-term value creation (Elamer & Boulhaga; Yu et al., 2024). Empirical studies also confirm the positive relationship between strong ESG performance and key financial indicators, including improved stock performance, effective risk management, and increased profitability (Barko et al., 2022). These findings have elevated ESG from a niche investment criterion to a mainstream strategic consideration. However, the lack of standardized ESG metrics and the need for advanced analytical models to assess ESG's multifaceted impacts on financial outcomes hinder the full realization of ESG's role in driving sustainable and responsible investment practices (Berg et al., 2022).

Most recent research has focused on methodological innovations in ESG measurement. For instance, Kenneth David et al. (2024) combined Bayesian Linear Regression with Neural Network techniques to uncover the relationship between ESG commitments and corporate innovation in China (Kenneth David et al., 2024). Lee et al. (2024) integrated ESG information into financial assessments, validating the necessity to consider ESG for financial assets and introducing a new perspective to develop investment strategies and decision-making processes (Lee et al., 2024). Ongoing research is essential to address existing limitations and explore new frontiers, particularly in developing a unified framework for

ESG reporting and integrating ESG considerations into finance paradigms. This review synthesizes the state of ESG research in finance. It highlights avenues for future exploration, fosters discourse on sustainable finance, advocating for strategic ESG focus on achieving financial success alongside societal and environmental stewardship. (Chouaibi & Affes, 2021; MacNeil & Esser, 2022; Weston & Nnadi, 2023).

2. Methodology

2.1. Bibliometric Analysis

Bibliometric analysis is a statistical tool that provides a quantitative overview of academic publications, highlighting research developments and predicting future innovations. This method condenses extensive research into accessible and reliable formats, quantitatively reviewing large collections of academic papers (Pessin et al., 2022). Bibliometric analysis is also particularly effective for examining large datasets over time, offering a detailed and unbiased assessment of academic texts (Mukherjee et al., 2022). Thus, this work employs bibliometric analysis to investigate the ESG theme within corporate finance and to explore the relationships among publications, citation counts, author productivity, and the evolution of critical terms, employing network mapping visuals to identify unexplored areas within the field (Donthu et al., 2021). R bibliometric package, VOSviewer 1.6.20, and Biblioshiny 2.0 are also utilized in this analysis (Farooq, 2023). These user-friendly, free tools facilitate the creation and visualization of literature collections and scientific concepts to provide insights into research patterns through network diagrams (Guleria & Kaur, 2021; van Eck & Waltman, 2010).

2.2. Research Questions (RQs)

The bibliometric study addressed the following inquiries:

RQ1: To what extent have ESG and corporate finance been explored?
RQ1.1: What trends are prevalent at the convergence of ESG and corporate finance?
RQ1.2: Which journals, articles, authors, and countries contribute significantly to this area?
RQ2: What themes dominate this specific field of study?
RQ3: How have the focal points and themes evolved?
RQ4: Where might future investigations into ESG and corporate finance lead?

To address RQ1, a performance analysis was conducted to identify leading entities in the research by assessing relevant metrics. This involved examining publication counts for productivity, citation numbers to gauge impact, and the prominence of sources and papers. For RQ2, co-citation analysis within scientific mapping revealed emerging trends and subjects. Keyword co-occurrence analysis was employed for RQ3 to identify evolving research themes. RQ4 utilized bibliographic coupling analysis to forecast potential research avenues, highlighting unexplored areas and future opportunities in the domain.

2.3. Bibliographic Database Selection

This research evaluated studies on the influence of Environmental, Social, and Governance (ESG) aspects on corporate finance, using Clarivate Analytics' Web of Science (WoS) for data gathering. The WoS is recognized for its rigorous indexing of literature in scientific and technical disciplines, offering valuable perspectives on critical scientific and technological sectors. The investigation revealed WoS's superior adherence to quality benchmarks compared to Scopus, resulting in fewer mistaken identifications among authors and keywords, partly due to the integration of Keywords Plus (Forliano et al., 2021). The PRISMA framework was utilized to enhance the reliability of the review procedure. As a methodical review approach, PRISMA aids in the meticulous selection, evaluation, and integration of literature through a structured 27-item checklist, thus refining the precision in screening and choosing databases (Salameh et al., 2020), making it a premier methodology in bibliometric research (Figure 1).

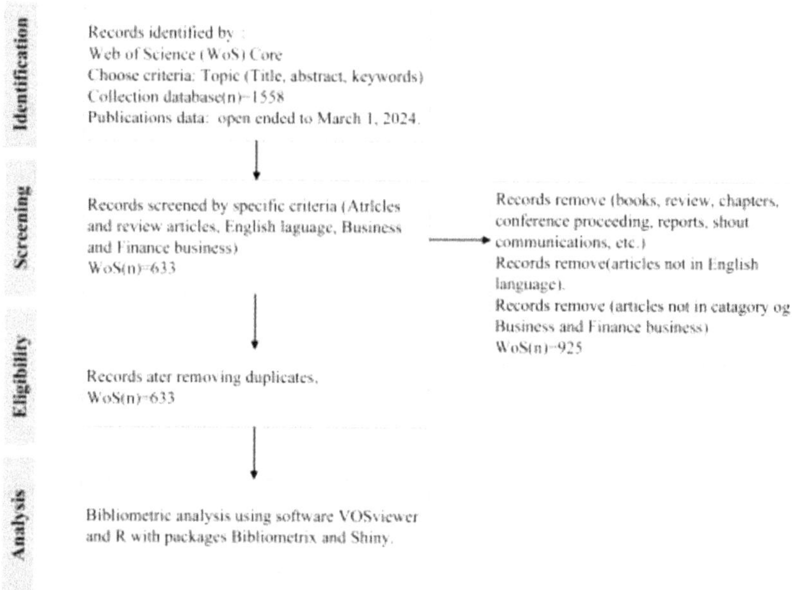

Figure 1: Flow diagram using the PRISMA method

2.4. Bibliographic Database Collection

Following PRISMA guidelines, inclusion and exclusion criteria were established to shape the database (Page et al., 2021). The research period concluded on March 1, 2024, with searches conducted within the WoS database, filtering by "Topic." Excluded documents included books, book chapters, reports, review articles, conference materials, and publications with early access. Only English-language articles that significantly contributed to understanding ESG and finance were included, with duplicates omitted for clarity. The bibliographic analysis focused on influential publications, article trends, citation numbers, journals, publishers, nations, and contributing authors within the targeted study area (Ülker et al., 2023). Searches utilized keywords relevant to ESG in finance (Nyantakyi et al., 2023), spanning from January 1970 to March 1, 2024, following a four-step procedure: database search, academic relevance screening, language preference, and subject categorization. A total of 633 articles were retrieved initially (Table 1).

Table 1: Web of Science search query

Search query		Results
Search date:	March 1, 2024	
Search topic:	"Environmental, social, governance (ESG)" and "financial performance" OR "sustainable finance" OR "socially responsible investing (SRI)" OR " Ethical investing" OR " Impact investing" OR " Green investing" OR " Responsible investing".	1558
Document Types:	Article or Review article	1469
Languages:	English	1446
Web of Science Categories:	Business Finance or Business	633
Final data		633

2.5. Bibliographic Data Analysis and Visualizations

For the bibliometric evaluation, the Web of Science (WoS) documents were compiled into a single file—previous studies employed Biblioshiny for analytical modeling and R Studio 3.0.1 for visual mapping. Data from multiple databases were consolidated into one dataset. R Studio commands facilitated this data amalgamation, which was then formatted into CSV files for use with VOSviewer (Donthu et al., 2021; Wang et al., 2022). This analysis examined the influence of ESG on corporate finance and research trends. Data visualizations were created using Biblioshiny and VOSviewer. Biblioshiny processed the data through commands, while VOSviewer provided a graphical interface for analytical tasks. The datasets underwent two forms of analysis: WoS data integration using Biblioshiny 2.0 and Microsoft Excel 2010, highlighting annual growth, citation patterns, and publication trends. Network analysis, including country collaborations, author co-citations, and keyword co-occurrence, was performed using VOSviewer 1.6.20 (Kumari & Singh, 2023).

3. Results

3.1. Publications Output

Table 2 presents the core data from WoS, including 633 articles from 179 sources from 2004 to 2024. Annual publication growth was 22.82 %, with an average of 22.92 citations per article, totaling 28,024 references. The analysis identified 1,647 author keywords and 954 index terms. There were 1,647 contributors, 104 single-author articles, and an average of 2.68 authors per paper. International collaborations accounted for 32.54 %.

Table 2: Summary of results after combining datasets from WoS

Description	Results
Timespan (Year)	2004:2024
Sources (Journals, Books, etc)	179
Documents	633
Annual Growth Rate %	22.82
Average citations per doc	22.92
Document Average Age	2.65
References	28,024
Document Content	
Keywords Plus	954
Author's Keywords	1647
Authors	
Authors	1454
Authors of single-authored docs	91
Single-authored docs	104
Co-Authors per document	2.68
International co-authorships %	32.54
articles	190

3.2. Number of Publications and Citations Per Year

A. Soppe's 2004 article "Sustainable Corporate Finance," published in the Journal of Business Ethics, represents the first study on ESG in finance identified in the WoS database. This work underscores integrating ESG principles into corporate finance (Soppe, 2004). Figure 2 shows the growth of ESG research in finance from 2004 to 2024. After a dormant period until 2011, there was a gradual increase, with a significant rise in publications starting in 2018. This reflects the financial industry's increased focus on sustainability and ethics. Publications peaked at 218 in 2023, dropping to 61 in early 2024. This trend highlights the growing importance of ESG factors in financial analysis and policy development, with ESG evolving from a marginal to a central research area, requiring detailed analysis to understand its impact on fiscal performance, risk mitigation, and investment strategy.

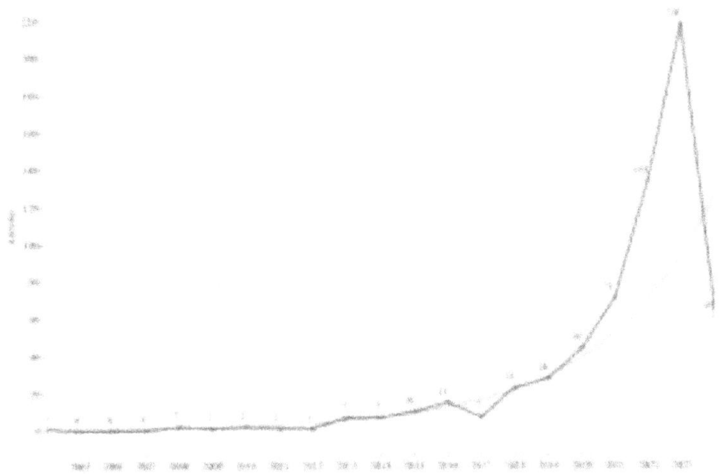

Figure 2: Trends of publications in the research of ESG in finance

3.3. Sankey diagrams: three field plots on Authors-Keywords-Sources

The three-field plot illustrates the connections among authors (AU), keywords (DE), and sources (SO) in ESG research within finance (Figure 3). This analysis highlights essential themes such as "ESG," "sustainable finance," and "financial performance," linked to high-impact sources like the Journal of Sustainable Finance & Investment and the Journal of Business Ethics. Prominent collaborative authorship emerges around themes like "corporate social responsibility," "sustainability," and "corporate governance." The convergence in prestigious publications highlights ESG's increasing influence and interdisciplinary nature in financial studies. As ESG integration deepens, it becomes a central focus in financial research, affecting theoretical frameworks and practical applications in financial markets.

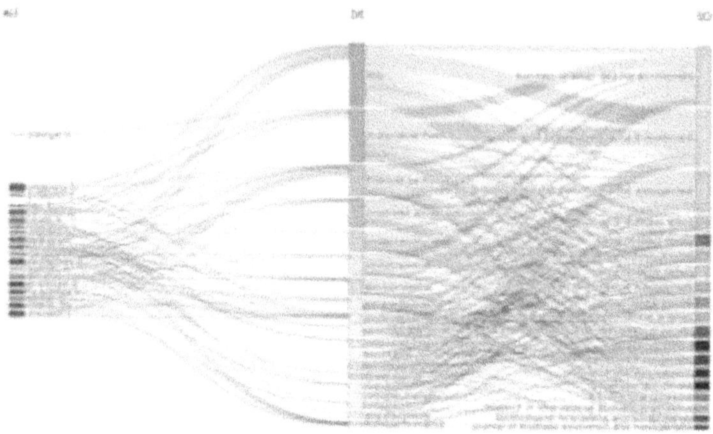

Figure 3: Three fold Diagrams or Sankey diagram

3.4. Distribution by Critical Countries

Table 3 contrasts countries based on their publication volume and research impact in ESG finance. Italy leads with 160 articles, accounting for 24.13 % of total publications. The United States sets the benchmark for research impact with 2,526 total citations and an average of 42.8 citations per publication. The United Kingdom and Germany follow with 1,585 and 1,439 total citations, respectively, underscoring their significant contributions. Australia shows a balanced scholarly presence with 71 publications and 1,069 citations. Despite fewer publications, Japan and Lebanon demonstrate high citation impact per publication, highlighting their research's profound influence. This analysis is crucial for understanding the global dissemination and impact of ESG research in finance, providing essential context for the current literature review.

Table 3: Countries with the most published and most influential in the research of ESG in finance

Most published countries			**Most impactful countries**		
Country	TP	Fre (%)	Country	TC	AC
ITALY	160	24.13 %	USA	2526	42.8
USA	132	19.91 %	UNITED KINGDOM	1585	33
CHINA	124	18.70 %	GERMANY	1439	38.9
UK	118	17.80 %	AUSTRALIA	1069	30.5
INDIA	99	14.93 %	ITALY	1033	14.2
FRANCE	77	11.61 %	FRANCE	952	38.1
AUSTRALIA	71	10.71 %	CHINA	752	16.7
GERMANY	60	9.05 %	INDIA	439	8.8
SPAIN	60	9.05 %	JAPAN	414	82.8
MALAYSIA	48	7.24 %	CANADA	382	23.9

Note: TP=total publications, TC=total citations, AC=average citations

3.5. Country-Level Cooperation

Country-level cooperation enhances academic exchange and accelerates knowledge advancement. Figure 4 illustrates global collaboration patterns in finance ESG research, revealing a dense intercontinental network with the US and the UK as crucial collaborators, highlighted by their mutual engagements. The UK's prominent connections with China and Italy signify its central role in European and Asian ESG research networks. Regionally, Australia and New Zealand's partnerships underscore localized cooperation, while the UK's alliances with countries such as Malaysia and France highlight its central role in global ESG discourse. These patterns emphasize the crucial role of international collaboration in advancing ESG research, which is essential for developing sustainable financial systems globally.

Figure 4: Global geographical distribution of papers and collaboration patterns

3.6. Distribution by Authors Productivity

Table 4 summarizes author productivity in ESG finance research, balancing publication frequency with citation impact. It lists authors with their publication counts (NP), total citations (TC), and bibliometric indices (h-index, g-index, and m-index). CHIAPPINI H leads with six papers since 2022. ZWERGEL B shows a significant citation impact, with 478 citations from four publications since 2015 and an h-index of 3. DORFLEITNER G has a high h-index of 4 from four publications, indicating consistent quality. The m-index highlights NASRALLAH N and AL AMOSH H for high annual impact rates. Early-career researchers like JALAL RNUD and BIRINDELLI G show promise with strong citation rates despite fewer publications. These metrics reflect the dynamic and impactful contributions to ESG finance literature, showcasing a vibrant scholarly community.

Table 4: Distributions of author's productivity

Element	NP	TC	h_index	g_index	m_index	FPY
CHIAPPINI H	6	21	2	4	0.667	2022
ZWERGEL B	4	478	3	4	0.3	2015
DORFLEITNER	4	375	4	4	0.4	2015
NIRINO N	4	186	3	4	0.75	2021
HUSSAINEY K	4	140	3	4	1	2022
CHOUAIBI J	4	125	2	4	0.5	2021
UTZ S	4	92	4	4	0.364	2014
NASRALLAH	4	73	4	4	2	2023
AL AMOSH H	4	58	4	4	1.333	2022
KHATIB SFA	4	58	4	4	1.333	2022

*NP-Number of publications, TC-Total Citations, TC/N- Total Citations per publications, FPY-First publication Year.

3.7. Co-Citations Analysis of Authors

Figure 5 showcases a VOSviewer network visualization of author co-citations in ESG research within finance, identifying 18 authors with at least 100 citations each. The network map reveals two clusters; the red cluster includes ten authors centered around 'Orlitzky, M,' with 177 citations (17 links, 1215 total link strength). The green cluster comprises eight authors, centered around 'Fama, EF,' with 199 citations (17 links, 1059 total link strength). Key nodes like Freeman, Porter, and Jensen show extensive cross-referencing, indicating foundational ESG research or seminal corporate finance works intersecting with ESG topics. The map highlights the importance of co-citation analysis in identifying influential works and interconnections shaping the intellectual landscape of ESG finance.

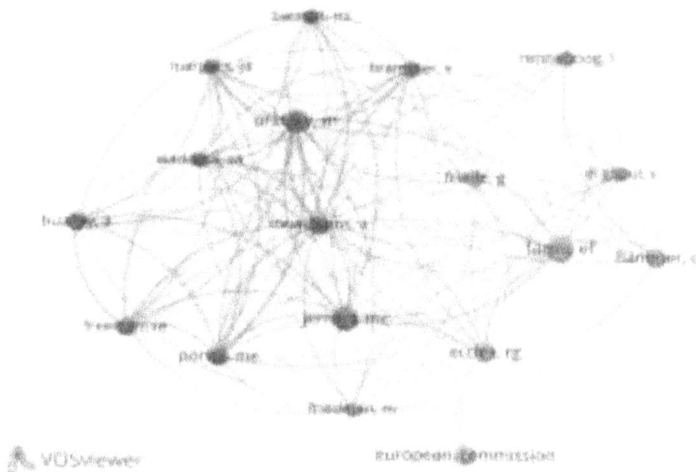

Figure 5: Visualizations authors co-citations

3.8. Distribution by Impactful Journals

Table 5 lists the most influential journals (Top 10) in ESG finance research, accounting for 43 % of the 633 publications and 8,084 citations. The Journal of Sustainable Finance & Investment leads this list with 49 articles since 2018, indicating a significant increase in ESG finance research. "Business Strategy and the Environment" has the highest citations (1704) and an h-index of 20 since 2014, indicating significant influence. The "Journal of Business Ethics," notable for its longevity since 2004, has 1592 citations. High m-indices for "Finance Research Letters" and "Technological Forecasting and Social Change" show strong annual citation rates despite their recent entries in 2020 and 2021. These metrics highlight journals significantly impacting the academic community and shaping sustainable finance discourse.

Table 5: Top 10 Most Influential Journals

Article	TC	NP	h_index	g_ index	TN (%)	FPY
Journal of sustainable finance & investment	824	49	16	27	7.74	2018
Business strategy and the environment	1704	41	20	41	6.48	2014
Corporate social responsibility and environment management	599	41	12	24	6.48	2019
Journal of Business Ethics	1592	19	15	19	3.00	2004
Finance research letters	357	19	9	18	3.00	2020
Sustainability accounting management and policy journal	415	14	7	14	2.21	2015
International review of financial analysis	157	14	5	12	2.21	2016
Journal of risk and financial management	206	12	7	12	1.90	2019
Research in international business and finance	182	12	5	12	1.90	2019
Global finance journal	549	10	6	10	1.58	2013

*NP-Number of publications, TC-Total Citations, FPY-First publication Year, TN (%)- the percentage of the total number of publications.

3.9. Citations Analysis of Journals

Figure 6, created using VOSviewer, illustrates the most influential citation sources in ESG finance research. Of the 179 sources surveyed, 18 meet the relevance threshold of at least eight citations. Significant nodes, such as the "Journal of Business Ethics" and "Business Strategy and the Environment," have garnered substantial citations, highlighting their crucial role in ESG research dissemination. The diagram categorizes three primary groups: The first group (red) emphasizes the "Journal of Business Ethics," with 19 articles and 1,592 citations (17 connections, 91 total link strength). The second group (green) centers on "Business Strategy and the Environment," encompassing 41 papers and 1,704 citations (17 connections, 128 total link strength). The third group (blue) is led by "Borsa Istanbul Review," which includes nine articles and 131 citations (11 connections, 28 total link strength). This visualization is vital for pinpointing key sources significantly influencing ESG research development.

Figure 6: Networking mapping of most impactful citations sources

3.10. Analysis of Highly Cited Publications

Table 6 lists the top 10 most-cited papers in finance ESG research, emphasizing their significant impact. These articles, accumulating 2049 citations and representing 20 % of total citations, underscore ESG research's importance. Fatemi, Glaum, and Kaiser's 2018 paper leads with 390 citations, examining disclosure's effects on the ESG performance-firm value nexus in the "Global Finance Journal." Flammer's 2021 "Journal of Financial Economics" article on corporate green bonds has a high citation rate of 97.25, reflecting a significant impact. Works by Li et al. and Xie et al. in the "British Accounting Review" and "Business Strategy and the Environment" focus on governance and ESG activities' roles in corporate valuation. Aouadi and Marsat's 2018 "Journal of Business Ethics" article on ESG controversies, with 269 citations, exemplifies the shift towards understanding ESG's financial impact. These foundational works provide a critical empirical basis for further research and submissions to journals like the "Journal of Corporate Finance."

Table 6: Top 10 most cited publications

Title	Authors	Year	Journal	TC	TC/Year
ESG performance and firm value: The moderating role of disclosure	Fatemi, A., Glaum, M., & Kaiser, S.	2018	Global finance journal	390	55.71
Corporate green bonds	Flammer, C.	2021	Journal of Financial Economics	389	97.25
The impact of environmental, social, and governance disclosure on firm value: The role of CEO power	Li, Y., Gong, M., Zhang, X. Y., & Koh, L.	2018	The British Accounting Review,	338	48.29
Do environmental, social, and governance activities improve corporate financial performance?	Xie, J., Nozawa, W., Yagi, M., Fujii, H., & Managi, S.	2019	Business Strategy and the Environment	319	53.17
The influence of firm size on the ESG score: Corporate sustainability ratings under review	Drempetic, S., Klein, C., & Zwergel, B.	2020	Journal of Business Ethics	318	63.6
Environmental, social and governance (ESG) scores and financial performance of mutilations: Moderating effects of geographic international diversification and financial slack	Duque-Grisales, E., & Aguilera-Caracuel, J.	2021	Journal of Business Ethics	292	73
Do ESG controversies matter for firm value? Evidence from international data	Aouadi, A., & Marsat, S.	2018	Journal of Business Ethics	269	38.43
Corporate social responsibility, firm value, and influential institutional ownership	Buchanan, B., Cao, C. X., & Chen, C.	2018	Journal of Corporate Finance	212	30.29
Environmental responsibility and firm performance: The application of an environmental, social and governance model	Lee, K. H., Cin, B. C., & Lee, E. Y.	2016	Business Strategy and the Environment	189	21
ESG practices and the cost of debt: Evidence from EU countries	Eliwa, Y., Aboud, A., & Saleh, A.	2021	Critical Perspectives on Accounting	188	47

3.10.1. Network Analysis of Authors' Keywords

This section analyzes trends in author keywords within 633 articles published from 2004 to 2024, identifying 1,647 keywords, with 33 occurring at least ten times using VOSviewer (Wang et al., 2022). Figure 7 illustrates the most prevalent keywords in ESG and corporate finance research. Node sizes reflect keyword frequency, colors indicate cluster strength, and lines show associative links. Five major keyword clusters were identified:

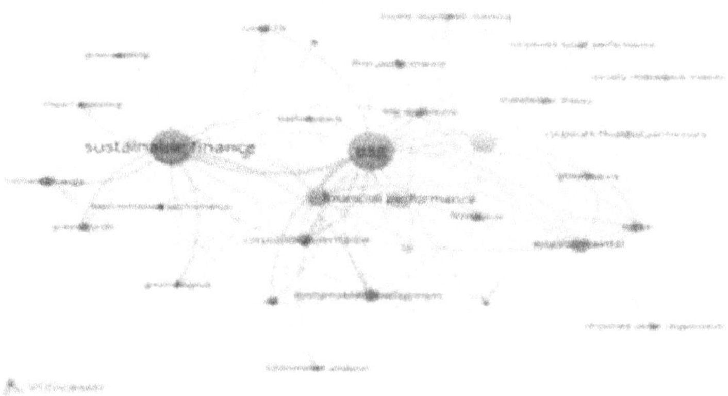

Figure 7: Authors' keywords co-occurrence network visualization

Red Cluster: Focuses on sustainable finance with keywords like 'climate change', 'green bonds', and 'impact investing'. It also notes concerns about 'greenwashing'.
Green Cluster: Centers on ESG's operational aspects with keywords such as 'COVID-19', 'ESG disclosure', and 'socially responsible investment'.
Blue Cluster: Addresses methodological and conceptual bases using 'bibliometric analysis' for 'CSR,' 'ESG,' and 'sustainable development', linking 'firm value' to sustainable practices.
Yellow Cluster: Focuses on ESG adoption outcomes, with 'corporate financial performance' and 'ESG performance' interconnected with 'socially responsible investment' and 'stakeholder theory'.
Purple Cluster: Distills ESG's core components—'environmental,' 'social,' and 'governance'—and their link to 'corporate social responsibility'.

These clusters show the multifaceted nature of ESG finance research, advocating for a holistic approach covering ethical investment strategies, performance metrics, stakeholder interests, and sustainability implications. The interconnected themes highlight the need for comprehensive econometric analysis to guide empirical research in corporate finance.

3.10.2. *Thematic Map of Authors' Keywords*

Figure 8 presents a thematic map highlighting the field's most relevant issues based on author keywords. The map, indicating internal (density) strength and external (connectivity) significance, features four quadrants, which are niche themes, motor themes, essential themes, and emerging or declining themes (García-Lillo et al., 2023). In the niche themes quadrant, 'executive compensation' and 'India' appear significant yet less developed and central in the literature. The motor themes quadrant, featuring 'integrated reporting,' 'legitimacy theory,' and 'business ethics,' indicates key research areas propelling the field. The primary themes quadrant prominently features 'ESG,' 'CSR,' 'environmental performance,' 'sustainable development,' and 'firm value.' Emerging or declining themes like 'portfolio choice,' 'performance measurement,' and 'investment decision' suggest new inquiries or waning topics. Themes like 'credit risk,' 'default risk,' and 'digital transformation' show evolving development despite gaining centrality. This thematic map informs the econometric literature review, highlighting the importance and development of ESG topics in finance and prioritizing central and well-developed themes while acknowledging the potential of niche and emerging themes for novel contributions.

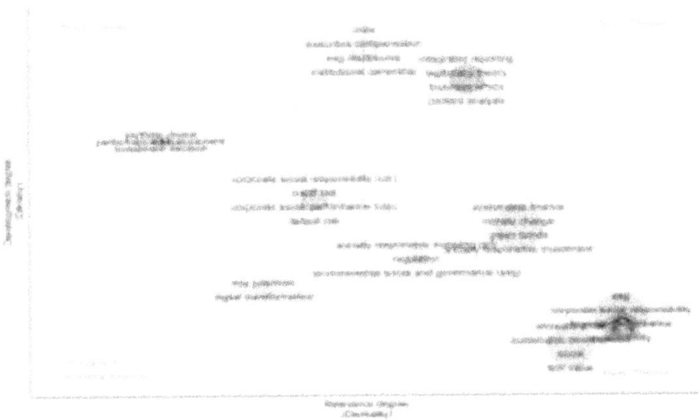

Figure 8: Thematic map

3.10.3. Thematic Evolution

The thematic evolution diagram (Figure 9) charts the development of crucial ESG research concepts over four periods, highlighting shifts in the financial sector's sustainability focus. During the initial phase (2004–2013), 'sustainable finance' and 'ethics' were foundational, indicating early integration into financial analysis. From 2014–2018, themes consolidated with a focus on 'CSR' and 'corporate governance', signifying deeper ESG integration into corporate strategy. Between 2019 and 2021, themes diversified, with 'firm performance', 'executive compensation', and 'impact investing' gaining prominence, reflecting a broader examination of ESG's impact on financial metrics. The latest phase (2022–2024) shows theme integration and refinement, with 'environmental performance', 'sustainability reporting', and 'risk management' as crucial topics, indicating evolved ESG understanding as critical to risk management and corporate accountability. The continuous presence of sustainable finance and rising ESG underscores their enduring central roles in the literature.

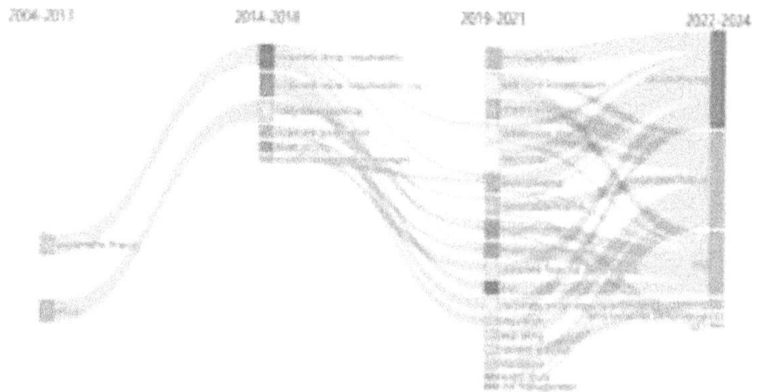

Figure 9: Evaluation of keywords in different periods

4. Conclusions

4.1. Discussions and Conclusions

Integrating ESG (Environmental, Social, and Governance) standards into finance has become essential for sustainable growth. ESG-focused research has significantly increased, with a surge post-2017 aligned with global sustainability efforts. Despite progress, gaps in ESG implementation persist, particularly in emerging markets. Addressing these gaps is crucial for sustainable economic advancement. ESG's shift from a peripheral to a central theme in financial discourse underscores its importance. Challenges remain, such as uniform ESG metrics and consistent reporting standards. Future studies should focus on unified ESG assessment methods and regulatory guidelines to enhance the finance sector's accountability and effectiveness in ESG integration, contributing to a more sustainable global financial ecosystem.

4.2. Limitations

This study has limitations due to its reliance on Web of Science databases, which may not capture the full breadth of ESG discourse. The focus on keyword searches and citation analysis might overlook seminal works that do not dominate citation networks. The study's temporal boundary may miss the latest emergent themes. Future research should expand data sources, incorporate interdisciplinary perspectives, and address emerging themes to strengthen ESG scholarship's robustness and relevance in tackling sustainability challenges in finance.

References

Barko, T., Cremers, M., & Renneboog, L. (2022). Shareholder Engagement on Environmental, Social, and Governance Performance. *Journal of Business Ethics*, *180*(2), 777–812. https://doi.org/10.1007/s10551-021-04850-z

Berg, F., Kölbel, J. F., & Rigobon, R. (2022). Aggregate Confusion: The Divergence of ESG Ratings*. *Review of Finance*, *26*(6), 1315–1344. https://doi.org/10.1093/rof/rfac033 %J Review of Finance

Chouaibi, S., & Affes, H. (2021). The effect of social and ethical practices on environmental disclosure: evidence from an international ESG data. *Corporate Governance: The International Journal of Business in Society*, *21*(7), 1293–1317. https://doi.org/10.1108/CG-03-2020-0087

Dmuchowski, P., Dmuchowski, W., Baczewska-Dąbrowska, A. H., & Gworek, B. (2023). Environmental, social, and governance (ESG) model; impacts and sustainable investment – Global trends and Poland's perspective. *Journal of Environmental Management*, *329*, 117023. https://doi.org/https://doi.org/10.1016/j.jenvman.2022.117023

Donthu, N., Kumar, S., Mukherjee, D., Pandey, N., & Lim, W. M. (2021). How to conduct a bibliometric analysis: An overview and guidelines. *Journal of Business Research*, *133*, 285–296. https://doi.org/https://doi.org/10.1016/j.jbusres.2021.04.070

Elamer, A. A., & Boulhaga, M. ESG controversies and corporate performance: The moderating effect of governance mechanisms and ESG practices. *n/a*(n/a). https://doi.org/https://doi.org/10.1002/csr.2749

Farooq, R. (2023). Mapping the field of knowledge management: a bibliometric analysis using R. *VINE Journal of Information and Knowledge Management Systems*, *53*(6), 1178–1206. https://doi.org/10.1108/VJIKMS-06-2021-0089

Forliano, C., De Bernardi, P., & Yahiaoui, D. (2021). Entrepreneurial universities: A bibliometric analysis within the business and management domains. *Technological Forecasting and Social Change*, *165*, 120522. https://doi.org/https://doi.org/10.1016/j.techfore.2020.120522

Fund, S. J. A. a. t. l. h. w. u. o. s. i. (2015). Sustainable development goals.

García-Lillo, F., Seva-Larrosa, P., & Sánchez-García, E. (2023). What is going on in entrepreneurship research? A bibliometric and SNA analysis. *Journal of Business Research*, *158*, 113624. https://doi.org/https://doi.org/10.1016/j.jbusres.2022.113624

Guleria, D., & Kaur, G. (2021). Bibliometric analysis of ecopreneurship using VOSviewer and RStudio Bibliometrix, 1989–2019. *Library Hi Tech*, *39*(4), 1001–1024. https://doi.org/10.1108/LHT-09-2020-0218

Kenneth David, L., Wang, J., Angel, V., & Luo, M. (2024). Environmental commitments and Innovation in China's corporate landscape: An analysis of ESG governance strategies. *Journal of Environmental Management*, *349*, 119529. https://doi.org/https://doi.org/10.1016/j.jenvman.2023.119529

Kumari, A., & Singh, M. P. (2023). A journey of social sustainability in organization during MDG & SDG period: A bibliometric analysis. *Socio-Economic Planning Sciences*, *88*, 101668. https://doi.org/https://doi.org/10.1016/j.seps.2023.101668

Lee, H., Kim, J. H., & Jung, H. S. (2024). Deep-learning-based stock market prediction incorporating ESG sentiment and technical indicators. *Scientific Reports*, *14*(1), 10262. https://doi.org/10.1038/s41598-024-61106-2

MacNeil, I., & Esser, I.-m. (2022). From a Financial to an Entity Model of ESG. *European Business Organization Law Review*, *23*(1), 9–45. https://doi.org/10.1007/s40804-021-00234-y

Mukherjee, D., Lim, W. M., Kumar, S., & Donthu, N. J. J. o. B. R. (2022). Guidelines for advancing theory and practice through bibliometric research. *148*, 101–115.

Nyantakyi, G., Atta Sarpong, F., Adu Sarfo, P., Uchenwoke Ogochukwu, N., & Coleman, W. (2023). A boost for performance or a sense of corporate social responsibility? A bibliometric analysis on sustainability reporting and firm performance research (2000–2022). *Cogent Business & Management, 10*(2), 2220513. https://doi.org/10.1080/23311975.2023.2220513

Page, M. J., McKenzie, J. E., Bossuyt, P. M., Boutron, I., Hoffmann, T. C., Mulrow, C. D., … Moher, D. (2021). Updating guidance for reporting systematic reviews: development of the PRISMA 2020 statement. *Journal of Clinical Epidemiology, 134*, 103–112. https://doi.org/https://doi.org/10.1016/j.jclinepi.2021.02.003

Pessin, V. Z., Yamane, L. H., & Siman, R. R. (2022). Smart bibliometrics: an integrated method of science mapping and bibliometric analysis. *Scientometrics, 127*(6), 3695–3718. https://doi.org/10.1007/s11192-022-04406-6

Salameh, J.-P., Bossuyt, P. M., McGrath, T. A., Thombs, B. D., Hyde, C. J., Macaskill, P., … McInnes, M. D. F. (2020). Preferred reporting items for systematic review and meta-analysis of diagnostic test accuracy studies (PRISMA-DTA): explanation, elaboration, and checklist. *BMJ, 370*, m2632. https://doi.org/10.1136/bmj.m2632

Soppe, A. (2004). Sustainable Corporate Finance. *Journal of Business Ethics, 53*(1), 213–224. https://doi.org/10.1023/B:BUSI.0000039410.18373.12

Tsang, A., Frost, T., & Cao, H. (2023). Environmental, Social, and Governance (ESG) disclosure: A literature review. *The British Accounting Review, 55*(1), 101149. https://doi.org/https://doi.org/10.1016/j.bar.2022.101149

Ülker, P., Ülker, M., & Karamustafa, K. (2023). Bibliometric analysis of bibliometric studies in the field of tourism and hospitality. *Journal of Hospitality and Tourism Insights, 6*(2), 797–818. https://doi.org/10.1108/JHTI-10-2021-0291

van Eck, N. J., & Waltman, L. (2010). Software survey: VOSviewer, a computer program for bibliometric mapping. *Scientometrics, 84*(2), 523–538. https://doi.org/10.1007/s11192-009-0146-3

Wang, S., Mao, J., Cao, Y., & Li, G. (2022). Integrated knowledge content in an interdisciplinary field: identification, classification, and application. *Scientometrics, 127*(11), 6581–6614. https://doi.org/10.1007/s11192-022-04282-0

Weston, P., & Nnadi, M. (2023). Evaluation of strategic and financial variables of corporate sustainability and ESG policies on corporate finance performance. *Journal of Sustainable Finance & Investment, 13*(2), 1058–1074. https://doi.org/10.1080/20430795.2021.1883984

Yu, Z., Farooq, U., Alam, M. M., & Dai, J. (2024). How does environmental, social, and governance (ESG) performance determine investment mix? New empirical evidence from BRICS. *Borsa Istanbul Review*. https://doi.org/https://doi.org/10.1016/j.bir.2024.02.007

www.ingramcontent.com/pod-product-compliance
Ingram Content Group UK Ltd.
Pitfield, Milton Keynes, MK11 3LW, UK
UKHW021847100926
8556IPUK00020B/1103

9 783631 929179